Readings on Islam in Southeast Asia

The **Institute of Southeast Asian Studies** was established as an autonomous organization in May 1968. It is a regional research centre for scholars and other specialists concerned with modern Southeast Asia, particularly the multi-faceted problems of stability and security, economic development, and political and social change.

The Institute is governed by a twenty-two-member Board of Trustees comprising nominees from the Singapore Government, the National University of Singapore, the various Chambers of Commerce, and professional and civic organizations. A ten-man Executive Committee oversees day-to-day operations; it is chaired by the Director, the Institute's chief academic and administrative officer.

Readings on Islam in Southeast Asia

compiled by

Ahmad Ibrahim
International Islamic University of Malaysia
Sharon Siddique
Institute of Southeast Asian Studies
Yasmin Hussain
Institute of Southeast Asian Studies

Social Issues in Southeast Asia
INSTITUTE OF SOUTHEAST ASIAN STUDIES

Published by
Institute of Southeast Asian Studies
Heng Mui Keng Terrace
Pasir Panjang
Singapore 0511

ISBN 9971-988-04-6 (hard cover)

ISBN 9971-988-08-9 (soft cover)

Contents

Foreword

Ethnic and religious factors have, in the last few decades, confounded many social analysts by refusing to disappear. The "liberal expectancy" among social analysts used to be that modernization would blur ethnic distinctions, achievement would replace ascription and particularistic criteria, and wide-ranging communication and education systems would homogenize populations. The "radical expectancy", on the other hand, was that differences in religion, language, and culture would be swallowed up, perhaps even across national boundaries, by emergent class consciousness. Instead, religion and ethnicity continue to cut across and envelope almost every facet of Southeast Asian life. Indeed, if anything, such divisions in many societies have become sharper, ethnic and religious interest groups more insistent, and opposition more politicized and strident. Much of this activity seems to be increasingly being played on the urban stage. And this at a time when the pace of urbanization in Southeast Asia is increasing rapidly, to the extent that by the turn of the century cities like Manila, Bangkok, and Jakarta could have populations of more than ten million each. In these settings Southeast Asian ethnic, religious, and linguistic complexities are likely to be even more challenging than in the past.

It was therefore only natural that among other aspects of the Southeast Asian social and cultural scene, the Institute should identify the study of contemporary religion as one of its key areas of interest. Southeast Asia is after all not only a home of all the major religions of the world — Islam, Buddhism, Christianity, and Hinduism — but the geographical spread of these is such that the bonds that bind their adherents at one and the same time defy and accentuate political and territorial divides and boundaries. The case of Islam is especially striking in this respect, as its followers are present in significant numbers in almost every Southeast Asian country, and in several of these across constraining political borders. Acting on this, a group of Southeast Asian scholars met in 1980 and proposed a project to increase our understanding of Islam in its regional context.

Towards this end, two clusters of issues were identified. The first of these was centred on the nature of Islam in the region, Islam and societal change, and Islam and education. The second concentration was to be on Islam and problems of economic development.

The first cluster in turn was to comprise three separate but related activities: (i) preparation of a basic reader containing significant contributions to the understanding of Islam in Southeast Asia; (ii) a research project on Islam and society in Southeast Asia; and (iii) another on Islam and higher education in Southeast Asia.

Whilst the second and third of these activities were to consist of a series of research papers to be presented and discussed at two separate workshops — and for these papers to be thereafter revised and edited for publication in book form — the first undertaking was to comprise a systematic selection of seminal contributions articulating the nature of Islam in the region, including its origins and development. It is this collection that forms the basis of the volume that follows.

The project on Islam stimulated considerable interest in not only other major religions of the region, but also issues relating to ethnicity and development, another of the Institute's long-standing and primary areas of research. Moreover, the experience gained in managing the project on Islam proved valuable in terms of co-ordinating comparative research involving numerous scholars from diverse backgrounds and disciplines. The Institute was thereby encouraged not only to plan parallel projects on Buddhism and Christianity in Southeast Asia, but also to think in terms of developing a longer-term *programme* of research that would encompass all its projects on contemporary religions, together with those that might grow out of the Institute's interest in ethnicity, urbanism, and related areas.

To facilitate this, in 1985 the Institute convened a meeting of senior Southeast Asian social scientists to discuss issues of social change in Southeast Asia, in order to identify firm areas of research and a sharper focussing of such research and associated activities. The group were unanimous in their conclusion that it was "essential and desirable" to encourage research of social issues in Southeast Asia, in particular religion, ethnicity, urbanism, and population dynamics.

To allow for proper planning and incremental research, the group felt that work in these areas could be most effectively developed within the structure and support of a *programme,* rather than as *ad hoc* projects. Accordingly, it was proposed there be established a programme of research to be known as "Social Issues in Southeast Asia" or SISEA. This programme would address itself to the nature, persistence, and impact of religions, ethnicity, urbanism, and population change in terms of their intrinsic dynamism and potential for societal conflict, co-existence or co-operation in the context of development, stability, and nation-building.

Additionally, SISEA would allow for the consolidation of the various publications emanating from the Institute's work in ethnicity, religion, urbanism, and population change within a single and integrated series, "Social Issues in Southeast Asia", with *Readings on Islam in Southeast Asia* being its inaugural number.

The preparation of *Readings on Islam in Southeast Asia* and the project on Islam as a whole have benefited greatly from assistance from several institutions and individuals within and outside the region, and from the financial support provided by the Konrad Adenauer Foundation of the Federal Republic of Germany. The Institute would like to record its appreciation of all such help and support and to express the wish that the various numbers of "Social Issues in Southeast Asia" will circulate widely amongst all concerned with the social dynamics of the region.

In wishing the volumes in the "Social Issues" series all the best it is clearly understood that responsibility for facts and opinions expressed in them rests exclusively with their individual authors, editors, and compilers, and their interpretations do not necessarily reflect the views or policy of the Institute or its supporters.

K.S. Sandhu
Director
Institute of Southeast Asian Studies

Preface

We initiated this project to publish a volume of selected readings on Islam in Southeast Asia with the desire that it should paint a portrait of the Southeast Asian Islamic mosaic, with an emphasis upon the contemporary (post-World War II) period. We also intended that the volume reflect the broad thematic interest of scholars who have contributed to our understanding of Islam in Southeast Asia — both indigenous and foreign, Muslim and non-Muslim.

With this goal in mind, we began the long process of selection, sifting through hundreds of books, monographs, and articles. Along the way we obtained advice from many sources, particularly sojourners at the Institute of Southeast Asian Studies. However, since the responsibility for the final selection rests with us alone, we will not name them individually but rather thank them collectively.

As we proceeded, we also began to address an imaginary audience. For what types of readers was this volume intended? One group of potential readers would be non-Southeast Asianists who would be interested in a one volume window into the world of Southeast Asian Islam. This group would include other area specialists, such as scholars researching Islam in North Africa or the Middle East, and also scholars whose main interest would be interdisciplinary comparisons, such as socio-religious change or political Islam. We also hoped that this book might be of use to teachers and their students, providing them with a reading list collapsed into one volume. Additionally we planned the bibliography to include not only all references within the selections, but also to include new materials, emphasizing the recently burgeoning literature in the Malay and Indonesian languages. Finally we hoped to provide a useful reference work for Southeast Asian scholars for whom the contents are familiar territory.

Slowly the volume began to take shape. An essentially linear historical development imposed itself. Naturally the beginning would be the coming of Islam to Southeast Asia — certainly not a simple process. We opted for articles which, in our estimation, provide the reader with the latest interpretations of this complex process. Our understanding of the coming of Islam to the region is based on painstaking reconstructions of events which are the cumulative achievement of generations of scholars.

We realized that the colonial period could be viewed from two perspectives — an insiders perspective contributed by colonial administrators/academics, and an outsiders perspective which is represented by contemporary attempts at reinterpretation. We have tried to give a flavour of this process, which is on-going.

This chronological development then carried us through to the post-World War II period, which ushered in the new nation-state era in Southeast Asia. Islam and nationalism or Islam and the political process emerged as an important theme, which carried its own chronological dynamic not only for the region as a whole, but for each emergent nation individually. Other themes, not so clear in their linear development, also emerged. Sociologists and anthropologists contributed to our understanding of the complexities of Muslim everyday life in Southeast Asia — stressing differences as well as basic similarities. In addition, we felt that the institutionalization of Islam could be viewed as a phenomenon distinct from, and perhaps complementary to, institutional politicization. This sphere is based on the belief that Islam is a complete way of life, and rejects the notion of a separation of the secular from the religious. Finally the theme of modernization and development in relation to the Islamic value system emerged as a significant area of scholarly concern.

It is impossible to justify our final choice of selections on any absolute criteria. The selection was governed by the interaction of the complex levels described above. All the authors whose work is represented in this volume have published widely, but there are others who have contributed to our knowledge just as significantly, who are not represented. Selections were chosen because they fit together to form larger pieces, interlocking to construct what we hope is one portrait of Islam in Southeast Asia. This portrait metaphor is particularly apt because, just as each artist paints what he sees to the best of his ability, so too have we. Others would do it differently, with equal validity.

Once this initial selection process was complete, we encountered a further constraint. Each selection had to be fitted — sometimes tailored — into the context of the entire volume so that their cumulative length could still be contained within the covers of a single volume.

Only then could we begin approaching authors and copyright holders to obtain their permission for us to reprint their already published material. Although we have acknowledged them all individually at the beginning of each selection, we would again like to thank them for their generous cooperation in our endeavour.

Because of the previously printed status of our selections, we did encounter some difficulties during the editorial process. Pages and footnotes have had to be renumbered, but we have scrupulously avoided re-editing the material. There are, therefore, inconsistences of style and spelling throughout the selections (and sometimes even within a single selection). We have used our energy to avoid the introduction of any new errors, and to render the published originals as accurately as possible. Editor's notes have been added when they appeared necessary.

We would like to thank the Konrad Adenaur Foundation for the generous grant which made this publication possible. In addition, there are three individuals who have helped us in our endeavour. We would like to thank Miss Isabel Chan who typed and filed the voluminous correspondence which developed between copyright holders, authors, publishers and ourselves, and Miss Eva Chung, whose keen eyes have caught many errors of typesetting and production which ours might have missed. Our greatest debt of gratitude is reserved for our editor, Mrs Triena Ong. Without her skill, patience, steadfast attention to detail, and dedication to high standards of production, this reader simply would not have been possible.

The compilers

Notes on Contributors

DATUK AHMAD IBRAHIM is currently holding the post of Shaikh Kulliyyah of Laws at the International Islamic University of Malaysia in Kuala Lumpur. His publications include *Family Law in Malaysia and Singapore* (1978); *Legal Education in Malaysia* (1980); *Islamic Law in Malaya* (1965); and *Law and Population in Malaysia* (1977).

ALFIAN is the Director of LRKN-LLIPI (the National Institute for Cultural Studies-Indonesian Institute of Sciences) in Jakarta. He has published a number of works on Indonesian political, social and cultural problems, Southeast Asian politics, and political science in Indonesia. He is the editor of *People: Perceptions of Culture (Persepsi Masyarakat Tentang Kebudayaan)* (1985).

AWANG HAD SALLEH is Vice Chancellor of the Northern University of Malaysia. He has published a number of literary books, academic books and textbooks. Among them are *Pelajaran dan Perguruan Melayu di Malaya Zaman British; dengan rujukan khas kepada Sultan Idris Training College* (1974); *Biru Warna* (1966); *Buat Menyapu si Air Mata* (1975); and *Merah, Kuning, Biru* (1966).

HARSJA W. BACHTIAR is Head of the Office of Educational and Cultural Research and Development, Department of Education and Culture, Jakarta. Among his publications are (with Stephen A. Douglas) *Indonesian Students: The Generation of 1966* (1970) and *The Indonesian Nation: Some Problems of Integration and Disintegration* (1974).

HARRY J. BENDA was Professor of History at Yale University at the time of his death in 1971. He is remembered for his many contributions to Southeast Asian history, some of which are *The Crescent and the Rising Sun; Indonesian Islam under the Japanese Occupation, 1942–1945* (1958); *Southeast Asian Transitions; approaches through social history* (ed. by Ruth McVey) (1978); (with John Bastin) *A History of Modern Southeast Asia; colonialism, nationalism, and decolonization* (1968).

B.J. BOLAND retired from his positions as Head of the Publications Department of the Royal Institute of Linguistics and Anthropology (KITLV) and Extraordinary Professor of Modern Islam in Indonesia at Leiden University in 1982. His publications include *The Struggle of Islam in Modern Indonesia* (1971) and a bibliography (together with I. Farjon) entitled *Islam in Indonesia: a bibliographical survey, 1600-1942 with post-1945 addenda*, KITLV, (1983).

NOEL J. COULSON is Professor of Oriental Laws and Dean of the Faculty of Laws at the University of London. His publications include *A History of Islamic Law* (1964) and *Succession in the Muslim Family* (1971).

M. DAWAM RAHARDJO is Director of the Institute for Economic and Social Research, Education and Information (LP3ES), Jakarta. He is the editor of *Profil Pesantren* (1974); *Pesantren dan Pembaharuan* (1974); and *Agricultural Transformation, Industrialization and Employment* (1984).

DELIAR NOER is Senior Lecturer, School of Modern Asian Studies, Griffith University, and part-time guest professor at IAIN, Jakarta. He is the author of *The Modernist Muslim*

Movement in Indonesia 1900–1942 (1973); *Mencari Jalan Keluar dari Kemelut Sekarang* (1974), and *Islam dan Politik di Indonesia (1945–1965)* (forthcoming).

G.W.J. DREWES retired from the University of Leiden in 1970, where he had been Professor of Malay and Bahasa Indonesia (from 1947) and Professor of Arabic (from 1953). He is the author of *Een Javaanse Primbon uit de 16de eeuw* (1954); *The Admonitions of Seh Bari* (1969); *An Early Javanese Code of Muslim Ethics* (1978); and *Directions for Travellers on the Mystic Path* (1977). A book dealing with the poems and prose of the 16th century Malay poet, Hamzah Fansuri, is awaiting publication.

HOWARD M. FEDERSPIEL is a Professor of Political Science at the Ohio State University, Neward Campus. Currently he is the Team Leader for the MUCIA (Mid-west Universities Consortium for International Activities) project on technical assistance to the University of North Sumatra, Medan. He is author of *The Persatuan Islam: Islamic Fundamentalism in Twentieth Century Indonesia* and numerous articles on Islam in contemporary Southeast Asia.

SIR RAYMOND FIRTH is Emeritus Professor of Anthropology at the University of London. He is the author of *Malay Fishermen: Their Peasant Economy* (1966); "Ritual and Drama in Malay Spirit Mediumship" (*CSSH*, 1967); and "Relations between Personal Kin (Waris) among Kelantan Malays" in *Social Organization and the Applications of Anthropology* (1974).

THOMAS M. FRASER, Jr. is Adjunct Professor (formerly Department Chairman) at the Department of Anthropology, University of Massachusetts. He is the author of *Rusembilan: A Malay Fishing Village in Southern Thailand* (1960); *Fishermen of South Thailand* (1966); *Culture and Change in India, The Barpali Experiment* (1970) and *Windward Road: Contributions to the Anthropology of St. Vincent* (1973).

JOHN FUNSTON is a senior analyst on Southeast Asia in the Office of National Assessments, Canberra, Australia. His publications include *Malay Politics in Malaysia: A Study of the United Malays National Organisation and Party Islam* (1980) and several articles on Malaysian politics and Southeast Asian international relations.

CLIFFORD GEERTZ is Professor of Social Science, the Institute for Advanced Study, Princeton, and Visiting Lecturer with rank of Professor in the Department of History at Princeton. Among his extensive publications are *The Religion of Java* (1960); *Islam Observed: Religious Development in Morocco and Indonesia* (1968); *Negara: The Theatre State in Nineteenth Century Bali* (1980); *Local Knowledge: Further Essays in Interpretive Anthropology* (1983); and *Works and Lives: The Anthropologist as Author* (forthcoming).

PETER G. GOWING was Director of the Dansalan Research Center at Dansalan College in Marawi City until his death in 1983. He wrote extensively on religion in the Philippines. Some of his most well-known publications are: *Mosque and Moro* (1964); *Islands under the Cross* (1967); *Mandate in Moroland; The American Government of Muslim Filipinos, 1899–1920* (1977); and *Muslim Filipinos — Heritage and Horizon* (1979).

S. HUSIN ALI is Professor of Human Development Studies at the Institute of Advanced Studies, University of Malaya. He is the author of *Social Stratification in Kampung Bagar* (1964); *Malay Peasant Society and Leadership* (1975); *Malays — Their Problems and Future* (1981); *Poverty and Landlessness in Kelantan* (1983); and editor of *Ethnicity, Class and Development — Malaysia* (1984).

A.H. JOHNS is Head of the Southeast Asia Centre, Faculty of Asian Studies, at the Australian National University. He is the author of *The Gift Addressed to the Spirit of the Prophet* (1965), and *Cultural Options and the Role of Tradition: A collection of essays on modern Indonesian and Malaysian literature* (1979).

MUHAMMAD KAMAL HASSAN is Professor and Head of the Centre for Fundamental Knowledge in the International Islamic University of Malaysia in Kuala Lumpur. He was formerly head of the Department of Islamic Theology and Philosophy at the National University of Malaysia. He is the author of *Muslim Intellectual Responses to 'New Order' Modernization in Indonesia* (1982).

CLIVE S. KESSLER is Professor of Sociology at the University of New South Wales. He previously taught social anthropology at the London School of Economics and at Barnard

College, Columbia University. He is the author of various works on Malaysian Islam, most notably *Islam and Politics in a Malay State: Kelantan 1838–1969* (1978).

THOMAS M. KIEFER is Instructor in Anthropology, Harvard University Extension, Cambridge, Ma., and the author of *The Tausug: Violence and Law in a Philippine Moslem Society* (1972).

KOENTJARANINGRAT is Professor of Anthropology at the University of Indonesia. He is the author of *Anthropology in Indonesia: A Bibliographical Review* (1975); *Kebudayaan Jawa* (1984); *Javanese Culture* (1984); (editor) *Villages in Indonesia* (1967); and (editor) *The Social Sciences in Indonesia* (1975).

ABDUL MAJEED MOHAMED MACKEEN, formerly Professor of Islamic Studies, University of Malaya, is at present a Member of the Royal Academy for Research into Islamic Civilization in Jordan. He is also consultant to the Faculty of Law, University of Malaya. His most recent publications include *Islamic Fiscal and Property Laws in Malaysia* (1985) and *The Administration of Islamic Law in Malaysia* (forthcoming).

CESAR ADIB MAJUL retired from the University of the Philippines in 1979. In recognition of his long service, he was given the titles of "University Professor" and "Professor Emeritus". His many publications include *The Political and Constitutional Ideas of the Philippine Revolution* (1957); *Mabini and the Philippine Revolution* (1960); *Apolinario Mabini: Revolutionary* (1964); and *Muslims in the Philippines* (1973).

A.C. MILNER is a Visiting Fellow in the Department of Pacific and Southeast Asian History, Australian National University. He is the author of *Kerajaan: Malay Political Culture on the Eve of Colonial Rule* (1982) and (with Virginia Matheson) *Perceptions of the Haj* (1984).

MOHD. TAIB OSMAN is Professor of Malay Studies at the University of Malaya. He is the author of *Modern Malay Literature* (1964); *Asas dan Pertumbuhan Kebudayaan Malaysia* (1974); and *Bunga Rampai Kebudayaan Melayu* (1983).

MOHD. ZAIN HJ. OTHMAN is Professor of Islamic Studies and Head of the Department of Islamic Studies, University of Malaya. His most recent articles include "Kebangkitan Islam di Asia Tenggara" (*Al-Islam,* 1980); "Kebincangan Bahasa Arab di Malaysia" (*Majallah Al-Arabi* [in arabic] 1980) and "Baitulmal Sebagai Institusi Kewangan" (*Islamica,* 1985).

CHANDRA MUZAFFAR, formerly lecturer in Political Science at the Universiti Sains Malaysia, Penang, is currently the President of Aliran Kesedaran Negara (ALIRAN). He is the author of *Protector?* (1979) and a number of pamphlets, essays and articles dealing with such themes as alternative concepts and approaches to development, human rights and democracy, national integration, and religion and social change.

JUDITH A. NAGATA is Professor of Anthropology at York University. Her recent publications include *Malaysian Mosaic: Perspectives from a Poly-ethnic Society* (1980) and *The Reflowering of Malaysian Islam* (1984).

NURCHOLISH MADJID is a researcher at the Indonesian Institute of Sciences (LIPI) in Jakarta. His most recent published work is *Khazanah Intelektual Islam* (1984) which he edited.

K.J. RATNAM is Dean of Graduate Studies at Universiti Sains Malaysia in Penang. He is the author of *Communalism and the Political Process in Malaya* (1965) and *Technology and Society* (1985).

M.C. RICKLEFS is Professor of History at Monash University. He is the author of *Jogjakarta under Sultan Mangkubumi, 1749–1792: A History of the Division of Java* (1974); *Modern Javanese Historical Tradition: A Study of an Original Kartasura Chronicle and Related Materials* (1978); and *A History of Modern Indonesia, ca. 1300 to the Present* (1981).

WILLIAM ROFF is Professor of History at Columbia University, New York. He is the author of *The Origins of Malay Nationalism* (1967) and editor of *Islam and the Political Economy of Meaning: Comparative Studies of Muslim Discourse* (forthcoming).

SAID RAMADAN is the Director-General of the Islamic Center in Geneva. His publications include *Islamic Law, its Scope and Equity* (1970), as well as numerous articles and pamphlets.

ENDANG SAIFUDDIN ANSHARI is currently residing in Bandung, Indonesia. His publications include *The Jakarta Charter of June 1945* (1979); *Agama dan Kebudayaan: mukaddimah sejarah kebudayaan Islam* (1980); and *Piagam Jakarta 22 June 1945, dan sejarah konsensus nasional antara nasionalis Islam dan nasionalis "sekular" tentang dasar negara Republik Indonesia, 1945–1959* (1981).

ALLAN A. SAMSON is a practicing attorney in San Francisco. He is also Executive Secretary of the *American Journal of Comparative Law* and a visiting Lecturer in Modern Islamic Law at the University of California School of Law at Berkeley. His book *Islam and Politics in Indonesia* will shortly be published in Jakarta.

SARTONO KARTODIRDJO is Professor of History at the Faculty of Letters, Gadjah Mada University. Some of his numerous publications include *The Peasants' Revolt of Banten in 1888* (1966); *Elite dalam Perspektif Sejarah* (1981); *Pemikiran dan Perkembangan Historiografi Indonesia* (1982); *Ratu Adil* (1984); and *Komunikasi dan Kaderisasi* (1984).

B. SCHRIEKE was a distinguished member of the Netherlands East Indies government until his death in 1945. He was a Professor at the Batavia Law School from 1924, and Director of Education from 1929. He is the author of *The Effect of Western Influence on Native Civilizations in the Malay Archipelago* (1929). In addition, collections of his articles were published posthumously.

SEDDIK TAOUTI is Special Assistant to the President of the Islamic Development Bank, Jeddah, an affiliate body of the Organization of the Islamic Conference. He was head of the Bank team that visited Kampuchea and Viet Nam to disburse aid made available by the Bank on the direction of the Islamic Foreign Ministers Conference.

P.M. DATO SHARIFFUDDIN, formerly Director of the Brunei Museum, is presently Executive Chairman, S.L. Apian (B) Sdn Bhd, Consulting Engineers and Designers.

SHARON SIDDIQUE is a Senior Fellow at the Institute of Southeast Asian Studies, Singapore. Her publications include (with Nirmala Puru Shotam) *Singapore's Little India: past, present and future* and (with Taufik Abdullah, co-editor) *Islam and Society in Southeast Asia* (forthcoming).

C. SNOUCK HURGRONJE was an outstanding Dutch Arabicist and Islamologist who began a long and distinguished career involving the Dutch East Indies with his appointment, in 1889, as Advisor on Arabian and Native Affairs. He left us with a legacy of voluminous writings on Indonesian Islam, the greater part of which were reprinted in Volume II of his *Verspreide Geschriften* (1923–27; 4 vols.). See also G.H. Bousquet and J. Schacht, eds., *Selected Works of C. Snouck Hurgronje,* edited in English and French (1957).

M.G. SWIFT was prior to his death in Kuala Lumpur in May 1984, Professor of Anthropology at Monash University. Among his publications are *Malay Peasant Society in Jelebu* (1965) and (with Maurice Freedman) *Rural Sociology in Malaya* (1959).

TAUFIK ABDULLAH is currently affiliated with the Indonesian Institute for Sciences (LIPI) in Jakarta. He was formerly the Director of the National Institute for Social and Economic Research (LEKNAS) (1974–78). His publications include: *Schools and Politics: The Kaum Muda Movement in West Sumatra* (1971); *Agama, Ethos, Kerja dan Perkembangan Ekonomi* (ed.) (1979); and *Sejarah Lokal di Indonesia* (ed.) (1978).

UMAR JUNUS has been lecturing at the University of Malaya since 1967. He is the author of *Sejarah Melayu: Menemukan Diri Kembali* (1984) and *Kaba dan Sistem Sosial Minangkabau, sebuah problema sosiologi sastra* (1984), as well as numerous articles in the field of linguistic anthropology.

W.F. WERTHEIM is Emeritus Professor at the University of Amsterdam. He is the author of *Indonesian Society in Transition* (1959); *East-West Parallels* (1964); *Dawning of an Asian Dream: Selected Articles on Modernization and Emancipation* (1973); and *Emancipation in Asia: Positive and Negative Lessons from China* (1983).

R.O. WINSTEDT began his long and distinguished career in the Colonial Civil Service with a posting to Perak in 1902. He left Malaya in the late 1930s to take up the post of Reader in Malay at the School of Oriental and African Studies in the University of London. During a career which spanned more than six decades (d. 1966) he authored numerous books and articles. Among them are *Malay Grammar* (1939); *The Malays: A Cultural History* (1947; reprinted 1972); *Kesusasteraan Melayu. Rampai-rampai* i–vi (1958); and *Malaya and its History* (1948).

Part One
Historical Perspectives

Introduction to Part One

The key word to understanding the history of Islam in Southeast Asia is complexity. Islam arrived in Southeast Asia — the geographical periphery of the Muslim world — through a process of peaceful co-optation which spanned centuries. There were few instances of military conquests, political upheavals, or forceful impositions of foreign power structures and societal norms. There are therefore no easy answers to the questions of "when", "why", "from where" and "in what form" did Islam first begin to make an impact on the societies of Southeast Asia. In fact, we are now beginning to realize that this Islamization process may have had no one definitive beginning, and also, that it certainly has had no end. The Islamization of the region is rather a continuing process which affects not only our present, but our future as well.

One can further increase the picture of regional religious complexity through the observation that Islam had not been the first great religion to flourish in the fertile soil of Southeast Asia. The religious history of the region is of itself complex. First, Hinduism, then Buddhism, Islam and later Christianity offered models which have molded the indigenous cultural-religious matrix for millenia. The degree of impact of these great religious traditions on indigenous Southeast Asian cultural patterns has varied from place to place and according to various time frames. Although these religious waves did follow each other in the rough historical sequence outlined, they by no means left clearly distinguishable layers of sediment upon Southeast Asian shores. There was instead a great mingling of religious traditions which is perhaps unparalleled in any other region of the globe. However, the view, prevalent particularly during the colonial period, that Islam was simply "a thin flaking glaze" upon the indigenous religious complexity of Southeast Asia, is no longer tenable. Islam made and continues to make a profound impact upon the socio-cultural, political and economic life of Southeast Asia.

In its spread throughout the region, Islam had to contend with the geographical complexity of the region as well. Cradled in the heart of island Southeast Asia from at least the 13th century, it grew and spread its influence throughout the archipelago. It began its climb up the Malayan peninsula, only to encounter Thai Buddhist culture of the Southeast Asian mainland. Islam pushed forward on its outer flank, spreading up the eastern side of the archipelago through the islands of what are today the Southern Philippines. Here its progress was halted by the arrival of the Spanish in Manila, and the religion under which they conquered: Catholicism.

Melaka, located in the geographical heart of the archipelago, was by all accounts a cosmopolitan trading city par excellence in the 15th century. But Melaka was more than a trading centre. During the 15th century, it was the socio-cultural and political centre for the indigenous Muslim proselytism of the region. Its fall to the Portuguese in 1511 marked the beginning of a new era in the history of Islam in Southeast Asia. For the next four and a half centuries, Islam was placed on the defensive. The gradual arrival of the colonial powers — the French in Indochina, the Dutch in the Netherlands East Indies, the British in British Malaya, and the Spanish in the Philippines signalled the erosion of independent indigenous Muslim socio-political and economic pre-eminence in Southeast Asia. Based on their direct colonial experience in the Middle East, and their collective memory of the Crusades, Islam was no stranger to the colonial powers. But Islam in Southeast Asia clearly intrigued colonial administrators and they spent a great deal of time and energy recording their observations of its supposedly unique character. At the same time, they were not prepared to underestimate its potential disruptive force, and each colonial power, in its own way, took steps to contain it.

One Southeast Asian phenomenon which became a source of fascination to colonial administrators was the ethnic complexity of the region. Indeed, Southeast Asia is unique in that it supports a population wherein ethnic heterogeneity has been peacefully maintained throughout the centuries. In a sense then, colonial administrators were correct in describing many "Islams" — Javanese Islam, Minangkabau Islam, Sundanese Islam, Achenese Islam, Buginese Islam, Malay Islam, and so on. Added to this complexity are pockets of Muslims drawn from other parts of the Muslim world who have made their homes in Southeast Asia — some for centuries — and contributed not only to the complexity of the religious matrix, but also to the maintenance of ethnic heterogeneity. Here one could count the Arabs (particularly from the Hadramaut) who came to trade, spread Islam, and eventually, to settle. Similarly there are various ethnic groups from India who migrated to the region — prominent among them were the Labbai (Tamil Muslims), the Mappilla (Malayalam-speaking Muslims from Kerala), the Bengali, the Gujerati and Urdu-speaking Muslims of North India and Pakistan.

EARLY ISLAMIZATION

As this book of readings emphasizes the contemporary period, it was necessary to limit the number of selections in Part One. Because of this constraint, no selections have been provided from the early descriptive travelogues. Instead, selections of an interpretive, reconstructive nature have been chosen in order to provide an overview of the complex questions relating to who, when, why, where from and how, Islam came to Southeast Asia. It is assumed that the interested reader can utilize the sources cited in footnotes and contained within the bibliography if he/she wishes to delve further into any aspect of the early history of the coming of Islam to Southeast Asia.

COLONIAL RULE

Greater emphasis has been given — in terms of the number of selections included — to the colonial period, which in itself is complex, spanning as it does several centuries of Southeast Asian history. In addition, the various colonial powers adopted different approaches to the interpretations of Islam within their territories, and evolved different solutions to its containment and administration. Colonial administrators and bureaucrats placed great emphasis on collecting indigenous texts and cultural artifacts, as well as describing Islam in *praxis.* In general, they seemed quite fascinated with the realm of *adat* (local custom) which they tended to view as contradictory to Islam, rather than complementary to it. Their attitudes and assessments in turn set the tone for colonial policies, and determined administrative procedures.

Assessing the writings of these colonial contributors has been the preoccupation of many post-independence scholars. Recent research has led to the discovery of new insights and information which, in turn, has caused a re-evaluation of the previously dominant colonial view of the position and character of Islam in Southeast Asia. In fact, it can be argued that a reconstruction of the Muslim history of the colonial period is an essential task if we are to base our contemporary understanding of Islam in the region on firm scholarly foundations.

Early Islamization

New Light on the Coming of Islam to Indonesia?

G. W. J. DREWES

What now have European researches contributed to this subject? It is obvious that in former times the spread of Islam in Indonesia and the Malay Peninsula should have been ascribed to Arabs. Seeing that Islam originated in Arabia it seemed self-evident to seek a link between this religion and the presence of Arabs wherever both Arabs and Islam were encountered. In Indonesia and the Malay Peninsula Arabs were found in many places. So it seemed a foregone conclusion that these were the ones who had brought Islam. But where the Arabs had come from was less clear. It had been observed that the Muslims in these areas followed the Shāfiʿī school of law, so they must have originated from a country where this was also the case. Thus Professor Keyzer, one of the earliest scholars of Muslim law in Holland, came to look for a link with Egypt, where the Shāfiʿī school has of old occupied an important place.[1]

The surprising thing about this explanation is that Keyzer, who was a professor at the Delft Academy for training civil servants for the Indies, apparently did not know that practically all the Arabs living in Indonesia originated from Hadramaut, and that the Shāfiʿī school of law is likewise the dominant one there. Otherwise he would probably have indicated Hadramaut, which, however, would have been just as incorrect, seeing that the immigration of Hadramis into Indonesia is of much later date than the advent of Islam.

Keyzer stood alone in this indication of Egypt as the country of origin of Indonesian Islam. Niemann (1861) and De Hollander (1861) spoke only of Arabs. Niemann did not venture an opinion on the dating of the advent of Islam; on the other hand De Hollander considered that there had perhaps already been Arabs in Java in the 13th century. Veth (1878) also spoke only of Arabs, who acquired influence for themselves by concluding marriages. The observation of Crawfurd (1820), who certainly mentioned Arabs, but also proposed "intercourse with the Mahomedans of the Eastern coast of India" as cause of the "superior instruction" of the Indonesians in religion, had apparently escaped them all.[2]

A step in the right direction was made by Pijnappel, the first professor of Malay at the University of Leiden. In a volume of this Journal, he devoted an article to the knowledge which the Arabs possessed of the Indonesian Archipelago prior to the coming of the Portuguese.[3] In this he based himself on Reinaud's *Relation des Voyages faits par les Arabes et les Persans dans l'Inde et à la Chine,* a booklet which appeared in Paris in 1845, containing the translation of a travel-story[4] from A.D. 851, then still ascribed to the navigator Suleiman. After having given a resumé of Suleiman's information on Indonesia, Pijnappel moves on to speak of Marco Polo and of Ibn Baṭṭūṭa, the Moroccan traveller who visited a large part of the then known world in the first half of the

Reprinted with slight abridgement from *Bijdragen tot de Taal-, Land-en Volkenkunde,* Deel 124 4e Aflevering (1968), pp. 433–459, by permission of the author and Koninklijk Instituut voor Taal-, Land-en Volkenkunde, Leiden, The Netherlands.

14th century (1325–1353), and thereby also included Sumatra. Pijnappel says that the question of whence and by which route the Arabs reached the Indonesian Archipelago would be of no interest to us were it not that the origin of their religion is closely connected with it, and that Persian influence seems to exist alongside Arab. He points then to the trade-route from the Persian Gulf along the western coast of India, he names Broach, Surat and Quilon (Kulam) as important commercial centres, mentions the Arab interest in Adam's Peak in Ceylon, where Adam is supposed to have done penance for 200 years after his banishment from paradise, and ends with the conversion to Islam of the king of Calicut, the "Zamorin", a name which also appears later on (e.g. in the Dutch East India Company's documents) referring to the rulers of this area.

Pijnappel ascribes the spread of Islam in the Indonesian Archipelago to these Shāfiʿī Arabs of Gujerat and Malabar, especially because these regions are mentioned so frequently in the early history of the Archipelago. The Persian influence would also be explained, partially at least, by this contact with the western coast of India.

Thus the preaching of Islam is still thought of as proceeding from Arabs, but these no longer come directly from the Arab countries, but from India, and in particular from the west coast — from Gujerat and Malabar. Neither the east coast, that is, the Coromandel Coast, called in Arabic Maʿbar (passage, corridor, i.e. between the mainland and Ceylon), North India nor Bengal come into consideration.

After Pijnappel came Snouck Hurgronje.

A colonial exhibition was held in 1883 in Amsterdam and on this occasion scholarly addresses were organized. One of the speakers was Snouck Hurgronje, who was then 26 years old and had taken his doctor's degree three years before; he took the topic: The Meaning of Islam for its Adherents in the East Indies. In this address Snouck first developed the proposition of the South Indian origin of Indonesian Islam. When Islam had once gained a firm hold in the port cities of South India, "the inhabitants of the Deccan, who resided in great numbers in the port cities of this island-world as middlemen in the trade between the Muslim states (i.e. the states of western Asia) and the East Indies, were as if in the nature of things destined to scatter the first seeds of the new religion. Arabs, especially those who passed for descendants of the Prophet under the name of Sayyid or Sharif, later found a welcome opportunity to demonstrate their organizational ability. As priests, priest-princes and as sultans they often put the finishing touches to the formation of the new realms".[5]

Hence the idea that Islam was necessarily brought by Arabs has been abandoned here. I should like to add the following.

In the study of Indonesian literatures one sees in the beginning a similar constraint in the idea that everything which is Muslim or has an Arabic title has to come from the Arabic. Later on a Persian origin was assumed for some writings, as people were struck by the numerous Persian words and names[6] encountered in Malay and Javanese stories. Famous Persian names also occur in Achehnese literature, of which Snouck Hurgronje gave a model summary in the second volume of his *De Atjèhers* in 1894, and this is why the writer warns against speaking of Persian influence on the Achehnese. For, he says, by far the majority of Achehnese romances show unmistakable signs of the same origin as the Malay. Very many are definitely based on Malay models, and as cradle of the bulk of romances in both languages one may certainly consider the same part of South India to which the popular mysticism and the popular religious legends of the Muslim peoples of the Indonesian Archipelago also point.

Snouck Hurgronje does not, however, further define which part of South India this is. On the contrary — a little further on he observes that he cannot for the time being indicate the section of South India where the threads linking the spiritual life of the Indonesians with that country come together. An investigation into the literature of the Muslim population of South India would be required in order to obtain a greater degree of certainty on these questions.

Unfortunately we have to admit that now, almost 75 years later, such an investigation has still not taken place, so that on the Indian side the position has remained unchanged. So it is no wonder that the Italian scholar Alessandro Bausani has again expressed the necessity for this research in an article on Persian words in Malay which appeared a few years ago.[7]

Bausani came to the conclusion that at least 90% of the Persian words in Malay indicate concrete objects, and not even 10% abstract or adjectival concepts, and that for only a limited number can definite borrowing from India not be established. But then he asks "which part of India?" — only to answer: "Ritengo che uno dei desiderata piu urgenti della filologia malese sia uno studio preciso e ben articolato dell'Islam sud-indiano" (*op. cit.*, p. 28). It is obvious that such research would not only be of importance for Malay philology, but also for determining the origin of Indonesian Islam.

Having touched on this subject in 1894 in his discussion of Achehnese literature, Snouck Hurgronje went into it more deeply in 1907 in his inaugural lecture at Leiden which is, in fact, entitled *Arabia and the East Indies,* but of which twelve pages are devoted to the relations of Indonesian Islam with India, and only a mere four to direct influence from Arabia, which only made itself felt when European commerce and shipping had gradually driven the Indians out of the Archipelago.

As the first of the fixed points important for reconstructing the advance of Islam in the Archipelago Snouck Hurgronje mentions the report on northern Sumatra, namely on Pase, to be found in the travel-tale of the Moroccan traveller Ibn Baṭṭūṭa who visited this place in 1345 on his journey from Bengal to China. The fact that he mentions only in passing in a note the report on North Sumatra by Marco Polo from about 50 years earlier will surprise many who recall that many a writer on this subject begins with the Venetian's information. Snouck Hurgronje had, however, already noted in his book on the Gayō country (of 1903) that the significance of Marco Polo's reports on Sumatra was in his opinion very much exaggerated.[8] It will become clear in the course of my lecture why Snouck Hurgronje rated the value of these reports so low. His scepticism is far from groundless.

Pursuing his argument he mentions three Muslim gravestones from the first half of the 15th century discovered in the Pase district, of which Ibn Baṭṭūṭa speaks. Amongst these is, remarkably enough, the "notice in stone" of the death of an ᶜAbbāsid prince, a great-great-grandson of the caliph al-Muntaṣir.[9] This "illustrious parasite" found his last resting-place in northern Sumatra in 1407. He had undoubtedly floated in from Dehli, where his father had lived for a long time at the expense of the maharajah of Hindustan.

Furthermore Snouck mentions that, as Van Ronkel had first observed, these three gravestones from northern Sumatra show a striking resemblance to the gravestone in Grěsik of Malik Ibrahim who died in 1418 and belongs to the eight or nine chief saints of Java who are recorded in tradition as the bringers of Islam. Moquette had then not yet made his discovery that these stones were imported ready-made, but without names and dates of death, from Gujerat.

Then Snouck proposes the year 1200 as the earliest date for the "first serious steps" toward inclusion of the Indonesian Archipelago into the territory of Islam; these steps are supposed to have been taken by Muslim merchants from India, with which the Archipelago had been in contact for centuries. Finally there follows Snouck's well-known explanation of the first penetration of Islam — which has in it nothing surprising for those who know how it has often happened in India and how Islam still gains ground in many areas — that is, by traders' and dealers' settling and marrying women native to the place where they have settled. So it was a penetration which proceeded peacefully and apparently soon led to the foreigners' becoming related to prominent families of the land and occupying important posts in the running of the port such as that of *shahbandar* or *běndahara.*

Before long more light would be thrown on the gravestones mentioned by Snouck Hurgronje. In 1910 Van Ronkel already expressed the surmise that the old gravestone found at Grěsik would prove to be of Indian origin.[10] In 1912 Moquette then came with the important discovery that many of the gravestones found in the Pase district as well as those of the grave-complex of Malik Ibrahim in Grěsik originated from Cambay in Gujerat. Thus relations with Gujerat were here placed beyond any doubt *for a certain period* — the gravestones referred to all being from the 15th century and later.[11]

Gravestones have also been discovered in

the Pase district with earlier dates than those of the 15th century mentioned above, e.g. that of Malik al-Salih, assumed to be the first Muslim ruler of Pase, who according to Moquette's reading of the Arabic epitaph died in 1297. This gravestone is of another type than those imported from Cambay. Nevertheless Moquette assumed an Indian origin for this stone too, although he added that it must have been placed on the grave some time after the death of the ruler.[12] Apparently he considered the gap in time between 1297 and 1407–1428, the years of the stones described by Snouck Hurgronje, too large to be able to decide in favour of importation at this early time. He evidently did *not* consider the striking difference in form so important.

Then comes the confusion. People ignore Moquette's hesitation expressed in his suggestion of later placement and conclude that the oldest known gravestone comes from Gujerat — so Islam also comes from Gujerat. This can, for example, be read in R. A. Kern's contribution in Stapel's large history of the Netherlands Indies (Vol. I, p. 313) and in the little book *De Islam in Indonesië,* in which the following words are found on p. 9: "The gravestones erected on Malik al-Salih's grave were brought in ready-made from Cambay. This is then, where we must look for the source of the spiritual and material links which joined Samudra to the world of Islam".

Later investigators could not help but discover the mistake in this theory, which over the years had come to be known as the specifically Dutch one, as if it was held by all Dutch scholars without exception. In 1951 there appeared a short article by G. E. Marrison in *J.M.B.R.A.S.* (pt. 1, pp. 28–37) in which it was argued, in agreement with the Malay tradition of a South Indian origin of Indonesian Islam, that Marco Polo describes Cambay in 1293 as a city still Hindu, and that Gujerat came under Muslim rule only in 1297. Marrison argues further that the Muslims had already been established for centuries in South India, without having gained political power, before the expansion of the Dihli Sultanate at the beginning of the 14th century. Here he points to the Moors of Ceylon, the Moplahs of Malabar and the Maracayars of the Coromandel Coast (Maᶜbar), which are ethnic groups of mixed blood whose members are still traders and seamen. The Moplahs claim to descend from Muslim immigrants from Iraq who had fled to India from the cruelty of al-Ḥajjāj toward the end of the 7th century; there is in northern Malabar a Muslim grave from A.H. 166/A.D. 782/'83 which makes such an early settlement seem not impossible.[13] Another tradition speaks of the conversion to Islam of the ruler of Cranganore, to the north of Cochin, in about 815 — another ruler who resigned his position, this time to be able to travel to Arabia and return as a preacher of Islam.[14] This ruler has the title Perumal, which according to the Ht. Raja-raja Pasai was also borne by one of the early rulers of Pase.[15] Finally Marrison argues that the Shāfiᶜī school of law was not the dominant one in Gujerat, but was in South India; that the whole *Ht. Raja-raja Pasai* has a background strongly coloured by South India (Tamils are mentioned in it repeatedly; both Tamil merchants and Tamil jugglers and wrestlers appear on its stage), and that the spiritual influence of Gujerat is not evident before the first half of the 17th century, when Nuruddin al-Raniri came to Acheh.

Consequently the study of Islam in South India appears to him absolutely essential.

Nowhere can it be seen from Marrison's article that he is acquainted with a book in which neither Gujerat nor South India are named as the source of Indonesian Islam, but Bengal. I refer to the English translation which appeared in London in 1944 of the book of Tomé Pires, the *Suma Oriental,* so very important for our knowledge of South-East Asia at the beginning of the 16th century.

Tomé Pires was a Lisbon apothecary who was sent out to India in 1511 at about the age of 40 as "agent for drugs". He had not been working a year at Cannanore and at Cochin on the west coast of South India when he was sent to Malacca by Alfonso d'Albuquerque in a more responsible position. During his posting at Malacca he made a trip of several months to the north coast of Java. In 1515 he was back in Cochin, where he completed the *Suma Oriental* — as the title-page of the English translation says: "An Account of the East, from the Red Sea to Japan". Because of his ability selected to go to China as head of a mission, he sailed via Pase and Malacca to Canton where he arrived in 1517. This was a journey from which he would never return. The reception in China was far from friendly; this, it seems, had something to do with the complaint which the ruler of Malacca, conquered by the Portuguese in 1511, had lodged with the Chinese emperor, his suzerain. There are hints that Pires, after being held captive for some years, was finally released and died in China as an exile at about the age of 70.

Apart from his professional interest in oriental drugs, Pires also shows much interest in every other item of trade, its origin, sale and destination. His book thus became an extremely important contribution to knowledge of the movement of commerce in the East at the beginning of the 16th century, and it is no wonder that Pires is quoted so often in Mrs M. A. P. Meilink's doctoral thesis.

Alongside interest in commercial products Pires also had an interest in the harbour-towns where these products were shipped from and in the petty harbour rulers who were in authority there, as well as in the life and activity of the people who lived there. On these things he gives all kinds of interesting information, and when he speaks from his own experience and observation there seems no reason to doubt his information. But one must not expect of him more than he can give. For a good deal of his historical data he had to rely upon his indigenous informants; hence what he gives on these is at best a reflection of the picture of the past which his informants possessed. This says nothing about the correctness of the picture — sometimes Pires is even demonstrably wrong, as for example, when he says that it was about 300 years ago that the kingdom of Cambay was seized by the Muslims from the heathens. In fact Cambay came under Muslim rule only in 1297,[16] and even in Pires' own time the trade was still mainly in non-Muslim hands, as he himself says. Another instance is when he reports that Pase still had a heathen king until about 160 years before then — hence till about 1355 — while we know from the gravestones of the earliest princes of Pase that Malik al-Salih, who died in 1297, was already a Muslim. And this being the case, what value is to be attached to his statement that the king of Aru was said to have "turned Moor before any of the others, even before the king of Pase" (*op. cit.* II:245)?

But Pires had more to say about early Pase, perhaps the cradle of Islam in Indonesia. He describes it as a rich city where many Moorish and Indian traders lived, among whom the Bengalis were the most important. He distinguishes further Rumis, Turks, Arabs, Persians, Gujeratis, Klings, Malays, Javanese and Siamese. The population consisted mainly of Bengalis or people of Bengali origin, however, and since the heathen king of the country had succumbed to the "cunning of the merchant Moors" the latter were supposed to have appointed a "Moorish king of the Bengali caste". The countryside was, however, still heathen, although Islam was progressing daily. Just as in Bengal the "law of the jungle" went here too. Whoever could topple the king would, providing he was Muslim, succeed in his place, without bringing about any disturbance in the city. Thus it happened that emissaries arrived in Malacca from Pase twice in three months in order to declare allegiance to the Portuguese in the name of the new king and to ask their help, "and they keep on coming to ask this as other kings succeed".

This information of Pires' is the starting-point of the argument that Islam in Indonesia was imported from Bengal, contained in the book which the Pakistani Professor S. Q. Fatimi devoted to this question in 1963.[17] Fatimi begins, as do many, from Marco Polo's report that in 1292 Perlak was already Muslim as a result of the religious fervour of the Muslim traders, but that the people of Samara, where he had to wait five months for favourable winds, were still heathen. He disputes the latter statement on the basis of the fact that a Chinese report from 1282 mentions the meeting of a Chinese traveller at Quilon with an official from Su-mu-ta (= Samudra), in which the former urged that the ruler of Su-mu-ta send envoys to China. That must have happened soon afterwards, and these envoys from Su-mu-ta bore the Muslim names Hasan and Suleiman.

In this connection Fatimi quotes with approval Professor P. E. de Josselin de Jong, who said in a broadcast on Radio Malaya that this Chinese report made it probable that Pase (Samudra-Pase is a dual entity) was already a Muslim state before Marco Polo's visit in 1292, although it had perhaps not yet officially adopted Islam. The Muslim community must already have been important, seeing that two of its members were assigned this foreign mission.

Some reflection is called for here. The identification of Marco Polo's Samara and Basma(n) with Samudra and Pase, which is already found in Valentijn's Description of the Indies, has always been a disputed point. Cowan pointed to this in his review of Kern's essay in Stapel's History of the N.I., in my opinion very rightly, and he came back to it again in an article in the *Tijdschrift van het Kon. Aardr. Genootschap,* Vol. LXVII.

Both Snouck Hurgronje and R. A. Kern doubted the identification of Basma(n) with Pase. Van der Tuuk and, following him, Schrieke, sought Basma(n) in Pasaman on the *west* coast of Sumatra,[18] which appears geographically unacceptable as this lies outside the searoute. Pelliot, though wrongly placing Pasaman on the south-west coast of Sumatra, acknowledged into objection, but added: "Polo attached to his description of 'Basman' details of the rhinoceros which can only be those of an eye-witness; as to his monkeys made up to look like pygmies nobody has yet offered an explanation . . . Although I am not positive on the point, it may be that Polo gave his description of the rhinocerous when speaking of a kingdom in Sumatra of which he had only heard, and from which his monkey-pygmies were said to come. In such a case, Pasaman would have a fair chance of being 'Basman', and that is the reason why I have adopted this spelling in preference to 'Basma'".[19]

Even so it remains strange to come across a place located on the west coast of Sumatra in an enumeration of harbour towns on the north coast. So Cowan wishes to identify *Basma(n)* with Peusangan at the mouth of the large river of that name, the valley of which forms the main link with the Gayō country of the interior. This Peusangan passes in Malay tradition as the place where Měrah Silu alias Malik al-Salih, the first prince of Samudra and founder of that city, came from. *Samara* according to Cowan is the present-day Samalanga, which is spelt Sam*a*r*langa in older works in Arabic script. Both places are situated on the north coast of Acheh (Samudra also lay on the north coast and there is still a kampong of that name). Why Marco Polo did not mention Samudra, is, Cowan says, a pointless question; he was on his way westward and had of sheer necessity to wait at Samara for a favourable wind.[20]

Further one can point to the fact that the use of the services of worldly-wise foreigners for overseas assignments of some weight is not unusual in Indonesia. This still happened in the 19th century. The father of Abdullah b. Abd al-Kadir Munshi, the author of the famous *Hikayat Abdullah,* who was of Arabo-Indian descent, acted as messenger of the ruler and the *raja muda* of Malacca to various little states in the Malay Peninsula and was entrusted with missions to Riau, Lingga, Pahang, Trengganu and Kelantan.[21] We need not conclude from this that the group to which they belonged was important and influential — they themselves had to inspire confidence and be equal to their task.[22]

The consequences of Cowan's identification for the appreciation of Marco Polo's report are clear. If Basma(n) is not Pase, then Marco Polo was never in Pase. The town was indeed not situated on the sea, but a certain distance upstream in the hinterland. If Samara is not Samudra, then all relevance to the Islamization of Samudra-Pase disappears — although this was a fact in 1297 in view of the gravestone of Malik al-Salih and, therefore, was considered to have come about between 1292 and 1297.

Meanwhile Fatimi is of the opinion that the year A.H. 696/A.D. 1297 after the "moving" of the Prophet which occurs on the gravestone should perhaps not be taken, as Moquette and everyone after him have done, as the year 696 of the Hijra, the Muslim era which begins with Muhammad's exodus to Medina, but as 696 years after Muḥammad's death. For the usual word *hijra* is not there, but instead *intiqāl*, a verbal noun deriving from *intaqala*, to emigrate, to pass over, and this same verb *intaqala* is used to indicate the death of Malik al-Salih. So the same word would have to be interpreted in the one sentence in two ways. If one does not accept this, Fatimi reasons, then one must assume, seeing that Malik al-Salih definitely died in the year 696 after the *intiqāl* of Muhammad, that his death occurred 696 years after the Prophet's death, hence in 1307. It is clear that this year supplies a more acceptable period for the transition from the abject heathendom said to have been encountered by Marco Polo to Islam, and so fits excellently into Fatimi's conception.

Nonetheless it is still surprising that the year should not have been calculated from the *hijra* but from Muhammad's death, and I do not believe that it is necessary to assume this. It is established that the word *intaqala*, with which the death of Sultan Mansur Shah of Malacca (died A.D. 1477) is likewise indicated on his gravestone (see *T.B.G.* Vol. LIX, 1921, p. 604), was used in the sense of "to pass over", "to die" in Arabic epitaphs in the Malay world. The reason for this is, it seems to me, obvious. People simply reverted to the Arabic original of the Malay term *bĕrpindah* as a refined expression of "to die", which literal rendering of an Arabic term must therefore have been already in vogue at that time. *Bĕrpindah* is in fact an abbreviation of *bĕrpindah kĕ-nĕgĕri yang baka*, the Arabic *intaqala ilā dār al-baqā'* (*dār al-ākhira*), to pass over (lit. move house) to the dwelling of eternity, the hereafter.[23] For the Malay reader with a command of Arabic it was quite clear that this "passing over" of the king meant something different from the "moving" (*intiqāl* = *hijra*) of the Prophet. So I stick to A.H. 696.

Fatimi derived further from the Chinese report of 1282 found in Parker[24] concerning the meeting of the Chinese and Sumatran travellers in Quillon in South India the fact that the title of the king of Su-mu-ta (Samudra) was *ta-kur*. This is apparently the same word as the Hindi *ṭhakur* (Skt. *ṭhakkura*) which means lord or master but which occurs in many North Indian languages, sometimes in other meanings,[25] and is also used as suffix after the name of Rajput nobles. In its anglicized form we know it in the name of the Bengali poet Rabindranath Tagore.[26]

Well then, Fatimi deduces from this title *takur*, too, that the Pase dynasty must have been of Bengali origin. With one exception I shall leave the remaining arguments which he produces, because the author himself notes that they are only conjectures "which in their present form require an imagination equal to that of the writer of the Hikayat, if they are accepted".[27] For Fatimi merrily juggles with place and personal names and he recoils least of all from wild conjectures. On one point, however, he is right: that is, where he points out that from ancient times, long before Islam, relations existed between Bengal and the Archipelago. There was sea traffic from the port of Tāmralipta in Bengal, as well as overland. It was from Bengal that the Śailendra realm received the form of Mahāyāna Buddhism which was dominant for centuries in the Archipelago. In about the middle of the 9th century the Sumatran Śailendra king Bālaputra Deva founded at Nālanda in Bengal a Buddhist monastery and set aside for its maintenance the five villages granted him by the then ruler of Bengal. The late Professor Bosch in 1925 devoted a fascinating and lengthy article[28] to the inscription from the great monastery of Nālanda in which this is laid down.

Bengal was overcome by the Muslims and Islamized in abut 1200, thus a century before Gujerat and South India. "It is not improbable", says Fatimi, "that this revolutionary change brought about a chain-reaction in North Sumatra, which was at the southern end of the Bay of Bengal" (*op. cit.*, p. 19). He considers this effect all the more acceptable, as the history of Islam in India mentions many great mystics who went to Bengal and there demonstrated great missionary fervour which even carried them to distant lands such as China. Why not then to Sumatra, which was so much closer, he wonders (*op. cit.*, p. 23).

With this ascription of Islamization to the preaching of Sufi holy men and great mystics Fatimi falls into line with Professor A.H. Johns, who wrote an article in the Journal of South-East Asian History of July, 1961 (Vol. 2, no. 2), entitled *Sufism as a Category in Indonesian Literature and History*, and in a later article returned to this subject yet again.[29]

Not wrongly in my view, Professor Johns opposes the conception he ascribes to both Schrieke[30] and Wertheim,[31] that the coming of the Portuguese may have contributed to a large degree to the spread of Islam in Indonesia. That process had, in fact, been going on for some centuries, and Islam was a growing power already before 1500. Professor Johns alleges that some local potentates even attempted to resist the spread of Islam by uniting with the Portuguese. One can indeed see in the instance of the heathen king of Sunda who signed a treaty with the Portuguese in 1522 an indication of the growing power of Islam on the north coast of Java before the Portuguese arrived.

It can, however, be seen from Pires' information that Pate Bubat, the Muslim lord of Surabaya who was involved in continuous strife with his heathen neighbours further to the eastward in Java, likewise sought friendship with the Portuguese, that Islam needed be no barrier to friendly relations with the Portuguese. The fact that the situation was different in the Moluccas, and that Muslim activity was intensified there, was due to the efforts of the Portuguese at Christianization.[32]

A century later the situation was no different. Writing on the Islamization of Macassar Noorduyn has stated that it was not prompted by political reasons and did not hamper friendly relations with the Dutch.[33] C. R. Boxer even observed that the real growth of Portuguese trade and influence in Macassar "occurred, oddly enough, after the Islamisation of Goa in the years 1605–07, and that, in later years, the rapprochement between the Muslim Macassars and the Catholic Portuguese was strengthened by their common dread of the growing Dutch power in Indonesian waters, and, more particularly, by their dislike of the Dutch efforts to monopolise the spicetrade of the Moluccas".[34]

However, when Professor Johns postulates a kind of world-wide Muslim mission, and in the spirit sees Muslim preachers going on board amid merchants with bales of produce "to attend to the spiritual needs of the craft or trade guild they were chaplain to, or to spread their gospel", then I cannot go along with him. It appears to me that in his efforts to expose what he calls "the internal dynamics" of Islam he has accorded the legendary tales of saints and preachers of Islam too great a significance. Since Snouck Hurgronje it is actually nothing new that Islam in Indonesia has had a strong mystical turn from the earliest times — and similarly with the significance of the mystical brotherhoods, although one must beware not to assume for Indonesia everything said by some to be associated with these in the Middle East. We know that Muslim scholars and saints travelled a lot, also in Indonesia, and not always for purely spiritual ends. Malay literature repeatedly mentions their arrival and the problems which were presented to them for solution. But nothing is known in Indonesia, to me at least, of "traders belonging to Sufi trade guilds, accompanied by their Sheikhs", and I cannot find in Professor Johns' paper any defense of this hypothesis. He does not produce new data which might have given his idea support.

No mention has been made above of the report from the History of the Sung Dynasty (960–1279), book 489, quoted by Groeneveldt in his well-known Notes on the Malay Archipelago and Malacca Compiled from Chinese Sources (*V.B.G.* Vol. XXXIX, 1876). This reads that it is five days' sailing from Java to the Tazi, which Groeneveldt wishes to take as Arabs on the west coast of Sumatra (*op. cit.*, p. 15 and note 2), whom he considered to have settled there very early.

An older report from the New History of the T'ang Dynasty (618–906), book 222, Chap. 2, contains a tale of a "prince of the Arabs" and a queen of Bali who was called Sima and may have come to the throne in 674.

It is understandable that those who would have Islam come direct from Arabia find these reports very important. But there is reason to doubt this, when one pays attention to what Groeneveldt says (p. 14, note 4), namely, that some Chinese authors confuse the west coast of Sumatra with Arabia, and one even has Muhammad make his appearance on the west coast of Sumatra. I support the view that the Chinese reporter, who was apparently telling a tall story about a land far, far away, simply made something out of it. Such an early settlement of Arabs in the Archipelago is confirmed nowhere else, though perhaps from time to time some Arabs may have strayed away from the usual Eastern trade route.

Neither have we yet mentioned the earliest Muslim inscription of Java on the renowned "stone of Léran", which is written in late Kufic script and according to Moquette contains the year A.H. 496/A.D. 1102. The name on the stone was read by Moquette as Faṭima bint Maimūn, a lady of whom nothing more is known; Ravaisse, however, read the name as: celle qui se garda du péché, qui fut à l'abri de la faute, la fille de Meimūn etc., and the date as 7 Rajab 475 = A.D. 1082.[35] Now this is a very early date for a Muslim gravestone in Indonesia. Moquette, who was very expert in the matter of gravestones, found it unacceptable that this inscription, shallowly incised in a soft type of stone, should have defied the damp tropical climate for so many centuries, so that he doubted very much whether this stone actually belonged in Java. He was inclined to assume that it had been brought to Java from an arid region, for example Arabia or that part of the world. In any case there is no connection with the second stone found at Léran which bears the chronogram 1313 (= A.D. 1391), and which in Javanese legend is supposed to cover the grave of a Putri Suwari together with the first mentioned stone. Neither is there any connection with the Malik Ibrahim mentioned on a gravestone at Grěsik from 833/1419, as legend would have it.

And thirdly there is also the stone of Trengganu, situated in the north of the present-day Malaya on the east coast. This is not a gravestone but an edict in which a Muslim ruler promulgated Muslim regulations in Malay and urged that they be observed. The inscription is the oldest Malay text in Arabic script; unfortunately the date is not established, as the stone is damaged at that spot. The English Malay scholar Blagden, who edited and translated the text, believes, rightly in my opinion, that the words *tujoh ratus dua* (702) could very easily be a *fragment* of a date, and thus by no means guarantee that the stone was erected in 702. Other words giving numbers could, of course, easily have followed the *dua* (2). Every scholar of Malay will back him up on this. Blagden himself decided in favour of the latest possible date, A.H. 788/789, = A.D. 1386–87; even so this is a full century before the Islamization of any state in the Malay Peninsula. Fatimi, however, settles for 702, = A.D. 1303. He constructs a second line of penetration of Islam in Indonesia, namely from China (where Arab colonies and Muslims were to be found centuries before) via Champa, which some consider to have been Islamized as early as the 11th century,[36] and the east coast of the Malay Peninsula to East Java. This penetration on the eastern flank would then explain both the very early year 1102 of the stone of Léran as well as the year 1303 of the Trengganu stone.

It seems to me a hypothesis for which too many uncertainties have been taken as firm facts. As far as East Java is concerned one can, for example, point to the fact that the Gujeratis called at Grěsik up to the beginning of the 15th century; Pires tells that a ship left by them would have stayed there for a long time after that. At about the same time Ma Huan wrote that the population in East Java was non-Muslim. So the Gujeratis had made no proselytes to speak of, though there will have been Muslims among them. The stone of Malik Ibrahim in Grěsik from 1419 is thus most probably that of a foreign Muslim trader. That is to say, Muslims did live in or come to Grěsik, but Islam had definitely not yet made much progress amongst the Javanese. This is evident only later in the 15th century, when there is mention of relations with South-East Asian Muslims, as appears from the marriage of a king of Majapait with a princess from Cěmpa (Champa).

Nevertheless it can be seen how difficult it is to speak with any certainty here from the thorough investigation which the French scholar L. C. Damais conducted on the gravestones of Trålåyå present at an Islamic burial-place just south of the spot where in all probability the kraton of Majapahit stood.[37] The stones have been known for a long time. They are mentioned, for instance, in the first edition of Veth's *Java* (1878). People had ascertained that there was Arabic script on them and L. W. C. van den Berg had read the inscriptions, and stated that the Arabic script was not beautiful, or at least much uglier than that on the stones of Grěsik and, therefore, had to be of a later date. As a consequence he had come to the conclusion that one was dealing with inscriptions which must have been made in comparatively recent times on stone fragments of old temples which happened to bear a date.

One will understand where the shoe pinches here: According to current Javanese opinion, the realm of Majapait fell in 1478, and in the second half of the 19th century no reason had been found to doubt the correctness of this dating. *Because* Majapait had thus not yielded to Islam before 1478, there *could* not have been any Muslim gravestones in Majapait from before 1478, and so the inscriptions on the stones of Trålåyå had to be of a later date.

In Brandes' edition of the *Pararaton* (1896) the Trålåyå stones and their years are likewise enumerated without, however, any mention of the Arabic inscriptions, but Rouffaer says cautiously in the article on chronology in the first edition of the *Encyclopaedie van Nederlandsch-Indië* (IV, 1905, p. 457): As long as the inscriptions of Léran, Trålåyå and Samudra have not been studied the earliest Arabic date to be found in the Archipelago is on the stone of Grěsik (that of Malik Ibrahim). In the second edition of the *E.N.I.* we again find, however, in the article on "Mohammedan Antiquities" (III, 1915, p. 203), which was written by Moquette and Hoesein Djajadiningrat, the idea of Van den Berg, just as in Krom's *Inleiding tot de Hindoejavaanse Kunst* (1920; second edition 1923).

Damais rejects this idea altogether. It would indeed be very remarkable, he says, if so often old stones from temples had been found which bore a year in such a way that a gravestone could be made from them with the year exactly in the place required.

The years on these gravestones are, with one exception, all in the Śaka era. They run, according to the decipherment of Damais, who was an experienced epigraphist, from 1298 Ś. to 1397 Ś., that is, from A.D. 1376 to 1475. One stone is of later date, i.e. from 1533 Ś, = 1611. The stone with a Hijra year is from A.H. 874, = 1391/92 Ś., = A.D. 1469/70. While the stones with Śaka dates all bear only verses from the Koran and pious formulas, the one with the Hijra year mentions the personal name Zainuddin — hence an Arabic name, but which could very well have been borne by a Javanese.

According to Damais' interpretation there were thus already Muslims of Javanese race in the capital of the realm in the time of Majapait's greatest prosperity under Hayam Wuruk. The influence of Islam in the interior, which until now could not be established before the year 1370 Ś. on the grave which is ascribed to the princess of Cĕmpa (a Muslim wife of one of the kings of Majapait), is thus already demonstrable more than 70 years earlier.

Seeing now that Islam must have penetrated the interior via the ports on the north coast of Java — perhaps mainly via Tuban, which although Muslim always remained on a good footing with Majapait — we must indeed accept (if we agree with Damais) that Islam had already gained a firm hold there in the 14th century, in about the middle or still earlier. Hence the long time between the earliest evidence of the presence of Islam in northern Sumatra and that of its presence in Java is considerably shortened.

To summarize my final impression after having read all these discussions, I come to the conclusion that their value lies more in that they have broken through the fascination with ideas which seemed well established, or even sacrosanct, than that they have provided acceptable new solutions. The only thing left of Marco Polo's report is that Pĕrlak was Muslim in 1292. From Malik al-Salih's gravestone, the year of which can indeed be kept as 1297, it appears that Samudra-Pase had a Muslim king in that year. But the basis for the idea that the Islamization of this state must have been completed between 1292 and 1297 has disappeared. It is at least uncertain whether Malik al-Salih's gravestone came from Gujerat, and according to Fatimi even wrong. Hence a Gujerat origin for Indonesian Islam comes to stand on a very rickety footing. But Pires' information that the land of origin was Bengal is, if only because of the difference in school of law, not immediately acceptable and what Fatimi produces to refute this argument cannot stand scrutiny.[38] Possibly Pires' informant was a Bengali from Malacca who claimed a Bengali origin for Islam in the Archipelago *ad maiorem gloriam* of his home-country. No support for this assertion can be found in Malay tradition or literature.

It is not impossible, though, that among the first Indian Muslims calling at Sumatran ports the Bengali element was much in evidence, since relations with Bengal were of long standing and this country was Islamized at an early date. But should these Bengalis have displayed proselytizing activities, then no traces of these have been left. On the other hand it is not without significance that the expert on religious matters is called *lĕbai* in Malay. As was pointed out by Van Ronkel[39] more than half a century ago, this clearly demonstrates the fact that not the Bengalis but rather a category of people known as *lĕbai* had a hand in the propagation of Islam in the Malay area.[40] Now Mal. *lĕbai* = Tamil *labbai* (written *ilappai*). It is irrelevant to the question under discussion whether one interprets this word as denoting the class of South Indian Shāfiᶜī Muslims called Labbai, who have their centre at Nagore on the Coromandel Coast, or as "merchant", "jeweller", according to its wider connotation. For in any case it bears testimony to the important rôle played by people from South India in the spread of Islam in the Archipelago.

Furthermore, Fatimi has produced no substantial arguments for his theory about two channels of Islamisation, a westerly and an easterly.

Marrison's article brings the matter back to

the line which was indicated by Snouck Hurgronje. Where Snouck Hurgronje speaks only of South India, Marrison narrows it, however, to the Coromandel Coast, although Islam obtained the supremacy no earlier here than in Gujerat. He rightly stresses the importance of the study of Islam in South India.

Bausani came to the same conclusion, but along quite a different path.

Fatimi points to the strong Sufi turn of Islam both in Bengal and in Indonesia. There is, however, no evidence in Malay literature of acquaintance with Bengali saints and mystics. Elsewhere too Indian Islam had a distinct mystical tinge and the Malay poetry of the 16th century Sumatran mystic Hamza Fansuri does give evidence of a close acquaintance with Arab and Persian mystics. But at that time the initial period of the spread of Islam lies far behind and the relations with the Muslims of the ports of the West Coast of India, where Arab and Persian influence was of long standing, were well-established.

In a nut-shell: the investigation has been reopened, but without new data is seems that the results will as yet be scanty. Resumption of the archaeological research in North Sumatra and painstaking study of Islam in South India — for which a thorough knowledge of Tamil is indispensable — appear to be primary requirements, as well as a revised and enlarged edition of Groeneveldt's *Notes . . . from Chinese sources.*

NOTES

1. Prof. S. Keyzer was the author of *Précis de Jurisprudence Musulmane par Abou Chodja*, Leiden, 1859.
2. G. K. Niemann, *Inleiding tot de kennis van den Islam, ook met betrekking tot den Indischen Archipel,* Rotterdam, 1861.
   J. J. de Hollander, *Handleiding bij de beoefening der land- en volkenkunde van Nederlandsch Oost-Indië,* 2 vols., Breda, 1861–1864.
   P. J. Veth, *Java, geografisch, etnologisch, historisch,* 3 vols., Haarlem, 1875–1882.
   John Crawfurd, *History of the Indian Archipelago,* 3 vols., Edinburgh, 1820.
3. D. J. Pijnappel, Over de Kennis, die de Arabieren voor de Komst der Portugeezen van den Indischen archipel bezaten, *BKI,* vol. 19, 1872, pp. 135–158.
4. Sauvaget, who republished the text and translation in 1948, showed that Suleiman was not the writer but was only an informant (*Relation de la Chine et de l'Inde,* p. XIX–XX). The writer is unknown.
5. Snouck Hurgronje, *Verspreide Geschriften* VI, p. 7.
6. Sometimes almost unrecognizably corrupted, as e.g. the "peculiar personal name" Meunua Djhō, regarded by Snouck Hurgronje (*De Atjèhers* II: 146 note 4) as having arisen from *benua Djohor,* the land of Johore, but explained by Bausani (Note sui vocabuli persiani in malese indonesiane, in *Annali dell' Instituto Universitario Orientale di Napoli,* Nuova Serie, Vol. XIV (1964), p. 31) as a corruption of Manučehr.
7. see note 6.
8. *op. cit.* p. 77 note. In a newspaper article written in 1899 (*V.G.* IV I: 403), however, he had mentioned Marco Polo at a breath with Ibn Baṭṭuṭā.
9. This must be a lapse; al-Muntaṣir died in 247/861. The last ᶜAbbās. caliph was called al-Mustaᶜṣim; his predecessor was al-Mustanṣir, who died in 1242. The latter was probably meant, but without further research it cannot be said whether the stone permits this reading; graphically there is only a slight difference.
10. *Tijdschrift Batav. Gen.* Vol. LII (1910), p. 599.
11. *ibidem* Vol. LIV (1912), p. 208; 536. See also his article Fabriekswerk in *Notulen Batav. Gen.* Vol. LVIII (1920), pp. 44–46. For that matter, the *Sĕjarah Mĕlayu* tells us that tombstones were imported from 'bĕnua Kĕling'; *vide* the story of the strong man Badang (*S.M.* ed. Djambatan 1952, p. 56).
12. *Rapporten van den Oudheidkundigen Dienst in Ned.-Indịë,* 1913, p. 9.
13. Cf. T. W. Arnold, *The Preaching of Islam*², London, 1913, p. 263, note 3.
14. Cf. Arnold, *op. cit.,* pp. 263–65, for a summary of this story as it is found in Zain al-Dīn's *Taḥfat al-Mujāhidīn.* Marrison does not apparently share Arnold's scepticism concerning the value of this tradition.
15. Namely Sultan Ahmad, in the Ht. Raja² Pasai called a great-grandson of Malik al-Salih, who was the father of the legendary hero Brahim Bapa mentioned in the Achehnese Hikayat Malém Dagang. Cf. H. K. J. Cowan, *De "Hikayat Malém Dagang",* 's-Gravenhage, 1937, pp. 35; 102–104.
16. On the conquest of Gujerat during the reign of Alauddin Khilji of Dihli (1296–1316), see: S. Krishnaswami Aiyangar, *South India and her Muhammadan Invaders,* 1921, p. 84.
17. *Islam comes to Malaysia,* publ. by the Malaysian Sociol. Research Inst. Ltd., Singapore 1963.

18. Snouck Hurgronje, *Het Gajō-land,* p. 77; R. A. Kern in *Geschiedenis van Ned.-Indië* ed. by F. W. Stapel, 1938, I, p. 310; Van der Tuuk in Von de Wall's *Maleisch-Ned. Wdbk.* under Pĕsaman; Schrieke, *Het Boek van Bonang,* p. 3 note 1.
19. *Notes on Marco Polo* (ouvrage posthume) I, Paris, 1959, p. 88. Pelliot was of the opinion that Basma could have originated from Basmā = Basman (*op. cit.,* p. 86), and that Port. Pacem (= Pase) could not be connected with this, because this name is only an example of the Portuguese tendency to nasalize final vowels, as was already noted by (*inter alios*) Blagden (in N. M. Penzer, *The Most Noble and Famous Travels of Marco Polo,* London, 1929).
20. Cowan's last remark is directed against Krom (*Bijdr.* Vol. 100 (1941), p. 17) who though finally deciding in favour of Samudra, was of the opinion that still "a lance could be broken" for Cowan's identification with Peusangan and Samarlanga.
21. *Hikajat Abdullah,* ed. R. A. Datoek Besar and R. Roolvink, Amsterdam, 1953, p. 8.
22. The Hindu ruler of Calicut (the Zamorin) sent a Muslim as emissary to the Tīmūrid Shāhrukh Bahādur (died 1447), which brought about the journey, known in Europe already in the 17th century, of ʿAbd al-Razzāq al-Samarqandī to Calicut to convert the Zamorin. This is described in his *Matlaʿ al-saʿdain wa-majmaʿal-bahrain.* See T. W. Arnold, *op. cit.,* p. 266; *The Căliphate,* Oxford, 1924, p. 113; *Enc. of Islam*[2], p. 91.
23. Cf. al-Bāqillānī (d. 1013), *Inṣāf,* ed. Muḥ. Zāhid al-Kawtharī, Cairo, 1369/1950, p. 55: .... *nubuwwāt al-anbiyā'* .... *lā tubṭalu wa-lā tankharimu bi-khurūjihim ʿani 'l-dunyā wa 'ntiqālihim ilā 'l-ākhira.* Death is only a *nugla min hāhunā,* a removal from this world, as Ghazālī says in 1. 20 of his poem on death (See: Johs. Pedersen, Ein Gedicht al-Gazālī's, in: *Le Monde Oriental,* Vol. XXV (1931) p. 235.
24. E. H. Parker, The Island of Sumatra, in *The Imperial and Asiatic Quarterly Review,* 3rd series, Vol. IX (1900).
25. Turner, *A Comparative Dictionary of the Indo-Aryan Languages.* No. 5488.
26. In *Hobson-Jobson,* p. 915 there is a quotation from the travels of Pyrard de la Val from 1610 which says that in the Maldives the nobles also attach *Tacourou* to their names. Perhaps we may connect this with the Bengali origin of the ruling family, which is mentioned by Ibn Baṭṭūṭa (Mahdi Husain, *The Reḥla of Ibn Baṭṭūṭa* Gaekwad Or. Series No. CXXII, Baruda, 1953, p. 204).
27. *op. cit.* p. 29.
28. In the *Tijdschrift van het Kon. Bat. Genootschap,* Vol. LXV (1925), pp. 509–588.
29. Muslim Mystics and Historical Writing, in *Historians of South-East Asia,* ed. D. G. E. Hall, London, 1961, p. 40.
30. As it would seem to me, in this respect more justice should be done to Schrieke, who certainly would not have endorsed the words of Wertheim quoted in the next note. In Schrieke's opinion Islam was a steadily increasing force in the Moluccas already before the coming of the Portuguese (mid 15th century), but the activities of the Roman-Catholic priests who followed in their wake contributed to the intensification of Muslim feeling. See his *Indon. Sociolog. Studies* I: 33.
31. *Indonesian Society in Transition.* The Hague, 1959, p. 1967: "one can sustain the paradox that the expansion of Islam in the Indonesian Archipelago was due to the Westerners". This opinion is likewise opposed by Syed Muhammad Naguib al-Attas in his book *Rānīrī and the Wujudiyyah of 17th Century Acheh.* Singapore, 1966.
32. H. Djajadiningrat, *Critische Beschouwing van de Sadjarah Banten,* thesis Leiden, 1913, p. 73; Pires, *Suma Oriental,* p. 196; Schrieke, Prolegomena, p. 155 (in *T.B.G.* Vol. LXV, 1925).
33. J. Noorduyn, De Islamisering van Makasar, *BKI,* Vol. 112 (1956), p. 262.
34. C. R. Boxer, Francisco Vieira de Figueiredo, A Portuguese Merchant-Adventurer in South East Asia, 1624–1667. *V.K.I.* Vol. 52 (1967), p. 3.
35. De oudste Mohammedaansche Inscriptie op Java, n.m. de Grafsteen van Léran, in: *Handelingen van het Eerste Congres voor de Taal-, Land- en Volkenkunde van Java,* Solo 25–26 December 1919. Weltevreden, 1921, pp. 391–399; Paul Ravaisse, L'Inscription coufique de Léran à Java, *T.B.G.* Vol. LXV (1925), pp. 668–703.
36. On Islam in Champa see the item "INDO-CHINA" by A. Cabaton in the *E.I.* A critical discussion of the question is given by Kōdō Tasaka in *Tōhōgaku* (Eastern Studies) of July, 1952, pp. 52–60.
37. Etudes javanaises I. Les tombes musulmanes datées de Trâlâyâ, in *B.E.F.E.O.* tome XLVIII (1956), pp. 353–415.
38. Thus Fatimi believes that he can conclude from the Achehnese term *balé' meudeuhab* that the Achehnese once belonged to the Ḥanafī school of law, because this expression is used to indicate the acceptance of a section of the teachings of the Ḥanafī school of law, because this expression is used to indicate the acceptance of a section of the teachings of the Ḥanafī school in some cases; see Snouck Hurgronje, *De Atjèhers* Vol. I, pp. 376 sqq.; Juynboll, *Handleiding Moh. Wet*[4], pp. 22, 23; 176. But Ach. *balé'*

does not mean "to return", as Fatimi (*op. cit.*, p. 34) assumes on the basis of Mal. *balik,* but "to change". *Balé meudeuhab* hence means no more than: to change rites, to follow another rite than the usual Shāfiʿī. There is no question of a "return".

On p. 38 great value is attached to a report in the highly unreliable *Annals of Acheen* (the chronicle published and translated by Dulaurier in the *Journal Asiatique* of 1839) that on Friday 1st Ramaḍān 601 (A.D. 1204) Sultan Johan Shah "came from the windward and converted the people of Acheen to the Muhammadan faith. He married the daughter of Baludri at Acheen and by her had a son, etc.". The fact that this "daughter of Baludri" must be understood as Ach. *aneu' baludari* = Mal. *anak bidadari,* hence a heavenly nymph, as H. Djajadiningrat already noted in *B.K.I.* Vol. 65 (1911), p. 142, note 3, certainly makes the report no less incredible than it already was. As is known, the *Bustan al-Salatin* ascribes the Islamization of Acheh to the founder of the realm, ʿAli Mughayat Shah, who died in 1522. Whether one doubts with Djajadiningrat the correctness of this report (*op. cit.,* p. 152 note 2) or not, the conclusion can be none other than that in Rānīrī's time (first half of the 17th cent.) in Acheh nothing was known of this early origin. The report concerning it will belong to the "learned conjectures of certain of the Achehnese" from a later period.

39. *T.B.G.* vol. LVI (1914), pp. 137–142. Note 9 on p. 5/6 of Fatimi's book, in which the views of Van Ronkel and T. W. Arnold on the derivation of *lĕbai* or *labbai* are assailed does no justice to either of them; moreover, the article on Java in the *E.I.* is ascribed to C.A.O. van Nieuwenhuijze, whereas its author is A. W. Nieuwenhuis. Van Ronkel did not derive Malay *lĕbai* from "*labaigem* or merchant". Evidently Fatimi has fallen a victim to a printer's error in the English edition of the *E.I.*, where indeed one finds (IV: 551 b) "*labaigem* merchant" (without "or"). This is obviously a misprint for "*labai,* gem merchant", as is shown by a comparison with the text of the German edition, where it says "*labai,* Juwelier". Neither did T. W. Arnold derive *labbai* from *ʿarabī.* He merely quoted popular opinion on the origin of this word by saying (*E.I.* IV:1) "Tamil, *ilappai,* said to be a corruption of *ʿarabī*".
40. In the *Hik. Hang Tuah* it is told that Hang Tuah knew the *bahasa Kĕling* and had acquired proficiency in this language owing to the fact he had been taught to recite the Qur'ān by a Kĕling *lĕbai* in Majapait. One may have one's doubts about the place, but the rôle of the South Indian merchant as a teacher of religion stands out clearly.

Islam in Southeast Asia: Problems of Perspective

A. H. JOHNS

Much has been written on the origins of Islamization in Southeast Asia, usually beginning with Pasai and other port towns along the northeast coast of Sumatra. Little is known of their early history, no more than is known of the beginnings of Islamic port towns along the north coast of Java. This is not the place or the occasion to discuss possible qualitative differences between these Muslim port cities and their non-Muslim predecessors on the one hand, or between them and the inland sacral centres such as Majapahit on the other, although it may be argued that the Islamic ethos brought about an increased measure of autonomy in secular activities. Be this as it may, there is no denying the vigorous role of secular and mercantile activity in the Islamic city as known in the heartlands of Islam, whether in the ports or in inland staging centres on traffic arteries or intersections.

With the coming of Islam to the city-state world of Southeast Asia, then, is it prudent to say that Muslim city-state equals Islamic city? Unfortunately, social historians of Islam do not give much attention to developments in our region, and the excellent collection of papers on the Islamic city edited by A. H. Hourani and S. M. Stern makes no reference to Southeast Asia.[1]

In his introductory chapter[2] Hourani constructs an ideal type of Islamic city, at the same time pointing out that it cannot be assumed that urban life in regions as diverse as Spain, Egypt, Syria, Central Asia, Iraq, Iran, and the Indian subcontinent — diverse in soil, climate, inheritance, and involvement in various commercial systems — should have taken the same form, and warning that the uneven distribution of research on the Islamic city in these widely differing regions creates the danger of imposing inappropriate models. The ideal type he proposes includes five components which might be common to many Islamic cities, although individually perhaps not exclusive to any one of them or necessarily characteristic of Islam.

These components are: a citadel or defence work; a royal city or quarter comprising the royal residence, administrative offices, and accommodation for the ruler's personal troops; a central urban complex with mosques, religious schools, and markets, with special places assigned for main groups of craftsmen or traders and the homes of the principal merchant and religious bourgeoisie; a "core" of residential quarters divided among resident foreign ethnic groups and religious minorities that enjoyed a degree of autonomy; and finally the outer quarters of "suburbs," where resided recent immigrants and temporary visitors to the city.[3]

There is nothing in this model irreconcilable with what we know, which is often little enough, of the Islamic port towns of Java and Sumatra already referred to or the later city-states of Malacca, Acheh, or Makassar. In each of them the presence of a fortress, royal compound, mosque and associated schools, commercial area, and the division of the residential parts of the city into quarters on the basis of ethnic groups — the kampong China, kampong Kling, kampong Java, and the like, each under its own captain — is sufficient to show that the concept of an "Islamic city" is a useful one and that, in any overall study of the Islamic city, such city-states deserve a place.

Such coastal city-states were centres for the diffusion of Islamic ideas to the peasant interior by means of kinship systems similar to those which had served to diffuse elements of Indic culture, adding a further colouring to the corpus of *adat* (a continually evolving code) already tinctured with Hindu-Buddhist beliefs. Though urban and peasant systems represent points on a continuum rather than mutually exclusive and alternative ways of life, the peasant end of the continuum is less likely to be intensely Islamic and more likely to reveal different levels of ideological tincture than the urban end.

The two most important Islamic city-states in the Malay world between the fifteenth and seventeenth centuries are Malacca and Acheh, and these approximate closely in structure and function to Hourani's model. There is a large body of writing in Portuguese relating to Malacca, and an even larger body of material in various languages relating to Acheh. To each state likewise can be attributed a significant corpus of writing in Malay. The most comprehensive account of this corpus is given in Sir Richard Winstedt's *A History of Classical Malay Literature.*[4] Unfortunately, although the work contains a wealth of material not duplicated elsewhere, the assumptions and expectations which have determined its structure are analogous to those which bedevil Southeast Asian history generally; that Malay is an undifferentiated category, that it has a classical period, in which is to be defined a golden age, that it is susceptible of a linear historical treatment, and so on. A glance at the table of contents shows that a historical frame of reference cannot be maintained. Since there is little in much Malay writing to indicate a date of composition, Winstedt is forced to use cultural content and genre as guides to periodization, and on this basis he assigns works to a Hindu, Transitional or Muslim period, regarding the Malacca sultanate (1400–1511) as the central "core" to which all that is worthwhile in Malay letters can be related.[5]

A little reflection reveals what has gone wrong. The same types of temporal and spatial discontinuity are apparent in Malay letters as in the pasts of various Malay city-states, whether on the Malay Peninsula, Sumatra, or Borneo. Just as the peasant base of the urban centres absorbed successive cultural tinctures, and not in uniform proportions or in any particular distribution or consistency, so the varying proportions of Islamic or Hinduistic material in a manuscript which may date at the oldest from the eighteenth century may tell us something about the society in which the story was popular, but they can tell nothing about its position on a temporal continuum indicated by the terms Hindu-Transition-Islamic because of the continuing presence of elements of both these and earlier traditions in differing strata of society.

Accordingly, just as in our survey of the past of the region we found it necessary to avoid broad categories and to distinguish between city-states and the peasant background out of which they rose and into which they were reabsorbed, so it is necessary to distinguish between works which can be ascribed to a court or bourgeoisie and those which belong to the folk tradition and at one stage or another were set down in written form; the latter require treatment and study rather different from that given to literature proper, although both may spring from the same cultural matrix. Such an amputation from the received body of Malay literature may appear radical, but it is necessary if we are to attempt to discover a clearer profile of Malay intellectual and literary life. The procedure in many cases is simple, but it reveals important perspectives that have often been overlooked. Every textbook tells us that Malay literature, at least until the time of Islam, is anonymous. But insofar as it is folk literature, of course it is anonymous, whether before Islam or after. And it is anonymous because it is folk literature, not because it is Malay. By the same token, if the first works in

Malay to which we can ascribe an author are Islamic, this once again is not because they are Malay but because they are Islamic; they hail from an Islamic city-state in which the various components of the Muslim city exist in a particular constellation and the activities of the *'ulamā'* play a significant role. And in Islamic learning, the foundations of every discipline are the authority on which any opinion or doctrine is based and its transmission.

A study of that body of writings which can be definitely associated with urban life in the Malay world reveals two foci of literary activity. In the first place there is the court. Under its aegis "chronicles" were compiled to legitimize the dynasty, record its family tree, and preserve its values and mores for the edification and example of later generations; and its library included stories of heroes, men of righteousness of before and after the call of the Prophet Muhammad, to be read as models of courage in times of crisis and around which hung an aura of sanctity, and *belles lettres* of various sorts.

Of a Malaccan court heritage, if heritage is not too grandiose a word, there is very little that remains directly, and not all that Winstedt thought derived from the Malaccan period is necessarily from Malacca. Even the Raffles manuscript of the *Sejarah Melayu*, the original text of which Winstedt believed dated from 1535, in fact is probably not earlier than 1612 and was compiled in Johore.[6] But if it presents a reliable picture of the cultural bric-a-brac extant a century earlier in a different place, then the Malacca court library could have included a version of the Alexander romance and epics of the heroes of Islamic tradition such as Muhammad Hanafiyyah and Amir Hamzah.[7]

In the second place there is the community of teachers of religion, the *'ulamā'*, to whose activities can be attributed the wide range of Muslim learning which became known in the Malay world. The exposition and administration of Islamic law, whether it concerns religious duties or the legal formulation of trade contracts, is a complicated but necessary chore in any Muslim society. Though we know little of the majority of these *'ulamā'* as individuals, as a class we know they existed and had a function and social disposition at least approximate to that of the *'ulamā'* in Hourani's model.

The great lacuna, of course, is in our knowledge of the bureaucratic processes of the state and details of business contracts and procedures. We lack a Malaccan or Achehnese equivalent of the Cairo Geniza, with its massive collection of trade contracts, marriage agreements, petitions to authorities, private letters, and even fragments of literary works, between the tenth and thirteenth centuries A.D.[8] Little of this kind of material survives except for a few blank forms for the manumission of slaves.

We are thus forced into a world of speculation. Yet there is one work which might be attributable to a Malaccan bourgeoisie, although later copies of it have been preserved only in court libraries. I refer to the *Hikayat Bayan Budiman* (Tale of the Wise Parrot), a fragment of which, now preserved at the Bodleian Library, may have found its way to Europe as early as 1598.[9]

It is perhaps the most remarkable work in old Malay secular literature. Although a rendering of a Persian work, there is nothing of "translationese" in the style: it is limpid and polished. The rhythmic character of its prose probably derives from the oral tradition, and the brief introduction setting out the parents and birth of the hero could reflect expectations conditioned by folklore, but it is none the less a work of considerable sophistication. A "miraculous" element such as the prescience of the parrot is used simply as a literary convention, not as a spectacle of wonder to hold interest. The setting is completely bourgeois; in the first demonstration of his wisdom, the parrot gives his master a business tip that enables him to buy up all the spikenard in Iran three days before a caravan arrives desirous of just this commodity, and thus to make a huge profit. The work shows a delicious irony in its asides at the morals of royalty and clergy, and its psychological insights are superb. One would expect it to be the property of a wealthy merchant family used to the finer things of life. One swallow, however, does not make a summer, and the vision of a wealthy Malaccan class of the third estate passing its leisure in the savouring of such works must be left as an alluring hypothesis.

That Acheh should be so often presented simply as a successor state to Malacca is another example of the distortions that occur when the past of Southeast Asia is viewed through the glasses of divisions created by the colonial powers. Malacca looms much larger in the past of twentieth-century Malaysia than Acheh in that of Indonesia, and thus it has a correspondingly greater role to play in the mythology of a modern nation. Yet in the seventeenth-century polity of city-states Acheh is not only much better known but on all available evidence it appears to have been the more important of the two, with a wider range of international relations and a far more clearly articulated religious intellectual life. It seems to have been a centre where a vigorous, intensely Muslim maritime kingdom, self-sustaining in trade as in religious life, could have developed. The number of religious works produced under its aegis, whether original or translations, is striking by Malay standards. Its role as gateway to the holy land for the *jawi*[10] pilgrims and students bound for Mecca, Medina, and centres of learning in Egypt and other parts of the Ottoman empire kept it in close contact with other Muslim port cities in the archipelago and made it a natural centre for an *'ulamā'*-bourgeoisie axis. Once again one can but hypothesize on the basis of Hourani's model, for only snippets of information are available. Of religious teachers, only four are relatively well known to us: Hamzah Pansūrī, (d. c. 1600), Shams al-Dīn (d. 1630), al-Rānīrī (d. 1657) and 'Abd al-Ra'ūf (d. 1690). Of al-Rānīrī it should be noted that he was a Gujerati scholar and prolific writer who won the favour of Sultan Iskandar Thani of Acheh in 1637 and led a witch hunt against the mystical doctrines of Hamzah Pansūrī and Shams al-Dīn.[11] Their works add up to a significant corpus of religious writing, which, although modest by Middle Eastern standards, gives some picture of the intellectual life of the city, its enthusiasms, shibboleths, and achievements, and provides a reference point for much transmission of learning to centres of Islam in other parts of the archipelago. While acknowledging this, one should be very cautious in assuming a linear development in Islam between one point and another. Rather, the same discrete character of the city-states of Southeast Asia is paralleled by autonomy and diversity in the distributions of emphases in their cultural and religious life. The point needs to be stressed since the expectations of Western historiography exert a kind of pressure to formulate generalizations based on larger units which appear to make sense yet somehow succeed only in obscuring the character of Islamization. Such a generalization, for example, is van Nieuwenhuijze's remark that Shams al-Dīn's mysticism in more than one respect "stands midway between the Indian and Javanese forms of Islamic mysticism."[12] It is simply not possible to plot a line of development between the forms of Indian and Javanese mysticism on which Shams al-Dīn can be allocated a place. The most that can be done is to compare his mysticism with that of a particular place in Java or the Indian subcontinent at a particular time. Neither India nor Java is a meaningful term in this context.

Islamic writing in Malay has not had a very good press. Winstedt complains bitterly about what he alleges to be the bad influence of the Arabic idiom on Malay and what he considers frequently unintelligible translations from Arabic in the tradition of *kitab* writing generally.[13] Hooykaas virtually excludes Muslim writing from his book *Over Maleis Literatuur* on the grounds that it is "more generally Islamic than Malay."[14]

In recent years Malay writing has been treated less patronizingly and with more insight.[15] The sad fact remains, however, that among Islamologists, Arabic religious writing of the seventeenth century does not have a good name, its authors being overlooked or regarded merely as transmitters of ideas better formulated and expressed elsewhere. This has two unfortunate consequences. The first is that the trained Islamologist is likely to regard Malay Muslim writing of the seventeenth century as at the lowest rank of a pecking order in a classification already well down on everyone's list. The second is that very little research has been done on the level of scholarship and writings of the Middle Eastern scholars under whom the *jawi* studied. The result is that the study of such Malay works has in great measure had to be the undertaken without that detailed study of the lines of transmission which can show a work in its proper perspective. The necessary infrastructure to make this possible is not yet available.

The seventeenth century, however, should be given its due. Perhaps its authors were not individually of the stature of the giants of Islam, but they were in close touch with the spirit and needs of their time. They belonged to the intelligentsia of their age, and they were guides to prince and pedlar alike. To them the Islamic world was one world, and they met one another on equal terms at Mecca, Medina, and other great centres of learning in the Middle East. Their writings are still human material, and within them can be discerned the pulse of human endeavour. And this is true even when Malay writing on Islamic matters has little to commend itself on the grounds of "originality."

We are thus returned to the role of a great tradition in attempting to assess and interpret the Muslim intellectual life of the Islamic city-states, taking as a fundamental point of departure that the holy cities of Mecca and Medina and University cities such as Cairo provide the norm, the core, the principle of order in all such activity, and supply that link with tradition that preserves the organic character of the Muslim world through a complex web of relationships between teacher and pupil, a network which in the seventeenth century was reinforced and enriched by the great Sufi confraternities.

Thus, important as it is to see what can be made of the writings of *jawi* authors at particular port cities, accepting them as they are in terms of their own environment, it is equally if not more important to study the lives and works of their Middle Eastern teachers, in which are to be found the norms and lines of transmission we require.

NOTES

1. A.H. Hourani and S.M. Stern (eds.), *The Islamic City* (Oxford, 1970).
2. *Ibid.*, pp. 9–24.
3. *Ibid.*, pp. 21–23.
4. R. Winstedt, "A History of Classical Malay Literature," *JMBRAS*, 31, 3 (1958).
5. *Ibid.*, pp. 129–132, 141, 152, and passim.
6. R. Roolvink, "The Variant Versions of the Malay Annals." *Bki*, CXXIII, 3 (1967): 311.
7. Winstedt, pp. 72–73.
8. S.D. Goitein, *Studies in Islamic History and Institutions* (Leiden, 1966), pp. 279–294.
9. Winstedt, pp. 95–98.
10. *Jawi* is the term used in Mecca for all pilgrims from the Malay world. It is both sufficiently specific and sufficiently general for our purposes.
11. Winstedt, pp. 113–122.
12. C.A.O. van Nieuwenhuijze, *Samsu'l-Dīn van Pasai* (Leiden, 1945), p. 239.
13. Winstedt, p. 6.
14. C. Hooykaas, *Over Maleis Literatuur* (Leiden, 1947), p. vii.
15. Over the past decade or so G.W.J. Drewes and P. Voorhoeve have been adding steadily to texts at our disposal and to knowledge of personalities. Nor should one overlook the important contributions and reassessments provided by al-Attas S.M.N. in *The Mysticism of Hamzah Pansuri* (Kuala Lumpur, 1970).

Islam and Malay Kingship[1]

A. C. MILNER

Every Malay considered himself to be living not under a divinely revealed law but under a particular Raja, an institution which, it will be seen, had deep roots in the Malay world's animistic and Indian-influenced past.[2] The Malay word often translated as "state" or "government", *kerajaan*, means literally "the condition of having a Raja". The Raja, not the Malay race or an Islamic *umma* (community) was the primary object of loyalty; he was central to every aspect of Malay life. It is not that he monopolized all military or economic power, but that those pursuing military or economic ends did so through the idiom of "Rajaship". It was said, for instance, of the rich and apparently powerful territorial chiefs of Siak, that "outside the *kerajaan* they are nothing".[3]

Malays referred to themselves as the slaves (*patik*) of the Raja, and the latter owned all the land in his territory.[4] The law, too, was said to be the Raja's "possession". The *Undang-undang Melaka* describes the reigning Sultan as owning (*mempunyai*) the laws, and the blend of Islamic and customary laws listed in the digest appears to have as its reference point the Raja. The laws gain their authority, it would seem, from having been laid down by the Raja and executed by his officials. The introduction to the *Undang-undang* explains that these customs (*adat*) "come down to us" from the time of Alexander the Great, and that it was his descendant, Sultan Mohammed Shah, the first Muslim ruler of Melaka, who first laid them down". These customs and laws were then, continues the text, handed down from ruler to ruler, and are in the possession of (*mempunyai*) the reigning Sultan. Finally, it is the Rajas' representatives (*ganti*) who are expected to administer these customs and laws.[5]

After the introductory paragraphs, the laws themselves are related. The first chapters concern sumptuary rules which regulate the costume, language and behaviour of the different ranks of royal subject and which exhibit the special position of the Raja. The circumstances allowing one to kill without the knowledge of the ruler and his ministers are next described, and the following chapters provide, for the ruler's officials, guidance in settling a wide range of disputes. Finally, in an appendix added at the order of a later Sultan, the reader (or listener) is warned that "Whosoever trangresses against what has been stated in the *Undang-undang* is guilty of treason against his Majesty".[6]

In the *Undang-undang Melaka*, therefore, law is presented as an aspect of Rajaship. The principles set out in this digest are often echoed in Malay writings. According to the so-called Trengganu stone, which dates back at least to the 14th century, the Ruler is "the expounder on earth" of laws;[7] the *Hikayat, Pahang* describes the Sultan of Pahang as "disseminating both Islamic and customary law",[8] and a Sumatran text portrays law (and

Reprinted in abridged form from *Journal of the Royal Asiatic Society of Great Britain and Ireland*, Vol. 1 (1981), 46–70, by permission of the author and the Royal Asiatic Society of Great Britain and Ireland, London, United Kingdom.

the Malay word here is *syariat*), together with customs and ceremonial, as being "in the hands" of the Raja.[9]

Although the Raja is presented as the focus of law, he is not generally portrayed as playing an active part in the legal process. To the extent that the ruler was involved actively in political life he was concerned primarily with what we might term ceremonial matters. Ceremony, like law, was "in his hands"; he was the focus of ceremonial occasions and the giver of titles which determined where a man sat and how he was to be attired. European reports confirm that these formal state functions held enormous importance for Malays,[10] and the Malay passion for titles was often noted. Even in the colonial period, a British official bemoaned the fact that Malay chiefs were "never content with the reality of power . . . they imperil it for the sake of empty titles".[11] Titles, however, were far from empty. In a community where, as a sociologist[12] has recently described it, men's lives were *public* rather than *private*, identity was encapsulated in a profound way in such apparently superficial emblems as titles. Moreover, titles had implications for the next as well as this life. Malay literature abounds with evidence of Malay concern for death status[13] and it is explained, in a text from East Sumatra, that the rank a man attains in this world "is honoured in the next".[13] Standing at the hub of the ceremonial structure which, in the Malay view, was the real substance of the Malay state, the Malay Sultan was thus able to suggest to his loyal subjects that their loyalty would be rewarded by God.[15]

This Malayo-Muslim polity, the Raja-centred, ceremonial, *kerajaan*, stands in strong contrast to the image of an Islamic state as a community of the faithful governed by *sharīʿa* law. The *kerajaan* also possessed deep roots in pre-Islamic times. It is not just that Indian and animistic elements were, and are, ingredients in Malay kingship, but the fragmentary evidence of pre-Islamic times suggests the Malay ruler's position was little altered by the arrival of the new religion.

The pre-Islamic ruler appears to have been the focus of political and spiritual life, at least in what has been called the Indianized period, and Malays drew upon Buddhist and Hindu writings to describe his position: the pre-Islamic founder of Melaka is portrayed in unmistakable terms in the Malay Annals as a *boddhisattva*,[16] the Buddhist enlightened being who renounces *nirvana* in order to remain in this world and assist the spiritual liberation of his fellow beings. The scant documentation from the early Malay empire of Srivijaya contained in the 7th-century inscriptions of South Sumatra, also reveals a *boddhisattva* figure offering his "loyal" subjects an "immaculate tantra" and "eternal peace".[17] The word translated as "loyal" is *bhakti* "devotion", and it suggests the devotion which Devotionalist Hindus (*Bhaktis*) expressed toward their teacher or *guru*; he was, of course, no ordinary teacher but assumed a God-like position in the eyes of his followers. Like a Malay ruler, and also in the fashion of a *boddhisattva*, his manner was often described as courteous and gentle and his words as "fragrant and beautiful"; moreover the guru is able to bestow on his devotees *anugerah* or divine graciousness.[18] This Sanskrit word *anugraha*, is precisely the term used by Muslim Malays to describe the gift of a prince.[19] The Indian element which is lacking in the early documentation of the Malay world is the dominance of a Brahmin class, the interpreters of the all-embracing *dharma*, the sacred law which is merely obeyed and implemented by the Indian king.[20] In the Malay world, as in other parts of Southeast Asia, the importation of Indian ideas was selective. Certain notions were accepted and persisted because they were intelligible and useful. It is not unreasonable, therefore, to conjecture that the ruler-centred polity, the *kerajaan*, existed, at least in embryo form, in the period prior to Indianization.

The development of the Malay *kerajaan* can never be described with certainty, but the *kerajaan* does not appear to have been radically altered by the arrival of Islam. The ceremonial structure of the Malayo-Muslim state, the titles and the rituals which displayed the worldly and spiritual achievements of Malays, were often of pre-Islamic origin; and the Muslim Sultan who suggested to his loyal subjects that they would be rewarded by God was echoing the Srivijayan ruler's promise of "eternal peace".

To emphasize the pre-Islamic origins of the *kerajaan*, however, is not to assume that Islamic political thinking was not taken seriously by

Malay rulers. On the contrary, the active part played by the Rajas is a feature of the Islamization process, a feature which suggests they found some aspect of the religion appealing. The prominence of rulers in the introduction of Islam is recorded in both Malay and European accounts. The *Malay Annals* describe the Raja, Sultan Mohammed Shah, as the first in the state to be converted, and relate that he then "commanded" all the people of Melaka "whether of high or low degree" to become Muslims.[21] A later Sultan of Melaka is described by a Portuguese writer, Tomé Pires, as "instructing" kings of other Malay states "in the things of Mohammed, because he knew all about them".[22] But Pires does not suggest that the Rajas were the first members of the community to adopt Islam. He relates that a large number of "Moorish merchants" existed in the region, and that many of them came to Melaka accompanied by "mollahs". The "mollahs" tried to convince the king "to turn Moor" and the king eventually came to "like them".[23] Muslim domination of the Indian Ocean trade in the years preceding Islamization is well known;[24] but at best we can make only an informed guess regarding what the Raja discussed with his "mollah" favourites.

The evidence suggests that Malay Rajas were attracted to two features of Islam. As we shall see, these are not features of which modern Muslim fundamentalists would approve: they consider that these features are not well grounded in the teachings of the Qur'ān. But the Islamic elements which interested the Malay rulers were characteristic of the medieval Muslim world. The elements the Rajas took from Islam both concern leadership. The first is the Persian tradition of kingship, a tradition which, it will be seen, had been assimilated into medieval Islam.

Malay utilization of this medieval Islamic tradition of kingship was expressed at the most obvious level in the adoption of titles and descriptive formulae from the Persianized Muslim world.[25] The Malay Rajas are often portrayed as having adopted Muslim titles immediately upon adopting Islam. On his conversion, Merah Silu, the ruler of Pasai, received the Arabic title, Sulṭān, and an assembly was held at which his chiefs and people proclaimed Merah Silu to be "God's Shadow on Earth" (*ẓill Allāh fī 'l-'ālam*).[26] Such titles are also displayed on coins. The coins from 15th-century Melaka, for instance, proclaim the ruler Sulṭān, Shāh, and "Helper of the World and of the Religion" (*Nāṣir al-dunyā wa 'l-dīn*),[27] in Kedah, Trengganu and Johor, the coins refer to the Raja as "Caliph" and the same title is found in a legal digest from Pahang.[28] Time and again Malay texts apply to rulers the formula "Shadow of God on Earth".[29] A Portuguese account of 16th-century Pasai, notes that the people of that state believed the "king" was the "one who governed on earth in place of God".[30] This theme is carefully developed in a range of Malay writings. The *Sejarah Melayu* explains that "a just prince is joined with the Prophet of God like two jewels in one ring. Moreover, the Raja is as it were the deputy of God. When you do your duty to the Prophet of God it is as though you were doing your duty to God himself".[31] The Pahang legal digest,[32] and the 17th-century text *Tāj al-sālatīn,*[33] also invoke the "two jewels in one ring" formula to explain the position of the Raja.

All three of these texts, the *Sejarah Melayu*, the Pahang laws and the *Tāj al-salāṭīn*, seek in the Qur'ān support for their claims on behalf of the Raja. The Qur'ān is not a comforting text, however, for those who cherish a Raja-centred polity, and the interpretation placed upon certain passages by these Malay authors angers many modern Muslims. In particular the Pahang laws translate *Sūra* XI, 30, as stating not that God placed Adam on earth as his representative, but that he had "placed the Raja on earth as his representative".[34]

The first observation which must be made about these new titles and formulae enhancing kingship is that they would not have been utilized initially to justify the ruler's position to the Malay community. The old Malay royal title, Yang di Pertuan, the "One who is made Lord",[35] or the Sanskrit, *rāja,*[36] which were retained after Islamization, were not obviously less spendid epithets than Sultan or Shāh. It is equally unlikely that the position of "God's Shadow on Earth", of the privilege of being linked to the Prophet like "two jewels in one ring", would be seen as radically superior to *boddhisattva*-hood.

If the new titles and formulae were no grander than the old ones however, they were also not inferior. They would not diminish the ruler's authority in the eyes of his old subjects, yet they would permit him to explain his position to the Muslim community in the port.[37] Like the inclusion of *sharīʿa* elements in the Malay legal digests they were an aspect of the ruler's response to the Islamization of the Indian Ocean trade route.

The fact that Islam possessed the ideological apparatus to contribute to Malay kingship, it must be admitted, is at first glance surprising. There is much in Islamic teaching to suggest that the adoption of Islam would challenge the basis of the Raja-centred *kerajaan*. The Malay polity, as we have seen, differed greatly from the image of a *sharīʿa*-governed community. Indeed Muhammad is quoted as having warned that "whenever a man accedes to authority he drifts away from God";[38] and when an Arab chief, after conversion, told the prophet, "You are our Prince", Muhammad replied "the prince is God, not I".[39] So strong is the tension between government and religion in Islamic doctrine that, in the view of one modern scholar, "Islam knows no kingship".[40]

The medieval Muslim world, however, certainly knew "kingship", and in acquiring titles and formulae from that world which would support the Raja's position, Malays were not choosing an obscure or heterodox version of Islam.

In the medieval period, as is well known, the *sharīʿa*-based community was only one political ideal in the Islamic world; another and important ideal was the Persian-inspired vision of a society articulated round the institution of kingship. Persian influence is evident first in the development of the institution of the Caliphate. Originally a prosaic rather than an imperial institution, the Caliphate began to adopt the characteristics of Persian monarchy at the time of the Abbasid regime, based at Baghdad, not far from the heart of the old Persian Empire. Persian notions of the "cosmic ruler", whose presence created a state of peace even among animals, encouraged the emergence of a new type of Islamic caliph.[41] The old Babylonian epithet, "God's Shadow, on Earth",[42] was attributed to him, and the "light of prophecy" was said to shine round the Caliph's forehead. His subjects kissed the ground before him, an honour once reserved for God, and he was believed to radiate divine blessings.[43] In the 'Abbasid period, then, there developed within the Islamic world an Imperial Caliph in direct line of succession to the pre-Islamic kingship of Iran.

By the time Islam was adopted in the Malay lands, however, spiritual and political leadership in the Muslim world had ceased to be the monopoly of one Caliph.[44] The Baghdad Caliph became only one of the Persianized monarchies in Islam. In the 11th century, the Saljuqs assumed a new and potent title, Sulṭān; they were soon, in the manner of the Caliph, also called "Shadow of God on Earth" and portrayed as fulfilling the role played by the Persian king of pre-Islamic times.[45] Later in the century, in India, the Delhi Sultans introduced the obligation of prostration before the monarch and the epithet "Shadow of God upon Earth".[46] During the 14th century similar honours were assumed by the Mārīnid ruler of Morocco,[47] and Muhammad b. Tughluq of Dehlī declared, "He who obeys the Sultan obeys God".[48] Before long even the relatively unimportant rulers of Bengal assumed, in the manner of the Saljuqs, the old Persian title Shāh,[49] and called themselves Khalīfa.[50] The ruler of 14th-century Madura in south-eastern India was also designated Shāh,[51] and the Sultan of Bījapūr was called "Shadow of God".[52]

On the eve of Islamization in the Malay world, therefore, there existed an expanding galaxy of Persianized Muslim Sultans, who — on the face of it — performed roles and possessed titles not far different from those of the pre-Islamic Malay Raja. The "mollahs" who accompanied Muslim traders coming to Pasai or Melaka would have brought news of these developments,[53] and, in a world increasingly dominated by Islam, it would have been tempting, and certainly not disadvantageous, for Malay Rajas to see themselves as members of the Muslim galaxy.

The Persian-influenced notions of kingship, then, were the first aspect of Islam which attracted Malay rulers. The second, but not necessarily less important feature of Islam which they appear to have discussed with the learned Muslims who visited their courts was Sufism or mysticism.

In a number of articles on Sufism in South

East Asia,[54] Professor A. H. Johns has demonstrated the danger of interpreting Islamization solely in political or commercial terms; both Malay and European documents indicate that spiritual questions were important matters of state for a Malay raja. It was his duty to obtain knowledge of the latest spiritual doctrines or techniques and to utilize them for the benefit of his subjects. Just as the pre-Islamic ruler was portrayed as a *boddhisattva* figure, caring for the spiritual welfare of his people, more recent Malay Rajas even summoned Christian missionaries to discuss with them the "world to come".[55]

The particular mystic doctrine which appears to have caught the attention of the Malay Rajas during the early period of Islamization was the doctrine of the "Perfect Man". The documentation regarding this matter is especially tenuous: Sufī questions would have been little understood by foreign writers and, as we shall see, reference to Sufīsm in Malay writings would often invite censorship on the part of later Malay copyists.

The Malay Raja's interest in the "Perfect Man", the saintly figure who has "fully realized his essential oneness with the Divine Being" and who, *boddhisattva* like, guides his disciples along the path he has trodden,[56] emerges gradually from the records of the 15th- and 16th-century Malay world. The Pasai chronicles, the *Hikayat Raja-raja Pasai*, imply that a 14th-century ruler of Pasai, one of the first Malay states to adopt Islam, gained magical power as a consequence of being Muslim. When an Indian yogi, skilled in magic arts, comes into the Sultan's presence and performs miraculous tricks, the yogi, overawed by the sanctity or *keramat* of the Sultan, falls to the ground.[57] *Keramat* is the Arabic word *karāma*, referring to the magical gifts of Muslim saints, men whose "ecstasy and rapture" are, in Professor Nicholson's words, an outward sign of their "passing-away" from the phenomenal self.[58] Contests in the performance of miracles, such as that occurring between the Pasai ruler and the yogi, were commonplace among Sufis.[59]

Further indications of the Malay Raja's interest in the "Perfect Man" are to be found in the *Malay Annals*. Sultan Mansur (1456–77), it is related, was particularly impressed by a Maulana Abu Bakar, a student of Maulana Abu Ishak, who, according to the text, was "very knowledgeable in the science of Tasauwuf" or mysticism.[60] Maulana Abu Ishak wrote a book, *Durr Mandzum*,[61] which his student took to Melaka and which aroused the interest of Sultan Mansur. This book has not been identified, but the Malay Annals explain it was written in two languages: *bahasa sifat*, plain language, and *bahasa zat*, the language of things as they are, that is, the esoteric language of mysticism.[62] The ruler of Melaka sends the *Durr Mandzum* to Pasai for explanation and is pleased with the result. He then asks the Pasai divines a question: "Do those in heaven and those in hell remain there forever?" The answer from Pasai is the orthodox one that they do remain in their respective places, but the Sultan of Melaka is not satisfied. He then obtains a second answer with which he is pleased: the *Malay Annals* do not record that answer.

Several scholars have observed that the Melaka ruler's question, and its probably esoteric answer, were an indication that Malays were acquainted with the work of the 15th-century mystic, Jili.[63] Jili ('Abd al-Kārim al-Jīlī, d. A.D. 1417) and his 13th-century predecessor, Arabi (Muhyī al-dīn b. al-'Arabī, A.D. 1165–1240), were certainly known in the 16th-century Malay world; they were quoted, for instance, in writings from Sumatra.[64] Together Arabi and Jili are responsible for the development of the notion of the "Perfect Man".

The appropriateness of the "Perfect Man" to Malay rajahood is obvious, and the *Malay Annals* provide further indications that the concept was influential in Melaka. Thus, in the midst of the Portuguese attack on the city in 1511 Sultan Ahmad is described as mounting his elephant, accompanied by his spiritual advisor, Makhdum Sadar Johan. The Sultan, it is explained, was studying the doctrine or technique (*ilmu*, Arabic *'ilm*) of the unity of God (*tauhid*, Arabic *tawḥīd*). The text continues: "And the King went forth onto the bridge and stood there amid a hail of bullets. But Makhdum Sadar Johan, clasping the saddle with both hands, cried out to Sultan Ahmad Shah: 'Sultan this is no place to study the unity of God, let us go home'."[65]

At one level this is an amusing incident but it may reveal something of the Sultan's spiritual preoccupations. Every Muslim believes in the unity of God (*tawḥīd*), but the concept holds a special meaning for the mystic. To the mystic, *tawḥīd* is understood as "the extinction of the ignorance of our essential and unmovable identity with the only Real",[66] preoccupation with *tawḥīd* is thus characteristic of the Perfect Man who fully realizes his "essential oneness with the Divine Being". The Perfect Man could be expected to be absorbed in the knowledge of *tawḥīd*, even in the midst of battle, and his saintly powers would protect him "amid a hail of bullets".

The possibility that Ahmad's father, Sultan Mahmud, had similar spiritual aspirations is implied in Tomé Pires's magnificent account of 15th-century Melaka. Sultan Mahmud is reported as announcing that the Islamic pilgrimage was unnecessary as "Melaka was to be made into Mecca".[67] We shall see that Mahmud's declaration aroused criticism among the Muslim community of the Port, but again it has a Sufi explanation. Some Muslim mystics believed that the pilgrimage was unimportant. The Ka'ba, they argued, might visit *them*, and in any case, outward rites were not "absolutely binding on one who has reached perfection".[68]

The possible content of the conversations between the Malay Rajas and their "mollah" favourites is emerging. The evidence, however, is not only meagre but one-sided, for if the mystics at the courts of Pasai and Melaka expressed their doctrines in writing, these works have not survived.[69] Yet a poem of a Sufi from North Sumatra provides one indication of the way a mystic confidant portrayed his Raja's position. The Sultan, Ala'ud-Din Ri'ayat Shah (1588–1604), is called a *wali*, and is termed both *kamil* and *kutub*.[70] In Arabic usage *walī* means a "saint", or what Nicholson describes as "the popular type of Perfect Man";[71] *kāmil* refers to divine perfection,[72] and *quṭb* indicates the head of all saints; "the virtual centre of spiritual energy upon whom the well-being of this world depends" and the "highest spiritual guide of the faithful".[73]

The above paragraphs have followed two somewhat difficult trails. The scent has not always been good; it has been masked perhaps by the activity of copyists. Two strands of Islamic thinking, however, appear to have appealed to the Malay Raja: Persianized kingship, and the mystical, concept of the Perfect Man. The preoccupations of the Malay Raja through time are evident; they are distinctly consistent. The ruler of the raja-centred *kerajaan*, who had once been portrayed as a *boddhisattva*, found attractive in Islam those ideas which enhanced kingship, and which permitted and assisted the monarch to fulfill the central role in the spiritual life of his subjects.

Just as Irano-Islamic kingship was not an obscure element in medieval Islam, so Malays of the period are not to be regarded as heterodox in their attachment to mystical Sufism. Sufis were not generally considered to be heretical; indeed, it has been observed that, from the 11th century onwards, Sufism "enlisted in its service a large proportion of the vital spiritual energies of the Muslim community".[74]

The idea of the Perfect Man, expounded by Arabi and Jili, was influential in the medieval period,[75] and scholars have suggested that the concept was sometimes linked to that of Caliph or of the Shi'ite Imām.[76] In India, where Sufism was prominent,[77] the Emperor Akbar was attracted to the work of Arabi and Jili, and Akbar appears to have applied to himself the concept of the Perfect Man.[78]

What is important to emphasize here is that, in the words of the late Professor Hodgson, the medieval Muslim world possessed "an intellectual spirit tolerating wide differences of tongue and clime, and welcoming everywhere all that was Muslim from anywhere".[79] In their selective acceptance of Islam, Malays were not necessarily seen as "bad Muslims". It is not to be wondered at that the elements of Islamic law they did adopt were of the orthodox Shāfi'ī school which was to be found in numerous places along the Indian ocean routes.[80] In medieval times, orthodoxy existed more or less peacefully beside mystical and Persian-influenced sentiments. Nor is it surprising that such Muslim travellers as the 14th-century Ibn Baṭṭūṭa, and the 15th-century Ma Huan, refrained from describing Malays as spiritually lax.[81] If *sharī'a* law was not strictly adhered to in Malay lands, its scope was often radically restricted in India and Western Asia. From 'Abbasid times onward, the sovereign was not so much subject to the *sharī'a* as given discretion to determine "how far the purposes of God for the Islamic community might best be effected".[82] Time and again one reads of the authority of *sharīʿa* having been encroached upon by royal authority.[83] *Qāḍīs*, from the time of the Persian *wazīr*, Naẓām al-mulk, were often seen, not as independent Islamic judges, but as deputies of the Sultan. Even in Arab lands the *qāḍī*'s jurisdiction was usually limited to private law, and in some communities indigenous custom was sufficiently powerful to remove family law also from the purview of *sharīʿa*.[84]

In emphasizing these encroachments on the sphere of *sharīʿa*, however, it must be remembered that those whom Professor Hodgson has described as the "shariah minded", those for whom the centrality and implementation of *sharīʿa* law was the highest aim,[85] were certainly present in the medieval period. The 14th-century thinker, Ibn Taymiya (Taqī al-dīn Aḥmad b. Taymiya, 1263–1328) was perhaps the most famous. But Ibn Taymiya's opinions landed him in prison and, in general, during these years, the "shariah minded" held a defensive rather than a dominant position in the Muslim world.[85]

This digression into Muslim history is important. It permits us to appreciate why Malays, retaining so much of their *kerajaan* political structure, were able, nevertheless, to consider themselves Muslim. To view Islam in the Malay world against the background of Muslim developments elsewhere also contributes to our understanding of the timing of Islamization. Arabs, it is known, frequented the Malay lands over many centuries prior to the adoption there of Islam.[87] But the news they brought of early Islam would not have been conducive to the interests of *boddhisattva*-minded Malay rajas. The Raja would be attracted neither by the pedestrian doctrine of the early Muslim ruler nor by the possibility of subjection to the Imperial caliphate of the 'Abbasids. The Malay ruler could, however, empathize with, and benefit from, the doctrines of the medieval Muslim world. At the point when Malay states adopted Islam, Malay political culture was compatible in some important respects with the prevailing political culture of the Muslim world. Moreover, acceptance of certain new Muslim doctrines allowed the Malay ruler, situated on commercial routes which appear to have been increasingly dominated by Muslim traders, to describe his ancient functions in terms which his new subjects would understand. In addition, through adopting Islam, the ruler was acquiring the most modern spiritual doctrines and techniques, and, at the same time, entering the Muslim galaxy which he would believe encompassed the greater part of the civilized world. Yet, if he had something to gain, he had nothing to lose. In accepting Islam, the ruler probably believed he was in no way threatening the basis of the Malay, Raja-centred, *kerajaan*. He was right only in the short term.

NOTES

1. This article is based on a lecture given to the Royal Asiatic Society in June 1979. I am grateful for comments and suggestions to Professor C. F. Beckingham, Dr. D. J. Duncanson, Mr. J. G. Bousfield, Professor P. de Josselin de Jong, Dr. R. F. Ellen, Mr. M. B. Hooker and Dr. R. McVey.

   [The names of Islamic rulers in Malaya, and Islamic technical terms used in specifically Malay contexts, are given in this article in the customary Malay romanizations, and without diacritical marks. Arabic titles of Malay works are rendered with diacritics in the forms used in manuscript catalogues. Names of rulers of Muslim countries outside Malaya, and Islamic technical terms in a general context, together with the titles of Arabic texts, are given in orientalist transliterations, and with diacritics.]
2. The various "layers" of Malay culture are analysed in a number of works by Sir Richard Winstedt; see, for instance, *The Malays* and *The Malay magician*, London, 1961.
3. H. A. Hijmans van Anrooij, "Nota omtrent het rijk van Siak", *Tijdschrift voor Indische Taal-, Land-, en Volkenkunde* (hereafter *TBG*), XXX, 1885, 312.
4. W. E. Maxwell, "The laws and customs of the Malays with reference to land", *Journal of the Malayan Branch of the Royal Asiatic Society* (hereafter *JMBRAS*), XIII, 1884, 79 and 91–2. Regarding the ruler's unlimited rights over his subjects ibid., 108.
5. Liaw Yock Fang, *Undang-undang Melaka*, The Hague, 1976, 62–4.
6. ibid., 176.

7. "Penuntu ugama Rasul Allah"; see H. S. Paterson, "An early Malay inscription from Trengganu", *JMBRAS*, XI, 1928, 255.
8. *Hikayat Pahang*, 3 and 78. The author is grateful to the Arkib Negara, Malaysia for permission to consult the recension of the Hikayat.
9. *Hikajat Ketoeroenan Radja Negeri Deli* (located in the Oostkust van Sumatra Instituut collection at the Instituut voor de Tropen, Amsterdam), 45. When Munshi Abdullah visited Pahang in the 1830s he was told that one who attempts to alter custom (*adat*) runs the risk of being punished by the supernatural power (*daulat*) of the former Pahang sultans. See Kassim Ahmad, *Kisah pelayaran Abdallah*, Kuala Lumpur, 1964, 40. See also the role of the Raja in the establishing of the Kedah Laws, Winstedt, "Kedah Laws", *JMBRAS*, VI, 1928, 15; and the comment in the *Malay Annals* regarding the part played by the ruler of Malacca in the compilation of law codes, Winstedt, "Sejarah Melayu", *JMBRAS*, XIV, 1938, 84–8 and 92.
10. See, for instance, "Bijdragen tot de kennis der Residentie Rio", *Tijdschrift voor Nederlandsch — Indië*, I, 1853, 412; H. Clifford, *Studies in brown humanity*, London, 1898, 176. For descriptions of Malay audiences, see *Singapore Daily Times*, 29 July 1875; W. H. Read, *Play and politics: recollections of Malaya*, London, 1901, 35; and "Journal kept on board a cruiser in the Indian Archipelago", *Journal of the Indian Archipelago*, VIII, 1854, 170.
11. R. J. Wilkinson, "Notes on the Negeri Sembilan", in Wilkinson, *Papers on Malay subjects*, Selected and Edited by P. L. Burns, Kuala Lumpur, 1971, 304. These "notes" were first published in 1911. See also the comments of the Reverend Favre: "A journey in Johore", *Journal of the Indian Archipelago*, III, 1849, 51.
12. R. Sennett, *The fall of Public Man*, Cambridge, 1977, Pts 1 and 2. See also the discussion in G. Lienhardt, *Divinity and experience*. Oxford, 1967, ch. IV.
13. See, for instance, Winstedt, "Sejarah Melayu", 121; A. H. Hill (ed.), "Hikayat Raja-Raja Pasai", a revised romanized version of Raffles Ms 67, together with an English translation," *JMBRAS*, XXXIII, 1960, 66.
14. *Hikajat Ketoeroenan Radja Negeri Deli*, 129.
15. ibid., 54. For indications in other texts that service to the Raja could bring benefits in the afterlife see Winstedt, "Sejarah Melayu", 144; Kassim Ahmad, *Hikayat Hang Tuah*, Kuala Lumpur, 1968, 319.
16. O. W. Wolters, *The fall of Srivijaya in Malay history*, Ithaca, 1970, ch. VIII.
17. The "Telaga Batu" inscription, lines 25 and 26 in J. G. de Casparis, *Prasasti Indonesia*, II, Bandung, 1956, 36, 45–6. See also the Talang Tuwo inscription in G. Coedès, "Les inscriptions malaises de Çrīvijaya", *Bulletin de l'École Française d'Extrême Orient*, XXX, 1930, 38–42.
18. M. Dhavamony, *Love of God, according to Saiva Siddhanta*, Oxford, 1971, 23.
19. R. J. Wilkinson, *A Malay-English Dictionary*, London, 1959. O. W. Wolters discusses the importance of Bhakti ideas in relation to Khmer kingship in "Khmer 'Hinduism' in the Seventh Century", in *Early South East Asia; essays in archaeology, history and historical geography*, edited by R. B. Smith and W. Watson, New York and Kuala Lumpur, 1979, 427–42.
20. For a helpful comparison of kingship in India and South East Asia, see L. Dumont, *Homo hierarchicus: the caste system and its implications*, London, 1972, 262–3. On Indian kingship, see I. W. Mabbett, *Truth, myth and politics in ancient India*, New Delhi, 1972, ch. VII.
21. Winstedt, "Sejarah Melayu", 84. Pires supports this account: see A. Cortesão (ed.), *The Suma Oriental of Tomé Pires*, London, 1944, 242. For the ruler's importance in the Islamization of two other states, see also Hill, *JMBRAS*, XXXII, 1960, 55; and P. L. A. Sweeney (ed.), "Silsilah Raja Raja Berunai", *JMBRAS*, XLI, 1968, 11.
22. Cortesão, op. cit., 251.
23. ibid., 240–1. Regarding the prominence of rulers in the Islamization process see R. Jones, "Ten conversion myths from Indonesia" in N. Levtzion (ed.), *Conversion to Islam*, New York, 1979, 129–58.
24. B. Schrieke, *Indonesian sociological studies*, The Hague, 1957 II, 232; M. A. P. Meilink-Roelofsz, *Asian trade and European influence*, The Hague, 1962, 20–1; M. A. P. Meilink-Roelofsz, "Trade and Islam in the Malay-Indonesian archipelago" in *Islam and the trade of Asia*, edited by D. S. Richards, Oxford, 1970, 145; and G .R. Tibbetts, "Early Muslim traders in South-East Asia", *JMBRAS*, XXX, 1957, 43.
25. Malay rulers adopted numerous other aspects of Irano-Islamic kingship. The genealogies of the Sultans of Melaka and several other Malay states commence with Iskandar Dhu 'l-Qarnayn; the Bendaharas of Melaka traced their descent to the *wazīr* of Saljuq Persia, Niẓām al-mulk, whose writings on kingship were often quoted in Malay works. The *Naṣīhat al-mulūk* ("Advice to kings") of the Persian-born al-Ghazālī was also translated into Malay (M. C. Ricklefs and P. Voorhoeve, *Indonesian manuscripts in Great Britain*, Oxford, 1977, 120). For a general note on Persian influence on Malay kingship see G. E. Marrison "Persian influence on Malay life", *JMBRAS*, XXVIII, 1955, 54–5.
26. Hill, *JMBRAS*, XXXIII, 1960, 57–8. See also the descriptions in Malay texts of the adoption of similar

titles by the Melakan ruler (Winstedt, "Sejarah Melayu", 84); and Patani ruler (A. Teeuw and D. K. Wyatt (eds.), *Hikayat Patani*, The Hague, 1970, 74–5); and the Kedah ruler (Dzulkifli bin Mohd. Salleh [ed.], *Hikayat Merong Mahawangsa*, Kuala Lumpur, 1973, 147; and J. Low, "Kedah Annals", *Journal of the Indian Archipelago*, III, 1849, 416).

27. W. W. Shaw and Mohd. Kassim Haji Ali, *Malacca Coins*, Kuala Lumpur, 1970, 2–4. Pires noted the title "Sultan" was also used in Pasai; see Cortesão (ed.), *The Suma Oriental of Tomé Pires*, 245. For mention of the title on Pasai coinage, see H. J. K. Cowan, "Bijdragen tot de kennis der geschiedenis van het rijk Samoedra-Pase", *TBG*, LXXVIII, 1938, 204–14.
28. W. W. Shaw and Mohd. Kassim Haji Ali, *Coins of North Malaya*, Kuala Lumpur, 1971, 12 and 34; J. A. S. Bucknill, "Observations upon some coins obtained in Malaya . . .", *JMBRAS*, I, 1923, 201; W. Linehan, op. cit., 50; J. E. Kempe and R. O. Winstedt, "A Malay legal digest compiled for 'Abd al-Ghafur Muhaiyu'd-din Shah, Sultan of Pahang 1592–1614 A.D. with undated additions", *JMBRAS*, XXI, 1948, 25. See also R. O. Winstedt and P. E. de Josselin de Jong, "The maritime laws of Malacca", *JMBRAS*, XXIX, 1956, 46; Raja Chulan bin Hamid, *Misa Melayu*, edited by R. O. Winstedt, Singapore, 1919, 13 and 23–4; and the letter from the ruler of Selangor, 1785, published in W. Marsden, *A grammar of the Malay language*, London, 1812, 147.
29. Teeuw and Wyatt (eds.), *Hikayat Patani*, 74–5; Liaw, *Undang-undang Melaka*, 64; Tardijan Hadidjaja (ed.), *'Adat Raja-Raja Melayu*, Kuala Lumpur, 1964, 60–1.
30. M. Dion (trns. and ed.), "Sumatra through Portuguese eyes: excerpts from João de Barros, *Decadas da Asia*", *Indonesia* (Ithaca N.Y.), 9, 1970, 140.
31. Winstedt, "Sejarah Melayu", 144.
32. Kempe and Winstedt, *JMBRAS*, XXI, 25.
33. Khalid Hussain (ed.), *Taj us-Salatin*, Kuala Lumpur, 1966, 49.
34. Kempe and Winstedt, *JMBRAS*, XXI, 25. The translation in the *Tāj al-salāṭīn* is more accurate; see Khalid Hussain, op. cit., 46. The *Tāj al-salāṭīn* does differ from Qur'ānic teaching in insisting that loyalty be given even to an unrighteous ruler; see L. W. C. Van den Berg, "De Mohammedaansche Vorsten in Nederlandsch-Indie", *Bijdragen tot de Taal-, Land- en Volkenkunde* (hereafter *BKI*), VI, 9, 1901, 14. *Sūra*, IV, 59, is also invoked in support of the Raja, see Winstedt, "Sejarah Melayu", 144; Khalid Hussain, op. cit., 50; and Hadidjaja, op. cit., 59 (cf. n. 29, above).
35. For a discussion of "Yang di Pertuan", see Wilkinson, *A Malay-English Dictionary*.
36. J. Gonda, *Sanscrit in Indonesia*, New Delhi, 1973, 621.
37. O. W. Wolters suggests that the Melakan ruler was trying to attract Muslim traders to his port as there had been a reduction in the Chinese trade. The *Sejarah Melayu*, he believes, was written partly to assist the Malacca ruler to "show himself to be an unmistakeable Muslim prince", see Wolters, *Fall*, 156–9 and 164.
38. S. D. Goitein, "Attitudes toward government in Islam and Judaism", *Studies in Islamic history and tradition*, Leiden, 1968, 16 and 20.
39. G. E. von Grunebaum, *Medieval Islam*, Chicago, 1971, 154.
40. Muhammed 'Aziz Ahmad, *Political history and institutions of the early Turkish Empire in Delhi*, Lahore, 1949, 323.
41. G. Widengren, "The Sacral Kingship of Iran", *The Sacral Kingship. Contributions to the central theme of the VIIIth International Congress for the History of Religions. Rome, April 1955*, Leiden, 1959, 250.
42. H. Ringgren, "Some religious aspects of the Caliphate", in *Sacral Kingship*, 746. Ringgren emphasizes that this is not the only possible origin of the epithet. On the relationship between Sassanian traditions and the concept of the "Shadow of God", see A. K. S. Lambton, "Justice in the medieval Persian theory of kingship", *Studia Islamica*, XVII, 1962, 97 and 119.
43. Ringgren, op. cit., 745–6.
44. A. K. S. Lambton, "*Quis custodiet custodes*: some reflections on the Persian theory of government", *Studia Islamica*, V, 1956, 127.
45. F. R. C. Bagley (trans. and ed.), *Ghazālī's Book of Counsel for Kings* (*Nasīhat al-Mulūk*), London, 1964, lvi and 45. A. K. S. Lambton, "The internal structure of the Saljuq Empire", *The Cambridge History of Iran*, Cambridge, 1968, V, 209 and *passim*. On the history of the title Sulṭān, see *Encyclopaedia of Islam*, IV, Part 1 (Leiden, 1934) 534–5.
46. Aziz Ahmad, *Studies in the Islamic culture on the Indian Continent*, Oxford, 1964, 170: K. A. Nizami, *Some aspects of religion and politics in India during the thirteenth century*, Aligarh, 1961, 96. On Persian influences on the Delhi state, see also 92–4. Just as was later the case in the Malay world, scholars in India and the Middle East sought support for these kingly pretensions in the Qur'ān. *Sūra* IV, 59, for instance, was often quoted; Bagley, op. cit., 104, Nizami, *Religion and politics*, 96.

47. *The travels of Ibn Battuta A.D. 1325–1354*, translated and edited by H. A. R. Gibb, Cambridge, 1958, I, 3. Gibb notes that Ibn Baṭṭūṭa refers to "all the temporal rulers" as "Sultans".
48. M. Mujeeb, *The Indian Muslims*, London, 1967, 33.
49. The independent Sultanate commenced in 1338 with Sultan Fakhr al-dīn Mubārak Shāh. Abdul Karim, *Social history of the Muslims in Bengal*, Dacca, 1959, 26. For the use of 'Shāh' elsewhere in the Muslim world, see *Encyclopaedia of Islam*, Leiden and London, 1934.
50. Abdul Karim, op. cit., 30 and 47. Jalāl al-dīn Muḥammad (1415–1432) was the first Bengal ruler to hold the title.
51. K. A. Nilakanta Sastri, *A history of South India*, Madras, 1966, 239.
52. 'Alī 'Ādil Shāh (1558–80); Iftikhar Ahmad Ghauri, "Kingship in the Sultanate of Bijapur and Golconda", *Islamic Culture*, XLVI, 1972, 4. Regarding the apparent devaluation of titles, see also I. Goldhizer, *Muslim studies*, London, 1971, 68; on the Persianization of government in Muslim lands, Lambton, *Studia Islamica*, XVII, 1962, 96–9; and K. A. Nizami, *Studies in medieval Indian history and culture*, Allahabad, 1966, 21.
53. The route which Islam took to the Malay world is still in doubt: G. W. J. Drewes, "New light on the coming of Islam to Indonesia", *BKI*, CXXIV, 4, 1968, 433–49. But it is clear that Malays were aware of, and sometimes influenced by, developments in many parts of the Muslim world; see, in particular, S. Q. Fatimi, *Islam comes to Malaysia*, Singapore, 1963.
54. See, in particular, his "Sufism as a category in Indonesian literature and history", *Journal of Southeast Asian History*, II, 1961, 10–23; and "The role of Sufism in the spread of Islam to Malaya and Indonesia", *Journal of the Pakistan Historical Society*, IX, 1961, 143–60.
55. See the tantalizing account of an interview between the missionary, W. H. Medhurst, and the Sultan of Trengganu in "Journal of a voyage to the east coast of the Malayan Peninsula", *Quarterly Chronicle of the Transactions of the London Missionary Society*, July 1830, 155. The ruler of Brunei also consulted both Christian and Muslim divines, see the report of Father Antonio Pereira, 1608, quoted in Nicholl, *European sources*, 89–90.
56. R. A. Nicholson, *Studies in Islamic mysticism*, Cambridge, 1921, 78.
57. Hill, *JMBRAS*, XXXIII, 74.
58. R. A. Nicholson, *The mystics of Islam*, London, 1975, 193. On *keramat*, see the entries in Wilkinson, *Dictionary*, and W. Marsden, *A Dictionary of the Malayan language*, London, 1812.
59. A. Schimmel, *Mystical dimensions of Islam*, Chapel Hill, 1975, 211.
60. *Sejarah Melayu, or the Malay annals*, edited by W. G. Shellabear, Singapore, 1950, 127. Conversion by a *shaykh* trained in Sufism was not uncommon; see, for example, the *Hikayat Merong Mahawangsa* (edited by Dzulkifli bin Mohd. Salleh, 113; and Low, *Journal of the Indian Archipelago*, III, 1849, 472.
61. The Shellabear text calls the book *Daru'l-mazlum*. Raffles 18 has "Durr-Mandzum"; Winstedt, "Sejarah Melayu", 127. For a discussion of the way the story is told in different recensions of the Sejarah Melayu, see R. Roolvink, "The answer of Pasai", *JMBRAS*, XXXVIII, 1965, 124–39.
62. Wilkinson, *Dictionary*, under *dzat*. But also see H. Overbeck, "The answer of Pasai", *JMBRAS*, XI, 1933, 254, n. 3.
63. Winstedt, *Malays*, 30; A. H. Johns, "Muslim mystics and historical writing", in *Historians of South East Asia*, edited by D. G. E. Hall, London, 1963, 41. For 'Abd al-Kārim al-Jīlī, cf. *Encyclopaedia of Islam*, second edition, sv. Insān al-Kāmil.
64. D. A. Rinkes, *Abdoerrauf van Singkel*, Leiden, 1909, 39 and 103; Syed Mhd. Naguib al-Attas, *The mysticism of Hamzah Fansuri*, Kuala Lumpur, 1970, 372, 406, 455 and 456. Johns, "Muslim Mystics", 41; P. Zoetmulder and W. Stohr, *Les religions d'Indonésie*, Paris, 1968, 336; G. W. J. Drewes, "Indonesia: mysticism and activism", in *Unity and variety in Muslim civilization*, edited by G. von Grunebaum, Chicago, 1971, 299–300. For Muhyī al-dīn b. al-'Arabī, widely known as "Ibn 'Arabī", author of *al-Futūḥāt al-Makkiya*, cf. *Encyclopaedia of Islam*, second edition, III, 708.
65. Winstedt, "Sejarah Melayu", 191.
66. L. Schaya, quoted by Schimmel, *Mystical dimensions of Islam*, 282.
67. Cortesão (ed.), *The Suma Oriental of Tomé Pires*, 253. Albuquerque also reported Sultan Mahmud's declaration, W. de G. Birch (ed.), *The commentaries of the great Alfonso Dalboquerque*, London, 1880, III, 82.
68. Schimmel, *Mystical dimensions of Islam*, 242.
69. The destruction of books sometimes accompanied accusations of heresy in the Malay world, see Johns, "Islam in Southeast Asia", *Indonesia*, XIX, April 1975, 45.
70. Quoted in Syed Muhammed Naguib al-Attas, *Rānīrī and the Wujudiyyah of 17th Century Acheh*, Singapore, 1966, 44.
71. *Studies*, 78 (cf. n. 56, above).

72. Wilkinson, *Dictionary*.
73. Schimmel, *Mystical dimensions of Islam,* 200. Sultan Muzafer, an 18th-century ruler of Perak, according to the Malay text, the *Misa Melayu,* was also considered a saint, see B.J.W. Andaya, *Perak, the abode of grace: a study of an eighteenth century Malay State,* Ithaca. New York, 1975, 305. On rulers as *wali,* see also Hijmans van Anrooij, op. cit., 280. The qualities of saints have much in common with those attributed to Malay rulers or to the devotionalist Hindu leader; saints were "recognizable by the loveliness of their speech, and fine manners . . . and perfect mildness toward all creatures . . .", see Schimmel, *Mystical dimensions of Islam,* 199.
74. H. A. R. Gibb, *Mohammedanism*, New York, 1962, 13.
75. M. G. S. Hodgson, *The venture of Islam*, Chicago, 1974, II, 334–5 and 462.
76. Hodgson, op. cit., II, 229; Schimmel, *Mystical dimensions of Islam*, 200; Allamah Sayyid Mohammed Husayn Tabataba'i. *Shi'ite Islam*, London, 1975, 114; Lambton, *Studia Islamica*, V, 1956, 137–8, 140.
77. Aziz Ahmad, *An intellectual history of Islam in India*, Edinburgh, 1969, ch. IV. For a comment on the predominance of Indians, Malays and Turks among the Sufi adepts in late 19th-century Mecca, see C. Snouck Hurgronje, *Mekka*, Leiden, 1970, orig. pub. 1888, 208–9.
78. Aziz Ahmad, *Studies in Islamic Culture*, 167.
79. Hodgson, *The venture of Islam*, II, 255, also 437.
80. N. J. Coulson notes that Shāfiʿī law predominated in Southern Arabia, East Africa and Southeast Asia, (*A history of Islamic law*, Edinburgh, 1964, 101). It was also important in South India; Snouck Hurgronje, *Mekka,* 183. On the predominance of Shāfiʿī law in the central lands of Islam before the rise of the Ottomans see D. B. MacDonald, "Mahommedan Law", *Encyclopaedia Britannica*, Eleventh edition, 1910–11.
81. For Ma Huan's account of states in Sumatra and on the Peninsula, see J. V. G. Mills (ed.), *Ma Huan: Ying Yai Sheng-Lan*, Cambridge, 1970, 108–24. Ibn Baṭṭūṭa certainly noted the extremely unorthodox behaviour of Muslims in the Maldives; see H. A. R. Gibb, *Ibn Battuta: travels in Asia and Africa 1325–1354*, London, 1929, 250. In Pasai, Ibn Baṭṭūṭa commented both on the presence of Persians and the ruler's adherence to Shāfiʿī law, see C. Defremery and B. R. Sanguinetti, *Voyages d'Ibn Batoutah*, Paris, 1858, IV, 230. A 17th-century Persian account notes that "the natives" of Aceh and Patani were "Muslims of the Shāfiʿī sect", and makes no mention of spiritual laxity in either place. J. O'Kane (ed.), *The ship of Sulaimān*, London, 1972, 175 and 218.
82. Coulson, *A history of Islamic law*, 130.
83. See, for example, C. L. Klausner, *The Seljuk Vezirate, a study of civil administration 1055–1194*, Cambridge, 1973, 44; H. A. R. Gibb and H. Bowen, *Islamic Society and the West*, Oxford, 1957, 1, pt. 2, 120; Afsar Umar Salim Khan and Mohammed Habib, *The political theory of the Delhi Sultanate*, Delhi, n.d., vi–x.
84. Coulson, *A history of Islamic law*, 132 and 135–6, see also C. Snouck Hurgronje, *The Achehnese*, Leiden, 1906, II, 271–9.
85. *The venture of Islam*, I, 318 and 351.
86. E. I. J. Rosenthal, *Islam in the modern national state*, Cambridge, 1965, 12–17. For an example of criticism of Persian influence in 13th-century Delhi, see K. A. Nizami, *Medieval Indian history and culture*, Allahabad, 1966, 21.

Islamization in Java: Fourteenth to Eighteenth Centuries

M.C. RICKLEFS

The extant literature on the introduction of Islam to Indonesia sometimes tends to consider the role of the recipients of the new faith as passive. Questions are asked about whence Indonesian Islam came, in what is probably an illusory quest for a single source, and what changes in the Islamic world outside Indonesia caused Islam to be adopted. This tendency to look at Java only from the outside may contribute to the lack of "new light" mentioned some time ago by Professor Drewes.[1] If one attempts to consider the issues from a vantage point within Javanese civilization as well, some aspects of the process of conversion may become clearer.

Java had long had a high culture predominantly Indic in form, but by the fourteenth century it was certainly not in any sense alien. For at least a millenium Javanese courtiers and literati had been absorbing Hindu and Mahayana Buddhist ideas. The resultant religious system was notable for its apparent lack of an exclusive sense of orthodoxy. Hindu and Buddhist temples stood side-by-side, and kings could be called the "Siwa-Buddha." King Hayam Wuruk (1350–89) of Majapahit, in whose reign the story of Javanese Islam began, was called "Siwa-Buddha" and "Nirguna to the Wisnuite."[2] Sectarian intolerance seems to have been foreign to Javanese thinking, as it seems also to have been in much of Southeast Asia.

Hindu and Buddhist cults in Java were almost certainly under the supervision of an elite including the royal family, its servants, and independent religious communities in the countryside. The concept of popular or "democratic" religion was probably as foreign as that of intolerance, but that is not to say the populace did not presumably gain some satisfaction from sharing in religious ritual. Documentation for this period, however, originates solely from literate (which is to say elite) circles, so that one's picture of pre-Muslim religious life at other social levels must depend to a large extent upon suppositions.

From the fourteenth century (still the "Hindu-Javanese period") survives the first evidence of the existence of Javanese Muslims.[3] To what extent was Islam in this period a fundamental and disruptive change in Javanese religious and social life? It has been suggested, upon what evidence is not clear, that in some areas of Indonesia Islam spread from the bottom of society to the top.[4] It is also commonly assumed that in Java Islam initially spread during a period of decline in the Hindu-Buddhist state system. And it is usually accepted that it spread to the north coast of Java through trading contacts and from there, rather later, to the interior of the island.

The first Islamic documents, a series of gravestone inscriptions from Trawulan and Tralaya in East Java, raise questions about all these assumptions. At the Trawulan site, the late L-Ch. Damais discovered one of the

Reprinted from Ricklefs, "Six Centuries of Islamization in Java" in *Conversion to Islam,* edited by Nehemia Levtzion, by permission of the author and Holmes & Meier Publishers, Inc. New York, N.Y.

oldest Islamic documents in Java, a gravestone dated Śaka 1290 (A.D. 1368).[5] The use of the Śaka era strongly suggests that this is the oldest surviving gravestone of a Javanese, rather than a foreign, Muslim. In the Tralaya graveyard were found stones apparently marking the graves of distinguished Muslim Javanese who were perhaps even members of the royal family; they are located near the site of the court of Majapahit and the earliest dates from Śaka 1298 (A.D. 1376), believed to be the period of Majapahit's glory.[6] This is not necessarily to say that Islam originated in Java in the court circles of Majapahit at the height of its power, a conclusion which is unsupportable by such fragmentary evidence and which some might feel is unlikely in itself. But it does suggest that some of the assumptions which have been widely accepted by writers on this subject not only have little or no evidence in their favor, but even contradict such fragmentary evidence as these gravestones.

It would be consistent with what is known of the pre-Islamic history of religion in Java, and with the evidence of these fourteenth-century gravestones from the Majapahit area, to suggest that Islam may have found favor among some members of the upper classes of Javanese society and that it may have spread at least in some areas, particularly in the interior of the island, through the patronage of the traditional elite. The much later Mataram court chronicles (the oldest extant versions of which date only from the eighteenth century) preserve the tradition that the Hindu king of Majapahit not only did not object to the practice of Islam, but even "confirmed" its practice.[7] The Portuguese observer Tomé Pires, who was in the Indonesian area in 1512–15, arrived too late to see the initial growth of Islam in Java. But it had spread to the Moluccas only a few decades before he wrote and it is of interest that he says that most of the people there were still "heathen"; the Muslims were the kings and a few of their followers.[8] This does not, of course, prove that the process in the more sophisticated Javanese kingdom was the same as in the Moluccas, but the evidence of the early gravestones suggests that there may have been a similarity.

It will be seen that the introduction of Islam brought few important changes to the religious life of the interior of Java, insofar as this is possible to judge. If, as is suggested here, Islam spread without elite opposition and perhaps with elite patronage, this state of affairs is not surprising. But why was the new faith adopted at all? To this question there can be no confident answer except in the unlikely event of some new and revealing source of evidence being discovered. But one may suggest that the adoption of a new religion would have been no extraordinary matter for the Javanese elite, who had long been able to adopt various Hindu and Buddhist cults apparently without a sense of conflict. Indeed, it would not greatly surprise this writer to discover that there were members of the fourteenth-century elite who regarded themselves as Muslim, Buddhist, and Hindu at the same time. The new faith may have been a means of tapping another source of supernatural energy. Reading the Qur'ān may have released another spiritual force, as Professor Zoetmulder has suggested that the reading of Old Javanese works of literature caused the god evoked therein to descend.[9] For such adherents Islam would have provided a new dimension to their religious practices. Needless to say, this would not have brought much understanding of the new faith or commitment to its formal requirements. This Islam would probably have been heretical by what were later regarded as the ideal standards of Islam in Arabia, just as the Islam of much of the Central Javanese literati and of the courts has been heretical by such standards down to the present day. To the question why Islam apparently began to be accepted in the interior of Java in the fourteenth century rather than at some other time, there can on present evidence be no answer. Such "conversions" are not likely to have been accomplished either by conquest or by pressure from a new ruling elite. The only plausible agent here is the occasional Muslim teacher.

The situation on the north coast of Java in the fourteenth century and after was different. There a series of trading ports developed as important entrepôt centers in the trade between the "Spice Islands" and the west of the archipelago, and as suppliers of rice to the great Malay entrepôt of Malacca after ca. 1400.[10] Evidence here is also scanty, but it seems reasonably clear that, as a part of the great network of shipping in the archipelago, these port cities differed in two important ways from the interior. First, they were in constant contact with Malay, Arab, Gujerati, Persian and other merchants, the majority of whom (including many of the Chinese) were Muslims. The number of such foreign Muslims actually residing in the north coastal ports probably increased after the Portuguese conquest of Malacca in 1511, which dispersed the Asian trading community of that city throughout a series of ports along the Java Sea and the western part of the archipelago. Thus, through trade the coastal Javanese had more constant access to knowledge about Islam, and their economic interests were closely connected with an international system of commerce reaching from the Moluccas to the Mediterranean which, at least by the fifteenth century, was predominantly in Muslim hands. Second, because their commercial prosperity depended on external trade, they may have had little interest in paying obeisance and taxes to a court farther inland, which probably played little role in their commerce except perhaps as a marginal source of rice and as a source and market for some luxury goods. Thus their most fundamental interests lay with a Muslim trading network and against a kingdom which, whatever the progress of Islam among its populace, was offically Hindu-Buddhist until its final collapse in the early sixteenth century.

That the coastal ports should have become Muslim at least by the end of the fifteenth century, for both economic and political reasons, is not surprising. Nor is it surprising that the Javanese Muslims of the coast have on the whole been more self-consciously Muslim than those of the interior. That is not to say, however, that they were necessarily more orthodox in doctrinal terms or in religious practice. Two sixteenth-century manuscripts containing Islamic mystical teachings survive because they were brought back by the first Dutch expedition to Indonesia (1595–97).[11] Both are probably from the north coast of Java and both are orthodox mysticism, but one of them (the "admonitions of Seh Bari") contains lengthy warnings against various heresies, which may suggest that heresy was not uncommon in Javanese coastal Islam.[12]

These coastal ports were probably fairly new as trading centers, with the exceptions of the very old ports of Surabaya and Tuban, and were perhaps less integrated into the Hindu-Javanese cultural system. According to the early sixteenth-century *Suma Oriental* of Tomé Pires, a generally reliable record so far as can be judged, many of the lords of these Javanese port cities were not Javanese but of Malay, Indian, Chinese, Arabic, and other descent. They were often at war with the Hindu-Buddhist king then still reigning in the interior, but at the same time they spoke of the affairs of court with awe, emulated its style, and paid great respect to the *tapas* (ascetics) who were almost certainly not Muslims.[13]

The men who rose to be coastal lords would in most cases have been Muslims before their arrival in Java; this did not, however, rule out their emulation of the non-Muslim Javanese aristocracy. For such coastal lords, the main cultural change they experienced would have been Javanization rather than Islamization. About the conversion of the Javanese elements in the population of these ports nothing reliable is known. There is no evidence either for or against the idea of Islam as a "revolution from below" anywhere on the north coast, but such a development would seem to have been as unlikely there as elsewhere in Java. Subjects most probably became Muslim because their lord was.

The history of Javanese Islam down to the present has been influenced to some extent by the distinction between the north coast and the interior. But Islam is probably more a symptom than a cause of this distinction. Islam has struck deeper roots on the coast, and has tended to be at its most self-conscious among trading communities. There has often been tension, and sometimes devastating warfare, between the coast and the interior. Although it is attractive to think of Islam as a causative factor in his conflict, it would probably be more correct to think of it as deriving from primary economic and political differences, with a rather more self-conscious Islam providing from time to time a convenient rallying banner for the coastal states.

The importance of political and economic rather than of doctrinal interests on the north coast is perhaps also confirmed by the history of Javanese-Dutch East India Company relations. It has sometimes been assumed, with extraordinary unconcern for the historical evidence, that the more self-conscious Muslims of the coast were the greatest enemies of the Dutch Protestants, while the less firm Muslims ruling the interior kingdom of Mataram more readily became the tools of the Europeans.[14] But this is simply not so. The greatest enemies of the Dutch were the Mataram rulers and princes, who were nevertheless confident enough of their own power to enlist Dutch armies when they seemed useful. That they underestimated Dutch power at times (and overestimated it at other times) does not change the fact that, with few exceptions, most of the major enemies of the Company—Sultan Agung, Surapati, several rebels of the Kartasura period 1680–1745), Pangeran Mangkubumi, Mangkunĕgara I, Pangeran Singasari, and Dipanagara—were rulers, princes, or protégés of Mataram. The areas which most readily accepted Dutch authority in the seventeenth and eighteenth centuries were those which had most to gain from peace with the Company's merchants and detachment from the claims of the central court: the north coastal ports and Madura. These were also the areas where Islam had penetrated most deeply.

In the course of the centuries, Islam spread throughout the Javanese population, until its adoption by the last large district, the "east hook," was accomplished in the late eighteenth century.[15] This process seems on the whole to have been peaceful, or as peaceful as it could have been in a period of Javanese history characterized by almost incessant warfare. Conversion by arms may have occurred when a Muslim dignitary defeated a non-Muslim, whereupon the vanquished and his people would presumably have embraced Islam.[16] During this period there were undoubtedly changes and developments within Javanese Islam, but in the present state of historical knowledge it is difficult to identify any very important developments. This writer, for instance, rather suspects that Islam was a more powerful influence in the life of the court in the seventeenth century than in the eighteenth. Royal titles, for instance, were sometimes in what looks like a rather more Muslim style,[17] and one encounters several letters from rulers and rebels stressing that it was Islam which made the Javanese one nation. But is it not yet possible to confirm this suspicion. One can picture the Islam of the seventeenth and eighteenth centuries as being in a fairly stable state, but in doing so one should not forget that this stability may prove to be illusory when more historical materials have been made available.

Javanese Islam in the seventeenth and eighteenth centuries was almost certainly mystical in its theological content, a natural development given the predominantly mystical thrust of previous religions in Java. Although there are documentary problems concerning the first centuries of Islam, certainly by the sixteenth century (and probably earlier) *ṣūfī* teachings had been known in Java.[18] But this mysticism often tended to cross the boundary into "pantheistic" heresy. Consistent with the monistic Javanese view of reality both before and since the introduction of Islam, many Javanese Muslims could only conceive of man as a drop in the ocean of God's existence.[19] The reality within man was no different from the divine reality, which was indwelling in man. The doctrine that man and God are one, in its most extreme form that there is no difference between God and the infidel (*kafir*), was and is a common belief in Java and occurs frequently in Javanese mystical texts.[20] There are traditions concerning the supposed martyrdom of teachers who revealed this doctrine of unity (Seh Siti Jĕnar, Pangeran Panggung, Ki Cabolek, and Seh Amongraga),[21] but in each case it seems probable that they were martyred not because of the heretical content of their teachings but because they had revealed the ultimate truth (Javanese *ngelmu gaib*) to the uninitiated. Here was the crucial point of theological confrontation between Islamic orthodoxy and pre-Muslim Javanese monism; could the doctrine of a transcendent God be accepted by Javanese mysticism, which assumed an immanent divinity? Such records as survive suggest that the result of this confrontation was only a limited acceptance of Islamic orthodoxy, at least in literate circles.

To what extent did Javanese feel that they had adopted a fundamentally new religious allegiance? Although little of the evidence concerning the coast has been studied, it seems probable that there some Muslims were conscious of having embraced a new system which superseded and to some extent even put an end to what they had believed before. Here it is, of course, more a question of a sense of religious identity than of theological orthodoxy. Whether these Muslims were all Orthodox (Sunnī) as now, or whether there were perhaps also representatives of the Shī'a is impossible to say.[22] But this and other such distinctions would perhaps have been understood by, and have seemed important to, only a very small circle of believers.

In the interior of Central Java, where the Mataram kingdom was centered, Islam was certainly not of an exclusive nature. There were Javanese who made the pilgrimage to Mecca, perhaps even in some considerable number. But they seem to have brought back little concern for orthodoxy and were perhaps most respected for the supernatural skills they were believed to have acquired.[23] Indeed, before the rise of the Wahhābī movement in the eighteenth century, Mecca itself may not have been a place to inspire much concern for orthodoxy among Indonesian (or other) pilgrims. The greatest ruler of the Mataram dynasty, Sultan Agung (1613–46) acquired the title of *sulṭān* by sending a mission to Mecca late in his reign.[24] But this and other signs of concern on the part of the Javanese to maintain some contact with the Middle Eastern sources of Islam did not cause them to abandon many older ideas. Pre-Islamic cultural legacies such as the *wayang* (shadow-puppet) theater continued to thrive, and the *wayang*'s most popular themes continued to be drawn from the Hindu epics known in Java since pre-Islamic times. The first of Agung's successors to follow him in using the title *sulṭān* was Sultan Haměngkubuwana I of Yogyakarta, who ruled over a century later (1749–92). But he was also likened to the Hindu god Wisnu in a chronicle written by his son, who in the same text compared himself to the Qur'ānic hero Joseph, known in Java in a highly elaborated romance called *Sěrat Yusup.*[25] Wisnu and Yusup were together considered to be appropriate similes for a sultan and his crown prince, whatever orthodox Hindus or Muslims elsewhere might have thought.

For the Central Javanese courts, Islam and religion generally may have been primarily a source of supernatural energy. There is a statement (which may be apochryphal) in a nineteenth-century version of the *Babad Tanah Jawi* which says, "At that time many Javanese wished to be taught the religion of the Prophet and to learn supernatural powers and invincibility."[26] Such supernatural energies were apparently used against the coastal powers, with whom the Mataram rulers of the seventeenth century were often at war. One of their most troublesome opponents was Sunan Giri, who ruled at Grěsik near Surabaya. The first Sunan Giri was supposedly one of the *wali sanga* (the nine apostles) who were said to have introduced Islam in Java, according to the eighteenth- and nineteenth-century chronicles. He and his successors possessed great spiritual and temporal influence. When Sultan Agung subdued Giri about 1636, he did so by putting his force under the command of the son of the last independent ruler of Surabaya (subdued by Agung in 1625), who was related to the family of Sunan Ngampel-Děnta, an even more senior *wali* than Giri.[27] Thereby was Giri's supernatural energy (and popular influence) undermined. Coastal Islam was perhaps equally concerned with the cultivation of spiritual energies. When the lords of Giri again opposed Mataram during the Trunajaya war (1675–80), the ruler of Giri prepared for his last fatal battle against the Dutch and Mataram armies with magic rituals. He is said by a Dutch report to have announced that he had spoken with the king of the spirits in the smoke of a fire, who had promised to protect each of his sons in battle with a thousand spirits.[28]

Of the main dramatis personae of Javanese history before the nineteenth century, perhaps the one who seems most self-consciously Muslim was Raden Trunajaya, who was killed in January 1680, after his unsuccessful rebellion against Mataram. He was from the adjacent island of Madura which had apparently adopted Islam later than Java's coastal port cities[29] but where Islam has struck deeper roots than in Central Java. In his last testament, a letter to Amangkurat II (1677–1703), Trunajaya admonished the king not to mingle with the Dutch Christians, who had joined Mataram to defeat Trunajaya. He feared Dutch rule would cause the Javanese all to be converted to Christianity, which was itself a comment on his view of the depth of the Javanese commitment to Islam. Rather, said Trunajaya, the king should take his court to Majapahit, "so the whole island of Java may know that Your Highness has established his court there."[30] Majapahit was, according to Javanese tradition, the last great Hindu-Buddhist kingdom of Java. This suggests that Trunajaya saw Islam as a part of the Javanese identity, which also included the glorious pre-Islamic past of Java but which (for him) did not include submission to Europeans.

It may now be possible to suggest some general historical conclusions on the conversion of the Javanese to Islam down to the end of the eighteenth century. Most Javanese had probably adopted the new faith, but it was an idiosyncratic Islam which flourished. It was mystical, much given to metaphysical speculation of a kind not greatly different from that of pre-Islamic days. Some Arabic texts were known in Javanese translation, including of course Arabic texts of the Qur'ān with interlinear Javanese translations or glosses.[31] But knowledge of Arabic was probably limited to a very small circle of religious teachers. These established religious schools called *pĕsantren,* "place of the *santri.*" In this period the term *santri*[32] meant merely a student of religion; only later did it acquire the meaning of a strict follower of Muslim religious practice, in which sense it is used by Professor Geertz. Although Java has never produced any indigenous Muslim scholars of international stature, some of these *santri* must have been learned in Islamic law and theology. But some *santri* apparently used texts of pre-Islamic as well as Islamic origin in their teaching (e.g. *Sĕrat Rama, Dewa Ruci, Bratayuda, Minta Raga,* etc.). The issues of orthodoxy and heresy which were important in some other areas of Indonesia, such as seventeenth-century Acheh,[33] seem not to have had much importance in Java. If one had wished to seek orthodox Islamic mysticism in seventeenth- or eighteenth-century Java, one would have been most likely to have found it on the coast. But if one had sought an austere, exclusive, puritanical orthodoxy, one would probably have found few adherents anywhere. The old culture grew and lived on in a more-or-less Islamic garb. For much of the populace of Central Java, the Goddess of the Southern Ocean undoubtedly was the most important spiritual force in their lives, as she is still today.

Javanese Muslims probably had little doubt that their faith was true and correct. The idea that many of them were "bad Muslims" would not have occurred to them. If some visitor or teacher told them their neglect of daily prayer or other formal transgressions required reform, most Javanese would probably have taken the view that each finds his own way to God. The tradition of religious tolerance in Java made any serious doctrinal conflict unlikely.

However deep the conversion of the Javanese did or did not go at this stage, seeds had been planted which were to produce bitter fruits. Being Muslims, the Javanese were potentially susceptible to pressures for greater Islamic orthodoxy. And since they were by nature committed to mysticism, relatively unconcerned about personal religious practice (except as ritual releasing supernatural energies or warding off baneful forces), and inclined to feel that the relation between one's soul and one's God was essentially an internal and secret matter, greater pressures for orthodoxy could produce among some Javanese a reaction against what might seem a distasteful intrusion into their spiritual life. This would lead by the twentieth century to a situation in which Javanese society would perceive itself as consisting of groups split on religious lines.

NOTES

1. G. W. J. Drewes, "New Light on the Coming of Islam to Indonesia?" *BKI* 124, no. 4 (1968), pp. 433–459. This article can be recommended to readers who wish to have a review of the extant literature on this question by one of the leading authorities on Indonesian Islam.

A new and important study of the materials on Javanese political history during the initial conversion period is H. J. de Graaf and Th. G. Th. Pigeaud, "De eerste Moslimse vorstendommen op Java: Studiën over de staatkundige geschiedenis van de 15de en 16de eeuw," *VKI* 69 (1974).

2. *Nāgarakĕrtāgama,* canto 1:1–2. See the edition and translation in Th. G. Th. Pigeaud, *Java in the 14th Century: A Study in Cultural History,* 5 vols. (The Hague, 1960–1963).
3. I am ignoring the late eleventh- or early twelfth-century tomb at Leran, since the date when this gravestone was imported to Java may be much later than the date of its inscription. In any case, it seems clearly to be the grave of a foreign, rather than a Javanese, Muslim. Foreign Muslims had probably been living, travelling, and dying in Java for centuries before there was any significant Javanese conversion to Islam. See J. P. Moquette, "De oudste Mohammedaansche inscriptie op Java, n.m. de Graafsteen te Leran," *Handelingen van het eerste congres voor de taal-, land- en volkenkunde van Java* (Weltevreden, 1921), pp. 391–399; Paul Ravaisse, "L'inscription coufique de Léran à Java," *TBG* 65(1925), pp. 668–703.
4. See G. W. J. Drewes, "Indonesia: Mysticism and Activism," p. 286, in G. E. von Grunebaum, ed., *Unity and Variety in Muslim Civilization* (Chicago, 1955).
5. L-Ch. Damais, "L'épigraphie musulmane dans le sud-est asiatique," *BEFEO* 54 (1968), p. 574. On the older stone at Leran see note 3 above.
6. Idem, "Études javanaises: I, les tombes musulmanes datées de Trálájá," *BEFEO* 48 (1957), pp. 353–415. See also idem, "L'épigraphie musulmane," p. 573.
7. See the texts in M. C. Ricklefs, "A Consideration of Three Versions of the *Babad Tanah Djawi,* with excerpts on the fall of Madjapahit," *BSOAS* 35, part 2, (1972), pp. 296–297, 304–305.

   At Trawulan there is also found the grave of a Muslim dignitary, dated Śaka 1370 (A.D. 1448), traditionally said to have been a queen of Majapahit, the Princess of Champa (*Putri Cĕmpa*). Damais ("L'épigraphie musulmane," pp. 573–574) also discusses this stone and the possibility that *Cĕmpa* is Jĕmpa in Aceh, not Champa. This latter suggestion is, however, probably incorrect. In the full *Babad Tanah Jawi* texts *Putri Cĕmpa* is also called the princess of *Dyarawati* or *Darawati,* which could only be on the Indochinese peninsula (although not necessarily Champa), not in Aceh; see M. C. Ricklefs, *Jogjakarta under Sultan Mangkubumi, 1749–1792: A History of the Division of Java* (London, 1974), p. 3 n. 9.
8. Armando Cortesão, ed. and trans., *The Suma Oriental of Tomé Pires and the Book of Francisco Rodrigues,* 2 vols (London, 1944), vol. 1, pp. 213–218.
9. P. J. Zoetmulder, "Die Hochreligionen Indonesiens," p. 273, in Waldemar Stöhr and Piet Zoetmulder, *Die Religionen Indonesiens* (Stuttgart, 1965); P. J. Zoetmulder, *Kalangwan: A Survey of Old Javanese Literature* (The Hague, 1974), pp. 173–185.
10. See M. A. P. Meilink-Roelofsz, *Asian Trade and European Influence in the Indonesian Archipelago between 1500 and about 1630* (The Hague, 1962).
11. G. W. J. Drewes, ed. and trans., *Een Javaanse primbon uit de zestiende eeuw* (Leiden, 1954); idem, ed. and trans., *The Admonitions of Seh Bari* (The Hague, 1969).
12. Drewes, *Seh Bari.* See especially pp. 42–45, 50–61, 74–87. The doctrines criticized include those of 'Abd al-Wahīd ibn Makkiya; Wibatiniya; Karrāmiyya; Mutangiyya; Ibn al-'Arabī; Shaikhs Sūfī, Nūrī, and Jaddī; and others whose origins are not explained.
13. Cortesão, *Suma Oriental,* vol. 1, pp. 173–200.
14. For example, see W. F. Wertheim, *Indonesian Society in Transition: A Study of Social Changes* (The Hague, 1959), p. 202. See also Drewes, "New Light," pp. 452–53.
15. See H. J. de Graaf, *Geschiedenis van Indonesië* ('s-Gravenhage, 1949), pp. 272–275. The Tĕnggĕr mountain area of Malang remains "Buddhist" to this day.
16. See the story about the conversion of Mataram reported in H. J. de Graaf, ed., *De vijf gezantschapsreizen van Rijklof van Goens naar het Hof van Mataram, 1648–1654* ('s-Gravenhage, 1956), p. 186.
17. Amangkurat II (1677–1703), for instance, used the title *Susuhunan Ratu Amangkurat Senapati Ingalaga Abdulrahman Muhammad Zainal Kubra,* whereas after Pakubuwana I (1703–1719) the rulers used the titles *Susuhunan Pakubuwana* (or *Amangkurat*) *Senapati Ingalaga Ngabdurahman Sayidin Panatagama.* No ruler between 1646 and 1755 consistently used the title *Sultan,* although there are a few occasions when it is mentioned. In 1719 a rebel prince took the title *Sultan Ibnu Mustapa Pakubuwana Senapati Ingalaga Ngabdurahman Sayidin Panatagama.*
18. The sixteenth-century MSS edited by Professor Drewes are both orthodox Sūfī works; see *Seh Bari* and *Javaanse primbon.* See also A. H. Johns, ed. and trans, *The Gift Addressed to the Spirit of the Prophet* (Canberra, 1965).

    For further discussion of the Sufis, see A. H. Johns, "Muslim Mystics and Historical Writing," pp. 37–49, in D. G. E. Hall, ed., *Historians of South East Asia* (London, 1961); idem, "Sufism as a Category in Indonesian Literature and History," *Journal of Southeast Asian History* 2, no. 2 (July, 1961), pp. 10–23; Drewes, "New Light," pp. 452–453; idem, "Indonesia; Mysticism and Activism."

19. See P. J. Zoetmulder, *Pantheisme en monisme in de Javaansche soeloek-litteratuur* (Nijmegen, 1935). On recent mystical teachings in Java, see Harun Hadiwijono, *Man in the Present Javanese Mysticism* (Baarn, 1967).
20. See Zoetmulder, *Pantheisme en monisme;* idem, "The Wajang as a Philosophical Theme," *Indonesia,* no. 12 (Oct. 1971), pp. 85–96.
21. These traditions are briefly described in Soebardi, "Santri-Religious Elements as Reflected in the Book of Tjentini," *BKI* 127, no. 3 (1971), pp. 346–348, with references to previous literature.
22. There are some hints of Shī'itic influence in Indonesian Islam but they are of a rather elusive nature. See Th. G. Th. Pigeaud, *Literature of Java: Catalogue Raisonné of Javanese Manuscripts in the Library of the University of Leiden and other Public Collections in the Netherlands,* 3 vols. (The Hague and Leiden, 1967–1970) vol. 1, p. 133; Zoetmulder, "Hochreligionen," p. 283.
23. See T. S. Raffles, *The History of Java,* 2 vols. (London, 1830), vol. 2, p. 3. One *haji* who claimed to have acquired magical powers is described in Ricklefs, *Jogjakarta under Sultan Mangkubumi,* p. 264.
24. H. J. de Graaf, "De regering van Sultan Agung, vorst van Mataram 1613–1645, en die van zijn voorganger Panembahan Séda-ing-Krapjak 1601–1613," *VKI* 23 (1958), pp. 264–268.
25. The text is *Babad Mangkubumi* (Leiden University *cod. or.* 2191). This matter is discussed in Ricklefs, *Jogjakarta under Sultan Mangkubumi,* pp. 80–82. A summary of a late-eighteenth-century Central Javanese *Sĕrat Yusup* is to be found in A. C. Vreede, *Catalogus van de Javaansche en Madoereesche handschriften der Leidsche universiteits—bibliotheek* (Leiden, 1892), pp. 26–31.
26. W. L. Olthof, ed. and trans., *Babad Tanah Djawi in proza: Javaansche geschiedenis,* 2 vols. ('s-Gravenhage, 1941), text p. 46, trans. p. 48.
27. De Graaf, "Sultan Agung," pp. 205–220.
28. *Dagh-register, gehouden int casteel Batavia vant passerende daer ter plaetse als over geheel Nederlandts India* ('s-Hage, 1896–1931), *1680,* pp. 323–324.
29. Cortesão, *Suma Oriental,* vol. 1, pp. 227–228, (Tomé Pires) says Madura was still "heathen" in 1512–1515.
30. H. J. de Graaf, "De opkomst van Raden Trunadjaja," *Djåwå* 20(1940), p. 86; see also idem, "Gevanǵenneming en dood van Raden Truna-Djaja, 26 Dec. 1679—2 Jan. 1680," *TBG.* 85, no. 2(1952), pp. 290–291.
31. See Pigeaud, *Literature,* vol. 1, pp. 81 ff. Many Arabic MSS from Java are registered in P. Voorhoeve, *Handlist of Arabic Manuscripts in the Library of the University of Leiden and other Collections in the Netherlands* (Leiden, 1957). Several early MSS of this type are to be found in British MSS collections; see M. C. Ricklefs and P. Voorhoeve, *Indonesian Manuscripts in Great Britain: A Catalogue of Manuscripts in Indonesian Languages in British Public Collections* (Oxford, 1977).
32. The etymology of this term is not clear. Zoetmulder, "Hochreligionen," p. 293, suggests that it comes from Sanskrit *śāstrī* (one who has studied the scriptures) but this is not entirely certain. It may be connected with Javanese *cantrik* (servant, pupil), which is also said perhaps to derive from *śāstrī* in J. F. C. Gericke and T. Roorda, *Javaansch-Nederlandsch handwoordenboek,* revised edition, ed. by A. C. Vreede and J. G. H. Gunning, 2 vols. (Amsterdam and Leiden, 1901), vol 1, p. 247. It is of interest here that the first edition of this dictionary, which sometimes contains older meanings which were regarded as obsolete in 1901 and were therefore dropped from the revised edition, defines *cantrik* as "a pupil of a *Buda*-priest"; J. F. C. Gericke and T. Roorda, *Javaansch-Nederduitsch woordenboek* (Amsterdam, 1847), p. 102.
33. See Denys Lombard, *Le sultanat d'Atjéh au temps d'Iskandar Muda, 1607–1636* (Paris, 1967), pp. 159–164.

Islamization of the Malays: A Transformation of Culture

MOHD. TAIB OSMAN

It is said that the main single contribution attributed to the Sufis in facilitating conversion to Islam in the Archipelago has been their ability to syncretise Islamic ideas with existing local beliefs and religious notions and their tolerance towards these pre-Islamic beliefs. But one should also bear in mind that Sufism continued to be practised long after the initial conversion. In this case, Sufism had nothing to do with the attempt to accommodate earlier beliefs, but had come to function as a pious practice for those who were attracted to its mystical approach to religion, even if its doctrines were regarded as heretical by some schools in Islam. The writings of the seventeenth century Indonesian Sufis in north Sumatra are a case in point. As A.H. Johns puts it in another paper, "in this instance (these writings are) not a matter of syncretism with primitive cults, but a deviation that was part of the Islamic tradition itself."[1]

This brings us to an important point in understanding the background of Islam among the Malays. The Sufis, and also other early propagators of Islam in the area, brought with them popular beliefs which, properly speaking, stand outside the strict teachings of Islam. Most of these popular elements arose not only when Islam spread from Arabia to Persia and then to India, but also through earlier Arabic contacts with the Egyptians, Hebrews and Christians in the west. Local elements tended to be added to the ever expanding Islamic civilization, and Islamic elements themselves were prone to be given new meanings and functions. It was inescapable that such situations should arise as Islam imposed itself on already established belief systems. The practice of mysticism helped to facilitate such processes. In the Archipelago, Islamic ideas came to be identified with existing beliefs. The spread of Islam also brought with it magical beliefs and practices popular among the Persians and Indian Muslims. Some of the texts on Islamic magic are still today regarded as *Kitab*, a term usually reserved for religious books. One of the most celebrated works held in high esteem by the Malay peasantry is *Taj-ul-Muluk*, which is often regarded as a standard reference for Islamic magic. Besides magic, *Taj-ul-Muluk* also contains chapters on curing illnesses. Besides the *Taj*, there are many other versions which deal with magic and cures for illnesses and they are collectively known as *Kitab Tib*. Saint-worship or the worship at the graveside of holy men, which is quite wide-spread in other Muslim areas, is another example of the product of Islamic mysticism. This complex of beliefs is known as *keramat*-worship among the Malays. Like other folk or popular belief traditions, there are many forms and versions of *keramat*-worship. However such beliefs and practices are informal aspects which have not been

Reprinted in abridged form from *Tamadun di Malaysia* (1980), 1–8, by permission of the author and Persatuan Sejarah Malaysia, Kuala Lumpur, Malaysia.

accepted or recognised formally. Hence they are on the periphery of Malay life, tolerated but not officially recognised by the learned or *ulama*.

The Malays today belong to the orthodox *Sunni* sect, but the total impact of Islamic culture had come from many different directions. Islamic Malay culture is actually woven from numerous diverse strands. The early propagators came principally from India, from the Malabar coasts and from Gujerat. Richard Winstedt, for example, suggests that conversion to Islam was facilitated by the fact that the early Indian missionaries were able to syncretise Islamic teachings with existing beliefs.[2] It is interesting to note in this connection that the Sanskrit terms for some religious notions have been applied to Islamic practices instead of adopting Arabic terms. Sanskrit words such as *puasa* for "fasting," *neraka* for "hell", and *shurga* for "heaven" are representative examples. Even the word for religion is taken from Sanskrit, that is *agama*. Sufism and popular Islamic elements were brought to the Archipelago from India to a much greater extent than from Persia or Arabia. However, whether they had come directly or indirectly, Persian influence on the culture of the Malays has been particularly strong, especially on the Malay royal courts. Malay court ceremonies, the title "Shah" for the Sultans or rulers, literature and ideas on statecraft and kingship, the literary style of court literature, religious literature of *Shi'ite* tradition, Sufi writings, and popular narratives, all bear indelible marks of Persian influence.[3]

In addition to the Indians and Persians, the Arabs also played a role in bringing to bear the influence of Islamic civilization on the Malays. By the seventeenth century A.D. there were already permanent settlements of Arabs in the Archipelago, and "wandering Arab traders, adventurers, and religious scholars had been a feature of Malay life for many hundred years."[4] As stated above, in the Philippines as well as in other parts of the Archipelago, the status accorded the "sayyid" (descendants of the Holy Prophet) enabled some to carve out kingdoms for themselves and ruled over the Malay subjects. As descendants of the Holy Prophet as they claimed themselves to be, they were regarded as having not only a charisma but piety and knowledge in religious matters. The Arabs were often involved in the local politics and with the esteem they were held by the local population they often ended up in the position of advantage. But still their contribution had been in the field of religious knowledge as suggested by William Roff:

> . . . the Malays had for centuries tended to look upon all Arabs, whatever their origin, as the direct inheritors of the wisdom of Islam, and on Sayyids in particular . . . as possessed of unexampled piety and religious merit.[5]

As opposed to the earlier propagators of Islam from India and Persia who were responsible for the spread of pantheistic mysticism and other popular elements of Islam, the Arabs had familiarised the Malays with the orthodox teachings of the religion. This does not mean that the Arabs had had no hand in the spread of popular Islamic beliefs and practices, for itinerant Arab mendicants performing magic and divination have been known in the Archipelago for a long time. In fact most of the *keramat* worshipped by the Malays are the graves or sites once connected with Arab traders or adventurers. And Arab merchants who travelled from village to village would often have semi-precious stones and talismen which they claimed had special magical qualities.

More important than the role of the Arabs in advancing orthodox teachings is the closer contact the Malays enjoyed with the Arab world during the last two centuries. Two phenomena should be singled out: the first is the "Wahhabi" reformation, a movement which swept the Arab world in the middle of the eighteenth century, and the second is the "modernist" movement started in the last century by scholars like Sayyid Djamal al-Din al-Afghani and Muhammad 'Abduh of Egypt. The main aim of the "Wahhabi" movement was to return to the purity of Islamic monotheism. Thus it campaigned and attacked vigorously any form of practice or belief that might have contaminated these ideals. The pre-Islamic survivals, magical practices and saint-worship which had come to attach themselves to the religious practices of the Muslims, were condemned and attacked. The influence of the movement in furthering the character of orthodoxy among the Malays had been quite considerable. The second movement too had its roots in the "Wahhabi" ideals, but the stress had been more on "modernistic" reforms. In Indonesia, the reform movements like *Muhammadiah* and others were not only interested in furthering the teachings of Islam but had built up organisations which also served the public by establishing schools and hospitals.[6] In the Peninsula, the reformers of the modernist school were referred to as *Kaum Muda* and they lashed away at both the Malay peasantry as well as the aristocracy for subscribing to the un-Islamic beliefs and customs of the past, which feature a great deal not only in the rituals and ceremonials but also in the everyday life of the people.

Of the cultural influence that Islam had brought to bear on the Malays, those in the field of literature have been the most profound. The literary heritage of the Malays has been exclusively written in the Perso-Arabic script, including those literary works carried over from the Hindu period. The connection of literary activity with the royal court is richly reflected in the literature. Treatises on duties of kingship and concepts of state are represented in books like *Taj-us-Salatin* (The Crown of Kings) and *Bustan-us-Salatin* (The Garden of Kings). Theologians who flocked to the royal courts translated and wrote works on Islamic jurisprudence, theology, and history. Even the state chronicles, which claimed a sacred origin for the ruling dynasties, were modelled on Persian or Indian works such as *Shah-Nameh* and *Akbar Nameh.* Islam also introduced a wealth of writings on mysticism to the Malay world. These writings do not represent attempts at syncretism with polytheistic beliefs. They are doctrinal exercises in the tradition of Islam. Tales of heroes were among the earliest stories to be introduced to the area. Winstedt claims that "the first task of the missionaries was to substitute for the Hindu epics tales of the heroes of Islam."[7] These hero tales fitted into the feudal structure of the society as did the *Mahabharata* and *Ramayanan* in the Hindu period. From the Muslims' lands of Persia and India came works bearing *Shi'ite* influence and spurious treatment of Islamic history and theology. Tales of the lives of the prophets based on popular legends, Sufi thoughts couched in simplistic terms, and treatises on magic and divination had been circulating in the Malay Archipelago since the early days of Islam. It is from these sources that popular Islamic notions were introduced to the Malay masses.

As far as the basic tenets of Islam were concerned, the impact of Islamic ideology had been felt in the royal courts as well as in the villages. But the total impact of Muslim civilization apparently had different meanings at the different social levels. Thus literature about statecraft or doctrinal discussions on points of theology would principally belong to the courtly circles, while popular religious literature and the romances would inevitably find their way to the masses. The point to be made is that the scholarly tradition of Islam was nurtured within the precincts of the royal courts[8] or if there was no royal patronage, there would have been schools established by scholars of repute and to these scholars the aspiring young students would flock to study religious knowledge. The *Pesantren* (as it is known in Indonesia) and *Sekolah Pondok* (as it is known in the Peninsula) used to be the centres of religious instruction. Although such schools later became the stronghold of the conservative scholars as against the teachings of the so-called "modernistic reformers", they had served for a long time as the point of reference for Islamic knowledge. The peasantry, on the hand, while subscribing to the basic tenets of Islam were quite often unaware of the scholastic traditions of religious knowledge.

The characteristics of the early period of conversion have to be contrasted with the subsequent trend towards orthodoxy and rigorous application of the Islamic teachings. Retentions of past beliefs still form a part of the Malays' belief system, and popular Islamic elements are still tolerated in everyday life. Yet, the Malays hasten to claim that they are good *Sunni* Muslims. Today, Islam is the declared official religion of Malaysia, although Malaysia itself is not a theocracy, and freedom to worship any other religion is guaranteed by the Constitution. In the component Malay states there had been established government departments which dealt with the administration of religious affairs in all aspects. In the period of British administration, religious affairs and local Malay customs were under the jurisdiction of the Sultans and these were administered through either a department, a council or the Sultan's office. But after 1948, every state in the Federation of Malaya had established a religious affairs department. Muslims in Malaysia are also subjected to Islamic law which is applied as "personal status law", and subjected to the jurisdiction of religious courts (*mahkamah syariah*) which are presided over by the religious judges. At the same time Islamic religious education in Malaysia has been given a new dimension with the establishment of religious faculties and departments in the universities.

In the light of these new developments, it is difficult to say that Islam has not transformed the cultural values of the people. Snouck Hurgronje had observed that conversion to Islam among the peoples of the Malay Archipelago was characterized by expansion rather than intensification. But such a statement seems to be applicable only to the early period of Islam in the Malay world. It does not give an accurate picture of Islam in its subsequent development. Nevertheless, a substratum of older beliefs and a cultural heritage (usually subsumed under the Arabic derived term *'adat*) has continued to exist among the Malays. To say that the Malays are eclectic in their religious observance is to miss the point. There are conflicts to be sure, but such conflicts can best be described in the way P.E. de Josselin de Jong views the position of customary law (*'adat*) and Islamic law (*syara'*) in a Malay community:

> (The conflict) is between two systems of ideals and practices, both of which were considered by the society concerned as being an integral of its culture, both applicable to the entire society, and both perceived as a system by inhabitants of that society.[9]

We may add, furthermore, that each system serves a different function in the total culture of the people. But since the fourteenth century A.D. onwards, it can safely be said that Islam had transformed the culture of the Malays. From then on, it is the Islamic belief and *ethos* that have become the foundation of the culture of the Malays.

NOTES

1. "Aspects of Sufi Thoughts in Indonesia," *Journal of the Malayan Branch of the Royal Asiatic Society,* XXVIII, 1 (1955), 70–77.
2. *The Malays: A Cultural History*, New York, 1950, pp. 35–36.
3. See G.E. Marrison, "Persian Influences as Malay life," *Journal of the Malayan Branch of the Royal Asiatic Society,* XXVIII (1955) pp. 52–69.
4. William R., Roff, "The Malayo-Muslim World of Singapore at the Close of the Nineteenth Century", *Journal of Asian Studies,* XXIV (1964), p. 80.
5. *Ibid.,* p. 81.
6. See Delia Noer, *The Modernist Muslim Movement in Indonesia, 1900–1942,* Singapore, Kuala Lumpur, 1973.
7. *The Malays: A Cultural History,* p. 145.
8. See Mohd. Taib Osman, "Raja Ali Haji of Riau: A Figure of Transition or the Last of the Classical Pujanggas?" in *Bahasa Kesusasteraan dan Kebudayaan Melayu: Essei-Essei Penghormatan Kepada Pendita Za'aba,* Kuala Lumpur, 1976, pp. 136–160.
9. "Islam versus Adat in Negeri Sembilan (Malaya)," *Bijdragen tot de Taal-, Land-en Volkenkunde,* CXVI, 1, (1960), p. 203.

An Analysis of the "Genealogy of Sulu"*

CESAR ADIB MAJUL

The term *tarsila* comes from the Arabic *silsilah*, which means a chain or link. It is used in the Muslim South as in other parts of the Indonesian and Malay world to refer to written genealogical accounts. One of the primary functions of the *tarsila* was to trace the ancestry of an individual or family to a famous personality in the past who was either an important political figure or religious teacher. This fact immediately suggests that *tarsilas* were not meant to remain purely historical documents or quaint remembrances of things past. On the contrary, they served to bolster the claim of individuals or families to hold political power or to enjoy certain traditional prerogatives or at least some prestige in their respective communities. Consequently, all sultans and leading datus had their respective *tarsilas*.

Obviously, if *tarsilas* were to serve their purposes, they had to be kept up to date. When written on perishable materials, such as paper, their contents were preserved by copying them on new paper. Thus, the age of the material used is no index to the age or authenticity of the accounts. However, it is commonly accepted that the use of the Malay language, especially in the earlier parts of *tarsilas*, is an index to their ancient character — at least for those parts in Malay. The use of this criteria is quite reasonable. Sulu was intimately involved in the trade which covered the Malay peninsula and Indonesian archipelago as far back as the 13th century, if not earlier. And, as is well-known, the *lingua franca* of the traders was Malay. This language was also extensively used in the Sulu court, just as it was in the courts of Malacca, Brunei, and so on. It was only during the 17th century, with the coming of the Spaniards to the Philippine archipelago and other Europeans to other parts of Southeast Asia that the Sulus gradually became isolated from other Malay lands. It was then that the use of Malay in the Sulu court began to decline.

The tradition of writing or having *tarsilas* among the Muslims in the Philippines probably derived from the Muslim principalities in the neighboring Indonesian islands which had an earlier history of Islamization. In turn, these principalities used as a model the earliest part of the *Sīrāt Rasūl Allah* (*The Biography of the Messenger of Allah*) as their model. This work was written by Ibn Ishāq (c. 85 A.H. — 151 A.H. or c. 704 A.D. — 768 A.D.). Its first paragraph, in the recension of Ibn Hishām, contains the genealogy of the Prophet Muhammad, tracing his descent from Adam — a total of 48 generations. The style here is not much different from that found in the Jewish Bible regarding genealogies.

It would be a mistake to look at the *tarsilas* of the South as purely genealogical documents. Actually, they may contain descriptions of some of personages mentioned, place names, and actual data regarding historical events in the

*Paper prepared for a Filipino Muslim History and Culture Seminar-Workshop, Department of History, College of Arts and Sciences, University of the East, Manila, October 20, 1977.

past. Some *tarsilas* even include mythological elements, some of which have now lost their meaning for us. In brief, *tarsilas* were meant to accomplish a few aims beyond the genealogical function. These aims will be discussed in greater detail later on.

II

We are all greatly indebted to Dr. Najeeb Saleeby for the collection, translation, and publication of many *tarsilas* from Sulu and Mindanao in the first decade of this century. We owe Saleeby even more, considering that many of these documents had been burnt or lost during the last days of the Japanese Occupation in 1945. This especially holds true for the Sulu documents belonging to the Kiram family and Haji Buto 'Abdul Bāqī of Sulu. Unfortunately, too, not a few *tarsilas* in the possession of some of the leading Muslim families in the upper valley of the Pulangi had been burned in 1972 as a result of fighting between government troops and secessionists in the area. Nevertheless, there still exist *tarsilas* among some families there — at least this is what we have been assured.

In the past, *tarsilas* were jealously guarded from the prying eyes of the curious, especially those of strangers. It took Saleeby, who was an Arab from Lebanon, years of friendship with the families of the sultans and chief datus to succeed in seeing the *tarsilas* and having them published. Yet, even he, missed some important ones, possibly because of mistrust. For example, he did not have the chance to see the ones from the Buluan and Tawi-Tawi areas. In any case the debt of Philippine Muslim scholars to Saleeby remains inestimable.

That the sultans jealously guarded their *tarsilas* does not mean that they did not divulge some of their contents to foreigners. For example, Alexander Dalrymple, who was in Sulu in 1761 and 1764 and who came to know the Sulu Sultan 'Azīm ud-Dīn (Alimudin) in Manila, learned from the Sultan and other leading datus many details of Sulu *tarsilas* which correspond to those published by Saleeby in 1908. Likewise, Thomas Forrest, who was in Maguindanao in 1775, was able to put down in writing the dictation of Faqir Maulana Hamza, a Maguindanao sultan, who was consulting his *tarsilas* on data concerning the history of Maguindanao. Moreover, the Sultan appeared to have known the genealogies of the sultans of Sulu and Brunei, to the extent of claiming that they, together with the sultans of Maguindanao, had a common Arab ancestor somewhere in the dim past. Significantly, some Maguindanao *tarsilas* make it a point to mention dynastic or marriage relations between the royal families of Maguindanao and Sulu. The Brunei *Selesilah,* likewise, makes reference to a marriage between the Brunei royal family and that of Sulu. John Hunt, who was in Sulu in 1814, appeared to have had indirect information regarding various Brunei and Sulu *tarsilas*, probably from his datu friends. Writing from memory, however, his account is a bit unreliable since he often confuses different sultans with one another and unnecessarily telescopes events. But anyone with a knowledge of Dalrymple's works and Spanish sources can easily recognize the misidentifications in the genealogy and historical events reported by Hunt. No less than seven varied sources must have been available to him. If he had reported them separately, according to specified sources, instead of lumping them together, he would have been of greater value to present scholars.

What follows is a description and analysis of the Sulu *tarsilas* published by Saleeby.

III

The so-called "Genealogy of Sulu" was published by Saleeby in 1907 in a chapter in his important work *The History of Sulu.*[1] It was supplemented, in the same chapter, by another *tarsila* entitled by him as "Sulu Historical Notes". For convenience, Saleeby also entitled various parts of the "Genealogy of Sulu" in accordance with subject matter. They are successively as follows: "Sulu author's introduction", "Descendants of Asip", "Descendants of Tuan Masha'ika", and "Original and later settlers of Sulu".[2]

The first part deals with the writer of the *tarsilas* while the second part is a *tarsila* having to do with the descendants of Asip, one of the ministers who came to Sulu with Raja Baguinda, a Sumatran prince. Incidentally, the writer of the *tarsilas* claimed descent from this minister. The other two *tarsilas*, namely, the "Descendants of Tuan Masha'ika" and the "Original and later settlers of Sulu", as well as the "Sulu Historical Notes" were written in Malay, attesting to their antiquity. It is believed that the "Sulu Historical Notes" which consists of four parts, was originally composed before the "Descendants of Tuan Masha'ika" and the "Original and later settlers of Sulu". All three *tarsilas* have many elements in common, but unlike the "Original and later settlers of Sulu", the "Sulu Historical Notes" does not deal either with the first sultan or his descendants.

Disregarding some differences, if not actual inconsistencies, between the above three *tarsilas,* and setting aside certain details which are not quite relevant for purposes of this essay, what follows is their summary:

During the time of Raja Sipad the younger, a son or descendant of Raja Sipad the older, a certain Tuan Masha'ika arrives in Jolo island, in the area now known as Maimbung. At that time, the inhabitants there are not Muslims but worshippers of stones of various sorts and tombs. On account of his qualities, probably regarding knowledge and skills, he is very much esteemed and respected by the people. In time, he marries a daughter of Raja Sipad. She bears him three children of which two, one male and one female, have Arab names. The name of the female, 'Aisha, is a typical Muslim name. One of the sons, Tuan Hakim, in turn, has four sons (Tuan Da'im, Tuan Buda, Tuan Bujang, and Tuan Muku) and a girl.

Not long after, people from Basilan (called *Tagimahas*) and another group called *Baklayas* settle in Sulu. They are followed by Bajaos supposed to have come from Johore. The Bajaos do not remain in one place but become scattered in various islands.

Some time after the arrival of the Bajaos, a certain Karim ul-makhdum, entitled Sharīf Awliyā, arrives in Sulu and eventually settles among the Tagimaha nobles in Buansa who then built a mosque. At this time, the people of Sulu begin to adopt Islam. Ten years later (it is not clear whether after the arrival of Karim ul-makhdum or after the building of the mosque), Raja Baguinda from Menangkabaw, Sumatra, appears with his followers, in Buansa. There is a fight between the Raja and his followers on one hand, and the Tagimaha chiefs of Buansa and their followers on the other. After this, peace ensues, especially when, it is said, it was found out that Raja Baguinda was a Muslim like the Buansa chiefs. Raja Baguinda appears to have become a chief in Buansa as evidenced by the report that five years after his arrival, he receives a gift of elephants from the Raja of Java. In any case, Raja Baguinda settles in Buansa and marries there. It is important to note at this point that one of the *tarsilas* mentions that during the arrival of Raja Baguinda, some of the Sulu chiefs (not from Buansa) were Tuan Buda, Tuan Da'im, and Tuan Bujang. These chiefs, it will be recalled, were grandchildren of Tuan Masha'ika of Maimbung.

Now, according to the "Original and later settlers of Sulu", it was while Raja Baguinda was in Buansa that Sayyid Abu Bakr, after having stayed in or passed through Palembang (in Sumatra) and Brunei, arrives and preaches Islam. The people then become more attached to Islam. Abu Bakr then marries Paramisuli, the daughter of Raja Baguinda, and ends by establishing himself as the first sultan. He lives thirty years in Buansa and upon his death, one of his sons, Kamal ud-Dīn, succeeds him as sultan.

The enumeration of sultans in the "Genealogy of Sulu" is as follows:[3]

1. Abu Bakr (Sultan Sharif)
2. Kamalud Din
3. Maharaja Upo
4. Pangiran Buddiman
5. Sultan Tanga
6. Sultan Bungsu
7. Sultan Nasirud Din
8. Sultan Karamat
9. Sultan Shahabud Din
10. Sultan Mustafa Shapiud Din
11. Sultan Mohammad Nasarud Din
12. Sultan Alimud Din I
13. Sultan Mohammad Mu'izzid Din
14. Sultan Isra'il
15. Sultan Mohammed Alimud Din II
16. Sultan Mohammed Sarapud Din
17. Sultan Mohammed Alimud Din III

Judging from the last name in this list of sultans, this enumeration of sultans was completed around 1808 since 'Azīm ud-Dīn III (Alimud Din III), No. 17 and last in the list, ruled and died in this same year. He was sultan for only 40 days. The earlier portions of the chapter must have been written much earlier. Some of its contents were even told to Dalrymple in 1761.

The above brief summary suggests various observations and conclusions:

1. The genealogy of Sulu asserts that the earliest inhabitants of Jolo island were centered in the area of Maimbung, in the southern part of the island. Their rulers were entitled "Raja Sipad", from the Sanskrit Raja Shripaduka, a title of Indian or Hindu origin. The second to arrive were the Tagimahas who came from Basilan and who settled in Buansa, in the northern part of the island west of the present Jolo town. The third to come were the Baklayas who settled in the northern part of the island east of Jolo town. They were followed by the Bajaos (and Samals) who distributed themselves all over the Sulu archipelago.
2. Tuan Masha'ika was one of the first foreign Muslims to come to the Maimbung area and, therefore, to Jolo island. That some of his children and grandchildren had Arabic names supports this view. Moreover, the "Sulu Historical Notes" state that "Masha'ika begot Mawmin". Now, the word "mu'min" (pl. mu'minin) is an Arabic term for "the faithful" or "believer". The phrase, therefore, means that Masha'ika begot Muslims. (However, it is possible that "mu'min" is used as a proper name and may actually refer to a son by that name.) Furthermore, the word *"mashā'ikh"* is one of the Arabic plural forms for *"shaikh"*, a title of respect. In South Arabia, the term *"mashā'ikh"* is also used for pious men or religious leaders to distinguish them from the "sayyids" or "sharīfs" who are descendants of the Prophet Muhammad. Of common knowledge, too, is the fact that the majority of Arabs who settled in the Indonesian archipelago came from South Arabia.
3. The account of the genealogy of Tuan Masha'ika that he was "born out of a bamboo and was esteemed and respected by all the people", not only reveals that his land of origin was unknown, but also serves to emphasize his greater knowledge *vis-à-vis* the people he came to live with. The other report in the "Sulu Historical Notes" that the parents of Tuan Masha'ika were sent to Sulu by Alexander the Great shows that the writer of the "Sulu Historical Notes" was acquainted, in one way or another, with the traditions of the Malacca sultans who claimed descent from Alexander the Great. Other Sulu traditions state that the rulers of Sulu were descended from Alexander the Great. This is simply a technique to bolster the claim for legitimacy to rule, for the rulers of Sulu were, in this case, claiming kinship with the Malacca sultans.
4. The coming of Karim ul-makhdum, suggests the coming of a Muslim to actually preach Islam. This is unlike the coming of Tuan Masha'ika to whom neither the preaching of Islam nor the building of a mosque is attributed. The word *"makhdum"*, in Arabic, means "master". In Arab lands, it is used as a converse of "server". However, in India and in the land of the Malays, the word came to be used as a title for Muslim religious teachers or scholars and pious men. That he was called "Sharīf Awliyā" suggests that people considered him a descendant of the Prophet Muhammad since this is what "Sharīf" connotes. That he was entitled "Awliyā", the Arabic plural for *walī* or saint, implies that he was a pious man.
5. The coming of Raja Baguinda from Sumatra and his establishment of a principality in Buansa creates a dramatic link between Sulu and a center of an older empire, that of Srivijaya, which was based on Sumatra. In personal terms, this means that Raja Baguinda was sort of claiming an uninterrupted sovereignty. His marriage with a local girl also means that his descendants who became sultans had rights to land in Sulu by virtue of bilateral relations. In brief, the Sulu sultans, who were descended from Raja Baguinda could not be criticized as representing a foreign dynasty since, after all, their ancestress

who married the Raja was a local girl. In effect, the links with Raja Baguinda who was asserted to be a Sumatran prince bolstered the claims of Sulu sultans to reign in Malay lands.

6. Sayyid Abu Bakr, who was entitled Sultan Sharīf, is also asserted to have been a descendant of the Prophet Muhammad. The word "sayyid" like "sharīf" connotes this. It has been held by some classical Muslim jurists that one of the qualifications for a *khalīf* was to belong to the Quraish or family of the Prophet. Clearly, then, the claim of the Sulu sultans to rule over Muslims is based on their reputed descent from the Prophet, through Sayyid Abu Bakr. But again, to strengthen their claims on the land without appearing fully as a foreign dynasty, the Sulu sultans claimed descent from the wife of the first sultan who, in spite of her being a daughter of Raja Baguinda, was considered a local girl. Indeed, her mother was a lady from Buansa.
7. In brief, the Sulu *tarsilas*, particularly those owned by the Sulu royal family, are not mere genealogical accounts made for antiquarian interests, but represent documents *par excellence* to support their claim of legitimacy to rule over Muslims as well as their claims to their right to the land. The tarsilas are also meant to show kinship and historical links between Sulu and older centers of empire.
8. Of great importance is that the three above-mentioned *tarsilas* try to explain the advent and the spread of Islam in Sulu. As such, they represent an affirmation that Sulu constituted an important part of the Islamic international community — that of *dār-ul-Islām*.

The problem can now be raised as to the authenticity or historicity of the personalities and accounts found in the *tarsilas* as well as to that of the chronology.

First of all, the elaborate and well-preserved tomb of the first Sulu Sultan, Sultan Sharīf, still exists on one of the slopes of Mt. Tumangtangis which faces Buansa. The tomb carries the elaborate titles of the Sultan; but, unfortunately, it gives no date. A stone slab nearby is pointed out as the marker of the grave of Kamal ud-Din, the second sultan. According to Spanish records, Spanish soldiers in 1638 destroyed one of the most revered tombs near Buansa. This tomb was a center of pilgrimages and was supposed to be that of a Muslim ruler who had come from other lands. Whether or not this tomb is that of Raja Baguinda remains an unsolved problem.

The fourth sultan, Pangiran Buddiman was known to the Spaniards in 1578. He was a brother-in-law of the Brunei Sultan Seif ur-Rijal and had a home in Brunei. The fifth sultan, called Pangiran Tengah, was also known to the Spaniards and the Jesuit Francisco Combes narrated a few things about him. This same priest also had various times conversed with Sultan Bongsu. In effect, all the sultans numbered from 4 to 17 in the "Genealogy of Sulu", had dealings with the Spaniards and some of them had even communicated with the Dutch and the English. However, that sultans from 4 to 17 are to be considered as historical figures only because of the existence of cross references in European sources, is no criteria why sultans from one to three cannot be regarded as historical figures. It is just unfortunate for scholars that the first three sultans had no dealings with or were unknown to the Spaniards who were simply not around. But, indeed, there are Spanish references to a Sulu ruler in 1521 who happened to be a father-in-law of the Brunei Sultan. This ruler might have been one of the earlier sultans. On the basis of other *tarsilas* or Sulu traditions not reported by Saleeby, it can be accepted that it was the first sultan who put the different peoples of Sulu, including those in the mountains in the interior, under one rule. Thus did Sulu begin to have the semblance of a principality or small state.

Unfortunately, none of the Sulu *tarsilas* contain any date. The same holds true for the Maguindanao *tarsilas*. The Brunei *Selesilah,* however, contains one and only one date. Scholars cannot, so far, be absolutely sure about, or conclusively prove, the existence of Tuan Masha'ika or Raja Baguinda. But this does not mean that they did not exist. On the contrary, to assume that they existed can explain a great deal of Sulu history. Actually, by cross references to other sources, historical or archaeological, the probability is that they actually existed. And more than this, they signify persons involved in the dramatic political and religious transformations in the history of Southeast Asia.

Professor Oliver Wolters in his brilliant book *The Fall of Srīvijaya in Malay History* describes a momentous event in the history of Southeast Asia which took place in 1397, a time coincident with the final dissolution of the Srīvijayan empire.[4] His researches revealed that around this year a prince of Palembang, Sumatra, threw off his allegiance to Java and incurred as a consequence, a brutal invasion. A source says that this prince escaped with a small following to found, after some adventures, a kingdom in Singapore, after which he or his descendants founded Malacca. Another source, however, mentions that the princely evacuation was of such great magnitude that "the sea seemed to be nothing but ships". It says: "So vast was the fleet that there seemed to be no counting. The masts of the ships were like a forest of trees; their pennons and streamers were like driving clouds and the state umbrellas of the Rajas like cirrus."[5] Referring back to this incident at the end of one of his appendices, Professor Wolters concludes that ". . . the years immediately before 1400 were a disturbed time in the western archipelago, and this is another, and perhaps more likely, time when small groups of adventurers migrated to Borneo and elsewhere."[6] One is tempted to ask whether it was not possible that Raja Baguinda was one of these Sumatran adventurers who came to the Philippines to found a principality. The "Sulu Historical Notes" and the "Original and later Settlers of Sulu", mention that he went to Zamboanga first, from where he sailed to Basilan until he decided to transfer to Buansa where he and his followers first had to fight the Tagimaha chiefs there before he could establish a principality. That the *tarsilas* say he came from Menangkabaw instead of Palembang is not of much consequence; for the central power in Sumatra in the few years before 1400 was located in Palembang. It does seem that some of the Palembang adventurers had founded not only the city of Malacca, which was to become the greatest emporium and Islamic center in Southeast Asia in the 15th century, but also a principality in Sulu which had become so important later on as to attract the Sharīf Abu Bakr. The Malays who left Palembang eventually for Malacca saw this principality as the heir to, or the continuity of, the empire of Srīvijaya — an assertion of Malay maritime supremacy in the area of the western archipelago. When the Sulus tried to build Sulu as the greatest trading center in their own area in the eastern archipelago, was not this a parallel of the action of those who founded Malacca?

There is an indirect evidence to further support the speculation that Raja Baguinda came to Sulu about 1397 A.D. or slightly later. This has to do with the *tarsila* report that, five years after his arrival, Raja Baguinda received a gift of elephants from the Raja of Java. This date can be placed at anywhere between, say, 1397 A.D. and 1405. Now, in 1410 A.D., the new ruler of Brunei, in the north of Borneo, formally requested the Chinese Emperor that he should not pay tribute anymore to Java (Majapahit) but instead to the Celestial throne. This request was approved by the Emperor.[7] All this means that before 1410 A.D., Brunei was tributary to Java. Most likely, the ruler who gave a gift of elephants to Raja Baguinda was not *the* ruler of Java (Majapahit) but one of the petty rulers of the numerous principalities that constituted the Javanese Empire. Widely-held traditions in Sulu state that the elephants came from the northeastern part of Borneo, an area where Brunei rulers exercised power. Thus, the gift came from the Brunei ruler who, or whose successor, stopped being in 1410 A.D. one of the petty rulers tributary to the empire of Majapahit. Consequently, Raja Baguinda must have received his gift not later than 1410 A.D.

In his work on Sulu, Saleeby calculated that Sayyid Abu Bakr arrived in Sulu around 1450 A.D. This calculation was based on his belief that the Sayyid was the same Abu Bakr who, according to the *Sejarah Melayu*, was in Malacca during the reign of the Malaccan Sultan Mansūr Shāh. Furthermore, Saleeby calculated that Mansūr Shāh had began to reign in 1400 A.D. Making allowance for various protracted stops in Palembang and Brunei, he concluded that Abu Bakr must have arrived in Sulu between 1436 A.D. and

1450 A.D. This calculation of Saleeby is not found in his above-mentioned book but in an unpublished essay entitled "The Establishment of the Mohammedan Church in Sulu and Mindanao: The Earliest Mohammedan Missionaries in Mindanao and Sulu."[8] However, after Saleeby had written his book and essay, a more definite and accurate chronology of the Malacca sultan emerged. Mansūr Shāh, the sixth Malacca sultan, is now known to have ruled from 1458 (or 1459) to 1477 A.D. Thus, the Abu Bakr who was in Malacca during this reign could not have been the Sayyid Abu Bakr whom Saleeby calculated had come to Sulu around 1450. However, in the above-mentioned unpublished essay, Saleeby calculated on the basis of the number of generations of succeeding Sulu sultans that Abu Bakr's reign had begun between 1407 A.D. and 1436 A.D. This calculation fits the well-thought out speculation that this father-in-law, Raja Baguinda, left Sumatra in 1397 A.D. and arrived in Sulu not much later. Incidentally, Alexander Dalrymple, using Isaac Newton's computation for the reign of princes, calculated that the Sulu sultanate under the first sultan was established about 1526 A.D.[9] But if it is considered that Dalrymple's list of sultans misses at least three of the earlier sultans and if 25 years instead of 20 is used for each generation, the sultanate might as well have been established in the first half of the 15th century. Indeed, the date of 1526 A.D. is wrong since Spanish records state that in 1521 there was already a ruler in Sulu who had enough prestige to have become the father-in-law of the Brunei sultan at that time.

Since the coming of Karim ul-makhdum to Sulu is stated by all *tarsilas* to have antedated that of Raja Baguinda by at least ten years, the date given by Saleeby, that is, about 1380 A.D., can be accepted for want of better reasons to support another date. Actually, the end of the 14th century and the early part of the 15th century had witnessed various *makhdūmīn* (pl. of *makhdūm)* coming to Java, Malacca, and North Borneo by way of India. That two or three places in the Sulu archipelago presently claim the grave of a *makhdūm* is not a contradiction. What poses a difficulty is when all of them claim their grave to be that of Karim ul-makhdum. My researches have shown that at least one other *makhdūm* came to Sulu in the first few years of the 15th century and that he was associated with Chinese traders or travellers. He is buried in Bud Agad in the interior of Jolo island and his name is different from that of Karim ul-makhdum.

As for Tuan Masha'ika, which is actually not a name but a title, not much can be said about the exact time of his coming beyond what is reported by the *tarsilas*. To seek a definite date of his arrival is an exercise in futility. The most that can be said about him is that since his grandchildren were already chiefs in Maimbung when Raja Baguinda came to Buansa about 1397 A.D., he must have come to Sulu by the first half of the 14th century. But if this is so, then he might not have been the first Muslim to have come to Sulu; although it is still entirely possible that he was the first Muslim to have come to Maimbung. The evidence for this is the grave of a foreign Muslim in Bud Dato, close to Jolo town, which bears the date of 710 A.H. (1310 A.D.). The name on the grave is that of Tuhan (Tuan) Maqbālū. However, is it possible that Maqbālū is the proper name of Tuan Masha'ika and that they are one and the same person? If so, then Tuan Masha'ika's grandchildren would have indeed been very aged chiefs of not less than 60 or 70 years when Raja Baguinda arrived. However, a peculiarity of *tarsilas* is that they tend to encompass events or, as some historians put it, telescope them. Indeed, the *tarsilas* do not say that the Maimbung chiefs who were descended from Tuan Masha'ika, fought against or greeted Raja Baguinda. The "Original and later settlers of Sulu" state tersely that they were chiefs living at that time, and this could mean at *around* that time. Certainly, they were not in Buansa, and they could have lived much earlier. Indeed, to say that they were chiefs living during the arrival of the Raja is a simple case of telescoping events as when many present-day students would, in the next few decades, say that they were living during the times of Manuel Quezon or the Commonwealth government, when actually they were born after World War II or the establishment of the Republic in 1946. Consequently, it would be rash to dismiss the possibility that the Tuan Maqbālū who died in 1310 A.D. is identical to Tuan Masha'ika.

V

Although the *tarsilas* in the "Genealogy of Sulu" are of great importance, there are also other important Sulu *tarsilas*. These can often serve to supplement the former. It is significant to note that some Tawi-Tawi *tarsilas* contain, for the same period of time, the names of other sultans not found in the "Genealogy of Sulu" as, for example, the name of Badar-ud-Dīn I. This sultan was known to the Dutch and the Spaniards and had written letters to them. He reigned from about 1718 to 1732 and was the father of well-known Sultan 'Azīm ud-Din I (known to the Spaniards and most Sulus as Alimudin) who was proclaimed sultan of Sulu on 1735. His name should have, therefore, been inserted between Sultan Muhammad Nasarud Din (no. 11) and Sultan Alimud Din I (no. 12) in the "Genealogy of Sulu". Other *tarsilas* insist that Alawadin, a brother of Sultan Kamalud Din (no. 2), succeeded him as sultan — something denied by the "Genealogy of Sulu". As a matter of fact, the elimination of the names of some sultans in a *tarsila* signify dynastic problems or controversies. Some names have been eliminated probably to prevent their descendants from becoming pretenders to the throne. In effect, some *tarsilas* can be quite selective in the enumeration of names. Saleeby was himself quite aware of this fact such that in his *History of Sulu*, he had to depend on other sources, notably certain *khutbahs* to have a more correct enumeration or succession of Sulu sultans. Now, a *khutbah* is normally a sermon delivered in Muslim Friday congregational prayers. Some of them, however, were composed specially to serve as prayers for the Prophet Muhammad and the first four so-called "rightly guided" khalifs as well as for all persons who had reigned, including the incumbent ruler, as sultans in Sulu. They were often repeated in the mosques to the extent of becoming fixed public knowledge. Thus, it was not easy to tamper with the names of the sultans enumerated in such formalized *khutbahs*. A peculiarity of such *khutbahs* is that they were written in literary Arabic by relatively learned teachers or religious leaders. Consequently, there was the conscious effort to mention the sultans by their Arabic names, whenever possible.

On the basis of the "Genealogy of Sulu", other Sulu *tarsilas*, a few *khutbahs*, seals of sultans found in their letters and now found in various archives, coins struck by them, and European historical references, especially Spanish, Dutch, and English, the following succession of sultans is presented. Their Arabic names as stated in the *khutbahs* as well as their common names will be specified.

1. Sultan Sharīf ul-Hāshim (Sayyid Abu Bakr)
2. Sultan Kamāl ud-Dīn
3. Sultan 'Alā ud-Dīn
4. Sultan Amīr ul-Umarā (Maharaja di Raja)
5. Sultan Mu'izz ul-Mutawadi'īn (Maharaja Upo)
6. Sultan Nāsir ud-Dīn I (Digunung, Habud)
7. Sultan Muhammad ul-Halīm (Pangiran Buddiman)
8. Sultan Batara Shāh (Pangiran Tengah)
9. Sultan Muwallil Wasīt (Raja Bongsu)
10. Sultan Nāsir ud-Dīn II (Pangiran Sarikula)
11. Sultan Salāh ud-Dīn Bakhtiar (Pangiran Bactial)
12. Sultan 'Alī Shah
13. Sultana Nūr ul-'Azam
14. Sultan Al Haqunu Ibn Walīyul-Ahad
15. Sultan Shahāb ud-Dīn
16. Sultan Mustafā Shafī ud-Dīn
17. Sultan Badar ud-Dīn I
18. Sultan Nasr ud-Dīn (Datu Sabdula)
19. Sultan 'Azīm ud-Din I (Alimudin I, Datu Lagasan)
20. Sultan Mu'izz un-Dīn (Datu Bantilan)
21. Sultan Muhammad Isra'īl
22. Sultan 'Azīm ud-Dīn II (Alimudin II)
23. Sultan Sharaf ud-Dīn (Datu Salapudin)
24. Sultan 'Azīm ud-Dīn III (Alimudin III)
25. Sultan 'Ali ud-Dīn
26. Sultan Shākirullah (Datu Sakilan)
27. Sultan Jamāl ul-Kirām I
28. Sultan Muhammad Fadl (Pulalun)
29. Sultan Jamāl ul-'Azam
30. Sultan Badar ud-Dīn II
31. Sultan Hārun ar-Rashīd
32. Sultan Jamāl ul-Kirām II (died in 1936)

The dates for the reigns of at least twenty of the above 32 sultans are known with certitude. The rest have to be calculated. The most comprehensive attempt at a chronology for the Sulu sultans is found in the work *Muslims in the Philippines*. It is too tedious to repeat the details here.[10]

VI

As mentioned earlier, some *tarsilas* contain mythological elements as well as incidents considered miraculous or normally impossible. It may be recalled that "Descendants of Tuan Masha'ika" say that he was born out of a bamboo. It also adds that he was not a descendant of Adam. The bamboo motif is quite common in many of the myths and traditions of the Malay peoples. The original meaning of such a myth is probably lost. However, it has certain functions, among which is to portray the beginnings of mankind or certain important historical figures whose ancestry are not traceable. Thus, to say that Tuan Masha'ika was born out of a bamboo is to state that his origins were unknown. Here, also, the bamboo motive may be understood as a literary device to indicate the starting point of a story. The account that Tuan Masha'ika was not descended from Adam only serves to emphasize that he was an extraordinary man *vis-à-vis* the people he had come to live with. In brief, he represented a different and superior culture.

It may be speculated that the report that Karim ul-makhdum came on an iron pot or vessel might mean that he came on a boat different from those used by the Sulu inhabitants at that time and that it was probably a boat that used metals in its construction. There are other *tarsilas* that narrate how the Makhdum came walking over the water. This is very interesting, for it suggests that the Makhdum was a member of a mystical (Sūfī) brotherhood *(tarīqat)* of the Qādirīya order. The reputed founder of this *tarīqat* was the famous Muslim mystic and saintly man called 'Abdul Qādir Al-Jīlānī (470 A.H. – 561 A.H. or 1077 A.D. — 1166 A.D.) to whom, it is believed, God gave the power to walk over the waters of rivers and seas. Even at present he remains the patron saint of fishermen and sailors in some parts of the Islamic world. Thus to say that Karim ul-makhdum walked on water is simply an allegorical or symbolic manner of stating that he belonged to the Qādirīya *tarīqat* which, up to the present, counts hundreds of followers. Actually, a study of many of the *makhdūmīn* who went to Malaya and Indonesia had been Sūfīs and to them had been attributed extraordinary or magical powers. This is probably one reason why Karim ul-makhdum had been called "Sharīf Awliyā", for such men had been considered saintly and full of Allah's blessings to the extent that they were supposed to have *barakah*, that is, the power to confer blessings on other people. Another *tarsila* report that the Makhdum had the mysterious power of ordering or communicating with people over long distances by bits of paper or cloth simply implies that he was literate.

To conclude, no history on the Muslims of the Philippines can be written without paying due regard to *tarsilas*. Their existence can also be a source of pride not only for the Muslims but for all Filipinos; for they represent the efforts of the human mind to understand the past within an ordered pattern — that of descent and sequence of events in time and space. Moreover, they have given part of the Filipino people a historical sense, without which their present would be unintelligible and their future blurred.

NOTES

1. Saleeby, Najeeb M. *The History of Sulu*. Manila, Filipiniana Book Guild, Inc. 1963.
2. The "Genealogy of Sulu" and the "Sulu Historical Notes" are found in *ibid*., pp. 30–36.
3. Cf. *Ibid*., p. 34. The names of the above seventeen (17) sultans are Saleeby's transcriptions from the Arabic Jawi script. Strictly speaking, not all follow the correct Arabic transcriptions of the names the way they are spelled classically. For example, the Tausug Sarapud Din is Sharaf-ud-Din in correct Arabic, which a learned man *('ālim)* in Sulu would normally use.
4. Wolters, Oliver, *The Fall of Śrīvijaya in Malay History*, Asia Major Library, Lund Humphries, London, 1970.

5. *Ibid.*, p. 76.
6. *Ibid.*, p. 190.
7. Brown, D.E. *Brunei: The Structure and History of a Bornean Malay Sultanate.* Star Press, Brunei, 1970, p. 133.
8. A copy was in the Beyer Collection.
9. Alexander Dalrymple, "Essay towards an account of Sulu", *The Journal of the Indian Archipelago and Eastern Asia,* Volume III, Singapore, 1849, p. 565.
10. See *Muslims in the Philippines* (U.P. Press, Quezon City, second edition 1973) pp. 14–24 for dates of the reigns of sultans and the bases for their statement.

Colonial Rule

Christiaan Snouck Hurgronje and the Foundations of Dutch Islamic Policy in Indonesia

HARRY J. BENDA

Ever since the arrival of the Dutch East India Company in Southeast Asia at the turn of the seventeenth century, the Dutch had encountered Muslim hostility in Indonesia. Time and again, the consolidation of their expanding power was threatened by local outbreaks of Islamic-inspired resistance, led either by Indonesian rulers converted to the faith of the Prophet or, at the village level, by fanatical *ulama,* the independent teachers and scribes of Islam. In spite of the ultimate subjugation of the greater part of the archipelago to Dutch control, Islam not only continued to spread among ever greater numbers of Indonesians, but from the eighteenth century on received fresh impetus from increasing contact with the centers of Islamic orthodoxy in the Near East. Every year thousands of Indonesian Muslims embarked on the Mecca pilgrimage, some of them remaining there for long periods of study and returning home as bearers of orthodox teachings which were gradually displacing the mysticism and syncretism formerly prevalent in Indonesian Islam.[1]

As a consequence, by the late eighteenth century Indonesian Islam was showing growing signs of restiveness which in the course of the nineteenth century exploded in a series of major upheavals. Thus in 1825, Prince Diponegoro rose in revolt against "infidel" colonial rule.[2] Though the so-called Java War was easily suppressed by the Dutch, village unrest, fanned by Muslim scribes, continued to plague the colonial government on Java, the center of Dutch power. The third quarter of the century witnessed the beginnings of an even more serious uprising, in Acheh in Northern Sumatra, that soon grew into full-scale military operations fought under the banners of an Islamic "Holy War."[3] This increasing militancy of Indonesian Islam caused growing concern among administrators ill prepared to cope with it. Traditionally, Dutch attitudes toward Indonesian Islam had been shaped by a contradictory combination of exaggerated fears and hopes — both born of a lack of adequate knowledge, if not of almost total ignorance, of matters Islamic.

Dutch apprehensions and misconceptions of Islam, especially of Muslim fanatics — the "priests" and "popes" of the early Dutch literature concerning the subject — reached back to the first contacts between Dutch and Indonesians in the seventeenth century.[4] Islam was thought of as a tightly organized religion, similar in many respects to Roman Catholicism, with a hierarchical clergy owing allegiance to the Turkish caliph, and wielding great powers over Indonesian rulers and their subjects, Muslims whose lives were believed to be regulated by Islamic law. Both in its international ramifications, including the danger of Indonesian appeals to Muslim rulers abroad, and in its hold over native life, Islam thus appeared as a formidable enemy. These

Reprinted from *The Journal of Modern History,* 30 (1958), 338–347, by permission of the University of Chicago Press.

fears had helped to shape a policy of alliance with the princes and aristocracy on Java, and with sultans, rajahs, and local chiefs on other islands, who, for political reasons of their own, were known to be either lukewarm Muslims or outright enemies of Islamic "fanaticism."

On the other hand, particularly in the nineteenth century, many Dutchmen both at home and in the Indies had great hopes of eliminating the influence of Islam by rapidly Christianizing the majority of Indonesians. These hopes were partly anchored in the fairly widespread, if facile, Western belief in the superiority of Christianity to Islam, and partly in the erroneous assumption that the syncretic nature of Indonesian Islam at the village level would render conversion to Christianity easier in Indonesia than in other Muslim lands.[5]

While not so closely allied with missionary enterprises as the Spaniards and Portuguese in Southeast Asia had been in previous centuries, Dutch governments at times were under strong pressure from Christian political parties in parliament. The Netherlands' constitution allowed Christian missions, both Roman Catholic and Protestant, to operate in Indonesia, and missionary work in the colony was subsidized by public funds. In spite of such government assistance, Christianity had been able to spread only very slowly — and even then only among Indonesians living in areas which had not previously been Islamized.[6]

Toward the close of the nineteenth century, Dutch fears, reinforced by the happenings of the last few decades, tended to predominate over the hopes concerning the future of Indonesian Islam. In the absence of an Islamic policy proper, the colonial government sought to place restrictions on Indonesian Muslims, especially Mecca pilgrims, who were held responsible for spreading agitation and rebelliousness in Indonesia. The result of these restrictive actions was, however, entirely negative. Although on Java large-scale rebellion under the banner of Islam ceased after the Java War, peasant outbreaks under local Muslim leadership increased in frequency. In Sumatra, the Dutch were involved in drawn out warfare against the fanatical Achehnese. A new course in matters Islamic thus became imperative for the future of Dutch rule in Indonesia.

Against this background, in 1889 an outstanding Dutch Arabicist and Islamologist, Christiaan Snouck Hurgronje, was appointed to the newly created office of Advisor on Arabian and Native Affairs. In addition to possessing initimate knowledge of Indonesian Islam — a sojourn, in disguise, had provided him with unique insight into the Indonesian haji-colony at Mecca — Snouck Hurgronje was one of the great colonial statesmen of the Netherlands. He brought to his office not only unrivalled expertise, indefatigable energy, and moral candor, but, at least equally important, a vision for the future evolution of Indonesian society in keeping with the best traditions of nineteenth-century liberalism. Snouck's understanding of the nature of Indonesian Islam, though open to some question, was invaluable in steering Dutch Islamic policies along a course which was, at least initially, successful. His principal achievement was no doubt the part he played in the political re-orientation which, together with improved military tactics, at long last led to the conclusion of the Acheh War.[7] Beyond this, Snouck's fame derived from the more general improvement in the relations between colonial authorities and most Muslim leaders in Indonesia. Especially on Java, a *modus vivendi* came before long to replace the hostility of former times. No wonder that to some of his contemporaries Snouck Hurgronje appeared as the almost legendary architect of a successful Dutch Islamic policy, the man who had inaugurated a new era in Dutch-Indonesian relations. Such, indeed, was his stature that he continued, as professor in Leiden University and as consultant on native affairs to the ministry of colonies, to exert a lasting, if ambiguous, influence long after his departure from Indonesia in 1907.

The formulation of an Islamic policy involved, above all, the substitution of sober facts for the motley of fears and hopes which had surrounded Indonesian Muslims for so long. In this respect, Snouck Hurgronje's masterly and scholarly analyses have remained an indispensable guide to the conditions of Indonesian Islam at the turn of the century.[8] Snouck countered Dutch fears concerning Islam at both the international and the local level by arguing, in the first place, that in the absence of a clerical establishment in Islam the so called "priests" and "popes" in Indonesia were no more members of a religious hierarchy than they were the executors of commands from the caliph of Constantinople. Since the caliphate was not vested with ecclesiastic powers of dictation in matters of dogma, the caliph was but the well nigh powerless symbol of the nonexisting unity of all Muslims. Pan-Islam, however dangerous as a vague ideology, was thus not a political reality identifiable with the caliphate. The Turkish government itself, Snouck made clear, had "deposited the panislamic program in the museum of [its] political antiquities."[9]

Second, the vast majority of Indonesian Muslims, and even the "priests" themselves, were not necessarily and a priori fanatics or sworn enemies of "infidel" rule. Snouck showed that the officials in charge of administering Islamic worship and religious justice were traditionally the subordinates, rather than the superiors, of native rulers, and that neither they nor their masters were as a rule addicted to Muslim "fanaticism." And even the unattached *ulama,* far from being as a group engaged in a sinister conspiracy, were — like their counterparts in other Islamic lands — independent and, as it were, otherworldly scribes and teachers, most of whom desired nothing better than to serve Allah in peace. Finally, Snouck destroyed the myth according to which the Mecca pilgrimage transformed thousands of peaceful Indonesian *hajis* into rebellious fanatics.

Realistically appraising the place of Islam in Indonesian society, Snouck furthermore showed that Indonesians, like other Muslims, did not owe sole allegiance to their religion. He was the first Dutch scholar to recognize both the importance of *adat,* or customary law, and the limitations which it imposed on the influence of Islam in the social and legal life of its Indonesian believers. In these matters Indonesian Muslims, he pointed out, differ in degree rather than in kind from their coreligionists in the Middle East. Everywhere and at all times the strict law of Islam had had to adapt itself to the traditional customs and mores, as well as to the political realities, governing the lives of its adherents. Thus, while Koranic law had gained acceptance in the realm of marital and family law, in almost all other matters the Indonesian *adat* had prevailed. However great, therefore, the authority exercised by either Islamic judges or independent teachers, in secular and political affairs Indonesians continued to be guided by their *adat* and to obey the traditional bearers of political authority.[10]

On the other hand, however, Snouck insisted that Islam was not to be under-estimated either as a religious or as a political force in Indonesia. For one thing, Snouck maintained — countering the false hopes held by some of his compatriots — that Indonesians, for all the "impurities" of the village Islam of the peasantry, considered themselves to be good and devout Muslims, profoundly attached to their own version of the faith. He therefore counseled against the unwarranted and optimistic expectations of large-scale conversions to Christianity.[11] For another, he even anticipated that the Islamization of Indonesia would be furthered, in extent as well as in depth, by the extension of the *Pax Nederlandica.* Not only was Islam likely to spread to hitherto pagan areas, Islamic orthodoxy was equally likely to wage increasingly successful war against social institutions opposed to its tenets — such as the matriarchal family in the Minangkabau region of western Sumatra — in succeeding decades.[12]

But while Snouck Hurgronje stressed the peaceful nature of the Islamic religion in Indonesia, he was by no means blind to the political potential of Muslim fanaticism. There was always the danger that some dedicated and doctrinaire believers, bent on carrying the demands of Muslim theologians to their literal political extremes, might turn into fanatic proponents of Islamic unity and world empire, inciting their followers to holy war against the "infidel" rulers of the Indies. There remained, in other words, cause for fear, but fear of a small minority — especially of fanatical *ulama* — dedicated to the notions of pan-Islam. They were the more dangerous because of the Islamic elements in the syncretic religion of the Javanese peasantry, which had "absorbed [its] ideas just sufficiently to doubt the continued legality of the European administration."[13] The enemy, then, was not Islam as a religion but Islam as a political doctrine, both in the shape of agitation by local fanatics and in the shape of pan-Islam, whether or not it was in fact inspired by Islamic rulers abroad like the caliph.

Snouck Hurgronje's recommendations for an Islamic policy follow logically from his analysis of Indonesian Islam. Broadly speaking, he envisaged a division of Islam into two parts, one religious, the other political. Toward the former, Snouck counseled in favor of toleration: a policy of neutrality toward religious life. If for no other reason than that the overwhelming majority of Indonesians were, and were likely to remain, Muslims, and convinced as he was that the Islamic religion as such formed no threat to colonial rule, he argued that its toleration was the *sine qua non* for pacification and stability. Suppression was neither wise nor necessary, let alone honorable for a country dedicated to religious neutrality at home. For similar reasons, no barriers should be placed in the way of the Mecca pilgrimage; such interference would, again, militate against the principles of personal liberty embodied in the Dutch constitution.[14] But while the government should respect the religious life of its Muslim subjects, it must not "platonically envisage all those trends that bear or tend to bear, a political character."[15] Any sign of incitement must, therefore, be resolutely met by force, and all interference in matters Islamic from abroad must be nipped in the bud.

Religious neutrality, including the lifting of all obstacles from the Mecca pilgrimage, would, if strictly observed, convince not only the majority of religious officials but also most, if not all, *ulama* of the honest intentions of the Dutch adminstration and would persuade them that they had nothing to fear from the colonial government as long as they abstained from political propaganda. Where, on the other hand, Muslim fanaticism had already reared its head or had, as in Acheh, gained the upper hand, Snouck insisted that drastic — if need be, military — action would be needed to restore Dutch authority and thus lay the groundwork for religious peace and for a *modus vivendi* between the colonial rulers and Indonesian Islam. The determined application of the twin policies of tolerance and vigilance should, finally, go hand in hand with Dutch support for and encouragement of those social elements least under the sway of Islamic fanaticism, the *adat* chiefs and rulers of the Outer Islands and the traditional aristocracy on Java.[16]

But, however important, neither pacification based on firm alliance with *adat* authority nor the attainment of a workable *modus vivendi* with Indonesian Islam was to Snouck Hurgronje an end in itself. They were, indeed, no more than the prerequisites for the healthy growth of Indonesian society. This growth, however, ultimately called for a new and bold colonial policy in Indonesia. Snouck's Islamic policy, that is to say, was only part of a larger scheme which went beyond the immediate needs to a wider vision of the future.

This larger vision was implicitly based on three central considerations. First, while Islam — whether in the syncretic garb of Indonesian village religion or in the sterner attire of Islamic orthodoxy — could be made to accept foreign overlordship, it could at best be expected only to acquiesce in coexistence between Christian rulers and Muslim subjects. In other words, as long as Indonesians, especially their leaders, remained Muslims, the colonial relationship could not give way to a lasting bond between Indonesia and the Netherlands.

Second, though *adat* institutions formed the traditionally most powerful barrier against Islam and though their representatives were thus the obvious allies of the colonial power, the *adat*, because of its intrinsic conservatism as well as local particularisms, could not be expected to stem the expanding influence of the dynamic and universalistic faith of the Prophet. Respect for the *adat* and recognition of its ability gradually to adapt itself to changing conditions had to go hand in hand with the sober realization that an accelerated rate of change was eroding its foundations too quickly to guarantee its survival. In short, blind support for the status quo of the traditional *adat* pattern, quite apart from inevitably widening the gulf between Muslims and Christian rulers, could not suffice for the long-term purposes of colonial administration. Invaluable though such support might be in the greater part of the Outer Islands, where Western influence and Dutch control were as yet peripheral, it was clearly inadequate for Java and some other parts of the archipelago, where the impact of colonial rule, together with economic and religious forces, had speeded social evolution.

Finally, and most important, in spite of the fact that in many areas of Indonesia Islam had been not only the beneficiary of the changes wrought by this evolution but was in fact expanding its hold at the expense of the *adat,* Islam held no keys to healthy social growth. It could not, in other words, generate from within itself the dynamics of a higher, modern civilization. Thus even if orthodoxy were ultimately to triumph over the syncretism and mysticism of the traditional village religion, even if it were to displace the Indonesian *adat* in the greater part of the colony, its victory would yet not constitute a victory for progress so much as for religious medievalism.

Yet — and this was the crux of Snouck Hurgronje's philosophy of colonialism — Indonesia, and Java first of all, would have to make the transition to the modern world of which it was increasingly becoming a part. Since a modern Indonesia by definition could be neither an Islamic Indonesia nor an Indonesia ruled by the *adat,* it would have to be a Westernized Indonesia. Dutch rule, then, was to be primarily justified, and ultimately judged, by the degree in which it had aided Indonesia's adaptation to the twentieth century.

The ultimate defeat of Indonesian Islam, the freeing of its adherents from what Snouck Hurgronje called the "narrow confines of the Islamic system."[17] was to be achieved by the association of Indonesians with Dutch culture. It was only natural that Snouck Hurgronje should focus his attention upon the Javanese aristocracy as the first and most obvious social class to be drawn into the orbit of Westernization. The aristocracy's higher cultural level, its proximity to Western influences brought about by contacts with the European administration, and, finally, its traditional aloofness from Islam, made it the logical beneficiary of Snouck's assimilationist schemes. According to Snouck, the Indonesian nobility, having lost their cultural and political moorings as a result of Dutch conquest, were clamoring for participation in Dutch culture. The Netherlands, he declared, had "assumed the moral duty of teaching [them] and of making them partners in our own [i.e., Dutch] culture and social life."[18] Such a partnership would close the gulf between rulers and ruled. No longer divided by religious allegiances, both would come to share a common culture and a common political allegiance. Though at first this community of interests would embrace only the Javanese elite, Indonesian society, rooted in the *adat,* would prove adaptable enough gradually to follow the path charted by its traditional leadership.

For association to become a reality, Western education had to be made available to ever larger numbers of Indonesians. In the final analysis, then, Western education was the surest means of reducing and ultimately defeating the influence of Islam in Indonesia. In competition with the attractions of Western education and cultural association, Islam could not but be the loser. Indeed, its decline was already observable. Whereas in 1890 Snouck had noted an increase in the number of Islamic theological training centers, twenty years later he triumphantly observed that Western schools were starting to win the race against their Muslim counterparts.[19] Even then, however, much remained to be done if Western civilization was to win the race against Islam in Indonesia.

Education was only the first step. It would have to be followed by granting the Indonesian beneficiaries of Western education a steadily increasing share in the management of the colony's political and administrative affairs.[20] Snouck was well aware that such a policy of Indonesianization would involve a sharp departure from past Dutch attitudes, governmental no less than private, toward the education of qualified Indonesians and their employment in the higher ranks of the colonial administration.[21] More than that — he knew that what was called for was, in essence, a gradual dissolution of the colonial status of the Dutch East Indies. But he was convinced that only such an imaginative break with the past would in the end build a lasting bridge between rulers and ruled.

Snouck prophetically warned that time was running out fast: the social evolution, on Java in particular, had been steadily gaining momentum for decades and could no longer be halted. The alternative to timely Dutch action, steering this evolution along an associationist channel, would be that its direction might pass by default into the hands of others inimical not only to the modernization of Indonesia but, indeed, to the continuance of Dutch rule itself.[22]

An appraisal of Snouck Hurgronje can be useful only if the positive as well as the negative aspects of his work are viewed in the context of his own times. Thus his lofty and impatient liberalism on the one hand, and his basically low esteem for Islam[23] on the other, were both rooted in nineteenth-century Western thought. Association itself was a typical product of the era's idealistic and confident hopes for bridging the gulf separating East and West. Again, the cultural milieu of the nineteenth century was doubtless responsible for Snouck's optimistic — if not arrogant — belief in the superiority of Western civilization and his inability to see the potential for growth in Islam and, though to a lesser extent, in Indonesian traditional culture. Not only were Snouck Hurgronje's views thus rooted in the temper of his times; they were in fact representative of a new era in Dutch colonial policy — the so-called Ethical Policy, which was officially inaugurated in 1901.[24] The liberal and humanitarian advocates of the new course shared with Snouck the conviction that the Netherlands were charged with a moral responsibility for the material and spiritual welfare of their Indonesian "wards." The new policy was to make native welfare its main concern, breaking with a past of colonial exploitation, whether governmental or private.

Like other contemporary Dutch reformers, Snouck believed that economic interests would allow themselves to be subordinated to considerations of welfare policies. Like others, too, his confidence in the possibility of steering Indonesian developments along Western lines made him neglect the serious and disintegrative effects which Westernization, including even the best-intended liberal reforms, was bound to have on Indonesian society.[25] Yet though in many respects Snouck Hurgronje was a typical representative of the ethical era, his courage and vision raised him far above most of his contemporaries. Few foresaw as clearly as he the ultimate demise of colonialism; fewer still were prepared to draw the logical and inevitable conclusions from this insight. In pressing for higher education of the Indonesian elite, for their association with Dutch culture, and for the rapid Indonesianization of colonial administration, Snouck virtually stood alone.

It was, indeed, not his associationist principles but his specifically Islamic policies which found immediate acceptance. In matters Islamic, Snouck was the recognized and virtually unchallenged expert of the ethical era. But while there can be little doubt that few Western, if not also Muslim,[26] scholars could match his intimate knowledge of the Islamic faith and its adherents in Arabia and in Indonesia, Snouck's plausible, yet facile, separation of religion and politics in Islam was, in the long run, unrealistic. It belied the very universalism of the faith which, not unlike medieval Christianity, does not recognize the existence of independent, secular realms of life. Even if this universalism had frequently been forced to compromise with divergent realities in most Muslim lands, its claims remained nonetheless intact. Separation of religion and politics, in other words, was at best a temporary phenomenon of Islam in decline. In an era of Islamic awakening, it could not survive for long, either in independent Muslim lands or in Islamic areas ruled by non-Muslims.[27]

The problematical nature of his neat but misleading compartmentalization was, perhaps, obscured by the fact that it seemed to correspond to the conditions of Indonesian Islam at the turn of the century. It was obscured, that is to say, by the spectacular successes following in the wake of the application of Snouck's Islamic policies. In Acheh vigorous military action against fanatical *ulama,* combined with Dutch support for *adat* chiefs, at long last brought about the termination of the war. Freed from this major political and military preoccupation, the Netherlands could now devote their resources and manpower to the pacification of large areas in the Outer Islands where they had hitherto exercised no more than nominal control.[28]

More impressive still were the results of the new policy of religious neutrality — in particular, the freeing of the Mecca pilgrimage — on Java. While no major Muslim-led revolt had threatened the center of Dutch power since the suppression of the Java War, the island had been plagued by incessant Muslim restiveness at the village level. The Islamic "New Deal" proffered by the sagacious adviser was accepted by many *ulama* who, in return for governmental non-interference in matters religious, acquiesced in rule by "infidels." This was a major victory for the colonial government, since the new *modus vivendi* with Islamic leaders significantly reduced the grass-roots commotion on the island. In fact, Snouck's policies continued to pay dividends, for some of the Muslim scribes and teachers remained dependable allies of the Netherlands until the end of Dutch rule in Indonesia.[29]

Snouck Hurgronje's stature as a colonial statesman thus rested on solid achievements. Even though he was not without bitter and vociferous critics,[30] in the eyes of many of his contemporaries the success of his policies seemed to vindicate the new course which he had, at times against stubborn opposition, so brilliantly and tirelessly advocated. Yet neither the undeniable fact that Snouck's name looms large in the history of the ethical era of Dutch colonialism in Indonesia, nor the record of the unwavering tributes paid him by so many administrators in the colony and political leaders at home, can be taken as a reliable guide in assessing his actual influence on the direction of colonial policy. In spite of the continued invocation of Snouck Hurgronje's name, Indonesian developments — not least among them Islamic developments — as well as Dutch colonial policy came before long to deviate so profoundly from Snouck Hurgronje's prognostications and recommendations that both seem to have been rendered largely irrelevant or obsolete as early as the first two decades of the twentieth century.[31]

NOTES

1. For a detailed discussion of syncretism and orthodoxy in Indonesian Islam, see G. H. Bousquet, "Introduction à l'étude de l'Islam indonésien", *Revue des études Islamiques,* II–III (1938), pp. 235–359, *passim*.
2. See J. M. van der Kroef, "Prince Diponegoro: Progenitor of Indonesian Nationalism," *Far Eastern Quarterly,* VIII (1949), pp. 430–33.
3. For a good account of the Acheh War in English, see E. S. de Klerck, *History of the Netherlands East Indies* (Rotterdam, 1938), II 342 ff.
4. See J. J. van de Velde, *De godsdienstige rechtspraak in Nederlandsch-Indië, staatsrechtelijk beschouwd* (Leiden, 1928), pp. 5 ff., and literature cited there. It was due to these early misconceptions that anomalies such as the so-called *priesterraad* (priests' council), used to designate religious judicial tribunals, stubbornly survived in Dutch official nomenclature until the end of the colonial regime.
5. In some missionary quarters these attitudes are apparently still held today. For a recent re-statement, replete with misconceptions about both Indonesian Islam and Dutch Islamic policies, see A. Rétif, "Aspects religieux de I'Indonésie," *Études* (1954), pp. 371–81.
6. W. F. Wertheim, *Indonesian Society in Transition: A Study of Social Change* (The Hague and Bandung, 1956), pp. 204–205. In fact, the colonial authorities, exercising the statutory right to determine the extent of missionary activities, barred Christian missionaries from areas known to be strongly influenced by Islamic "fanaticism." The statute governing and restricting the admission and activities of missionaries was often hotly debated in the Dutch parliament, imposing upon the ministry of colonies no less than on colonial administrators the difficult task of balancing the ardor of Christian spokesmen at home against the dictates of a moderate policy aimed at not arousing Muslim sentiment in the colony.
7. For a brief discussion, see H. J. de Graaf, *Geschiedenis van Indonesië* (The Hague and Bandung, 1949), pp. 440 ff. Snouck Hurgronje's crucial contribution to the Dutch victory over Acheh, long overshadowed by the military achievements of General van Heutsz (later Governor General of the Indies), is emphasized in K. van der Maaten's well-documented study, *Snouck Hurgronje en de Atjeh Oorlog* (Leiden, 1948; 2 vols.).
8. The summary of Snouck Hurgronje's work in the text is based on his voluminous writings on Indonesian Islam, the greater part of which were reprinted in the two parts of Volume II of his *Verspreide Geschriften* (Bonn. Leipzig, and Leiden, 1924–26; 6 vols). References are limited to points of special significance, while the broad outline is generally based on the following essays: "Over

Panislamisme" (1910; I, 364–80): "La politique musulmane de la Hollande" (1911; Vol. IV, Pt. 1, pp. 225–306): and "Dee Islam in Nederlandsch-Indië" (1913; Vol. IV, Pt. 2, pp. 361–91). For a recent selection from Snouck Hurgronje's scholarly writings, see G. H. Bousquet and J. Schacht (eds.), *Selected Works of C. Snouck Hurgronje, Edited in English and French* (Leiden, 1957).

9. Snouck Hurgronje, "Over Panislamisme," pp. 372–73.
10. For a recent discussion, see J. Prins, "Adat-law and Muslim Religious Law in Modern Indonesia." *Welt des Islams,* N.S. I (1951), 283–300.
11. "Even in those parts of Java in which orthodox Islam has gained the least grip upon the population ... the Hindu *pandit* would experience as great difficulties in communicating with simple peasants as would the Christian missionary; yet the Muslim *kiyayi* or ... teacher, if he deigns to stoop to this lowly creature, is assured of a deferential hearing." Snouck Hurgronje, "Het Mohammedanisme" (1911), *op. cit.,* Vol. IV, Pt. 2, p. 206.
12. Snouck Hurgronje, "Advies over codificatie van het Adatrecht" (1893), *op. cit.,* Vol. IV, Pt. 1, p. 271. Snouck also noted that Islamic orthodoxy paradoxically appeared to thrive in the Central Javanese principalities and in Batavia, in spite of the fact that the former were the very center of the pre-Islamic Hindu-Javanese civilization, while European influence had been most profound in the latter (*Ibid.,* p. 270). Cf. also C. A. O. van Nieuwenhuijze, "Moslims leven en Indonesische levenssfeer," *Wending* 4 (1949), p. 140.
13. Snouck Hurgronje, "Over Panislamisme," p. 375.
14. For an elaboration of this problem, see Snouck Hurgronje's "De hadji-politiek der Indische regeering," *op. cit.,* Vol. IV, Pt. 2, pp. 173–98.
15. "La politique musulmane de la Hollande," p. 279.
16. This policy of support for the secular *adat* authorities was the substance of Snouck Hurgronje's advice with regard to the situation in Acheh. For a brief summary, see his "Eene onbezonnen vraag" (1899), *op. cit.,* Vol. IV, Pt. 1, pp. 371–86. Cf. also A. J. Piekaar, *Atjeh en de oorlog met Japan* (The Hague and Bandung, 1949), p. 5. A fuller treatment can be found in Snouck Hurgronje's larger work, *The Achehnese* (Leiden, 1906), I, xvi ff.
17. "La politique musulmane de la Hollande," p. 294.
18. *Ibid.*
19. Compare Snouck Hurgronje's observations in "Rapport over de Mohammedaansche godsdienstige rechtspraak" (1890), *op. cit.,* Vol. IV, Pt. 1, p. 102, with those in "La politique musulmane de la Hollande," p. 294. See also I. J. Brugmans, *Geschiedenis van het onderwijs in Nederlandsch-Indië* (Groningen, 1938), pp. 6–7.
20. "La politique musulmane de la Hollande," p. 300.
21. *Ibid.,* pp. 289 ff. While Snouck welcomed the educational work of Christian missions in Indonesia, he deplored their confessional bias, which rendered missionary education "with the Bible" unacceptable to most Muslims.
22. *Ibid.,* p. 301.
23. For an example of Indonesian Muslim leaders' resentment of what they felt to be Snouck Hurgronje's deprecation of Islam, see Haji Agus Salim's article, "De slulering van de vrouw," written in 1926 and reprinted in *Djedjak langkah Hadji A. Salim: Pilihan karangan utjapan dan pendabat beliau dari dulu sampai sekarang* (Djakarta, 1954), p. 174.
24. For a brief but succinct discussion of the "Ethical Policy," see A. Vandenbosch, *The Dutch East Indies: Its Government, Problems and Politics* (Berkeley and Los Angeles, 1944), pp. 63–73.
25. Cf. B. Schrieke, "Native Society in the Transformation Period," *The Effect of Western Influence on the Native Civilizations of the Malay Archipelago,* ed. by B. Schrieke (Batavia, 1929), pp. 237–47. The best contemporary discussion of the impact of Western forces on Indonesian society can be found in Wertheim, *passim.*
26. It is indicative of Snouck's prestige among Muslim scholars that in 1911 the University of Cairo offered him a chair in Arabic, which he declined. See van der Maaten, I, 52 ff., for comments on Snouck's stature in the Near East.
27. One of the most scathing comments by a leading Indonesian Muslim on Snouck's arbitrary division can be found in an article written by Mohammad Natsir in 1939. See "Oleh-oleh dari Algiers: Prof. Bousquet tentang 'Testamen Prof. Snouck Hurgronje dalam teori dan praktek,'" reprinted in his *Capita Selecta* (Bandung and The Hague, 1955), pp. 164–65.
28. See Wertheim, pp. 65 ff., and J. S. Furnivall, *Netherlands India: A Study of Plural Economy* (Cambridge and New York, 1944), pp. 236–37. Snouck Hurgronje played an important part in the expansion of Dutch power in the Outer Islands. He designed a short treaty — the so-called "Korte Verklaring" —

which facilitated the establishment of Dutch suzerainty over the territories nominally ruled by Indonesian potentates. See also J. M. Somer, *De Korte Verklaring* (Breda, 1934), pp. 238 ff.

29. See Wertheim, p. 201.
30. On the occasion of Snouck's seventieth birthday, on February 8, 1936, the daily newspaper *Algemeen Handelsblad* carried the following appreciation: "There are few people in the Netherlands who have aroused such bitter enmity and such deep and warm friendship among their contemporaries and their compatriots" (quoted in van der Maaten, II, 177). Snouck's principal opponents were to be found among the political leaders of the clerical parties in the Netherlands parliament, who countered his ideas of cultural association by strenuous pleas for the Christianization of Indonesia. At times conservative members also criticized Snouck for his "idealistic" visions. See W. H. Vermeulen's chapter, "Oost-Indië in het Nederlandse parlement, 1891–1918," in W. J. Welderen Rengers and C. W. de Vries, *Schets eener parlementaire geschiedenis van Nederland* (The Hague, 1955), IV, 319–21 and 353–54, resp.
31. The writer has discussed later developments in his book, *The Crescent and the Rising Sun: Indonesian Islam under the Japanese Occupation, 1942–1945* (The Hague and Bandung, 1958), pp. 32–99.

Jâwah Ulama in Mekka in the Late Nineteenth Century

C. SNOUCK HURGRONJE

A sheikh from the Lampong district (South-Sumatra) who had lived twenty-five years in Mekka, told me the following story which in its principal feature is undoubtedly true, although this or that detail concerning events in the home he had for so long not visited might need to be corrected. In his youth the Islamising of his home was long completed but there was not apparent any vigorous religious life. His family had always been one of the most important of the neighbourhood; he claimed even in the society of former officials to be descended from the Sultans of Banten. Decayed from various causes his family owed the winning back of its former greatness and comfort in the last fifty years to having joined the Dutch government in its wars with Palembang and the introduction of their government in the Lampong district.

In his youthful days a hajji was the greatest of rarities; his eldest brother was among the first to go on pilgrimage to Mekka. Ambition, and "*Wanderlust*" aroused in our Sheikh as a boy the desire to go on pilgrimage, he thought vaguely that the government officials disapproving of such plans caused his father to delay the journey at least for a year. At last, however, he reached his aim, and once settled in Mekka, the young Lampongman would not go away, but having completed the customary studies, was accepted by the venerated Khatîb Sambas) in the Qâdirite *tarîqah* and took out a licence as pilgrim-sheikh. Some of his countryfolk lived in his house, in particular a countrywoman who became his wife. She however, has passed her best days and our sheikh enjoyed as second wife the daughter of the divine Mènschâwî[1]).

He was the first pilgrim sheikh for his countryfolk, until then they were "led" by the same mutawwif as the Benkulese. He now worked energetically by correspondence and other means to increase the Lampongese contingent to the pilgrimage. He now stated with satisfaction if not without sorrow for the loss of his own monopoly that now four sheikhs with their widespread families, helpers, etc. profited from the pilgrims from his native land; besides himself one Lampongese and two Mekkans. His own helpers were mostly countryfolk or at least Malays. Also there lived now in Mekka a comparatively important colony of Lampongese, many of whom studied successfully. Owing to this, experts in Moslim law, and protagonists of Moslim life in the Lampong districts are much more numerous than was the case thirty years ago.

The Pan-Islamic movement was not without influence on our Sheikh and all Lampong in Mekka was touched by the same hope. During the Russo-Turkish war (1877–8) fervent prayers were offered up in the house of our Sheikh for the success of the Moslim arms, and no one contributed more willingly

---

Excerpted from C. Snouck Hurgronje, *Mekka in the Latter Part of the 19th Century*, trans. J. H. Monahan (1970 ed.; Leiden: E. J. Brill, 1888), by permission of E. J. Brill, Leiden, The Netherlands.

to money-subscriptions for the war than he. In his native land, meanwhile, the political element of Moslim enthusiasm had not spread energetically. There had always been people opposed to European rule, but his family were not in sympathy with them. The Sheikh often reflected how things would have gone if one had not eagerly welcomed the Dutch; if one had drowned the petty squabbles which divided the Jâwah at home by the noble war-cry of Islam: had one gathered under the colours of the Sultan of Banten, Palembang, or even Achèh and expelled the Belanda (= Welanda, Olanda) then many millions of Jâwah would form together a great Moslim Empire, which other members of the race would continually have joined. Whilst in such mood, letters often reached him from home which, particularly when they came from his nearest relatives, breathed quite a different spirit. A very near relative, who was chief of a district, told continually of new alterations in the administration, expressed his pleasure at the good relations between himself and the assistant-resident, once even sent him the drawing of a medal given to him by the government for meritorious service, etc. Such letters roused the Sheikh, normally not *wild* in his views, to a fury of fanaticism in which he cursed one of his elder relatives who had fallen in battle against Palembang, and called him a "martyr to the Devil".

Once there came an outburst: that District Chief wrote him that the Dutch sustained in Achèh one defeat after another principally because they could not stand the climate, nor sustain the wiles of the Achèhnese. His sense of honour would not allow him to remain inactive under such circumstances and, through his Dutch superior as intermediary, he had offered to the "Great Lord" (Governor-General) himself to take the field with 300 welltrained Lampongese against the northern foe. For this reason he had asked the Government to let him have 300 breech-loaders. He now begged his relative, settled in Mekka, to buy him an excellent "Stamboul" sword, to sprinkle Zemzem-water over it, and to say prayers over it in the *Haram* so that Allah might make it a sword of victory!

Our Sheikh's answer to this naive epistle must have come like a thunderbolt to the house of the District Chief. Instead of the usual form of greeting "Peace be with thee" this opened with the words customary when in cases of doubt as to the propriety of the religious sentiments of the person addressed: "Peace be to him who follows the True Guidance!". Then followed a far-reaching discourse as to the relations between Believers and non-Believers, that the latter should everywhere be subject to the former and that it is contrary to God's Word if Moslims abandon their own territory, without desperate combat, to the Unbelievers. He described the tragic position into which the Jâwah lands were fallen owing to laxity in religious things, and insisted that stronger faith would have meant greater zeal and union, in which case without doubt an irresistible Moslim Jâwah empire would have developed instead of the *kafir* government. In conclusion he expressed the hope that his relative might forsake the ways of the Infidel, and further, in his neighbourhood, the pure Moslim sentiment. But should the Sheikh ever hear that his former friend had gone to Achèh to help to triumph the armies of Satan, so vowed he that every day before the threshold of the Kaabah his prayers would rise that God might leave the corpse of the renegade unburied on Achèh soil. What has been told hitherto I heard from the Sheikh's mouth without making local enquiries, but the answer of the District Chief I read myself. He ruefully confessed his error but pleaded as excuse his ignorance of religious things. He had found means to withdraw his offer in a suitable form, and for the future would pray for the triumph of Moslim arms.

Such native officials are usually little informed as to the contents of religious books. Even when they, as often happens, are less well-inclined towards the Government than our Lampongese, or when they, from superstition, venerate the mystic Sheikhs in the highest degree.

From intercourse with many Lampongese, who came to Mekka specially for Hajj, I gathered that now one can get there a fairly thorough training in the "three branches" although such scientific centres do not exist there as in the highlands of Padang, in Palembang or in Achèh. From this typical example one can see how the Hajj serves indirectly as a channel through which currents of intensive Moslim life find their way to the Jâwah lands. In general, the scientific elements of the Jâwah colony in Mekka play a greater part than people of the type of the Lampongese sheikh. If I wished to give an in some measure exhaustive description of these circles, as they existed during the time of my stay, I should often be obliged to repeat the same thing in other words, for the career and activity of one of the learned differ from those of others only in name and unimportant details. For a general view it will suffice if we visit a few prominent men and question them and their friends and pupils as to their past and mode of life.

* * *

The "Nestor" of the Jâwah professors, *Juneid*, comes from Batavia, was already ripe in years, and had made somewhat deep studies, when he travelled fifty years ago to Mekka, never to return home. Among his teachers was the Muftî Jamâl, known only by name to the present generation, and if a celebrated contemporary of Juneid who belonged with him to the Jâwah colony, is mentioned to-day, one adds as prefix the significant word "blessed": *Khatîb Sambas* (from Borneo) learned in every branch, who as Sheikh of the order, has initiated so many Jâwah in the Qâdirite *tarîqah; Abdulghani Bima* (from Sumbáwa) almost declared a saint; the emotional but somewhat learned and very fanatical *Isma'il Menangkabo* (from Sumatra) concerning whom the opinions of his countryfolk vary greatly; and many others who have come less prominently on the stage, belong rather to the past. Only *Juneid* still lives and shows himself when possible at the family festivals of learned or fashionable countryfolk who gladly entrust to him the naming of a child, the concluding prayer of a *qirâjah* or the leading of a *dhikr* although his voice is becoming indistinct owing to the weakness of age and the lack of many teeth. In former years he taught Arab grammar and Law in his house to students coming from the province of Batavia, and probably to other Jâwah (i.e. from Bali and Sumbáwa) who use Malay as a scientific language. He strove, however, to bring his pupils as speedily as possible to the reading of Arabic books, as to the fully arabised Sheikh, the Batavian dialect was but a clumsy instrument of tuition. Then, he gave lectures on all branches, sometimes at home, sometimes in the *Haram*, and more advanced Jâwah, who as beginners had used a tongue other than Malay, could also attend these lectures. Juneid won such great reputation, that without any request from his side, he was named for a part of the annual gift of corn for professors. For many years he has been obliged to renounce his lectures; teachers of no less capacity have continued his work.

He had two sons by an Egyptian wife: *Sa^{c}id* and *As^{c}ad*. Both enjoyed a fairly Arab education, learnt however the elements of the science, besides from their father, from his contemporaries among the Jâwah (Abdulgháni Bima etc.). Later, the Shafi^{c}ite professors, Mustafa Afifi, Ahmed Dahlân, and the now long dead Madah and èn-Nahrâwî, whose lectures most Jâwah students attended, were their teachers. Since the father's need of rest, the sons took over a part of his activities as a teacher: Sa^{c}id died a few years ago at an age of about forty five. As^{c}ad, about forty, still teaches the Batavian and other students who gather round him. The most learned and highly spoken of Jâwah respectfully kiss the old Juneid's hand and address him publicly and privately as their *Tuwan Guru* (Lord Teacher).

A daughter of Juneid is married to the Batavian divine *Mujtaba* who has passed nearly the half of his forty years in Mekka. Mujtaba had also begun his early studies before his first pilgrimage and uses the finer Malay tongue with more skill than his father-in-law. After having made his studies more profound with help of Juneid and the Arab professors, (particularly, Nahrâwî, Madah and Hasab Allah) he began himself to teach in Mekka, but did not lose the opportunity to hear an occasional lecture given by his old teachers. He did not lack pupils, and his friends and relatives at home willingly supplemented the proceeds from his small estate there, to make an adequate income. This quiet life, however, could not satisfy him permanently, and for many years he has belonged to the migratory elements of the Jâwah colony. Every few years he leaves Juneid to take care of his (Juneid's) daughter and visits his two wives in Batavia where he stays a year or so, puts his local affairs into order, sells books and other goods from Mekka, and devotes his leisure hours to the interests of those countryfolk eager for knowledge. His behaviour in social intercourse is affectedly modest and "high-toned": before answering a question he stares for a moment in front of him, and then, according to the questioner's race, he brings out in elegant Malay or Arabic a formal discourse. He never negatives or corrects outright the opinions of another, a *rectissime sed potius contrarium* is the sharpest censure which can come from his wise lips. This manner immensely impresses the Jâwah, and although, owing to his frequent journeys Mujtaba has been unable to secure a place in the foremost rank of learned Jâwah, he is a very popular figure among his countryfolk.

* * *

We will proceed to consider the Sundanese divines in Mekka and pause a moment by some. Two attract our attention owing to the great number of Priangan youths around them. Both Muhammed and Hasan Mustafa are known here by the name of their native place in Priangan, Garut, as if by a surname. *Muhammed Garut* is fairly old and came first to Mekka not as a primary student but as a teacher thirsting for more thorough study. He sat at the feet of Egyptian and Daghestani professors, and found in their circle the most hopeful Jâwah as his comrades. The bustling life of the Holy City during the holidays caused him sometimes to follow the example of his countryfolk and pay a visit to his native land: thus he also was a link in the communicating chain between Mekka and Java. At times here, at others there, he taught with many "blessings" in all theological branches. For the last ten years he has lived uninterruptedly in Mekka, and presents from relatives and disciples have enabled him to build his own house on the slope of the mountain which rises behind the Qushâshiyyah quarter. For about six years he daily held a couple of lectures on grammar and *fiqh* but his principal interest is in mysticism. Sixty or seventy Javanese and Sundanese in Mekka obey him like "corpses in the hands of the washers", and many pilgrims annually barter pious offerings for "blessings".

Hasan Mustafa was Muhammed's pupil in Java, and came first to Mekka about 14 years ago, to hear the lectures of the elder Jâwah divines and to attend in the *Haram* the lectures of Hasab Allah, Mustafa ᶜAfîfî, Abdallah Zawâwî etc. For about ten years he has taught himself, and some of the text-books written by him, (including one on Arabic prosody) have been published in Cairo. In his house, one always found after sunrise and in the afternoon, several dozens of Javanese and Sundanese, listening to his words: at other times he studies himself in the *Haram*. A few years ago he returned to Java, not meaning however to stay longer there than to put his affairs in order.

Now we come to the province of Banten, the inhabitants of which are numerously represented in all classes of the Jâwah colony. The most highly esteemed leaders of the intellectual movement originate in most cases from Banten. As doctor of divinity the Sheikh *Muhammed Nawáwi*, vulgo Sheikh Nawáwi Banten, who does all honour to his name taken from the celebrated author of the principal Shafiᶜite manual of Law, overtops all others. His father, Omar ibn Arabi was district-*penghulu* (i.e. director of the mosque etc.) in Tanara (Banten) and himself taught his sons, Nawáwi, Tamim and Ahmed, the elements of Holy Science. The brothers got further instruction from Hajji Sahal, then a famous teacher in Banten, later they went to Purwakarta in Krawang, where Radèn Hajji Jusuf attracted travelling students from the whole of Java, particularly from the West. They made the pilgrimage whilst quite young, after which Nawáwi remained about three years in Mekka, and as he returned home, with rich "scientific" booty, the plan was already ripened within him, permanently to settle himself in the neighbourhood of the House of God, which plan soon came into execution.

For thirty years he has now been incessantly active in Mekka to improve his own knowledge of Moslim science in every direction, and, as leader, to smooth the path of study for the Jâwah. At first he studied under the now departed great ones of the previous generation, Khatîb Sambas, Abdulgháni Bima etc., but his real teachers were the Egyptian Yûsuf Sumbulawênî and Nahrâwî, besides Abd èl-Hamîd Daghestânî (died a few years ago) whose lectures he used to attend, in company with many other divines almost to his life's end. Formerly he taught himself at every available hour, but during the last 15 years his literary work has left only the forenoon for that purpose. Every morning, between 7.30 and 12 noon, he gives about three lectures, calculated according to the requirements of his numerous pupils. He readily receives boys, who first begin with grammar, as well as ripe pupils, who have themselves at home a small lecture-hall. These latter however, as also some of the Sheikh's household (e.g. his youngest brother Abdullah, sixteen years old, whom he has entirely brought up) take a part of the elementary tuition off his shoulders.

Nawáwi is a significant example of the difficulties which a Jâwah must overcome in oral use of the Arabic tongue. After a thorough preliminary training, he has lived thirty years in the Arab city; he can recite the Qur'an, which he knows by heart, perfectly, and in reading aloud an Arabic text the consonants come out correctly. But as soon as he uses the colloquial language in every day life, he forms half Javanese constructed sentences, and hurls about the gutterals Ḥâ, Khâ, ᶜAin, and Qâf in despair. These four sounds cause the Javanese the most trouble, and as the Khâ is comparatively least trouble many of them use this instead of the two others, and for that reason are often laughed at by the Mekkans. The answer to the customary question which a Mekkan addresses to decently dressed Jâwah, "How long hast thou already studied here?" may run *qarêt fi 'l-haram sabᶜah senîn* "I have studied in the *Haram* seven years". This sentence is yelled after the members of the Jâwah colony, in their own corrupted Arabic, by the streetboys thus: *Kharêt fi l-kharam sabᶜah senîn* which means: "For seven years I have *polluted* the Kharam".

It was scarcely favourable to Nawáwi's fluency in speaking Arabic however, that his only wife should be a countrywoman, who according to his intimates, "wears the breeches" and successfully opposes his desire for a second marriage. Against this must be balanced his extraordinarily active association with the Arab divines of Mekka. But in any case the brilliant gifts of our learned divine are expressed more with the pen than with the tongue, and he has the defect, which is often found linked with disorder in speech, of utterly neglecting his outer appearance. If the ritual law of Islam had not made cleanliness a duty he would be positively dirty. His body sparsely covered with dirty, colourless clothes, with a "sweat-cap" on the head, he lectures upon the Holy Text, in a large room on the ground floor of his house; and even his street-garb, according to Mekkan ideas, scarcely accords with the dignity of his social position. His bent body makes his little figure yet smaller, he goes along the street as if the whole earth were a gigantic book, in which he reads. When I once asked him why he never lectured in the *Haram*, he answered that the ugliness of his clothes and of his outer man did not accord with the distinguished appearance of the Arabic professors, and when I remarked that less learned countryfolk did not refrain from lecturing there on that account he replied, "If they have attained such high honour, then assuredly they have earned it".

From such expressions, one need not necessarily conclude that the man is really modest, and also the manner in which he described himself in a preface as "The dust of the feet of those striving for science", does not prove much. In reality however he actually distinguishes himself by that quality. He accepts the handkiss from almost all Jâwah living in Mekka without false compliments as an obvious tribute to science, and never refuses an enquiry as to the Divine Law. In social intercourse of any kind, he rather joins courteously in the conversation, than dominates it, and never starts any scientific discussion without cause given by others. An Arab, who did not know him, might pass a whole evening in his society without noticing that he was the author of about twenty learned Arabic works. His moral influence is very important and far-reaching but his personality is entirely in the background. Under his inspiration, more and more Sundanese, Javanese and Malays turn to the thorough study of Islam, and the politico-religious ideals of Islam gain, in their most highly developed form, increased circulation. But Nawáwi is no man's father-confessor. It is only natural that the man should rejoice in the difficulties caused by Achèh to the Government, and, in conversation, disagree with those pensioned officials who hold that the Jâwah lands must necessarily be governed by Europeans. The resurrection of the Banten sultanate, or of an independent Moslim state, in any other form, would be acclaimed by him joyously whether or not the insurrection followed according to the Holy Law or took the form of undisciplined fanatical bands. For himself however, he would seek no political role, nor counsel such to others. It would however be impossible for him to do as was once done by his father, and is now done by his brother, Hajj Ahmed, in succession to his father: serve the infidel government even as *pĕnghulu*.

Personal ambition leads Nawáwi only to activity in the literary sphere. Formerly he gave plenty of work to the Cairo press, and lately he is said to have had a great Commentary on the Qur'an printed by the young newly established Mekkan Press. As examples of Nawáwi's works published in Cairo may be mentioned: in the grammatical field a Commentary to the Ajrûmiyyah 1881, a treatise on style (*"Lubâb al-bayân"*) 1884; in the field of doctrine *Dharî^c at al-yaqîn*, the title of a commentary on the well known work of Senûsî, 1886, a commentary entitled *Fath al-mujîb* on Ad-durr al-farîd, written by Nawáwi's teacher an-Nahrâwî (printed 1881) and three books in which apart from the principles of dogmatic, the five religious divisions of the Law, i.e. the "Five Pillars of Islam", are treated. To this must be added some devotional works which are read out in solemn assemblies: two commentaries on the poetic *Môlids* (Biographies of Muhammed) by Barzanjî; a commentary upon the work by the same writer upon the legendary Journey to Heaven, and a commentary upon a poem in which are given the "most beautiful" names by which one can call Allah, the Prophets and the Saints. Nawáwi has written two great commentaries dealing with the whole body of Law; in a commentary on the Manâsik of Sharbînî (printed 1880) he deals with the rules for the pilgrimage; and in two small commentaries on works of Hadramî divines (*Sulûk al-jâdah,* 1883, *and Sullam al-munâjâh* 1884) he deals with various questions as to ritual.

In mysticism our divine follows, as one might gather from the characteristics described above, the line of Ghazâlî; like the professors of the *Haram*, Nawáwi exclusively introduces his students to the works of Sûfî's with whom ethic preponderates over the occult elements of mysticism. He does not counsel his students to join a *tarîqah*, but does nothing to prevent them from doing so. From many conversations which I have had with Nawáwi, it was clear to me that he found in the penchant of his ignorant countryfolk for the mysterious, under prevailing conditions, reason to turn an even more tolerant eye upon the errors of the tarîqah than is done by the present-day Arab divines[2]. When the Arab opponent of the tarîqahs which are widely spread over Java, Sèyyid Othmân bin Yahya in Batavia, sent him a violent polemic against this pernicious system, for approval, he did not refuse to support the Sèyyid with flattering words; but this latter inferred therefrom a closer agreement with his opinion on the part of Nawáwi than what actually existed. Othmân bin Yahya indeed takes the field against *tarîqahs*, which he does not exactly describe by name but only in venomous sermons, and *insomuch* as the latter touch upon a mystic order, Nawáwi can only agree. But in the *application* of a criterium agreed to by both, their ways go far apart, a point which the polemical brochure did not touch upon.

However that may be, the mysticism practiced by Nawáwi himself is the moderate, ethical Sûfism of Ghazâlî in the more formalistic shape which it adopted in later times. His literary activity again evidences this, for in 1881, there was printed a commentary by him on Ghazâlî's Bidâyat al-hidâyah and 1884 a commentary upon a mystic poem of Zein ad-dîn al-Melêbârî (the grandfather of the author of the same name, mentioned above).

Nawáwi's brother next in years, *Tamim* has not made such thorough studies as the Sheikh but is said to have a good Arabic style, and to speak good Arabic. Formerly he was a pilgrim-sheikh, and before the steamer had gained supremacy over the traffic, he earned good money as pilgrim-agent in Singapore. I have not been able to learn why the Government forbids his stay in Banten, his homeland. Financially crippled he now lives in Penang. Nawáwi, for several years has also been a pilgrim-sheikh, although his disciples consider the traffic unworthy of his scientific attainments. If one can believe them, Nawáwi's relatives, whilst he was on visit to Medina, took advantage of a new regulation imposed upon the guild of mutawwifs, to buy a license in the name of the divine, in the well founded hope that his revered *name* would be a good *omen* for the business. Even if the Sheikh was not entirely in ignorance of the transaction, it is certain that he neither directly nor indirectly has anything to do with the exploitation of foreign pilgrims; for that he has no time, no inclination and absolutely no skill. Also he has no instinct for making money or even for a comfortable, let alone luxurious, life; although rich gifts rain upon him he lives with extreme simplicity, and writes his books at night by the glow of a little, pewter, petroleum lamp (*mèsrajah*) which other people only use when showing a visitor out. His wife seems to have a greater sense for realities, and undertakes some rather important business. It is thanks to her care that the guests whom the Sheikh invites to meals on holidays, lack nothing although the Professor himself behaves as if in a strange house.

The Sheikh *Marzúqi*, a relative of Nawáwi, has a much more distinguished appearance and also speaks Arabic better than he. In Mekka he attended the same professors as Nawáwi, and despite the slight difference in their ages, he studies also under Nawáwi himself. A real bird of passage, while I was there he had for the fifth time returned to Mekka after long journeys, and now lived, since about nine years, quietly in the Holy City, engaged at home, after each of the five daily salâts, with the teaching of his numerous pupils. He spoke Malay better than Nawáwi and was perhaps on the whole a better teacher although he had not read half the books which Nawáwi had in his head. He was brother of the Qâdirite order (which no doubt helped him whilst on his travels) and thus was very intimate with Abdul ̓Karim below mentioned. Not long after I left Mekka, he went away again, it was said to visit friends, and do business at home. I think however, that the last was only a pretext to quiet the suspicions of Government officials. Formerly he visited, all through, not only Banten but, for instance, also Siam and Bali, both lands in which Moslims are in a minority. He is said now to have visited Penang and Deli: the well-to-do Sultan of Deli seems willingly to receive visits from pious Jâwah, or sherîfs from Mekka.

Sheikh *Isma'il Banten* also on account of his descent, takes a prominent position, and as scion of the Banten sultans (who count as séjjids) is addressed by his countryfolk as "Tubagus". His sister was the wife of a Regent, his father-in-law was appointed Regent in the time of the English. He was first taught by his father Hajji Sadili, who took him with him on the pilgrimage, whilst a small boy. After returning from this Hajj he followed exactly the same course of study as the Sheikh Nawáwi i.e. was taught by Hajji Sahal in Banten, and later travelled to Purwakarta in Krawang to the learned Hajji Yusuf[3]). Most of the elder people, who later made a reputation for learning in Banten, have visited this school.

Isma'il was still young when he came for the second time, and for a long stay, to Mekka. Here Nawáwi's teachers were also his, except that he studied dogma and mysticism under a Hanafite Professor, ès-Sèjjid èl-Kutubî. After a few years of study he returned to Banten, and there taught the *"âlât"* (instrumental subjects in the degree that it is absolutely essential to the Jâwah for the understanding of the "three subjects" (Law, Dogmatic, Mystic). According to Arab notions he went much too fast towards this goal, impelled by his genuine Javanese penchant for mysticism, as also the scantiness of his Arabic knowledge. Sundanese, who had studied with him, formerly in Banten, and then came to Mekka, told me with good-humoured scorn that the *Tubagus* explained the difference between the masculine and feminine form of the Arab demonstrative pronoun *hâdhâ, hâdhihi* (this) as if *hâdhâ* meant the nearer lying, *hâdhihi* the thing farther off[4])!

He interrupted his tutorial activities now and then by travel to Mekka, and settled down there permanently about thirteen years ago. Plantations which he possessed at home, and wealthy relatives gave him a considerable income. His relatives presented him with three houses in Mekka, in one of which he lived himself. Whilst healthy, he studied regularly with two professors in the *Haram*, and himself gave two lectures at home daily, his pupils being also students of Nawáwi. His descent, pious character, and benevolence to those in need, gained him in popularity what Nawáwi gained in prestige, but in late years he has been continuously in ill-health, and only receives intimate friends. While he was well, his house, particularly in the month Rabî^c al-awwal, which saw the birth of Muhammed, formed a centre for social unions of the Jâwah. The Prophet's birthday (*Mulud*) is still more warmly celebrated in Java than in Mekka. Indeed the whole month *Mulud* is there so crowded with festivals and holidays that one can scarcely accept all the invitations showered upon one. Javanese in Mekka, who were travelling home at the beginning of the year, often told me how glad they were to be able to pass the joyous Mulud month at home. Their colony in Mekka sticks to this custom as far as possible and there scarcely passes an evening without a gathering, in 5–10 Jâwah houses, of large companies of Jâwah and their Arab friends to hear *môlids* in Muhammed's honour, and then gourmandize together. The well-to-do *Tubagus* was not inactive in these things, and even now he calls his friends together a few times in the Mulud month, without however being able himself to participate in the feast.

There are dozens of the younger West-Javanese divines who partly owe their preparation for the lectures of the *Haram* to Nawáwi and who now when they remain in Mekka, can take the younger students so far that Nawáwi can start with them at once *in medias res*.

Thus, for instance, Arshad ibn ^c*Alwan* from Tanara who went to school to Nawáwi's father, and later learnt from Nawáwi, his brother Tamim, and from Marzuqi. In Banten, he also sat at the feet of Hajji Sama'un in Pandeglang[5], and of the Arab professors in Mekka his principal teacher was Hasab Allah. One counts it as a sign of high endeavour on his part, that he even studied the Arab medicinal art under a scholar from Hadhramaut, and during a four years stay in Banten, he had often to give medical advice. For some time he functioned in Serang as member of the Muhammedan court ("priesterraad"). In 1885 he had made three more pilgrimages and both eagerly studied and taught. Now he is said to have gone home again. A second *Arshad, son of As'ad* from Banten, has left Mekka at about the same time as the first named. His father having gone to Batavia, Arshad first studied there, then in Mekka, under guidance of Abdulghani, later under that of Nawáwi and the Arab professors. He speaks Malay excellently but Arabic very badly. A swarm of Malays, Sundanese and Javanese, flocked to his lectures. The thirty-year-old *Ahmed Djaha* from Anyar (Banten) is both extremely modest and thoroughly learned. He has passed nearly half his life in Mekka, and did his means allow it, he would willingly pass some years in the Azhar University in Cairo. He mingles with less learned contemporaries without the least affectation, and the Javanese boys regard it as a pleasure to study with him, indeed they whisper, with youthful exaggeration, that Sheikh Ahmed is really more learned than Nawáwi, the Sheikh *per exeellentiam.*

NOTES

1. Muhammad Mènshâwî completed his studies at the famous Shafi'i center, the Azhar mosque in Cairo and privately he taught many Javanese in the art of Qur'an reciting. For further reference see Snouck C. Hurgronje, *Mekka in the Latter Part of the 19th Century,* Leiden: E. J. Brill, 1970; p. 185.
2. Ibid. p. 204.
3. The following and others were mentioned to me as pupils of Yusuf: Sheikh Abu Bakar, who also studied in Mekka twenty years ago, and since then has himself had a big school in Pontang (Banten), Hajji Hamim, Muhammed Ash'ari (later in Bogor), Banten further boasts of the following divines who have studied for a time in Mekka: Hajji Othman in Undar-andir, who lived for about eight years in Mekka, and whose tutorial activities have suffered continued interruption by official duties since his appointment as *penghulu*; Muhammed Sadili in Serang, upon whose counsel the Regent is said to lay great weight, and who is said to drill the children of the neighbourhood in the salât as if they were soldiers; Hajji Mahmud in Terate and Hajji Muhammed Qasid in Bêdji (Tjilegon). This Qasid, also called Wasid, was the ringleader of the recent riots in Tjilegon.
4. The languages of Indonesia have no grammatical gender.
5. This divine is said to have had his school in the village of Kadu Marna.

Malay Beliefs and Religion

R.O. WINSTEDT

For though the Malay is an orthodox Sunni of the school of Shafi'i, there were Shia' elements in the form of Muhammadanism he learnt originally from India. These elements were a crude pantheism, a Gnostic concern with mystic names and formulae and the worship of innumerable saints. The reverence for saints permitted offerings at the graves of ancestors, founders of settlements, rulers, religious teachers and even before rocks and trees. Immediately after his enthronement, for example, a Sultan of Perak is supposed to pay a pilgrimage to the graves of former rulers. As for mystic names and formulae, in Hindu days the Malay had invoked nature-spirits and deities by every possible designation so that an incantation might not go astray. It was therefore no break with tradition to invoke Allah by all His Excellent Names and to replace *Om* the Hindu word of power with the Arabic *Kun* "Let it be" and with the *Basmala*, whose recital can attract fish from all the seas, make the barren fruitful, lay the tyrant low and bring honour and salvation. The Malay's new teachers taught him how the appropriate Arab text written on an amulet at the right astrological moment in scented rose-water musk and saffron with a recitation of the proper formula would save a woman from all attempts on her virtue even by the black art and would protect a man from bullet, spear, pestilence and shipwreck. The hexagonal seal of Solomon attracted the interest once bestowed on the Laksamana line, which Sita in the Ramayana crossed to her undoing.

As for mysticism even the court of mediaeval Malacca was so interested that on two occasions envoys were sent to Pasai to propound hard problems for solution. Sultan Mansur Shah sent an offering of gold and two slave-girls to any one in Pasai who could tell if those in heaven and those in hell abide in their respective places forever. Later Sultan Mahmud sent two cockatoos and a knife inlaid with gold for any Pasai theologian who could solve the paradox that whoever believed God had created and bestowed His gifts from all eternity was an infidel and whoever disbelieved it was an infidel. The answer to the first problem Malays found in the popular *Insan al-Kamil* or Perfect Man of al-Jili, who held that the sufferers' power of endurance being a divine gift extinguished the fire or else that their torment was changed to pleasure. To the second question the Malay knew two answers, the orthodox one that spirit *(ruh)* is not eternal but created, and the unorthodox one that the word of creation merely raised what was already existent though not manifest.

In its chances and changes the Muhammadanism of the Malays has followed the movements of the Muslim world. There has been the recurrent conflict between the transcendentalism of orthodox theologians, for

Excerpted from R.O. Winstedt, *The Malays: A Cultural History* (1961 ed.; London: Routledge & Kegan Paul PLC, 1947), by permission of the publishers.

whom God is in heaven, and popular mysticism, which starting from animism inclines towards a pantheism that finds Him closer than the veins of one's neck.

Malacca in the 16th century and Acheh in the first half of the 17th saw the same compromise and harmony between orthodoxy and Sufism that then characterized Islam in the Near East, a compromise of which the Malays owing their new religion to India were hardly conscious. As the centre of Malay commerce after the Portuguese capture of Malacca in 1511, Acheh attracted to its capital men of profound learning of the mediaeval type, missionaries of Islam from India, Arabia and even Egypt. While the orthodox preached the necessity of ritual and doctrine for man's communion with his Maker, the exponents of a Sufism derived from India and from 17th century Medinah disallowed any distinction between God and man, denied that there was any receiver or offerer of prayer and declared that one who offers prayer is not a monotheist. Two of Acheh's foremost heterodox mystics were Sumatran Malays, Hamzah of Barus (c. 1600) and Shams al-din of Pasai (d. 1630), and their mystic doctrines became known throughout the Malay world. For the orthodox Allah is omniscient but for Hamzah He is identical with man and the universe. Sole and absolute He contains all being and all worlds, subject and object, lover and beloved, heat and cold, good and evil, the Ka'abah and the heathen temple. Following ibn 'Arabi, Hamzah accepts Allah or Being as not only sole but bound by necessity, so that it is not the arbitrary will of God but the necessity of His Being that makes one man a Muslim and another not. God is a sea, immobile, without ripple but with potential waves, that stirred by his creative word have come to represent this world of appearance but always have the reality of the sea. Absolute Being is identical with the spiritual essence of man, wherefore it is said in the Kuran, "Wheresoever you turn, there is the face of God". For the mystic who attains wisdom or gnosis (*ma'rifat*), the veil between lover and beloved falls away.

Shams al-din also employs the image of sea and waves and surge. Man's Being for him is God's Being, the individuality of man being no more than a name. Man's outward body is no more than a wave and life no more than surge in God's infinite sea. For Shams al-din all but God is the reflection on a screen by the hand that moves the puppets. The outstanding features of his speculations are the doctrines of the Unity of Existence and of the Perfect Man, the mirror by which God is revealed to Himself and therefore the final cause of creation. "In more than one respect his system stands midway between Indian and Javanese forms of Islamic mysticism."

Then in 1637 there arrived in Acheh from Rajputana a famous interpreter of Ghazali's orthodox mysticism, one Nur al-din ibn 'Ali from Ranir in Bikanir, the author of the *Bustan al-Salatin* and other works, who compared himself with a cup-bearer circulating the wine of the Prophet. For him there was no doubt about the answer to the second question Sultan Mansur Shah had put to the theologians of Pasai. Spirit for him was not eternal but created, and he condemned the pantheistic identification of man and the world with God. The heretical works of the two Sumatran mystics he got burned. Fortunately some of them escaped the fire. For the skill with which these Malays with a vocabulary lacking in abstract terms were able to grasp and introduce Sufi mysticism to their world is very remarkable, and though their ideas were not original, in no other field has the Malay mind ever displayed such intellectual ability and subtlety. For Shams al-din Islamic theology meant metaphysical speculation in which the importance of intellectual processes is stressed above that of emotion. But the ordinary Malay, untrained to distinguish between orthodox and heterodox, was content to seek a vent for spiritual emotion in mystic reverie induced by Yogi postures, by closing the eyes and noting the breath in the nostrils, by the interminable counting of rosaries or the repeated chanting of his profession of faith. Metaphysics were above his head, and his proofs of the identity of God and man were based on such crude evidence as the quaternity of the first Caliphs, the Archangels, the founders of the schools of Islamic law, and the letters that in Arabic spell the name of Muhammad and the word Allah. Man he conceived to be a microcosm, whose backbone corresponded to the pillar of God's throne, his bile to fire, his phlegm to water, his belly to the ocean, his spirit to a bird. To the mystic union of the lover and the beloved he attached a literal and carnal meaning, and his medicine-man, who had already grafted Hindu beliefs on to primitive animism, welcomed a new weapon for his spiritual armoury, giving to the love-charm called since Hindu times the arrow of Arjuna the new name of the Arrow of Gnosis, that made lover and beloved one.

> In the name of God, the Merciful, the Compassionate!
> I boil and steam this sand from my beloved's foot-print
> To be a dart made powerful by Allah,
> Whose will I am bringing to pass;
> I take this sand through my knowledge (*ma'rifat*) of Allah.
> If I shoot at a mountain, it falls;
> If I shoot at rock, the rock is riven,[1]

and so and so on, as in the Hindu charm already quoted above. To guard his life during sleep the Kelantan peasant draws a deep breath and recites:

> I am the real Muhammad!
> It is not I who speak, Muhammad is speaking.
> First spirit was created, then the body.
> This evening is as the womb of my mother;
> Only if it is destroyed, can I be destroyed!
> My being is Thy being,
> My being is one with Thy being!
> I retreat into the enclosure,
> "There is no God but God! Huwa,"
> The womb of my mother, the Light of Muhammad,
> Until daybreak to-morrow.[2]

Only if Allah and Muhammad are parted, can I and my beloved be parted! Only if Allah and Muhammad suffer harm, can I suffer harm! These are frequent vaunts in Malay adjurations. As I have written elsewhere, "One is reminded of the Hermetic discourse known by the name of Poimandres, wherein the initiated claims complete knowledge of the name and nature of God and complete equality with Him and addresses Him — 'if anything happen to me in this year, this month, this day or this hour, it will happen to the great God also'." A Persian heretic, Mansur Hallaj, would say to one man, "Thou art Noah", to another, "Thou art Moses", to a third, "Thou art Muhammad". And the same crude mysticism inspired the Malay magician, who, when planting the main post of his fishing-stakes, would cry that it was resting against the pillar of God's throne, that Allah was handing it down and Muhammad receiving it. An old Perak charm-book advises the lover that over a posy of flowers for his mistress he should recite, "*I* am Allah, the Divine Reality, Who blesseth all the worlds". Hardly more covert is the threat of a Kelantan exorcist to malignant genies that the organs of the patient they are afflicting are the habitations of the four Archangels and the first four Caliphs and that on the patient's feet move Allah and His Prophet. In the Bhagavad-Gita it is written of the Eternal Spirit "everywhere are Its hands and feet", and many of the Indian missionaries of Islam failed to rise above a literal interpretation of metaphysical mysteries. It is not, therefore, surprising that the extrovert mind of their disciple, the Malay medicine-man, borrowed the crudest of pantheist ideas to fortify and comfort his patients in their hour of need.

Malay theologians, however, at the end of the 18th century followed as usual the fashion of the Near East, which then turned back to the orthodox mysticism of al-Ghazali. 'Abd al-Samad of Palembang spent ten years (1779–1789) translating his famous work "The revival of religion" (*Ihya Ulum al-din*) into Malay, and Daud ibn 'Abdillah ibn Idris of Patani also translated it along with al-Ghazali's "Book of Secrets" (*Kitab al-asrar*) and his "Book of approach to God" (*Kitab al-kurbat ila Allah*), his work being published at Mecca in 1824.

But already about the middle of the 18th century the Near East had experienced the Wahhabi reformation with its hatred of animism (and the Muslim counterpart, pantheism) and its condemnation of all pagan survivals in Muslim culture and of the idolatrous worship of saints. Fifty years later it reached India and a century ago led in Sumatra to the white-clad Padri rising in protest against heathen notions of relationship and inheritance that are still cherished under the Minangkabau matriarchy. The Wahhabi movement, allied with political ends, was behind the idea of Pan-Islamism. But that notion of a far-flung Muslim theocracy, though taken up by the Sublime Porte to enhance its political prestige, made little or no appeal to Malays, whose loyalties were still parochial. Nor had it a long life. For one of the consequences of the first world-war was the extinction of the Turkish Caliphate.

Another was the seizure of Mecca by a Wahhabi king. The triumph of this fundamentalist diminished the status and comfort of Indonesian Shafi'is in the Holy City and diverted more Malay theological students to the al-Azhar university at Cairo. There Muhammad 'Abduh (d. 1905) had preached a modernism already popular in some Malay circles for its puritan ideal of religion freed from superstition and its advocacy of a scientific education for the transformation of djinns into microbes. But having no translations of European works on logic and philosophy, these modernists saw nothing wrong in brushing aside historical evidence in order to exalt their Prophet. And a new cult of Muhammad not only became a convenient counterblast to the Christian exaltation of Christ but brought the Malay back to the Perfect Man and Sufism. In Malaya, however, as elsewhere the orthodox Muslim authorities remained so rigidly conservative that 1934 saw the burning of a tract on free will because it had been compiled at the instance of a Malay modernist from the Egyptian university. Even now Malay orthodoxy dislikes the acceptance of interest from banks, companies and co-operative societies. And in fact, Malay modernism has owed far less to conservative al-Azhar than to the secular education imparted by Dutch and English to lay pupils whose ignorance of theology has compelled them to air their advanced views only by such external signs as the adoption of European clothes, the use of the Roman alphabet and the exaltation of a vernacular they know above Arabic of which they have no knowledge. Generally, however, Malaya lagged well behind Java in adopting these changes. For a while the Malays dallied with the Ahmedia movement, started in the Panjab in 1900 by Mirza Ghulam Ahmed Kadiani, who in spite of a modernist outlook held that Christ did not die on the Cross but migrated and is buried at Srinagar in Kashmir, and who himself claimed to be a Mahdi, the incarnation of Jesus and Muhammad. Later the Malay became interested in the Muhammadiah party of Netherlands India, modernists who are feared and distrusted by the traditionalists or Islamiah party. The Muhammadiah party would interpret the Kuran in the light of modern knowledge and aim at the physical and intellectual advancement of the race. With such an ideal the Sufi is hardly in accord. So in a bid to command popular support, these modernists took the word *tasawwuf* the "mysticism" of the Sufi with its age-long appeal to Indonesian mentality and applied it to a system of ethics bearing on practical life. Needless to say, this system in the eyes of traditionalists is not Sufi mysticism at all, however great its pragmatical value.

Throughout the Muslim world the second world war had startling repercussions. Even before it, the Islamic theory of the brotherhood of all believers had been reinforced by the spread of democratic ideas, and the war was to discover the prestige of Malay royalty so undermined that in Sumatra Sultans were murdered in defiance of the immemorial sanctity of an anointed king. Never before the war did one meet a peninsular Malay who would profess neutrality towards all religions or was inclined to extol his Hindu past as a golden age of freedom and self-government. Never before the war could one imagine a Malay woman speaking from a public platform or sitting in a legislative council. After it nationalist aspirations extinguished or at any rate silenced objections to female education; and the Malay woman, who never tolerated purdah, entered the political arena.

NOTES

1. See [Richard Winstedt, *The Malays: A Cultural History* (London: Routledge & Kegan Paul, 1961)], Appendix A [for the Malay original].
2. *Ibid*.

The Ulama in Acehnese Society

ALFIAN

The strength of that unity under Islam was clearly shown during the Acehnese war against the Dutch, known as the *Aceh War*[1] which started in 1873 and lasted for nearly forty years. The *ulama* were instrumental in turning it into a religious holy war. With Islam as their common ideology they fought their common enemy, the Dutch *kafirs* (unbelievers), fiercely. Partly through their use of the poetic folktale about the holy war, the *Hikayat Prang Sabi,* the *ulama* were able to stimulate and maintain the fighting spirit of the people. Their emotion was cleverly cultivated through the promises conveyed along the lines of the *hikayat* that their ultimate sacrifice, *syahid* (holy death) in the battlefield, would be abundantly rewarded by *Allah* in the afterworld.[2]

But the Dutch finally won the war, largely due to the superiority of their modern weapons and the new policy suggested by Snouck Hurgronje which was closely executed by General van Heutz.[3] Contrary to the thesis of Snouck Hurgronje, Siegel saw that the rise of the *ulama* during the war was not motivated by their desire to wrest power from the *uleebalangs*.[4] In fact, after the *ulama*, under the leadership of Teungku Chik di Tiro, liberated certain regions from the Dutch they returned them to the *uleebalangs*. This suggests that the strong unity which existed during the war among the different sectors of Acehnese society was significantly helped by the behavior of the *ulama* in resisting the temptation seriously to cut or damage the political power of the *uleebalang*, though they could easily have done it through the use of their dominant position at that time.

However, after the war the relationships between the two groups became increasingly bad which finally led to a bloody conflict not long after Indonesia's independence in 1945. The origin of this clash seems to be traceable change in Dutch colonial policy at the turn of this century into which Snouck Hurgronje's Islamic policy was integrated.[5]

The Dutch eliminated the *sultan*, then the symbolic figure of Aceh, from his top position in the power structure. In accordance with Snouck Hurgronje's Islamic policy the role of the *ulama* was to be significantly curbed by limiting their activities to strictly religious matters. Under the new colonial administration the *uleebalangs* were to govern the Acehnese through their Dutch-supported authority as *adat* chieftains. Aceh then was divided into two types of administration: the regions surrounding the capital city, Kutaradja (now Banda Aceh), with about 50 *uleebangships*, were under *direct rule* of the Dutch; other regions with about 100 *uleebalangships* under *indirect rule* or *zelfbestuur*.[6] In practice, however, the distinction between the two had almost no meaning, largely because the effect of the new colonial policy appeared to have made most of the *uleebalangs* more or less totally dependent on the Dutch.[7]

As has been previously mentioned, there was no strong common ties between the *uleebalangs*

Reprinted in abridged form from *Southeast Asian Journal of Social Science* Vol. 3 No. 1 (1975), 27–41, by permission of the author and the *Southeast Asian Journal of Social Science*.

and the common villagers in their regions. For one thing, the *uleebalangs* did not own most of the land in their regions, and that had made the majority of peasants freeholders of their own land. At that time the wealth of the *uleebalangs* came largely from their control or monopoly of market (commerce) in their regions. They especially made substantial profits from the flourishing pepper trade at that time.[8] At any rate, lord-peasants relationships like in a true feudal system that had never existed in Aceh.

Since the basis of their power in Acehnese society was not that strong the *uleebalangs* were bound to seek it somewhere else. It then became obvious that the security of their power seemed largely from the guarantee of Dutch support. Some of them used this new security to enrich themselves. It was then during this colonial period that a number of *uleebalangs*, notably those in the densely populated areas of Pidie, became large scale owners of land. Some of them owned one third up to one half of the rice fields in their regions. Though in theory people could complain to the *controleur*, the Dutch administrator above the *uleebalangs* about the conduct of their *uleebalangs* "in practice such appeals were futile at best and dangerous at worst".[9] The Dutch did take certain actions against a few of the conspicuously corrupt *uleebalangs* such as by replacing them.[10] But this seemed to have little influence in halting the process of dissatisfaction toward them as a group which developed among the villagers.

In fairness to the *uleebalangs*, some of them did show serious sympathy to the cause of the oppressed common people under colonialism, and that even led them to become actively involved in the Indonesian nationalist movement. *Teuku*[11] Nya' Arief and Teuku Muhammad Hasan were two of the most notable ones among them. Teuku Nya' Arief showed his open sympathy with Indonesia's nationalist movement, even during his membership in the Dutch-controlled *Volksraad* (People's Council). He actively helped the efforts of various social and religious organizations, especially their educational institutions. Teuku Muhammad Hasan was the first Aceh representative (*konsul*) of the Java-based Muhammadiyah movement, a modernist Muslim organization primarily interested in religious and socio-educational reforms. When he stepped down from that position he was replaced by yet another *uleebalang* by the name of Teuku Cut Hasan.[12] Significantly different from their corrupt fellows, those who took the side of the people and, for that matter, became strongly nationalist, were by and large progressive and better educated *uleebalangs*. However, they were not able to erase the feeling of dissatisfaction that had already developed among the peasants toward all of them as a group. As a result, there was fertile soil for the *ulama* to re-emerge. Once again they were to receive strong support from the population when they launched their new reform movement which started in the 1920's and culminated in 1939 in the establishment of *Persatoean Oelama Seloeroeh Atjeh* (All Acehnese Ulama Association), better known under its abbreviation *POESA* OR *PUSA*, in 1939.

The apparent delay in the re-emergence of the *ulama* to a prominent position was due to a number of factors, and one of them was the effect of the Dutch (Snouck Hurgronje) Islamic policy which had significantly curbed their activities. The most important factor, however, seems to be the heavy loss suffered by the *ulama* during their holy war against the Dutch. Most of their leading figures lost their lives in the various battlefields, and unlike *uleebalang* the title of *ulama* was not hereditary which made it even harder to replace them. Some of the children of the *ulama* did follow the step of their fathers, but like anyone else only after they had proven themselves worthy of that title, through *meudagang* in one of the *dayahs*. The war had apparently destroyed most of these traditional religious schools, largely because their *teungkus* (religious teachers), the *ulama*, had been deeply involved in it. Therefore, for many years afterwards the Acehnese were to feel the absence of those prominent *ulama*. This prompted many of them to send their children to various religious schools again, in and outside Aceh, and with that the process of renewal speeded up significantly.

A large number of Acehnese went to religious schools in Minangkabau (west Sumatra), some went to Java, while a few even went as far as Egypt. In Minangkabau, the majority of them entered schools which were run by modernist Muslim, especially the *Thawalib* schools which had been flourishing since the conclusion of the *Aceh War*. These modernist Muslim schools had a strong political tint, since many of their teachers and students were actively involved in the anti-Dutch nationalist movement.[13] Some of them who went to Java also entered modernist Muslim schools such as the ones run by Muhammadiyah. The few who went to Egypt seem to have also been influenced by the modernist Muslim movement there. Thus, when they returned to Aceh from all those places they also brought with them the ideas of modernist Muslim (Islamic modernism) which had eventually made them politically anti Dutch colonialism and religiously reformists. Subsequently, they were to play a major role in the re-emergence of Acehnese *ulama*.

But, and interestingly enough, they appear to have not been persuaded to bring with them the various organizations of modernist Muslims they had encountered outside to Aceh. Muhammadiyah, for example, which came there in the 1920's was apparently brought by the Minangkabaus, who for many years also remained its main supporters. The few Acehnese who joined and even played an active role in it were the *uleebalangs*. That probably was one of the reasons why the *ulama* refrained from joining it. This attitude was not only limited to Muhammadiyah, but extended to all other outside-based organizations.[14] These organizations, including the educational-oriented ones, were parts of the Indonesian nationalist movement. Therefore, the Dutch were bound to suspect them of being involved in politics, and that might have created a certain fear among Acehnese *ulama* to join them. If that was so, then the Dutch Islamic policy did appear to have a certain effect in curbing the behavior and activities of the *ulama*.

Whatever was the true reason, Acehnese *ulama* at that time did seem to prefer to act by and for themselves. The first serious sign of their re-emergence was the establishment of new religious schools in the 1920's. The first one to become famous was the school of Teungku Abdul Wahab which was established in 1926 at Seulimeum, Aceh Besar (Great Aceh) regency. Two other famous ones were *Madrasah Al-Muslimin Peusangan* of Teungku Abiurrahman Meunasah Meucap, established in 1930 at Matangglumpangdua, North Aceh, and *Madrasah Saadah Adabiah* of Teungku M. Daud Bereueh, established in 1931 at Blang Paseh, Pidie. There were also some religious schools connected with or even affiliated with religious schools outside Aceh. The *Madrasah Al-Irsyad*, established in 1927 Lhok Seumawe, North Aceh, was a branch of the same school in Surabaya (Java), while the *Thawalib* (1928) at Tapak Tuan, South Aceh, was known to have connections with a school under the same name in Minangkabau. Another school which also became famous at that time was *Madrasah Iskandar Muda* which was established by a well-known *uleebalang*, Teuku M. Daud Panglima Polem, though he did not run it by himself.[15]

Many of those who returned to Aceh upon completion of their studies at several religious schools outside were to become teachers of these new religious schools, and partly through them the ideas of modernist Muslim movement were to develop there also. But most of the leading figures in these new schools, especially because they were the founders, were still basically Aceh-trained *ulama*. As such, Islamic modernism which came to Aceh from Minangkabau, Java, Egypt and elsewhere was bound to make a certain adjustment to the thinking of these prominent *ulama*. Consequently, the modernist Muslim movement which eventually developed in Aceh was to have some differences with those found outside, say with the Muhammadiyah, for example, though basically they were about the same. Needless to add, the re-emergence of the *ulama* as a movement in Aceh was inspired and influenced by the ideas of Islamic modernism. As a result, they were politically anti Dutch colonialism which subsequently caused them to have an unfriendly image of the *uleebalangs* as a group. Religiously, they became reformists which led them to feel not at ease with traditional *ulama* who still had a significant influence in Acehnese society.

The climax of their success under Dutch rule was marked by the establishment of the previously mentioned *All Acehnese Ulama Association*, *PUSA*, in a gathering held at *Madrasah Al-Muslimin Peusangan* on the fifth of May 1939. Teungku M. Daud Beureush was then elected as the first chairman of the organisation. Another important decision of the gathering was about the need to establish a school for the sole purpose of training future religious teachers for their various religious schools. This was seen as an effort to harmonize and standardize their curriculum. In addition, this newly planned school was also to provide its students with certain secular subjects, so that they would be able to meet the needs caused by the development of Acehnese society or the progress of the modern world. That school was finally established at the end of 1939 at Sigli, Pidie, and was named *Normaal Islam Instituut*. The first director of the School and also one of its principal teachers was T.M. Nur El-Ibrahimy, a graduate of Al-Azhar, Cairo, and son-in-law of Teungku M. Daud Beureueh. Another important teacher was a certain Muhammad, a former student of the Law School in Jakarta, who taught secular subjects including Dutch and English languages. Not long after its formation *PUSA* became a member of *Majlis Islam A'la Indonesia*. (All Indonesia Islamic Council), a federation of various Islamic organizations in Indonesia, and by that action it began to take an active part in Indonesian nationalist movement.[16]

Immediately after its birth *PUSA* established new branches all over Aceh and it received strong support almost everywhere, except in South Aceh where the people already had long traditional ties with Minangkabau and Tapanuli. PUSA was especially strong in North Aceh, Pidie and Aceh Besar where the above mentioned new religious schools were centred. Interestingly enough, a few *uleebalangs* were also among its strongest supporters. One of them was Teuku Muhammad Amin, a businessman, who played a very active role as a member of its central board. In fact, the ruling *uleebalang* of Peusangan, Teuku Muhammad Johan Alam Syah, was very instrumental during the process which led to the first establishment of *pusa*, since he was the one who guaranteed it to the Dutch and continued to protect it. Many other *uleebalangs* had also assisted this organization, especially during the establishment of its branches all over Aceh, usually by becoming its advisers.[17] Such favorable cooperation offered by the *Uleebalangs*, however, substantially failed to erase the unfavorable image toward them as a group which appeared to have developed within the circle of *ulama*.

NOTES

1. The *Aceh War* is discussed, among others, in Mohammed Said, *Atjeh Sepandjang Abad*, Djilid Pertama, Medan, Diterbitkan oleh Pengarang sendiri,1961; Anthony Reid, *The Contest for North Sumatra: Atjeh, The Netherlands and Britain 1858–1898*, Kuala Lumpur Singapore, Oxford University Press,1969.
2. See Ali Hasjmy, *Hikajat Prang Sabi* mendjiwai Perang Atjeh *Lawan Belanda*, Banda Atjeh, Pustaka Faraby, 1971.
3. Snouck Hurgronje's advice concerning the war can be found, for example, in E. Gobee and C. Adriaanse, eds., *Ambtelijke Adviezen van C. Snouck Hurgronje, 1889–1936*, vol.1, The Hague, Martinus Nijhoff, 1957. See also *footnote* 5 below.
4. James Siegel, *op. cit.*, p. 71.
5. Discussions on the new Dutch colonial policy and Snouck Hurgronje's Islamic policy can be found in Harry J. Benda, *The Crescent and the Rising Sun: Indonesian Islam under the Japanese Occupation 1942–1945*, The Hague and Bandung, van Hoeve, 1958, Chapter 1; Alfian, *Islamic Modernism in Indonesian Politics: The Muhammadijah Movement during the Dutch Colonial Period (1912–1942)*, Ph.D. dissertation, University of Wisconsin, 1969, Chapter II.
6. A. J. Pickaar, *Atjeh en de Oorlog met Japan*, 's Gravehague — Bandung, van Hoeve, 1949, p. 7.
7. James Siegel, *op. cit.*, p. 87.
8. Anthony Reid, *op. cit.*, pp. 14–17.
9. James Siegel, *op. cit.*, p. 87.
10. A.J. Piekaar, *op. cit.*, p. 8.
11. *Teuku* is the hereditary title of *uleebalang*.
12. A.J. Piekaar, *op. cit.*, pp. 11–12. See also T.M.A. Panglima Polem *Memoir [Tjatetan] T.M.A. Panglima Polem*, Kutaradja, Alhambra, 1972; "Mengenang: Seorang Pembela Rakyat dan Tokoh Perjuangan Nasional Tig Zaman", *Harian Mimbar Umum*, 24 Oktober 1974.
13. Some of the studies on modern Muslim movement in Indonesia are: Deliar Noer, *The Modernist Muslim Movement in Indonesia, 1900–1942*, Singapore, Kuala Kumpur, Oxford University Press, 1973; Taufik Abdullah, *School and Politics: The Kaum Muda Movement in West Sumatra [1927–1933]*, Ithaca, Modern Indonesia Project, Cornell University, 1971; Alfian, *op. cit.*, Howard F. Federspiel, *Persatuan*

Islam: Islamic Reform in Twentieth Century Indonesia Ithaca, Modern Indonesia Project, Cornell University, 1970.

14. A.J. Piekaar, *op. cit.*, pp. 13–24.
15. See Ismuha, "Lahirnja 'Persatuan Ulama Seluruh Atjeh' 30 Tahun Yang Lalu", *Sinar Darussalam*, No. 14 dan 15, Djuni dan Djuli 1969, pp. 43–47 and 33–40; Jajasan Pembina Darussalam, *10 Tahun Darussalam dan Hari Pendidikan*, Darussalam, Jajasan Pembina Darussalam, 1969, pp. 371–72.
16. Ismuha, *op. cit.*, *Sinar Darussalam*, No. 14, Djuni 1969, pp. 45–47.
17. A.J. Piekaar, *op. cit.*, pp. 18–24.

Islam, Adat and Communism on the West Coast of Sumatra

B. SCHRIEKE

The political myth of the West Coast of Sumatra has been for a hundred years the struggle between the *adat* party and the religious party,[1] a struggle which may, indeed, present new aspects, but nevertheless determines the view taken of administrative problems. While in a former period the stereotype was *adat* versus religion, and no one analyzed the social forces which brought about the conflict, in more recent times the slogan, *kaum muda,* that is to say, the younger generation, has been added as a powerful phrase giving a satisfactory explanation of all difficulties.

The absorption of former 'revolutionary' tendencies by society. The religious life also shows signs of development, however. In Rao the old conditions are still found, though even there these are the products of the period of the *padris,*[2] but the fierce turbulence of those days has been moderated by the evolution of a society which has absorbed the erstwhile revolutionary elements. In the Lubuk Sikaping district the administration of the *padris* and that of the *adat* were reconciled in the Besar nan IX, The Big Nine, which consisted of the five lords (*datuk*) and the four gentlemen (*manku*). Sundatar has in addition to the *rajah adat* a general chief of religion, just as Rao and its dependencies, the region of the Besar nan XV, has, besides the secular head at Padang Nunang, another chief as religious head, with representatives in Rokan, on the East Coast of Sumatra, and Pakantan in Mandailing. The village of Mahat, in Suliki, shows the rudiments of this in two dignitaries above the village head, the *rajah adat* and the *rajah ibadat,* both of whom are of little practical significance any more, however. Religious offices and religious teachings have got into a rut there which would cause great annoyance to more educated persons.

The profession of priest has fossilized into a hereditary *adat* position once more. When people with knowledge of the holy books come into such a district and call attention to the decay of religion or to errors that have crept in, they too are nowadays called modernists, however outmoded their erudition may be.

And yet the phenomenon is many decades old. That it has not yet penetrated to a region of this kind is simply due to the comparative isolation of the area.

Above 1890 the lively propaganda of the *Naqshibandiyyah* Brotherhood alarmed the administration. It rained instructions: it was ordered that in the regular reports the official interest in the intensification of religious life had to be shown, and the instrument of the *adat* had to be set to work against the religious reformers and zealots. The community, however, absorbed this spiritual current as well.

The *Naqshibandiyyah* now enjoys official approval — it promotes peace and order. The first opposition of the religious modernists, whose aims in this respect ran parallel with the rigidly orthodox views of the older teachers, was antagonistic to the heretical 'innovation'

Reprinted in abridged form from *Indonesian Sociological Studies, Selected Writings of B. Schrieke, Part One* (2nd ed.; The Hague: W. van Hoeve Publishers Ltd., 1955), by permission of the publishers.

of the *tariqahs*. New distrust — but in religiously old-fashioned Talu, Lubuk Sikaping and Rao we also find the *tariqahs* pining away under the pressure of the materialistic spirit of the times.

One factor which, apart from the natural dislike of the conservative section of the population for the new and unknown, lurked in all such new conflicts, was the fact that the traditional social system did not furnish a satisfactory place for the authority of the free religious dignitaries, that the prestige of the religious teachers extended beyond the *adat* relationship. And then there was the professional jealousy between the *adat* priesthood and the new element which availed itself of part of the 'voluntary offerings' prescribed by religion.

We have already dealt with the struggle against matriarchic heredity law, which began during the days of the *padris* and was carried on under the leadership of Ahmad Chatib at Mecca about 1894 and then again greatly disturbed the civil authorities. The social causes and points of contact, such as the forming of one-family households, were discussed at the same time.

'Neutrality' in matters of religion,[3] which in practice often expressed itself in a silent struggle against the religious teachers, drove the latter — often quite involuntarily — to assume a reserved attitude, sometimes even a hostile one, towards the authorities, who were unbelievers: an attitude which it was quite easy to rationalize from the standpoint of religion. Hence all resistance against the government easily found religious teachers who were both able and willing to attach to it the ideology desired by a religious-minded population. For instances of this we need only turn to the taxation troubles of 1908 and 1918 and the attack on Padang Panjang of 1915, although the latter was rooted simply in the easily understandable personal resentment of a single *tariqah* sheik.

However, all the above was put in the shade by the struggles carried on by the *kaum muda* and the *kaum kuno*[4], though this conflict — which reached its high watermark in 1919 — has lost much of its virulence owing to the developments of recent years. Apart from a few die-hards on either side, the antithesis between the two religious groups has become less sharp. They have become more or less reconciled to each other, as it were, and if now and then the smouldering hostility bursts anew into flame, that is due for the most part either to hidden professional jealousy of a newcomer trying to make a place for himself in the community or to the fact that some latent social conflict of long standing has come to a head.

Kaum muda became so easily acceptable as a slogan because its many-sided meaning covered every sort of modernism whether religious or political. Hence it is a grave mistake to suppose that it was only the religious *kaum muda* who played a part in the communist propaganda.

It was the most respected *Naqshibandiyyah* sheik who carried on propaganda for communism on a religious footing at Chupak, in Solok.

In Muara Sipongi, in South Tapanuli, there was also an old-fashioned *Naqshibandiyyah* teacher who was well known on account of his knowledge of charms and performance of magic and whom the famous Mohammed of Padang Panjang used as a tool by means of which to introduce communism *via* a *Sarekat Pandaraman*. The object of the society was at first said to be to collect money so as to enable the indigent to enjoy a religious retreat characteristic of that order. Later the aim was defined as mutual aid and the support of all needy and oppressed persons. The society was to be popularized by his pupils.

In Sungai Sarik, in Pariaman, the propagandist was Sidi Djemadi, a respected teacher of religion belonging to the *Shattariyyah* and known for his proficiency in secret knowledge. In Ulakan it was Labai Kadir, also a member of the *Shattariyyah*. At Pulau Tello the propagandist was even a supporter of the pacifist *Ahmadiyyah*.

In Tanah Datar the practitioners of the secret teaching of invulnerability did good business in those times of unrest. In this connection, too, the communist leaders knew how to adapt themselves to social conditions in their agitation to 'resist', only 'resist', as Semaun cried at the *Sarekat Islam* Congress in 1916.

Kaum muda and communism. The greatest religious teachers of the *kaum muda* — Hadji Rasul, Sheik Djambe', and Hadji Abdullah Ahmad — were hostile to communism. The last of these three was challenged by Hadji Muhammed Nur Ibrahim, when not yet a fugitive, to debate with him in public. Sheik Djambe' had to beg repeatedly in November, 1926 to be allowed to speak against communism in public. (After which the opinion the *demang* concerned had of him changed.) Hadji Abdullah Ahmad and Hadji Rasul[5] tried to persuade Hadji Bahauddin of Sawah Lunto of the error of his ways, as they had previously tried to persuade Hadji Datuk Batuah. Hadji Rasul washed his hands of the school of the *Sumatra Tawalib,* when it proved to be going in the wrong direction. Sheik Djambe' expelled Ramaja and Muchtar (the latter not a communist) from his *surau,* or college, when they began mixing politics with religious instruction. Hadji Rasul was abused for his anti-communist views in the communist newspapers, such as *Njala,* and at the communist meetings, for example at Pajakumbuh, and was also blamed for the exile of Hadji Datuk Batuah.

But the distrust felt by the native administration — and hence also by the European civil service which took its cue from it — in regard to the *kaum muda* remained as great as ever, and so no use was made of the willingness of the important religious teachers to take a stand against the communists. Sheik Ibrahim from Parabek, who was not a partyman nor even a convinced follower of *muda,* went so far as to request that his lessons in religion might be regularly supervised, so as to save him in the name of Allah from being suspected. On 3 November, 1924 he had already expelled both Sadruddin — who later became a section leader — and Rustam from his school for religious instruction because of their communistic propensities. The notes made by Sadruddin, which were seized in Benkulen, contained fierce attacks on Hadji Rasul and Sheik Ibrahim of Parabek, as well as against Sheik Djao and the *Mohammadiyyah* at Padang Panjang because of their anti-communistic views. The society just mentioned had, indeed been founded by Sheik Djao as a bulwark against the threatening communistic stream. Yet for all that it was regarded with distrust by both the *adat* chiefs and the administration.

On one occasion when Sheik Djambe' gave a lecture in Pariaman on religion and was asked at the end of his talk for the meaning of a verse from the *Koran* constantly quoted by the communists in their propaganda against the Dutch rule, he was even forbidden to give an answer. And yet, as early as 1924, *Persatuan Guru Agama Islam,* the association of modernist religious teachers, had declared itself opposed to communism and stated that that doctrine could not be brought into line with Islam. Support from that quarter, thus, was not made use of. The persecution to which the teachers of religion who did not support communism were subjected, particularly in Padang Panjang, finally drove even them to keep silent and hold themselves aloof.

Religious elements in communist propaganda. Nor was there anything specifically modernistic in the propaganda of the communists which was religious in tone. To realize this one need only read the anonymous leaflet sent from the West Coast to a number of teachers of religion in South Tapanuli, in Jambi, and presumably, in Minangkabau as well.

> Let no one speak ill of the communists, for whosoever does that is a *kafir,* an unbeliever. There are, after all, four ways in which a man may invalidate his being Moslem: (a) by doing a thing of which he has no knowledge, (b) by not doing a thing of which he has knowledge, (c) by, lacking knowledge, being unwilling to learn from those who know, (d) by speaking ill of those who do right.
>
> *Re* (a): Those who speak ill of the communists without having first become communists and without knowing anything about communism, do that of which they have no knowledge.
>
> *Re* (b): Although it is well known that one should not speak ill of a thing one does not know, nevertheless people speak ill of communism and thus do not do that of which they have knowledge.
>
> *Re* (c): Although people do not know what the aims of communism are, yet they are not willing to ask for information from those who know, and thus they join those who know not and yet are unwilling to learn from those who do know.
>
> *Re* (d): By speaking ill of the communists, who really desire what is right, a man becomes guilty of speaking ill of those who do right.
>
> The communists really do desire what is right, namely that religion, *adat,* and prosperity should all be improved.
>
> 1 Has not Allah said, "Do not obey the commands of the *kafir*"? And what do we do?
>
> 2 Our *adat,* which used to govern us, yea and what not, have been ruined by the government and the capitalists.

3 Now we work only for the benefit of the capitalists, not for the benefit of ourselves and our families.

In all these matters the communists seek to bring improvement. The hour has almost struck!

Whoever joins those who do right, does right himself. Whoever joins the ranks of those who do wrong or give it their approval, does wrong himself!

The communists wish to do right but are prevented from so doing by the capitalists. Whoever does not join the communists and whoever speaks ill of them are themselves capitalists.

Whoever, when the time shall have come for the fight against the Dutch, is not a communist, has ranged himself on the side of the *kafirs*. Otherwise he would have become a communist. Think it over.

It is plain to see that there is nothing modernist in all this. We have here a document written after the manner of the religious teachers and intended simply as a means of inciting the people against the unbelieving government. That was the spirit which animated all propaganda. It was no use to touch on the points of difference between the *kaum muda* and *kaum kuno*, only an appeal to Mohammedan feelings as such and speculations on religious antitheses and instincts were appropriate when making propaganda. Suitable texts[6] from the *Koran* which could be taken out of their context and twisted to suit the propagandist purpose were used to strengthen the oft-repeated argument. For has not social psychology taught us[7] that a powerful suggestive influence is exerted by such repetition of "a simple statement of emotional facts, whether true or false"? The masses believe only what they want to believe, namely, that which accords with their wishes and desires.[8] It was only too well known that religion was the weak spot in communism and hence it was imperative to show clearly that communism and religion, communism and *adat* were one and the same.

Identification of the Antichrist with capitalism and of communism with the Messiah. The images selected to be used were therefore taken from familiar conceptions. The capitalists were the *Dajal* of which the religious teachers preached — the appellation applied to the eschatological figure of the Mohammedan Antichrist and a term of abuse in common parlance. This identification at the same time suggested the redemptive advent of the *Mahdi* — the Messiah.[9] Thus the gospel of the eschatological ideal republic also was made 'communized' and incorporated in propaganda!

The catchword 'capitalism'. We have already called attention to the effect of the catchword 'capitalism'. Once more it is social psychology which has taught us that uncomprehended foreign words are so powerful as catchwords because each of us can load them with his or her own effects.[10] For, as Lowell remarks, "Public opinion is usually the flattering substitute for private opinions and public emotions".

That catchword 'capitalism' became even more effective when 'translated' into the Minangkabau language, as *kapi,* the Minangkabau equivalent to *kafir* or unbeliever, plus *setali,* the Dutch twenty-five cent piece. Thus two 'complexes' could react to the word *kapisetali,* namely, the feelings against the unbelievers, the *kapi,* and the feelings against the scrape-penny, the money-grubber, the skinflint *par excellence,* the tax-demanding government. It was also these complexes that the above-mentioned anonymous piece of writing sought to stimulate.[11]

Modern religious schools. We have already quoted Delaisi on the political myth as follows:

> The masses interpret events of the present day by the aid of traditional conceptions. They are prone to forget the facts, which do not tally with generally accepted ideas; they bear in mind only those which concern them.

There was, indeed, some outer justification for suspecting the religious *kaum muda* of sympathy with the communists. For did not these *kaum muda* — like their Arab co-religionists on Java in the past in the struggle of the *Irshad* against the supremacy of the *sayyids* — demand the recognition of the equality of all men before Allah, on the authority of the *Koran*? And did not this sound suspiciously like the ideal of *sama rata sama rasa*, equality for all?

More important, however, was the religious teaching at the school of the *Sumatra Tawalib* at Padang Panjang. Just as the communist leaders had managed to get a hold on the students of the teacher training school, so also had they succeeded in enticing the pupils of the theological school to a course on communism. Thanks to the influence of Hadji Datuk Batuah, the school was later driven in the direction of communism. As a matter of fact the aim of the propaganda carried on in both the institutions was the same, namely, to introduce communism into the villages *via* the students.

For the rest, the school of the *Sumatra Tawalib* had been established, on the one hand, because religious education was lacking in the government schools and, on the other, because the outcome of government instruction was disappointing, since the graduates of the Dutch vernacular schools (*Hollands-Inlandse scholen*)[12] found it hard to obtain employment and were still always in an inferior position to the young people who had passed through the European schools. And now came the graduates of the Padang Panjang educational institution, who had already been infected during their school days with communistic ideas, and the community was unable to furnish jobs for them all, in spite of the fact that the school of the *Sumatra Tawalib* was highly reputed because of the competent religious teachers who had taught there (the late Zainuddin Labai, Hadji Rasul) and that the system of instruction there was, as is fashionable these days, more or less adapted to modern requirements. The graduates found it hard to make a living, the little schools they established soon went downhill, payment of school fees was irregular. Quite a number of pupils did certainly come to them after leaving the government schools when these increased their fees; they tried evening and afternoon lessons for government school pupils, but the struggle for existence remained difficult. The ideas inculcated while they were at school were given a real basis in the circumstances of their lives, and 'communism' seemed to be in accordance with the spirit of the times — society was ripe for it. And so it came to pass that many former students of the school of the *Sumatra Tawalib* became propagandists of communism, as did also many elementary school teachers, graduates of the training school. That communist leaders like Ramaja, who had religious convictions, were more apt to belong to the *kaum muda* than to the old-fashioned trend of thought, is, of course, natural enough.[13]

The political myth of the West Coast. This was, however, not the point of vantage from which the native administration and parts of the European administration looked at the state of affairs. 'The political myth' remained: distrust of the teachers of religion — although there were exceptions — and particularly of the *kaum muda.*

The guru ordinance of 1925. And then a remarkable thing happened. While the government was for political reasons still hesitating to declare the *guru* ordinance in force on the West Coast — the ordinance which merely demanded from the religious teachers that they should keep the government informed as to their activities — it was suddenly decreed in various places that a man must ask official permission for giving religious instruction. Great was the dissatisfaction among the teachers of religion, who felt very much injured because their age-old rights were ignored, particularly because some of their number who had been able to teach for years unquestioned were now refused the necessary permit on the ground that 'the *penghulus*' did not wish them to have it. In places where this had not been heard of within the memory of man, it appeared with equal suddenness that there existed an *adat* which placed the religious teachers under the tutorship of the *penghulus.*

The traditional apparatus of adat set in motion against religious teachers. Here, too, the lack of expert knowledge made itself felt and the native administration, the education of whose members was usually not adapted to modern needs, was given free play. The apparatus of *adat* was set in motion after the traditional manner against bold teachers of religion with somewhat advanced ideas who were suspected of being communists because they were *kaum muda.* Petty nagging, which naturally aroused embitterment among the victims, was regarded as the course of wisdom.[14] For instance, teachers who were highly respected in their villages and whose only fault was that they belonged to the modern religious group were bothered in the following way: when they wished to give a party in connection with some domestic event such as a baby's first bath or the wedding of a sister's child, or when their pupils wanted to honour them by coming in procession to offer them a sacrificial animal, the authorities devised transgressions of *adat* law in order to put a stop to the festivities or disorganize them and then punish the persons concerned 'in accordance with the *adat*'. The most hateful thing in all this was that the people recognized the hand of the administration in it. Love for the *adat* was certainly not strengthened by such doings!

GLOSSARY

Adat: Custom especially as (a source of) customary law.
Datuk: Distinguished title.
Ibadat: Religious duties.
Kaum kuno: 'The old fashioned group', people of conservative (religious) tendencies.
Kaum muda: 'The young growing', people of modernist (religious) tendencies.
Sarekat (or serikat): Association.
Sayyid: Descendant of Mohammed through Fatimah and Ali.
Tariqah (or tarikat): Moslem mystic brotherhood.
Surau: (Religious) school.
**Ahmadiyyah* is the name given to the followers of Ahmad Qadiani (or Kadiani). The doctrines of Ahmadiyyah agree on the whole with those generally taught by Islam. The most striking differences concern only the Christology, the vocation of the Mahdi and the djihad (holy war). They believe that Jesus migrated to Kashmir in India to preach the gospel in that country. Regarding the vocation of the Mahdi and the djihad the Ahmadiyyah teach that the task of the former is one of peace, and that the djihad must be conducted with peaceful means and in all circumstances sincere obedience must be given to the government.
**The *Naqshibandiyyah, Shatteriyah* and the *Chadariyyah* were the three popular orders (tariqah) in Indonesia at the beginning of the century. Each of these tariqah have ties with the sheikhs in the Middle East.

NOTES

1. B. J. O. Schrieke, 'Bijdrage tot de bibliografie van de huidige godsdienstige beweging ter Sumatra's Westkust' (Contribution Towards a Bibliography of the Contemporary Religious Movement on the West Coast of Sumatra), *TBG*, LIX (1919–1921), pp. 249–261.
2. *Padris*: A sect of religious revolutionaries striving after the abolition of the *adat* and all Minangkabau popular customs contradictory to Islam. The doctrine of the Prophet according to them had to be imposed upon the people — if need be by means of violence. The movement, stimulated by hadjis who had witnessed the reforms of the Wahhabits in Mecca, was suppressed by the *adat* party with the help of the Dutch (1821–1839). [Editorial note]
3. *Cf. TBG*, LIX (1919–1921) 259, n. 1.
4. An analysis of this may be found in Schrieke, "Bijdrage tot de bibliografie van de huidige godsdienstige beweging ter Sumatra's Westkust", *TBG* LIX (1919–1921). On the *kaum muda* movement in its earliest phase the reader should consult the report by Drvan Ronkel, *Rapport betreffende de godsdienstige verschijnseler ter Sumatra's Westkust, samengesteld door den ambtenaar voor de beoefening der indische talen Dr Ph. S. van Ronkel,* Batavia: Landsdrukkerij. See Schrieke, *Indonesian Sociological Studies,* The Hague: van Hoeve, 1955, pp. 126–129.
5. Thus also the communication from the resident of Sumatra's West Coast, dated 20 February, 1924, no 108, confidential.
6. The leaders possessed little handwritten compendiums of *Koran* and *hadith* (sayings and deeds of the Prophet) quotations.
7. *Cf.* Carl Timm, *Zeitschrift für Völkerpsychologie und Soziologie*, II (1926), 361 f.
8. Graham Wallas says in his *Human Nature in Politics,* (first edition, 1908; third edition, 1920; reprinted, 1924), 98 f.: "The empirical art of politics consists largely in the creation of opinion by the deliberate exploitation of subconscious non-rational inference." *Cf.* Steven Reynolds and B. and T. Wolley, *Seem So! A Working-Class View of Politics* (1913), 127 f. See also n. 11 below.
9. The traditional descriptions of the tremendous powers of the Antichrist (*Dajal*) must not be interpreted literally, for they convey a prophecy of the immense power of capitalism.
10. We have the war to thank for a whole series of studies in this field in which are analyzed both the war psychosis and — especially — the war propaganda of the various nations: secrets, methods, and effect.

See amongst others H. D. Lasswell in *Bibliography of Recent Literature on International Propaganda* (Publications of the American Sociological Society, XXXII, 1926).

11. "The necessity of explaining these problems, viz the basic principles of a rigid socialist social philosophy, to great masses of the people who lacked all preconceived ideas except that of immediate repression, compelled their popularization, their formulation in a few easily understood axioms which by constant repetition, that is, by an appeal to faith, could be impressed upon the masses. The sovereign power of the slogan is the other important basis of radicalism which is required for socialist propaganda. . . The vague emotional world and the unstable will of the radical masses clutch at such slogans and see in them an expression of that indefinable something which moves them without finding clear definition": Curt Geyer, *Der Radikalismus in der deutschen Arbeiterbewegung* (1923), 40 – 41, 42 – 43. *Cf.* H. Sultan "Zur Soziologie des modernen Parteiensystems", *ASS*, LVI (1926), 124–125; Alfred Meusel, "Der Radikalismus", *Kölner Vierteljahreshefte für Soziologie,* IV (1924), 46; A. Fischer, "Psychologie der Gesellschaft", in Kafka, *Handbuch der vergleichenden Psychologie,* II (1922), 419; Roffenstein, "Zur Psychologie der politischen Meinung", *Zeitschrift für Völkerpsychologie und Soziologie,* III (1927), 405–406.
12. See Schrieke, "The Educational System in the Netherlands Indies", *Bulletin of the Colonial Institute* (Amsterdam), II, (1938–1939), 14. [Editorial note]
13. *Cf.* above, pp. 126–129.
14. The following data are taken from an official report.

Adat and Islam: An Examination of Conflict in Minangkabau

TAUFIK ABDULLAH

Except for some fragmentary accounts[1] the early history of the Islamization of Minangkabau is still unrecorded. The first historically known religious center was Ulakan, a small town on the west coast, north of Padang. The first *ulama* of this center was Sjech Burhanuddin, who died in 1704 and who was regarded in Minangkabau tradition as the first ulama who spread the religion to the interior. There are many indications, however, that Sjech Burhanuddin was not the first ulama to introduce Islam to Minangkabau, and he himself travelled to Atjeh in order to study under the famous Sjech Abduurauf of Singkel. But he seems to have been the first important ulama to establish a religious center, which eventually became the sole authority in religious matters. The earliest branch of Burhanuddin's school was established by his pupils at Pemansiangan, Kapeh-kapeh (Padang Pandjang). In religious matters the position of the *tuanku* (religious teacher) of Pemansiangan[2] was second only to that of Sjech Burhanuddin, the Tuanku of Ulakan. Besides instructing the new branch of his school, the Tuanku of Ulakan was able to teach the so-called four tuanku, each of whom represented the different religious "sciences" and disciplines. These four pupils came from several parts of Minangkabau, and when they finished their studies they returned to their own regions and established new religious centers. Thus, before the death of the Tuanku of Ulakan there were already several religious centers in the interior, with Ulakan as their source of authority.[3] As the *"kalifah"* of the *Sjatariah-tariqah,* it is no wonder that after his death the grave of the Tuanku of Ulakan was made into a holy place. Until the rise of the Padri movement it was still anathema to the religious teachers in Minangkabau to question the religious authority of Ulakan. In the late 18th century Marsden noted that Minangkabau was regarded "as the supreme seat of civil and religious authorities in this part of the East. . ."[4] By that time there were already dissident elements in the interior resisting the religious center on the coast.[5]

A common and critical problem faced by all universal religions is how to adjust the existing environment to the religious doctrine. It should be noted, however, that those who brought Islam to Minangkabau, like any other *sufi*-oriented "missionaries", were more concerned with the purity of an individual's heart than with the religious correctness of his actions. In this case the indifferent attitude toward the Islamic duties which Marsden noted[6] is understandable. The crucial problem at the early stage of Islamization was the re-structuralization of adat in order to "interpret the heterogenetic change . . . as orthogenetic."[7]

The earliest impact of Islam was accordingly reflected in the new formulation of adat as

Reprinted in abridged form from *Indonesia* Vol. 2 (1966), 1–23, by permission of the author and Cornell Modern Indonesia Project, Ithaca, New York, U.S.A.

the ideal pattern of behavior, to the end that the outside elements might be thoroughly absorbed into the existing order as part of a coherent system. It is very difficult to know how this reformulation of the whole structural pattern of the society was attained. In the first place there was no recognized source of adat prior to the coming of Islam, except in the scattered information provided in the tambo and the popular sayings (*pepatah adat*). Secondly, the real "codification" of adat began only with the introduction of the Arabic script.[8] Furthermore, the logical foundation of the adat formulation was also based on the Islamic "logical law" (*mantik*).[9]

The Minangkabau attitude toward adat is based on the juxtaposition of the imperative continuity of the system — *tak lakang dipaneh, tak lapuak dihudjan* — and the recognition of the importance of change — *sakali aia gadang, sakali tapian barubah* ("when flood comes, the bathing place moves"). Thus it is implicit in adat that it should be always renewed and adjusted to the situation — *usang-usang dipabaru, lapuak dipakadjang* — while a permanent tension within the system itself is created by the need to reconcile the basic value with the changing situation. To handle this contradiction the system is arranged in such a way that its unavoidable revaluation can be smoothly undertaken, adat being divided into several categories, in which the permanent and the changing elements, the general principles and the local variants, are given their proper place.

There are four classes of adat, namely the *adaik nan sabana adaik* (adat which is truly adat), *adaik istiadaik* (adat of ceremonials), *adaik nan taadaik* (adat which has become adat), and *adaik nan diadaikkan* (adat which is made adat).[10] This hierarchical categorization of adat is a device for overcoming the tension between what should be and what is. The adaik nan sabana adaik is considered to be eternal, since it is also identical with natural law. In the later adat codification a new dimension is added to this class of adat, that of supernatural law,[11] for although Islamic doctrine was not intended to replace local practices, it was from the outset put in the highest adat category. The Quran and Hadith and the natural laws were accordingly viewed as the eternal principles that guide human spiritual and secular activities and from which actual practices and lesser values should emanate.[12]

Another term applied to the traditional norms of life is the *tjupak nan duo* — the two measures (*tjupak* is a standardized bamboo measure). The tjupak nan duo consists of the *tjupak usali* and the *tjupak buatan,* the former being the original standard, the source of all values and practices, from which the tjupak buatan derives its regulations. The tjupak usali in adat is the ideal pattern of behavior, while the tjupak buatan is the realization of the ideal in actual life, which should also be in conformity with the environment.

In view of the fact that early Islamization in Minangkabau was mostly directed toward the tariqah-practices and the reformulation of the existing order, the coming of Islam did not seriously threaten the basic foundation of Minangkabau society. Instead of cultural loss the new elements meant cultural enrichment; but, ironically, they also contributed another dimension to the ongoing internal conflict. The existing tension between continuity and change, between the "great tradition" and the local variations in adat, was compounded by the contradiction inherent in Islamic doctrine. Leaving aside the eternal dilemma in religious doctrine between the unity and separation of the natural and supernatural, Islam also had to deal with the tension between its ideal universality and a real parochialism. The Islamic standard of conduct recognizes this problem, being based on the two opposing poles of obligatory and prohibited actions — *wadjib* and *haram* — on which reward and punishment are based. Since most human actions fall outside these two categories two more are added, those of recommended and objectionable (but not forbidden) actions — *sunat* and *makruh* — and a third of those which are neither bad nor good: the indifferent actions, or *djain.*[13] In practice as well as in theory the application of these law categories is based on the Quran and Hadith, the Prophetic tradition. In order to deal with those circumstances which cannot be found in the two highest authorities, reasoning is employed as a third important source. New circumstances, it is maintained, should be decided either by analogy (*qyas*) or by the consensus of the *ulama.*

The position of reasoning is certainly one of the most crucial problems in Islamic doctrine. How, for instance, can man's responsibility to the transcendental power — God — be reconciled with his duty to his community? The process of Islamization in Minangkabau began with the minimum requirement of both responsibilities. It put more stress on the recognition of the eternal values, of the Omnipotent God and His Messenger. By avoiding the potential conflict between the self and the universe at the earliest stage of its introduction, Islam was able to restructure the social value pattern so that the Quran and Hadith were given the highest place. It is within this context that we should understand the claim by the earliest sources of Minangkabau adat that "adat is based on religion, religion is based on adat" — *adaik basandi sjarak, sjarak basandi adaik.*[14] Since in this sense there is no paradox in the ideal pattern of behavior between adat and religion, there is also no difference between adaik nan sabana adaik and the teachings of the Quran and Hadith.

Like the notion of the Minangkabau World — the Alam Minangkabau — as the integrative concept for all opposing institutions and systems of Minangkabau society, a *nagari* is also held to function as a smaller universe. It can be legally called a *nagari* if it has a *balai* (council hall), *musadjik* (mosque), *labuah* (road), and *tapian tampek mandi* (public bathing place). The mosque is the place to perform religious duties, and the balai is the place where secular and administrative matters are discussed. Only with the existence of these two institutions can a settlement be properly called a community, in which one's responsibility to his society and to the supernatural being can be integrated. Both duties should be performed and perfected with and within the community. As ruling institution — the nagari-council — the *balai* should classically symbolize the integration of the two components, adat prescription and religious law. The members of the balai are the *urang patuik,* the "exemplars", a composite elite consisting of the *penghulu* (or "adat-chief") and his staff, the *alim ulama* (the religious dignitaries), and the *tjadiak pandai* (the "neutral" intellectuals).[15] The *tjadiak pandai,* whose membership in the council is based on merit,[16] are selected by the common consent of the community and theoretically act as a "neutralizing" factor.

In a larger scope — while the antithesis between the royalty and the commoners prevailed — a new phenomenon emerged within Minangkabau society after the coming of Islam. The religious centers under the leadership of the tuanku began to become religious enclaves within the community. Despite continuing jealousies and doctrinal conflicts between them, the mobility of the religious pupils from one *madrasah* (school) to another, made the small, scattered religious enclaves into a potential challenge to the royalty as the symbol of the "great tradition." These religious centers were parts of the commoners' community when viewed vis-à-vis royalty, but they were also challengers of the social structure as a whole in that, leadership of the enclaves being inherited either spiritually from teacher to pupil or genealogically from father to son, the religious communities followed a paternal line of inheritance that was unlike the commoner but like the royal family system.[17]

The potential institutional conflict between the two claimant representatives of a "great tradition," the one based on the past and the other on the expertise of the universal religion, had little impact on the society as a whole until the end of the 18th century. The prestigious institutions never confronted each other directly. Nevertheless, the political power of the king was gradually undermined on the coast, and at the same time the religious authority of Ulakan was threatened by the rise of many religious centers in the interior. Minangkabau society at the turn of the 19th century can be described as in a period of transition, with many symptoms of social disintegration beginning to manifest themselves in the form of social demoralization and deterioration.[18] While the traditional sacral power of the king had been greatly undermined, the religious centers were too occupied with their own contemplative practices to provide an effective substitute. This stalemate between the old and a still weak and ineffective new was abruptly ended by the Padri movement.

The Padri movement, which took shape with the coming of the famous "three hajis" from Mecca in the early 19th century, was deeply influenced by the initial success of the Wahabi movement in Arabia at that time. Like the Wahabists, the Padri also directed their attacks first of all against deterioration.[19] But if in the Middle East Wahabism with its puritanical attitude had a "salutary and revitalizing effect",[20] in Minangkabau it became the inspiration for a dynamic force, impatient in transforming its environment, aiming at the destruction of what it considered a *djahiliah* — syncretic and unenlightened — society and at the creation of an Islamic one, by coercive measures if necessary. Consequently, this movement was, especially in its early stages, more interested than previous forms of Mingangkabau Islam in eliminating the distinction between man's responsibility to God and to the society.[21]

The success of the Padri movement is inconceivable if — as Schrieke suggests — it was simply a "revolution" of religious leaders who had been frustrated by living in a society which provided them no place in its social hierarchy.[22] The first leader of this movement in the valley of Alahan Pandjang, for instance, was one of the most powerful penghulu and a member of the ruling *Radjo Ampek Selo* (Kings of the Four Seats) of that region. Moreover, the protector of one of the pioneers of the movement was a penghulu.[23] The memoirs of a moderate Padri illustrate the way the Padri approached the entire membership of the *urang patuik*, which often resulted in growing numbers of new converts from that composite elite.[24] Not rarely the first to accept the Padri doctrine were the non-religious leaders, while on the other hand some of the most important leaders of the Padri were the old religious teachers.[25]

The Padri revolution was preceded by a growing feeling of detachment from their existing social environment on the part of some members of the *urang patuik*. In the process of searching for a means of social renovation they found Islam the most obvious choice, due to the incessant flow of rejuvenating ideas brought by the returning haji and to the position it had already acquired in the realm of Minangkabau adat. It is ironic that the Padri, in attempting to resolve the tension between the doctrine they believed in and their environment, unintentionally created a new issue — the social schism between the Padri and the non-Padri defenders of the old order. Progress toward a reconciliation of these forces was abruptly disturbed by the involvement of the Dutch in 1821.[26] The eventual rally against the Dutch in the last stages of the Padri War (1830's) temporarily overcame the schism,[27] only for it to reemerge under the encouragement of the domestic policy pursued by the alien regime.

The most significant impact of the Padri episode was the greater assimilation of religious doctrine within Minangkabau adat as the ideal pattern of behavior. Adat was "recodified", and the position of religion as the system of belief was strengthened. In the new codification religious doctrine became more clearly identified as the only basic standard of behavior. In daily life it was expected that adat regulations should be manifestations of religious designs: *agamo mangato, adat mamakai* (religion designs, adat applies). Within the new codification a sharper contradiction was made between the *adat islamiah* and *adat djahiliah*. *Adat islamiah* is adat which is in accordance with the religious doctrine, while *adat djahiliah* is adat which is contrary to religion. Adat djahiliah is defined as adat "which is forbidden in the adaik nan sabana adaik."[28] This distinction is identical with the distinction between "right" and "wrong", or, in religious terms, between *hak* and *bathil*, between *darl islam* and *darl harb*.

The working harmony of adat and Islam within the social system under the new codification is symbolized in the architectural style of the mosques. In the Minangkabau interior, especially in Lima Puluh Kota, Agam, and Solok, the roofs of the mosques are divided into three stories, as the symbol of the three social groups (*urang tigo djinih*) according to adat, namely the penghulu, the *imam-chatib* (the religious dignitaries), and the *urang banjak* (the mass). In some regions, such as Tanah Datar, the mosques are divided into four or five stories, which also reflect adat-symbols. The mosque of Lima Kaum, for instance, has five stories which symbolize the five *kampung* of the nagari.[29] Moreover, the mosque, especially the *surau* of every kampung, serves not only as the place for religious performances but is also an educational institution. The surau in many cases can also be regarded as the channel of socialization for boys, giving them a place which is not available in their mother's houses, and providing a solution to the uncertain position of the unmarried men.

The deepening absorption of Islam into the Minangkabau social fabric can be clearly seen in the mushrooming of religious schools, which in the post-Padri period were no longer isolated "enclaves" in their environment.[30] Verkerk Pistorius points out that the prestige of the religious teachers in almost every field was then far greater than that of the "native chiefs." They not only preached to the people but also aroused them from their "lethargic environment" to "strive for a high and noble life."[31]

The position of the religious teachers as the intelligentsia was not without opposition, however. The traditional professional division of religious dignitaries into adat-religious functionaries and religious teachers had not altered; but in the new situation, under the political dominance of the alien power, their traditional "antagonism" entered a new stage.

In the middle of the 19th century a wave of religious rejuvenation resulted in an attack against the entrenched tariqah, the Islamic mystic schools. This movement directed its attack especially against the hitherto most influential tariqah-school, the Satarijah, which now "began to be regarded as an old fashioned and much corrupted form of mysticism", and the school was at last forced "to make place for the tariqahs now most popular in Mecca, such as Naqshibendite and Qadirite."[32] It was the more orthodox-oriented Naqshibendite (*Naqshabadijah*)-*tariqah* school that came to Minangkabau[33] as a further step toward the perfection of the Islamic society. In its conflict with the older *tariqah* school the most sensitive issues were usually those concerning the beginning and the end of the fasting month and the problem of the *qiblah* — the direction faced while praying in the mosque.[34]

By attacking the old tariqah-schools[35] the leaders of the Naqshabandijah also directly challenged the adat-religious functionaries, since most of them belonged to the old school and were interested in maintaining the religious status quo. Hence the traditional contradiction between the two religious functionaries, the teachers and the officials, was intensified, and in the process the new school made itself a challenger to the whole establishment as it existed under the custodianship of the members of the nagari council. In some *nagari,* for instance in Suliki and Pariaman, this conflict resulted in the establishment of a separate nagari-mosque. This was a question which could not be decided by the religious law but by adat regulation,[36] since according to adat there could be only one common mosque for a nagari.

After the subjugation of Minangkabau as the result of the Padri War, Dutch policy sought to contain the influence of the religious teachers — and the Mecca returnees (*haji*) as well[37] — by alienating them as far as possible from the people's daily affairs and by upholding the authority of what they considered to be the legitimate "native chiefs." The effect of this policy was not only to rigidify the traditional leadership pattern, which centered around the balai, but also to create a separate group whose vested interest resided in the maintenance of the new status quo. As a sociological phenomenon this group was usually called — with an unfortunate choice of words — the *kaum adat*, the adat-group. This meant the detachment of one component from the whole context of the Minangkabau system, resulting in an imbalance of change in the society, a disequilibrium made the greater by the fact that the newly acquired status quo tended to ossify. This situation undoubtedly contributed much to the intensification of the conflict between the upholders of the status quo, the so-called custodians of adat, who had the support of the outside power, and the religious teachers who were the agents of incessant change.

Ironically, instead of enhancing the position of the representatives of adat, Dutch policy resulted in the erosion of the penghulu's traditional prestige. As elsewhere,[38] in Minangkabau the Dutch government based its policy on the manipulation of the existing political system — without, if possible, disrupting it — for the benefit of its economic-oriented motives. But in Minangkabau a new problem arose, since there was no functional supra-nagari organization available for such purposes. A nagari was a community *par excel-*

lence where real political and judicial powers resided.[39] A major problem for the colonial authorities was, therefore, the establishment of the required supra-nagari organization. After the failure during the Padri episode of the extension into the interior of the coastal Regency system supported by an "aristocratic" officialdom, a new system of nagari-federation was introduced. This nagari federation was headed by a "native chief" who not only acted as the representative of the European administration — being responsible for the collection of the coffee crop and the enforcement of the government's corvée[40] — but in reality also functioned as the highest adat authority of his region. Furthermore, at the nagari level some adjustments were made to meet the federation's needs: in effect the government invested in some "newcomers" — since the appointment of these "native officials" depended entirely on the government's preference — an authority and prestige much higher than that of the members of the traditional balai. In other words, the position of the penghulu and the balai as the traditional ruling group was gravely undermined. Unintentionally, a new kind of "professional" antagonism was introduced into Minangkabau society, that of the traditional penghulu versus the government-appointed "native officials."[41]

The encroachment on the authority of the penghulu and the unprecedented and unpopular function given them as managers of the government's corvée resulted in the erosion of their prestige. This process was furthered by the growing numbers of people who claimed the title of penghulu, their multiplication being a direct response to the policy of exempting penghulu from the corvée obligation.[42] Many wealthy families installed new penghulu by paying off the adat ceremonial obligation, and this eventually resulted in excesses. The sociological consequence of this tendency was the further dispersion of deference at a time when traditional deference was already eroding.

The alienation of the religious leaders, especially the religious teachers and the haji, and the ossification of the status quo, which had been attuned to the government's rather than the people's needs, were among the most important factors creating an atmosphere of stagnation and apathy in some parts of the society.[43] It was this temporary stalemate which was at last attacked by the "adat" revivalist movement and the "religious" orthodox reformation at the beginning of the 20th century. The former movement wanted to purify Minangkabau adat as a whole from outside influence, especially that of Atjeh on the coast. The orthodox reformation movement, which was especially active in the interior, directed its attack against the whole existing order, the tariqah schools as well as the matrilineal inheritance law.

These opposing movements — both were the staunchest of enemies[44] — were the first expressions of social reformation by urban "intellectuals" at a time when the traditional pattern of leadership was in decline. The opportunity to capture this leadership came especially after the failure of the scattered anti-tax rebellion of 1908.[45] This syncretic and rustic response to an unprecedented situation was led by penghulu and tariqah leaders, especially those of the Satarijah-school, and was the last battle fought for the restoration of the old order. Its failure not only resulted in the obligation of the people to pay money-taxation, but also paved the way for urban dominance. The end result was the transformation of the pattern of leadership, which now transcended the nagari boundaries. In other words, the nagari had now ceased in every sense to be an independent unit.

Another important impact of the urban phenomenon was that it tended to minimize the potential and actual conflicts between adat and Islamic inheritance law. In Minangkabau, property is divided into two categories, ancestral and self-earned. Ancestral property — usually land, house, etc. — may not be inherited by persons outside the maternal family. This semi-sacral property cannot be sold or pledged unless in an extreme emergency, such as marrying off an unmarried girl, paying for a funeral, redeeming debts, repairing the adat-house; and this can be done only by the consensus of all adult members of the family and by consultation with the penghulu. The position of a man regarding such property is more like that of a manager than a possessor. He has the right to use it but has no right to dispose of it or for that matter to pass it on to his own children.

Exception can only be made by gift — *hibah* — for which general agreement is also required. The real problem as far as inheritance is concerned is that of self-earned property, usually called *pusaka rendah*. The question is whether it is necessary for a person to make the hibah in order to pass on such property to his own children. According to adat, if he does not make the hibah it is his maternal family which has the legal right to this property. But according to the sjariah, first priority should be given to one's children, and thus hibah is unnecessary. It is *haram* — strictly forbidden — to inherit a property which is not religiously lawful.

This problem, as has been suggested earlier, has been partly solved by the individualizing tendencies created by the urban phenomenon. It is generally accepted in theory that the disposal of self-earned property depends entirely on the owner's will. It is assumed that even without a will of the deceased, the sister's children or other members of the maternal family have no right to claim the property. A problem may arise, however, if the self-earned property is itself the result of the investment of ancestral property, since such property also functions as a family-treasury. Furthermore, how should property be divided if it is accumulated in partnership with one's children and one's sister? In many cases the question of inherited property deals with these kinds of problems. The source of tension, accordingly, should not be seen as arising from the particulars of each case but as resulting from the need to formulate a general rule that can be taken as a valid inheritance law.[46]

According to Hazairin, the conflict between Islamic inheritance law and that of adat could not be solved as long as the ulama based their judgment completely on the codified *fikh*. The true inheritance law of Islam is based on clear bilateral principles, he claimed, the fikh being the result of an *idjmak* of the ulama, whose interpretations of the Quran and Hadith were certainly colored by their own social structure.[47] Obedience to the codified fikh was one of the characteristics of the early orthodox reformation, which tended to include all properties into one category so it should be regulated according to the fikh, which thoroughly ignored the possibility of the maternal ancestral property.[48] In short, in Hazairin's view the issue is not the conflict between religion and adat per se but rather the inadequacy of the codified fikh in dealing with a particular local situation.

In view of *taqlid* — blind obedience to whatever was written by the earlier ulamas — it is understandable that the modernists did not attack this sensitive problem in the early stages of development. The cleavage between the modernists and the orthodox was mostly due to their attitudes toward law, the conflict between idjtihad and taqlid. The modernists were more concerned with the rediscovery of the true Islamic spirit than with law for its own sake. They opposed the other-worldly attitude of the tariqah schools as well as the taqlid of the orthodox ulama. By establishing modern schools, publishing books and magazines, and holding *tabligh* — the public religious gatherings — the modernists attempted to create a situation in which their goals could be smoothly achieved. As the representative of its "own time" the modernist movement reached its peak at the end of the second decade of the 20th century. From this time on, various other dimensions of the internal conflict would play an important role in the social development of Minangkabau.[49]

NOTES

1. Ph. S. van Ronkel, "Een Maleisch getuigenis over den weg der Islam in Sumatra", *B.K.I.*, 75 (1919), pp. 363–378.
2. *Tuanku* is one of the highest titles of the religious teachers. The teacher who is considered to be higher than tuanku is called *sjech*. See: Hamka, *Ajahku*, Djakarta, 1958. p. 26 (note).
3. Ph. van Ronkel, "Het Heiligdom te Oelakan", *T.B.G.*, 56 (1914), 281ff. See also: Sjech Djilal-eddin, *Verhaal van den aanvang der Padri-onlusten op Sumatra*, ed. by Dr. J. J. de Hollander, Leiden, 1837, pp. 3–7.
4. W. Marsden, *History of Sumatra*, London, 1783, p. 343.
5. Sjech Djilal-eddin, *Verhaal*, pp. 15, 47.

6. Marsden, *History*, p. 346.
7. Gustave E. von Grunebaum, *Modern Islam: The Search for Cultural Identity*, New York, 1964, p. 20.
8. Ronkel, *Rapport betreffende de Godsdienstige verschijnselen ter Sumatra's Westkust*, Batavia, 1916, p. 15.
9. Hamka, *Adat Minangkabau Menghadapi Revolusi*, Djakarta, 1962, p. 27. See also the method of writing employed in Dt. Batuah Sango's *Tambo Alam Minangkabau*, Pajakumbah (n.d.).
10. For a brief explanation of these terms, see: A.H. Johns, (ed. and trans.) Introduction to the *Rantjak Dilabuah*, Ithaca, 1951.
11. J. C. van Eerde, "De adat volgens Minangkabausche bronnen," *Wet en Adat*, I/II, pp. 209–220.
12. It is interesting to note that when the Dutch government wanted to introduce Western criminal law into Minangkabau the same method was applied, including in the category of the *adaik nan taadaik*, which can be changed in accordance with the social and local environment. See: Ph. van Ronkel, "De invoering van ons Strafwetboek ter SWK naar aanteekeningen in een Maleische handschrift", *T.B.B.*, 46 (1914), pp. 249–255.
13. The English translation is based on H. A. R. Gibb, *Mohameddanism*, London, 1953, pp. 100–101.
14. E. Francis, "Korte Beschrijving van het Nederlandsch grondgebied ter Westkust van Sumatra", T.N.I., II, i (1839), pp. 113–114.
15. A. L. van Hasselt, *Volksbeschrijving van Midden Sumatra*, Leiden, 1882, p. 189.
16. Francis quotes from an old adat source to the effect that "The appointment of the 'king' and other 'chiefs' should be decided by a common agreement and the choice of the people or the *'anak buah'*, and that all problems should be solved according to *Sjarak* and *Adat*"; "Korte Beschrijving", p. 105.
17. Ronkel, "Het Heiligdom van Oelakan", *T.B.G.*, 56 (1914), pp. 281–316.
18. See: V. d. H., "De oorsprong van de Padri", *T.N.I.*, 1, 1837, also: Sjech Djilal-eddin, *Verhaal, passim.*
19. Schrieke, by comparing what the Wahabists did in Arabia and what was done by the Padri in Sumatra, concludes that the Padri should not be considered as Wahabists. B. Schrieke, "Bijdrage tot de bibiliografie van de huidige godsdienstige beweging ter Sumatra's Westkust", *T.B.G.*, 59, 1920, pp. 254–256. Cf. Ph. S. van Ronkel, "Inlandsche getuigenissen aangaande de Padri-oorlog", *I.G.*, 71, 1915, p. 1259. "They were Padri, but above all Moslems of the Minangkabau blood." However, it should not be forgotten that up to a certain point there was a synchronization between the development in the Middle East and that of Minangkabau. For instance, in 1829 a new wave of religious reformation came to Minangkabau which claimed that Wahabism was no longer attractive in Mecca because it had become obsolete. See E. Kielstra, *B.K.I.*, 37, pp. 368–369, also M. Radjab, *Perang Padri*, Djakarta, 1954, pp. 101–103. In Arabia the Wahabist power had been weakened by the 1820's.
20. H. A. R. Gibb, *The Modern Trends in Islam*, Chicago, 1947, p. 27.
21. Radjab, *op. cit.*, pp. 3–34. Cf. Jeanne Cuisinier, "La guerre des Padri (1803–1838–1845)", *Archives de sociologie des réligions*, IV, 7, 1959, pp. 70–88.
22. Cf. Schrieke, *T.B.G.*, 59, pp. 252, 260.
23. Francis, *T.N.I.*, I, p. 99.
24. Sjech Djilal-eddin, *Verhaal, passim.*
25. H. J. J. L. Ridder de Steurs, *De vestiging en uitbreiding van Nederlanders ter Westkust van Sumatra*, Amsterdam, 1849, vol. II, pp. 63–64.
26. See for instance the memoirs of Tuanku Imam Bondjol, included as an appendix in Steurs, *Vestiging*.
27. C. Westenek. "Iets over land en volk van Minangkabau," *K.T.I.* (1912), pp. 641–654.
28. Ronkel, *Rapport*, p. 7.
29. (Een Majeijer in het Nederlandsch beschreven), "De masdjid's en inlandsche godsdienstscholen in de Padangsche Bovenlanden", *I.G.*, I, 10, 1888, pp. 312–333. The writer also points out the different style of mosques in the Bodi Tjaniago and the Koto Piliang regions.
30. A. W. P. Verkerk Pistorius, "De Priester en zijn invloed op de samenleving in de Bovenlanden", *T.N.I.* (1869), ii, pp. 423–452; Van Hasselt, *op. cit.*, p. 59.
31. Verkerk Pistorius, *T.N.I.* (1869), ii, p. 449.
32. C. Snouck Hurgronje, *The Achenese*, Leiden, 1906, vol. II, p. 8. The Satarijah was corrupted — according to Snouck Hurgronje — because its adherents in Indonesia "have been so long left to themselves . . . But besides this, both Malay and Javanese have made use of the name of Satariah as a hallmark with which to authenticate various kinds of village-philosophy to a large extent of pagan origin", pp. 18–20. On Satarijah, see "*Shat*tariya" in H. A. R. Gibb and J. H. Kramers, *Shorter Encyclopedia of Islam*, Leiden, 1953, pp. 533–534.
33. Schrieke, *T.B.G.*, 59, pp. 562–567.
34. Schrieke, *T.B.G.*, 59, pp. 263–265.

35. On the numerous tariqah-schools, see: R. L. Archer, "Muhammedan Mysticism in Sumatra", *J.R.A.S.M.B.*, XV, ii, pp. 10126; see also Ronkel, *Rapport*.
36. Ph. S. van Ronkel, "De twee moskeeën en de adat", *Koloniaal Tijdschrift*, vi (1917), pp. 1589–1599.
37. C. Westenenk, "De Inlandsche bestuurschoofden", *K.T.*, II, (1913), p. 833; Van Hasselt, *Volksbeschrijving*, pp. 60–61.
38. See: B. Schrieke, "The Native Rulers", in *Indonesian Sociological Studies*, vol. I, The Hague, Bandung, 1955, pp. 167–201.
39. B. J. Haga, "Influence of the Western Administration on the Native Community in the Outer Provinces", in B. Schrieke (ed.), *The Effects of Western Influence on Native Civilization in the Malayan Archipelago*, Batavia, 1929, p. 74.
40. C. Westenenk. K.T., II (1913), pp. 828–830.
41. Cf. H. W. Stap, "De Nagari Ordonantie ter Sumatra's Westkust", *T.B.B.*, 53 (1917), pp. 699–765.
42. Van Hasselt, *Volksbeschrijving*, p. 190.
43. Cf. "Sumatra's Westkust. Een beschouwing van den tegenwoordigen toestand aldaar door een ambtenaar bij het Binnenlandsch Bestuur", *I.G.*, ii (1886), pp. 1575–1581.
44. See: Schrieke, *T.B.G.*, 59, pp. 262–280.
45. See: W. J. Kroon, "De invoering van belastingen op Sumatra's Westkust", *T.B.B.*, li and lii (1916), pp. 342–351, 503–509; lii (1917), pp. 170–179; also: G. A. N. Scheltema de Heere, "De belasting-invoeren op Sumatra's Westkust", *I.G.*, xlv (1923), pp. 122–156.
46. On this problem see for instance, J. Prins, "Rondom de oude strijdvraag van Minangkabau", *Indonesië*, vii (1953–1954), pp. 320–329. For a comment by a Minangkabau leader before the Second World War, see: H. A. Salim, "Adat contra Islam", 1934, reprinted in *Djedjak Langkah Hadji Agus Salim: Pilihan Karangan Utjapan dan Pendapat Beliau Dari Dulu Sampai Sekarang*, Djakarta, 1954, pp. 176–189.
47. See: Hazairin, *Pergolakan Penjesuaian Hukum Islam dengan Adat*, Djakarta, 1956.
48. It is interesting to ask whether or not the conflict between these two laws was intensified because of the historical circumstances, such as the patronizing of the penghulu at the expense of the other members of the elite. Josselin de Jong, for instance, has argued that the Minangkabau family system originally followed a pattern of unilinear double-descent; *Minangkabau*, pp. 82–91.
49. On the modernist movement in Minangkabau see: Schrieke, *T.B.G.*, 59, pp. 278–325; Ronkel, *Rapport*, p. 16ff; Hamka, *Ajahku*, p. 76 *et passim*; and Deliar Noer, *The Rise and Development of the Modernist Movement in Indonesia during the Dutch Colonial Period (1900–1942)*, unpublished Ph.D. thesis, Cornell University, 1963, pp. 47–85.

The Peasants' Revolt of Banten in 1888: The Religious Revival

SARTONO KARTODIRDJO

THE NATURE OF THE SUBJECT-MATTER

The rebellion of 1888 dealt with in this study occurred in the district of Anjer in the extreme north-west of Java. Although it flared up during a relatively short period — from the ninth until the thirtieth of July — the social ferment which preceded the outbreak of the revolt must be traced back to the early 'seventies. This revolt was only one of a series of risings which took place in Banten during the 19th century and it was also an instance of the social convulsions which were sweeping across Java. The records of the Colonial Office for the last century tell of many risings and attempts at insurrections by the peasantry.[1] Millenarian movements, a concomitant of social unrest and turmoil, appeared in various parts of Java, while religious revivalism manifested itself in the mushrooming growth of religious schools and mystico-religious brotherhoods throughout Java. In fact, the nineteenth century was a period of social unrest accompanying social change, brought about by the growing impact of the West. An increasing modernization of the economy and the polity could be observed. The whole transition from traditionality to modernity was marked by recurrent social upheavals, akin to the insurrection of 1888 in Banten. The risings, which occurred in almost all the residencies of Java and in the Principalities,[2] exhibited common characteristics. They were traditional, local or regional, and short-lived. As social movements they all lacked modern features such as organization, modern ideologies, and nationwide agitation.[3] Most of the peasant uprisings were local and disconnected. The peasants did not know what they were fighting for; they had a vague desire to overthrow the government, but did not feel consciously that they were taking part in a social revolutionary movement. There was certainly no realism in the aim professed by the rebels. It is very likely that even the leaders lacked the understanding of politics to make realistic plans in the event of success. These risings were therefore doomed to failure and the same tragic sequel of repressions followed all the outbreaks.[4]

The significance assigned to this type of revolt is not so much related to its impact on the political development, as to the fact that its endemic occurrence during the 19th century can be regarded as a manifestation of the agrarian unrest which formed an undercurrent of the political mainstream during the period of the *"Pax Neerlandica"*.[5] Up to the time of the fall of the Dutch regime, there seemed to be a constant simmering of widespread discontent just below the surface. Most contemporary writers regarded the risings as an outburst of fanaticism or a riot against an unpopular tax. They were mostly content to ascribe the risings to either religious or economic factors. In fact, various

Excerpted from Sartono Kartodirdjo, *The Peasants' Revolt of Banten in 1888* (Verhandelingen van het Koninklijk Instituut voor Taal-, Land-en Volkenkunde Deel 50 ('s-Gravenhage: Martinus Nijhoff, 1966), pp. 1–4 and 140–147, by permission of the author and Koninklijk Instituut voor Taal-, Land-en Volkenkunde, Leiden, The Netherlands.

grievances came to a head during such disturbances: economic and social as well as religious and political.

In the context of contact between Western and Indonesian culture, peasant risings can be regarded as protest movements against intruding Western economy and political control, which were undermining the fabric of traditional society.[6] With the introduction of money economy, wage-labour, and central administration, a general breakdown of the traditional economic and political structure was brought about.[7] The disturbance of the old equilibrium of traditional society undoubtedly caused general frustration and deprivation, which feelings, once communicated, grew into widespread restlessness and excitement. This was bound to erupt whenever it could be focused under a leadership capable of directing the aggressive potency either against certain hostile objects or towards the realization of millenarian ideas. In regions where religion played a dominant role, religious leaders easily succeeded in assuming leadership in popular movements by couching their millenarian message in religious terms. Consequently, the insurrectionary movements they launched can be safely identified as religious and millenarian movements as well.[8]

This study is concerned chiefly with insurrectionary movements in what has always been the most disturbed region of Java, namely Banten.[9] Compared with peasant rebellions in other countries and of other periods, the rebellion of 1888 in Banten was not of great stature. This revolt has been chosen as subject-matter, not so much for its consequences, but rather as a typical symptom of social change and its concomitant, social unrest, which loomed large in 19th century Java. Furthermore, an attempt will be made to investigate problems which conventional historians have considered less significant, in order to make Indonesian history more comprehensive. Indispensable for this purpose is broadening the scope of the problems, not the topic — and refining the relevant methodology.

The term "Peasant revolt" needs some clarification. It does not denote that the participants are exclusively peasants. Throughout the history of peasant rebellions, the rebel leaders were very rarely ordinary peasants. They belonged to wealthier or more eminent groups of rural inhabitants, and were religious leaders, members of the old nobility or people belonging to the rural gentry, people therefore, whose status facilitated the assessment of a movement's goal and who could function as a symbolic focus of identification. It is only in a limited sense that any rebellion that occurred in Indonesia in the 19th century may be said to have been a peasant revolt, pure and simple. The role played by other groups in the rebellions will be examined later on. The leaders formed an élite group, which developed and transmitted the time-honoured prophecies or vision of history concerning the coming of the *Ratu Adil* — the righteous king — or the *Mahdi*. In many cases, it was the religious leaders who gave this prophecy a popular form and translated it into action by inciting the masses to revolt. Peasants furnished the numerical strength in the movements, but the organizing leadership was in the hands of the rural élite. As we shall see, the religious teacher or the mystic leader figured prominently in almost all the large-scale — relatively speaking — uprisings on record.

THE RELIGIOUS REVIVAL

One aspect of the problem raised in this study is centred on the religious background of the Banten revolt. The latter part of the 19th century was a period of religious revivalism and it is naturally interesting to inquire to what extent this stimulated the insurrectionary movement in Banten under study. The conditions prevailing in the socio-cultural environment of Banten as described in previous chapters undoubtedly prepared a fertile soil for the rise of religious revivalism. Not only were the people inveterate adherents of the Islamic religion; the disruption of traditional order and its concomitant, enduring social restlessness, favoured the increase of religious activities. As will be shown, this process contributed greatly to the acceleration of the preparations for the rebellion. In this connection it should be pointed out that religious protest movements are a product of the same social forces that sustain rebellious attitudes. The stage of development reached in the 'eighties suggests that the religious movement strove to sanction political aspirations. One encountered political deprivation on the one hand, and traditional reaffirmation on the other. The majority of the religious élite, deprived politically, acted as a protest group, opposing the newly-introduced institutions. Seen from this point of view, the religious revival in Banten can be identified as a religio-political movement, which accommodated various social strains. In the Banten of the 19th century, the religious revival and the other kinds of social movements obviously had notable points of resemblance, particularly in their millennial appeals and lower-class base. The rebellions that have been dealt with up to now were tinged with religion; nevertheless they can hardly be designated as religious movements, simply because religious institutions and communities did not play any part in these movements. It will be shown that during the religious revival religious bodies were conspicuously prominent and became centres of political protest. Although it must be assumed that at this stage the religious movement provided an outlet for the discontent and frustration, which would otherwise have occasioned social disturbances, the movement appeared to take a revolutionary course. The resentment against forceful domination by the Dutch and the powerful anti-foreign hostility underlying the general unrest, now found another outlet in an allegiance with extremist religious movements. As a result the movements not only gained in vigour, but were also provided with a more effective institutional device, namely the *tarekat.* As we shall see, the religious revival became a means of recruiting men for the rebellion rather than a pure religious movement.

For several decades a large part of Java was swept by a religious revival that demonstrated a tremendous increase in religious activities such as the observance of daily prayers, undertaking pilgrimages, furnishing traditional Muslim education for the young, establishing branches of *tarekats,* the widespread distribution of sermons, etc. In the late 1850s, Holle observed that orders had still to be issued by regents, urging the people to observe their religious duties more strictly.[10] A few years later, a religious revival manifested itself in the increasing number of religious schools and pilgrims.[11] Furthermore, the erection of numerous mosques and small prayer-houses can also be regarded as a sign of more vigorous religious practices. Referring specifically to heavily Islamic areas, our informant pointed out that the people held the *hadjis* in high esteem at that time and that the *hadjis*, with their great prestige, could exert their influence to induce people to fulfil their religious duties far more conscientiously.[12] To what extent this aspect of religious awakening endangered the colonial regime will be subjected to special consideration. In searching for the external stimuli of the religious revival, many students of Indonesian Islam have overlooked the fact that the Russo-Turkish war — known in Indonesia as the so-called *perang Rus* — had a tremendous impact on the minds of Muslims living in "countries below the wind".[13] The Indonesian people were eager to learn of its development, and any victory on the side of the Sultan of Rum was enthusiastically celebrated with prayers and *sedekah.*[14] Besides this instance of embryonic Pan-Islamism, we have to take into account the wide communication system in the Muslim world, established by the pilgrimage, which meant that news concerning the Muslim community could reach its most remote corner. In this connection it must be remarked that religious revivalism in many parts of the Muslim world commenced almost simultaneously with the imperialists' scramble for colonial territories in the latter half of the 19th century. It is generally assumed that a correlation exists between the expansion of colonial powers and Pan-Islamism or the religious revival.[15] The question is whether this contention holds as regards the development of Islam in Indonesia in general and in Banten in particular.

An examination of the general development of Pan-Islamism and the religious revival indicates that they were both saliently marked by essentially anti-Western characteristics during this period. The conquests of Western Imperialism were rapidly advancing; in this critical period, thoughtful Muslims became fully aware that the Muslim world was in growing peril of falling under Western domination. Faced with Western encroachment, Muslims in large parts of the world of the crescent manifested militant fanaticism engendered by feelings of hatred against the infidel conquerors.[16] It is not surprising that the exacerbation of fanaticism and militant spirit in the Middle East and North Africa during the second half of the 19th century developed religious reverberations among the Indonesian Muslims. A closer contact between the widely separated sections of the Muslim world was facilitated by the pilgrimage which constantly increased with improved communications and transit. We shall confine ourselves to Indonesia in examining the various forms and phases of the religious revival.

In general, there was a certain reaction to westernization in the revival of religiosity, but there were clearly various types of responses and different degrees of speed of adjustment. One must keep in mind that the liberalistically tinged policy of the Dutch concerning religion left room for a wide range of religious movements, from peaceful, accommodative ones to radical, aggressive ones. Which of these emerged depended largely upon the socio-cultural setting and the power position of the religious élite in this context. In this connection the predominant fear among European civil servants of all movements with a conspicuously religious orientation can be traced back to a *hadji*-phobia.[17] It must be admitted that, because no distinction is made in Islam between a religious and a political community, every religious protest movement easily turns into a political one. It is generally known that religious fraternities in many parts of the Muslim world were caught in this kind of religio-political movement. In this connection the *hadjis* constituted a potential danger to the colonial ruler insofar as they could assume leadership in a movement. As has been explained previously, the salient characteristic of the radical wing of religious movements in the second half of the 19th century was a strong condemnation of Western domination and vehement attacks on newly-introduced institutions.[18] Since the protesting groups were conquered societies, whose religious protest derived from a distinct religious tradition, the movement tended to move in the direction of conflict. These extreme forms of religious movements resisted adjustment,[19] and occupied an important place in the struggle for a sense of dignity and self-respect in the face of a situation of deprivation and discrimination.[20] As a student of Islam put it, "any existing inferiority was felt to be only external, that is, in terms of physical power, and not spiritual".[21] There were, on the other hand, religious groups that emphasized peaceful acceptance of Dutch rule and furthered accommodation to the new political system. The result was factionalism and conflicting groups in the development of the religious movements. A reference to specific movements in a later part of this section may be of use in analyzing this problem.

With regard to Banten in the 1880s, the *tarekats* developed into the most predominant revivalist groups. At their inception the *tarekats* were in essence religious revivalist movements, but they gradually developed into politico-religious bodies. They formed institutional devices for political extremism. They took up a strong position against the process of westernization and were determined to defend traditional institutions against Dutch influence and encroachment. Driven by xenophobia, they resorted to violence against Dutch overlords and also against fellow Muslims who collaborated with the Dutch. The development of this vigorous protest can be interpreted in terms of both the external social conditions and the specific stimuli prevailing in the Banten of the 'eighties.

As for the *Sufi* disciplines, we know with certainty that they were an early importation in Indonesia and dated back to the 16th or the beginning of the 17th century.[22] The Satariah *tarekat* was originally propagated in Atjeh by Abdurra'uf of Singkel.[23] From the 17th century onwards, the Satariah movement travelled from Atjeh to West Java and from there to Central and East Java. It was Sjech Abdul Muhji of Karang, a disciple of the said Abdurra'uf, who established the Satariah *tarekat* in West Java.[24] A famous Kadiriah mystic was Hamzah al-Fansuri, who visited various places, including Banten, as a wandering dervish.[25] Especially as regards Banten, contact with Mecca had already been established in the first half of the 17th century by repeatedly sending missions to Mecca to attempt to gain information on religious matters.[26] During the latter part of that century, Banten was reputed as a centre of Islamic orthodoxy, where religious scholarship and a religious way of life were highly esteemed.[27] There are strong indications that the Kadiriah order had penetrated Bantenese Islam before the 19th century,[28] but it had not yet gathered any vital momentum. Viewed against this historical background, the development of the Kadiriah order in Banten during the latter part of the 19th century distinctly marked a revival in the true sense of the word.

To return to the consideration of the characteristics of the religious movement: an interesting feature was the development of cleavages which were prolongations of those to be found in the core region of the Muslim world — the religious bureaucracy against those established as religious teachers or as heads of brotherhoods, rivalries between various *tarekats,* factionalism in a *tarekat.* The revivalist activities led by brotherhood leaders were regarded with some suspicion and hostility by the official *ulama.* As its strength lay in its popular appeal, the brotherhood tended to become the basis of association for religious protest movements. The rivalry between the various fraternities in some regions frequently sapped their vigour and vitality to a large extent. In addition, the emergence of modernistic reformist movements later deepened the split between the religious revivalist movements.[29]

The colonial government created an institutional religious structure made up of a hierarchy of professional men of religion, with recognized functions and powers.[30] This group of official religious men commonly lent themselves to the Dutch colonial policy in repressing manifestations of activity by the brotherhoods in particular, and in stemming the tide of religious revivalism in general. They were induced to echo or sustain the secular ideas introduced by the colonial government. With the secularization the *ulama* as pre-eminent exponents of the Islamic religious heritage were divided into "secularists" and "revivalists"; the first group was granted formal status within the framework of the colonial bureaucracy, while the second group was denied it by the Dutch and continued to exist almost exclusively because of the devotion and support of the rural population. In facing the menace of this secularization, the latter group had to resort to the alliance of religious brotherhoods which, as a rigid form of social organization, became an instrument of protest movements and rebellions. It was to be expected that the revivalists would remain a strong traditional force, attempting to ensure a return to the cultural values prevailing during the sultanate and a return to their religious rehabilitation as well.

It would, of course, be an error to assume that doctrinal controversies were the main source of the conflict between the secularists and the revivalists. From the explanation given above it is plain that certain basic contributing factors were responsible for the split between the religious movements. The conflict was closely related to other aspects of the struggle for power among religious leaders on the one hand, and of that between the religious and the secular élite on the other.[31] Modern trends threatened traditional institutions and traditional groups naturally resisted the progressive encroachment of the alien overlord vehemently. Especially as regards Banten, the conflict was deepened by the existence of a tradition of revolt which sometimes enlivened religious controversies. All in all, the religious movements in the second half of the 19th century involved a strong emphasis on group conflict. Seen in the sociocultural setting of Banten in this period, the continued and even sharpened emphasis of revivalist groups on vigorous and even violent protest movements is not surprising. After "secular" protests had proved entirely inadequate, the affirmation of religious goals simultaneously with the affiliation with brotherhood movements revitalized the religio-political effort to re-establish the traditional order. Of great significance is the fact that the fraternities promoted group cohesiveness and group identification, which could intensify the religious strife. Small wonder that members of the brotherhoods became intensely involved in the conflict.

We shall deal with the main manifestations of the religious revival, with special reference to Banten, in the light of the general trends briefly sketched above. The first sign of revivalist sentiment was the continually increasing number of pilgrimages in the 19th century. The flourishing of this pious activity was of great importance not only for the spreading of innovations throughout the Muslim world, but also for the spreading of a corps of religious élite. For this reason, Mecca can be regarded as the heart of the religious life of Indonesia. [32] The second visible sign of the spirit of revival was the phenomenal growth of religious schools, which functioned as nurseries for militant participants of the revival movement. Other evidence of revived Islamic piety was given by the many newly-built mosques, which were jammed with worshippers during the Friday noon congregational prayers. Evidently, there was a conspicuous renewed interest in and a rigid fulfilment of religious duties. Itinerant *sjechs* or preachers found great audiences everywhere, and there was a growing demand for printed sermons and other religious publications. Of course, cases of pious ostentation were also known, such as the wearing of Arabian garb or the voluminous cloth draped around the head. For a few years, the so-called "Last letter of the Prophet" circulated widely; it urged people to fulfil their religious duties more strictly in preparation for the "Day of Judgment". Lastly, the most vital aspect of the religious movement was undoubtedly the revival of Islam mysticism, as embodied in the *tarekats*.

In discussing the religious revival, we must keep in mind that it may be understood within the context of the social movement in Banten. In its last phase before the outbreak of the revolt in 1888, the revival movement brought about the emergence of charismatic leadership, militant partisanship, effective recruitment organization and animating ideology, all essential ingredients of a forceful revolutionary movement. The pulse of the social movement should be measured by the intense expressions of religious revivalism which unmistakably underlay it. In this connection the progressive penetration of Westernism may be viewed as an accelerating factor, stimulating the emergence of religious revival.

NOTES

1. In the records, different terms were used to denote this category of disturbances. They were clearly distinguished from large-scale insurrections with war-like proportions, like the Atjeh War or the Java War. The terms used are: *onlusten* in Vb. Jan. 13, 1859, no. 15; *ongeregeldheden* in Vb. Dec. 16, 1864, R[13] Kab.; *complot* in Vb. Oct. 2, 1865, E[15] Kab.; *samenscholingen* in Vb. Oct. 8, 1866, C[12] Kab.; *woelingen* in Vb. Nov. 27, 1871, no. 20; *onrust* in MR 1886, no. 90[a]; *rustverstoring* in MR 1888, no. 413. In this study, no clear distinction is made between these two categories of risings, since they have many characteristics in common; both are traditional and regional, in contrast to modern national movements. They must also be considered as differing from palace revolutions or wars of succession.
2. The numerous rebelions in Java during the period from 1840 until 1875 are listed by de Waal (1876, pp. 228–229). According to him, only in 1844, 1847, 1860, 1863, 1871 and 1874 did no uprising occur. This list is incomplete, some risings have been omitted, e.g. 1864 in Klaten; 1865 in Tjirebon, Tegal, Jogjakarta, and Kedu; 1872 in Pekalongan. Movements with a specific character are separately described. This is an indication that the colonial government was already aware of the significance of this kind of movement. De Waal was for some time Secretary of the Central Government in the Netherlands East Indies, so that he had access to official documents.
3. In this study, Hobsbawm's distinction between archaic, and urban or industrial movements is used; see Hobsbawm (1963, p. 6). These modern characteristics can be found in modern social movements as meant by Heberle, e.g. labour movement, farmer movement, Naziism, Zionism, Communism. His concept of the social movement is so broad as to include also nativistic movements and peasant movements. See Heberle (1949, p. 6).
4. The suicidal nature of peasant revolts in Java is inherent to the magico-religious form in which their strivings were expressed. Here we come across the real difference between these and modern, political movements with their secular ideology and effective organizational devices. We have to bear in mind, however, that there is a continuum from pre-modern religious revolts to full-fledged secular revolutionary movements. The Banten revolt of 1888 should be localized somewhere in the continuum. See Talmon in *AES*, Vol. III (1962), pp. 125–148.
5. The *'Pax Neerlandica'* refers to the period of Dutch colonial rule in Indonesia during which peace and order could be enforced throughout the Archipelago; the so-called pacification of many parts of the Outer Provinces had already come to an end.

6. The explanation of peasant movements or millenarism in terms of a clash between colonial power and traditional society can be found in many studies, e.g. Bodrogi (1951), Balandier (1953), Emmet (1956), Worsley (1957), Köbben (1959), Pieris (1962), Lanternari (1963). It is relevant to this study, since it refers to conditions created by colonialism and to events, processes and tendencies contributing to the rise of anti-Western currents.
7. It suffices here to refer to existing standard works on the transformation from traditionality to modernity, e.g. works written by Burger (1949–1950), Schrieke (1955), Wertheim (1959).
8. Very helpful in searching for the identity of peasant revolts and social movements in Java in the 19th century, are recent inclusive studies on millenarian movements by Guaraglia (1959), Mühlman (1961), Thrupp (1962), Lanternari (1963). As far as movements in Indonesia are concerned, these works do not refer to data with regard to other 19th century movements, except those presented by Drewes (1925). The material of this study is intended to provide new data for cross-cultural comparison of special aspects of these movements.
9. Most of the rebellions in Banten were mentioned or described in the works of Roorda van Eysinga, Vol. IV (1832), pp. 87–88; Francis, Vol. II (1856–1860), pp. 51-78; de Waal, Vol. I (1876) p. 219–222; see also articles in *TNI* (1859), no. 1, pp. 135–187; *TNI* (1870), no. 2, pp. 325–341.
10. See Missive from Holle to the Governor General, Aug. 12, 1873, no. 125, in Vb. June 3, 1874, no. 31; Holle also referred to other religious activities of the regent as head of the *umat* in his region, e.g. giving sermons, controlling the treasury of the mosques, discussing dogmatic problems, etc. These activities were regarded as transgressing their authority. According to article 17 of the Instruction for regents in government regions (*Staatsblad* 1867, no. 114), regents were entitled to supervise the religious officials, and to compile the list of *hadjis, kjais* and *gurus,* all under the contemporary heading "priests" (sic).
11. See the list of pilgrims, covering the period between 1852 and 1875, in de Waal, Vol. I (1876), p. 245. See also the list for the period 1879–1889, in Report on the pilgrimage of 1889, in Vb. Jan. 24, 1890, no. 53. Cf. Vredenbregt in *BKI,* Vol. CXVIII (1962), pp. 91–154. See the list of the numbers of disciples of religious schools, in de Waal, Vol. I (1876), p. 252.
12. See Missive from Holle to the Governor General, Aug. 20, 1873, no. 126, in Vb. June 3, 1874, no. 31. Special reference was made to the *hadji* in Prijangan, where the religious movement gained momentum in the early 1870s. As regards the prestige and position of the *hadji* in Indonesia, they varied from region to region; see Summary of the reports of residents, in Vb. June 3, 1874, no. 31.
13. The Russo-Turkish War, also known as the Crimean War, 1856. Its impact was also reflected in Malay and Sundanese literature; the so-called *"tjarita perang Rus"* gives a description of it. See Missive of Holle, Aug. 20, 1873, no. 126.
14. The "Sultan of Rum" here means the Sultan of Turkey; evidence of this popular notion is also given by an Indonesian version of the hagiography of the founder of the Kadiriah *tarekat,* Abdulkadir Djaelani; see Drewes and Poerbatjaraka (1938), p. 55.
15. See van den Berg's "Pan-Islamisme", in *De Gids* (1900), no. 4; Snouck Hurgronje, in *VG,* Vol. I (1923), pp. 363–380; also his *"Mekka"* (1931), pp. 244–245. For Pan-Islamism in the 1890s, see Snouck Hurgronje, in Gobée and Adriaanse, Vol. II (1959), pp. 1615–1717. Especially as regards the correlation between Pan-Islamism and the Sufi orders, see Snouck Hurgronje, *VG,* Vol. III (1923), pp. 189–207.
16. For the general development of the awakening of the Muslim world and its outstanding anti-Western character, see Stoddard (1921).
17. This *hadji*-phobia was clearly reflected in various reports, e.g. Missive of Holle, Aug. 20, 1873, no. 126; Missive of the Assistant Resident of Pandeglang, June 29, 1876, no. 864/8, in Vb. Feb. 10, 1877, K^2; Missive of the Resident of Prijangan, March 31, 1886, no. 3030, MR 1886, no. 262, and its counterpart, Brunner's article, in *Java Bode,* Sept. 4 and 7, 1885. For *hadji*-phobia in the post-rebellion period, see Snouck Hurgronje, *VG,* Vol. II (1924), pp. 424–425; see also his letter to the First Govt. Secretary, Aug. 1890, in Gobée and Adriaanse, Vol. III (1965), pp. 1919–1923.
18. For general accounts about the reactions of the Muslim world against Western penetration, see von Grunebaum (1962), pp. 128–179; also Werner Caskel, in von Grunebaum, ed. (1955), pp. 335–360. Esp. as regards Indonesia in the 19th century, see Benda (1957), pp. 9–31; Wertheim (1959), pp. 195–235.
19. Von Grunebaum (1962), pp. 128–179; Werner Caskel, in von Grunebaum, ed. (1955), pp. 335–360.
20. Their sensitivity concerning their dignity was once expressed in Malay as *"tanda diaku"* (sic); see the statement of the Head *Panghulu* of Bandung quoted by Holle in his missive of Aug. 12, 1873, no. 125.
21. Werner Caskel, in von Grunebaum, ed. (1955), p. 340.
22. For a general account of religious life and Sufism in Indonesia in the 16th and 17th century, see Rinkes (1909), Kraemer (1921), Drewes and Poerbatjaraka (1938), van Nieuwenhuijze (1945), Schrieke (1956); see also Johns, in *JSAH,* Vol. II (1961), pp. 10–23.

23. Rinkes (1909).
24. For a life history of Sjech Abdul Muhji, see Rinkes, in *TBG,* Vol. LII (1910), pp. 556–589.
25. Kraemer, in *Djawa,* Vol. IV (1924), p. 29; Drewes and Poerbatjaraka (1938), pp. 10–11.
26. Djajadiningrat (1913), pp. 50–52, 126, 187. Mention is also made of the granting of the title of sultan to the chief of the Bantenese kingdom for the first time in 1638.
27. Drewes, in *Djawa,* Vol. VI (1926), p. 83.
28. The evidence consists of the following facts: the first Sultan of Banten was called Sultan Abulmafachir Mahmud Abdulkadir; the last name refers to the founder of the Kadiriah *tarekat*; see Drewes and Poerbatjaraka (1938), p. 11, also H. Djajadiningrat (1913), p. 51; the latter author also mentions the name of a certain trader, Hadji Dulkadir, also known in Banten as *"djuragan Kadiriah"*, i.e. a Kadiriah trader; see H. Djajadiningrat (1913), p. 263. Furthermore: the wandering mystic Hamzah al-Fansuri must have visited Banten in the course of his travels; in any case his mystical teaching, the Wudjudiah, was well-known in Banten, see Drewes and Poerbatjaraka (1938), p. 12.
29. For an extensive account of the attitude of modernistic groups, more conversant with Western culture and receptive to Western progress, see Hourani (1962), esp. as regards the ideas expressed by Jamal ad-Din al-Afghani and Muhamad Abduh.
30. Van den Berg, in *TBG,* Vol. XXVII (1882), pp. 1–47.
31. The conflict between the various segments of the élite in traditional Muslim society was related not so much to doctrinal matters but rather to a power struggle; see Pigeaud (MS, 1943–1945), p. 126.
32. Snouck Hurgronje (1931), p. 291.

Bourgeois Currents in Religion[1]

W. F. WERTHEIM

'Every new period in the history of civilization obliges a religious community to undertake a general revision of the contents of its treasury,' wrote Snouck Hurgronje.[1] Islam in Indonesia did not escape this process of renewal.

At the beginning of the present century the upper stratum of Indonesian society came into closer touch with the civilisation of Western Europe. Its ways of thought and feeling were strongly influenced by contacts with individual Westerners, by education, familiarity with European literature and European travel. Cultural elements derived from European bourgeois civilisation, such as Western individualism, rationalism, naturalism, bourgeois morals, obtained a hold on the Indonesian nobility, especially the younger ranks.

This process of acculturation took place largely outside the boundaries of Islam. In particular the nobility of Central Java, though Moslem in name, had always maintained its attitude of reserve towards the stricter forms of the Faith. In *kraton* (court) circles in Solo and Jogjakarta 'Javanism' prevailed: it was a syncretic religion in which Hindu and pre-Hindu elements still played an important part. In Central Java the stricter forms of the Islamic faith were found among the city traders; the nobility were inclined to deprecate this strict conformity to the Islamic law. Bousquet describes how an aristocrat from Central Java reacted to his question, whether he approved of the plans for founding a Moslem University, in the same aloof and puzzled way as if a French aristocrat had been asked whether he approved of the foundation of a Marx-Lenin Institute.[2] Apart from a general tendency among aristocrats to observe religious duties less rigorously than petty traders do, it was also Dutch policy which had helped those elements inclined to reject Islam in its stricter form, to rise to the top.

It is thus understandable that modern ideas influenced the younger generation of Javanese *pryayis* without their feeling any inner need to confront these ideas with Islam as a religion. The letters of Raden Adjeng Kartini,[3] the highly cultured daughter of a regent, a young woman of modern ideas who died at an early age and who is in some ways regarded as a precursor of the nationalist movement, exhibit a spirit of free-thinking liberalism similar to that of free-thinking Christians; she shows tolerance also in religious matters and believes that her religious and moral principles can be found in every faith. Nevertheless she calls herself a Mohammedan and traces her modern liberal opinions regarding religion back to her own faith just as the Moslem peasant projected his *adat* on to the Islamic faith. She writes that she did not find it possible to examine the principles of the Islamic faith more deeply, however, since the scribes reserve the Holy Scriptures to themselves and deny the layman access to it.

Excerpted from W. F. Wertheim, *Indonesian Society in Transition, A Study of Social Change* (2nd ed., rev.; The Hague: W. van Hoeve, 1959), by permission of the author and the publishers.

The utterances of other Westernised Indonesians of the early years of this century are even more negative regarding Islam.[4] Time and again one finds expressions of opinion in that period which completely reject the Faith, seeing the Islam of tradition either as a brake on all progress, or as a corruption of the great Hindu-Javanese culture of former times. The first nationalist society on Java, the *Budi Utomo,* a movement of younger Indonesians of Western education, adopted a more or less indifferent attitude towards religion.

When Western ideas and bourgeois culture began to stir the Indonesian middle class as well, this comparative indifference could not continue. Islam was a valuable asset to many Indonesian traders or teachers. They witnessed its decline in public esteem and saw it losing its recruiting power owing to the tendency of those who became acquainted with Western ideas to regard it as a backward religion, without real value for the modern age. There was a strong tendency among the young, especially, to turn away from Islam and to regard its customs, at best, as traditional folklore. The Christianity proved to have an attraction for certain young people among the educated class; others among the younger intellectuals turned to theosophy which was, in a way, related to Hinduism. Still others were completely indifferent to religion.

Thus it was realised that if Islam was to retain its hold on the people, it would have to rehabilitate itself. In Indonesia its adaptation to the modern world found its expression first and foremost in the *Muhammadyah* movement, the aim of which was to purify the Faith of traditional admixtures and formalism, both of which had caused it to be stigmatised as backward. It was chiefly inspired by the Egyptian reform movement led by Muhammed Abduh, who had tried to bring the Faith into harmony with modern rational thought. As the Christian Reformation had preached 'back to the Bible', so Muhammed Abduh and his disciples preached 'back to the Koran and the true Islamic faith.' In both instances it was a matter of loosening the grip which tradition had on the Faith and creating the freedom necessary for a return to the source of religion, in search of values better fitted to the modern age.

In Indonesia, the *Muhammadyah* sought likewise to create a more modern and more personal kind of religious experience. Subjection to the authority of tradition and the lawgivers was no longer the ideal of religion; the individual had the right to scrutinise and criticise the tradition in the light of the true sources of Islam. The purely formalist manner of religious observance caused Islam to lose its hold on the spirit. The Friday sermon in Arabic was never understood. The mumbling of the Koran in Arabic, which children had been obliged to learn at the Koran schools in former years, as a sort of incantation, was too far removed from the requirements of modern living as was also the religious teaching of the *'pesantrens'* (the institutes of higher religious learning). The *Muhammadyah* no longer sought to approach the human mind by imposing authority and invoking tradition, but rather by appealing to reason. It took up the fight against all kinds of practices — for example in the field of marriage and funeral rites — which were regarded as harmful superstitions. The Friday sermon was henceforth given in the regional tongue and its contents were sensibly adapted to the needs of daily life. Religious teachers of modern education tried, by lecturing in small discussion groups, to bring the Islamic faith and its ethical philosophy closer to believers, both men and women. The movement cooperated in the foundation of schools where the same subjects were taught as in the government schools according to the same rational methods of the West, and where religious teaching was included as a separate subject. It was active in other social fields, too, helping in the establishment of hospitals, libraries, homes for the blind and others of the needy, organising a scout movement, concerning itself with girls' education. In short, the movement entered those fields in which the Christian missionaries had been working for some time. Indeed the desire to compete with the Christian mission and keep a place reserved for the Islamic faith in the hearts of believers (the young in particular) played a great role in this process of renewal. And in this way there developed a certain outer resemblance between Islamic and Christian activities.

The similarity went further. The attitude of modern Moslems to life resembled that of many modern Christians. Mohammed was no longer worshipped as a worker of miracles, but as a human being. His miracles, such as the Ascension, were often interpreted as symbolic.[5] Love of the Prophet from whom one sought consolation in one's difficulties was a typical feature of modern Mohammedanism. The descriptions of his character often show a striking resemblance to the description of Christ: it was even suggested by missionaries in India, where similar developments were discernible, that the figure of Mohammed had been painted 'in colours drawn from a Christian paint box.'[6]

The reformed ethical teaching also showed a similarity with modern Christianity. Islam was no longer fatalistic, turning aside from the things of every day life.[7] Asceticism (abstinence) which had survived as an undercurrent in the Faith, was rejected. Modern Islam believes in progress and in science as the means of achieving it. From the individual is now required an inner purity of heart in relations with others, modesty, tolerance of his fellows, conscientious service and industry. The *Muhammadyah* believes in the possibility of shaping human character by practice and of improving behaviour.

Kenneth P. Landon therefore writes with justice that 'there will be more difference between conservative and liberal Moslems or between conservative and liberal Christians than between liberal Moslems and liberal Christians.[8] But he is incorrect when he attributes this similarity to the simple adoption by Moslems of the Christian ethic and the Christian ecclesiastical customs for their own use. The new attitude to life is neither typically Christian nor typically Moslem. It is the attitude of the urban trader of the first years of the present century. In this ethical philosophy and faith one can trace that typical bourgeois individualism and rationalism, which regards mankind not as a totality but as a collection of individuals. Just as the city dweller resists the authority of the feudal nobility and the feudal tradition, so, too, he resists the authority of the recognised scribes and the religious tradition. He lives in a world which offers opportunities to the energetic, conscientious individual: he is full of confidence. He sees no sin in acquiring earthly possessions: he can become a virtuous Moslem by devoting himself diligently and honestly to his business. He has duties, not to mankind as a whole, but to his individual fellow creatures. The Prophet, too, is a fellow creature to whom he turns for comfort if he feels lonely and isolated in his urban environment.

The modern Moslem projects this attitude to life on to his faith as nineteenth century bourgeois Christians grafted it on to theirs. The virtues he ascribes to the Prophet are all those he can think of — the typically bourgeois virtues. They are no more typically Moslem than they were ever typically Christian. The modern age needed a new Islam and a new Prophet just as every new era has created a new Christendom and a new Christ.

The main reason why the average middle class Indonesian did not go over to Christianity but remained Moslem was that he felt strong traditional emotional ties with Islam such as most Europeans feel with Christendom. Moreover, in a colonial country there was all the more need to distinguish oneself from the foreign overlords. What this Indonesian really needed was to be able to call himself a Moslem without having to feel ashamed of his faith in the presence of Westerners — to profess a faith which harmonised with the modern age and his own aspirations as a man of his time.

Modern Islam became a religion which made few positive claims on the conduct of its adherents,[9] but rather afforded them the gratification which belonged to a life of reasonable prosperity and permitted them to go through life with an attitude of tolerance and pleasurable satisfaction with their own progressive ambitions.

Besides the *Muhammadyah* movement, the *Ahmadyah* movement, imported from India, was also rather influential as a bearer of liberal enlightened ideas. Though its following was not nearly as large as that of *Muhammadyah,* the Lahore branch of it in particular had a qualitative advantage in that it had a good deal of influence among the younger intellectuals.[10]

The people's movement *'Sarekat Islam'* which had rapidly blossomed forth during World War I also displayed many bourgeois traits. The movement had been originated by Indonesian traders as a counter-balance to the strong Chinese middle class. During the first years the middle class background of the movement was noticeable, not only in its activities, but in its ideology as well. The movement laid stress on the virtues of honesty and sobriety. But the most typical bourgeois trait was the stress it laid upon industry. In a government report[11] an interesting parallel was drawn between modern trends in Islam and the Reformation of the sixteenth century, notably the Calvinist trends, which embodied the new ethics of the rising middle class in Western Europe.

Whereas labour, according to traditional popular attitudes (as during the Middle Ages in the West), was considered a necessary evil at best, at the first *Sarekat Islam* Congress in 1916 the improvidence and negligence of the Indonesians were strongly criticised.[12] At the second Congress in 1917 it was stated that religion commands people to exert themselves in allowed professions, such as agriculture, handicrafts, trade etc. and strictly forbids laziness, idleness, resignation to poverty and living from the charity of others. 'Religion prescribes all the people to acquire knowledge and to practise the sciences.[13]

The eighteenth century *Wahhabi* movement, which had embodied a protest of the agrarian communities against the modern luxuries of town life, and had also preached a way back to the primary sources of Faith and to simplicity, had some traits in common with Lutheranism. Both religious movements, *Wahhabism* and Lutheranism, were, on the whole, regressive,[14] though showing a few traits already of an incipient bourgeois mentality such as Luther's approval of the conscientious discharge of the ordinary duties of daily life. But it is an interesting parallel that both movements also paved the way for a progressive bourgeois religion, originating in town life and accepting wholeheartedly its spiritual implications. The return to the Bible and the return to the Koran proved to be temporary retreats to the sources of religion to find new interpretations, better adapted to the demands of modern life than the traditional ones. Just as Luther became a precursor of Calvinism, the *Wahhabi* sect paved the way for the so-called *new-Wahhabi* movements of Muhammed Abdul and *Muhammadyah,* which were also reflected at the *Sarekat Islam* Congresses.

Though in the *Sarekat Islam* propaganda much was made of the 'interests of the people', there are many signs that the union was really mainly concerned about the interests of the rising middle class, the 'Third Estate'. The demands made in connection with education were more in accordance with the interests of this middle class than with those of the poor *tanis* (peasants) and coolies.[15] It is understandable, therefore, that *Sarekat Islam* soon set about opposing the privileges of the feudal nobility and the power of the native officials, as well as the colonial caste system and the large Western entrepreneurs. It did this by appealing to the broad mass of Indonesian Moslems. But the enormous support the movement obtained in no time convincingly shows the extent to which the mass of Moslem peasants regarded the Faith as a unifying force. It became thus obvious that Islam had assumed the role of a pre-nationalism.

At the same time it became clear that now that the peasant mass had begun to stir, it would continue to do so and would no longer seek protection from Western influence by a flight into the past, and by rejecting all that was new (as had been the case with the Samin movement[16] at the close of the nineteenth century). The Indonesians were now striving to combat the West with its own weapons. Organised political action provided a means to this end, and it was, also, a means which showed that the two powerful classes of former times — the *pryayis* and *kyahis* — were losing their authority over the masses.[17] From now a new type of leader, mainly urban intellectuals, would succeed in making use of the Islamic and nationalist impetus. The *kyahis* could only retain their influence by joining the movement.

Even Christianity, formerly used by the colonial power as a means to win support among parts of the population, became a weapon which could be directed against the rulers as well. The protest against aristocratic rule and traditional authority also arose among Christianised populations. For the central Batak country this process has been vividly described by van Zanen in his dissertation.[18] The missionaries in this territory (mainly Germans of the Rhenish Mission) were rather authoritarian and paternalistic in outlook. They had found the Batak country an agrarian society and wanted to keep this society free from the materialist tendencies of which they disapproved in Western society, and to imbue the Christian Bataks with higher spiritual values. But the Bataks themselves, especially the younger people, gave a quite different interpretation to their new religion. They were also affected by the awakening of Asia and by the revolutionary developments in Europe during the first decades of this century. The education they had enjoyed at missionary schools could not fail to evoke individualistic tendencies, which made themselves felt in economic life and social attitudes as well. Despite the continuous warnings of the missionaries they were increasingly being affected by a capitalist spirit which made them apply themselves to commercial crop cultivation and trade. Batak dynamics found their expression in a call for *'hamadjuon'* (progress), which became little less than a magic formula. People craved for higher education, material wealth and higher social prestige, to emulate the Europeans. The young Christian Bataks, too, established a union (the *Hatopan Kristen Batak*) which had, in the eyes of missionaries, rather revolutionary leanings. Since the missionaries tried to block such wayward activities, the young Bataks clashed against the authority of the white missionaries and against the aristocratic order of society. They did not like being told by European missionaries, which Western cultural elements were fit for consumption in Indonesia and which were not. Rationalism proved to appeal to the younger Indonesian Christians more than the thin infusion of Western culture, which the European missionaries wanted to spoonfeed them.

Thus, Christianisation proved quite inadequate to stem the rising tide of nationalism. Within Christian communities, the clash between modernism and traditionalism presented itself in a specific shape, which was but a variety of the general pattern.

Thus it seemed as if the bourgeois developments of former centuries in Western Europe were to repeat themselves in Indonesia. But there was a tremendous difference, springing from a divergent combination of time factors. Whereas the Third Estate in Western Europe had ample time to consolidate its position before a Fourth Estate raised its claims, in Asia the latter closely follows the former. In Indonesia, especially in the Islamic field, the enormous following the *Sarekat Islam* had been able to raise was soon to prove a threat and not simply a support to the bourgeois Moslems. The small man's aspirations went much further than those of the urban traders, who had founded the *Sarekat Islam* in the beginning.

NOTES

1. C. Snouck Hurgronje, *Mohammedanism. Lectures on its origin, its religious and political growth and its present state,* New York/London, 1916, p. 138. See further B. Schrieke, 'Bijdrage tot de bibliografie van de huidige godsdienstige bewegingen ter Sumatra's Westkust' (Contribution to the bibliography of the contemporary religious movements on the Westcoast of Sumatra), in *Tijdschrift voor Indische Taal-, Land- en Volkenkunde* (Journal for Indian Philology, Geography and Ethnology), Vol. LIX, 1919–1921, p. 281.
2. G. H. Bousquet, 'Introduction à l'étude de l'Islam Indonésien', in *Revue des études Islamiques,* 1938, p. 259. 259.
3. Raden Adjeng Kartini, born 1879, died 1904. Her letters were published in English in *Letters of a Javanese Princess,* London, 1921.
4. Cf., for example, *Onderzoek naar de mindere welvaart der Inlandsche bevolking op Java en Madoera* (Investigation into the diminished welfare of the native population of Java and Madura), Batavia, 1905–1914, Vol. IXe: 'Inlandsche stemmen over de laksheid van den Inlander' (Native voices concerning the Native's indolence).
5. G. F. Pijper, *Fragmenta Islamica. Studiën over het Islamisme in Nederlandsch-Indië* (Fragmenta Islamica. Studies about Islamism in the Netherlands Indies), Leiden, 1934, p. 148/149.
6. 'The Jesus of History replaced, in liberal circles, the Christ, and the qualities ascribed to him are so similar to those now ascribed to Muhammed, that Christian missionaries are wont to say that the modern character of the latter has been painted 'in colours drawn from a Christian paintbox' (W. C. Smith, *op. cit.,* p. 67). My colleague from Leiden, C. C. Berg, who was so kind as to read this chapter critically, draws my attention to the possibility that other Islamic schools of thought, such as the *Shiah* and the *Ahmadyah* movement, also had an influence on the development described in the text.
7. Cf. K. P. Landon, *op. cit.,* p.191, and R. L. Archer, *loc. cit.*

8. K. P. Landon, *op. cit.*, p. 192.
9. K. P. Landon, *op. cit.*, p. 192.
10. See for a description of the *Ahmadyah* movement G. F. Pijper, 'De Ahmadyah in Indonesië' (The Ahmadyah in Indonesia), in *Bingkisan Budi* (The mental gift. Collection of articles presented to Dr. P. S. van Ronkel), Leiden, 1950, p. 247.
11. *Mededeelingen omtrent onderwerpen van algemeen belang* (Informations about subjects of general interest), Weltevreden, 1920, p. 6ff. The pertinent section, which gives an evidence of a thorough acquaintance with Max Weber's theories on sociology of religion, is to be attributed to the able sociologist D. M. G. Koch.
12. *Sarekat-Islam Congres* (1st National Congress), 1916, p. 29 ff., 69 ff.
13. *Sarekat-Islam Congres* (2nd National Congress), 1917, p. 43, 120.
14. See R. H. Tawney, *Religion and the rise of capitalism*, Pelican Books edition, Harmondsworth, 1938, p. 95 ff.
15. *Mededeelingen omtrent onderwerpen van algemeen belang*, 1920, p. 11.
16. This movement is discussed in W.F. Wertheim, "Nationalism and After", in *Indonesian Society in Transition: A Study in Social Change*, The Hague/Bandung, 1964, Chapter XI.
17. Cf. *Herinneringen van Pangeran Aria Achmad Djajadiningrat* (Memoirs of P.A.A. Djajadiningrat), Amsterdam/Batavia, 1936, p. 285 ff.
18. A. J. van Zanen, *Voorwaarden voor maatschappelijke ontwikkeling in het central Batakland* (Conditions for social development in the central Batak area), Leiden, 1934, p. 65 ff.

The Development and Nature of the Modernist Movement in Indonesia

DELIAR NOER

In our discussion of the various organizations, whether social and educational or political, we have touched on the characteristics of each organization, the varied tendencies they stressed in spreading their ideas, characteristics and tendencies which were shaped by the personalities who led the respective organizations and by the milieu in which the organizations operated. One might obtain the impression that there was not one movement in Indonesia, but several movements, each with distinct characteristics of its own. The existence of non-cooperative parties (e.g. Sarekat Islam after 1921, and Persatuan Muslimin Indonesia) and co-operative parties (e.g. Partai Islam Indonesia), the existence of pro-nationalist (Persatuan Muslimin Indonesia) as well as seemingly anti-nationalist (e.g. Persatuan Islam), organizations, and the existence of the tolerant Muhammadijah beside the intolerant Persatuan Islam, all point to a variety of movements.

Yet this variety did not mean the absence of agreement on the part of the reformist organizations. On the contrary, in spite of the varied attitudes, tendencies and policies, the basic principles of their ideas, which reflected the nature of the reforms they championed, were sufficiently in agreement that it can indeed be said that they all constituted one movement.

To understand this apparent contradiction, we must first recall and understand the position of Islam, and the way Islam was being practised by traditionalists up to the turn of this century.

First of all Islam was considered by the great majority of the Indonesian people as a national identity. The word *bumiputera* (literally: son of the soil or earth) was applied in general to Muslims, while Christians, though natives, were considered aliens.

THE TRADITIONALISTS

The traditionalists were also mainly concerned with pure religion, *din* or *ibadah;* Islam was for them mostly *fiqh,* jurisprudence. In this connection they recognized *taqlid,* and rejected the validity of *idjtihad.* Many of the traditionalists were also concerned with *sufism* (mysticism).

In spite of their claim to be followers of *madzahib* (schools of law) — mainly the *madzhab* (school) of Sjafi'i —, they did not in general follow the teachings of the founders of the *madzahib* but confined themselves mainly to teachings of later *imam* or persons of knowledge, who in many cases deviated from the teachings of the founders. The traditionalists in Indonesia were following the established *fatwa* rather than the method of arriving at the *fatwa.* In the Minangkabau area where the matrilineal system was still strongly upheld, *faraidh* (law of inheritance)

Excerpted from D. Noer, *The Modernist Movement in Indonesia 1900–1942* (Kuala Lumpur: Oxford University Press, 1973), by permission of the author and the publishers.

which is part of *fiqh,* gave way to *adat* on inheritance in many cases.

In *sufism* many of the traditionalists often fell into practices which were close to *sjirk,* associating God with beings and objects. They venerated *keramat* (shrines, graves of saints), gave offerings to spirits, held *slametan* or *kenduri* (feasts) as offerings, and used *azimat* or charms to protect themselves from evil genii or bad luck — which all in all resulted in the watering down, at least, of *tauhid,* the oneness of God. In general, 'accretions from the culture of the various peoples in the Middle East and India were mixed with new accretions from the indigenous (animistic and Hinduized) beliefs and practices in the country'. Whether this mixture of ideas and practices was compatible or not with Islam as delivered by Muhammad, the Prophet, appeared to be unquestioned by them.

This unquestioning traditionalist attitude often led to blind obedience since in both *fiqh* and sufism, the teacher (*kijahi* or *sjech*) was regarded as infallible. In this situation Islam and its interpretation was monopolized by the *kijahi* or *sjech* rather than being shared by its individual followers as well. The *kijahi's fatwa* was final and should not be argued with.

The highly elevated and infallible position of the *kijahi* or *sjech* created a system of education (in the *pesantren* or *surau*) in which learning by heart rather than understanding was the main object. The students did not dare to express a different view from the *kijahi's.* Teaching at the *pesantren* or *surau* was, and this was also true for advanced students, a one-way communication from teacher to student, not a discussion in which the students might have a chance to sharpen their mind and contribute to learning. The textbooks used were those used generations before, and the courses taught were purely religious. For advanced education the traditionalists usually went to Mekka.

The *pesantren* or *surau* were not formally organized. There was no system of classes, no curriculum, no periodic assignments. Too much depended on the 'natural' progress made by the student without any guarantee as to what stage he could reach after a certain period of study. In addition, the continuance of the existence of a *pesantren* depended to a large extent on the *kijahi* personally, his death often resulted in its closing.

Because of their main concern with purely religious questions, the traditionalists in general did not participate in political affairs but left these to others like the *adat* group and the *prijaji.* This did not mean, however, that they were all content with the colonial condition. On the contrary; many of them were against the Dutch, but instead of making the necessary systematic preparations to end the Dutch rule, they adopted a negative attitude. They isolated themselves in the *pesantren* or *surau,* or went to Mekka to spend the rest of their life in the Holy City; or through their secret, mystical orders, they built up a following which could resort to violence in order to drive away the Dutch. This following was, however, limited in size, and rarely extended outside the locality. There existed also a strong inclination among them to expect help from the caliphate in Istanbul. They had no thought of strengthening themselves instead by founding an organization which might build up a national following, thereby enabling them to put pressure on the Dutch.

Many of the traditionalists became religious officials, a position in which they found satisfaction either with the idea that they were devoting themselves to the cause of Islam by acting as guardians for the application of its purely religious aspects, or with the secure and recognized positions as officials. In this case, personal interest played a role, and those who entertained this idea favoured, together with the *prijaji* and those *adat* chiefs who were on good terms with the Dutch, the political *status quo* of the country.

THE REFORMISTS

The reformists, on the other hand, were concerned with the nature of Islam in general. To them Islam is compatible with the demand of time and circumstances. Islam also means progress, it will not hamper the search for knowledge, the development of science, the position of women.[1] Islam is a universal religion, the basic teachings of which had been revealed to known and unknown prophets[2] who were sent to all nations and whose works were completed by Muhammad, the last Prophet and Apostle for all mankind.

This idea, according to the reformists, is embodied in the *sjari'ah,* the law, which can be divided into two divisions of which the second also consists of two sections. There is first the real *din,* the real religion or *ibadah* (ritual) of which the purpose is often not explained (not *ma'qul*) but the method of execution is defined. On this question 'everything is prohibited except that which is commanded'; thus the specific rituals, like *salat* (prayer service), in which *bid'ah* is not tolerated.[3]

The other division is concerned with worldly matters. The first section of this division has a religious character in the sense that it is based on Allah's commandments, but contrary to the *din* or *ibadah* above, these commandments are *ma'qul.* The purpose is explained but their execution is 'left to us in accord with the period and circumstances in which we live, as long as it will lead us to that purpose'. There is, for example, the order to take care of orphans, to respect parents, to clean the teeth, — matters, the method of execution of which is in large measure left to the individual.[4]

The other section is concerned with 'purely worldly matters which might exist and might arise with or without any religious commandment'. On this question 'everything is permissible unless expressly prohibited by religion'. The limits of this wide scope of ideas and activities consist of *had* (limitations). A simple example is the permissibility of eating and drinking any kind of foods and drinks except the *had* mentioned in the Quran which include among others, pork, intoxicants, blood,[5] or that one should not be immoderate or prodigal.[6]

In the eyes of the reformists, the traditionalists did not pay attention to the above-mentioned division of *sjari'ah.* In the realm of *din,* the reformists said, the traditionalists had fallen into *bid'ah* practices to such an extent that accretions to the religion were considered as if they had been derived from the practices of the Prophet. Many of the traditionalists, especially the *tarekat* people, entertained ideas and carried out practices which ran counter to *tauhid,* the oneness of God. On the other hand, the reformists argued, in purely worldly matters, the liberty of reasoning among the traditionalists was obstructed to the extent that any adaptation of Western methods, as in education, or any resemblance to Western habits, as in clothing, was considered *haram* or taboo. In the worldly realm, the reformists accused the traditionalists of adopting an attitude which hampered their own progress, and in general the progress of Muslims. They were, especially in the early years of the reformist movement, in a condition of *djumud* (inertia) because they were content with their traditional methods and practices, isolated themselves in the *pesantren* and *surau,* and showed every indifference toward the progress made by the outside world.

This leads us to the problem of liberty of thought, a problem closely related to the idea of *idjtihad* and *taqlid.* The reformists considered that Islam 'respects man's reason and protects it from possible suppression' as could be derived from the Quran and *Hadits.*[7] However, they also recognized that liberty of reasoning can also create ideas which might lead one astray from the right path. This is exemplified by the existence of pantheistic ideas, the innovation of religious practices incorporated in the rituals, the veneration of *keramat* (shrines) and the creation of certain performances to honour heroes, saints and such like people — performances which are not based on religion but are close to religious services. According to the reformists, freedom of reasoning and thought might thus lead one to a noble idea as well as to evil, and therefore religion is needed to direct the power of reasoning along the path of righteousness.[8] In this connection statements of the Prophet have often been cited:

> Ponder over the creation of God, not over His essence. On religious matters, leave them to me. As far as your worldly problems are concerned, you know more about them [than I do].[9]

The reformists furthermore considered that religion would become a mere 'fossil', if independent reasoning is 'allowed to dismiss all standards, to abandon religious principles' adding that man's soul needs 'religion as a criteria, a judge, an absolute standard to decide what is right or wrong'. Religion is, therefore, not an object which is to be judged by independent reasoning. In this connection they have maintained that science has left many problems unclarified, problems which compel man to acknowledge the existence of a Supreme Being.[10]

These limitations, according to the reformists, do not run counter to the completeness of Islam which they view as

> . . . a way of life giving equal rights and equal duties to all mankind . . . a code for the upholding of ethics . . . for regulating the relations between man at home, in society, government and the state . . . the relations with people of other faiths . . . the relations with people of other countries, for giving guidance to the fulfillment of the physical and spiritual needs of man in order to attain the highest aspirations of mankind.[11]

Reformism in Islam in Indonesia lies, therefore, much deeper than what can be observed from the activities and ideas displayed on the surface. It is concerned with the rediscovery of what the reformists consider as the basic principles which are eternal and which can survive the changes of time and place. Time, milieu and innovations caused the basic principles to become less clearly visible and covered them with other ideas; moreover, these accretions often gained popularity and were imbued with such authority that eventually they were often referred to as representing Islam.

The reformists thus made an attempt to recover the basic principles by means of eliminating all the accretions as regards *din*, religion, and of releasing individuals from *djumud,* inertia, as regards worldly affairs. Their idea was to break through all the accretions and the *djumud* in order to discover and find the content, the core, the essence of religion (Islam) which, they believe, is the light of guidance in this world.

This return to these basic principles, which they generally call the return to the Quran and *Hadits,* at a glance means a return to the old ages, for as has been said by the reformists themselves, it is the Prophet and the Shahabah (Companions of the Prophet) who should be taken as examples in one's actions. The Prophet and the Shahabah lived in the remote past with which the present world is unfamiliar except through the words of scholars and through the pages of historical books. But their contents and the basic principles are fit for all times and places. Islamic teachings which they have advocated, do not accommodate themselves to circumstances nor do they need to be adjusted to modern thought. The basic principles, the essence (of Islam), are eternal which means that they are always modern.

In this sense, the reformists can also be called modernists, for their ideas and thoughts are always subject to further investigation by themselves or by others. They themselves will not stop the re-examination, study and re-investigations of their findings, for all progress and advancement is liable to reconsideration, to *idjtihad.*

Viewed in this light, the basic principles which they turn to, contain within themselves the idea of modernism. With these principles as a basis, thoughts and practices develop, and methods, however foreign they may appear, are applied, as long as they are compatible with the basic principles.

In this light let us discuss the characteristics of the reformist, or modernist, movement (on which we have elaborated in the previous chapters). The modernists recognized only the Quran and *Hadits* as the basic sources of their ideas and thought. They maintained that 'the gate of *idjtihad'* is still open and rejected the idea of *taqlid.* This does not mean that they condemned the founders and other *imam* of the *madzahib,* however, the *fatwa* and opinions of these *imam* as is the case with any other idea, are subject to further examination. In the minds of the modernists, the validity of any *fatwa,* idea or practice should in principle be judged on the basis of the Quran and *Hadits.*

Idjtihad has brought the modernists to pay regard to opinions rather than to personalities or leaders. The modernist teacher, often still called *kijahi* or *sjech,* did not enjoy the infallible position of the traditionalist *kijahi.* He did not monopolize the knowledge of Islam or any other knowledge, — but merely releases it to the public which has the same right as he to discuss it.

Discussions on Islam were therefore not confined to the *pesantren, surau, langgar* and mosques, but were brought out to the open through newspapers and periodicals, and — through *tabligh* — in theatres and public squares. With the rise of the modernists, Islam was given as an additional course, though outside the curriculum, in schools established by the (Dutch Indies) government, for which the instructors were modernists. Religious observances became part of the scouts' training and were introduced in social institutions like orphanages and the houses for the poor, in clinics and hospitals, and in some cases also in hospitals founded by the government. Through the modernist organizations, Islam became an organized social force operating at the national level in which women also participated and contributed their full share.

Throughout the period of this study, the modernists readily adopted the organizational and educational method and ideas of the West, including those of Christian missionaries, so long as these were not in violation of the principles of Islam. The establishment of educational, social and political organizations, scout movements, missionaries, and the adoption of the educational system certainly point to recognition by the modernists of the advantages of Western methods and techniques. In the educational field, *Al-Azhar* of Cairo was certainly not taken as a model, for this Muslim institution continued to maintain the traditional line. The Muhammadijah and the Persatuan Islam went so far as to establish a counterpart of Dutch government schools in Indonesia, except for the colleges. The two organizations founded H.I.S.,* Schakelschool,** MULO,† H.I.K.,‡ A.M.S.§ — the only difference was that religion was taught as a compulsory subject at these reformist institutions and that the students, in particular those at the modernist boarding schools, were subject to religious disciplinary regulations. Hadji Abdulhalim of Madjalengka claimed to have been influenced by Rabindranath Tagore's Shantiniketan in founding the Santi Asrama.

The modernists also recognized the benefit of scientific education which the Dutch had introduced into their (Dutch) schools in Indonesia, and science was incorporated into the curriculum of the modernist schools. Arabic was not the only recognized medium for augmenting one's knowledge; in addition to it, European languages, including Dutch, English, German and French, also found their way into the curriculum. There was a decrease in the publication and the use of Arabic textbooks, except on religion; instead these were more and more written in Indonesian. Djawi, i.e., Malay in Arabic script, and Pego i.e., Javanese in Arabic script, made way for Latin characters. This was most obvious in the publication of books, pamphlets, brochures, newspapers and periodicals for the public at large.

The adoption of the Western system of education gave to the students some idea as to the stages of their study whereas the traditionalist system at the *pesantren* or *surau,* we will remember, had no fixed time limit. The modernist institutions, moreover, stressed understanding rather than learning by heart. For advanced training, the graduates of these institutions went more and more to Egypt, and from there, to Europe. Some of them continued their studies at Dutch established institutions, like A.M.S. and the law school in Djakarta.

The modernist movement was able to prevent, at least partly, the 'emancipation' from their religion of Indonesians who were trained in Dutch schools. In this connection, the activities of the Jong Islamieten Bond which consisted mainly of students and graduates of Dutch institutions were largely responsible. The youths in this organization remained devoted Muslims and strengthened the movement by providing part of its leadership.

In the beginning the modernists, like the traditionalists, were also concerned with pure religion. Both *fiqh* and *sufism* drew their attention. Some social aspects of Islam also drew the attention of the modernists at the early stage of the rise of the movement, but these were confined to those closely related to pure religion, like the law of inheritance in the Minangkabau area, marriage regulations and the educational field. Gradually this attention spread to the political aspect as well.

This broadening of the call of the modernists produced a conscious conviction among many of the Muslims in Indonesia that in Islam, there is unity of religion and politics. The Quran and *Hadits* became, in the mind of the modernists, not only sources for religious ideas and practices, but for social and political ideas as well. It was when this conviction of the unity of religion and politics in Islam was expressed in words and in deeds, as was reflected in the activities of the Muslim political organizations, that reaction came from the Dutch as well as from other Indonesian groups, including the religiously neutral nationalists.

In this event, the modernists considered it a natural development that they should pursue a national (Indonesian) and a nationalist policy — i.e. pursuing independence. This was more so because of the consolidation of Dutch control over the area comprising what was called the Netherlands Indies.

NOTES

1. *Al-Munir*, Vol. II No. 24 stated *inter alia* that the *sjari'ah* discusses women in general within the framework of mankind, there is no discrimination against them; only on certain minor questions which are exclusively concerned with womanhood, does the *sjari'ah* make specific regulations'. Further examples used in this connection were the right of women to have direct communication with God, to act independently of her husband, the recognition of the property right of wives. Even Madjlis Tardjih, the *fatwa* body of the Muhammadijah, was prepared to accept women members if there were recognized women *ulama*. See *Moment Verslag Congres ke-28 Muhammadijah di Medan* (Jogjakarta: Muhammadijah, 1939), p. 19.
2. Q 10:47, 2:164, 35:24, 40:78.
3. A. Muchlis [pseud. M. Natsir], *Islam dan Akal Merdeka* (Tasikmalaja: Pusat Pimpinan Persatuan Islam Bagian Penjiaran, 1947), p. 72. On this and the following few paragraphs, the writer has also secured further clarifications from Abdul Kadir Hassan, head of the Pesantren Persis of Bangil, in a letter dated 25 March 1962.
4. Natsir, ibid.
5. Q 5:3, 90.
6. Q 7:31, 5:87.
7. Natsir, op. cit. p. 7, 9. Q 56:58–72, 6:97–98.
8. Natsir, op. cit. p. 16.
9. Ibid. pp. 18–21.
10. Ibid. pp. 33, 35.
11. Mohammad Natsir in *Pembela Islam*, No. 44 (n.d., approximately March (1932), p. 3. Natsir used *Is* as his pseudonym for this article.

EDITORS' NOTE

* H.I.S. stands for Hollands Inlandse School [Dutch speaking native (elementary) school].
** Schakelschool is the Dutch language elementary school.
† MULO stands for Meer Vitgebreid Lager Onderwijs (junior high school).
‡ H.I.K. stands for Hollands Inlandse Kweekschool (training school for native teachers).
§ A.M.S. stands for Algemene Middelbare School (lit. General Secondary School) — Senior High School.

Kaum Muda-Kaum Tua: Innovation and Reaction amongst the Malays, 1900–41

WILLIAM ROFF

But it was not mainly, or most importantly, through the columns of newspapers and journals that the *Kaum Muda — Kaum Tua* conflict was fostered at the village level. More often it arose as a result of the interests of the villagers themselves. It needed only one Haji to return from the Middle East with reformist ideas, one religious teacher to study at a *Kaum Muda madrassah* in Singapore, Perak or Penang, to divide a village into two embittered factions.[1] And while the main disputes centred round those religious questions already referred to, social questions related to them became easily involved, both as a result of independently arising social change (through the extension of popular, Western-oriented education, the introduction of rubber growing for cash and a changing economy), and as a result of the wider implications of *Kaum Muda* ideas. Arguments about whether it was permissible for a Muslim to wear European dress, and whether the taking of interest from post-office savings banks and rural co-operative societies was lawful or not, divided people along the same lines as arguments about the holiness of the local *keramat* (spirit shrine) or whether a teacher had correctly interpreted a verse of the Kuran. In short, to be *Kaum Muda* came to mean espousal of modernism in any form; to be *Kaum Tua* was to be in favour of all that was traditional, unchanging and secure.

In a volume of essays originally published in the *Police Magazine*, and collected in 1935 under the title *The Malayan Kaleidoscope*, Haji Abdul Majid[2] wrote that there was hardly a village in Malaya where the Malays did not argue and discuss the teachings of the *Kaum Muda*, and went on: 'The "*Kaum Tua*" or Old Party, from among whom have been recruited the religious officials of the country, try to insinuate in revenge that the *Kaum Muda* are undesirable Communists, which they decidedly are not'[3]. The politicization of the image of *Kaum Muda* began to make itself evident only in the mid-1920's, notwithstanding the political implications inherent in reformist ideas prior to this time. Other writers have referred to the role played by Islamic reform in Indonesia as a kind of prenationalism.[4] The same may be said of reformism in Malaya, but with the important qualification that unlike the Indonesian movement, it never succeeded in elaborating, either organisationally or programmatically, a political nationalism capable of attracting mass support. The principal reasons for this I shall suggest in due course, but that there are not lacking signs that, in other circumstances than those prevailing, it might have done so, is clear from an examination of the writings of the polemical wing of the reformist movement in the 1920's. These are to be found primarily in two periodicals published in Cairo by Malay and Indonesian students at the University of Al-Azhar, *Seruan Azhar* (1925–28) and *Pilehan Timour* (1927–28).[5]

As with earlier newspaper and journals,

Reprinted in abridged form from K. G. Tregonning (ed.), *Papers on Malayan History* (*Journal of South East Asian History* [Singapore: *Journal of South East Asian History*, 1962]), pp. 162–192, by permission of the author and the *Journal of South East Asian Studies*, Singapore.

Seruan Azhar and *Pilehan Timour* were much concerned with those topics of primarily religious and social concern already dealt with at some length in this article. What now made its appearance for the first time (as far as Malaya was concerned) was a new and aggressive spirit of overt political discussion. This discussion centred round three main ideals, Pan-Islamism, Pan-Malayanism (union between Indonesia and Malaya), and anti-colonial nationalism. The first of these was the least realistic in political terms, and the shortest lived, hinging as it did on the hopes aroused by the conquest of the Hajaz by the Wahhabi ruler Ibn Saud in 1924, and the ill-fated attempts to resurrect the Caliphate and organise a rejuvenated Islamic world, which finally came to grief with the failure of the proposed Islamic World Congress, to have been held at Mecca in 1926.[6] Representatives were sent to Mecca by the Cairo Union of Malaysian students (led by Mokhtar Loutfi), and at least two delegates travelled from Malaya itself.[7] International Islamic unity as a political ideal to be expressed in Pan-Islamism had little force or influence in Malaya, in spite of an undoubted interest in the progress, welfare and government of the Middle-Eastern countries, but there was, nevertheless, at this time, amongst the reformist-oriented element, a certain amount of excitement at the possibilities held forth by the idea of an Islamic renaissance which would command the respect of the West.

More important, in the long run, was the growth of the idea of closer union between Malaya and Indonesia. Though not worked out in any detail, or indeed proceeding beyond sentiment and exhortation, some sort of the political association between the two areas became a recurring theme in the columns of *Seruan Azhar*. The journal's first editorial, written by Mahmoud el Jounousij, made an appeal for the peoples of Sumatra, Java, Borneo and Malaya to 'unit with one heart for progress and prosperity.[8] Much was made of the possession of a common religion and a common language, and numerous articles compare the present state of economic development, education, and political life under the separate colonial regimes.[9] From this developed discussion of colonial rule as the major obstacle to true progress and reform, and it is in this area of discourse that the most outspoken political protests against the *status quo* occur. In an article entitled 'What is the Advantage of Freedom?', the Malay writer Abdullah Ahmad wrote, concerning the educational systems of Malaya and Indonesia, 'We do not deny that education is necessary for freedom, but we do not believe that education which is given in countries under colonial rule can contain the seeds of freedom. The knowledge that is given to peoples under foreign influence has no other purpose than to impoverish their intellect and lead them to lick the soles of their masters' boots'.[10] In general, it is true, criticisms of the British colonial system are much less harsh than those of the Dutch[11] (in this connection, one should recall the repression of the rebellions in Sumatra and Java in 1926–27), but in comparison with the carefully apolitical reformism of the earlier years, the views expressed by the two Cairo journals introduced a new and more violent tone into the propaganda of the reformist movement in Malaya.[12]

I have tried to describe the conflict in Malaya between the Islamic reformers and, on the one hand, the religious hierarchy and the traditional elite, on the other the rural *ulama* and the predominantly conservative elements in Malay peasant society, and to suggest the way in which these conflicts carried wider implications of social and political change. That these implications existed is, I think, clear, but it would be a misreading of Islamic reformism in 20th Century Malaya to suppose that it was itself directly responsible for fostering or initiating widespread social or political protest. It never succeeded, for example, in creating a mass movement similar to either the non-political *Muhammadiah* or the activist Sharikat Islam in Indonesia, in spite of much discussion of the need for unity and association, and it seems never to have created real anxiety on the part of the British.[13]

The reasons for this failure of reformism to provide a coherent and sufficiently appealing philosophy of action for developing Malay society are various and complex, but some attempt must be made to disentangle them. In dealing individually with the various factors involved, I do not suggest that they were not inter-related. The reverse rather was the case, for as with all social processes, analysis of the parts must ultimately make possible their synthesis into a meaningful whole, meaningful in the terms of the society under discussion.

In the first place, reformism itself, especially in the first two decades of the 20th Century, saw its task as one with primarily religious and educational, and not at all political ends. That is to say, it endeavoured to substitute for rudimentary and repetitious theological learning, clouded in a haze of doctrinal misunderstanding and superstitious practice, a new kind of Islamic teaching based on intelligent re-appraisal of the truths contained in the Kuran and Traditions, combined with a programme of modern education properly adapted to the pressing needs of the world into which the Malays were emerging. This, if properly applied and received, would, it was believed, result in a rejuvenation of the Malay Islamic community, enabling them to stand on their own feet. In pursuing this aim, however, the *Kaum Muda* rapidly found itself in conflict with all the forces of traditionalism, strengthened as a result of British Malay policy — the rural *ulama* and much of peasant society, the religious hierarchy in the States, and the traditional ruling class. Reformism in Malaya, as elsewhere, was primarily an urban-centred phenomenon, appealing to a small middle class which found in the more rationalistic and individualistic ethic of modernism something which chimed with their needs and aspirations, which indeed gave them a rationale for, as well as an ability to compete in, the somewhat anarchic world in which they found themselves. Traditionalism, as exemplified in the rural *ulama* and peasant society, with its customary religious and magical beliefs, and a value system oriented to a rural and still largely subsistence village economy, was inevitably antagonistic to, or at the least distrustful of, the new ideas inherent in reformism. British policy towards the Malays, based on the assumption that the great majority were destined to remain within the traditional agricultural society, relied on the importation of Chinese and Indian labour and entrepreneurship for the development of the country's resources, and did much to fence off the Malays from the harshnesses of social and economic change, inhibiting, in the process, the growth of an economic middle class susceptible to the potential radicalism of the reform movement.

I have already referred [14] to the effects of the elaboration, with British support, of a professional religious hierarchy in the Malay States during the first decades of colonial rule, a phenomenon virtually coeval with the rise of reformism, and in effect disruptive of reformist attempts to organise their activity on a more systematic and persuasive basis. The identification of the religious hierarchy not only with rural-centred Islam but with the traditional ruling class who supported and legitimised them, resulted in an alliance of traditional forces which it was virtually impossible to breach in force.[15] Any attack on the hierarchy was, by extension, an attack on the traditional elite, a situation only compounded by *Kaum Muda* criticism of the Malay aristocracy for their failure to provide a more dynamic and less selfish leadership. Finally, in this immediate context, reformism had to face the State system, which for long was to sunder all Malay attempts, from whatever source, to create a wider unity in terms of religious, ethnic or class interests.

This, then, was broadly the situation up to the late 1920's by which time a number of new forces had entered upon the scene. The most important of these was the growth of two new groups within Malay society — the Western-trained elite and a young Malay-educated intelligentsia — neither of which placed Islam at the centre of their concerns, the first deriving its inspiration from explicitly Western socio-political values and organizational forms, the second from the cultural (especially literary) and politically activist movements in Indonesia. Squeezed, as it were, between these two groups, the reformists were forced increasingly onto the defensive, a process assisted by the strong 'pro-Malay' reaction evinced by the second group in the early 1930's against the Arab and Indian Muslim elements in Singapore and Penang, which for long had provided leadership for the Muslim communities there.[16]

The Western-trained elite, in its upper echelons, was very largely drawn from the Malay aristocracy and its connections, as a result of British policy on the provision of higher education and facilities for entry into the Civil Service by way of the 'Malay Officers

Scheme'.[17] Experience in administrative organisation and procedures, and with the social and political philosophies of the West, combined to produce a class of Malays who, both from their hereditary origins and from their new status, felt themselves entitled to and capable of leadership. In addition, the extension of ordinary secondary school English education (the number of Malays attending English-medium secondary schools trebled between 1920 and 1930)[18] meant a great increase in the number of Malays capable of holding clerkships and similar posts in the State and Federal services, and widened the base of the Western-oriented class. Developments in the Federated Malay States in the late 1920's and early 1930's, tending towards what was described as a 'restoration' of States' rights and the prestige of the Malay Rulers, and accompanied by liberalisation of promotion prospects within the Civil Service, led to increasing participation by Malays within the process of government and administration. At the same time, newly awakened, locally-domiciled Chinese demands for a greater share in the direction of affairs in the country they now regarded as their home, gave rise to a defensive reaction on the part of the Western-educated Malays in particular, and to a restatement by the British of their traditional 'pro-Malay' policy in the allotment of opportunity and position.[19] In the late 1930's, a series of Malay Unions was formed within the Federated, and subsequently the Unfederated States of the Peninsula, quasi-political organisations of a markedly conservative character with a programme largely concerned with the expression of 'Malaya for the Malays' sentiment — an ideal which expressed not anti-colonialism but fears of domination by locally-domiciled communities of alien origin, principally the Chinese. The leadership of the Unions, which combined for a pan-Malayan conference in 1939, and held a larger and more comprehensive one the following year, was largely in the hands of the Western-educated aristocratic elite. Politically they were mild in tone, and conciliatory (even dependent) in their attitude towards British rule, but their following was considerable, and represents both the appeal inherent in leadership of this character, and organizational technique which could not be matched by other groups.

More radical, but on the whole less coherent feelings were expressed by the Malay-educated intelligentsia, mainly schoolteachers and journalists, who, in the 1930's, formed the first genuine political-nationalist Malay party. In 1922 the Government had opened Sultan Idris College for Malay teachers, at Tanjong Malim in Perak, the only institution then or subsequently to offer a secondary education in the vernacular, and it was from graduates of this institution that a new and more truly autochthonous spirit in Malay life derived. It expressed itself first in a wave of literary activity, mainly in the form of short novels, much influenced as to theme and content by the publications of the recently established *Balai Pustaka* in Indonesia, and exploring, in however jejune a way, the conflicts of values and situational problems then facing many Malays.[20] Literary and debating societies sprang up at the College, members of the staff, as well as students, contributed to controversies in the vernacular press, and a growing interest was taken in events in Indonesia. After the failure of the Communist rebellions in Java and Sumatra in 1926, a number of Indonesian revolutionaries escaped to Malaya,[21] where they were brought into contact with some of the graduates and students of Sultan Idris College. When Sukarno's *Partai Nasional Indonesia* was formed in 1927, several of the latter, led by Ibrahim bin Haji Yaacob, became members and resolved to fight for Malayan independence and a closer association with Indonesia.[22] Little attempt, however, was made at this stage to elaborate any strategy of action, and it was not until 1937, after much secret discussion, that Ibrahim Yaacob and Ishak bin Haji Muhammad formed the *Kesatuan Melayu Muda* (KMM — Young Malay Union), with exiled Indonesians as the remaining officers and a following recruited mainly from the students of Sultan Idris Training College, the Agricultural College at Serdang, and the Trade School in Kuala Lumpur. Sutan Djenain, one of the original refugees from the collapse of the 1926 rebellion in Java, acted as liaison between the KMM and the Malayan Communist Party (virtually an entirely Chinese organization). The political platform of KMM was vague, and never elaborated in any contemporary document. Its chief components were a generalised anti-colonialism (expressed in the slogan 'non-cooperation'), independence for Malaya, and union of Malaya within a Greater Indonesia (*Indonesia Raya*). As the Pacific War approached, Ibrahim Yaacob made contact with the Japanese, and was assisted with Japanese money to purchase the daily newspaper *Warta Malaya*, in which the rather confused revolutionary tendencies of the party found some expression. In December 1941, 150 of the leaders and members of KMM were arrested by the British, and put in jail in Singapore, where they still were when the city fell to the Japanese in February 1942.[23]

For the Western-oriented elite, as for the young Malay intelligentsia, the conflicts between the Islamic reformers and their traditionalist opponents were either anachronistic or irrelevant. It is, nevertheless, significant that many Malays in 1937 regarded KMM, which had no vestige of religious content, reformist or otherwise, as '*Kaum Muda*', and therefore something to beware of as a threat to the established order. This helps to explain the Sultan of Perak's remark, quoted at the beginning of this article,[24] categorising *Kaum Muda* as 'those who devote their time mainly to the material side of life'. What in fact had happened was that religious reformism, as a vivifying force in Malay society, had been overtaken by secular and political movements which found their rationale in a specifically non-Islamic approach to developmental problems, and were better equipped by reason of either their authoritarian heritage or their political orientation to elaborate a more decisive form of nationalism. Reformism, during the 1930's and subsequently, found itself moving closer to its erstwhile religious opponents, both because of the common situation in which they were placed *vis-a-vis* secular nationalism, and as a consequence of a diminution in the fires of dispute through improved religious education and the dying off of an older generation. The inheritors of this closing of the ranks may perhaps be seen today, in political terms, in the shape of the Pan-Malayan Islamic Party, which still attempts, in the face of considerable odds, to formulate the ideal of the *Dar'ul Islam*, the Islamic State, ruled by Muslims in accordance with Kuranic Law.

NOTES

1. In the Selangor village of Jeram in the late 1920's a dispute developed between *Kaum Muda* and *Kaum Tua* factions over the question of whether or not participants should stand up at the mention of the Prophet's name during the *Maulud Nabi* ceremony. (Literally 'Prophet's Birthday', the ceremony, which consists mainly of readings from biographical works about Muhammad, is used very widely on other occasions than that of the birthday proper). The disruptive effects of the dispute were considerable, the adherents of each side refusing to pray with the others in the mosque, or to attend weddings and other ceremonies held by the opposition. Though such faction fights were often, as in this case, patched up after a time, they were not uncommon in Malay villages, as one of the unsettling effects of new ideas.
2. Haji Abdul Majid bin Haji Zainuddin, *The Malayan Kaleidoscope* (Kuala Lumpur, 1935). Abdul Majid was educated at the English public-school type Malay Residential College, Kuala Kangsar, later becoming the Malay language teacher on the staff there. In 1923 he was appointed Pilgrimage Officer at Jeddah, spending part of the year there and the rest in Malaya as a Liaison Officer with the Political Intelligence Branch of the Federated Malay States Police, posts he held until the mid-1930's. In addition to *The Malayan Kaleidoscope* he wrote *The Malays of Malaya* (Singapore 1928) under the pseudonym 'One of Them', a number of educational works on the Malay language, and contributed frequently to both the English and the vernacular press. In 1940 he started, with his son Haji Abdul Latiph as editor, the monthly magazine *The Modern Light* (1940–41), described as 'the first Malay national organ in English'. His outlook, as expressed in all his writings, was very pro-British, and he was greatly attracted by the Lahore branch of the Ahmadiya movement.
3. *Op. cit.*, p. 23.
4. Notably W. F. Wertheim, *Indonesian Society in Transition* (The Hague/Bandung, 2nd ed. 1959), p. 215; and, with greater analytic sophistication, Harry J. Benda, *The Crescent and the Rising Sun* (The

Hague/Bandung, 1958), pp. 43, 46, 57 and *passim.* Cf. also B. Schrieke, "The Causes & Effects of Communism on the West Coast of Sumatra", in *Indonesian Sociological Studies,* Pt 1 (The Hague/Bandoeng, 1955).

5. The prime mover (and financial backer) in starting these journals would appear to have been Haji Othman bin Abdullah, a Minangkabau-born Malay from Malacca, who studied in Mecca for five years before going to Al-Azhar in 1925. According to Othman, there were some 400 Indonesian and Malay students in Cairo at this time, 100 of them from the Peninsula — though this figure is probably rather high. (Interview with Haji Othman bin Abdullah, Kuala Lumpur, December 1960.) The editorial staffs of the magazines were mainly Indonesian (notably Ilias Ja'coub, Mahmoud el Jounoesija and Mokhtar Loutfi), but several Malays, Later well-known, were amongst them (notably Ahmad Lutfi and Abdullah Ahmad), and there were in addition correspondents in the Malay States. Both magazines were banned by the Dutch in Indonesia, and *Pilehan Timour* stopped publication by order of the Egyptian Government in October 1928.
6. See *Seruan Azhar,* I, No. 9 (June, 1926).
7. Syed Hassan bin Ahmad Al-Attas and Syed Abu Bakar Al-Attas, representing the Sultan of Johore, *Seruan Azhar, loc. cit.*
8. *Seruan Azhar,* I, No. 1 (October, 1925).
9. See, for example, *Seruan Azhar,* II, No. 17 (February, 1927), pp. 245–6; II, No. 20 (May, 1927), pp. 383–5; II, No. 21 (June, 1927), pp. 403–6; and III, No. 25 (October, 1927), pp. 490–1.
10. T. Abdullah [Ahmad], 'Apa-kah Faedah Merdeka?' ['What is the Value of Freedom?'], *Seruan Azhar,* III, No. 25 (October, 1927), pp. 492–3. Cf. also Radin Soenarno, 'Malay Nationalism, 1900–1945', *Journal of Southeast Asian History,* I, No. 1 (March, 1960), pp. 8–9, where further quotations from this article are given.
11. See *Seruan Azhar*, II, No. 22 (July, 1927), pp. 421–5, in which, on the one hand it is held that the Malays have greater autonomy than the Indonesians, in that there are Malay Residents (sic) and Assistant Residents in the Malayan Civil Service, and on the other that the prosperity and ease of life in Malaya explains Malay political apathy.
12. The fostering of the political component in the *Kaum Muda* image at this time was undoubtedly assisted, though this is difficult to document, by the association between reformism and Communism in the Minangkabau region of Sumatra (see B. Schrieke, *op. cit., loc. cit.*), an area which had close ties and frequent communication with Malaya. Sheikh Tahir bin Jalaluddin, as already noted was in fact arrested by the Dutch in 1927, while on a visit to Bukit Tinggi, in Sumatra, and imprisoned for several months on suspicion of 'subversive activities', though nothing appears to have been proved against him.
13. The most outspoken of the reformist journals, *Seruan Azhar* and *Pilehan Timour,* though violently anti-colonial and banned by the Dutch in Indonesia, were allowed free entry into Malaya throughout their life.
14. See, e.g., the Abstract of Minutes of the Selangor State Council [SCM] from 1884 onwards, which give a clear indication of the process that was at work. In June 1884, the Council decided to appoint a State Kathi (religious magistrate) 'to decide disputes involving questions of Mohammedan Law and Custom' (SCM, 14/6/84); the appointment of Assistant Kathis for the Districts was ratified the following year (SCM, 22/10/85); Regulation XI of 1894 provided penalties for the offence of adultery by Muslims (SCM, 17/12/94); the Muslim Marriage and Divorce Registration Enactment was passed in 1900 (Sel. VII, 1900; SCM, 10/5/100); and a 'Mohammedan Laws Enactment' was passed in 1904 providing penalties for a variety of offences against Muslim Law (Sel. III, 1904; SCM 29/2/04). The Federated Malay States Courts Enactment of 1905 (FMS XV, 1905) included provision for religious courts and legislated for their composition and jurisdiction. Although the initiative for some of this activity came from the Residents, this was by no means always the case, and the committees of Council which deliberated on religious matters were formed from the Malay members. See also Perak Council Minutes, 1877–82, printed in R. J. Wilkinson (Gen. Ed.) *Papers on Malay Subjects, History,* Pts III and IV (Kuala Lumpur, 1907 and 1909), *passim.*
15. Hamka's comment on this situation was: "As a result of Malay feudalism, the "Rajas of Islam" supported the ulama of the old school, who preached implicit faith in themselves in order that the peasants should remain loyal to them, therefore to the Rulers therefore to the English!', Hamka, [Haji Abdul Malek bin Abdul Karim Amrullah], *Ajahku: Riwajat Hidup Dr. Abd, Karim Amrullah dan Perdjuangan Kaum Agama* (Djakarta, 1950), p. 60.
16. Abdul Rahim Kajai, an energetic journalist and writer, coined at this time the slogans 'DKK' and 'DKA', '*Darah Keturunan Kling*' ('Indian-descended') and '*Darah Keturunan Arab*' ('Arab-descended'), to express this hostility; they soon became familiar currency.

17. The Malay Residential School, later the Malay College, Kuala Kangsar, was founded in 1905 explicitly to provide English public-school type education to Malay boys 'of gentle birth', with a view to their entry into the ranks of the Government administrative service. Subsequently conditions of entry were liberalised somewhat, but there was still a high percentage of the well-born and well-to-do.
18. J. M. Gullick, 'The Malay Administrator', *Merdeka Outlook* (some copies titled *The New Malayan*), I, No. 1 (May, 1957), p. 80.
19. For a good account of the constitutional and administrative changes of this time, see Rupert Emerson, *Malaysia: A Study in Direct and Indirect Rule* (New York, 1937), pp. 153–93; for a succinct expression of the Malay/Chinese dispute, in the Malay press, see *Al-Ikhwan,* V, No. 6 (January, 1931) which excerpts from both English and vernacular newspapers.
20. Some discussion of this activity can be found in Za'ba [Zainal Abidin bin Ahmad], 'Recent Developments in Malay Literature', *Journal of the Malayan Branch of the Royal Asiatic Society,* XIX, Pt. I (February, 1941), pp. 8–10 and *passim.*
21. Chief among them were Tan Malakka, Sutan Djenain, Alimin, and Djamaluddin Tamin; see Ibrahim Yaacob, *Sekitar Malaya Merdeka* (Djakarta ?, 1957), p. 20.
22. *Op. cit.*, p. 21.
23. A factual account of the history of *KMM* is given briefly in *op. cit.*, pp. 24–37; Cf. also the same author's *Nusa dan Bangsa Melayu* (Djakarta, 1951), pp. 59–63.
24. See above.

Part Two
Contemporary Concerns

Introduction to Part Two

One divide which separates the past from the present in terms of contemporary Islam in Southeast Asia is World War II. The defeat of the colonial powers by the Japanese Imperial Army ushered in a new era in Southeast Asian history. Even though the period of Japanese Occupation was short (1941–45), it quickly became apparent that even with the Allied victory over Japan, post-war Southeast Asia would not return to colonial domination. Independent nation-states were carved out of former colonial territories, and Islam played a leading role in the independence movements of several.

The year 1985 — 40 years after the end of the Japanese occupation and the advent of the modern era of nation-states — seems an appropriate time to assess the large accumulated corpus of scholarly writings on Islam in contemporary Southeast Asia. In terms of geographical distribution the research is not uniform. For example, little research has been published on Muslim minorities in Burma, or the Indochinese states of Vietnam, Laos and Kampuchea. Relatively more research has been undertaken in the six ASEAN countries of Indonesia, Malaysia, Thailand, the Philippines, Singapore and Brunei Darussalam. These six states can, in turn, be divided into the three with Muslim majorities in their populations (Indonesia, Malaysia and Brunei) and the three with Muslim minorities (Thailand, the Philippines and Singapore).

Most research has been conducted on Indonesia and Malaysia. In both countries the role of Islam in the emergent nation-state ideology and political process has been well documented. The importance of Indonesia as a Muslim country quite transcends its regional significance because Indonesia, both in terms of geographical size and population, is the largest Muslim country in the world. Brunei, in contrast, with a population of around 200,000 is one of the smallest, and one of the newest — Brunei only became fully independent on 1 January 1984. Research on Thailand and the Philippines has centred on the fact that the Muslim minority in both these countries is also largely concentrated in the southern provinces and thus forms a majority within certain territories of these states.

If one surveys research undertaken, particularly on Islam in the six ASEAN countries, two important factors emerge. First is the inter-disciplinary character of this research. Contributions have been made by historians, political scientists, legal experts, economists, sociologists, anthropologists, as well as Islamic scholars. Those scholars with a primary interest in Islam — whether indigenous to the region or foreign — form a relatively small group who are rather well-integrated in the sense that they are aware of each other's contributions to the extent that debate is generated, and ideas shared across disciplinary and geographical boundaries.

Second, there seems to be a trend toward an increase in both the quantity and quality of such research, and a gradual expansion of the contributions by indigenous scholars. More research is therefore appearing in indigenous languages and thus research on Islam is beginning to reach a wider local audience. English continues to be the avenue through which indigenous and foreign scholars alike, communicate their work to an international audience. We can expect this trend to continue, and also to pick up momentum. As more qualified students graduate from the expanding university systems of Southeast Asia, and as more avenues for publication open up due to local interest, the corpus of scholarly material on Islam in Southeast Asia will continue to grow.

If one takes stock of current research and surveys published works, there seem to be four main foci of research interest. Each of these research areas have become the focus of one of the four sections of Part Two of this volume.

POST-INDEPENDENCE POLITICS

This was perhaps the major focus — in terms at least of quantity — of the research of the last few decades. As independent countries began to emerge out of the ashes of colonial domination, the role of Islam within the newly emergent nation-states became a crucial factor. This dealt with Islam within the state ideological frameworks, as well as Islam within the newly-formed political party structures. This process has been closely monitored by scholars over the past 40 years, and will probably continue to be a key focus for research in the future.

THE INSTITUTIONALIZATION OF ISLAM

With independence came self-government, and the aspirations of at least certain sections of the Muslim populations for Islam to be reflected in state institutional structures. This of course derives from the recognition that Islam is more than a religion in the narrow sense of the term. Islam provides a blueprint for political, economic, social, legal, educational and administrative organization.

Research in this field is of a more recent and restricted nature, but given the fact that the institutionalization of Islam will be of growing concern in the decades to come — reflected in such issues as Islamic banking, Islamic legal systems and the expansion of national-level Islamic bureaucratic structures — it will certainly gain ground as a focus of scholarly research.

SOCIO-CULTURAL SETTINGS

This area acknowledges the continuing importance — first stressed by colonial commentators — of ethnic and cultural diversity which is now encompassed in the newly emergent nation-states. Weekes (1978) in his world ethnography of major Muslim ethnic groups (those over 100,000 individuals) lists 23 Muslim ethnic groups which are found in Southeast Asia, and many of them have been the subject of exhaustive research. Key foci within this area, in addition to the topic of ethnicity *per se,* have been elements of religious practice including magic, ritual, and *adat,* key religious institutions and religious functionaries, and differences in rural and urban settings. There has also been some debate on the development of conceptual categories appropriate to describing inter- and intra-ethnic variations.

PERSPECTIVES ON MODERNIZATION

It is within the fourth area, perhaps, that scholars writing on Islam in Southeast Asia have anticipated an area of research which Western scholars have, for decades, devalued within their own socio-cultural milieu. This is the relationship between religious value systems and the development process. Such themes as the role of religion in modern life, the role of Islam in a modernizing society and the role of religious values in developing societal norms have been subjects for applied research. In fact, the "secularization theory", which dominated most scholarly work on the relationship between religion and development in the West for decades was never considered a plausible topic in Southeast Asia. There was a recognition that intellectuals had a role to play in the articulation of a value system on which to base, or through which to sieve, competing elements thrown up in the disruptive course of rapid socio-economic development. Because regional political leadership seems committed to a fundamental recognition of religious legitimation (viz., Mahathir's Islamization programme, Suharto's articulation of the Pancasila State), this research area also seems likely to expand in future.

Post-Independence Politics

The Struggle of Islam in Modern Indonesia (1950–1955)

B. J. BOLAND

The first split in the Masjumi [the name being a contraction of *Muslimin Indonesia*] had already taken place in July 1947. A number of members under the leadership of Wondoamiseno and Arudji Kartawinata re-established the old *Partai Serikat Islam Indonesia* (P.S.I.I.) in order to take part in the left-wing cabinet of Amir Sjarifuddin, while the Masjumi went into opposition.[1]

More serious, however, were the tensions between the progressive left wing of the Masjumi consisting of "religious socialists" and its conservative group of *kiyai*s and *ulama*s. These tensions would lead to a break which put its mark on the struggle within the Islamic community in the new Indonesia.

The difficulties began to come into the open about the time of the recognition of Independence and the formation of the federal R.I.S. [United Indonesian Republic]. As has been said, the Masjumi programme of December 1949 breathed a somewhat different spirit.[2] The emphasis had apparently shifted from formulations concerning religious principles to a number of practical questions concerning the transition from the Republic of Indonesia ("Jogja") to the R.I.S., which would include the whole territory of the former Dutch East Indies. Such questions included, for instance, membership of the United Nations, the setting up of a Diplomatic Service, the formation of a Constituent Assembly and preparations for general elections. The programme also contained a number of socio-economic demands concerning, for example, the transformation of the colonial economy into a national economy and the care of victims of the fighting.

With regard to the Constitution of the R.I.S. — a product of the negotiations with the Dutch — it was stipulated (even before this new Constitution took effect!) that its contents would have to be studied, and that a new Constitution would be drafted in agreement with the ideals of the people. It is a fair guess that a number of Islamic leaders genuinely believed that these "ideals of the people" would result in a more or less Islamic state. Furthermore, the position of the various "states" within the R.I.S. would have to be reconsidered. Another contribution of the Republic to the R.I.S. would be compulsory religious instruction in state schools, and the equalization of teachers of religion with other teachers. One point probably also originating from *kiyai* and *ulama* circles, concerned the "protection of the rights of women in marriages to be contracted in accordance with their own religion" (read: separate marriage laws for the Muslims as well as for the Christians and others?).

Apart from these points, the programme of 1949 did not include any formal demand to carry out the teachings of Islam in state and society. Did some Masjumi leaders realize that

Excerpted from B.J. Boland, *The Struggle of Islam in Modern Indonesia* (1982 reprint, Verhandelingen van het Koninklijk Instituut voor Taal-, Land-en Volkenkunde Deel 59 [The Hague: Martinus Nijhoff, 1971]) pp. 45–54, by permission of the author and Koninklijk Instituut voor Taal-, Land- en Volkenkunde, Leiden, The Netherlands.

Indonesia included important non-Muslim areas, so that they could no longer put forward all sorts of formulas and slogans originating from conservative *kiyais* and *ulamas*? In this Assembly at any rate the Party Council (*Madjlis Sjuro*) — with its many religious leaders — was degraded to being merely an advisory body, while the Party Executive (the "politicians") took the lead. A revealing comment from an important Indonesian source runs as follows: "This change meant that the *ulamas* withdrew and no longer developed their activities in the struggle, because every problem was henceforth considered only from a political point of view, without the guidance of religion".[3]

This comment expressed the formal reason for the withdrawal of the Nahdatul Ulama (N.U.) from the Masjumi in April 1952, and the reshaping of the N.U. into a political party. The book on Wahid Hasjim — originating from N.U. circles, like Wahid Hasjim himself — admits that this split was also influenced by injured feelings and tactical considerations.[4] The immediate cause was certainly the struggle for the post of Minister of Religion in the Wilopo cabinet (April 1952). Criticism of Wahid Hasjim's policy led to the choice of the Muhammadijah leader Fakih Usman whereas, N.U. circles continued to claim this post for Wahid Hasjim.[5]

Together with the P.S.I.I. and some smaller parties the N.U. set up a co-ordinating organization, the *Liga Muslimin Indonesia* (League of Indonesian Muslims), which, however, did not amount to much, probably because of the coming elections, which were frequently announced and then postponed, finally to be held at the end of 1955.

Just as the period of the fight for freedom (1945–1950) can be typified as the period of relative unity-in-the-struggle, so the years 1950–1955 can be characterized as the period of strife between the parties. The real issues of this struggle were as much positions, jobs and commercial interests (e.g. import and export permits for friends of the parties in power) as ideological questions. As far as the latter aspect is concerned, the Muslims clashed with the "secular" parties, in particular the Nationalists (P.N.I.) and Communists (P.K.I.). But at the same time a hidden struggle, or at least competition, arose between the Islamic parties themselves. In July 1955 the four most important Islamic parties — Masjumi, N.U., P.S.I.I. and the Sumatran *Pergerakan Tarbijah Islamijah* (Perti, the "Movement for Islamic Education") — apparently agreed to suspend all attacks on each other until the elections.[6] The P.K.I. had made a similar sort of agreement with the P.S.I.I. in April 1955, probably to prevent itself from being regarded as anti-religious.[7] The election campaign is described in detail by Herbert Feith.[8] He concludes that "the Great Debate was between the P.N.I. and the Masjumi" . . . while "the Communist Party did in a way constitute a third main party".

This "Great Debate" has often been simplified into the choice between a state based on the Pantjasila or a state based on Islam. Actually the Islamic parties did not succeed in convincing people that their opinions were not in conflict with the Pantjasila ideals. Both the Masjumi and the N.U. gave the impression that they were aiming at an Islamic State, whatever that might be. From the beginning of 1953 the conflict became sharper, because President Soekarno openly threw himself into the arena. In a speech on January 27th, 1953, at Amuntai (South Kalimantan/Borneo) he said: "The state we want is a national state consisting of all Indonesia. If we establish a state based on Islam, many areas whose population is not Islamic, such as the Moluccas, Bali, Flores, Timor, the Kai Islands and Sulawesi, will secede. And West Irian, which has not yet become part of the territory of Indonesia, will not want to be part of the Republic."[9] For months this speech of Soekarno's was talked about. It may fairly be concluded that the definite break between the Masjumi and President Soekarno dates from this moment. The chief spokesman for the Masjumi in this matter was Isa Anshary.

Looking back, some Muslim informants are prepared to admit that the struggle for a so-called Islamic State was largely an empty, emotional battle of words for the label of the state. This certainly applied to a number of *kiyais* and *ulamas* who were used to thinking and speaking in a religious terminology, but who were too little at home in politics to grasp the problems of modern statecraft. This type of leader played a great role in the N.U., though the Masjumi too included important spokesmen and writers who advocated a realization of Islamic principles in politics.

The difference between the Masjumi and the N.U. developed into a conflict which dominated (and probably still dominates) to a large extent the struggle within the Islamic community in Indonesia. For this reason special attention must be given to these two parties.

With regard to the Masjumi it can be said on the one hand that many of its members and leaders were modern Muslims who took Islam seriously as a religio-political and social entity. The ideals of an Islamic State or the realization of Islamic principles in politics clearly flourished within this circle. And these ideals were quite clearly formulated by some Masjumi adherents. On the other hand, however, many Masjumi leaders were modern intellectuals with a realistic view of politics as "the art of the possible". It can be concluded that under the leadership of the "religious socialists" (as Kahin called them) the Masjumi "was the Islamic party considered best able to deal with the secular problems usually associated with socioeconomic development". In order to prevent a misunderstanding of the word "secular", it must be added "that both modern and traditional Muslims believe that Islamic doctrine provides the basis for all human action".[10]

Viewed sociologically, the adherents of the Masjumi were originally to be found in particular among the urban traders and independent employers and among intellectuals descended from them. Their religion has sometimes been described as an urbanized Islam, or an Islam of areas with "a cosmopolitan, urban and commercial character developed through centuries of cultural contact and trade".[11] It was the same circle of "middle-class people — merchants, tradesmen, landowners, small manufacturers, school-teachers, clerks, etc." — in which reformist ideas coming from Egypt (Muh. ᶜAbduh, Rashīd Riḍā) first met with a response.[12] Therefore many adherents of the reformist Muhammadijah movement would be politically organized in the Masjumi.

According to the Statutes of the Masjumi, applying after August 1952, the party was based on Islam and its goal was "the realization of the doctrine and law of Islam in the life of the individual, in society and in the Republic of Indonesia as a State, directed toward that which pleases God".[13] The concrete meaning of such formulas is, however, difficult to gauge. To what extent are these formulas intentionally vague, and therefore multi-interpretable within the Islamic community itself? In how far were these phrases used in order to win over potential supporters, such as, for instance, sympathizers with *Darul Islam* ideas? On the other hand, in how far did some Masjumi leaders have in mind modern ideas of democracy and social justice — in other words, principles which are not specifically and exclusively Islamic — when they talked of "Islamic principles" as being the basis of the state?

The Nahdatul Ulama (N.U.) was of old the association (later the political party) of teachers of religion and "scribes" (*kiyai*s and *ulama*s who had close connections with the countryside and the religious schools (*pesantrèn*s) established there. Set up in 1926, the N.U. can be considered the successor of the Nahdatul Wathan (= *watan*), the "Awakening of the Fatherland", founded in 1916 in Surabaja by Abdul Wahab (in 1945 a member of the Party Council of the Masjumi) and K. H. M. Mansur. The aim of this older organization was to defend the authority of the four orthodox schools of law (*madhāhib*, sing. *madhhab*) against the reformer Soorkati. It is remarkable that Mansur (who had studied in Cairo) afterwards went over to the Muhammadijah, while Abdul Wahab (who had spent some years in Mecca) played a great part in the N.U.

According to article 2 of the N.U. Statutes of 1926, the aim of this association was: "To uphold one of the schools of law of the four *Imāms* — Imam Muh. bin Idris Asj-Sjafi'i, Imam Malik bin Anas, Imam Abu Hanifah An-Nu'man or Imam Ahmad bin Hanbal — and to do everything which would be beneficial to Islam".[14] Over against the modernists (*ahli bid'ah*), they liked to call themselves the *ahli sunnah wal djama'ah,* that is, the people who keep to the *sunna* (usage) of the Prophet, in community with the one great *umma* or *djamāᶜa,* in short the orthodox (in the sense of "orthoprax"[15]). Beside this official, theological characterization, the N.U. can be typified as being more moderate towards the Javanese way of life and Javanese religious practices than the "puritan" reformers. Partly for this reason the N.U. became a typically Javanese party, whereas many Javanese considered the Masjumi "too fanatical", that is to say, too rigorously Islamic.

When the N.U. entered politics in 1952, article 2 of the Statutes was formulated as follows:

"The Nahdatul Ulama is based on Islam and its aim is:

a. to uphold the law of Islam, in accordance with one of the four schools of law: Sjafi'i, Maliki, Hanafi and Hanbali;

b. to bring about the application of the precepts of Islam in society".[16]

Also according to article 1 of the by-laws of the N.U., membership was dependent on recognition of the authority of one of the four schools of law.[17] This meant that reformists or modernists who advocated a return to the Qur'ān and Tradition in order to study these sources in an independent way as required in modern times (the so-called "new *idjtihād*") could strictly speaking not become members of the N.U., and therefore remained or became members of the Masjumi.

Probably the Masjumi tried to nullify the possible results of this N.U. propaganda for the orthodox schools of law. In December 1954 the Masjumi declared that it respected these schools of law completely, but wanted to be a political party uniting people of various opinions and schools of law.[18] Nevertheless the success of the N.U. in the 1955 elections may well be due to the (tolerant) orthodoxy displayed in its defence of the four schools of law. For many voters the N.U. was emotionally the truly Islamic party, with leaders whom they could trust to maintain Islamic principles unabridged. Were not many of these leaders the teacher (Ind. *guru*) of many voters, who followed their teachers as thankful pupils (Ind. *murid*)? On the other hand, many voters might have considered the Masjumi a dubious party in many ways, as its leaders often used an intellectual language and a modern terminology which made too little contact with the traditional pious.

The resolutions and the action programme of the N.U. drawn up in 1952 give the impression that its religio-political formulations were less clearly Islamic than those of the Masjumi. Probably it was easier simply to quote available formulas, for example, those of the Pantjasila and the 1945 Constitution. For instance, the N.U. wanted "to press the government to intensify instruction in the Pantjasila to be given in an orderly and fundamental way, in particular instruction concerning the (first) pillar of Belief in God, to which clearly too little attention is being paid".[19]

According to the Action Programme of 1952, the N.U. would strive for the application of religious precepts, as interpreted according to one of the four schools of law. The N.U. wanted "a National State based on Islam, a State which guarantees and protects the fundamental rights of man, that is, the freedom to adhere to a sound religion (*agama jang sehat*) and the freedom to have and to express ideas and opinions which do not cause harm to others . . ." The political course of the N.U. was aimed at *As-Shulchu* (Ar. *aṣ-ṣulḥ* = peace, reconciliation, solidarity, settlement, accommodation, compromise; cf. Sura 4:128), as "the normal basis of contact with every kind of group as long as this is not detrimental to Islam and its struggle". Furthermore it was stated — obviously an adoption from the preamble of the 1945 Constitution — that the N.U. desired "a state upholding the rule of law (Ind. *negara hukum*) and based on the sovereignty of the people in the sense of mutual deliberation, led by wise policy executed in the representative bodies of the people . . .".[20]

The N.U. has sometimes been characterized as a typically government-minded party. Because of its extreme readiness to join any cabinet, it was often accused of opportunism. "The NU leaders were 'solidarity makers', wielders of symbols, both traditional and nationalistic."[21] The colour and atmosphere of the N.U. were certainly conservative when it became a political party. It gave the impression of being dominated by *kiyai*s and *ulama*s. According to Herbert Feith, "The Nahdatul Ulama leadership included virtually no one with modern-state-type skills".[22]

It is worth recalling how Wahid Hasjim, in November 1953, explained his choice for the N.U. He admitted that originally the N.U. did not satisfy his desire to join a *radical* party; nor was the N.U. a party with many *intellectuals* — "looking for graduates within the N.U. is like looking for an ice-cream seller at one o'clock in the morning!" — but from the beginning the N.U. somehow turned out to have an appeal for the people. "While in the course of ten years a youth movement of another Islamic group only made gains in 20 places, all close together, that of the Nahdatul Ulama came to cover 60% of the whole territory of Indonesia." Contemplating such results, Wahid Hasjim decided to choose the N.U., because it was clear "that the Nahdatul Ulama offered great possibilities for the uplift of the Islamic community in Indonesia".[23]

The elections — in September 1955 for Parliament and in December 1955 for the Constituent Assembly — resulted in a great disappointment for the Islamic parties. Both in the spoken and written word, Islamic leaders had continuously stressed that Indonesia was a Muslim country. At least 80%, and according to others 90% or even 95%, of the population were considered Muslims since they called themselves Muslims and wanted to be Muslims. Moreover, *ulama* conferences in Java and elsewhere had declared — through *fatwā*-like resolutions — that for a Muslim it was forbidden (*ḥarām*) to vote for a non-Muslim or for a Muslim who did not have the intention of putting Islamic law into practice.[24]

In spite of all this, the four Islamic parties — Masjumi, N.U., P.S.I.I. and Perti — obtained together only 43.5% of the total number of votes at the elections for Parliament. A disinterested observer might conclude that in a country such as Indonesia it is no mean achievement if 43.5% of the population consciously vote for an expressly Islamic party, that is, a party which "has the intention of putting Islamic law into practice". Muslim leaders, however, seem to have taken it for granted that everyone who wanted to be called a Muslim would vote for an Islamic party.

At the elections of September 1955 the nationalist P.N.I. was returned as the biggest party, with 22.3%. The fourth party was the Communist P.K.I. with 16.4%, a success which many had not expected after the Communist set-back in the Madiun revolt of 1948. Numbers 2 and 3 were the Masjumi and the N.U. with respectively 20.9% and 18.4%. The P.S.I.I. turned out to have become a small party (2.9%); the Perti was hardly of any importance (1.3%). The elections of December 1955 "showed great similarity with the result of the parliamentary elections, with an over-all trend for all medium- and small-sized parties to lose votes, and for the four largest parties to gain them".[25] The numbers of votes for Parliament and Constituent Assembly, as well as an analysis of the election campaign and of its results, are given by Feith.[26] Some interesting conclusions are, for example, that the Masjumi, apart from West Java, got the greatest numbers of votes from the islands outside Java, whereas the N.U. turned out to be a typically Javanese party. Further, beside the Socialist Party, not the N.U. but the Masjumi appeared to have many adherents in the army. And as far as Java was concerned, the N.U. in East Java obtained roughly three times as many votes as the Masjumi and in Central Java twice as many, whereas in West Java (with its Sundanese, not Javanese, population) the Masjumi got three times as many adherents as the N.U.

Contrary to the expectation of many inside and outside the Islamic parties, the Masjumi support turned out to be not much bigger than that of the N.U. The explanation heard immediately after the elections was that the Masjumi had acted too much as an urban party of the better educated, with a centralized election campaign, and had certainly under-estimated the personal influence of N.U. leaders (*kiyais* and *ulamas*) in the *kampungs* and the *désas*. That was probably what Wahid Hasjim had understood better! And to explain the success of the N.U., it has to be said that the Indonesian feeling about the relationship between teacher and pupil (*guru-murid*) was perhaps still more important than the general connection of the N.U. with orthodoxy and peasantry that has usually been stressed.[27]

Through this election result it became apparent that the political struggle of Islam in Indonesia for the time being had failed. In the representative bodies the necessary majority had not been obtained, so that it would not be possible to realize certain Islamic principles in state and society by democratic means. Hence the year 1955 may be considered the end of the first period in the modern history of Islam in Indonesia. The attention and energy of Islamic leaders during these first ten years had in particular been directed towards politics. The struggle had been felt as a struggle for a free Indonesia which was hoped would become at least a clearly Muslim country, if not an official Islamic State. In other words, the Islamic *da^cwa* (the call to men to walk in God's ways) had been carried out especially in the field of politics. But from now this *da^cwa* would have to be more or less transferred to other fields, as free Indonesia had turned out to be *not yet* a truly Muslim country — let alone an Islamic State!

NOTES

1. Cf. George McT. Kahin, *Nationalism and Revolution in Indonesia,* Ithaca, N.Y. 1952, pp. 209ff.
2. The text of this programme is to be found in *Sedjarah Hidup K.H.A. Wahid Hasjim dan Karangan Tersiar,* ed. by H. Aboebakar, Djakarta 1957, pp. 365–367.
3. Wahid Hasjim, p. 478.
4. Wahid Hasjim, p. 563.
5. Cf. Herbert Feith, *The Decline of Constitutional Democracy in Indonesia,* Ithaca, N.Y. 1962, pp. 233–237.
6. According to J. W. M Bakker S.J., in *Het Missiewerk,* 1956, 4, p. 228.
7. Feith, *The Decline,* p. 359.
8. Feith, *The Decline,* pp. 353–366.
9. Quoted by Feith, *The Decline,* p. 281.
10. Allan A. Samson, *Islam in Indonesian Politics,* in *Asian Survey,* December 1968, Vol. VIII, no. 12, pp. 1002–1003.
11. Samson, *Islam,* p. 1002.
12. Cf. G.W.J. Drewes in *Unity and Variety in Muslim Civilization,* ed. by Gustave E. Von Grunebaum, Chicago 1955, p. 301.
13. Wahid Hasjim, p. 405.
14. Wahid Hasjim, p. 505.
15. Cf. W.C. Smith, *Islam in Modern History,* Princeton 1957, p. 20: "The word usually translated 'orthodox', *sunnī,* actually means rather 'orthoprax', if we may use the term. A good Muslim is . . . one whose commitment may be expressed in practical terms that conform to an accepted code".
16. Wahid Hasjim, p. 509.
17. Wahid Hasjim, pp. 511–512.
18. Wahid Hasjim, p. 377.
19. Wahid Hasjim, p. 493.
20. Wahid Hasjim, p. 494.
21. Feith, *The Decline,* p. 234.
22. Feith, *The Decline,* p. 234.
23. Wahid Hasjim, pp. 740–741. The successful youth movement referred to is the present-day ANSOR, founded in 1934. "Ansor" is the Indonesian pronunciation of the Arabic *anṣār* (*al-anṣār* were the Medinan helpers of the Prophet when he arrived at Medina in A.D. 622). The basis and aim of this ANSOR are to be found in *Anggaran Dasar dan Anggaran Rumah Tangga Gerakan Pemuda ANSOR,* Djakarta 1964. The history of ANSOR and its predecessors is sketched in Wahid Hasjim, pp. 547–559.
24. Wahid Hasjim, p. 758.
25. Feith, *The Decline,* pp. 449–450.
26. Herbert Feith, *The Indonesian Elections of 1955,* Interim Report Series, Cornell University, 1957.
27. Compare W. F. Wertheim, *Indonesian Society in Transition,* The Hague 1969², p. 345.

27a. See the recent standard work by C. van Dijk, *Rebellion under the Banner of Islam; The Darul Islam in Indonesia,* The Hague 1981, ADDENDA, p. 283 below.

Religion and Politics in Malaya*

K. J. RATNAM

Until the end of World War II (and, with some modifications right up to 1957, when Malaya achieved its independence), British administration in the Malay States was based on a system of indirect rule.[1] A characteristic feature of the agreements between the British Crown and the Malay rulers, on which the system was based, was that the latter had full authority on matters concerning the religion and customs of the Malays. This naturally helped to soften the impact of British rule, and the fabric of Malay society was generally left undisturbed. The non-Malays, not being seriously affected by this arrangement, found little cause for complaint. Further, at least before the war, they were essentially a transient population and did not involve themselves to any great extent in local political affairs. Another important feature of this period was the absence of representative institutions. This helped to keep political competition between the communities to a minimum; consequently, the Malays had fewer anxieties about their political status vis-à-vis the other communities, particularly since the non-Malays had not by this time begun to enjoy the rights of local citizenship.[2]

It is only since the immediate preindependence period that religion has come to assume any serious political significance in Malaya. The factors that gave it this significance are not difficult to understand.

As soon as independence was imminent and the process of drawing up a new constitution was set in motion, a vigorous controversy developed over those features of the constitution that would determine not only the broad framework of government but also the manner in which political and economic power should be shared between the different communities.[3] A viable equilibrium had to be found between the need to provide certain safeguards for the Malay community (which, as the indigenous community, had been accorded a "special position") and the necessity, at the same time, of guaranteeing full citizenship rights to the non-Malays, who, by this time, had become a part of the settled population.

The Malays had two important preoccupations, both arising from their desire to safeguard their political pre-eminence in the country: first, they wanted the constitution to serve as an instrument that would give Malaya certain external features of a Malay state: second, they wanted to secure political and economic advantages that would help them improve their position in relation to the other communities. Islam, being regarded as a chief component of Malay identity, naturally became involved in the efforts to promote the first goal. In the event, there was not much difficulty in having it established as the state religion[4] although it was necessary to assure the sultans that the creation of a state religion would not undermine their own status as

---

Reprinted from R. O. Tilman (ed.), *Man, State and Society in Contemporary Southeast Asia* (New York: Praeger Publishers, 1969) pp. 351–361, by permission of the author and the editor.

heads of the faith in their respective states. It was, however, not the intention of those responsible[5] for establishing Islam as the official religion of the Federation that Malaya should thereby become a fully theocratic state. Care had to be taken not to provoke any new fears among the non-Malays, and one way of doing this was to emphasize the purely symbolic content of the constitutional provision in question, while guaranteeing that other faiths would not in any way be made to suffer disabilities.[6] Thus, it is stated in clause (3) of article 11 of the constitution that every religious group has the right, "(a) to manage its own religious affairs; (b) to establish and maintain institutions for religious or charitable purposes; and (c) to acquire and own property and hold and administer it in accordance with law." As regards educational rights, clause (2) of article 12 states: "Every religious group has the right to establish and maintain institutions for the education of children and provide therein instruction in its own religion, and there shall be no discrimination on the ground only of religion in any law relating to such institutions or in the administration of any such law; but federal law may provide for special financial aid for the establishment or maintenance of Muslim institutions or the instruction in the Muslim religion of persons professing that religion."[7]

Although it was not intended that Malaya should become a theocratic state, it was unavoidable that the mere fact of establishing Islam as the state religion, in combination with the strong undercurrent of communal politics in the country since independence, would generate conflict over the practical consequences that should or should not be implicit in such a provision. Put simply, there has been a continuing agitation from some sections of the Malay community that the purely symbolic value attached to the constitutional provision that elevates Islam to its national status is not satisfactory. Leaders of the Pan-Malayan Islamic Party (PMIP), for example, have been steadfast in maintaining that article 3 of the constitution (which establishes Islam as the state religion) has turned out to be nothing but a dishonest political maneuver by the Alliance, and that if their own party came to power they would see to it that genuine "Islamic principles of administration" were adhered to.[8] On more specific matters, controversy has ranged from matters like the adequacy or otherwise of government financial support for Islamic religious schools and the recognition of qualifications obtained in them to whether alcohol should be served at state functions and whether it is proper for Muslim girls to participate in beauty contests.[9]

Although a decade has now passed since Malaya achieved its independence, the feeling has persisted among the Malays that "Malay nationalism" still has an important role to play in the country. Not surprisingly, this nationalism derives its inspiration from the belief that the Malays are the true "sons of the soil" and that Malaya therefore is, or should rightly be, a Malay country. The goals of Malay nationalism are, therefore, at least partly based on communal antipathy toward the non-Malays, and are, to this extent, a result of the frustrations felt by the Malays in having to accommodate themselves to a multiracial society where they are slightly outnumbered. Despite the attainment of independence, they feel unable to claim full ownership of the country and resent being inhibited in their efforts to promote their own language and culture. An important residue of nationalist aspirations thus continues to be of relevance in determining the political outlook of the Malays.

Given this continuing importance of "nationalist" appeals, one can see why many Malay political leaders (notably those in the PMIP) have attempted to bring about a more effective political unification of their community. It is also not difficult to understand why these attempts should have included references to the religious identity of the Malays, since this clearly constitutes an important source of communal solidarity. But before we go on to evaluate the substance of religious appeals, it may be useful to have a brief account of the UMNO and the PMIP, the two main contenders for Malay support. Such an account will enhance our understanding of the main postures that have been adopted in appealing to the Malay communal vote, and will also give some indication of the role played by religion in Malayan politics.

The United Malays National Organization (UMNO) is both the oldest and the most prominent political party in Malaya. It was founded in 1946 to lead Malay opposition to the Malayan Union scheme. It harnessed the emerging nationalist sentiments of the Malay community[10] and succeeded in unifying that community on a scale that was surprising in the light of prewar experience. As a result of the party's activities (which involved the mobilization of mass protest on a large scale), the Malayan Union scheme was withdrawn and replaced by the more pro-Malay Federation of Malaya Agreement.[11] Thus, during its early years, the UMNO was without question a party that dedicated itself solely to the cause of protecting Malay interests by firmly opposing the claims of the non-Malays to increased political rights. Indeed, so strong were its suspicions of the non-Malay communities that it chose to allow its president, Dato' Onn (who could have claimed considerable personal credit for the popularity of the UMNO and the withdrawal of the Malayan Union Scheme), to resign from the party rather than accept his proposal, made some two years after the Malayan Union Scheme had been withdrawn, to allow non-Malays to become associate members of the UMNO.[12]

However, by 1952, when municipal elections were first held in the country, the UMNO had lost some of its earlier intransigence. It was willing to form a partnership with the Malayan Chinese Association (MCA) in Kuala Lumpur, where the first elections were held, in order to defeat Dato' Onn's newly launched Independence of Malaya Party (IMP). But this was purely a local election alliance, in which the primary concern did not involve the formulation of a common platform: the chief aim of the two parties was to maximize their chances of success by presenting a united front against the IMP and by apportioning seats in such a manner between themselves that UMNO candidates would be put up in Malay wards and MCA candidates in Chinese wards. Success at this and subsequent municipal elections, however, encouraged the two parties to consider their partnership more seriously, and this led in 1953 to the formation of the Alliance Party. Just before the first federal elections in 1955, the Malayan Indian Congress (MIC) was brought into the fold.[13]

With the formation of the Alliance, the UMNO unavoidably had to moderate its earlier outlook to accommodate its non-Malay partners. From being a party whose horizons did not go beyond serving Malay interests, it became a party which, while retaining this characteristic, nevertheless had to satisfy certain non-Malay demands. While it originally saw Malay and non-Malay interests as necessarily in conflict with each other, the UMNO now had to view these admittedly divergent interests as being capable of accommodation within a common framework of intercommunal partnership.

The PMIP is undoubtedly the most extreme communal party in Malaya. Although its name might indicate a preoccupation with religion (and Islam undeniably constitutes an important cornerstone of its appeal), it is a communal party in a more general sense, in that its activities cover all aspects of Malay welfare.[14] It is unwilling to concede that the non-Malays have a legitimate place in the country and sees its goal of protecting Malay rights primarily as an effort to stave off the "non-Malay threat." The party's support is concentrated in the predominantly Malay states in the north and northeast, the most tradition-bound and economically backward areas in the country, where it has been able to put its religious and anti-Chinese themes to profitable use. It also has the advantage of being the UMNO's only serious rival, as a result of which it automatically becomes the chief beneficiary of Malay dissatisfaction. It is, however, worth pointing out that although the PMIP's uncompromising stand on communal issues gives it a basic core of support and enables it to profit from Malay protest, the same stand is also an important weakness in that it virtually rules out all chances of the party's coming to power at the national level. Not only will non-Malay support never be forthcoming,[15] but even Malays in the more advanced states of western and southern Malaya will find many of the party's present attitudes repugnant.

A convenient and effective way of assessing the significance of religion in Malayan politics would be to focus attention on the importance of religious appeals during elections. This could be done by looking at the relevance of religious issues in election campaigns and by evaluating the role played by religious elites in mobilizing party support.[16]

The main debate on religious issues has tended to be between the PMIP and the UMNO. At first glance, this may appear a little curious: If the religious theme is essentially a part of Malay nationalism, how is it that the conflict on religious issues has not been between the PMIP and the strongest non-Malay party, but rather between the two main Malay parties in the country? The explanation lies almost entirely in the fact that the chief contenders for support in the rural areas, where the population is predominantly Malay, have been these two parties. It would certainly be unrealistic to conclude that the non-Malay parties in the country are any less opposed to the PMIP's platform, or that they do not fear any increase in that party's support; at least during elections, they have had to concentrate on winning seats in the areas where their candidates were contesting (that is, in the predominantly non-Malay urban areas), and attacks on Malay religious extremism would not have been too relevant to the issues that separate them from their opponents.[17] Further, non-Malay politicans have also felt reassured that the UMNO, not only because of its electoral rivalry with the PMIP, but also because of its partnership with the MCA and the MIC and its belief that the PMIP's obscurantist policies are not in the best interests of the Malays, will do their work for them. These leaders have perhaps also realized that the UMNO's attacks on the PMIP will be far more effective than attacks by non-Malay parties.[18]

As pointed out earlier, one of the PMIP's chief complaints has been that the adoption of Islam as the state religion has not in itself been sufficient either to elevate the status of that religion adequately or to produce the desired practical consequences. In this connection, the party has bitterly attacked the UMNO, allegedly the custodian of Malay interests, for having overlooked an important element of Malay welfare and identity, namely religion. In a similar vein, the UMNO has also been accused of sacrificing spiritual advancement for material progress of dubious promise, and, in any case, of being unqualified to represent Malay interests because of its collaboration with "infidels." The party's alleged disregard for the tenets of Islam was further conveyed by the PMIP during the 1964 elections in the form of certain specific accusations — for example, that the Alliance government had allowed Chinese to rear pigs near Malay homes, and that the Tungku had danced the twist with girls who had been competitors in a Koran-reading competition during Ramadan, the Muslim fasting month. It was reported that the PMIP had also, in the course of its door-to-door campaign, warned Malay voters that they would be going against the dictates of Islam if they voted for non-Islamic parties or even parties (like the UMNO) which worked in close collaboration with non-Muslims.

The UMNO's response to these tactics and allegations has rested on two main arguments. First, it has maintained that the PMIP's interpretation of the Koran is perverse and likely to damage not only the prospects of peace and harmony in the country but also the future progress of the Malay community. The PMIP's attempts to create a religious basis for communal unification and Malay political protest have frequently been condemned as both unnecessary and irrelevant when the true interests of the Malay community are considered. Several examples have been given of the party's irrational and obscurantist approach. During both the 1959 and 1964 elections, it was alleged that the PMIP had made rural Malay voters swear on the Koran that they would vote for its candidates. Apparently votes were solicited on the grounds that the contest between the PMIP and the UMNO was not merely one between the candidates of the two political parties but between "messengers of the prophet" and "infidels." The party was alleged to have insisted that it was *haram* (forbidden) for Muslims to cooperate politically with non-Muslims, and a great deal of attention was given to its alleged "whisper campaign" in the less sophisticated areas of Kelantan that those who supported political parties that had non-Muslims in them (for example, the Alliance) would be regarded as infidels who, in addition to suffering various other calamities, would have their marriages annulled in heaven. In Kelantan and Trengganu, the PMIP was accused of having made use of talismans, chain letters, and even love charms.[19] It was linked with the circulation of certain allegedly "seditious" pamphlets, which contained quotations from the Koran and Hadith and which purported to serve as "guides for Muslims during elections."

This kind of politics, the UMNO has argued, is not merely obscurantist — it is also likely to endanger the future of democracy and communal harmony in the country by giving the Malay community the false impression that it is at odds with its political environment. This view was expressed with unmistakable firmness by the Prime Minister, who, in the course of an election rally in 1964, observed:

> I have warned the PMIP before to cease inciting the people [to fight] each other. This time I will take stronger action. If they dare defy me, go ahead. I'll fight back. I will arrest those who want to destroy the unity of our people. Democracy should be pursued through persuasion. That is the essence of democracy. We cannot force people into accepting our point of view, leave alone incite them to wage a holy war against those who are not members of the PMIP.[20]

At another rally he had this to say:

> [The PMIP's] policy is particularly dangerous because there are almost the same number of Malays and Chinese living in Malaysia. No party should ever play the game of religious and communal politics. If ever the people accept the policy and propaganda put out by the PMIP and other Opposition parties, then there will be trouble and chaos in the country. Malaysia might even end up worse than Cyprus.[21]

The second argument used by the UMNO in countering the PMIP's allegations has been that it is at least as concerned as its rival in promoting the interests of Islam, and that, unlike its rival, it has solid achievements to back its claims. In this connection, great political capital has been made of the vast sums of money that have been spent by the federal and (Alliance-controlled) state governments in building mosques and small prayer houses. The PMIP, in contrast, has been said to be unable to boast of any similar achievements in Kelantan, where it has been in power since 1959; it had come to power there by posing as the champion of Malay rights and Islamic principles of administration but had promoted neither during its period in office. In its campaign pamphlets issued during the 1964 elections, the Alliance also claimed credit for promoting such things as Koran-reading competitions (which are held, not infrequently, at state, national, and international levels), religious education, and pilgrimages to Mecca.

Turning now to the role played by religious elites in political campaigns, the first thing to note is that the local (that is, sub-state) rather than the national elites constitute the most relevant groups. High-ranking religious officials seldom pronounce on political issues and do not generally become involved in partisan activity. At the village level, however, local religious elites are often active in promoting the interests of the party of their choice. Secondly, the activities and influence of these elites should, ideally, be studied in relation to those of other local elites (particularly the local administrative elites, like the *penggawa*s, *penghulu*s, and *ketua*s *kampong)*, because they operate in a common milieu and either compete with or complement each other's activities. It is, however, well beyond the scope of this paper to attempt a general discussion of all categories of local opinion leaders.

The political influence of religious elites is by no means widespread throughout Malaya, but, by and large, is confined to those areas where the competition between the UMNO and the PMIP is keenest. In areas where the PMIP is weak, or where the population is unresponsive to religious appeals, these elites are naturally reluctant to embark on serious political activity; such activity would be unrewarding. Also, in the absence of any PMIP threat, there would not be the same incentives for the UMNO to conduct its campaign through persons whose main value would lie in their ability to counteract the PMIP's appeal. It is, therefore, not surprising that the rivalry for the support of religious leaders has been keenest in Kelantan and Trengganu (and, to a lesser extent, also in Kedah and Perlis); these states provide fertile ground for religious propaganda, and they have witnessed a close rivalry between the UMNO and the PMIP.

Among local religious elites, four groups may be mentioned: religious schoolteachers, imams, *mubhalirs,* and gurus. In some ways, those in the first group have only an indirect political influence; they do not campaign openly during elections,[22] but, because of their contact with parents, are able to exert a certain degree of influence. There are, however, other ways in which they have made their political importance felt. Together with Malay schoolteachers, they have constituted an important pressure group that has endeavored to goad the government into adopting more "positive" measures in promoting Malay as the national language. The influence of this pressure group has, needless to say, been enhanced by the fact that, between them, its two component units represent the areas of Malay culture (namely, language and religion) that are politically the most sensitive and therefore receive considerable attention from those who want to promote a more explicitly Malay identity for the state, and who wish to confirm Malay preeminence in the country's political life.

The next two groups, the imams and the *mubhalirs,* are part-time officials of the State Religious Councils and are, to that extent, semigovernment servants. As such, they are precluded from active political participation, particularly when their state government is not controlled by the party they wish to support. But the religious significance of their duties, and the fact that they come into frequent contact with the people, gives them a fair amount of political influence, particularly in the more traditional rural areas. In Kelantan, where they were active during the 1964 elections, both the UMNO and the PMIP were agreed that the support of these groups was an important factor in deciding the outcome of the elections.

The final group, the gurus,[23] are in many ways the most influential. They are private religious teachers who enjoy informal recognition as the main spiritual guides of the communities in which they operate. While the other groups mentioned are civil servants of one kind or another (and, to that extent, perform duties that are at least partly of a routine kind), the relationship between the gurus and the communities they serve is highly personalized. They have closer and more intimate contact with the people than the other groups have, and, being the main stalwarts of the traditional society, naturally have an easy rapport with the rural population in the less developed states, notably in Kelantan. They are regarded with some reverence as men with a genuine spiritual calling who have dedicated their whole lives to unfolding the true meaning of Islam. Not being government servants, they also have the advantage of being more free than the other groups to participate actively in political campaigns.[24]

In Kelantan, the PMIP clearly enjoys the active support of the majority of the religious elites discussed above and it owes its success to this fact. In the other states, the situation is less one-sided; in fact, the UMNO often has a slight edge, but this is not of equal significance, because in these states the religious elites are both less active and politically less influential. The difference, as indicated earlier, can be best explained in terms of the more traditional nature of Kelantan society, which has helped to sustain the influence of traditional opinion leaders. Because of the continuing importance of traditional values and relationships, there are also more religious leaders in Kelantan than in the other states. Although the PMIP, in its efforts not to be outdone by the Alliance, created an elaborate election organization in 1964 based on a functional decentralization of responsibility right down to the village level, it was apparent that this was aimed at bolstering the morale of rank-and-file members, by giving them individual duties to perform, and partly at preventing the Alliance from having an advantage by being the only well-organized party in the rural areas. It was evident during the campaign that the PMIP relied less on its formal organization than on individuals outside it (namely the religious leaders) for the success of its campaign.

In conclusion, it is worth emphasizing that religion does not derive its political significance in Malaya from the conflict between different faiths. The issue must be viewed primarily as a component of the more general rivalry between the Malays and the non-Malays. Religious appeals for political ends are confined to the Malay community and are, in the main, directed at unifying that community by emphasizing its separate identity and interests. Religious and anti-non-Malay slogans almost always go hand in hand and are aimed at persuading the Malays to be more vigilant in safeguarding their pre-eminence in the country's political life and, as a corollary, to be less compromising in their relations with the other communities.

But one cannot completely dismiss economic underdevelopment and the continuing pulls of traditionalism as being irrelevant. As shown in the preceding pages, these factors at least influence the forms and the content of political persuasion, in that religious appeals and the use of religious elites in political campaigns are more rewarding in the less-developed and tradition-bound areas of the country. However, the most crucial factors that explain the political importance of religion are to be found not in the traditional versus modern but rather in the Malay versus non-Malay continuum. The conflict between traditional and modernizing interests might have become the dominant factor only if the Malays had constituted the entire population (or at least a very substantial part of it), or if the communal differences between the Malays and the non-Malays had failed to assume much political significance. In actual fact, however, intra-communal differences have tended to be very overshadowed by the more serious conflicts *between* the Malays and non-Malays.

NOTES

* This paper was presented in slightly different form at the Twenty-seventh International Congress of Orientalists (Ann Arbor, Michigan, August, 1967) and is published here by permission of the author. ["Malaya" is a shorthand term employed here to mean the eleven peninsular states of western Malaysia.]

1. The Straits Settlements of Singapore, Malacca, and Penang were administered as a colony. The Malay states were divided into two categories: the Federated Malay States (comprising Perak, Pahang, Selangor, and Negri Sembilan) and the Unfederated Malay States (made up of Kedah, Kelantan, Trengganu, Perlis, and Johore). As implied by the names given to the two categories, British rule was more direct in the former group of states.

   There was a brief period after the war when indirect rule was abandoned: between 1945 and 1946, when there was a military administration, and between 1946 and 1948, when the ill-fated Malayan Union proposals were in operation. (The Malayan Union was abandoned mainly as a result of Malay opposition. Although this opposition was aimed primarily at the drastic liberalization of citizenship rules that allowed vast numbers of non-Malays to become citizens, an important factor was the severe reduction in the prerogatives of the sultans, including their control over religious affairs.)
2. In the Straits Settlement, however, no political distinction was made between Malays and non-Malays, since all were equally regarded as British subjects.
3. The Malays constitute just under 50 per cent of the total population of Malaya, which stands at about 8 million. The Chinese constitute about 38 per cent and the Indians about 12 per cent. Although no single community forms a clear majority, it is important that the indigenous population is slightly outnumbered by the non-indigenous. The Muslim population (which includes all Malays), however, slightly outnumbers the non-Muslim.
4. The Malay character of the state was also promoted by certain other provisions, such as the preservation of the sultanates, the creation of the post of Yang di-Pertuan Agong (the Supreme Head of the Federation), and the acceptance of Malay as the national language.
5. In effect, the Alliance, headed by the United Malays National Organization (UMNO), on whose recommendations the entire constitution was based.
6. The major festivals of all main religious groups, for example, are declared public holidays.
7. There is one exclusive safeguard that Muslims enjoy. This is contained in clause (4) of article 11, which states: "State law may control or restrict the propagation of any religious doctrine or belief among persons professing the Muslim religion."
8. Although this assertion is frequently made, the PMIP has never been explicit about the actual content of "Islamic principles of administration."
9. In late 1966, there were protests from certain Malay organizations about the impropriety of Malay girls taking part in beauty contests. The Penang Malay Youth Patriotic Organization, for example, set up a special "Banning of Beauty Contests" Committee and urged the Islamic religious authorities in the country to take action on this matter, stating: "We are protesting against participation in such contests by Muslim girls purely on religious grounds. . . . It seems to us that Muslim girls in this country are beginning to get enthusiastic over beauty contests. Some of them have even gone beyond the religious limits and trespassed Islamic and cultural decorum." (*The Straits Times*, November 3, 1966.) But these

protests failed to find receptive ears in the highest circles. The Prime Minister failed to see anything in Islam that forbade the participation of Muslim girls in these contests (*The Straits Times,* December 20, 1966), while the Minister for Education (who is also the Secretary-General of the UMNO), commenting on criticisms that had been leveled against a Malay school teacher who had participated in a beauty contest, observed: "Anyone who is pretty and has the potentialities is entitled to take part in a beauty contest. . . . As for her posing in a bikini, all I can say is that she was exercising her constitutional rights." (*The Straits Times,* October 17, 1966).

10. These sentiments, although directed at the colonial government, were provoked to a large extent by fears of non-Malay domination.
11. Among other things, the Federation of Malaya Agreement restored the sultans of their prewar status, imposed more stringent regulations regarding the eligibility of non-Malays to become citizens, and gave official recognition to the "special position" of the Malays, which entitled them to certain privileges in recruitment to the Civil Service, the awarding of scholarships, and the issuing of business licenses.
12. After his resignation from the UMNO. Dato' Onn founded the noncommunal Independence of Malaya Party (IMP). When this party failed, he reverted (but without much success) to his original role as a champion of Malay rights through Party Negara, another party which he helped to found.
13. The Alliance Party is thus made up of three component units, and individual membership is confined to these units. It exists only at different coordinating levels (constituency, state, and national) and comprises delegates from the member bodies. Although the party represents intercommunal ideals and contests elections as a single unit, its strength lies basically in the support given directly to its constituent organizations.
14. The fact that the Muslim population is almost entirely made up of Malays has no doubt made it easier for the PMIP to play this dual role.
15. In 1964, the non-Malays constituted about 45 per cent of the total electorate.
16. For a detailed account of these aspects of the campaign in 1964, see K. J. Ratnam and R. S. Milne, *The Malayan Parliamentary Election of 1964* (Kuala Lumpur: University of Malaya Press, 1967).
17. It should be made clear that the effective contest in most urban constituencies tends to be between candidates from different non-Malay parties.
18. Since there is no risk of non-Malays being attracted by Malay communal propaganda, it is only the Malay voters who have to be persuaded not to endorse the PMIP's extremist platform. Given the importance of communal politics in Malaya, non-Malay attacks on Malay communalism, particularly in Malay-dominated areas, may backfire by producing greater communal solidarity among the Malays. Malay leaders are therefore more likely than others to receive a sympathetic hearing when they campaign against the PMIP's extremism.
19. The talismans apparently urged Muslims in the country to wage a holy war against non-Muslims. The love charms were allegedly sold to unsuspecting kampong women with the warning that they would not produce the desired consequences in the case of those who voted for the Alliance!
20. Quoted in Ratnam and Milne, *op. cit.,* p. 122. A few PMIP men were, in fact, arrested in 1964, under a law that prohibits incitement to communal hatred.
21. *The Straits Times,* March 31, 1964, quoted in Ratnam and Milne, *op. cit.,* p. 124.
22. The reference here is only to government religious schoolteachers. Private religious schoolteachers have been known to campaign vigorously, usually on behalf of the PMIP.
23. Referred to as *tok* gurus in Kelantan and *tuan* gurus in the other states.
24. In fact, it was the gurus who were alleged to have been responsible for distributing the talismans referred to earlier. They were also believed to be the ones who most actively encouraged, and played on, religious superstitions.

The Military and Islam in Sukarno's Indonesia

HOWARD M. FEDERSPIEL

During the period of Guided Democracy (1957 to 1965) the Indonesian armed forces — and the army in particular — served as an important instrument in the resolution of several outstanding national problems. In its military role it checked a major rebellion in the Outer Islands in 1958 and ultimately, in 1962, brought the insurgents back to recognition of the central government. It was successful in ending the *Darul Islam* rebellions that had been active in several areas of the countryside, in one case for over a decade, by energetic counter-insurgency campaigns. It aided the resolution of the West Irian problem in Indonesia's favor in 1962, by mounting preparations for an invasion of the territory and by dispatching numerous pre-invasion commando attacks to signal Indonesian intentions of taking the territory by force if necessary. In the anti-Malaysia campaign from 1963 to 1965 its regular units guarded the Borneo frontier and its special units gave training to infiltrators and saboteurs who were dispatched to disrupt Malaysia. In the non-military realm the Indonesian army provided officers to operate confiscated Dutch businesses when these were nationalized in 1957. Finally, it operated the State of Emergency Administration from 1957 to 1963 while martial law was in force throughout the nation and maintained a security watch-dog role thereafter.

Throughout the period the army was politically important and regarded as such by the other political participants, including President Sukarno. The army command structure, which paralleled civilian government organization throughout the country, was to all intents the actual government while martial law was in effect. Even after martial law's repeal, the territorial army commands frequently retained controls on political life in many areas, in some cases dominating, and in other cases interfering in, the running of government and the political affairs of the area. Service officers, particularly those of the army, were appointed to administrative positions throughout the governmental hierarchy, thereby giving the military another means of influencing the administration and the political system. Military officers were recognized as a functional group and given 43 seats in the appointed Consultative Assembly the same year. In each cabinet they controlled the portfolios of the defense ministries and several other ministries as well. Finally, in the so-called policy-making bodies — actually advisory — such as the Supreme Advisory Council and the National Council, army membership and influence was significant.

Throughout the period two principal underlying problems confronted the Indonesian army: internal factionalism that seriously affected its political and military effectiveness, and the fear of governmental failure to build a stable Indonesian state. The two

Reprinted in abridged form from *Pacific Affairs* Vol. 46 No. 3, (1973), 407–420, by permission of the author and the University of British Columbia, Vancouver, Canada.

problems were related in that basic unity was lacking on several key matters, particularly the relationship between Java and the Outer Islands, the ideological format of the state philosophy and the nature of economic and social development that the government was to pursue. The failure to reach decisions on these matters during the Constitutional Period (1950 to 1957) threatened the political stability of the nation, and these unresolved issues were reflected within the military.

The army services regarded President Sukarno as essential to the operation and advancement of the Indonesian state and to the unity of the armed services. They found in him a symbol of unity for a divided nation, an arbiter among various factions and a national spokesman with vision to create a strong and prosperous Indonesia. The manner in which Sukarno took control — in virtual partnership with the army (which was eroded only after 1962) — gave the armed services a strong identification with him. This identification was enhanced by the procurement of new military equipment from the Soviet-bloc nations even when Sukarno's military policies became less acceptable to many army officers in the 1963–1965 period. Within the army, with its factionalism, it was essential that there be someone in authority to whom all factions could pay allegiance and Sukarno served that purpose until October 1, 1965 when he allowed several army generals to be massacred.

The army leaders and Sukarno agreed that a common national ideology was needed to form a national consensus, but they differed substantially on the content of that ideology. At the beginning of the period there was not much disagreement, for both were reacting to the ideological chaos of the Constitutional Period and each wanted a concept that nearly all Indonesians could accept as a basic philosophic statement. That concept was contained in the *Manipol/Usdek* declarations in 1959 which called for a return to the values of 1945 when Indonesia embarked on the final stage of its efforts to win independence from the Dutch. By midpoint in the period it was clear there was a pronounced difference in attitudes, however, for by then Sukarno clearly favored a Marxist, ultra-nationalist line with all elements combining to form a "revolutionary coalition," while the military in general wanted a nationalist, yet non-communist direction where its identity was preserved. But throughout the period Indonesian military leaders followed Sukarno's ideological lead and even re-cast their own ideological pronouncements to conform in tone and form to Sukarno's utterances as the latter moved steadily toward ultra-nationalism. The slaughter of six leading generals on October 1, 1965 by Communist groups, however, so shocked the army leadership that the latter group recovered rapidly and acted to preserve its own security and to moderate the national ideology and the policies of government.

The Army leaders were forced to take a policy position on religion — and more specifically on Islam (statistically the major religion of Indonesia) — for it was part of the problem that hindered unity in the nation and in the army. Doctrinaire Islam, which sought the reordering of Indonesian values to correspond with those of the Islamic Middle East, had become the ideological backbone of an entire sector of Indonesian political movements in the early part of the twentieth century.[1] The insistence of many proponents of this group — but by no means all of them — that their particular doctrinal beliefs and ritual should become the principal underpinning of the Indonesian state was a point of major controversy before and after Indonesian independence was won in 1949. Large numbers of Indonesians, most only superficially Muslim, opposed the changes in indigenous values that the doctrinaire Muslims advocated. The issue was finally debated in the Constitutional Period on whether Indonesia should become an "Islamic State" — which the doctrinaire Muslims favored — or remain a secular state with freedom of religion guaranteed. The political activity that developed around this issue produced a polarization of attitudes preventing a resolution of the problem. The issue was further complicated by the defection of several groups from the Republic who established insurrectionary movements in the name of Islam, and finally by the Outer Islands rebellions in 1957 and 1958 with which the *Masjumi Party,* one of the standard-bearers of doctrinaire Islam, became associated.

Given its factionalism, some of which centered on different attitudes concerning Islam, the military leadership had generally favored a secular state during the Constitutional Period. Almost without exception, military officers gave their support to Sukarno's *Pantja Sila* doctrine, the leading expression of secularism in that period, which recognized five major points (belief in God, nationalism, democracy, humanitarianism and social justice) of national aspiration and had been a slogan of the Revolution. The army mission was based on a concept of territorial warfare evolved during the Revolutionary Period (1945 to 1949) where religion was regarded merely as a factor contributing to the morale and morals of individual fighting men.[2] A letter signed by the Armed Forces Chief of Staff, and accompanying a 1962 handbook for religious service issued by the armed services, spoke directly to this point. It noted that the role of religion in the armed forces was based on references to religion in the 1945 Constitution, on the *Pantja Sila,* on the army code of honor (*Sapta Marga*) and finally on the importance of religious belief in the morale and moral efforts of the army members.[3]

There seems to have been no real agreement regarding the extent to which Islam was to become a promoter of morale and moral values among military personnel. One group, led by General Abdul Haris Nasution, the Armed Forces Chief of Staff and Minister of Defense, wanted propagation of doctrinaire Muslim religious beliefs and ritual among armed services personnel as a means of assuring a common ethical and moral guide and standard of behavior. This viewpoint was expressed by Major General Sungkono in a 1962 speech when he stated that the army leadership wanted a fighting force that was highly motivated, not knowing the meaning of surrender, without, however, departing from the limits of decency and high ethical standards. Religion, he noted, was the means of assuring that propriety by the Indonesian fighting forces.[4]

The opposing group was not a formal faction, but rather a grouping of officers who expressed loyalty to various non-Islamic value systems. Armed service officers came from a wide variety of Indonesian areas and tended to reflect the values of the subcultures in those areas. In some of those subcultures, particularly that of the dominant and highly influential Javanese, doctrinaire Islam was not an important motivating factor, but rather a cause of irritation because doctrinaire Muslims there sought to change the sub-culture to accord with their own Islamic value system. Consequently, while General Nasution's attitudes and pronouncements regarding the importance of Islam usually were not challenged, neither did they always receive the attention he wanted, particularly among some of the senior territorial commanders who operated their commands relatively independent of central army authority.

The Nasution policy for spiritual development of the armed forces largely used the instruments already available — the chaplain service (*imam militer*). spiritual commemoration day and the issuance of religious handbooks — but new emphasis was given to them. From 1957 to 1965 the army chaplain service was under the leadership of Colonel Muchlas Rowi, a protégé of Nasution, who made a conscious effort to increase the scope of doctrinaire Islamic values in the army. In an article written in 1962 he expressed his philosophy that the *imam militer* were to be competent in matters of religious ritual and doctrine and knowledgeable about life in general. Their task was to relate their religious message to the lives of armed service personnel and to society.[5] This viewpoint was confirmed by the chaplains when they met at Tjipajung in June 1962 and adapted the motto *"taqwa, wira, karja."*

> The basis of life for an *imam* must be fear of God (*taqwa*), the establishment of a firm relationship with God, and a firm belief to defend the efforts of life. Since *imams* cannot be excluded from participating in all activities of life, their actions must originate in this proper spirit of leadership. *Wira* represents that spirit of leadership. Clearly duty (*wira*) means that *imams* must be able to lead in the armed forces, but as religious persons they are necessarily faced with particular problems of upholding virtue, and values of the religious community. *Karja* has the meaning of working for the establishment of the worship of God and to perform service for society.[6]

Since, presumably, this outlook was more activist than those of Rowi's predecessors, additional staff was required to execute the new policy. Consequently in 1961 and 1962 three groups of *imam militer* were brought into the army to supplement those already in the service. To assure that they received proper indoctrination they underwent a special course at the Al-Azhar Mosque in Kebajoran, an institution whose leadership was in accord with the religious and political views of General Nasution.

A major concern of the chaplain service was the preparation and distribution of religious materials to meet the spiritual concerns of members of the armed forces. In 1961 the Mandala Command, as part of its preparations for the invasion of West Irian, issued a small handbook on Muslim prayer and worship in times of combat.[7] In 1962 the Army Spiritual Center issued a 247 page handbook containing the religious obligations recognized in doctrinaire Islam,[8] and in 1964 a pamphlet was issued by the same office outlining the purpose of the feast day of *Hari Raya* (*Id al-fitr*) and the religious obligations necessary at that time.[9] All these publications were specially directed to members of the armed forces and their families. Significantly all of these works dealt almost exclusively with matters of ritual worship and religious belief in the narrow sense. Political obligations and even national policies were scrupulously avoided. Such a stance was not unusual among doctrinaire Muslim groups outside the military, for they often issued such technical studies, also without reference to political matters, but also wrote other works which expressed political and social viewpoints. Certainly some *imam militer* did issue pronouncements containing social and political commentary, but these were always made outside the context of the military and aimed at exhortation of civilian Muslim groups.[10] Within the military, then, Rowi's activist approach seems to have been limited to matters of worship. As a secular institution the military leadership apparently saw no need to explain or justify its viewpoint or policy in religious terms — and here General Nasution was in agreement — but preferred to state its position through the pronouncements of its leaders speaking in nationalistic terms.

One possibility for increasing the Islamic content of army life did not materialize, if, in fact, it was ever meant to. The Army Staff and Command College (SESKOAD) at Bandung may have originally been a target since Major-General Soedirman, a generally respected theoretician on military affairs, and a devout doctrinaire Muslim believing that Islam could play an important role in society and in the military, was made commandant in 1957 and held the position throughout the period of Guided Democracy. Statements made elsewhere[11] indicate he believed that doctrinaire Islamic values should be part of army life, but there is not evidence to indicate that he attempted to incorporate them into Army doctrine, which was the work of SESKOAD. The SESKOAD publication, *Karja Wira Jati*, which reported on the major studies made at the school, carried several articles during that period which took a rather critical position regarding Islam's importance to the army. One such study written by Brigadier-General Sudjono in 1964 noted that religion had been a divisive factor throughout Indonesian history and had often prevented national unity. He concluded that only by common acceptance by all Indonesians of Sukarnoist doctrine could religion, and particularly Islam, be released from that politically divisive role and contribute properly to Indonesian culture.[12] In another study, Lieutenant-Colonel Herlan Prawiradiwirja discussed the spiritual input into the armed services as consisting of *Pantja Sila* and other Sukarnoist doctrines, without any mention of Islam whatsoever.[13] Finally, when the official army mission was modified in 1964 and again in 1965, there was no stress in either document on the importance of Islam, even though General Soedirman participated in the deliberations. He appears to have drawn a distinction between his views as military theoretician and his views as a proponent of Islam, the true mark of a secularist. Such an attitude was consistent with those of General Nasution who seldom said much about Islam when he spoke as Chief of Staff or Minister of Defense or when addressing the general public. It was only when addressing a Muslim audience that he propounded specific views on Islam.

Nasution's interest in making Islamic

values important to personnel in the armed services does not seem to have made any great impact on the Indonesian armed forces in the 1960's. If doctrinaire Islam was to be successful it had to be a proselytizing religion, given the non-Islamic value-systems of large numbers of army personnel. Most commanders would not encourage an energetic Islam for obvious reasons of military solidarity and effectiveness. Furthermore, there were other ideologies influencing the armed forces during this period that competed with Islam. Sukarnoism, of course, had official sanctions and had to be given some attention by all responsible military officials, including the chaplains. Communism, as well, was making its impact felt on the armed forces during this period and was winning the loyalty of particular officers and enlisted personnel; for example, in units from areas where Communism was influential, such as central Java. Such counter-ideology, of course, impeded the success of the chaplains in strengthening doctrinaire Islam within the armed forces.

There seems to have been a general consensus among senior army officers favouring encouragement of those groups and activities in broader Indonesian society that had some prospect of accomplishing political and social goals complementing those of the Indonesian army. Both the army headquarters in Djakarta and the various territorial commands acted as decision-makers with regard to military-sponsored drama groups, a labor organization, a woman's association, a veteran's organization and a para-military youth organization. Army overtures to Muslims then, must be seen in this perspective, i.e., as only one of several activities sponsored and coordinated by the army.

The general aim of the military involvement with Muslims centered about General Nasution's belief, shared by some senior officers, that a strong Muslim influence could serve as an ideological and political counter weight to ultra-nationalist and Communist political efforts. To achieve these goals the army concentrated on the development of a religious propaganda center near the capital, an attempt to create a semi-official coordinating agency of all Indonesian Muslims, and sponsorship and encouragement of activities where Muslim unity efforts could take place.

General Nasution's aspirations in organizing Muslims in Indonesian society as a political ally of the army were centered principally around activities at the Al-Azhar Agung Mosque in Kebajoran, a suburb of Djakarta. The theme here was Muslim unity, a point emphasized by Major-General Soedirman in a 1962 speech there. He lamented that Muslims had not achieved unity in Indonesia, and stated that he could find few real obstacles in the religion itself preventing them from doing so. He reviewed the cause of schisms among Indonesian Muslims and found that insistence on interpretation of doctrine was a principal cause of disunity and really constituted a disservice to Indonesian Muslims. He concluded by stating that Muslim unity was a necessity for Indonesian Muslims, a point in line with Nasution's views that the Muslims could be the army's ally in Indonesian politics.[14]

The project at Kebajoran centered originally on the personality of Dr. Hamka[15] and his ideas concerning the development of Islamic culture in Indonesia. Deeply impressed by the Islamic modernist thinkers of Egypt (particularly Muhammad Abduh, Rashid Rida and Lufti al-Manfaluti), he attempted to imitate their efforts and reinterpret Muslim scriptures in the light of conditions in modern Indonesia. Even after Dr. Hamka was imprisoned by Sukarno in 1964 his influence remained; his *Tafsir al-Qur'an,* a general commentary on ethics and morals in life, continued to be a regular feature in *Gema Islam.*

At Kebajoran attention was given to the development of drama and art with Islamic themes, even though there was a common belief among Indonesian Muslims that drama was not really a proper pursuit sanctioned by Islamic law. Muslim concern with drama and other art forms was general among Indonesian Muslim societies at this time, as witnessed by Muslim drama activity in Surabaya and Jogjakarta as well as in Djakarta. Significantly the themes of these dramas were limited to historical incidents relevant to Islam, such as events in the life of the Prophet but never on contemporary themes of Indonesia. The army was generally in favor of drama as a vehicle for political and social indoctrination to counter Communist-promoted drama which presented values contrary to those of the army. The army consequently promoted a variety of non-Communist drama, not merely that of Muslim groups. The Brawidjaja Territorial Command, for example, sponsored *ludruk* theatre troupes in East Java.[16] At Kebajoran the army's concern was particularly apparent because Junan Helmi Nasution, an army chaplain, was a moving force in this endeavor and personally wrote many of the dramas presented.

A periodical titled *Gema Islam,* which had several army officers of Nasution's group on its governing and editorial boards, began functioning at Kebajoran in 1962. *Gema Islam* outlined the activities taking place at Al-Azhar Mosque, reviewed Muslim activities in Indonesia in general and promoted writing by Muslims in good standing in Indonesian society. The writing centered generally on progress reports in areas of Muslim concern, such as education, mosque activity, the pilgrimage and missionary activities. There was a constant effort to include news from all parts of Indonesia, apparently as a means of promoting a national consciousness among readers, rather than merely the regional emphasis apparent previously in similar periodicals.

The armed forces officers connected with this enterprise at Kebajoran wrote occasionally, always on Islamic subjects — drama, morals and ritual — but almost never on army policy. Bahrum Rangkuti, a naval officer, wrote articles in *Gema Islam* on the development of Islamic culture in Indonesia. In addition to his dramatic efforts, Junan Helmy Nasution wrote articles in a number of journals on Islamic history. Beginning in 1965 with the publication of *Angkatan Bersendjata,* the official daily organ of the armed forces, Lieutenant Colonel Esa Edris and Junan Helmy Nasution, alternated in contributing a weekly column titled *"Chotbah Djumaat"* (Friday Sermon) which sometimes dealt with the role of Islam in an Indonesian nation. Esa Edris usually wrote on the importance of traditional Muslim ethics, morals and values as a guide to Indonesian society, while Junan Helmy Nasution dealt with the importance of Muslim adherence to national causes.

Another army effort at Kebajoran was aimed at making contact with Muslim youth and influencing them along ideological lines acceptable to the army leadership. Lieutenant-Colonel Esa Edris was in charge of this liaison role with Muslim youth and centered his activities on promoting traditional Muslim values — the importance of loyalty to family, religious precepts and nation. This life-style was promoted to prevent what Esa Edris and many doctrinaire Muslims believed were the degenerate styles of life introduced from the West and by the Communists.[17] There is little evidence to show that Esa Edris instigated Muslim youth activity in the 1963–1965 period when they engaged in polemics with Communist groups and undertook general activity intended to promote a non-Communist political force and undermine Communist strength. But army spokesmen did not disapprove these activities and, significantly, early in 1965 when Sukarno moved against one such Muslim youth organization, the *Himpunan Muslimin Indonesia* (HMI), the HMI turned to General Nasution for protection. He was successful in preventing proscription of several local branches although Sukarno insisted that the national organization be suppressed for anti-Sukarnoist activities. It would thus seem that such groups were encouraged by the military but that the links were not firm and support was not clear.[18]

Aside from Kebajoran the Nasution group was involved in an attempt in 1962 to establish an Islamic Council (*Madjlis Ulama*)[19] as a coordinating council of all Muslim groups in Indonesia in good standing with the government. While efforts were made to recruit leading Muslims from all factions, the move was visibly connected with the military. Its first meetings were held at the offices of the chief chaplain for the Greater Djakarta Military District and Colonel Muchlas Rowi, a Nasution aide, was among its organizers. While there was some initial response in organizing other *Madjlis Ulama* throughout the country, enthusiasm quickly waned and after 1963 it was almost entirely forgotten, except for occasional references in the speeches of certain Muslim spokesmen.

The army was also prominent in promoting particular Muslim projects or national projects in the general interests of Muslims. Thus, army officers supported and participated in a commission to improve conditions for Indonesians undertaking the annual pilgrimage to Mecca.[20] Again army officers were prominent on the committees established in 1962 to raise funds and construct the *Mesdjid Istiqlal* (Independence Mosque) which was to be the largest mosque in the world and was a part of Sukarno's efforts to make Djakarta an international capital of the Third World.[21] The army also gave verbal support — if overall enthusiasm was lacking — for the efforts of traditionalist Muslims to host an Afro-Asian Islamic conference in Djakarta in early 1965.[22]

At times army friendship with Muslim groups was carefully used to promote a particular political viewpoint. In the early days of Guided Democracy various territorial commanders assembled regional conferences of Muslim scholars and prompted them to issue statements supporting the central government and condemning the autonomist aspirations of the Outer Islands groups. In the latter days of the era some commanders prompted Muslim groups to issue statements supporting Sukarnoist doctrines, apparently as a move to rival Communist enthusiasm in that activity. Throughout the period army officers attended the major Muslim meetings, and promoted, through formal addresses and in informal conversation, general statements that supported certain national causes that the military favored.[23-24]

The army's effort among Muslim groups was only partially successful for Muslim unity was never achieved and Muslims did not develop into a strong civilian grouping backing army policy. The split between the two doctrinaire groups that had been apparent since the 1920's continued. The traditionalist group — represented primarily by the *Nahdatul Ulama* — had allied itself to Sukarno in 1957 and cooperated with him throughout the period of Guided Democracy. With their share of high government posts and some access to Sukarno by their leaders they were not disposed to cooperate closely with the military which they may have regarded as striving to assume a pre-eminent position at their expense. Consequently, while not unfriendly to military leaders, traditionalist Muslims concentrated on their own efforts to win influence with Sukarno. The modernist group found all political activity difficult in this period because of its involvement in the Outer Islands rebellion in the late 1950's, its general opposition to Sukarno's *Pantja Sila* concepts in the Constitutional Period, and its open anticommunist position. Much of its top leadership was in prison and modernist Muslims who became politically active were usually arrested. Consequently modernists concentrated on non-controversial educational and social welfare projects and gave verbal support to government policies when such statements were called for. Modernists did cooperate to some degree with the army but only in the context of those non-controversial activities.

The Armed Forces' efforts to promote Muslim activism along lines favorable to the military influenced Indonesian development in three inter-related ways. First it gave new direction to Muslim thought at a time when Muslim goals had proven to be unacceptable to Indonesian society and helped redefine Muslim values that were acceptable to the national secular feeling that had emerged in Indonesia. The viewpoint that Islam had to operate in the context of the secular national state was not limited to the armed forces leadership; many Muslims held this opinion. But army efforts to foster this viewpoint in a period of political disarray for Muslims gave direction to the tendency and aided its further development. Second, armed forces efforts to win Muslim support for its political leadership proved to be part of the larger loose coalition of army allies which impeded the take-over of Indonesian society by the left and made possible the eventual army challenge to Sukarno in 1965. Muslims constituted an important part of this coalition but only because of armed forces efforts in aiding Muslims in that period. Finally, the rapport between Muslims and the army built up in the Sukarnoist era was to carry over into the succeeding New Order (*Orde Baru*) period and help make possible the military-directed government that emerged. It is not that the army converted all Muslims and convinced them of the rightness of army-directed policy, for it did not. Rather, it convinced large numbers of Muslims that army aims were not against their own interests, as evidenced by army aid and friendship in the Sukarnoist era.

NOTES

1. The major Islamic movements of Indonesia can be classed as doctrinaire since each seeks to perpetuate values of orthodox Islam as developed in the Middle East. Within the doctrinaire community a differentiation can be made between traditionalist (*kaum tua*) groups, such as the *Nahdatul Ulama,* which follows the *Shafi'i* law code and the modernists (*kaum muda*), such as *Masjumi,* which stressed basic religious sources in the development of a new Islamic law. Doctrinaire Muslims probably constitute 30 to 40 percent of Indonesia's population while nominal or syncretic Muslims, who have only partly accepted Islamic values and usually are opposed to the doctrinaire Muslim organizations, constitute 40 to 60 percent.
2. Restatements of the official army mission in 1964 and 1965 did not change this viewpoint on Islam, although certainly Sukarnoist ideology increased appreciably, which implied that the role of Islam in national affairs was to be more circumscribed.
3. "Surat Keputusan Kepala Staf Djenderal A. H. Nasution," 24 October, 1961.
4. Al-Bahist, "Kronik dan Komentar Islam," *Gema Islam* I, No. 8 (May, 1962), 5.
5. "Kursus Dinas Imam Militer," *Gema Islam,* I, No. 12 (July 15, 1962), 26.
6. The use of these three terms shows a blending of religious and military terminology and assigning a religious connotation to all three. *Taqwa* is an Islamic legal term indicating fear of God. *Wira* is a military term connoting a soldier's duty and responsibility to his unit and country. *Karja* is a term indicating service done for others and for country, not exclusively military, but adopted by the military as a symbol of its efforts toward the nation. *Ibid.*
7. Indonesia, Angkatan Darat, Komando Mandala, Rawatan Rohani Islam, *Shalot Dalam Tugas Tempir, Pembebasan Irian Barat.* Djakarta, 1962.
8. Indonesia. Angkatan Darat, Pusat Rawatan Rohani Islam, *'Idul Fithri dan Zakat Fithrah.* Djakarta, 1964.
9. Indonesia. Angkatan Darat, Pusroh Islam, *Pedoman Agama Islam untuk TNI.* Djakarta, 1962.
10. See following pages.
11. See following pages.
12. Brigadier General Dr. Sudjono, "Dharma Bhakti TNI AD sebagai alat revolusi dalam mentjapai Masjarakat Sosialis Indonesia Pantjasila," *Karya Wira Jati,* IV, Nos. 13–15 (January-July 1964), 91–94.
13. Lieutenant Colonel Herlan Prawiradiwirja, "Tentang Sistim Pendidikan Angkatan-Darat kita," *Karja Wira Jati,* II, No. 7 (1962), 244–245.
14. Brigadier General Soedirman, "Chotbah 'Idulfithri, March 18, 1961 dilapangan SESKOAD, Bandung," *Gema Islam,* I, No. 4 (March 1, 1962), 8–11.
15. Dr. Hadji Abdulmalik Karim Amrullah.
16. See James L. Peacock, *Rites of Modernization.* Chicago, 1968, pp. 40–50.
17. Mohammad Isa Idris, "Persoalan pemuda remadja kita sekarang," *Gema Islam,* I, No. 8 (May 15, 1962), 9.
18. "Menudju Da'wah Islamyah jang lebih sempurna," *Gema Islam,* I, No. 8 (May 15, 1962), pp. 14–15; *Angkatan Bersendjata,* April 1, 1965; 1; *Ibid.,* September 14, 1965, p. 2.
19. Al-Bahist, "Kronik dan Komentar Islam," *Gema Islam,* I, No. 11 (November 15, 1962), p. 4.
20. *Penjuluh Agama,* XI, No. 4 (April 1963), pp. 4–7.
21. "Mesdjid Istiqlal," *Gema Islam,* I, No. 2 (February 15, 1962), 18–19.
22. *Angkatan Bersendjata,* September 15, 1965, 1.

23–24. See for example *Penjuluh Agama,* XI, No. 3 (March 1963), 4.

The Politics of Islamic Egalitarianism

CLIVE S. KESSLER

Underlying the political division in the Kelantanese countryside [therefore] were significant socio-economic factors. For that reason support for the PMIP cannot simply be portrayed as an outbreak of archaic religious fanaticism. On the contrary, it represents a real response to real and contemporary issues. But to assert that support for the PMIP reflects underlying class tensions in the countryside, and that it is based upon a not unrealistic assessment of antagonistic interests in rural society, does not mean that PMIP supporters necessarily see (or that outside observers may see) that political stance as an explicit act of class-conscious strategy. On the contrary, and as this analysis of the PMIP's appeals will illustrate, the interests espoused by the PMIP are presented through Islam as 'the common interest of all the members of society, put in an ideal form.' The PMIP may thus present itself 'not as a class but as the representative of the whole of society . . . confronting the one ruling class' because it does effectively, if in very general terms, represent 'the common interest of all [the] non-ruling classes.' The pressure of circumstances in Kelantan, and throughout Malaysia, has not yet required that it define itself as the representative of the 'particular interest of a particular class' (Marx and Engels, 1947:40–1).

This section offers [but] a brief analysis of the Islamic political appeal in Kelantan, and of the way in which it generates and employs a notion of 'the common interest of all the members of society, put in an ideal form.* It indicates how that appeal is generated by the tension between the terms of an implicit Islamic social theory and the social experience of the Kelantanese peasantry. It shows how the strength of that appeal derives from the ability of an Islamic idiom of political discourse to transform the nature of political demands — to allow the presentation of sectional interests in a universalistic and thus morally sanctioned fashion. By its ability to effect that translation, the Islamic idiom permits one of the contending parties in a conflict-ridden situation to present itself as the vehicle of popular interests and of the 'general will'; in consequence, it also facilitates the casting of the other party into the role of protector of those sectional and hence immoral interest which have rejected and detached themselves from the purported general interest. The Islamic idiom may thus furnish the cement of collectivist solidarity to the party which, appealing to popular interests, succeeds in presenting itself as the vehicle of a morally sanctioned general interest; it thus inhibits perception of, and also action upon, potential political differences (primarily those of class, such as those separating the middle and lower peasantry) between supporters of the popular party. Since it encompasses those differences with a broader popular unity, the party fails to develop as the articulator of 'the particular

Reprinted in abridged form from H. W. Mason, et al. (eds.), *Humaniora Islamica* Vol. II (1974), 237–252, by permission of the author and the editors.

interest of a particular interest of particular class.'

In earlier discussions (especially 1972 & n.d.) I have pointed out that there is an almost inevitable tension between the social experience a believer seeks to apprehend and the religiously-furnished terms for its apprehension. In Islam this tension or dissonance is particularly acute because of the explicitness of Islam's claim to possess a comprehensive and adequate social theory congruent in all respects with whatever vicissitudes the Faithful may undergo. For them Islam is the, and the only, sociological religion, and this at least in part is in their eyes the reason for its superiority over other religions. Yet, far from being adequate to the explanation of all sociological facts and far from being smoothly and automatically consonant with all human experience, Islam requires of the Faithful a considerable effort as they strive to apprehend and formulate experience in a manner congruent with the terms of their religious culture. Because experience does not automatically conform to, or readily display consistency with, those ideal terms, believers must ever strain to construe experience as approximating to that ideal form; and occasions wherein, if only momentarily, experience can be rendered congruent with the Islamic terms through which all experience should ideally and readily be apprehended become central and valuable, indeed sacred, moments to believers more often beset with a disquieting dissonance between experience and its cultural forms.

For the social theory of Islam is in some respects problematic;[1] and the effort to reconcile idealized Islamic views of the nature of man and society with the inescapable facts of political life engender a tension which in such 'sacred' moments may be evoked and also transcended. For politics is about social division and sectional interest, about rivalry and antagonism, and it is precisely these facets of social life which Islam (though it may acknowledge them) finds difficult to reconcile with the dominant terms of its social theory. As I have argued, Islamic social theory is predominantly ethical and individualistic: its focus is upon the individual, and it looks to the possibility of his behaviour being at some future time actuated by higher principle rather than being conditioned, as generally happens, by baser interests. The means by which it attempts to realize that possibility — to render that future possibility imminent — are almost exclusively hortatory. Further, this theory, grounded in Quranic egalitarianism, construes the nature of obligation, even social obligations, in a moral and asocial way. For obligations, including those of social import, do not so much derive from the nature of social life or inhere in particular social statuses, but rather attach themselves to men in virtue of their common and divinely created humanity. More than a theory, the Islamic view is a vision of the kind of society which would and ideally should emerge quite automatically if men would only act in accordance with those higher principles of personal disinterest which Islam urges. This vision is profoundly individualistic in the sense that it remains largely blind to the existence and significance of organized groups in society mediating between the individual and the total community. Its stress is upon the mutual obligations linking, on the one hand, a total and ideally conceived community and, on the other, a morally depicted individual, stripped of any particular social status and construed as the sole significant yet atomistic component of a society and of social theory. This unmediated polarity of what might be termed a disaggregated, or in C. B. MacPherson's term (1962:1) "dissociated," individual, on the one hand, and of the total yet unactualized moral community, on the other, generates the main points of tension, in the individual experience of Muslims, between social theory and social reality.

The key issues of Islamic social theory and the central moral dilemmas confronting Muslims in charting the course of their social behaviour touch upon the basic opposition between personal interests and the common interest, between privately interested action and moral and personally disinterested commitment. For those former interests, given the morally idealistic nature of this individualistic-communitarian theory, are rooted in what is but should not be, while the latter virtues call upon the individual to act in terms of what should be but has not yet come into being. In Islam (as in other religions, but more pointedly) the antinomies are presented as the opposition between sincerity and reason, on the one hand, and deceit and personal desire on the other. This theory, with its extreme bifurcation of the individual and the community, of the actual and the ideal — theory a which yet calls for the reconciliation of what it sets up as polar opposites — vest moral worth in the unactualized ideal community, allowing individuals to share in that moral worth to the extent they behave as if they lived in the ideal rather than the actual social world. Inherent in this position is a grave distrust of private ends, a suspicion that they are the product of baser desires which threaten to seduce men away from the reasoned recognition of their joint interests with, and moral obligations towards, their fellow men.

For the Kelantanese, as for certain other Muslims elsewhere (cf. Siegel, 1969:102–4; Rosen, 1978; and, in slightly different terms, Geertz, 1960:72–6, 238–41, and Jay, 1969: 66–7, 177) this moral tension is expressed in terms of the opposition between *nafsu*, or the animal desires of the flesh and the consequent temptation towards a morally unregulated pursuit of private ends, and *akal*, or the intelligent and reflective control whereby the individual, weighing his own motives and interests with a degree of detachment, holds his desires in check to the extent that they may corrode his moral bonds to other individuals and to the community as a whole. Anything which would seem to be prompted by the attempt of *nafsu* to undermine the tenuous dominance of *akal* is therefore to be deplored and resisted: wilful and selfish actions are seen as humanly unworthy, animalistic and even violent, and are interpreted as the socially and morally subversive machinations of Satan.

In this context the notion of sincerity takes on a particular meaning which merges with that of disinterest. For in this lexicon, sincerity does not connote (as it tends to in English usage) an honest recognition and explicit declaration of where one's interests and inclinations lead one, but refers rather to an unburdened state of mind in which one may properly approach one'e fellow man. It connotes not simply a lack of dissimulation concerning motives, whatever they may be, but implies that those motives themselves are morally proper. Sincerity is a state of mind, a precondition for and predisposition to disinterested behaviour; its hallmark is a kind of equanimity or lack of tension attained through a prior and successful attempt to bring self-regarding inclinations under control. Only after acknowledging that one's own insistent interests or *nafsu* may cause disharmony and conflict may one approach others in that moral and disinterested fashion, born of humanly-possessed but divinely-inspired *akal*. Through *akal*, consideration may prevail over a selfishness that amounts to violence.

This notion of sincerity may be contrasted with the English usage, which suggests an even brutally forthright frankness — not the renunciation of private interests and ends but the explicit acknowledgement of their irresistibility. It was something like this latter notion which seemed, to many Kelantanese, to be involved in the Alliance Party's approach to them. The Alliance claimed to be sincere, but made itself morally unacceptable by the very terms in which it proclaimed its sincerity. In a speech at the laying of the foundation-stone of a mosque during a Kelantan by-election, the then Deputy Prime Minister, Tun Abdul Razak, made the following forthright declaration to the electors of the district:

> It is said that we of the Alliance Party harbour ill-will against the people of Kelantan, and that we refuse to help this state to progress from its backward condition. This is not true. We have only the best of intentions towards all the people of Kelantan and all the Malay people. There is nothing that we would like more than to be able to help you. But, alas, as things now stand we cannot. I shall be completely frank and sincere (*ikhlas dan jujor*) with you. We cannot help you until you turn the PMIP out of power in this state and elect an Alliance party government in its place. The reason is simple: we cannot help you until you enable us to help you. We can only help those who help us. We can only provide projects to those who vote for us. This is sincere talk. Those are our terms and that is our offer.

Such a position was incomprehensible to the Kelantan electors, or rather, in terms of what they understood by it, Tun Razak's protestation was self-contradictory. In coming with his own terms and in attempting to drive a bargain, Tun Razak was seen as being not merely intransigent but also violent. By his refusal to acknowledge the kind of people and commitment he was confronting, and by refusing to admit that there were fundamental differences of interest and allegiance separating his listeners from him, Tun Razak was seen as committing some kind of moral and social violence. He was, in his listeners' terms, being anything but sincere. With an undisguised measure of inflexible self-interest he was offering them a mosque and other benefits provided they forgot about their fundamental principles and simply concentrated upon the undeniable attractions of what he offered them. In short, Tun Razak's appeal was seen by his listeners as an appeal to *nafsu.* To them his behavior was that of *nafsu,* and his appeal was that others should relate to him on that same basis.

This tension between the ideal and the actual, between private and shared interests, does not simply generate a simplistic, binomial moral calculus; on the contrary, *akal* and *nafsu* become the key terms of a whole moral vocabulary and of a whole grammar of recognized but morally unequal political motives. The political vocabulary and understandings of the Kelantanese are rich in dichotomous contrasts, all of which are at the highest level encompassed within the opposition of *akal* and *nafsu.* Among them are terms which contrast against their opposites the political actions of *kepentingan* ('interest') of those who *kira perut sendiri* ('care only for their own stomachs') and who *kira harta benda saumor* ('forever evaluate things in exclusively material terms'). These people still 'sleep' *(tidor)* in a condition of unenlightened darkness *(jahiliyya);* their actions are antithetical to the actions of those engaged in *pejuang* (a 'campaign' or 'cause'). Such causes recall those *jihad* (or 'righteous battles') of the Prophet Muhammed himself in being *suchi* (that is to say, 'holy', but holy in the sense of being waged by those who have brought physical *élan* and moral purpose to the cause by leaving selfish and private interests behind). It is but these latter efforts, to which private and material interests have been subordinated, which manifest and are informed by *tauhid* and *hedayah* (the 'unity' born of properly disinterested 'true guidance').

To the electors of Kelantan, it was the PMIP which was the party of *akal* and of *nasehat* ('moral guidance'), while the Alliance and its representatives appealed but to private and material interests and urged upon them an almost utilitarian individualism of political calculation. The Alliance leaders, of course, claimed to be *ikhlas dan jujor* ('frank and sincere'), but those protestations were belied by other actions. The Alliance held out the promise of development projects aplenty and of material advancement if only the Kelantanese could bring themselves to elect an Alliance government to power in the state. But these appeals concentrated upon the undeniable attractions of what was being offered, and ignored the important questions of why they were being offered and why such offers had repeatedly been refused in the past; the Alliance's approach was seen as a deceitful, indeed violent, attempt to bury moral scruple under a pile of material but Satanically immoral inducements. It was seen as an appeal to *nafsu* — as an attempt on the Alliance's part to do a morally uniformed deal between its own inordinate *nafsu* for power and the ever-present and tenuously-controlled *nafsu* of the Kelantanese for worldly goods and comforts.

The Alliance's blindness to the limits of its own notion of sincerity prevented it from seeing that the way it presented itself to the Kelantanese peasantry served only further to alienate them, strengthening therefore their allegiance to the PMIP. The whole Alliance effort to persuade the Kelantanese of the advantages of modernity was thus brought into disrepute. All the claims of miles of roads built by the Alliance federal government, of mosques erected, of land projects opened and of the value in money of all these efforts — the naked statistics of its quantified claims suggested that the Alliance was but a party of *nafsu.* The material benefits already enjoyed by the Alliance functionaries, and the promise of benefits held out to the Kelantanese should they change their allegiance, suggested that the Alliance was not simply a party of an immoral materialism, but also one whose materialism was based upon an equally immoral competitive individualism heedless of a shared and higher social interest. To the Kelantanese, the Alliance not only itself manifested the Satanically immoral side of human nature, but also appealed to that same *nafsu* in them. This appeal to their 'worst selves' amounted to a contemptuous and thus politically disastrous judgment by the Alliance upon the Kelantanese, who chose instead to continue supporting a party which appealed to, and provided them with the opportunity occasionally to actualize, their Islamically moral 'better selves.'

The Kelantanese chose what they regarded as justice and 'the virtues which Allah will reward' (cf. Ibn Khaldun, 1958: I, 323) over material advantage. In making that choice they were voting in accordance with what they saw as their own interests. But the terms in which their demands were cast transformed the appearance of those interests: they were made to appear, not as the sectional interest of a group in society, but as a moral imperative of society as a whole — as the common interest 'put in an ideal form' and embodied in values represented 'as the only rational, universally valid ones' of all the members of society. As Julien Benda noted (1969: 34 – 6), 'A passion whose sole motive is interest is too weak to contend with another which combines interest and pride', and hence political convictions may display a 'realism of a particular quality, which is an important element of strength in them: They are *divinized* realism.' So, at least, it has been in the case of the PMIP.

Once questions of interest have been cast in the mould of *nafsu* and sincerity, an antagonism between two sectional interests is transmuted into a conflict between the very moral foundations of social life and those who seemingly choose to disregard them. The unmediated polarity of public and private interests permits one of the contending parties to pre-empt and present itself as the claims of the public good. This antagonism presents itself as a conflict between legitimate social imperatives and illicit private interests. Islam thus makes possible the presentation of moral claims upon unresponsive authority; it facilitates not simply the expression of neglected popular interests, but the demand for redressive justice as a general social interest. A social theory which portrays relations between the public and private domains in moral and idealistic terms both enables and requires sectional interests to be advanced as overall social needs. It permits neglected sectional interests legitimately to reject as morally unresponsive political authorities which appear as but protectors of privileged sectional interests. Put in other terms,[2] the Islamic idiom affords the means for a critique of the individualistic and competitive assumptions of the kind of 'modernizing' capitalist development which so often, in circumstances similar to Kelantan, has against the interests of the peasantry advanced those of a nascent bourgeoisie.

In making their stance with the PMIP the Kelantanese, in exemplary but intermittent acts, would momentarily approximate to those ideal standards of principled and disinterested Muslim behaviour which as worldly and calculating peasants they are at other times far, even in their own estimation, from displaying. Islam thus represents their potential but mostly unactualized ideal selves, and the PMIP for them embodies the *pejuangan Islam* ('the cause of Islam') because it evokes, though but transiently and sporadically, their Islamically-informed but generally unfulfilled ideal selves. In Kelantan, idealized Islamic notions of the nature of man and society have come to constitute an 'inverted world consciousness' (Marx, 1970:131) providing temporary or illusory fulfillment to the unfulfilled and spiritual recompense to the materially deprived. It is the very tension between experience and the Islamically-furnished terms for its construal which has made this possible. The Islamic vision of the just society, consisting of individuals motivated by principle rather than immediate material interest, has provided the terms through which people may momentarily experience themselves as morally worthy and dignified human beings. In these moments of political intransigence the Kelantanese in their own eyes attain that perfection which Islam enjoins upon them, and thus also exempt themselves from the attempt to live the lives of the just in what they see, by ideal standards, as an unjust society.

Much of the argument between the Alliance and PMIP has turned upon whether it is possible in the modern world to build a society and live in accordance with 'Islamic social theory.' Without rejecting what it termed 'Islamic social principles', the Alliance would claim it was not possible, and thus appealed to the Kelantanese not to attempt what it said was the impossible task of living and acting politically in accordance with what was imagined to be Islamic theory. This appeal, however, presented itself as a challenge to those who believed that such a theory existed and was capable of being acted upon. Instead of acting in accordance with what the Alliance told them was a realistic assessment of their mundane interests, the Kelantanese chose rather to act upon their own implicit and Islamically-informed theory of political behaviour. In so doing, they acted in accordance with a theory which the Alliance claimed could not be acted upon in the real world. Thereby, perhaps paradoxically, they produced real political consequences and revalidated for themselves a view of man and society which the Alliance claimed was politically inapplicable. In effect, they proved the Alliance wrong, to their own satisfaction at least, by enacting that theory, making thereby a practical and symbolic assertion of its applicability. Efforts to convince the Kelantanese of the irrelevance of Islamic social theory to their lives foundered with the Alliance's electoral defeats.

NOTES

* A more extended version of the argument presented here, together with details of the historical and ethnographic context, are to be found in C.S. Kessler, *Islam and Politics in a Malay State: Kelantan 1838–1969* (Cornell University Press, Ithaca, N.Y., 1978), especially Chap. 11 "Religious Ideas and Social Reality", pp. 208–234.

1. This contention is argued on historical and sociological grounds in Kessler (1972: esp. pp. 35–40) where it is argued that, far from determining or directly reflecting social reality, the Islamic social vision was elaborated in disapproving defiance of existing social and political realities. Thus, far from there having existed any close and determinative relation between Islamic social theory and social practice (as many classically-inspired scholars, adopting Islam's own sociological preconceptions, have implied) the Islamic social vision has stood in dialectical opposition to Islamic social practice, and has therefore been capable of invocation as an ideology of political protest, especially by the *ulama* in times of crisis. Islamic social theory was not the sociological blueprint of societies which have actually existed, but an ideal of social justice nourished in opposition to the social and political realities of classical Muslim society. For this reason, the contention of the classically-inspired scholars that a close, determinative relation of social theory upon social reality renders Islam a 'special case' for the sociology of religion collapses. Islam, like all religions, collides with social reality — but more so than others, because of its unique claims of possessing an adequate social theory. Islam is thus a 'special case' only in the diminished sense of evidencing in extreme, not unique, fashion the more general dissonance between social theory and social reality by which all the world-religions are beset.
2. This precise and perceptive formulation was suggested to me by Hester Eisenstein.

Indonesian Islam since the New Order

ALLAN A. SAMSON

Cooperation among the army, student organizations, and Islamic groups in decimating the Communist party in the aftermath of the attempted coup of September 30, 1965, indicated to many that Islam would gain a legitimate place of political importance in the New Order. Indeed, many Islamic leaders came to feel that Islam was the most important civil force in society. Its major antagonists, the PKI* and Sukarno, had been eliminated. With the destruction of the Communist party and its millions of supporters, the Islamic parties comprised the largest single political force. Such cooperation was short-lived, however, as non-Islamic groups and much of the military believed that the Islamic parties still clung tenaciously to their goal of an Islamic state, and remained on guard against any attempt to rekindle ideological disputation.

Although Islamic figures affirmed their support for Pancasila, secular groups criticized such support as being based on political expediency. "The Muslim parties still want an Islamic state," a secular leader emphasized. "Make no mistake! They can't oppose the armed forces openly on this, but they're waiting for the right moment to bring up the issue again" (this quotation comes from a personal interview). Muslim leaders claimed the issue was dead. Pancasila, they claimed, could be accepted and supported according to the norms of Islam. In this regard, it was particularly stressed by Muslim leaders that the first sila, belief in Almighty God, inspired the four other silas. Nonetheless, suspicion on the part of non-Islamic groups toward Muslim intentions was often intensified by phrases such as "*Pancasila yang diridhoi Tuhan*" ("Pancasila which is blessed by God"). Secular groups interpreted such statements as attempts to introduce the Jakarta charter in a covert manner (see *Pedoman,* August 6, 1969).

Ideological debate continued in the post-1965 period, albeit on a plane of lower comprehensiveness and immediacy. In part, this was a reflection of ideological concern operating at both the levels of unifying symbol and imperative demand. At the first level, Islamic concern with ideology in the New Order was broadly symbolic, providing identity and solidarity. At the second level, it was also a reaction against military determination not to allow the rehabilitation of Masyumi (which had been dissolved by order of Sukarno in 1960) nor to allow the participation of the major Masyumi figures in the newly established Partai Muslimin Indonesia. At this level, ideological concern took on more intense proportions, reflecting the frustration felt by many modernist supporters of Masyumi. It did not reach the level of imperative demand, as was the case in the 1959 Constituent Assembly debates, but was in its own way a defensive reaction against clear military hegemony and the frustration engendered by the political weakness of Islamic modernism. Nahdatul

---

Reprinted in abridged form from K. D. Jackson and L. W. Pye (eds.), *Political Power and Communications in Indonesia* (Berkeley: University of California Press, 1978), pp. 196–226, by permission of the author and the Regents of the University of California, Berkeley, California, U.S.A.

Ulama's ideological concerns were broadly symbolic; it could affirm its theological dedication to an Islamic state, Shari'ah, or the Jakarta charter without sacrificing its accommodative policy and the limited influence it had gained at the periphery of political influence. Similarly, for the accommodationists in Partai Muslimin (Mintaredja, Agus Sudono, H. M. Sansui, Djaelani Naro, Imron Kadir), ideology was interpreted in a broadly symbolic manner as pertaining to a loose, personal religious identity.[1] Ideology was far more important for the reformists and fundamentalists in Partai Muslimin, for whom it possessed both symbolic and political importance. Consequently, when the political goals of the Masyumi-supporting majority of Partai Muslimin were thwarted and obstructed, their reaction was phrased in the meter of religio-ideological demands.

Post-1965 debate revolved around the demand of the Muslim parties that a statement emphasizing the obligation of Muslims to follow Islamic law be given legal force. This obligation was stated in the Jakarta charter of June 22, 1945, which, with the exclusion of the Islamic law statement, was made the preamble of the 1945 constitution. The Islamic parties demanded that this statement be reinserted and given legal force. They expressed this view in the March 1968 meeting of the People's Deliberative Assembly in which the ideological direction of the state was discussed. Their proposal would make it incumbent on all Muslims (be they nominal or intense adherents) to follow Islamic law and would link the state to religious observance and practice. The state would then have the responsibility of enforcing Islamic law. It was this topic which aroused such strong feeling during the 1959 Constituent Assembly debates on the return to the 1945 constitution. With the state responsible for the enforcement of religious observation, many feared that the Islamic political parties and their affiliated organizations would be catapulted to predominant political influence. Muslim religious and political leaders interpreted the Jakarta charter not as a permissive rule, but as one which must be enforced by the state (*Api Pantja Sila,* April 15, 1968). Such an eventuality left even many Muslims apprehensive.

Throughout 1968 and 1969, the Islamic parties sponsored "Jakarta charter Commemoration Day" programs to be held each June 22. Fanfare and wide press coverage accompanied preparation for the event during the preceding month. Organizational impetus was held by Partai Muslimin associated groups, but Nahdatul Ulama also supported the effort, which served to tighten ideological solidarity (albeit temporarily) among the generally divided Islamic ranks.

Three views of the Jakarta charter were expressed by Islamic groups:

1. The statement that the Jakarta charter "inspires" the 1945 constitution could be accepted without attempting to further define or modify it. With this, the issue would be deliberately downplayed, possibly avoiding a renewal of acrimonious debate. Symbolic satisfaction would thus be provided for some but not for all.
2. The Jakarta charter should be made the preamble to the 1945 constitution (which would essentially mean reinserting the deleted phrase into the text of the document). This would signify a symbolic victory for Islam in that Shari'ah would officially be recognized by the state.
3. The Jakarta charter should be made a part of legislation in article 29 of the constitution, thereby giving Shari'ah legal force and designating the state as being responsible for its implementation. This option was feared most by nominally and non-Islamic groups who opposed any attempt to force implementation of Islamic law.

The first view was acceptable to the political leadership of Nahdatul Ulama, for whom the retention of minor political influence and control of the religious bureaucracy was preferable to ideological confrontation. Once the expression of symbolic concern was made, Nahdatul Ulama was content to continue its accommodationist policy. Masyumi-Partai Muslimin reformists favored the second or third options which implied state recognition, and possible enforcement, of Islamic law. As in 1959, their ideological demands were intensified by the political obstruction they encountered at the hands of the government. Whether governmental agreement to the participation of the Masyumi figures in Partai Muslimin would have diluted the ideological demands of the reformists in the Jakarta charter debates is conjectural. That Partai Muslimin was not permitted to develop in this direction clearly makes the question an academic one. Military determination to "domesticate" Partai Muslimin, however, was predicated on the interpretation that a vigorous, politicized Islamic modernism writ in the image of Masyumi would itself evince an ideological concern far exceeding the realm of the broadly symbolic. Governmental strategy was to encourage Partai Muslimin's accommodationists while obstructing its reformists and fundamentalists. To this effect, the military-fomented internal coup within Partai Muslimin in October 1970 resulted in the leadership of H. M. Mintaredja, who urged accommodation to secular authority and a devolution of religious concern from the political to the personal.

In effect, the government was following the policy of Snouck Hurgronje, the eminent Dutch Islamologist of the late nineteenth and early twentieth century, who urged that Islamic religious activities be encouraged and political activities restricted. Nahdatul Ulama's leadership could accept these restrictions, but the situation was a frustrating one for reformists, who argued that the political weakness of Islam was attributable only to external obstruction and did not reflect Islam's actual numerical strength in society. The disparity between Islam's political weakness and the tendency of reformists leaders to overestimate their numerical and social strength intensified the political dimensions of the Perjuangan Ummat Islam. By 1971, all of this served to intensify a perception of politics which defined political participation as unremitting struggle, ideology as imperative demand, the "Islamic struggle" as a zero-sum political competition, secular political power as only semi-legitimate, and the ummat Islam as a politically exclusivist concept.

The decisive victory of government-sponsored GOLKAR** in the 1971 national election, in which the Islamic parties received 27 percent of the votes cast, gives further evidence of Islam's minority position in politics. This total represents a noticeable decline from the 43 percent of the vote Islamic parties received in the 1955 national election. The Islamic parties sustained a political defeat, a fact which may finally indicate to the Islamic parties and leaders that Islam is but one of several political forces in Indonesia, and by no means the largest one. If so, the failure to achieve political goals can no longer be attributed to "behind-the-scenes" machinations of secular groups, and a more pragmatic assessment of Islam's actual political strength may therefore curb unrealistic expectations and demands.

Ideology as imperative demand was of immediate concern when political failure was attributed to manipulation by non-Islamic groups who were deemed unrepresentative of Indonesia's supposed Islamic majority (the "myth of the numerical majority"). However, an election which shows Islam to be no more than a political minority may change political self-perception within the ummat Islam and perhaps lay the groundwork for an internal reassessment. Could such a realization lead to a diminution of ideological expectations and demands on the part of the ummat Islam? Ideology has been of immediate concern to Islamic parties — both as symbolic unity and imperative demand — and the response of Islamic modernism to political failure has been couched in terms of ideological defense. Is it plausible to anticipate a reassessment in which religious defense is eschewed for the more prosaic articulation of definite social and economic interests? More generally, the question could be asked whether a politicized Islam is capable of relinquishing religio-ideological demands. Are Islam and ideology so inextricably linked that — paraphrasing the Qur'an — each is as close to the other as man is to the vein in his neck, or can political problems be faced in political terms? If secular political authority is perceived as legitimate, the political demands and expectations of Islamic organizations may be readjusted downward and the incidence of ideology as imperative demand in response to political failure may also diminish. To predict, however, with any degree of certainty that this will occur is clearly impossible; politicized Islam has been on the defensive and frustrated for too long to be able to posit a calculated response on its part. What is evident, however, is that for the first time in this century, Islam has been shown by the results of a national election to be a distinct political minority — a fact which cannot help but be a sobering experience for Muslim leaders, and one which may call for a readjustment of strategy.[2]

Such a readjustment has been made most easily by Nahdatul Ulama's accommodationist leadership and by the accommodationist faction of Partai Muslimin — the very groups which currently exercise leadership. Partai Muslimin's accommodationist faction, which was the least disposed to a rigid ideological stance, was always on the defensive in internal party debate. Its perception of politics as the attainment of definite social and economic interests, rather than the expression of religious demands, received slight welcome from fundamentalists and reformists. With the accommodationists on the defensive within the party, diminution of ideological intensity remained unrealized. The Indonesian military's frank interference in Partai Muslimin's affairs has greatly altered this political equation. The thrust of both Sukarno's and Suharto's restrictive policies toward Islam, however coercive they may have been, appear to have succeeded in preventing the reification of Islamic symbols at the expense of national symbols. Islamic political parties were weakened by Sukarno but could maintain a political confidence based on belief in their comprising a numerical majority. Given the results of the 1971 election, this confidence is no longer merited.

Ideology will certainly retain its relevance as a unifying symbol so long as the Islamic and Javanese *weltanschauungen* remain counterpoised. Ideology as imperative demand, however, may decline in importance, for it is the response to the frustration engendered by perceiving one's own groups as a natural majority, beset by covert, unethical forces.

For Partai Muslimin's military-supported accommodationists, the results of the election demonstrated what they had long suspected — that the expanse of Islam's political goals had to be reduced. I have previously noted that reformist policy was pragmatic and realistic if many of the important political goals and demands of the Islamic parties were achieved. However, given reformist leaders' overestimation of Islam's actual social strength, failure to achieve political goals was attributed to plots by a well-placed anti-Islamic minority rather than to Islam's own minority status. Accommodationists urged a reassessment of Islam's actual social and political strength and a new strategy to follow therefrom. The ideal Islamic society could not be achieved through political means. Politics was not the pursuit of the ideal but the art of the possible, and the clear political primacy of military and secular political power made accommodation necessary. This necessitated, they contended, a relinquishing of Islam's ideological goals, its dreams of political victory, and the emphasis of Islamic groups on perjuangan as religio-political struggle.

This sentiment was expressed by Mintaredja in a criticism of the "formal political approach" previously carried out by the Islamic political parties. An approach which emphasized ideological struggle, he maintained, was "out of date." Politics was a wordly concern and could be differentiated from religion; material advantage should be sought:

> Where is the proof of the Perjuangan Ummat Islam during the twenty-five years we have been free? It seems the public is already bored waiting for the results of the struggle which have been promised by leaders who only consider formal ideological struggle important. This [formal political approach] is empty; what is awaited by the public and the Ummat Islam especially are the [material] results of the political struggle. To achieve this result . . . we need to implement development in all fields, especially in the field of the economy . . . .
>
> Partai Muslimin Indonesia does not desire to carry out the formal political approach as formerly. Partai Muslimin Indonesia has already decided . . . to cooperate with the armed forces and get in line with the development group [program-oriented order]. In other words, Partai Muslimin Indonesia will carry out a political material approach without forgetting its base, namely Islam [Mintaredja 1971:48].

If it is to overcome reformist and fundamentalist suspicions of religious laxity and political opportunism, such a policy would have to bring noticeable benefits in its wake. In particular, this would connote economic improvement, in view of the fact that the social base of support for Indonesian Islamic modernism continues to lie in the commercial and trading strata of Indonesia's cities and towns. A quid pro quo between the government and modernist groups would necessitate governmental policies that benefit (or at least do not harm) Islamic entrepreneurial groups. Only such development might promote a willingness on the part of many reformists to reassess strategy and agree to accommodation.

In early 1973, the government ordered the nine existing political parties (excluding GOLKAR) to "fuse" into two basic parties which were to serve as an issue-oriented "loyal opposition" matched against GOLKAR. This plan was intended to curtail the influence of the ideologically based party system. The four Islamic parties fused to form the PPP (Partai Persatuan Pembangunan, Development Unity party). Idham Chalid of Nahdatul Ulama and H. M. Mintaredja of Partai Muslimin became chairman and vice-chairman respectively of the PPP. The four Islamic "component parties" were then instructed to divest themselves of their political identity and revert back to a more basic socioreligious orientation. Although this was unpopular with the Islamic rank and file, it would appear to have the effect of successfully depoliticizing Islamic activities, so long as governmental policy is not perceived as threatening or injurious to religious and material interests.

Another potentially important consequence of the election may be a cultural reflorescence within Islam in which faith may come to be defined in terms of a religious and cultural rather than a political commitment. In this sense, the belief that Islam is on the political decline may, as Lev notes, "effect a kind of cultural liberation" (Lev 1972:262). Even before the election, a number of younger Islamic figures formerly associated with Himpunan Mahasiswa Indonesia opened a serious social and theological debate among knowledgeable Muslims by contending that the personal affirmation of Islamic faith need not imply support for an Islamic political party. Led by the former chairman of HMI, Nurcholish Madjid, this group posited compartmentalization of religious belief from political affairs — one in which Islamic norms would influence the broad ethical values of society but remain within the purview of personal, as opposed to political, commitment. Such a model affirmed the concept of an ummat united by religious sentiment, but deliberately eschewing a political identity. These ideas were first articulated publicly in 1970, but have received considerable attention since the 1971 election.[3] These younger figures have by no means won the established Islamic political leaders over to their side; even within their own organizations, they have generated much opposition to their position. What they have done, however, is to propose a rethinking, a re-examination, of the Islamic religiopolitical traditions and its relevance to modern society.

All of the preceding, then, may serve to rechannel the Islamic emphasis on politics into religious and cultural directions. The policies desired by figures as diverse as Snouck Hurgronje and Sukarno may now be realized by the actions of the Suharto government. The irony presented by its restrictive actions is that in the long run they may have the unintended consequence of promoting a rethinking on the part of Islam's younger generation, a generation which is not committed to the religiopolitical issues and struggles of the 1950s that so mobilized their elders. The critical variable was the result of the election. Whereas governmental restrictiveness was perceived as anti-Islamic repression when Islam was felt to comprise a "natural political majority," the elections demonstrated that Islam did not comprise such a majority. The committed struggles of the 1950s still bulk large in the memories of many, but as younger figures increasingly come to articulate their views, an Islamic consciousness may develop which "derives moral guidance from Islam, but faces political problems in political terms" (Bellah 1970: 161). Such a development need not necessarily mean the loss of religious importance; indeed, it could ultimately strengthen the ethical and moral influence of the faith.

NOTES

1. Nahdatul Ulama's view of ideology differed from that held by Partai Muslimin's accommodationists in that it was felt to pertain to a social, as well as to a personal, identity.
2. Although Islamic organizations lost out to secular leaders for control of the nationalist movement due to the greater skill and expertise of the latter, the claim to societal primacy could still be maintained so

long as a majority of the population was felt to be Islam-oriented. The results of the recent election would appear to weaken this conviction.

3. See Madjid 1970. See also the journal *Arena* on the speech by Madjid, "Menyegarkan Faham di Kalangan Ummat Islam Indonesia," October 30, 1972, given at Taman Ismail Marzuki. For critical comments, see Rasjidi 1972 and Anshari 1973.

EDITORS' NOTES

* PKI. Partai Komunis Indonesia or Indonesian Communist Party.

** GOLKAR. Golongan Karya (Functional Groups).

The Politics of Islamic Reassertion: Malaysia

N. JOHN FUNSTON

The most significant manifestations of current Islamic revivalism in Malaysia are the emergence of numerous dakwah organisations and a number of new government policies which have given greater emphasis to the importance of Islam. Most of Malaysia's dakwah organisations date from the late 1960s and early 1970s, and indeed even the term dakwah itself had only a limited and specific usage prior to this. It should be noted from the outset that although 'dakwah' (literally, to call or invite) is loosely translated as missionary activities, in the Malaysian context this refers more to the task of making Muslims better Muslims than converting the non-believer. All dakwah groups are committed to at least the first of these two goals, but beyond this there is considerable diversity over objectives, in effect reflecting conflict over the nature of Islam itself. The most fundamental cleavage is between private dakwah organisations committed to establishing a fully Islamic society in Malaysia, and government dakwah organisations which adhere to official policy upholding the need for a secular state.

The largest and most important of the private dakwah organisations is the Muslim Youth Movement of Malaysia (*Angkatan Belia Islam Malaysia*, or ABIM). A brief report on the organisation prepared for ABIM's eighth general assembly in July 1979[1] notes that its formation was first proposed at the annual general meeting of PKPIM [National Union of Malaysian Muslim Students] in August 1969. It came into being two years later. Three reasons for its establishment are noted:

> Firstly, to provide a platform for the graduating students from the respective Universities and Colleges who had been active in *da'wah* activities to continue their Islamic activities; secondly, to fill the vacuum due to the lack of organisation to cater for the interest of Muslim youths at all levels in the Malaysian society; and thirdly, to generate an Islamic Movement as the path to Islamic revival in Malaysia.[2]

Numbers have rapidly swollen from the 153 people attending the inaugural meeting. ABIM now claims 35,000 members, drawn from a broad cross-section of occupations, in 86 branches throughout the country. It is engaged in a wide variety of activities. One of its first initiatives was the establishment of a school, run largely by volunteer labour, to assist 'drop-outs' from the government system. Training camps in Islamic leadership are held at several different levels throughout the year. Islamic study groups are the main focus of regular branch activities. ABIM publications include a Malay language monthly magazine, *Risalah* (restricted by the government to distribution among members), an English language monthly, *Perspective,* launched in September/October 1979, and

Reprinted in abridged form from Mohammed Ayoob (ed.), *The Politics of Islamic Reassertion* (London: Croom Helm, 1981), pp. 165–189, by permission of the author and the publishers.

several books. Islamic books from throughout the world are also sold, and an Islamic Library maintained currently holding some 3,000 volumes. ABIM has been associated with a number of economic co-operatives, one of which currently operates a retail goods shop in Kuala Lumpur, and has established a charitable trust. Finally, it also participates in, or sometimes organises on its own, numerous talks, forums and seminars, from the local to the international level, on Islamic affairs.

ABIM's central message is the importance of Islam as *deen*, a self-sufficient way of life that holds the key to all of man's problems. Ritualistic aspects of Islam, such as the form of clothing worn, are held to be only of secondary importance, a view that contrasts with the strong emphasis most other dakwah groups give to this. The stress on Islam as *deen* makes ABIM the most directly political of all the dakwah groups. This is expressed particularly in calls for the introduction of Islamic legal, educational and economic systems, and political reforms that would end corruption and the misuse of power, and guarantee basic political freedoms. ABIM also takes seriously the bonds of international Muslim brotherhood, asserting that the role of Islam in Malaysia cannot be separated from the fate of Muslims throughout the world.[3]

The details of what an Islamic legal system would look like in the Malaysian context have not yet been spelt out comprehensively. Some of the social ills which, however, have been specially noted for condemnation, and could presumably be legislated against, are trading in alcoholic drinks, taking drugs, gambling, beauty contests and prostitution. It is specifically noted, however, that non-Muslims will be free to implement their own religious laws, and ABIM's president, Anwar Ibrahim, has expressed the view that certain aspects of Muslim personal law (including those relating to *khalwat* — an unmarried couple in close proximity — and *zina* — adultery) should only be applied to non-Muslims with their prior agreement.[4] There is also a commitment to gradualism in such matters. Though the introduction of an Islamic legal system is officially one of ABIM's aims, Anwar has asserted that, 'that's not the issue now. People should be made to understand what Islam is; there's no point harping on Islamic government, Islamic law when people have no opportunity to understand'.[5]

Issues such as these, though important, are stressed less than the Islamic commitment to justice (*keadilan*) in all spheres, particularly in the economy and in politics. The Malaysian economy, it is claimed, benefits only a small group of local and foreign capitalists at the expense of the rest of the population. Islam offers a middle path between this and an equally unacceptable socialism. Among the specific reforms considered necessary are the establishment of non-exploitative credit institutions and land reform to ensure that all who work the land gain an equitable share of its bounty. Politically, the two major issues touched on have been corruption and the lack of political freedom. ABIM leaders were amongst those who, in the early 1970s, initiated complaints against the former Selangor *Mentri Besar* (Chief Minister) Datuk Harun Idris, later followed by Datuk Harun's trial and conviction on a number of charges associated with corruption. They have continued to allege that corruption among Malaysia's top political leaders remains one of the gravest problems facing the nation. ABIM criticisms of restrictions on political freedoms gain a sharp edge from the organisation's own experiences, most notably the two-year detention without trial of Anwar Ibrahim following anti-government student demonstrations in December 1974.

The other major strand in ABIM ideology is its commitment to Muslim internationalism. ABIM leaders are frequent international travellers, participate in a number of international Islamic forums and host visits by Muslim leaders to Malaysia. In spite of such links ABIM denies it has ever received funds from abroad, since 'we know this could be used against us'.[6] At least 20 per cent of the monthly *Risalah* is concerned with Islamic developments outside Malaysia. Much attention is given to the needs of oppressed Islamic minorities in countries as diverse as the Soviet Union, China, Thailand and the Philippines, and the struggle of the Palestinians. The other main focus is on welcoming the present strengthening of the Muslim world and looking for further ways to support this. Recently, ABIM has been a strong supporter of the Iranian revolution. While this has caused some alarm in government quarters, Anwar Ibrahim (who met with Ayatollah Khomeini shortly after the latter's triumphant return to Iran), has not endorsed all Iranian developments, and stressed in his address to the 1979 ABIM general assembly that such support does not mean 'we support similar actions [by Muslim revolutionaries] in Malaysia . . .'.[7] Indeed ABIM leaders recognise that the situation in Malaysia is unique and have rejected the possibility of transplanting any foreign model. A final aspect of the ABIM's international program, though mentioned only occasionally, is its opposition to allegedly anti-Muslim organisations such as Zionists and Freemasons.

From the earlier discussion of post-May 1969 developments it will be apparent that ABIM criticisms of government policy are in several respects justified, and these, together with ABIM's views on international Islam, strike a responsive chord amongst a large section of the Malay population. ABIM is not, however, totally opposed to the government and has cooperated with it in sponsoring Islamic activities on a number of occasions. While there is a very uneasy relationship between the two sides, and the government has acted in a number of ways to limit ABIM activities, the organisation derives its importance, at least in part, from its image as a moderate if uncompromising critic of the government. The two remaining factors largely responsible for ABIM's importance are the prestige of its president, Anwar Ibrahim, and its avoidance of party politics.

Anwar Ibrahim, son of a former UMNO [United Malays National Organisation] parliamentarian, pursued a course in Malay Studies at the University of Malaya during the second half of the 1960s, and at the same time became leader of the two major contemporary Malay student organisations, PKPIM and PBMUM [University of Malaya Malay Language Society]. He was to the fore during the heady days of Malay student opposition to former Prime Minister Tunku Abdul Rahman and government policies on the Malay language and economics, and was successful in establishing a considerable reputation as a mass orator and a determined government critic. On graduation he declined many lucrative opportunities to join the bureaucracy or either of the two major Malay political parties. Instead, he continued to play an active role in youth organisations, involving himself particularly in the founding of ABIM and its school. He has had extensive contact with most government leaders, in spite of tensions, since the 1960s. In December 1974, at the time of student demonstrations in support of Malay peasants suffering acute economic hardship in Kedah, he was arrested and held without trial under Malaysia's Internal Security Act. The government case against him (not officially released, but widely circulated among the Malay community) focused on alleged anti-government activities conducted since 1969 and made only a general reference to background involvement in the 1974 event. He was unconditionally released twenty-two months later. Anwar's position is also enhanced by the contact he has with non-Malays and non-Muslims. Aided by an English-medium education, he has an easy rapport with non-Malays and has had extensive contact with them in the course of various youth and political activities, particularly while head of the coordinating body for all youth groups, the Malaysian Youth Council, in the early 1970s. While many non-Malays remain suspicious of his objectives, he commands respect and has a large circle of friends among them.

ABIM's constitution specifically prohibits it from involvement in any party political activities, and members who have actively participated in party politics have not been allowed to hold official positions. This has given it credibility as an organisation able to speak on behalf of all Muslims without being compromised by the vested interests of the two major Malay political parties, UMNO and PAS [Pan-Malayan Islamic Party]. ABIM has strongly criticised both these parties, but ideologically it has much in common with PAS and there is some evidence that recently it has shifted from a policy of more or less equidistance to one that is much closer to PAS. Anwar spoke at a rally organised by PAS and gave the party a qualified endorsement, before state elections in Kelantan in March 1978. During the PAS general assembly in September 1979, a former ABIM deputy-president was elected vice-president and other ABIM members gained positions on the executive committee. It remains to be seen whether, as a result of these developments, ABIM can continue to maintain its image of political neutrality.

ABIM has so far probably not convinced many non-Malays that Islam provides a solution to Malaysia's many problems. (It has also not actively sought to convert non-Malays to Islam.) But it has increasingly sought to emphasise that its own approach places a lower priority on race than that given by the government and that Islam upholds justice irrespective of race or religion. The presidential address at the ABIM general assembly in July 1979 was entitled 'Islam — Solution to the Problem of a Multi-Racial Society'. While this did not discuss vexed communal issues that have polarised Malaysian society (such as language and education), it did at least emphasise the Islamic commitment to social equality and justice for all. Whether or not non-Malays see merit in these views, they do serve to undercut a prominent theme in government criticism of the dakwah movement, namely the argument that the demands of dakwah groups are often unacceptable to non-Muslims and a grave threat to inter-communal harmony. In terms of actually exerting political influence the support of non-Malays is not, of course, essential, because of the decisive governing role acquired by Malays since May 1969.

ABIM receives a great deal of support from Islamic student organisations attached to all tertiary institutions in Malaysia, commonly linked in PKPIM. Students are discouraged from joining ABIM until after graduation, but PKPIM activities are closely co-ordinated with ABIM, and there is widespread support for ABIM activities among the Malay student body. These organisations, membership of which considerably exceeds ABIM in number, are not generally recognised as separate dakwah entities (perhaps because of their close relations with ABIM), though a large part of their activities are concerned with dakwah.

There are, in addition, a great number of smaller dakwah groups, advocating a much more fundamentalist Islam than that pursued by ABIM. The two best-known groups are *Darul Arqam* and *Jamaat Tabligh.* Darul Arqam was founded in 1969, and now has three centres in Kedah, Trengganu and Selangor. The main operational base is in Selangor, at a village close to Kuala Lumpur. Here an attempt has been made to re-create the life style adhered to during the earliest years of Islam, adopting ancient Arabic forms of clothing and discarding Western innovations such as television sets and chairs. At least some of its followers appear to believe that the end of the world as we know it is imminent, and that the Imam Mahdi will be resurrected to establish universal Islamic rule.[8] Not in other respects directly political, it is attempting to establish a model that can be used for 'Islamising' further areas of Malaysia. Jamaat Tabligh is a Delhi-based missionary organisation which initially gained adherents from Malaysian Muslims of Indian descent and has recently started to gain some Malay support. It is a much less open organisation, places heavy emphasis on rituals, and requires all its followers to undertake missionary activities at least a few days each month. Its political ambitions relate essentially to a desire to 'convert' politicians, which is considered sufficient to ensure that they will not thereafter act unjustly. The combined membership of both these organisations probably does not exceed 10,000.

Organisations of this nature are strongly anti-Western, anti-material development and anti-infidel. In one case this has been carried to the extreme of actually desecrating Hindu temples. On 19 August 1978 five men were caught breaking into a temple by guards, and in the ensuing fight four of the intruders were killed. It was subsequently revealed that, since early August, no less than 28 temples throughout the peninsula had been desecrated. Those responsible were all Malays, most were well educated (at least two had some university training), and all had apparently been associated with extremist dakwah groups. Another four such incidents occurred in May 1979.

There is also at least one underground dakwah movement that seeks the creation of an Islamic government by winning over senior personnel in the administration and the army.[9] The movement has caused some alarm among bureaucratic circles, but appears to have only a very small following. Its future potential must also be doubted, as the social background of the target group — English-educated, conservative and economically well-off — is not conducive to the acceptance of radical Islamic doctrines.

Acting, in part, to offset such extreme elements of the dakwah movement, and for other reasons associated with the aftermath of 13 May 1969, the government has also been extensively involved in dakwah activities over the past decade. As noted, the necessary machinery to intervene in religious affairs was established in 1968, with the launching of the Malaysian National Council for Islamic Affairs within the Prime Minister's Department. Conceived initially as an organisation with very limited powers to co-ordinate the various state Islamic bureaucracies, its activities expanded rapidly during the early 1970s to encompass also instruction on Islam, publication of Islamic materials, an Islamic Research Centre and, in January 1974, an Islamic Missionary Foundation (*Yayasan Dakwah Islamiah*). Its importance was also emphasised by the appointment in 1973 of a Deputy Minister to oversee its activities. Early in 1974 it underwent a change of nomenclature, becoming the Malaysian Council for Islamic Affairs, and a new body, established by the Council of Rulers, became the Malaysian National Council for Islamic Affairs and took over most of the co-ordinating functions previously vested in the Prime Minister's Department. Apart from dakwah activities carried out under the aegis of these two organisations, nearly every federal government department now has its dakwah section. In December 1978 the government made a special effort to support the dakwah movement by holding a 'dakwah month'.

Such activities extend also to the state level, where dakwah sections have become an established part of the religious bureaucracy. The Sabah government was one of the first to act, establishing a dakwah organisation which claimed to have converted some 100,000 non-Muslims — a figure questioned by many — in the early 1970s. Dakwah departments in other states, however, have focused on Muslims rather than non-Muslims.

Government dakwah agencies, it has already been noted, differed from the non-government dakwah groups in stressing largely the moral and spiritual teachings of Islam. Further, in the words of one observer, government missionaries

> seldom showed a critical attitude towards government policies. Rather, they generally raised aspects of Islam that supported the position of the government, or touched on Islam in a general manner, such as emphasising that it endorsed progress, or that it was suitable for all times, or that it was the religion of Allah. A few government missionaries who went beyond these limitations were considered unsuitable or too radical, and were eventually shifted to other positions or forbidden to teach.[10]

Supporting this, government leaders have repeatedly warned the nation of dangers from the non-government dakwah groups, and stressed the need for a 'moderate' approach to Islam. Indeed at times the government was obviously concerned that its own dakwah activities might increase the general level of religious fervour and thus make Malays more susceptible to dakwah extremists. The dakwah month introduced in 1978 was expected to become an annual event, but did not take place in 1979.

Developments relating directly to government dakwah movements should also be seen within the context of other government programs. As part of the post-May 1969 efforts to mobilise people through ideology the government sought to define and foster the emergence of a new national identity. There were several initiatives directed towards this goal, including the proclamation of a national ideology, the *rukunegara,* which has belief in God as one of its pillars, and a five-day, government-sponsored National Cultural Congress in August 1971. One of the three major conclusions of the Congress was that Islam should be recognised as an important part of Malaysian national culture. It also suggested that more should be done to spread Islamic moral values, that the significance of Islam in founding the modern era in Malaysia should be widely taught, and that Islamic and civil law should be unified under a basically Islamic structure. Also, by mid-1971 UMNO had completed a revision of its own ideology and announced a new commitment to according spiritual development an equal place with material development. This policy was strongly reasserted, and reinforced, when UMNO and PAS joined in coalition at the beginning of 1973.

In addition to expansion of the government dakwah movement, several other results of this new policy were evident. Radio and television (both government monopolies) increased the number of programs devoted to Islam, and the call to prayer for two of the five obligatory Muslim prayers broke programs daily on the Malay medium channel, with scenes from Malaysian Islamic life featured as the visual background. A much sterner attitude was also taken towards influences that were considered likely to lower the morals of society. Rock concerts, 'X'-rated movies, and the entry of hippies were all banned; penalties for drug offences were substantially increased; and an attempt was made to rule that dresses for school girls should reach ankle-length (though the government later retreated from its full implementation). Steps were also taken to reform Islamic education. A high-level committee was established in late 1974, and as a result of its recommendations plans to improve the Islamic syllabus in all government schools and to make Islam a compulsory subject for all Muslims, were announced in October 1979. In at least one tertiary institution, the University of Technology, Islam became a compulsory topic for Muslim students. And at a symbolic level the Red Cross was renamed the Red Crescent.

It should, however, be emphasised that steps such as these did not, with the possible exception of Sabah, pose a threat to other religions. The only organisation in Peninsular Malaysia specifically concerned with converting non-Muslims, the Malaysian Muslim Welfare Organisation *(Pertubohan Kebajikan Islam Malaysia)* was more involved in welfare than proselytising activities. A private organisation, but with close government ties (it was established by former Prime Minister Tunku Abdul Rahman in 1960), by 1974 it reported a cumulative total of 20,000 conversions. Religious freedom remains a reality, apart from a long-standing prohibition against non-Muslims attempting to convert Muslims. The government, while acting to enhance the significance of Islamic principles in the legal system, has rejected attempts to make Islamic law the basis of Malaysian law.

Another field in which Islamic affairs have been given higher priority is foreign policy. Malaysia has moved somewhat closer to the Islamic world community, evidenced particularly by the growing exchange of government leaders between Malaysia and the Middle East, Malaysia's support for the Islamic Secretariat (the first Secretary-General of which was Tunku Abdul Rahman), and other initiatives such as the hosting of the Fifth Islamic Foreign Ministers' Conference in 1974. Government leaders have looked hopefully to the Middle East as a source of trade, investment and economic aid, but so far there has been only a small growth in these areas. Malaysia has, however, identified itself with the less revolutionary Islamic states, and has largely reassured neighbouring Thailand and the Philippines, both of which are sensitive about the position of their own Muslim minorities, that the new policy will not be allowed to prejudice regional relations. At the May 1977 Islamic Foreign Ministers' Conference in Tripoli Malaysia co-operated with Indonesia to prevent the seating of Muslim representatives from Southern Thailand, and to soften a resolution condemning the Philippines.

The Islamic revivalist movement is not, of course, the only significant development taking place in the Malay community. There remains, for instance, an enormous desire for material advancement among Malays (the poorest of Malaysia's three major ethnic groups), and the ready employment opportunities available to Malay graduates have served to still much religious fervour. The number of Malays graduating from tertiary institutions who continue to play an active role in Islamic organisations remains relatively small.

None the less the growth of the revivalist movement is an extraordinary phenomenon and has wide implications for many spheres of Malaysian life. The concluding section seeks to draw out more systematically the political significance of the events just described, and to identify other areas in which Islamic revivalism has impinged on the political process.

* * *

The most obvious political consequence of Islamic revivalism, and certainly the one given most prominence in the international press, is its implication for communal relations in Malaysia. Members of extreme dakwah organisations at best seek to avoid contact with infidels, and at worst are openly hostile. The dangers were dramatically illustrated by the case of the Hindu temple desecrations, which predictably provoked a strongly hostile response from the Indian community. Even ABIM, probably the most liberal of the dakwah movements on this issue, has not yet spelt out a precise formula for the place of non-Muslims in Malaysia. Until this happens, it is understandable that non-Malays would be deeply concerned. None the less, ABIM leaders are fully conscious of the fragility of Malaysia's communal balance and have no desire to upset this. They were quick to express opposition to the temple desecrations and, as earlier indicated, have emphasised that the Islamic principle of justice applies equally to non-Muslims. Non-Malays should also be reassured by the government's concern and awareness of the problem: since 13 May it has been well prepared to deal with any outbreak of communal violence.

The major problem in assessing the political significance of Islamic revivalism is to weigh the increased dangers of communalism against the positive role of dakwah organisations as government critics. Without these groups, ABIM and its allies in PKPIM in particular, few voices would be raised about the continuing hardship endured by many in rural areas, or against restrictions on political freedom and the problem of corruption. Virtually the only other organisations to speak on these matters are minority opposition political parties, and these can easily be dismissed as having their own particular axe to grind. The movements perform a public service by raising these issues, and at the same time serve, in effect, as an important safety-valve.

Apart from these two major areas, Islamic revivalism has also had a number of other important implications. It is perhaps almost a truism to note that it has made Islam once again an important issue of political debate and led to increased government intervention in Islamic affairs. As in the past, debate has centred on one interpretation of Islam that focuses on its devotional and moral sides, and another which proclaims the relevance of Islam also in fields such as politics and economics. Similarly, as has often occurred in the past, dakwah members have criticised state control of Islamic affairs, in particular the right of states to determine who teaches Islam within its own boundaries by restricting it to those issued with an official letter of approval (*tauliah*).[11] Given the constitutional and legal position Islam occupies, these issues will not be solved in the short run, and the future of the debate will hinge on the continuing importance of the dakwah movement.

The increased government intervention in Islamic affairs is likely to remain a feature of Malaysian politics for some time. The two broad considerations that have prompted this intervention — the government's desire to increase its legitimacy among Muslims, and its concern to ensure that the energies of the dakwah movement are channelled into politically acceptable activities — should remain salient for many years. An enlarged religious bureaucracy will also help ensure that the momentum is maintained. These activities will, however, continue to be constrained by the government's firm commitment to a secular state, and its fear that too much sponsorship of Islam might strengthen the non-government dakwah.

Islamic revivalism has also had far-reaching effects on the intra and inter-party disputes of UMNO and PAS. During 1977 elements within UMNO, led by members of the Youth wing, capitalised on the concern with Islamic matters by launching a major attack on the alleged dangers of Freemasonry in Malaysia. This appears, in fact, to have been an indirect attack on senior UMNO leaders and members of the judiciary who were either freemasons or had some links with the movement. The attacks on the judiciary were designed to discredit it prior to the sentencing of Datuk Harun Idris, former Mentri Besar of Selangor, on a number of corruption charges. Datuk Harun was leader of UMNO Youth for many years and retained their loyalty even after corruption charges were pressed against him. The innuendo against senior UMNO leaders, on the other hand, needs to be seen in the context of the intra-party conflicts which have racked the party since the death of Prime Minister Tun Abdul Razak in January 1976. Those promoted under Tun Razak were the objects of a concerted campaign aimed at ousting them launched by two factions in the party, one led by Datuk Harun's supporters in UMNO Youth, and another by older UMNO leaders who had been largely edged aside since May 1969. In 1976 the factions launched their opposition on the platform of 'anti-Communism' and in 1977 shifted to anti-Freemasonry.[12] This attack was finally neutralised in 1978 when the government promised to conduct a full enquiry into the issue.

Within PAS, serious intra-party differences emerged in 1972 when a large percentage of the rank and file opposed steps taken to establish a coalition with UMNO. Party president, Datuk Mohammed Asri b. Hj. Muda, adroitly deflected criticisms by extended homilies on the party's Islamic struggle in his addresses to general assemblies. Later intra-party conflicts in Kelantan erupted over the issue of alleged corruption and were generally not specifically related to Islam. One outcome, however, was the formation of a new Islamic party, *Berjasa (Barisan Jamaah Islamiah Malaysia,* Islamic People's Front of Malaysia), early in 1978. Berjasa won 11 seats in the March 1978 Kelantan state election (as against 23 won by UMNO, and 2 by PAS), but its promising start was squandered by subsequent acute internal factionalism, and it now appears unlikely that it will play an important political role in the future.[13]

Since PAS was expelled from the National Front it has continued to stress the Islamic aspect of party ideology, though in a manner that is now directly critical of the government, and has attempted to gain support from members of non-government dakwah groups. As already noted in reference to ABIM, there has recently been some evidence of success. This has been a matter of major concern to the government, which has openly declared that a major reason for its Islamic program is to undercut PAS.[14] While a refurbished PAS may pose a threat in the long term, this is unlikely to emerge in the next few years. In spite of ABIM's endorsement, PAS experienced a shattering defeat in the March 1978 Kelantan state election (noted above) and in the July national election when it won only 5 of 154 seats.

Two other reasons for the government's pursuit of its present Islamic policies are related to its fear that the dakwah movements may stand in the way of Malay economic development, and to its attempt to make Malays immune to the allurements of Communism. With regard to the first of these concerns, there is little evidence so far of dakwah groups committed to such a goal gaining wide support. Groups such as ABIM are certainly not opposed to economic development *per se* and, as previously mentioned, the desire for material advancement in the wider Malay society remains strong. Malay resistance to Communism probably will be strengthened by the dakwah activities, though the number of Malays who have been attracted to Communism in the past is almost negligible.

The final area of relevance is that of foreign affairs. There has, as already noted, been a shift in emphasis towards closer relations with the Islamic world (particularly towards its less revolutionary members), though this has so far had few significant political or economic consequences. It has been marginally more difficult to maintain good relations with neighbouring countries in the face of PAS and ABIM criticisms of Thai and Philippine policy towards their Muslim minorities, but the government has made it clear that Islamic issues will not be pursued at the expense of regional co-operation.

NOTES

1. Cenderamata Muktamar Senawi Ke 8, Angkatan Belia Islam Malaysia, 18 hb–20 hb. Sya'aban 1399/ 13 hb.–15 hb. Universiti Kebangsaan Malaysia, Julai 1979, pp. 4–5.
2. Ibid., p. 4.
3. ABIM has formally spelt out its ideology in a number of 'Declarations'. For the third of these (which

does not differ in substance from the earlier two), see 'Perisytiharan 24 hb. Syaaban 1398', ibid., pp. 22–4.

4. *Asiaweek*, 24 August 1979, p. 31.
5. Ibid., p. 30.
6. Ibid., p. 23.
7. Sdr. Anwar Ibrahim, President ABIM, 'Islam — Penyelesaian Kepada Masalah Masyarakat Majmuk', Kuala Lumpur, nd., p. 29.
8. *Asiaweek*, 1 June 1979, p. 58.
9. Information on the underground dakwah is necessarily difficult to obtain, but the broad outline of the activities the group referred to has been confirmed by several well-placed informants. In April 1980 the existence of another extremist underground movement in Kedah was reported. See *Far Eastern Economic Review*, (11–17 April 1980), pp. 24–5.
10. Mohammed Abu Bakar, 'Kebangkitan Islam dan Proses Politik di Malaysia', Kertaskerja untuk Persidangan Antarabangsa Pengajian Melayu, Universiti Malaya (8–9 September 1979), pp. 19–20.
11. For ABIM's view on this matter see: 'Report on the Asian Muslim Youth Seminar on Da'wah', Kuala Lumpur, (24–8 February 1977). Organised by: Muslim Youth Movement of Malaysia and World Assembly of Muslim Youth. With the co-operation of Malaysian Foundation of Islamic Da'wah and Pusat Islam Malaysia, p. 131. It appears however that several of the dakwah organisations have ignored the requirement of a tauliah, and in some cases their action has been supported by leading figures in the state religious bureaucracy.
12. I have discussed post May 1969 factionalism within UMNO in N.J. Funston, *Malay Politics in Malaysia. A Study of the United Malays National Organisation and Party* (Heinemann Educational Books [Asia] Ltd., Kuala Lumpur, 1980), pp. 240–2, and footnote 157 on p. 291.
13. There is a useful account of the rise and subsequent troubles of Berjasa in Kamarudin Jaffar, 'Malay Political Parties: An Interpretative Essay', Institute of Southeast Asia Studies, *Southeast Asian Affairs 1979*, (Singapore 1979).
14. *Far Eastern Economic Review*, 9 February 1979, p. 23.

Moros and Khaek: The Position of Muslim Minorities in the Philippines and Thailand

PETER G. GOWING

This essay examines some of the factors — ethnic, social, historical, religious, and so on — which currently mark the Muslims of the Philippines and Thailand as people apart, deserving of patient consideration and special accommodation in their respective countries. Though they are separated by more than 2,012 kilometres of land and sea, and are citizens of two quite different nations, the situations of the Filipino and Thai Muslims are so strikingly similar that it is both appropriate and instructive to look at them together. Hopefully, our examination will contribute to an understanding of why significant numbers of Muslims in the two countries are engaged in secessionist struggles against their governments. That this is a matter of more than academic interest will be obvious to anyone who observes the Southeast Asian scene. For the fact is that tension and violence between Muslims and non-Muslims in the Philippines and Thailand have steadily escalated in recent years, contributing to instability in the region and adversely affecting the economies of both countries. The inter-relationships of the five member states of the Association of Southeast Asian Nations are directly affected, for each of them has highly volatile majority/minority problems, and the outbreak of communal trouble in one of the neighbouring states inevitably has repercussions in the others. Furthermore, the Muslim nations of the Middle East — from whence comes much of the oil energizing the industries, commerce, and communications of the Philippines and Thailand — are watching the present travail of their Muslim brothers in those lands with sympathetic concern and, occasionally, with overt expressions of support.

Professor Wilfred Cantwell Smith, in his classic study of *Islam in Modern History,* points out that the Muslim minority in India is facing a problem virtually unprecedented in Islamic history: how to live as *equals* with non-Muslims in the same state. Historically, Muslims have seen Islam as a closed system — embracing *all* aspects of the lives of Muslims, making no distinction between "secular" and "religious" — and one of their fundamental convictions has been that Muslims can never be fully Muslims without a state of their own. "Muslims," writes Professor Smith, "have either had political power or they have not. *Never before have they shared it with others."* In the past, when Muslim communities had been conquered by non-Muslims, the Muslims could at least hope and strive for freedom. But the tens of millions of Muslims in India now find themselves as citizens of a secular state, made up overwhelmingly of non-Muslim fellow citizens, in which freedom of religion is protected by law. The problem arises from the fact that many Indian Muslims continue to see Islam as a closed system, and despite certain concessions which are made in law to meet some of their

Reprinted from *Southeast Asian Affairs 1975* (Singapore: Institute of Southeast Asian Studies), pp. 27–40.

Islamic customs, they feel that they are less than fully Muslim because they are not politically part of an Islamic social order. Nor can they realistically hope and strive for a change in their situation. They are in a position of being forced to reconcile what many of them regard as basically irreconcilable: the demands of their common citizenship with non-Muslims in the Republic of India, and the demands of Islam which in their view presuppose membership in a closed community (*umma*) obedient to Islamic law (*shari'a*). That many Indian Muslims find reconciling the demands of Indian citizenship and faithfulness to Islam very difficult cannot be denied, and this difficulty has been one of the major reasons for continuing tension between Muslims and non-Muslims in India.

The Muslim minorities in the Philippines and Thailand find themselves in a position comparable with that of the Indian Muslims. They, too, are caught in the dilemma of having to reconcile the demands of their rather traditionalist conception of faithfulness to Islam with the demands of citizenship in modern states in which non-Muslims predominate and in which freedom of religion is protected. However, unlike the Indian Muslims, who are scattered in communities all over the country, the 2·2 million Filipino Muslims and the 1·5 million Thai Muslims are placed in a more complicated dilemma. Theirs is compounded by the circumstance that both groups are concentrated in the southern provinces of their respective countries, in areas contiguous to predominantly Muslim Malaysia and Indonesia. The fact that many Muslims in the Philippines and Thailand believe it to be impossible to reconcile their present national citizenship with full adherence to Islam explains in part the existence of vigorous Muslim separatist movements which are gripped in guerrilla warfare with government forces in these two countries. The separatists seek independence, though some favour eventual union with Malaysia. But the reality is that their homelands are now internationally recognized as part of the national territories of the Philippines and Thailand, and there is little likelihood that the separatists can succeed in actually taking those southern provinces out of the two countries.

It is the thesis of this essay that, in the final analysis, the Filipino and Thai Muslims, like their Muslim brothers in India, will simply have to find ways of reconciling the seemingly irreconcilable. Their situation as citizens of the Philippines and Thailand is not likely to change, and they will continue to be expected to participate fully, in co-operation with all other citizens, in the goals of nation-building and development. But it is clear that if they are to do so more effectively than in the past, they will have to solve some of the problems special to themselves as Muslims, including fundamental problems of Islamic theology, law, and morals. They will probably find little in Islamic precedent to help them. Instead, they will have to rely largely on the experience of modern-minded Muslims elsewhere who are facing similar situations, and on their own creative ingenuity, to find solutions, in the light of God's wisdom, which will allow them to rest easy in their conscience as Muslims. Still, as Professor Smith has so aptly stated with respect to the Muslim minority in India:

> . . . all Muslims together are in fact in a comparable situation within mankind. The relative independence of civilizations has in our day died. Each of man's cultures is called upon to evolve a new ingredient: compatibility. The West has perhaps most to learn in this regard, but no civilization is exempt. In the past civilizations have lived in isolation, juxtaposition, or conflict. Today we must learn to live in collaboration. Islam like the others must prove creative at this point, and perhaps it will learn this in India.

Maybe it will learn this, too, in the Philippines and Thailand.

For their part, the governments and non-Muslim peoples of the Philippines and Thailand must recognize, understand, and make appropriate allowances for the special difficulties the Muslim minorities have in adjusting to their role as full and responsible citizens. Filipino and Thai Muslims are, after all, citizens through no choice of their own, of nations which they had no hand in establishing and by which, as a matter of historical fact, they were conquered. Thus they do, in a very real sense, feel

> . . . a stranger and afraid
> In a world I never made.

The canons of human decency, and the prerequisites of peace and stability in Southeast Asia, require that Filipino Christians and Thai Buddhists and their governments do a better job than in the past of helping the Muslims to see themselves as full partners in national development and entitled to a full share of the national patrimony of their respective countries. This will tax all of the reserves of patience, goodwill, and generosity which belong to peoples avowedly Christian and Buddhist — but the alternative is a continuation of the debilitating tensions and conflicts which have for too long prevailed in the southern parts of the Philippines and Thailand.

INTEGRATION FOR CONSOLIDATION

The political incorporation of the Muslim areas into the Philippines and Thailand was, in both cases, the end result of centuries of struggle. Beginning in the last quarter of the sixteenth century, the Spaniards fought the "Moro Wars" for three hundred years before the Muslim sultanates in Mindanao and Sulu grudgingly acknowledged Spanish sovereignty. And, in the first two decades of this century, the Americans, succeeding to Spanish sovereignty, were obliged to wage a number of costly military campaigns to "pacify" Filipino Muslims. The Spanish and American forces used in the military subjugation of the Muslims were manned, to a large extent, by Filipino Christians — and by 1920, effective government of the Muslim area was in the hands of Filipino Christian administrators in accord with the American "Filipinization" policy looking towards the self-government of Filipinos in a Commonwealth (1935) and eventually a Republic (1946).

Siamese efforts to subjugate the small Malay states of the northern Malay Peninsula began earlier — back in the late thirteenth century during the reign of King Ramakhamhaeng of Sukhothai. But it was not until the nineteenth century, after much bloodshed and intrigue, that Thailand (then called Siam) came to exercise more than nominal sovereignty in the area. By virtue of the Anglo-Siamese treaties of 1904 and 1909, she was obliged to give up her claims of suzerainty over four Malay states which were then incorporated into British Malaya, but she was given tacit recognition of her authority over the territories and Malay peoples north of the agreed-upon border.

For a mixture of nationalist, developmental, and security reasons, twentieth century governments in both the Philippines and Thailand have sought to consolidate their hold on the Muslim inhabited southern provinces. The overall aim of their policies and programmes is best summarized by the word "integration". The first step was administrative integration, designed to bring the Muslim areas into the national political systems centralized in Manila and Bangkok. Because the Muslims had no experience with those systems, it was believed necessary to put them under Filipino Christian and Thai Buddhist government officials. In both countries, the traditional leaders of Muslim society were virtually bypassed in the establishment of the national political structures in their areas, though a few, especially in the Philippines, came eventually to participate in local and national political life through election or appointment to public office. But, until the 1950's, the Muslim provinces of the southern Philippines were still under governors appointed from Manila and most of them were Christians. To this day, there are no Muslim governors in the southern provinces of Thailand.

Along with administrative integration, there has been government concern for economic integration, and for the involvement of the southern provinces in the development goals of the two nations. The first care was to see that governing the southern provinces would not be burdensome to the national treasuries. Thus, taxes in one form or another began to be collected, and duties were imposed on trade coming from across international borders. Then there has been the wish to gainfully exploit the natural resources of the Muslim areas and harness them to the national economy. In the southern Philippines, this had meant mainly that sparsely settled but rich agricultural lands in Mindanao and Sulu were surveyed, titled, and made available to large numbers of Christian homesteaders from the northern and central provinces of the country. The process began well before World War II but has accelerated since the war as population pressures in the north have proven acute. All the while, Filipino Muslim anxieties over the alienation of lands they regard as theirs, and their cultural involvement in a system of clan ownership of land as over against individual title ownership, have been overriden, giving rise to explosive problems in Muslim relations with non-Muslim settlers.

Parts of southern Thailand have long been exploited for tin, though the Muslim villagers have been mostly farmers and fishermen. In the twentieth century, the area has shown itself amenable to the commercial production of rubber and coconuts. Partly for the purpose of developing plantations for these and other cash crops, and partly to introduce an ethnic mixture into the predominantly Malay south, the Thai Government has sponsored, since World War II, the resettlement of thousands of non-Muslims from other parts of the country in the more sparsely inhabited interior districts of the southern provinces. Thai Muslims fear that, in time, they will be submerged in their own homeland by non-Muslims and that this is the government's real plan.

The motives behind Philippine and Thai efforts at the cultural integration of their minority peoples — including the Muslims — are quite complex. Certainly a prime motive has been a natural wish to forge national unity in order to counter the centrifugal forces of traditional regionalism and tribalism. In addition, there has been an ill-defined urge to a sort of *mission civilisatrice* on the part of the Christian and Buddhist majorities, respectively, toward the non-Christian and non-Buddhist peoples of the two countries. There is no question that the minority peoples, except, perhaps, the Chinese, are generally regarded by the majority peoples as more or less backward and unprogressive. Muslims find this implication of integration policies and programmes particularly offensive.

In both the Philippines and Thailand, the Muslims, of all the minority peoples subjected to government integration objectives, have demonstrated themselves to be more determined and better organized to resist. Hence, greater pressure has had to be applied to them. This pressure has been applied far more restrainedly in the Philippines than in Thailand, however. The Philippines, after all, is (the present martial régime hopefully not for long withstanding) a secular democratic state committed to the principles of separation of church and state and freedom of religion. So, government officials have been somewhat responsive to complaints about aspects of integration raised by Muslims on the basis of religion. The Commission on National Integration, established in 1957, is the government agency with prime responsibility for receiving and interpreting those complaints. Still, the integration activities of the government, including the expansion of the public school system in the southern provinces, have long been seen by many Muslims as a grand conspiracy to dilute the distinctiveness of their society and gradually move it toward the adoption of Filipino Christian social and economic patterns. These Filipino Muslims are not likely to give up soon looking for an alternative to that. Some have opted for secession.

The Kingdom of Thailand is not a secular state, but throughout the twentieth century, the laws of the country, including all of the Constitutions since 1934, have permitted freedom of religion in terms similar to those in most secular democratic states. The King, who is titular head of the Buddhist religion in Thailand, is also the "patron" of the non-Buddhist religions in the country. Still, Thai Muslims have had much to fear for their culture and way of life (seen by them as integral to their religion) from the integration policies and programmes of the Thai Government. The danger is present even now, but it was greater during the two periods (1938–44 and 1947–57) of the premiership of Field Marshall Phibun Songkhram. A chauvinist dictator, Phibun sought to Siamize all the non-Buddhist minority groups in the nation. Beginning in 1940, certain cultural "rules" were introduced and enforced. Oddly, these rules included such things as wearing western dress, along with brimmed hats, by both men and women. People were to use forks and spoons and to sit on chairs at tables when they ate. The Muslims in the south were discouraged from wearing Malay dress and were obliged to adopt Thai names if they sought admission to government schools or employment in government service. The Malay language was prohibited from being taught in the public schools or used in transactions with government officials. Restrictions were placed on the practice of Islam, and the special provisions for the application of Islamic law relating to marriage and inheritance were abolished. The more obnoxious of these rules were relaxed when Phibun was overthrown in 1944, but the Thai Muslims were already thoroughly aroused against the government. Their feelings rose to fever pitch as the winds of Malay nationalism blew in the immediate post-war period. Muslim leaders who petitioned or criticized the government were imprisoned or liquidated. In 1948, armed revolt broke out in the provinces of Pattani and Narathiwat, and while it was quickly put down (with much bloodshed), it resulted in many hundreds of Thai Muslims fleeing over the border into Malaya for safety. Large numbers of them are still there, from whence they support continuing dissidence and separation in their homeland.

The difficulty which both the Philippines and Thailand have in meeting their integration objectives among Muslim minorities is compounded by the activities of some inept, corrupt, and abusive government officials to whom the administration of integration programmes and funds are committed. It is compounded, too, by the misdeeds and perfidy of some unscrupulous citizens, both Muslim and non-Muslim, who exploit sensitive situations and manipulate people purely for their private interests. But, having said this, we must also acknowledge that the cause of the difficulty goes much, much deeper. It is rooted in the negative attitudes which the majority peoples have developed with regard to the Muslim minorities, *and* vice versa. It is rooted, as well, in the very nature of the Islamic consciousness of Filipino and Thai Muslims. To these matters we turn our attention now.

NEGATIVE ATTITUDES

In the Philippines and Thailand, the Muslim minorities are popularly referred to as *Moros* and *Khaek* respectively. Both terms have pejorative connotations and symbolize the general dis-ease of the Muslim position *vis-à-vis* the majority peoples. Filipino Muslims were first called Moros by the Spaniards in the sixteenth century, after the Islamized North African Mauritanians (Moors) who, under Arab leadership, had conquered and ruled in Spain for eight centuries. The name stuck, but, over the centuries, it turned from being a left-handed compliment into a label of contempt as the Filipino Muslims stubbornly resisted conquest and then "Filipinization". In the popular mind, "Moro" came to connote a people who were ignorant, treacherous, violent, polygamists, slaves, pirates, and so on. In the 1950's, reacting to this negative connotation and reflecting the post-war resurgence of Islam which they were then experiencing, many Muslims began to insist on being called "Muslims" or "Filipino Muslims". They became very sensitive to being called "Moros". Non-Muslims soon learned to be cautious in their use of the term, at least in front of Muslims.

Interestingly enough, in the past three years or so, as fighting between Muslims and Christians dramatically escalated in the southern Philippines, the label "Moro" has come back into common use — on both sides! The tragic conflict has given the Muslims new confidence and self-awareness, and they openly declare themselves to be *Bangsa Moro* (the Moro Nation) as distinct from the *Bangsa Pilipino*. The separatist movement now identifies itself as the "Bangsa Moro Republic". In fact, in the southern Philippines, "Moro" is fast becoming a national designation overriding the old group distinctions of "Tausug", "Maranao", "Maguindanao", and so forth. And even Christians and other non-Muslims loyal to the separatist cause can be Moros. The first issue of *Mahardika,* the clandestine newspaper of the Moro National Liberation Front, declared:

> From this very moment there shall be no stressing the fact that one is a Tausug, a Samal, a Yakan, a Subanon, a Kalagan, a Maguindanao, a Maranao, or a Badjao. He is only a Moro. Indeed, even those of other Faith who have long established residence in the Bangsa Moro homeland and whose goodwill and sympathy are with the Bangsa Moro Revolution shall, for purposes of national identification, be considered Moros. In other words, the term "Moro" is a national

> concept that must be understood as all-embracing for all Bangsa Moro people within the length and breadth of our national homeland.

The term *Khaek* lends itself to no such reconstruction. In the Thai language, it literally means "visitor". But, for at least a century, the term has also been used to refer to dark skinned foreign visitors or immigrants and, in that connotation, has been popularly applied to Indians and Malays residing in Thailand. The Muslims of southern Thailand, being Malays, are also called "Khaek", which they deeply resent for they are neither foreign visitors nor immigrants. They have inhabited the lands they occupy for many centuries. Officially, they are called "Thai Muslims", but even this designation is offensive to some, particularly the separatists. To the latter, "Thai" means "Siamese", and though there are a number of Indian, Pakistani, Chinese, and Siamese Muslims in Thailand, the vast majority are of the Malay race. The separatists — and some who are not separatists — want to be known simply as "Malays" or "Malay Muslims". They charge that the government's policy of calling them "Thai Muslims" is a deliberate attempt to blur their identity as an altogether different people from the rest of the Thai nation.

There is ample evidence in the Philippines and Thailand that negative attitudes towards the Muslim minorities do exist among the majority peoples. Perhaps nothing contributes more to the breakdown of the integration efforts of the two nations *vis-à-vis* the Muslims than the persistence of the pejorative popular stereotypes of "Moros" and "Khaek". These stereotypes are, in part, the inheritance from centuries of conflict between the Muslim and non-Muslim peoples; and, in part, the result of simple prejudice against people of a different religion and culture who, from a national point of view, appear to be stubborn and unprogressive. It is likely that there are elements of "scapegoatism", of atavistic fears (on the part of Filipino Christians), and of feelings of racial superiority (on the part of Thai Buddhists) mixed into such prejudice.

A study of ethnic attitudes in five Philippine cities located outside the Muslim area was recently conducted by Dr Rodolfo Bulatao, a respected sociologist at the University of the Philippines. A "systematic random sampling" of some 1,700 respondents was asked to class various Philippine ethnic groups according to fourteen categories: intelligence, industriousness, friendliness, generosity, progressiveness, peacefulness, cleanliness, and so on. Filipino Muslims were rated low in every category except thrift and physical strength, and they were the least favoured as employers, neighbours, and sons-in-law. The questionnaire included twenty-six statements with which respondents were to agree or disagree. The statement which attracted the strongest and most universal agreement was "The Philippines should be proud of being a Catholic country", while there was universal disagreement with the statement "The Muslims are making an important contribution to national development". Only 5·5% of the respondents felt that the religious rights of the Muslims should be recognized as one of the features of integration. "Perhaps the most important conclusion to be drawn," writes Professor Bulatao, "is that a gap exists between protestations of national unity at the level of national or regional leadership and the attitudes of ordinary people across ethnic boundaries, particularly those that set apart Chinese and Muslims."

The present writer is unaware of any such comprehensive survey of ethnic attitudes conducted in Thailand, but, all indications are that the observation of a British journalist who visited Thailand in 1947 is still valid: "Siamese colonialists openly scorn their Malay subjects as a race of illiterate and degenerate peasants." In 1966–67, Professor M. Ladd Thomas of the University of Northern Illinois surveyed the attitudes of some 108 non-Muslim Thai Government officials at work in the southern provinces. A large majority of his respondents regarded Muslims as less hardworking and less intelligent than Buddhists. Moreover, he found that those officials who had the most exposure to Thai Muslims tended to have the lowest opinion of them. Professor Thomas found that, in south Thailand, the negative attitudes of the bureaucrats were accompanied by correspondingly offensive behaviour on their part which, he concluded in something of an understatement, "may pose serious obstacles to political integration of the Thai Muslims."

Filipino and Thai Muslims sustain equally unflattering attitudes towards the majority peoples of their two countries — and this mutual antipathy continues from generation to generation. But, from the Muslim side, the antipathy is not simply a matter of inherited hostilities and prejudice, it is more profoundly a matter of religion: the inherent (in their view) antipathy of *dar al-Islam* (the "abode of Islam") and *dar al-Harb* (the "abode of war", that is, the non-Muslim nations). Filipino Christians and Thai Buddhists both protest that their current contests with the Muslim minorities are not religious warfare. The governments in both countries say they are fighting Muslim "bandits" or Muslim dissidents led astray by communist insurgents. They say that the issues are political and economic, and have nothing to do with religion, the freedom of which is guaranteed. But the Muslims who are fighting government forces in the southern Philippines and Thailand insist that they are engaged in *jihad* (holy war) in defence of Islam, and that the issues are religious. The crux of the matter is, of course, that in the Muslim view Islamic "religion" covers an infinitely broader range of affairs than ritual and doctrine. The negative attitudes of non-Muslims leave them ill-disposed to understand why the Muslims see their struggle as religious. Indeed, these attitudes prevent the non-Muslims from taking the Islamic faith of the Muslims seriously, and make them easy prey to the suspicion that Muslims use their difference in religion as an excuse to pursue interests which have nothing to do with religion. While such a suspicion is justified in a few instances, it is not justified as a generalization for the core of Muslim strugglers-for-freedom. The truth is, Filipino and Thai Muslims are victims of a costly misreading, by non-Muslims, of their Islamic consciousness.

ISLAMIC CONSCIOUSNESS

The Filipino and Thai Muslims live in quite a different world from that of either of the majority peoples in their respective countries. Filipino Christians, Thai Buddhists, and the Muslims are each oriented toward a different wider community from which they draw their religion, culture, law, values, and view of history. The Filipino Christians owe much to the West — to Spain which brought the Roman Catholic faith and many influences in language, music, art, law, and others; and to America which brought the English language, democratic institutions, and the "Hollywood" life-style. Thai Buddhists owe much to China, to India, and to Ceylon and other parts of the Theravada Buddhist world. But the Muslims of the southern parts of the Philippines and Thailand have their roots in the Malay world, and owe much to the Islamic civilization of Arabia and the Middle East. One cannot study the histories of the Mindanao and Sulu sultanates or of the old kingdom of Pattani and other Kra Isthmus states without discovering the dynastic, political, and trade relationships which, for centuries, existed between them and the rest of the Malay world, and the larger Islamic world beyond. One cannot travel in the Muslim areas of the Philippines and Thailand — each located just over the border on opposite ends of Malaysia — without noting that the arts and manufactures, music and dancing, language and literature, dress and life-ways are similar, if not practically identical, to those of neighbouring Malaysia and Indonesia. Nor can one stay long in the Philippine and Thai southern provinces without being aware that a great deal of commerce and communication — legal or otherwise — is still carried on between the Muslim inhabitants and their kinsmen and partners across the international borders. Indeed, those borders were more or less imposed by Western colonial powers and had the effect of imposing Philippine and Thai nationality on people who were, and are, integral to the Malay world.

Like so many other underdeveloped modern nations, both the Philippines and Thailand have been preoccupied since the Second World War with problems of economic, scientific, and educational development; international trade; foreign relations; and constitutional and political upheaval. Meanwhile, their Muslim minorities have been growing even more firmly fixed in their Islamic consciousness. They have constructed many new mosques, established many new religious schools, organized many new Islamic societies and associations, sent many more of their number on the *hajj* to Mecca, and welcomed expanded contacts with fellow Muslims from many other Muslim lands. Government efforts to wean the Muslim minorities away from the Malay and Islamic worlds and integrate them into the modern Philippine or Thai worlds have fallen short of success partly because of the impediments presented by their deepening Islamic consciousness.

This consciousness can be described — and should be understood — in terms of psychological identity, the Islamic ideal of *umma,* and the concept of *dar al-Islam.*

PSYCHOLOGICAL IDENTITY

Ordinary Filipino and Thai Muslims may not have a very sophisticated knowledge of the classical theology, philosophy, and legal formulations of Islam, and they may even *confuse* some pre-Islamic superstitions and customary practices (*adat*) with the essentials of Islam, but most of them do know the basic teachings and duties of their faith. They are conscious that their religion sets them apart from all other men, binds them together as a community, and, at least ideally, governs all aspects of their lives. Most important, there is no question about the psychological disposition of the ordinary person to be Muslim, which is, in the final analysis, the only valid criterion (even in Islamic law) by which their degree of "Muslimness" can be judged. At the same time, among the Filipino and Thai Muslims, there are a number of persons who have a solid learning in Islam, and from these persons come those who are recognized as *'Ulama,* that is, religious leaders qualified to pronounce on religious and legal matters affecting the community.

Islam, whatever their doctrinal grasp of it, provides the Filipino and Thai Muslims with, at the very least, a psychologically crucial view of the meaning of their existence. It shields them from the unbearable thought that their individual lives are fleeting and insignificant, and links them to a larger and more enduring purpose: the Will of Allah, as they understand it ("Islam" and "Muslim" come from the same root in Arabic meaning "submission"). And this constitutes a faith-ideology which is vital to their existence and which gives meaning to their lives. Any threat to this ideology would be intolerable and would represent a kind of "psychological death" which would be harder to contemplate than biological death. Historically, both Filipino and Thai Muslims have suffered much "biological death", in many bloody encounters with non-Muslims, defending the independence of their homelands (seen as *dar al-Islam*) and life-ways (seen as sanctioned by the Qur'an and Islamic custom). Unable to prevent the physical conquest of their homelands and their incorporation into the Philippine and Thai nations, the Muslims have nevertheless continued to struggle, in every way open to them, against threats to their psychologically-anchored Islamic identity.

The Moro National Liberation Front in the southern Philippines and the National Liberation Front of the Pattani Republic in southern Thailand are best understood as products of the strong Islamic identification of the Muslim minorities. They do not represent a phenomenon in Islam unique to Southeast Asia. Among traditionalist-minded Muslims in other parts of the world are many who turn to movements — some of them fanatical — which help them come to grips with such forces as colonialism, secularism, modernism, communism, and so forth, which threaten their all-embracing faith-ideology.

THE UMMA IDEAL

From an Islamic viewpoint, the fundamental concern of all such movements is to preserve, or to recover or restore as much as possible, the *umma,* the Islamic social community, in which the Divinely-ordained faith-ideology, with its accrued doctrines, customs, and laws, may find full expression. All Muslims belong, by virtue of being Muslims, to the world-wide, spiritual, non-territorial *umma* of Islam, no matter where they live. But, theoretically, each individual Muslim, in order to feel himself fully Muslim, seeks to be part of an *umma* on the local level, that is, he feels the need to belong to a local community which maintains the essentials of an Islamic social order. Thus, to illustrate, we find the noted Filipino scholar, Cesar A. Majul, addressing his fellow Muslims as follows:

> The fundamental question now facing individual Muslims in the Philippines is

> whether they still desire to have or preserve a Muslim community in the country — a community that will testify to the Oneness of Allah and the Prophethood of Muhammad and who will adhere to the fundamentals of Islam. This question is not the same as that as to whether the Muslims want to exist as individuals or not. The question, to be repeated, is whether the Muslims want to preserve their existence as an *ummah* .... It is inconsistent and not canonically possible for an individual to claim that he can still be a Muslim and not advocate the existence of a Muslim community .... Moreover, Allah has commanded the believers to act as a community or as a nation .... It has been clearly demonstrated that no one can be a good Muslim unless he works for the unity and cohesion of the Muslim community as well as its social well-being.

Any understanding of what has been happening among Filipino and Thai Muslims in recent years is inadequate if it fails to grasp that their activities aim at preserving such aspects of *umma* as remain to them in their respective areas, and recovering, if possible, those aspects of *umma* which they believe they have lost.

DAR AL-ISLAM

In the past, the Muslim areas of the present-day Philippines and Thailand were clearly *dar al-Islam,* that is, they were territorially part of the "abode of Islam". But their conquest by non-Muslims put those areas in an ambiguous position from the standpoint of Islamic law (*shari'a*). Filipino and Thai Muslims are, as we have noted, members of the spiritual, non-territorial, world-wide *umma* simply by being Muslims, and those living in communities more or less isolated from non-Muslims can achieve *umma* on the local level. But there is a question as to whether their homeland areas are still to be regarded territorially as part of *dar al-Islam* or as lost to *dar al-Harb* (the "abode of war", the territory of non-believers). This question is important to Muslims because it affects how they see their relationship to the non-Muslim governments under which they live. In the traditionalist view of Islamic law, if a Muslim country is conquered by non-Muslims who then, by their policies and actions, turn it into *dar al-Harb,* it is lawful for the Muslim "prisoners" to oppose the non-Muslims and fight them in every way possible.

Islamic law recognizes that a country which passes into the hands of non-Muslim conquerors does not *ipso facto* become *dar al-Harb.* It becomes so under three conditions: (1) when the legal decisions of unbelievers are regarded and those of Islam are not; (2) when the territory in question is not contiguous to a country which is *dar al-Islam* — in other words, it is completely surrounded by *dar al-Harb* territory; and (3) when no Muslim, or non-Muslim subject of a Muslim state, can live there in the same security as under the previous Muslim government.

Of these conditions, Muslim jurists regard the first as the most important, and some hold that as long as a single legal decision of Islam is observed and maintained, a country once Muslim cannot be said to have become *dar al-Harb.* The more general view is that if Islamic laws are enforced for Muslims, then the country retains its character as *dar al-Islam.* Muslim jurists also generally agree that another test of *dar al-Islam* is whether Muslims are able to hold their Friday assembly prayers and *Id* observances in places where they are not liable to be molested.

A number of the Filipino and Thai Muslims feel that because their non-Muslim governments allow sufficient freedom of religion, and make sufficient provision for the observance of some Islamic customs and laws, their areas are, therefore, still part of *dar al-Islam.* They are, thus, inclined to co-operate with their governments, and their concern is to press peacefully for an expansion of Islamic privileges and to protect the Islamic interests of the Muslim citizens. Many others feel that the Muslim areas are now in an intermediate position between *dar al-Islam* and *dar al-Harb,* and that there is danger of their slipping into the latter. In the Philippines, this intermediate position is sometimes called *dar al-Aman* (or *Darul Aman*), the "abode of peace", meaning that in the Muslim areas, Islam is, for the sake of trust and safety, protected to some extent by the laws and policies of the non-Muslims.

It is in the light of this *dar al-Islam/dar al-Harb* dichotomy that many of the issues which the Filipino and Thai Muslims raise with their national governments should be seen. Their past and present anxieties over such matters as official recognition of the dignities of their traditional leaders, the appointment of Muslims to government posts in their own areas, the security of their lands from alienation, respect for their religious customs, official cognizance of Islamic and *adat* law (particularly in domestic and inheritance affairs), and so on, should be understood as part of their general concern to preserve, or restore, their homelands as *dar al-Islam.* Although few Filipino and Thai Muslims would articulate their situation to non-Muslims in quite these terms, the fact is that their secession movements spring from their fear that government policies and programmes aimed at integration have the effect of turning their homelands into *dar al-Harb.* Moreover, this phraseology is found in Article III, Section 4 of the "Constitution and By-Laws of the Muslim Independence Movement of the Philippines" drawn up by ex-Governor Udtog Matalam of Cotabato and his followers in June 1968.

> That it is the duty and obligation of every MUSLIM to wage JIHAD, physically or spiritually, to change DARUL AMAN (present status of the Muslim communities) to DARUL ISLAM (Islamic territory) and prevent it from becoming DARUL HARB (hostile territory to the MUSLIM).

TOWARDS COMPATIBILITY

It is axiomatic in physics that when an irresistable force meets an immovable object, something has got to give. The Muslim minorities of the Philippines and Thailand are, in a sense, "immovable objects" confronting the seemingly "irresistable forces" of Philippine and Thai national destinies. Today, as so often in the past, their respective confrontations are violent, and, eventually, something has simply got to give.

Hopefully, the giving will be on both the Muslim and non-Muslim sides. The Filipino and Thai Muslims have natural human rights regarding their religion, customs and traditions, living space, and economic resources. They are entitled to have these rights recognized by their fellow citizens in the two countries. On the other hand, the Muslims must understand that, for better or worse, the forces of history have brought them and their homelands into union with the Philippine and Thai states. They belong, whether they like it or not, to the national concept of the two countries, and the nationalist sentiments of the majority peoples are unlikely to tolerate secession. Moreover, the Muslim areas in both lands are regarded as vital to their economic development and political security. So, if the present unhappy state of affairs is not to continue, Muslims and non-Muslims are going to have to work harder for compatibility.

In countries where cultural, religious, and linguistic minorities have long histories of their own, the cause of compatibility is probably best served if official policies allow, in an openly democratic spirit, cultural and religious pluralism. The Constitutions newly promulgated in the Philippines (January 1973) and Thailand (October 1974) affirm such a spirit in the two nations. At the same time, Filipino and Thai government legislators and administrators would be well advised to recognize that the Muslim minorities possess certain legal, educational, and social interests for which special accommodation ought to be made, though, of course, not in such a way as to affirm Muslim solidarity and against the rights and freedom of other citizens.

This essay cannot presume to put forth anything like a plan for achieving compatibility between Muslims and non-Muslims, but, perhaps, it would be appropriate, in the light of what has been said so far, to suggest briefly a few of the ingredients which might be included in such a plan.

On the side of the Filipino Christian and Thai Buddhist majorities, and the governments in which they predominate, the *sine qua non* of compatibility would seem to be responding positively to the deeply felt fears of the Muslim minorities. Former Senator Mamintal Tamano, speaking on behalf of fellow Muslims in the Philippines, though he could have been speaking for the Thai Muslims as well, summarized those fears under four headings:

(*a*) Fear of being alienated from their religion.

(*b*) Fear of being displaced from their ancestral home.

(*c*) Fear of having no future in their country because they really do not participate in its government nor share in the economic benefits derived from the exploitation of its natural resources.

(*d*) Fear of losing cherished values, customs, and traditions.

A positive response to these fears would begin with an appreciation of the fact that they are genuine, long-standing, and deserving of serious consideration and action. Elements in positive action would include the following:

(1) Ensure that the public schools throughout the nation contribute to inculcating in their pupils an attitude of respect and appreciation for the religion, culture, and histories of all the peoples who make up the nation, including the Muslims; and ensure that the public communication media contribute to a wholesome attitude in inter-group, inter-religious relationships.

(2) Take the necessary measures in law — and enforce them — with regard to securing for the Muslims (and other minority peoples) their traditional lands and living space.

(3) Provide in law for the enforcement, by separate religious courts organized and supported by Muslims, of the Islamic personal law system in cases involving Muslims only. Laws should also provide for the protection of religious education, observances, and traditions.

(4) Give serious attention to the desire of many Muslims for some measure of autonomy for their areas, including the possibility of establishing a form of federal relation to their respective national governments. The subject is worthy of full discussion. Especially worthy of respect is the demand of Muslims that more of their number be properly trained and appointed to responsible government posts, especially, though not exclusively, in the Muslim areas.

(5) Pay heed to the claims of Muslims that they have not received a just share of the national economic patrimony. Most likely, it will be found that such claims are not completely accurate and that the Muslim provinces participate more or less equally with other comparably endowed provinces in the economic underdevelopment of the two nations. But, to the extent that such claims are accurate, remedial steps should be taken.

(6) Set the national house in order. Let there prevail an atmosphere of honest, efficient, and fair-minded government. Officials, wherever they serve, who are abusive, corrupt, negligent, or inept should be removed. And those officials or citizens guilty of crimes against Muslims or any other group, should be brought to justice.

(7) Develop long-range planning for the Muslim areas for their economic, social, and educational advancement. And, most important, recruit the participation of a broad spectrum of Muslim leaders, young and old, traditionalist and modern, into the planning process. Let them become persuaded of the soundness of the plans formulated, and *let them* do the work of securing the support and co-operation of the Muslim peoples.

(8) Establish and maintain effective channels of communication between the Muslim peoples and government at the highest levels.

Of course, much has already been done along these lines in both the Philippines and Thailand. Both nations now have Muslim advisory councils at the national level (Thailand's was established in 1949, and the Philippines' in 1973). Both are accelerating programmes of economic upliftment in the Muslim areas, along with improvements in health and education (for example, there is now a major state-supported university in each area). In both countries, special provisions are made for the application of parts of the Islamic personal law system for Muslims, and the Philippine Government is now studying a sophisticated *Proposed Draft of the Administration of Muslim Law Code of 1974*, submitted in April 1974 by a special research staff of qualified Muslim attorneys commissioned by the Office of the President. The governments of both countries now provide for periods of formal orientation for non-Muslim civil and military officers assigned for duty in the Muslim areas. Unfortunately, these and other such measures, most of which have only recently been undertaken, appear to be motivated more by a desperate desire to bring order to steadily deteriorating situations than by a genuine respect for, and understanding of, the Muslims' faithful adherence to their religion. The nub of the matter is attitude. Success in making Muslims happy and contributing citizens will, in the long run, depend on a fundamental reconstruction of the presently negative attitude of non-Muslims.

But it is not just the Filipino Christians and Thai Buddhists who have responsibility to work towards compatibility. The Filipino and Thai Muslims have their obligations in this regard as well. Their hardest task — and only they can do it — is to fully *accept* themselves as citizens of the Philippines or Thailand as well as Muslims, and to reconcile the obligations of both their national and religious loyalties. This will undoubtedly mean revising the notion that one can be fully Muslim only as a member of a closed society structured and ordered under Islamic law. As a matter of fact, there are very few Muslim countries which adhere to such a view nowadays, to the consternation of some of their more traditionalist-minded citizens.

In this connection, it is worthwhile noting that the Jam'iyatul 'Ulama, an organization of conservative Muslim religious leaders in India, has offered a theological and juridical basis for its support of Indian nationalism in the Islamic concept of *mu'ahadah* or "mutual contract". The concept derives from the early years of Islamic history in the city of Medina where the Prophet Muhammad devised a civic contract between his Muslim group and the large Jewish community in the city. In the view of the Jam'iyatul 'Ulama, the Indian Muslim minority, through its elected representatives, has entered upon a mutual contract — *mu'ahadah* — with non-Muslims to establish the secular Republic of India. That contract is the Indian Constitution. It is, therefore, the *Islamic* duty of Indian Muslims, says the Jam'iyatul 'Ulama, to keep faith with the Constitution and to work out within the national life such personal and social aspects of the total Islamic pattern as can be implemented, and such socio-economic and administrative aspects as they can democratically persuade the nation to adopt. Much the same idea has been suggested to Filipino Muslims by Atty. Michael O. Mastura, Muslim descendant of Maguindanao sultans, who also declares: "One thing is clear: our task today is to align the religious loyalty of the Muslims and the public policy needs of the country."

If the Filipino and Thai Muslims can accomplish this admittedly gigantic task, then other aspects of their contribution to compatibility should fall easily into place. They will more easily recognize and purge those among them who pursue their private interest to the injury of the common good. They will put the resources of their faith and community at the disposal of worthy national, as distinct from purely communal, goals. They will cultivate the highest moral and spiritual virtues expected in Islam, not simply for their own benefit as Muslims but for the national benefit as well. Above all, they will work for a new climate of confidence and trust between citizens of all faiths.

Other nations, especially Muslim nations, have a role to play in promoting the compatibility of Muslim and non-Muslim communities in the Philippines and Thailand. It is not wrong for the Filipino and Thai Muslims to appeal to them for support — indeed, it is perfectly consistent with the Islamic concept of *umma.* But it would be wrong for those nations to respond in a way which undermines the national sovereignty of the two countries involved. All indications are that the Muslim nations well understand this. It is clear that Indonesia and Malaysia officially are determined to exert their pacific influences in the context of ASEAN, though the Malaysian Government apparently has difficulty in controlling the support which some sectors of its population give to the Muslim secessionist movements in the Philippines and Thailand. (Moreover, the position of Malaysia is further complicated by the fact that the Philippines has not withdrawn her claim to Sabah, and Chin Peng's Malayan Communist terrorists find sanctuary in South Thailand where they have allegedly joined forces with Thai Muslim secessionists.) With the notable exception of Libya, which advocates a more aggressive policy, the other nations of the Islamic world beyond Southeast Asia seem ready, on one hand, to affirm their moral solidarity with the just cause of the Muslim minorities and, on the other hand, to encourage the governments of the Philippines and Thailand to find political and peaceful solutions to problems with the Muslims within the framework of their respective national sovereignty and territorial integrity. They offer to help with financial support for their Muslim brothers, but only in consultation with the two governments concerned.

In the final analysis, the position of the Muslim minorities in the Philippines and Thailand is the unenviable one of being between the hammer of vigorous guerrilla-backed secessionist movements and the anvil of national unity. The anvil will long outlast the blows of the hammer, but, for the human beings caught in between, the suffering is terrible. The secessionist movements will weaken, atrophy, and disappear as soon as Muslims and non-Muslims succeed in coming to terms in the context of national unity.

The Forgotten Muslims of Kampuchea and Viet Nam

SEDDIK TAOUTI

TRANSIT THROUGH HANOI

"It is unusual to think of the Quran and the Crescent when evoking the countries of Southeast Asia, which are fundamentally coloured by Buddhism and by ancestor and spirit worship. Yet in Burma, in Thailand, in Cambodia, and to a lesser degree in Viet Nam, islands of Islamised populations have been settled for several centuries."[1]

It was in March 1981 that an official of UNESCO passed on to me a request from the Government of Viet Nam, in which assistance was requested for the reconstruction of 25,000 class rooms destroyed by typhoons. We were asked to make a contribution for the regions which were inhabited by Muslims.

It was thus through UNESCO that I was able to obtain a visa to enter Viet Nam.

I was received by the authorities of the Ministry of Education. I explained during meetings with them that I came in response to a request presented to UNESCO, and that I represented an institution one of whose aims was assistance to the Islamic communities in non-Muslim states.[2] The Vietnamese authorities explained that the two typhoons, to which reference had been made, had destroyed 25,000 class-rooms and that they desired assistance in the reconstruction of these schools.

This assistance was to be used for the import of corrugated sheets for the roofing of the destroyed class-rooms.

They also requested assistance for the obtaining of construction materials for a secondary school which would service the Islamic community of Ho-Chi-Minh City, the ancient capital of South Viet Nam, where according to them, there were numerous Muslims.

They suggested that I should visit areas inhabited by Muslims and that I speak freely with the members of this minority.

During the course of conversations with the authorities and particularly during talks with the Vice-Minister of Education, I informed them that the second phase of my mission related to the Islamic community in Kampuchea. This information was welcomed by the leaders in Hanoi, and this facilitated my mission.

I must also recall that immediately after my arrival I had visited the Embassy of Kampuchea, where after hearing the objectives of my mission, Ambassador Kong Korn gave me a visa and assured me that he would inform Phnom Penh of my arrival.

MISSION TO KAMPUCHEA

Ever since the overthrow of the Pol Pot regime in January 1979 there are only two weekly flights from Hanoi and Ho-Chi-Minh to Phnom Penh; they are on Mondays and Fridays. The return flights take place the same day.

I left Hanoi on 3 April 1981, and after a stop-over of one hour at Ho-Chi-Minh, landed

Reprinted from *JOURNAL Institute of Muslim Minority Affairs* Vol. 4, No. 1 & 2, (1982), 3–13, by permission of the editor.

at Phnom Penh Airport at 12.30 hours. There was no problem about police or customs formalities, and thanks to the Vice-Minister of Health who was travelling on the same flight, and to whom I had explained the object of my visit, I was conducted to the Samaki Hotel where I was able to obtain a room.

Towards 4 p.m. I received a visit from Mr. Moa Hun of the Middle-East African Division in the Ministry of Foreign Affairs, and he informed me that the message from Ambassador Kong Korn at Hanoi had just arrived, which was why I had not been received at the Airport.

The first official meeting was with Mr. Ho Nam Hong, Vice-Minister of Foreign Affairs. The meeting was very cordial and the Vice-Minister told me that he was ready to organise any appointments which I might desire with the authorities or with the Muslims. He asked me to promise that I would return again to visit all the localities inhabited by Muslims.

My second visit was to Mr. Chan Ven, Minister of National Education, and Mayor of the capital. I explained to the Minister that, having been sent by an Islamic institution, I was there to examine the possibility of aid to the Muslims of Kampuchea.

The meeting lasted more than an hour. Reference was made to the Pol Pot regime which had driven out city populations, destroyed pagodas, mosques, banks and other establishments and exterminated intellectuals: "The Khmer Rouges destroyed the entire infrastructure of Kampuchea, starting from almost all the educated persons and intellectuals, then by attacking the buildings and all the other installations necessary for the life of the country". In all this devastation Muslims, it was agreed, had suffered the most.

The Minister assured me that all assistance received from the Islamic Development Bank would be used exclusively for the Muslims who lacked essentials in all sectors. Any form of aid would be welcomed.

He gave me a statistical report on the literate population at the primary school level. This came to 1,304,225 children out of whom 764,811 were in the first year. This effort which had been started only two years ago, was more than remarkable, as school textbooks were written by hand by a group of teachers for all levels of education.

Under the Pol Pot regime schools had been closed or had been abandoned, and the buildings and school materials destroyed. No children went to school from 1975 to January 1979. Thus, all the children between the ages of 6 to 10 had never been to school and were all in their first schooling year. With them also were those aged from 10 to 15, that is to say, those who had been to school for 1, 2, 3 or 4 years, but who had been driven out and had therefore forgotten everything.

On Sunday, 5 April, I had a long meeting with Mr. Matli or Mohammad Ali, Vice-Minister of Agriculture, who is one of the representatives of the Islamic minority in the Government. He told me that the President of the community was Dr. Abdul Kayoum who represented the minority on the highest body, the National Union Front.

The meeting with the Minister took place in the presence of Mr. Attman Ibrahim, a former student of Al-Azhar between 1963 and 1968, and Mr. Mohammed Wan Wan, in-charge of religious affairs in the National Union Front. The meeting lasted more than two hours, during which a full picture was drawn of the situation of the Islamic community under the former colonial, Sihanouk, Lon Nol and Pol Pot regimes, its structure, its leaders, its militants. I was given the names of those resistants who died as martyrs for Islam under the different regimes.

The Muslim population of Kampuchea I was told was approximately 800,000. But more than 70% has been exterminated.

Out of 113 mosques, only 20 remained, the rest having been destroyed. Even these 20 mosques were only recently put back into a state of repair.

I was given the names of former religious chiefs like the Mufti Hadj Abdullah, Hadj Slimane Chekri and Hadj Slimane Fekri. Each mosque had its *imam.* More than 300 teachers were involved in teaching religion to community members. There were some well-known *sheikhs,* 9 holders of Al-Azhar diplomas, 5 from the Islamic University of Medina, others who had received their education from the Al-Mohammadiya University of Kalenten in Malaysia, as well as some trained in India.

From all the above only thirty eight survived, the rest having been exterminated by the Pol Pot regime: of the Azharis only two remain.[3]

WITH THE ISLAMIC COMMUNITY OF PHNOM PENH

Accompanied by Moa Hun, Mohammed Wan Wan and Attman Ibrahim we went to the locality inhabited by the Islamic minority at Kilo 7 on the road out of Phnom Penh.

We were welcomed by Ali Yacoub, President of the locality, Smail Youcef and Taleb Idris, *imams* at the only mosque which is still standing. I was also able to visit the site of the two mosques which were destroyed.[4]

The mosque where we met dates back to 1813 but was reconstructed and repaired over 50 years ago. About 40 to 50 of the faithful meet for daily prayers. On Fridays it is full and many have to pray in the court-yard.[5] The mosque had only one copy of the Quran in Arabic.[6] A young boy, 13 years old, by the name of Mohammed Ghali who had survived the extermination, recited some verses of *Sura Baqara*. The reception was more than warm, and the Imam expressed his joy at receiving us his Muslim brothers.

Currently the total population of the city is estimated at 250,000, of which 20,000 are Muslims.[7]

The country had 500 doctors, only 40 survived; among the survivors is Professor My Samedi, a Muslim and currently Director of the faculty of Medicine at Phnom Penh.[8]

I was able to visit the extermination camp at Toul Sleng. It is in a former high school which used to have 2000 students and which was transformed by Pol Pot into a torture house, prison and cemetery. The visit was a nightmare for me as it is for all those who pass by this site and who can easily see the still visible traces, the torture instruments used on those who entered this camp, men, women and hundreds of children, chains everywhere, electric and bath-tub torture instruments, and instruments for pulling nails, etc. The blood spots are still visible. I will not say anything of the ditches where human corpses were heaped on top of each other.

RECONSTRUCTION

The current government of Kampuchea is not recognised by any of its neighbours, nor by the United Nations. Its only relations are with Viet Nam. However, after the discovery of the genocide conducted by the Pol Pot team between 1975 and January 1979, the United Nations asked UNICEF to undertake an assistance campaign. I had long discussions with an expert who was among the first to arrive, and who had travelled widely over the country.[9]

He was present when the first refugees who returned from the countryside tried to install themselves again in the city. All of them were sick, very weak and under-fed, unable to walk, and they found nothing on arrival. According to this person, only the toughest were able to survive during the four years of the Pol Pot government.

Nevertheless, I myself found in a very tranquil capital, with people going about their business. In the last two years the efforts made by the survivors are remarkable. The authorities work relentlessly, helped by all the citizens. More than 1,000,000 hectares of fields were cultivated and a good crop was expected. Men and women were working day and night to repair different sectors of the country, to clean the city, to repair the water pipes and electricity and to provide material and personnel services, etc.

The schools are being constructed by the local population themselves with simple, locally available materials.

I was also able to visit several city markets where vegetables, fruit, fish and other articles were on sale. The vendors were mostly women.

I was suprised by the high number of women every where. The number of widows is in tens of thousands. I visited schools. In one of them, for example, there were 18 young women out of 23 teachers. All of them were widows, and some, like the Directress, had lost both husband and children.

At Kilo 7, in the Muslim locality, I also saw class rooms reconstructed with wood and branches, and also a mosque on the site of a previous one blasted by the former regime.

The UNICEF is coordinating all U.N. activities with 8 experts who are in position. The FAO representative is helping to restart agricultural activities. The High Commission for Refugees has three experts who are incharge of the reception and the installation of the refugees returning to the country — 185,000 refugees from Thailand, 115,000 from Viet Nam, and 20,000 from Laos. Out of this total of 320,000, around 20% are Muslims.

Although the Islamic community of Kampuchea suffered from a real genocide during the period from 1975 to January 1979, now the members of the community freely practice their religious duties, and the current Government is making serious attempts to give them representation at all levels.

The needs of these people are simple: class rooms, clothing, sewing machines, copybooks, pencils and school materials for students, religious books, cyclostyling facilities for text books, medicine etc.

Finally, on the last day of my visit, a dinner was given to me by the Vice-Minister of Foreign Affairs. My visit had brought a ray of hope to the Muslims and to the authorities in general. I pray that these hopes are not belied. The country has suffered greatly, but has been unable to bring its suffering to the world's notice because of political reasons.

My second visit to Kampuchea took place in June 1981. Its aim was to announce the decision of the Bank to give assistance to the Muslims, and to study the means of channeling this assistance consisting of US$1,000,000.[10]

THIRD VISIT TO KAMPUCHEA

My third visit to Phnom Penh occurred on Monday the 25th January, 1982 at 11.30 hours. We were received by three Government officers. One of them took our passports in order to get them stamped with entry visas. As soon as we were settled in, we drew up the programme of our visit together.

The same day at 3 p.m. we met the members of the committee established to receive assistance from the I.D.B.[11]

On Tuesday 26 January we left the capital on a Land Rover for Kimpong Cham, the provincial capital of the province of the same name. It is the most populated of the 18 regions of Kampuchea, and is situated at 125 km. from Phnom Penh.

We stopped at the village of Prek Kcham to cross the river. This village is only 30 km. from the capital but it took us more than an hour to reach because of the poor state of the road. While we were waiting for the ferry some young spectators surrounded us, and in reply to our questions they told us that some of them were Muslims, that the village had four mosques and two Quranic schools for 100 and 50 children respectively, yet the village had only one copy of the Quran.

Finally, after five hours, our vehicle reached the city of Kompong Cham. On arrival, our guide explained to the hotel keeper that we were Muslims with particular dietary requirements. To our astonishment the hotel keeper replied that he himself was a Muslim, and when I gave him a copy of the *Ama* that I had with me, he read some of the verses with great pleasure.

Muslims are numerous in this province. The last census conducted some months ago, reveals a figure of 66,793 Muslims out of a total population of 1,073,645.

The Ministry of Planning informed us that the total population of Kampuchea was 6,5000,000, with a Muslim population of 190,000.

We visited a reconstructed mosque, and the *imam* informed us that the province had 63 mosques, yet copies of the Quran were rare. In the mosque which we visited there was only one copy available.

The *imam* was Him Sem or Ibrahim Hocine, the *bilal,* Aboubaker B. Dris, the *ustad,* Abderrahmane B. Briss. We also visited the Quranic school, where boys and girls recited the Quran. The school has been constructed of palm branches. A child of 10 to 12 years of age recited some verses of the Quran for us.

We were told that in this region under the Pol Pot regime more than 300,000 had been killed. The next day we visited the common ditches and saw masses of human bones with horror.

We were also told that several Muslims had returned to the town after having lived in refugee camps in Thailand.

We also met an old*ustad,* Mohammed Youssof Chamseddine who had come from the commune of Stung near Kompong Cham where he had taught the Quran for 40 years. His son has then taken on the relay. He told us that his village had four mosques, and that there were 400 children in the school, but that they had no copy of the Quran. He also told us, "I carry the Quran in my head and in my heart."

THE PROSPECT

The majority of Muslims come from the Cham ethnic origin. It is difficult to establish when the Cham were introduced to the Quran; some specialists have estimated that the Muslim faith penetrated the Cham society during the period of the Zong dynasty in China (960–1280). Following the discovery of two kufic inscriptions, specialists have been able to affirm that a Cham Muslim community existed already in the tenth century. It would appear that it is through their relations with Malays that the Cham became Muslims. It is also necessary to recall the remark of Georges Maspero who in his book, *The Kingdom of Champa,* demonstrates that the Cham, after the fall of their state in 1470, saw some of their community members take refuge in Cambodia, where they were all Muslims. The hypothesis which follows is that it was after 1470 that Islam suddenly installed itself among the Cham people following their contacts with the Malays.

According to a study made by a UNICEF expert, the religious hierarchy among Kampuchea Muslims is composed of a spiritual chief of the entire community, the *mufti.* Below him there are three office-bearers: the *tun kalik,* the *vadjak* and the *tuan pake.* Below that again, at the level of the mosque, comes the *hakim* (or *Ke Vat*), and the *imam.* The *khatips* are incharge of saying the prayers and of directing the faithful. As for the *bilal,* he is incharge of religious discipline.

Muslim ceremonies are observed and respected; the month of Ramadan (*boulan oek*) and the month of the pilgrimage (*boulan oek hadjih*) and the month of God (*boulan ovlah*). *Melut* a rite of initiation for children, and *tamat,* another ritual honouring those who have become experts on the Quran were practiced until recently.

Events linked to the war have not favoured the blossoming of Islam in Cambodia over these past few years. This is all the more true for the dark Khmer Rouge period when bloody repressions took place against ethnic minorities.

Information about this genocide is somewhat incomplete and biased. It is however clear that between two-thirds and three-fourths of the Muslims were killed individually or collectively, and only because they were of the Muslim faith.

Certain statements made recently by *hakims* to foreign observers give the impression that the systematic massacre of Muslims followed from anti-religious fury. This was perhaps due to the fact that belief in Allah could never be compatible with blind submission to the Angkar, the supreme organisation of the Khmer Rouges.

Even though they are generally assimilated with the rest of the essentially Buddhist Khmer population, the greater part of the Cham Muslims live in the region of Tonle Sap and on the Mekong river banks. They are also settled in the province of Kampot and around the capital. Most of them are fishermen, farmers and livestock merchants.

Today they are trying to start their lives again. Materially, in the first instance, as most of them were totally ruined. Slowly they must rediscover the means to enable their families to live, and their dispersed and wounded community to survive, like the other Khmers.

Though they are a part both of the religious and ethnic minority simultaneously, the Cham have no problems with their Buddhist neighbours. Both elements live in harmony.

The survival of the Muslim Cham community in Cambodia is assured in a traditionally tolerant Buddhist milieu. It is only fair that the Muslim Cham community, and the Buddhist Khmer majority should together turn over a new page in the history of their country. Yet it is equally true that the recent history of the Muslim Cham community remains unknown to other than a few specialists, and that it deserves to be better known.

MUSLIMS IN VIET NAM

A sizeable Muslim community lives in the Socialist Republic of Viet Nam. They are settled in three different regions: in the centre-east in Ho-Chi-Minh city, in the south-west at Tay Ninh, and on the frontier with Kampuchea at An Giang.

The oldest of these communities is installed on the coastal planes of central Viet Nam, in the former Annam, in the region of Thun Hai. This region is more than 300 km. north-east of Ho-Chi-Minh city, formerly Saigon.

The first person who told us about this sizeable community was a FAO expert,[12] who had the occasion to visit this farming region several times. He told us that he had visited mosques, and met several readers of the Quran. The members of this community also belong to the Cham ethnic group. It was this ethnic group which created the Kingdom of Champa, a kingdom which reached its zenith during the 6th and the 13th centuries, before being destroyed by the Vietnamese in 1470. I got some information about this ethnic group from Phan Duc Duonc, Deputy Director of the Ethnographic Institute of Hanoi, and Phuan Newyen Long, specialist in the study of minorities and particularly the Cham. According to them, the Cham in this region are either Brahmins or Muslims, the latter represented a third of the population of 40,000 according to the 1964 census; the figures today are not precisely known.

I also spoke on the subject of Vietnamese Muslims with Phan Lac Tuyen, Director of the Centre for Social Research in Ho-Chi-Minh city, and particularly with his Assistant, Mahmoud, who is of Cham origin. According to them this community practices a particular type of Islam, as it is totally isolated from the rest of the world, and has no contact with the exterior. Matriarchy is practiced; the girls family receives the husband, who then leaves his own family.[13]

HO CHI MINH CITY MUSLIMS

A sizeable Muslim community lives in this major city of South Viet Nam. Members of the community come from different origins; alongwith the Cham there are a large number of Indonesians, Malays, Indo-Pakistanis, Yemenis, Omanis, and North Africans. Before the re-unification of Viet Nam in 1975 there were in all more than 60,000 Muslims. The greater part, however, fled. Today, it is estimated that about 10,000 remain, all of them Vietnamese citizens.

We arrived in Hanoi on Friday, 22 January 1982 and thanks to the authorities we were able to leave for Ho-Chi-Minh city the next day. Our flight landed at 9 a.m. A representative of the Peoples Committee received us. The city was preparing itself for the Tet festival. We informed the representative that we were nevertheless keen to meet the leaders of the Muslim community.

On the first day we visited three mosques, and attended lessons for the teaching of the Quran to children. The next Sunday under the guidance of the *bilal,* we visited four other mosques. In one of these mosques we found members of the community preparing a feast for the afternoon, with a competition for the best recitation of the Quran by boys and girls. We made a particular request to those Muslims whom I had already met during my last mission in June 1981 to invite four representatives from each of the mosques of Ho-Chi-Minh city, to participate in meeting in the Jamia mosque at 66 Dong Du Street.

The meeting was well-attended. We lunched with the members of the Committee. Then performed the *asr* prayers with about a hundred of the faithful. Each mosque was represented by more than four persons, as well as by all the locals. Together we established a committee composed of the Presidents of the different mosque committees.

It was named as the Mosque Coordination Committee[14] of Ho-Chi-Minh city which was to hold a monthly meeting to study the problems of different mosques. Based on this Committee, we set up a permanent Bureau.[15]

The headquarters of this Bureau are at Phu Nhuam,[16] which besides being a very central location also represents a locality inhabited by a large Muslim community. Its head, Haj Apdal Haliem, is recognised by the city authorities as President of the community. The mosque in the locality is very active and the annexed school gives Quranic education to a large number of boys and girls. There is a second mosque also, and the Islamic Bank has given assistance of US $200,000 for the purchase of material for the construction of a school for local Muslim children to be attached to this mosque. The Vice President of the Bureau is also Director of a small mosque with an over-crowded Quranic school, which deserves particular attention. The Secretary directs the mosque called the Masjid Rahim. The most beautiful mosque in the city is at 66 Dong Du Street.

Several sets of books in Arabic and Malay were distributed to the *imam* and the members of the mosque. In addition we delivered 500 books of *Ama* according to the Baghdadia method. We also sent by air mail a packet of 1500 of these books for free distribution to the students of different Quranic schools.

The minutes of the meeting and of the establishment of the Committee and the Bureau were drawn up in Arabic and in Vietnamese, and signed by the 13 members chosen, as well as by the two members of our mission. We asked the Bureau members to give a copy of the minutes to the local authorities, so as to inform them, and for legalising the text as this meeting had taken place without either the presence or the authorisation of the Vietnamese authorities.

In addition to these two communities, there is the community which lives on the frontier with Kampuchea. It is a large community. It appears that the city of An Giang is in majority Muslim. These Muslims are in regular touch with their compatriots in Ho-Chi-Minh city, as well as in Kampuchea. They are all of Cham origin, but are more outward looking than those who live in the centre of Viet Nam. Their language is close to that of the Muslims of Kampuchea. Both use the Arabic alphabet for writing.

I must acknowledge that the Vietnamese authorities asked me to visit all these communities, and that it was only because of a shortage of time that I was unable to do so.

I cannot end this over-view of Islam in Viet Nam without mentioning the Hanoi mosque.

It is historical and well planned, and if it is small, it has nevertheless a large covered court, toilets with running water, high, very visible minarets and lodgings for the concierge.

According to Dr. Abdelhamid Mansour, who knew the site on his arrival in 1979, it was used as the police station for the area. It was thanks to the intervention of the then Ambassador of Iraq, Nabil Nadjem Salah, that the authorities vacated the premises. The Ambassador had it repaired, carpeted, and used to pray every Friday alongwith some other diplomats.

However, despite this renovation, it still needs extensive repairs. Its roof is old, its electrical wiring needs to be redone fully, and it requires repainting. It is true that the authorities are doing nothing, but they are not stopping Muslims from repairing it either. The concierge is a Muslim of Pakistani origin, as is his wife. There is an important foreign Muslim colony here: besides 4 Yemeni students and three Palestanian students, there are diplomats from Malaysia, Indonesia, Algeria, Pakistan, Egypt, Iraq, etc.

NOTES

This report is based on my talks with members of the Kampuchean and Vietnamese communities in Saudi Arabia, Malaysia, in the refugee camps in Thailand and finally in the interior of Kampuchea during three trips which I undertook to that country and Viet Nam between May 1980 and January 1982.

The initiative for these contacts was, I must confess, taken by the Kampuchean Muslims, a delegation of whom visited the Islamic Development Bank and the Secretariate of the Organization of the Islamic Conference in April 1980 to seek moral and material support.

Following this visit a joint commission of the IDB and the OIC visited Malaysia and Thailand to meet with refugees fleeing from Kampuchea. I was member of this commission. In May 1980 the Eleventh Foreign Minister's Conference held in Islamabad approved a resolution requesting the fraternal government of Malaysia to facilitate the entry of Kampuchean Muslim refugees. The IDB sanctioned a subsidy of half a million dollars for this purpose. Details of further assistance are mentioned in the report itself.

Besides the above mentioned sources I have also consulted *Period of Resurrection,* a 117 page report by a Belgian journalist, Jacques Danois, published by the UNICEF; published documentation (May, 1980) on the Muslims in Kampuchea made available by PERKIM, an Islamic welfare organization of Malaysia headed by Tunku Abdul Rahman, former Prime Minister of Malaysia and the first Secretary-General of the OIC; Maria Antonietta Macciolchi, "Cambodia — with the Survivors of the Genocide, if Any," *Nouvel Observateur,* Sept 12, 1981; Marc Riboud, "Second Death of Angkar", *Paris-Match,* Feb 12, 1982 and etc. Numerous personal interviews conducted with the victims and the refugees also form an invaluable base for this report:

1. "Cambodia — Land of Islam", *Sud Est Asie,* March 1981.

2. The Islamic Development Bank headquartered in Jeddah, Saudi Arabia, and an affiliate of the Organization of the Islamic Conference.
3. "It is difficult to explain why the followers of Ieng Sary and Pol Pot attacked the Muslims so forcefully during their dark domination over Cambodia. It is as difficult to explain as the extermination of Buddhist monks, of intellectuals and of city dwellers.

   What ever may be the reason, the Cambodian Mohammadans both in their capacity as Mohammadans, as well as in their capacity as Cham, were systematically massacred. All witnesses agree to this.

   In their effort to exterminate all religions, the more so a faith which was foreign to the sub-continent and which also coincided with an ethnic minority, the Khmers Rouges started marking out the Muslims right from the beginning. Thus religious dignitaries were their first victims.

   The minutes of the popular tribunal which was held at Phnom Penh in 1979 to judge the war crimes of the followers of Pol Pot and Ieng Sary are full of bloody details and duly attested affidavits testifying to the plain and simple extermination of the Cham. Dramatic cases are cited of villagers assembled by the Khmers Rouges and asked to consume food ostensibly containing pork. Those who refused to eat it and or who showed their disgust were often taken away and executed:" Jacques Danois, *Period of Insurrection,* op. cit.
4. During my two later visits I was able to note that the two mosques had been hurriedly reconstructed, and that the prayers are performed regularly, particularly those of *Maghreb* and *Isha.*
5. During my second trip, I arrived at the mosque just 30 minutes before the Friday prayers, and was able to verify that infact it could not contain all the faithful. The majority had to pray outside. At my arrival the Imam could not stop himself from informing his country-men who I was and from where I had come.
6. The Imam took out an object which seemed to be very precious, well-folded and placed on a cushion near where we were sitting. It was the only copy of the Holy Quran in Arabic as all holy books were totally destroyed under the Pol Pot regime.
7. Danois, op. cit.
8. When Pol Pot came to power there were three Muslim doctors: Zakaria Abdelhamid who fled on the day the city was occupied by the Khmers Rouges, another doctor who was assassinated, and a third, Abdel Kayoum, who hid himself among the countryside by concealing his identity.
9. In addition to the representatives of the United Nations, and the Red Cross about ten American and European organisations are assisting the population of Kampuchea. About 70 foreigners live in Phnom Penh.
10. This sum was allocated as follows: $800,000 for the reconstruction of mosques to which classrooms were annexed; $200,000 for school materials including scientific and religious books in Arabic and Malay.
11. During this meeting I informed the Committee set up to receive assistance from IDB that three Arabic typewriters and school material weighing 14,079 kg, including 7000 copies of *Ama* had been dispatched. Later, I was informed that these supplies reached Phnom Penh on Feb 21, 1982.
12. Dr. Abdelhamid Mansour.
13. Experts have found an inscription in Chinese carved on a stone, which indicates that the chief of the community used to pronounce the phrase *Allah u Akbar* when slaughtering animals.
14. The composition of this committee is as follows: Haj Apdal Haliem, representing the mosque of Nam Ky Khoi Nghia; Moussa Misky representing the mosque of 66 Dong Du Street; Hidir Sane Houane, representing the mosque of 45 Nam Ky Khoi Nghia; Sy Ossamaine, representing the mosque of 459 Tran Hung Dao; Haj Osmane B. Abdessama, representing the mosque of 343/356 Le Quang Liem, Abdelkarim Oryugen Orguc Hiem, representing the mosque of 641 Nguyen Trai; Tuan Yousouf, representing Masjid Musliminin District 8, Haj Ha Lim, representing the Nurul Islam mosque Binh Thanh; Haj Mah Mod, representing the Haya Tul Islam mosque District 10; Aissa Abdel Wahab, representing the Nutul Islam mosque District 3; Mohamed Abdu Latif, representing the Mu Ba Rak mosque District 4; Soulimane B. Younis, representing the Khay Ri Yah mosque District 4; Mohamed Salah, representing the Nurul Ihsan mosque Phu Nhum.
15. The Bureau is composed of the following: Haj Apdal Haliem, President; Tuan Yousof, Vice-President; Hidir Sane Houane, Secretary; Moussa Misky, Treasurer.
16. Address-52 Nam Ky Khoi Nghia, Ho Chi Minh City.

The Institutionalization of Islam

The Concept of Progress and Islamic Law

NOEL J. COULSON

'All innovation is the work of the devil'. These alleged words of the founder Prophet of Islam, Muhammad, do not merely reflect the innate conservatism and the deep seated attachment to tradition which was so strong among the Arab peoples who formed the first adherents of the faith. They also express a principle which became a fundamental axiom of religious belief common to Islamic communities everywhere — namely, that the code of conduct represented by the religious law, or *shari'a*, was fixed and final in its terms and that any modification thereof was necessarily a departure and a deviation from the one legitimate and valid standard.

Among Muslim peoples, therefore, it is what we may call the traditional or classical Islamic concept of law and its role in society that constitutes a most formidable obstacle to progress. Western jurisprudence has provided a number of different answers to the question of the nature of law, variously finding its source to lie in the orders of a political superior, in the breasts of the judiciary; in the 'silent, anonymous forces' of evolving society, or in the very nature of the universe itself. For Islam, however, this same question admits of only one answer which the religious faith itself supplies. Law is the command of Allah, and the acknowledged function of Muslim jurisprudence, from the beginning, was simply the discovery of the terms of that command.

Having thus been discovered, the religious code of conduct (thus formed) was a comprehensive and an all-embracing one, wherein every aspect of human relationships was regulated in meticulous detail. Moreover, the law, having once achieved perfection of expression, was in principle static and immutable: for Muhammad was the last of the Prophets and after his death in 632 A.D. there could be no further direct communication of the Divine Will to man. Henceforth the religious law was to float above Muslim society as a disembodied soul, representing the eternally valid ideal towards which society must aspire. In classical Islamic theory, therefore, law does not grow out of or develop along with an evolving society as is the case with Western systems, but is imposed from above. In the Islamic concept, human thought, unaided, cannot discern the true values and standards of conduct: such knowledge can only be attained through divine revelation, and acts are good or evil exclusively because Allah has attributed this quality to them. Law, therefore, precedes and is not preceded by society; it controls and is not controlled by society. If in Western systems the law is

Paper contributed to the International Seminar (June 3–9, 1963) on "Cultural Motivations to Progress and the Three Great World Religions in South-East Asia" sponsored by the University of the Philippines and the Congress for Cultural Freedom.

Reprinted from *Quest*, pp. 16-25, by permission of the author.

moulded by society, in Islam exactly the converse is true. The religious law provides the comprehensive, divinely ordained and eternally valid master plan to which the structure of state and society must ideally conform.

Obviously, therefore, the clash between the dictates of the rigid and static religious law and any impetus for change or progress that a society may experience poses for Islam a fundamental problem of principle. The Muslim countries of the Near and Middle East have sought the solution in a process which may be generally termed legal modernism, and it is the purpose of this paper to appreciate in broad outline the nature and efficacy of the solution which has thus been proferred. To do so I propose that we should focus our attention upon one particular legal reform introduced in Tunisia in 1957. This was the outright prohibition of polygamy, which represented a complete break with the legal tradition of some 13 centuries standing. I have chosen this particular case not because polygamy is one of the most pressing social problems in Islam today — it is generally not so — but because, firstly, it is concerned with the status of the family where the influence of the traditional religious law has always been strongest; secondly, because it highlights the various issues involved in legal reform which are common to Muslim communities the world over, and finally because it is one of the most extreme and significant examples of this process of legal modernism which may not only radically alter the shape of Islamic society but may well affect the very nature of the religion of Islam itself. Our approach to the subject must be essentially historical; for it is only in the light of past tradition that the significance of legal modernism and its potential role in the future development of Islamic peoples may be properly assessed.

Traditional Muslim jurisprudence is an example of a legal science almost totally divorced from historical considerations. Islamic orthodoxy sees the elaboration of the law as a process of scholastic endeavor completely independent of and in isolation from considerations of time and place, and the work of individual jurists during the formative period is measured by the single standard of its intrinsic worth in the process of discovery of the divine command. Master architects were followed by builders who implemented the plans; successive generations of craftsmen made their own particular contributions to the fixtures, fittings and interior decor until, the task completed, future jurists were simply passive caretakers of the eternal edifice. The picture of the elaboration of the system of Allah's commands thus presented lacks therefore any true dimension of historical depth. Recent researches by scholars, however, have shown that the genesis of Islamic religious law lay in a complex process of historical growth intimately connected with current social conditions and extending over the first three centuries of Islam.

The first steps in Islamic jurisprudence were taken in the early years of the second century of the Muslim era, around 750 A.D., by scholars working in various centres of which the most important were to prove those of Kufa in Iraq and Medina in the Hijaz. For these scholar-jurists, the fundamental axiom of Islam — that of total submission to Allah — indicated that all human relationships were subject to regulation by the divine command. Their aim, therefore, was to elaborate such a system of law as would express, in terms of the rights of men and their obligations, the will of Allah for Muslim communities, a system which was to be called the *shari'a*. But for these loose fraternities of legal scholars, whom we may refer to as the early schools of law, this activity entailed nothing more than the assessment of existing legal practice in the light of the principles embodied in the Qur'an. Now the Qur'an does not contain, in any sense, a code of law. It merely sets out to reform, in a limited number of particulars, the existing customary law, by precepts which often suggest rather than command, which are predominantly ethical in tone, and which amount in all to some one hundred verses. The Qur'anic legislation, in fact, amounts to little more than the preamble to a code of conduct for which succeeding generations were to supply the operative parts.

Accordingly, there was a wide scope for the use of reason — or *ijtihad* as it came to be called — in the formulation of the doctrine. And it is not surprising that this accepted freedom to speculate led to considerable divergence of doctrine in the different localities; for outside the limited field covered by the Qur'anic precepts, the thought of the scholars was naturally influenced by the particular social conditions prevailing in their locality, and local customary practice was accepted as part of their ideal scheme of things, unless some explicit principle of the Qur'an was thereby flagrantly violated. We may take one outstanding example of such divergence.

The law of Medina held that every woman, minor or adult, could contract a marriage only through her guardian (for this purpose a close male relative such as the father or the paternal grandfather). If the guardian did not conclude the contract on her behalf, the marriage was a nullity. Furthermore, the guardian possessed the power to give his ward in marriage regardless of her consent or otherwise — and again this applied whether the female concerned was minor or adult. These rules were natural enough in the traditionally tribal and patriarchal society of Medina where the inferior status of woman and the interests of tribal pride in marriage alliances combined to place the power to contract a marriage in the hands of the male members of the tribe. But in Kufa the rules are fundamentally different. Here the adult woman is completely free to contract herself in marriage without the intervention of any guardian, and can never be given in marriage without her free consent. These rules in turn were conditioned by the particular social climate of Kufa, where the cosmopolitan atmosphere resulting from very mixed population of a new town in a predominantly Persian milieu, naturally accorded to woman a greater freedom and a higher legal capacity.

For the greater part of the 8th century, therefore, Islamic law was represented by a number of different legal systems built by human reason around the common stock of the Qur'anic rules — systems designed to fit the varying conditions of the different localities.

This practical approach however, was not to remain for long unchallenged. The opposition materialised in the form of a group who sought to enlarge the area of law specifically regulated by the divine command. This they did by appealing to the authority of the Prophet of Islam. Such legal decisions as the Prophet himself had given, they argued, must be regarded as divinely inspired and it was these Prophetic precedents, and not the custom of a particular locality, which represented a positive manifestation of the divine will, and which formed the only acceptable supplement to the Qur'anic relevations. So formulated, the appeal of this thesis was irresistible, and the zeal of its exponents resulted in the discovery and collection of a great mass of reports and alleged rulings of the Prophet which were termed *hadith* and which, modern research suggests, represent not what the Prophet actually did say or do, but what this group were convinced, in all good faith, that he would have said or done in the circumstances envisaged. Prior to this time, all indications suggest, the 'Establishment' in the early schools of law had regarded the Prophet as a human interpreter of the Qur'an, a primus inter pares because he was closest in time and spirit to the Qur'an, but nonetheless a human and therefore fallible interpreter. The 'Establishment' however, could now no longer maintain the validity of their own human reason in the face of what was now asserted by the doctrinaire opposition group to be divinely inspired conduct and they reacted by gradually expressing their own doctrines in the form of *hadith* from the Prophet.

From this point onwards Muslim jurisprudence evolved a legal theory which expressed to perfection the notion of *shari'a* law as a divinely ordained system. This theory asserts that there are two material sources of law and two only. The primary source is, naturally enough, the very word of Allah himself as expressed in the Qur'an, and the second source lies in the body of precedents established by the Prophet and recorded in the *hadith* known collectively as the *sunna* of the Prophet, these precedents represent material divine in its content if not in its form, the function of which is to explain, interpret and supplement the general Qur'anic precepts. Questions which are not specifically answered in these two sources, and new problems which might arise, are to be solved by a disciplined form of reasoning by analogy known as *qiyas* — that is to say, deducing from parallel cases regulated by the Qur'an and the *sunna* the principles to be applied to these new cases. This theory therefore achieved a synthesis of divine revelation and human reason in law, but before it came to be generally accepted, the basic conflict of principle involved produced further schools of law in addition to those which already existed.

The first systematic exposition of this novel theory of the sources of law was the work of the great jurist al-Shafi'i, who died early in the third century of Islam. Initially there was strong opposition to his thesis in the established schools of law in Kufa and Medina, which both continued to support a far wider use of human reason in the formulation of the law than Shafi'i's insistence upon the restricted method of analogical deduction allowed. Accordingly, the immediate and convinced disciples of al-Shafi'i formed a group, and on the basis of his teachings elaborated a body of doctrine which differed considerably from that recognised by the schools of Kufa and Medina. On the other hand, there were extremist elements who refused to accept the validity of any kind of human reason at all in law, rejected the use of analogical deduction and purported to rely exclusively upon the Qur'an and the *sunna* as sources of law. In the late third century of Islam this group formed the Hanbali school taking their name from the founder of the movement Ahmad b. Hanbal, and their particular jurisprudential principles are responsible for many distinctive and individual features of their positive law which stand in sharp contrast to the law of the other schools. One such particular feature calls for consideration here since it is highly relevant to the question of polygamy.

Contract law in general, according to the views of the majority of Muslim jurists, consists of a series of individual and strictly regulated types of contract. Once a person enters into one of these defined contractual relationships, certain rights and obligations must of necessity result, and it is in general not permissible for the parties to modify or avoid these results by mutual agreement expressed in the form of a stipulation in the contract.

As applied to contracts of marriage, this principle means that the marital relationship, the result of the contract, is defined by the law in terms of the rights and obligations which accrue to and upon the husband and wife respectively. One of the rights which the law ascribes to the husband is the right of polygamy, the right to take additional wives up to the maximum of four concurrently. Should, therefore, the parties agree by stipulation in the contract that the husband will not take a second wife during the continuance of this marriage, they have attempted to deny what the law regards as an essential right of the husband. This they cannot do. The stipulation is void and does not bind the husband. If he breaks it and takes a second wife the first wife has no remedy. This approach, which largely negates any concept of contractual freedom does not arise from any dictates of the Qur'an. It is simply the result of the liberal *ijtihad* of the early jurists, based upon local practice and influenced strongly by the concepts of Roman law current in the former provinces of the Roman Byzantine Empire. Now for the early Hanbali lawyers such juristic speculation was, as we have seen, devoid of any authority. Relying exclusively upon the Qur'an and the *hadith* and in particular upon the Qur'anic text: 'Muslims must honour their stipulations', they held that the courts must give effect to any stipulation which the parties to a contract might mutually agree upon, provided only that such a stipulation did not involve anything expressly forbidden by the law and was not manifestly contrary to the particular contractual relationship in question. The effect of this principle in contracts of marriage is obvious. It is not expressly forbidden, nor is it manifestly contrary to the institution of marriage that a man should have only one wife. If then the husband is in agreement to take a second wife, Hanbali law will regard this stipulation as enforceable — not in the sense that the husband will be prevented from marrying a second wife, but in the sense that if he does the first wife will be able to claim a dissolution of her marriage.

As opposed to the Shafi'i and Hanbali schools, whose law was formally derived from the sources laid down in the legal theory, the early schools of Medina and Kufa had already developed a corpus of positive law before the legal theory was formulated. These two schools now became known as the Maliki and

Hanafi schools respectively, taking these names from outstanding representative scholars; and although they eventually adopted Shafi'i's theory of the sources of law, they retained this pre-established body of positive law and simply harmonised it by devious means, with the dictates of the legal theory. For the Malikis and Hanafis the legal theory was a formal and post facto rationalisation of existing doctrine and the result was the doctrines which had in fact originated in particular local customs and individual juristic reasoning were now represented as expressions of the divine command. And the same holds good, in fact for Shafi'i and Hanbali law for the purported Prophetic precedents which were the corner stone of their law were in reality largely expressions of local precedents and the views of particular scholars. For example, we referred previously to the fact that Medinise law required every woman to be given in marriage by her guardian, while the law of Kufa allowed an adult woman to contract her own marriage without the intervention of her guardian. Hanafi law conserved the Kufa tradition and Maliki law the Medinise tradition, and since the latter was now expressed in the form of a hadith from the Prophet, it was taken over by the Shafi'i and Hanbali schools. Accordingly wherever today in Islam the Hanafi school prevails, as it does in the Indian sub-continent an adult woman has the capacity to conclude her own marriage contract but has no such capacity where the Shafi'i school prevails, as it does in South East Asia — a distinction which stems from particular social circumstances obtaining in Kufa and Medina in the 7th century A.D.

The final stage in the historical evolution of the classical Islamic concept of law was perhaps the inevitable result of this idealistic identification of each and every term of the law with the command of Allah and the growing rigidity which this entailed. The material sources of the divine revelation the Qur'an and the sunna, were fixed and final in their form. There were obvious limits to the exploitation of this material by way of interpretation and analogical deduction and by the beginning of the 19th century the belief gained ground that this task of exploitation, by way of *ijtihad* had been completed and that nothing further remained to be done. Perhaps the chief contributory factor to this process of ossification was the development of the principle of *ijma,* or the consensus of the legal scholars. In the search to ascertain the will of Allah, which is the essence of Muslim jurisprudence, the *ijtihad* of individual scholars was a human and therefore fallible process. Its results could constitute only probable interpretations of Allah's will. But jurisprudence asserted that where a rule was the subject of general agreement by the scholars this was proof positive of its correctness and it thus represented an incontrovertible expression of the divine will. This principle obviously precluded further discussion on the points so settled. Furthermore, where differences of doctrine between the various schools persisted, the notion of *ijma* was carried to the point where it was held to cover these differences as equally possible and equally legitimate interpretations of the law but at the same time to deny the right to adduce any further solution. And it was because the jurists had thus agreed to differ that the four schools of law were regarded as equally orthodox definitions of the will of Allah. In each school, therefore, the current body of law embodied in their authoritative legal manuals written in the early mediaeval period came to be regarded as the final and perfect expression of the system of Allah's commands. The role of future jurists was to be confined to the consolidation of this doctrine. There was no longer any need or scope for *ijtihad,* and ultimately this attitude was expressed as an infallible consensus of opinion that 'the door of *ijtihad* was closed'. Henceforth all jurists were known as followers or imitators, bound by the doctrine called *taqlid* to follow the law expounded in the authoritative manuals.

As part of this body of crystallised law the doctrine of polygamy was fundamentally common to all the schools. In permitting polygamy the Qur'an had stressed the desirability of the husband being able to provide for his several wives and of his treating them impartially. But, naturally perhaps under the prevailing social conditions, the import of these precepts had been minimized by interpretation, and they were generally regarded as imposing merely moral obligations upon the polygamous husband. For their breach the law did recognise certain limited sanctions. The wife might be relieved of her duty of cohabitation or the husband might be subject to minor forms of punishment. But the obligations were not construed in any way as restricting the exercise by the husband of his undisputed right of polygamy. In this as in all other respects, the law was now artifically set in a rigid mould — not, I may suggest, as the result of any incontrovertible axiom of the Islamic faith, but as the outcome of a complex historical process springing from the desire to set upon each and every detail of the law the stamp of divine approval. So it was, then, that the classical Islamic concept of law finally emerged as that of a law totalitarian in its terms and immutable, its authenticity guaranteed by the infallible *ijma.* It was a concept of law which was to dominate Muslim thought until these last few decades of our own century.

In modern times the problem presented by the clash between the dictates of a legal system based upon the state of society in early mediaeval times but allegedly unchangeable and the demands of contemporary Muslim society naturally became acute. By the present century the criminal and commercial law of the *shari'a* had almost entirely been abandoned in the Middle East in favour of codes of law based upon Western models. In the realm of family law, however, which was always regarded as a particularly vital and integral part of the religious faith, such an extreme solution was not acceptable. Turkey, it is true, abandoned *shari'a* family law outright in 1927 and adopted in its place the Swiss Civil Code. But it is a significant fact that over the past forty years, when such intense thought has been given to this problem, no single Muslim country has as yet seen fit to follow this example. Instead, conscientious endeavours have been made to adapt the *shari'a* to the needs of modern society. This is the process of legal modernism, and we will now attempt to briefly outline its principal features as they have developed in the Middle East.

Due to the strength of the classical concept of law, the reformers at first strove to remain within the bounds of the traditional doctrine of *taqlid,* or imitation, and to base their reforms upon juristic principles recognised as legitimate by classical jurisprudence. The basis of their work was the doctrine of *siyasa,* which defines the position of the political authority vis a vis the *shari'a* law. This doctrine asserts that while the political authority has no legislative power to modify or supersede the *shari'a* he nevertheless has the power and, indeed, the duty, to make supplementary administrative regulations to effect the smooth administration of law in general.

Two main types of such administrative regulations attracted the attention of the reformers. Firstly there was the power of the sovereign to define the jurisdiction of his courts. In general, argued the reformers, this allowed him to codify the *shari'a* and in particular, where there was a conflict of opinion among the jurists on a given point, to adopt and embody in the Code that particular opinion among the existing variants which he deemed most suitable for application. Conflict of opinion within the *shari'a* is, as we have seen, reflected by the existence of four distinct schools of law, whose varying doctrines are regarded as equally legitimate expressions of Allah's law. It was therefore open to a Hanafi ruler in the Middle East to select, and to order his courts to apply, the doctrine of one of the other schools on a given point. It was on this juristic basis that the *Ottoman Law of Family Rights* in 1917 took a first step towards the limitation of polygamy by 'selecting' the Hanbali doctrine governing stipulations in marriage contracts as better suited than the Hanafi doctrine to the needs of the time. The Hanbalis, as we have noted, were the only school who allowed a wife to claim dissolution of her marriage if the husband married a second wife in breach of a prior agreement not to do so.

The widespread use of this principle since 1917 has resulted in many changes in the law as traditionally applied in the Middle East. Peoples who are officially Hana is are now governed by codes of law which represent an eclectic amalgam of the doctrines of all the four schools.

The second limb of the doctrine of administrative regulations successfully utilised by the reformers was the recognised right of the sovereign to confine the jurisdiction of his courts, in the sense that he might set limits to the competence of the *shari'a* tribunals by forbidding them to entertain certain types of cases on procedural grounds.

For an example of the subtle application of this principle in legal modernism we may turn to a sphere of the family law other than that of polygamy — the topic, namely, of legitimacy. The one aspect of legitimacy in *shari'a* law which concerns us here is its importance in regard to succession. For the legitimate child is by law indefeasibly entitled to the bulk of the deceased father's estate, while the illegitimate child is barred from any right at all. Where a child is born to a widow, whether or not such child is to be regarded as the legitimate child of the deceased husband will depend upon whether or not the law will presume that the child was conceived during the husband's lifetime. The law therefore lays down a maximum period of gestation — which it presumes may possibly elapse between the conception of a child and its birth. If a child is born to a widow within this period it will be presumed the legitimate child of the deceased husband. This maximum period of gestation laid down in the authoritative manuals was two years according to the Hanafis, four years and upwards according to the other schools. From the standpoint of modern medical knowledge of gestation the harsh and inequitable results of this rule were obvious. In particular the bulk of a deceased Muslim's estate might pass to a child who could not be his own child.

An Egyptian Law of 1929 therefore enacted in terms that no disputed claim of legitimacy would be entertained by the courts where it could be shown that the child concerned was born more than one year after the termination of the marriage between the mother of the child and the alleged father. In short the jurisdiction of the courts in matters of legitimacy was confined to hearing cases in which the factual situation involved was in accord with modern medical opinion. The rule of traditional *shari'a* law was not, as such, contradicted or denied: but by a procedural device the courts were precluded from applying that rule.

By such methods far-reaching modifications were effected in the *shari'a* law as traditionally applied. And formally at any rate the reforms had been accomplished within the framework of the doctrine of *taqlid*: for it was the law as expounded in the mediaeval texts which was still accorded an exclusive and binding authority. The limitations of such methods, however, are readily apparent, and eventually the desired reforms could not be supported by any shadow of traditional authority. At this stage the reformers had perforce to abandon any pretence of *taqlid.* They came to challenge the binding nature of the mediaeval manuals of law and the interpretations of the original sources which were recorded in them; they claimed the right to step beyond this corpus of juristic speculation and to interpret afresh the Qur'an in the light of modern needs and circumstances; in short they renounced the duty of *taqlid* and claimed the right of *ijtihad.*

This approach was, of course, met with the argument from traditionalist elements that it contradicted the infallible *ijma* and as such was tantamount to heresy. But its supporters argued with some force that either such *ijma* did not exist at all — it being manifestly impractical to ascertain the views of each and every legal scholar throughout the far-flung territories of Islam in the 9th century — or, alternatively, that if it did exist it was not binding, for it amounted to the arrogation by a self-constituted human authority of a legal sovereignty which belonged only to Allah. However, although scholars like Muhammad Abluh in Egypt at the turn of this century and Iqbal in Pakistan had already advocated a dynamic re-interpretation of the Qur'an as the basis for comprehensive legal reform the reformers were very conscious of the fact that their activities constituted an outright break with the practical legal tradition of ten centuries standing and so their first steps in this novel direction were somewhat hesitant and tentative.

Their approach to the problem of polygamy centered upon the Qur'anic suggestions that a husband should be financially able to support his several wives and that he should treat them impartially. In 1953 the Syrian Law of Personal Status interpreted the requirement of financial ability as a definite condition limiting the exercise of the right of polygamy. With this was coupled an administrative regulation which required all marriages to be registered and further required the permission of the court as an essential preliminary to such registration. Accordingly the result was that a court would not give its permission for a second marriage unless it was satisfied that the husband was financially able to support a plurality of wives.

It may of course be argued that the only practical result of this reform was to make polygamy the privilege of the rich. Yet the real importance of the Syrian reform lies in its juristic basis and the fact that a novel interpretation had been given to the text of the Qur'an. Thus unlocked, the 'door of *ijtihad*' was swung fully open by the *Tunisian Law of Personal Status* in 1957. This law interpreted the Qur'anic injunction regarding impartial treatment of co-wives in the same way as the Syrians had interpreted the requirement of financial ability — namely as a legal condition precedent to the very exercise of the right of polygamy and which would naturally apply regardless of financial standing. But it was now no longer within the discretion of the court to permit a polygamous marriage on the ground that it was satisfied that this condition would be fulfilled. For the law goes on to state that in the circumstances of modern society it is impossible for a husband to treat several wives impartially to their mutual satisfaction: in technical language there is a conclusive or irrebuttable presumption of law that this essential condition precedent is incapable of fulfillment. Polygamy therefore was prohibited outright.

Such is the phenomenon of the current evolution of an allegedly immutable law in the Muslim countries of the Middle East. Two considerations must be borne in mind. In the first place these reforms are not put forward as deviations, occasioned by practical necessity, from the ideal Islamic law, i.e. *hila,* but as contemporary expressions of that ideal law. And in the second place there is no uniformity in the method of legal modernism or in its results throughout the Middle East, and it is apparent that the process will tend, initially at any rate, towards a growing diversity in Islamic legal practice conditioned by the varying reactions of the different areas to the stimuli of modern life. This is made quite clear, even on the one question of polygamy, by the three most recent modernist enactments of Islamic law. The Moroccan law of 1958 merely gives the court the power to intervene retrospectively by way of dissolution of the marriage where a polygamous husband has in fact failed to treat his wives impartially. The Iraqi law of 1960 goes only a little further than the Syrian law in decreeing that the permission of the court is necessary for a second marriage and that such permission will only be granted when the husband has the necessary financial status and when 'no inequality of treatment is to be feared.' Finally the *Muslim Family Laws Ordinance,* promulgated in Pakistan in 1961, makes the permission of a duly constituted Arbitration Council necessary for a second marriage under pain of penal and other sanctions, and states that such permission will only be given where the Council is satisfied that the 'proposed marriage is necessary and just.' As to when a second marriage will so be considered 'necessary and just,' it is obvious that the consent or otherwise of the existing wife will be extremely relevant but such factors as the sterility, physical infirmity or insanity of an existing wife are specified as circumstances which may be taken into account.

We are now perhaps in a position broadly to appreciate the significance of the Tunisian reform in the context of the phenomenon of legal modernism.

In its simplest forms the problem facing Muslim jurisprudence today is the same problem which it has always faced and which is inherent in its very nature — namely the need to define the relationship between the standards imposed by the religious faith and the mundane forces which activate society. At the one extreme is the solution adopted by classical jurisprudence a divine nomocracy under which religious principles were elaborated into a comprehensive and rigid scheme of duties to form the exclusive determinant of the conduct of society. The other extreme solution is that of secularism, adopted by Turkey, which relegates religious principles to the realm of the individual conscience and allows the forces of society an unfettered control over the shape of the law. Neither of these solutions, it would appear, can be acceptable to contemporary Muslim opinion generally. For while the former is wholly unrealistic, the latter must inevitably be regarded as unIslamic. Obviously the answer lies, therefore, somewhere between these two extremes, in a concept of law as a code of behaviour which is founded upon certain basic and immutable religious principles but which, within these limits, does not neglect the factor of change and allows the adoption of such new standards as may prove more acceptable to current Muslim opinion than indigenous tradition. Law, to be a living social force, must reflect the soul of a society. And the soul of present Muslim society is reflected neither in any form of outright secularism nor in the doctrine of the mediaeval text books.

In its efforts to solve the problem of the clash between the dictates of the traditional law and the demands of modern society legal modernism as it appears in its most extreme stage in the Tunisian reform, rests upon the premise that the will of Allah was never expressed in terms so rigid or comprehensive as the classical doctrine maintained but that it enunciated broad general principles which admit of varying interpretations and varying applications according to the circumstances of the time. Modernism, therefore, is a movement towards a historical exegesis of the divine revelation and as such can find its most solid foundation in the view of the early historical growth of *shari'a* law which we described earlier in this paper. For recent scholarship and research have demonstrated that *shari'a* law originated as the implementation of the precepts of divine revelation within the framework of current social conditions, and in so doing it provides a basis of historical fact to support the ideology underlying legal modernism. Once the classical theory is seen in its true historical perspective, as a stage only in the evolution of the *shari'a*, modernist activities no longer appear as a total departure from the one legitimate position, but preserve the continuity of Islamic legal tradition by taking up again the attitude of the earliest jurists of Islam and reviving a corpus whose growth had been artifically arrested and which had lain dormant for a period of ten centuries.

It cannot be said, however, that legal modernism has yet reached the stage where it provides a completely satisfactory answer to the problems of law and society in present day Islam. Traditionalist elements condemn some of the modernist activities as the unwarranted manipulation of the texts of divine revelation to force from them a meaning which accords with the preconceived purposes of the reformers objectively determined: and this, argue the traditionalists, is in substance if not in form, nothing less than the secularisation of the law. Modernist jurisprudence does in fact often wear an air of opportunism, adopting *ad hoc* solutions as a matter of expediency, and does not as yet rest upon systematic foundations or principles consistently applied. 'Social engineers' the modernists certainly are, inasmuch as their activities are shaping the law to conform with the needs of society. Yet if Islamic jurisprudence is to remain faithful to its fundamental ideals, it cannot regard the needs and aspirations of society as the *exclusive* determinant of the law. These can legitimately operate to mould and fashion the law only within the bounds of such norm and principles as have been irrevocably established by the divine command.

Looking to the future, therefore, it would appear to be the primary task of Muslim jurisprudence to ascertain the precise limits and implications of the original core of divine revelations. And this perhaps will come to involve a re-orientation of the traditional attitude towards the reported precedents of the Prophet, not only as regards their authenticity, but also as regards the nature of their authority if their authenticity is duly established. And it would seem axiomatic that when the precepts of the divine revelation have been so established they must form the fundamental and invariable basis of any system of law which purports to be a manifestation of the will of Allah.

It cannot be denied that certain specific provisions of the Qur'an, such as that which commands the amputation of the hand for theft, pose problems in the context of contemporary life for which the solution is not readily apparent. But generally speaking the Qur'anic precepts are in the nature of ethical norms broad enough to support modern legal structures and capable of varying interpretations to meet the particular needs of time and place. And on this basis it would seem that Islamic jurisprudence could implement, in practical realistic and modernist terms, its basic and unique ideal of a way of life based on the command of Allah. Freed from the notion of a religious law expressed in totalitarian and uncompromising terms, jurisprudence would approach the problem of law and society in a different light. Instead of asking itself, as it has done since the tenth century and still generally does today, what concessions must be wrested from the law in the face of the needs of society, its new terms of reference would be precisely the opposite; to determine what limitations religious principles set upon the frank recognition of social needs.

But however considerable the problems that still face Islamic jurisprudence may be, legal modernism has at least infused new life and movement into *Shari'a* law and freed its congealed arteries from a state fast approaching that of rigor mortis. The era of *taqlid*, of blind adherence to the doctrines of the mediaeval scholars, now appears as a protracted moratorium in Islamic legal history. Stagnation has given way to a new-found vitality and potential for growth.

The Position of Islam in the Constitution of Malaysia

AHMAD IBRAHIM

When the Reid Constitutional Commission was drafting the Constitution for the Federation of Malaya it considered the question whether there should be any statement in the Constitution to the effect that Islam should be the State religion. The Commission in its report[1] said:

> There was universal agreement that if any such provision were inserted it must be made clear that it would not in any way affect the civil rights of the non-Muslims. In the memorandum submitted by the Alliance it was stated—'the religion of Malaysia shall be Islam. The observance of this principle shall not impose any disability on non-Muslim natives professing and practising their religions and shall not imply that the State is not a secular State'. There is nothing in the draft Constitution to affect the continuance of the present position in the States with regard to recognition of Islam or to prevent the recognition of Islam in the Federation by legislation or otherwise in any respect which does not prejudice the civil rights of individual non-Muslims. The majority of us think that it is best to leave the matter on this basis, looking to the fact that counsel for the Rulers said to us 'It is Their Highnesses' considered view that it would not be desirable to insert some declaration such as has been suggested that the Muslim faith or Islamic faith be the established religion in the Federation. Their Highnesses are not in favour of such a declaration being inserted and that is a matter of specific instruction in which I myself have played very little part'.

Mr. Justice Abdul Hamid, the Pakistani member of the Commission,[2] however felt that as the recommendation of the Alliance Party was unanimous, it should be accepted, and he suggested that a provision to the following effect should be inserted — 'Islam shall be the religion of the State of Malaya, but nothing in this article shall prevent any citizen professing any religion other than Islam to profess and practise and propagate that religion, nor shall any citizen be under any disability by reason of his not being a Muslim'.

He said:

> A provision like the one suggested above is innocuous. Not less than fifteen countries of the world have a provision of this type entrenched in their Constitutions. Among the Christian countries, which have such a provision in their Constitutions are Ireland (Article 6), Norway (Article 1), Denmark (Article 3), Spain (Article 6), Argentina (Article 2), Bolivia (Article 3), Panama (Article 36), and Paraguay (Article 3). Among the Muslim countries are Afghanistan (Article 1), Iran (Article 1), Iraq (Article 13), Jordan (Article 2), Saudi Arabia (Article 7) and Syria (Article 3). Thailand is an instance where Buddhism has been enjoined to be the religion of the King who is required by the Constitution to uphold that religion (Constitution of Thailand, (Article 7). If in these countries a religion has been declared to be the religion of the State and that declaration has not been found to have caused hardships to anybody, no harm will ensue if such a declaration is included in

Reprinted in abridged form from M. Hashim Suffian, et al., (eds.), *The Constitution of Malaysia, Its Development: 1957–1977* (Kuala Lumpur: Oxford University Press, 1978), pp. 41–68, by permission of the author and the publishers.

the Constitution of Malaya. In fact in all the Constitutions of Malayan States a provision of this type already exists. All that is required is to transplant it from the State Constitutions and to embed it in the Federal.

The Rulers of the Malay States at first opposed the enactment of such a provision in the new Federal Constitution because they were told by their constitutional advisers that if the Federation had an official religion, the proposed Head of the Federation would logically become the Head of the official religion throughout the Federation and it was thought that this would be in conflict with the position of each of the Rulers as Head of the official religion in his own State. However it was explained by the Alliance Party that it was not intended to interfere with the position of the Rulers as Head of Islam in their own States and that the intention in making Islam the official religion of the Federation was primarily for ceremonial purposes, for instance to enable prayers to be offered in the Islamic way on official occasions such as the installation of the Yang di-Pertuan Agong, Merdeka Day, and similar occasions.[3] This explanation was accepted by the Rulers and accordingly Article 3 of the Federal Constitution enacts that Islam is the religion of the Federation. In conformity with previous practise the Article goes on to say that other religions may be practised in peace and harmony in any part of the Federation. In recognition of the representations made by the Rulers, Clause (2) of the Article states:

> In every State other than States not having a Ruler the position of the Ruler as the Head of the Muslim religion in his State in the manner and to the extent acknowledged by the Constitution of that State and, subject to the Constitution, all rights, privileges, prerogatives and powers enjoyed by him as Head of that religion, are unaffected and unimpaired . . . .

And in order to assure the non-Muslims that their civil rights are not affected Clause (4) provides that nothing in the Article (that is Article 3) derogates from any other provision of that Constitution.

Even before Merdeka it was found necessary in practice for the Malay States to act in concert in certain religious matters, for example in determining the first and last day of the fasting month. In 1949 the Conference of Rulers appointed a Standing Committee consisting of the Keeper of the Rulers' Seal as Chairman and two representatives from each Malay State to advise the Conference on religious matters with a view to achieving where possible uniformity throughout the Federation, and also to advise the Conference on matters specifically referred to it. In theory it was open for each Ruler to act separately in such religious matters but it was felt that there should be some uniformity and that the Yang di-Pertuan Agong should be given authority to represent each Ruler in certain acts, observances, and ceremonies. Accordingly it is provided in Clause (2) of Article 13 that 'in any acts, observances or ceremonies with respect to which the Conference of Rulers has agreed that they should extend to the Federation as a whole each of the other Rulers shall in his capacity of Head of the Muslim religion authorise the Yang di-Pertuan Agong to represent him'. The various State Constitutions have been correspondingly amended. This provision has been used for determining the commencement of fasting in Ramadan and the dates of the Hari Raya Puasa and the Hari Raya Haji. Another instance is the authority given by the Rulers to the Yang di-Pertuan Agong to issue *tauliahs* or letters of authority to religious teachers for the Armed Forces after the individual teachers have been duly chosen separately by the Rulers of the States.

Although Islam is the religion of the Federation, there is no Head of the Muslim religion for the whole of the Federation. The Yang di-Pertuan Agong continues to be the Head of the Muslim religion in his own State and it is provided that he shall be the Head of the Muslim religion in Malacca, Penang, in the Federal Territory, and in Sabah and Sarawak.[4] Each of the other States has its own Ruler as the Head of the Muslim religion in that State. The various State Constitutions moreover provide that the Ruler of the State may act in his discretion in the performance of any functions as Head of the Muslim religion, but it would appear that the Yang di-Pertuan Agong may only act on advice in performing his functions as Head of the Muslim religion in Malacca, Penang, the Federal Territory, Sabah, and Sarawak.

While the Constitutions of the Malay States

provide that the religion of the State shall be Islam, this is not the case in Penang and Malacca. Neither the Federal Constitution nor the State Constitution provide that Islam is the State religion of either Malacca or Penang. In Sabah Islam has been formally declared as the religion of the State by a recent amendment to the State Constitution[5] but there is no similar provision in Sarawak. The position therefore is that Islam is the State religion in all the States of Malaysia except Malacca, Penang, and Sarawak. It may be noted that the former restriction that the function of the Conference of Rulers of agreeing or disagreeing to the extension of any religious acts, observances or ceremonies to the Federation as a whole shall not extend to Sabah or Sarawak has been removed.[6]

Article 8(2) of the Federal Constitution provides that:

> Except as expressly authorised by this Constitution, there shall be no discrimination against citizens on the ground only of religion, race, descent or place of birth in any law or in the appointment to any office or employment under a public authority or in the administration of any law relating to the acquisition, holding or disposition of any property or the establishing or carrying on of any trade, business, profession, vocation or employment.

The Constitutions of the Malay States contained provisions that require that only a person of the Malay race who professes the religion of Islam can be appointed to be the Mentri Besar, but after Merdeka these provisions have been amended to enable a Ruler to appoint a non-Muslim as Mentri Besar provided that in the Ruler's judgment he is likely to command the confidence of the majority of the members of the State Legislative Assembly.[7] The Constitutions of the Malay States still provide that the State Secretary shall be of the Malay race and profess the Muslim religion.[8] These provisions which existed in the State Constitutions prior to Merdeka Day are saved by Article 8(5)(e) of the Federal Constitution.

The Rulers of the Malay States and therefore the Yang di-Pertuan Agong who is chosen by the Rulers among themselves must necessarily be Malays professing the religion of Islam, but there is nothing in the Federal Constitution which provides that the Prime Minister or any Minister or Federal high official must be a Muslim.

Article 11 of the Federal Constitution provides that every person has the right to profess and practise his religion and subject to Clause (4) to propagate it. Clause (4) provides that State law may control or restrict the propagation of any religious doctrine or belief among persons professing the Muslim religion. No person shall be compelled to pay any tax, the proceeds of which are specially allocated in whole or in part for the purposes of a religion other than his own. Every religious group has the right to manage its own affairs, to establish and maintain institutions for religious or charitable purposes and to acquire and own property and hold and administer it in accordance with law.

Provision has been made in the State laws in Malacca, Penang, Negri Sembilan, Perak, Kedah, Kelantan and Sabah[9] to restrict the propagation by any person of any religious doctrine or belief other than the religious doctrine and belief of the Muslim religion to any persons professing the Muslim religion and to make it an offence to do so. It may be noted the offences are cognizable by a civil court and not by the Shariah courts. State law also prohibits the teaching (except in one's own residence and in the presence only of members of one's own household) of any doctrine of the Muslim religion without written permission; and the teaching or expounding of any doctrine or the performance of a ceremony or act relating to the Muslim religion in any manner contrary to Muslim law.

Article 12 of the Federal Constitution provides that there shall be no discrimination against any citizen on the grounds only of religion, race, descent or place of birth (a) in the administration of any educational institution maintained by a public authority and in particular the admission of pupils or students or the payment of fees; or (b) in providing out of the funds of a public authority financial aid for the maintenance or education of pupils or students in any educational institution, whether or not maintained by a public authority and whether within or outside the Federation. Clause (2) of this Article formerly provided:

> Every religious group has the right to esta-

> blish and maintain institutions for the education of children and provide therein instruction in its own religion and there shall be no discrimination on the ground only of religion in any law relating to such institutions or in the administration of any such law; but Federal or State law may provide for special financial aid for the establishment or maintenance of Muslim institutions or the instruction in the Muslim religion of persons professing that religion.

This has recently[10] been amended to read as follows:

> Every religious group has the right to establish and maintain institutions for the education of children in its own religion, and there shall be no discrimination on the ground only of religion in any law relating to such institutions or the administration of any such law; but it shall be lawful for the Federation or a State to establish or maintain or assist in establishing or maintaining Islamic institutions or provide or assist in providing instruction in the religion of Islam and incur such expenditure as may be necessary for the purpose.

It is not clear what changes are designed to be effected by the amendments except to make it unnecessary to have a Federal or State law to provide for financial aid for the maintenance and assistance of Islamic institutions and Islamic religious education. The amendment may however be interpreted to mean that religious groups cannot establish schools except for the education of children in their own religion, but then it is difficult to understand why there cannot be discrimination in such institutions on the ground only of religion. The words 'and provide therein instruction' have been omitted, but again it cannot be intended that no instruction in the religion can be given.

It may be noted that the powers under Clause (2) of Article 12 now extend to the whole of the Federation including Sabah and Sarawak.[11]

In the various States there is a Council of Muslim Religion known by various names whose principal function is to 'aid and advise the Ruler on all matters relating to the religion of the State and the Malay custom'. In such matters it is the chief authority in the State but is required to take notice of and to act in accordance with the Islamic law, Malay custom, and the written laws of the State. The power of the Council varies from State to State but generally it may issue *fatwas* on any matters referred to it, it has power to administer *wakafs,* it has power to act as the executor of the will or administrator of the estate of a deceased Muslim and it may hear appeals from Muslim courts.

There also exists in each State a Department of Religious Affairs responsible for the day-to-day administration of matters relating to the Muslim religion headed in each case by a lay administrator. Some of the members of the Department are also members of the Council and there is a close relationship between the two. There is legislation in each State for the administration of Muslim law and these provide for the setting up of Kathi's courts for the adjudication of disputes relating to Muslim family law and the trial of Muslim offences. They also provide for the registration of Muslim marriages, divorces, and revocations of divorce.

In most States apart from the lay head of the Religious Affairs Department the highest religious official is the Mufti whose principal function is to issue *fatwas* or to assist the Council of Religious Affairs to do so. In some States the prerogative of appointing the Mufti is exercised by the Ruler, although in other States he is appointed by the Ruler on the advice of the Ruler in Council or of the Council of Religion.

Although the Alliance Party had insisted that Islam should be declared in the Constitution as the official religion of the Federation, it did not ask that the Constitution should also declare, as did the Pakistan Constitution, that the State shall be an Islamic State. In the White Paper dealing with the Constitutional proposals (Legislative Council Paper No. 42 of 1957)[12] it is stated:

> There has been included in the proposed Federal Constitution a declaration that Islam is the religion of the Federation. This will in no way affect the present position of the Federation as a secular state, and every person will have the right to profess and practise his own religion and the right to propagate his religion, although this last right is subject to any restrictions imposed by State law relating to the propagation of any religious

doctrine or belief among persons professing the Muslim religion.

The position of each of their Highnesses as head of that religion in his State and the rights, privileges, prerogatives and powers enjoyed by him as head of that religion will be unaffected and unimpaired. Their Highnesses have agreed however to authorise the Yang di-Pertuan Agong to represent them in any acts, observances or ceremonies agreed to by the Conference of Rulers as extending to the Federation as a whole.

At present there is no head of the Muslim religion in either Malacca or Penang though in Penang the Government obtains advice in matters relating to the Muslim religion from a non-statutory Muslim Advisory Board. Since the Governors of the new States may not be persons professing the Muslim religion it is proposed that the Yang di-Pertuan Agong should be the head of religion in each of these states and that the Constitution of each should include provisions enabling the Legislature to regulate Muslim religious affairs and to constitute a Council to advise the Yang di-Pertuan Agong in such affairs. These Councils will be concerned solely with Muslim religious affairs and they will not be entitled to interfere in any way with the affairs of people of other religious groups; and the position of the Yang di-Pertuan Agong as head of the Muslim religion will not carry with it authority to intervene in any matters which are the concern of the State Governments or to require the State Governments to make financial provision exclusively for the benefit of the Muslim community.

If it is found necessary for purposes of coordination to establish a Muslim Department of Religious Affairs at federal level, the Yang di-Pertuan Agong will after consultation with the Conference of Rulers, cause such a Department to be set up as part of his establishment.

Early in 1958 a Muslim member introduced in the Federal Legislative Council the motion 'That this Council is of opinion that the serving of alcoholic drinks at all functions of the Federal Government ought to be prohibited'. In the event the following amended resolution was adopted 'That this Council is of opinion that the serving of alcoholic drinks to Muslims at all official functions of the Federal Government ought to be prohibited'. The Hon. Datuk Haji Yahya expressed the feeling of many Muslim leaders when he stated in his speech in favour of the original motion:

> It would be sufficient if I remind our Islamic Government that it is pointless for the independent Federation Government to recognize itself as an Islamic Government if the teaching of Islam and the laws of Shara' are neglected and the honour of Islam sacrificed through actions forbidden by the Hukum Shara', one of which is to spend the revenue of the Islamic Government on things forbidden by the Almighty Allah, which could be avoided although the expenditure is meant for functions of non-Muslims. We have been officially recognized as an Islamic State. The State must therefore respect the rules of Islam and Islamic laws, as far as possible. I believe at any function given by an Islamic Government the function can go on smoothly without alcoholic drinks. An Islamic Government is a pure Government and if we challenge the sanctity of its laws, I am sure this is one way for our government to be condemned by the Almighty Allah who has the power to bring down tragedies to our country.

On the other hand the Prime Minister, Tunku Abdul Rahman, deplored the bringing in of religion and he went on to state, 'I would like to make it clear that this country is not an Islamic State as it is generally understood, we merely provide that Islam shall be the official religion of the State.[13]

It can be seen that the jurisdiction given to the State and to the Shariah courts is limited. Even in regard to the subjects included in the item in the State list,[14] there are many federal laws which limit the scope and application of State laws. For example in the field of succession, testate and intestate, account has to be taken of the Probate and Administration Act[15] and the Small Estates (Distribution) Act,[16] with the resullt that the Kathis are only given the function of certifying the shares to be allotted to the beneficiaries under the Muslim law. In the field of the criminal law in particular the jurisdiction of the Shariah Courts is very limited. It has jurisdiction only over persons professing the Muslim religion and it has jurisdiction in respect of offences as is conferred by Federal law. The Muslim Courts (Criminal Jurisdiction) Act, 1965[17] provides that such jurisdiction shall not be exercised in respect of any offence punishable with imprisonment for a term exceeding six months or with any fine exceeding 1,000 dollars or with both. Thus for example the Shariah Courts are unable to exercise jurisdiction in respect of the *hadd* offence of *zinah,* where the punishment is fixed by the Holy Quran and the Sunnah.

Under the present constitutional structure the Sultan in theory may act in his discretion in the performance of his functions as Head of the Muslim religion[18] and the Sultan does have a great deal of influence on the appointment of the religious officials, especially the Mufti, and the direction of religious affairs in the State. The Sultans too are very jealous of their position as heads of the Muslim religion, so much so that we find that, through the influence of the respective Sultans, Kedah and Pahang have not participated in the National Council for Islamic affairs. *Fatwas* which are based on other than the orthodox doctrines of the Shafii school require the approval of the Sultan. Legislation however can only be exercised by a Bill passed by the Legislative Assembly and assented to by the Sultan[19] and to that extent the elected Ministers and members of the Legislative Assembly can influence the administration of Muslim law in the States. It might be noted that the Yang di-Pertuan Agong in the exercise of his functions as Head of the Muslim religion in Penang, Malacca, Sabah, and Sarawak has to act on advice[20] and here the influence of the Prime Minister and the Federal Ministers are more significant. The Sultan does continue to play an important part in the issue of *fatwas* or rulings on the Muslim religion and law. Under the various State enactments relating to the administration of Muslim law the power to issue *fatwas* is given to the Mufti, Fatwa Committee, or the Majlis Ugama Islam. In issuing such *fatwas* the person or body issuing the *fatwa* is required ordinarily to follow the orthodox tenets of the Shafii school, but where the public interest so requires the *fatwa* may be given according to the tenets of the other schools, but only with the special sanction of the Sultan.[21]

A further step to co-ordinate the administration of Islamic affairs was taken on 17 October 1968 by the establishment by the Conference of Rulers of the National Council for Islamic Affairs.[22] Its members are (a) a Chairman appointed by the Conference of Rulers (usually the Prime Minister is appointed); (b) a representative of each State in Peninsular Malaysia appointed by the Ruler concerned and in the case of Malacca and Penang by the Yang di-Pertuan Agong; and since July 1971 a representative also from Sabah and Sarawak, appointed by the Yang di-Pertuan Agong with the approval of the head of State in those States, after considering the advice of the Islamic Religious Council of the State concerned and (c) five persons appointed by the Yang di-Pertuan Agong with the consent of the Conference of Rulers. The functions of the National Council are (a) to advise and make recommendations on any matter referred to it by the Conference of Rulers, by any State Government or State Religious Council and (b) to advise the Conference of Rulers, State Governments, and State Religious Councils on matters concerning Islamic law or the administration of Islam and Islamic education with a view to imposing, standardizing, or encouraging uniformity in Islamic law and administration. It is expressly provided that the Council may not touch on the position, rights, privileges and sovereignty, and other powers of the Ruler as head of Islam in his State. Despite this safeguard, two States, that is Kedah and Pahang, have not agreed to appoint representatives to the Council.

The Council has a Committee of Muslim scholars known as the Fatwa Committee which considers matters pertaining to Islamic laws. The Committee comprises the Muftis of all the States which are members of the Council and five other Muslim scholars appointed by the Yang di-Pertuan Agong.

The Council has set up a number of Committees to co-ordinate and increase the efficiency of Islamic religious activities in all the States. They are:

(a) a task force to study the collection, administration and distribution of monies from *zakat, fitrah, Bait-ul-mal* and *wakaf;*

(b) a Committee to study the conditions of the Shariah courts and the position of Kathis;

(c) a Committee to study and streamline the laws pertaining to marriage and divorce; and

(d) a Committee to fix the First Day of Ramadan and the First Day of Shawal and to arrange Islamic Calendars.

The National Mosque is under the administration of the Council and so is the Islamic Research Centre. There is a separate organization dealing with Islamic missionary activities.

In Malaysia too it is the Constitution which is the Supreme law and it is significant that the definition of law which is contained in the Constitution does not mention Islamic law.[23] It is true that after Merdeka the Federal Parliament cannot make laws dealing with the law of Islam (except now for the Federal Territory) as Islamic law is a State responsibility but the State Legislatures can make laws and the laws cannot be held void because they contravene the Islamic law. The Civil Law Act, 1956, in effect makes the English common law and rules of equity the basic law to which recourse must be had if there is no written law in force in Malaysia. There are examples of laws made before Merdeka Day which contain provisions contrary to the Islamic law. In the case of *Ainan* v. *Syed Abubakar*[24] for example it was held that section 112 of the Evidence Ordinance (now the Evidence Act) applies to the exclusion of the Islamic law on the question of the legitimacy of a child. In *Tengku Mariam* v. *Commissioner for Religious Affairs, Trengganu*[25] the High Court held and the Federal Court was prepared to hold, that it was bound by the decisions of the Privy Council from India to hold that a *wakaf* for the benefit of the family of the deceased is bad, despite the validity of such a *wakaf* under the Islamic law. Post-Merdeka laws made by Parliament can only be made applicable to Muslims under the provisions of Article 76 of the Constitution, that is, they must be accepted by the States. The Guardianship of Infants Act, 1961, for example may apply to Muslims in a State if it is accepted by the State with the proviso that any provision in the Act which conflicts with the provisions of the Islamic law will not apply to Muslims. Despite this, in *Myriam* v. *Ariff*[26] it was held that the Guardianship of Infants Act, 1961, was applicable to enable the court to give the custody of a child to the mother even though the mother had married a stranger, if the court is satisfied that it is to the welfare of the child to grant such custody to the mother. The decision itself might perhaps be supported under the Islamic law but the learned Judge in his judgment said:[27]

> In my endeavour to do justice, I propose to exercise my discretion and have regard primarily to the welfare of the children. In doing so it is not my intention to disregard the religion and custom of the parties concerned or the rules under the Muslim religion but that does not necessarily mean that the court must adhere strictly to rules laid down by the Muslim religion. The court has not I think, been deprived of its discretionary power.

In the case of *Anchom* v. *Public Prosecutor*[28] the Court of Appeal of Johore rejected an argument that the Offences by Mohammedans Enactment was void as it 'purports to revise, enlarge or amend the Mohammedan law' contrary to the Johore Constitution. As McElwaine C.J. said: 'The offence of which these persons were convicted would, had it been witnessed in its entirety by four witnesses, have been the crime of *zinah* punishable under Mohammedan law by sentencing to death'. The Offences against Mohammedans Enactment on the other hand provides that the offence of illegal sexual intercourse may be punished by fine or imprisonment. The Court of Appeal held that it had no power to construe the Constitution of Johore or to declare the law to be *ultra vires* the Constitution. Poyser C.J. in his judgment makes the significant remark:

> I would add only that the Mohammedan law was never adopted in its entirety by the State of Johore . . . in recent years too the majority of Enactments probably contain provisions which are not in accordance with the Mohammedan law. Enactment No. 47 of 1937 is one of such Enactments, for under Mohammedan law the penalty for adultery is death but under the Johore law only imprisonment and fine.

The same point has been forcefully made in criticisms of the various enactments for the administration of Muslim law in the States of Malaya—that is, that the *hadd* punishments provided under the Islamic law have been set aside and this therefore makes the laws not Islamic and makes it sinful for the Kathis to enforce the law. The point has been made that no human legislature or agency can tamper with the laws of God. But the dichotomy in the administration of the law in Malaysia continues.

NOTES

1. Report of the Federation of Malaya Constitutional Commission 1957, Kuala Lumpur, 1957, paragraph 169, p. 73.
2. Ibid., p. 100.
3. M. Suffian Hashim, 'The Relationship between Islam and the State in Malaya', *Intisari*, Vol. 1, No. 1, p. 8.
4. Federal Constitution, Article 3, as amended by Act A206 and Act A354.
5. Constitution of Sabah, Article 5A, added by the Constitution (Amendment) Act, 1973.
6. Constitution (Amendment) Act, 1976 (Act A354).
7. See for example Constitution of Selangor, 1959, Part II, Article LI and LIII.
8. See for example Constitution of Selangor, 1959, Part II, Article LII.
9. Malacca Administration of Muslim Law Enactment, 1959, s.157(2); Penang Administration of Muslim Law Enactment, 1959, s.157(2); Negeri Sembilan Administration of Muslim Law Enactment, 1960, s.159(2); Kedah Administration of Muslim Law Enactment, 1962, s.160(2); Kelantan Council of Religion and Malay Custom Enactment 1966, s.68(2); Sabah Administration of Muslim Law Enactment, 1977, s93A.
10. Constitution (Amendment) Act, 1976 (Act A354).
11. Ibid.
12. Federation of Malaya Constitutional Proposals, 1957, Kuala Lumpur, 1957, pp. 18–19.
13. Official Report of Legislative Council Debates, 1 May 1958, Columns 4631 and 4671–2.
14. The Federal Constitution sets out the subjects which are in the State list which includes:

    1. Except with respect to the Federal Territory, Muslim Law and personal and family law of persons professing the Muslim religion, including the Muslim Law relating to succession, testate and intestate, betrothal, marriage, divorce, dower, maintenance, adoption, legitimacy, guardianship, gifts, partitions, and non-charitable trusts; Muslim *wakafs* and the definition and regulation of charitable and religious trusts, the appointment of trustees and the incorporation of persons in respect of Muslim religious and charitable endowments, institutions, trusts, charities and charitable institutions operating wholly within the State; Malay customs; *Zakat Fitrah* and *Bait-ul-Mal* or similar Muslim revenue; mosques or any Muslim public place of worship; creation and punishment of offences by persons professing the Muslim religion against precepts of that religion, except in regard to matters included in the Federal List; the constitution, organization and procedure of Muslim courts, which shall have jurisdiction only over persons professing the Muslim religion and in respect only of any of the matters included in this paragraph, but shall not have jurisdiction in respect of offences except in so far as conferred by federal law; the control of propagation of doctrines and beliefs among persons professing the Muslim religion; the determination of matters of Muslim Law and doctrine and Malay custom. Federal Constitution, Ninth Schedule, List 2(1).
15. Act 97.
16. Act 98.
17. No. 23 of 1965.
18. See for example Constitution of the State of Johore, Second Part, Article VII(2).
19. See for example Constitution of the State of Johore, Second Part, Article XXXI.
20. Federal Constitution, Article 40.
21. See for example the Perak Administration of Muslim Law Enactment, 1965, s. 42.
22. See *Malaysia Year Book*, 1973 p. 57ff.
23. Federal Constitution, Article 160.
24. [1939] M.L.J. 209.
25. [1970] 1 M.L.J. 222.
26. [1971] 1 M.L.J. 265.
27. Ibid., at p. 269.
28. [1940] M.L.J. 22.

Islam or the Panca Sila as the Basis of the State

SAIFUDDIN ANSHARI

In answering the question why the Islamic Group accepted the results of the meeting of August 18, 1945, General Soedirman[1] writes:

> The situation of the country at the time was still dangerous. With the Allied Army surrounding [sic] us, allowing the Dutch Colonialists, to return and to recolonialize our country, and with the Dai Nippon Army still completely dominating our country, the dangers threatened our state and nation, as stated by Bung Karno in his opening speech of the meeting of August 18, 1945.[2]

A very similar tone is heard in the following remarks of Harun Nasution:

> The day of the revolution were not the appropriate time [for the Islamic Nationalists] to press on with the realization of their Islamic ideas. For them the defence of the Independence of Indonesia must have the first priority. This idea is implied in the speech of Kasman Singodimedjo in the Constituent Assembly where he explained why Islamic groups did not raise a protest when the Islamic provision was removed from the Jakarta Charter on August 18, 1945. That particular time, he said, in view of the Japanese defeat and landing of the Allied Forces, was inappropriate for deep discussion of the matter.[3]

That was why the Islamic group put aside their own principles on the philosophy of the state and the constitution, "hoping that in the future, if the situation would permit them, they would deliberate over it again (Soedirman)."[4]

It was mentioned earlier that Soekarno had emphasized the temporary character of the 1945 Constitution, promising:

> Later on in the future. . . if we live in a safe and orderly state, we will gather the elected representatives of the people together again, who will enable us to make the more complete and perfect constitution.[5]

Prawoto Mangkusasmito remarks that:

> These very living thoughts of Soekarno — who was at the time really a great, authoritative and beloved national leader — were being held by the Islamic group as a 'national promise' which at the same time pacified and appeased their tempestuous hearts. The attention was then concentrated on the struggle against the Dutch, both physically and diplomatically.[6]

The general election finally took place more than 10 years later, on December 15, 1955,[7] and President Soekarno inaugurated the Constituent Assembly on November 10, 1956. The Islamic parties obtained 230 seats; while the other parties (Nationalist, Protestant, Catholic, Socialist and Communist) obtained 284. The ratio between two groups was, therefore, around 4 to 5. On the basis of the results of the general election it is evident,

Excerpted from Saifuddin Anshari, *The Jakarta Charter 1945* (Kuala Lumpur: Muslim Youth Movement of Malaysia, 1979), by permission of the author and the publishers.

therefore, that the Islamic faction was not properly represented in either the Investigating Committee (25%), or in the Preparatory Committee (12%); it was only in the Committee which had composed the Jakarta Charter that the Islamic group had been represented adequately.

In order to be able to follow the debates on the basis of the state in this new Constituent Assembly some very important events in the period 1945–1955 must be kept in mind. On January 27, 1953 President Soekarno made a startling statement at Amuntai, South Kalimantan, saying:

> The state we want is a national state of all Indonesia. If we establish a state based on Islam, many areas whose population is not Islamic, such as the Moluccas, Bali, Flores, the Kai Islands, and Sulawesi, will secede. And west Irian which has not yet become part of the territory of Indonesia, will not want to be part of the Republic.[8]

This speech invited the severe protest of the Islamic group. M. Isa Anshary was the first one to express his objections. He regarded the President's statement "to be undemocratic, unconstitutional, and in conflict with the ideology of Islam which is professed by the great majority of Indonesian citizens."[9] The protest was then followed by the *Nahdlatul Ulama Party* (Ulama Association Party), the *Gerakan Pemuda Islam Indonesia* (Islamic Youth Movement of Indonesia), the *Front Muballigh Islam* (Islamic Missionaries Front) of North Sumatra, *Perti* (Islamic Education Party) of Central Sumatra and a number of other Muslim organizations.[10]

> The G.P.I.I. stated that the President had exceeded his constitutional limitations, that his speech had sown seeds of separatism and that it represented a taking of sides by the head of state with groups opposed to the ideology of Islam.[11]

The Secular Nationalist leaders, in their turn, defended President Soekarno. "They argued for the special prerogatives of President Soekarno as a man who was a revolutionary leader and inspirer of his people as well as a constitutional head of state."[12] They then made Isa Anshary the target of severe attack; and the latter, in turn, responded to them and repeated his protest. Natsir and Sukiman, the prominent leaders of the Masyumi, tried to minimize the issue, assuring the people that "the disagreement resulted from a confusion of terms and that the matter was an internal one of the Moslem Community and not to be discussed in exaggerated terms outside it."[13]

Attempts were made to such a clarification of the certain key terms in the discussion. A Dahlan Ranuwihardjo, the Chairman of the *Himpunan Mahasiswa Islam (H.M.I.,* the Muslim University Students Association) wrote a letter to President Soekarno, "asking clarification of the relationship between a national state and an Islamic state, and between the Panca Sila and the Ideology of Islam."[14] President Soekarno then gave a general lecture on *"Negara Nasional dan Cita-cita Islam"* (The National State and the Ideals of Islam), on May 7, 1953 at the University of Indonesia. Toward the end of his speech he remarked:

> Concerning the position of the Panca Sila and Islam, I cannot tell more than that, and citing Brother the great leader of Masyumi, Muhammad Natsir in Pakistan. . . [who] said that the Panca Sila and Islam are not in conflict with each other, and even similar to each other. . . . Listen to Brother Natsir answering the question of Ranuwihardjo.[15]

The President then quoted a significant passage from the address which Natsir had delivered a year earlier before the Pakistan Institute of World Affairs, Karachi:

> Pakistan is a moslem country. So is my country Indonesia. But though we recognize Islam to be the faith of the Indonesian people, we have not made an expressed mention of it in our Constitution. Nor have we excluded religion from our national life. Indonesia has expressed its creed in the Panca Sila, or the Five Principles, which has been adopted as the spiritual, moral and ethical foundation of our nation and our State. Your part and ours is the same. Only it is differently stated.

The President then said: "Brothers, voila monsieur Muhammad Natsir."[16]

In connection with the *Nuzul al-Qur'an* celebration in May, 1954, M. Natsir returned to the same issue by discussing *"Apakah Panca Sila bertentangan dengan al-Qur'an"* (whether the Panca Sila is in conflict with the Qur'an).[17]

"The formula of the Panca Sila seems to Muslims not as *a priori*, a 'strange thing', which is in conflict with the Qur'an", he said, "however that does not mean that the Panca Sila is already identical or covers all Islamic teachings."[18] At the other part of his explanation he stated:

> The formula of the Panca Sila is the result of the deliberation of the leaders in the phase of Independence's struggle when it rose to the top in 1945. I believe that in such a situation, those leaders who gathered together, the majority of whom were adherents of Islam, would certainly not confirm any formula which was supposedly in conflict with the fundamental teachings of Islam.[19]

Natsir, who considered the Panca Sila as a formula of five ideals of virtue (*lima cita kebajikan*), continued:

> No one of those who composed it has the monopoly on its interpretation nor may he fill it just according to his personal wish. Every *putra Indonesia* (lit.: son of Indonesia) feels having the right to share in filling the formula.
> We do hope that, while seeking for its contents. . . the Panca Sila will not be filled with teachings which are against the Qur'an, the Divine Revelation which has become the *darah dan daging* (lit.: blood and flesh; the nature) for the majority of these Indonesian people.[20])

During the same month, President Soekarno gave a lecture (on the Panca Sila) which contained elements which, according to many, were in direct conflict with the teachings of Islam:

> Indonesian's nation is still at the *stadia agraria, an agrarischevolk.* Open once again the book of Huxender, *Economisch toetstand van den Inlandsch bevolking.* You will find in it his figures which point out that at least 72% of the Indonesian nation lives from agriculture. That is the old agriculture, not the modern one. A nation which is still at the *stadia agraria* must be mystical and religious.[21]

The *Ulama* and *Muballighin* of Makassar protested this statement on June 8, 1954:

1. According to Islamic law it is *haram* (forbidden) for a Muslim to pronounce such words;
2. It is *haram* for a Muslim to obey and accept it as his own creed.[22]

President Soekarno repeated his interpretation of the first *Sila* of the Panca Sila at a meeting of the "Movement of the Panca Sila's Defenders" *(Gerakan Pembela Panca Sila)* at the State Palace on June 17, few days after the protest from Makassar:

> Many of the nations which have left the phase of agraria and have entered the phase of industrialism, have left their religiosity as I have said before, for they live in the realm of certainty (kepastian). Even in this very phase the 'isms' which do not acknowledge the existence of God. . ., [such as] atheism came into being.[23]

Of interest in this connection is also the report which Takdir Alisjahbana gives of Sutardjo's interpretation of Panca Sila and his criticism of Natsir's 'Western' ideas:

> Sutardjo, a member of the Greater Indonesian party, attacked Mohammad Natsir, leader of the Islamic *Masyumi* Party, for being far too Western in his ideas, and demanded that the Prime Minister remind Natsir of what the Panca Sila really meant. But if we go on and listen to Sutardjo's own description of what *he* means by the Panca Sila, a very *idiosyncratic* interpretation emerges. Belief in one Almighty God turns out to mean Unity with God as expressed by the concept of Divine Love *(Cinta Asih);* Popular Sovereignty means *Panunggalan Kawula Gusti* or the Union of God with His Servant; and Social Justice becomes the family ideal and the traditional system of mutual help within the village community. . . .
> Quite clearly, Sutardjo's Panca Sila is simply a synthesis of indigenous Indonesian and Hindu cultural ideals, often called "Janavism", which totally rejects the ideas of a man like Natsir, who attempts to think rationally and realistically about the world in the framework of a modernized Islam.[24]

These few data from 1953 and 1954 give some impression of the situation and atmosphere in which the Constituent Assembly began its work in November 1956. At the beginning three proposals for the basis of the state came to the fore: the Panca Sila, Islam, and the Social Economy. The First one, the Panca Sila's proposal, was supported by the *Partai Nasional Indonesia (P.N.I.,* 116 members), *Partai Komunis Indonesia (P.K.I.,* including *Republik Proklamasi* faction, 80), *Partai*

Kristen Indonesia (*Parkindo,* 16), *Partai Katolik,* (10) *Partai Sosialis Indonesia* (*P.S.I.,* 10), *Ikatan Pendukung Kemerdekaan Indonesia* (*IPKI,* 8), and many other small parties; with a total of 273 representatives. The second option, Islam, was supported by *Majlis Syura Muslimin Indonesia* (*Masyumi,* 112 members), *Nahdlatul Ulama* (N.U., 91), *Partai Syarikat Islam Indonesia* (*P.S.I.I.,* 16), *Persatuan Tarbiyah Islamiyah* (*Perti,* 7) and four other small parties, with a total of 230 members in the Constituent Assembly. The third proposal, the Social Economy was supported by 9 members only, 5 of them belonging to the *Partai Buruh* (Labour Party) and 4 to the *Murba* Party.[25]

Because of the very limited support of the third option, it is fair to say, as Takdir Alisjahbana does, that:

> . . . the debates on political and philosophical principles, inevitably provoked in the writing of any Constitution, revealed the Constituent Assembly as a whole as divided into two: one group wanting an Islamic basis for the state, the other demanding the acceptance of the Panca Sila.[26]

It should be noticed here that what was meant by the "Panca Sila" was either Soekarno's "Panca Sila" or any other form of it, *except* the Jakarta Charter, although the latter was, as we have seen before, actually the first official formulation of the Panca Sila.[27] This is evident e.g. from Soewirjo's statement:

> I would not like to discuss the order of the *silas* or the arrangement of its words. For the *Partai Nasional Indonesia* this is not the matter of principle. The *P.N.I.* does not mind if the order of its *silas* and the arrangement of its words are changed, revised or perfected. The principle for us is the content, the teaching of Panca Sila.[28]

Not only do we see in the discussion of the Constituent Assembly references to several different forms of the Panca Sila, but also a variety of interpretations of specific terms and widely different emphases. For Roeslan Abdulgani (a *P.N.I.* leader), e.g. the most fundamental *sila* was obviously the *sila* of *Kebangsaan* (Nationalism), as a reaction against colonialism.[29] Arnold Mononutu, a Christian member of the *P.N.I.,* laid emphasis on the first *sila* from a Christian point of view: "*Ke-Tuhanan Yang Maha Esa* is for us the fundamental one and the source of the other *sila.* Without *Ke-Tuhanan Yang Maha Esa,* the Panca Sila becomes a materialistic philosophy."[30] The views of Soekarno concerning the *Ke-Tuhanan Yang Maha Esa* clause have been discussed above. In his address in the Constituent Assembly on November 12, 1957, M. Natsir criticized Soekarno's remarks in his speech for the *Gerakan Pembela Panca Sila,* quoted above:

> The summary of that [Seokarno's] idea in the simplest form is: One who is still living in the phase of the agrarian needs God, but as soon as he became an industrialist he does not need God any more. The idea of God has become a relative one according to the development of social life from one phase to another.[31]

"Where will revelation as the source of faith and belief in God then be placed?" Natsir asked. "How can we maintain in this way the idea of revelation which is independent upon any temporal influences such as agrarian, nomadism and industrialism?" Furthermore he emphasized that for a secularist the principle of *Ke-Tuhanan* is merely a man-made principle which therefore is subject to change and has nothing to do with *wahyu* (revelation).

> Such views in fact were championed by the Marxists, who say that it is the structure of economy and society which determines the views of life, religion, philosophy and culture of a society.[32]

Meanwhile Isa Anshary criticized Soekarno's "theory of compression" which was dissolved within the notion of "gotong royong"[33]: "Mr. Chairman, we the Islamic factions resist and reject the *Ke-Tuhanan Yang Maha Esa* in such interpretation."[34]

There seems to be ample reason for the remarks of Notonagoro: "Among the contents of the five *silas,* we would say that the sila of *'Ke-Tuhanan Yang Maha Esa'* is the most difficult one, for it is the most problematic of them all."[35] And W.B. Sidjabat observes:

> . . . that the interpretation of the first 'sila' stated by Soekarno and others do not specifically reflect the Islamic concept of God. The orthodox Muslims. . . are certainly far from being satisfred with that interpretation. Their dissatisfaction can be well understood in the light of the confusion of the first principle of the 'Panca Sila.'[36]

"For us, the supporters of the Panca Sila, religion is something supreme and sacred. That is why we hold religion in highest esteem," Soewirjo, the President of *P.N.I.*, argued. "Exactly because religion is supreme and sacred we do mind whether religion is to be used as the basis of the state." He quoted the statement signed by Soekarno and Hatta on September 14, 1957:

> That the Panca Sila which is inserted in the Preamble of the Provisional Constitution of Republic of Indonesia of 1945 is the real guarantee for whole people of Indonesia to live continuously, freely, justly and prosperously.[37]

The other side, however, was convinced that the Panca Sila in and by itself did not mean much: it could be interpreted as Masjkur stated, in many different ways:

> The Panca Sila is an empty formula which still needs contents. If the *Ke-Tuhanan Yang Maha Esa,* the first *sila* of the Panca Sila is filled by the people who consider a stone as God, the Lordship in the Panca Sila then will be filled in with a stone. If it is filled in by tree worshippers, it will be filled in with a tree.[38]

Masjkur remarked that both Islam and the Panca Sila desire a just and prosperous state, a democratic government, a life of a world economy which is formed in a family spirit, a happy life of the nation's household having high ethical values. Islam has the clear teachings in those matters, he said; but from which sources does the Panca Sila want to derive its teachings?[39]

M. Natsir stated on the above-mentioned date in the Constituent Assembly:

> Of course, nobody denies that there are good ideas in the Panca Sila. Yet the explanations given by its supporters indicate that they themselves cannot decide what are its true contents, its proper sequence, its source, its nucleus, and interdependence of its components. Because these are not clear, the difficulties will then gradually increase. Since the basis of our state needs to be clear and distinct so as not to confuse the nation, it is difficult for our group to accept something which is vague.[40]
>
> ....
>
> Panca Sila as a state philosophy is for us obscure and has nothing to say to the soul of Muslim community which already possesses a definite, clear, and complete ideology, one which burns in the hearts of the Indonesian people as a living inspiration and source of strength, namely Islam. To exchange the Islamic Ideology for Panca Sila is, for Muslims, like leaping from the solid into empty space, into a vacuum.[41]

To the supporters of the Panca Sila then Natsir appealed:

> Your intended *silas* exist in Islam, not as a sterile 'pura concept' but as a living value which has real and distinct substances. By accepting Islam as the philosophy of state the defender of the Panca Sila will not lose anything at all. Both the supporters of the Panca Sila and the adherents of religion will have a living philosophy with distinct and strong contents. No one of the five *silas* formulated in the Panca Sila will fall and be lost by your accepting Islam as the basis of the state. In Islam the certain norms are found where the 'pure concept' of the five *silas* has substance and moving soul and spirit. And in a similar manner the supporters of the 'Social Economy' could find in Islam the progressive concept of social economy.[42]

The only alternative for the supporters of Panca Sila, according to M. Isa Anshary, is to let the Panca Sila live with other fellow *silas*, 1001 *silas* which are widespread in the pages and teachings of Islam.[43] Unless protected in this way, he said, "the Panca Sila will be swallowed by the giants of imperialism and communism."[44]

"The election of 1955 had not brought victory to any one of the main streams in Indonesian society," Boland remarks. "A balance of power had come about which was to make a political compromise necessary, both in Parliament and in the Constituent Assembly."[45]

The Constituent Assembly then tended to seek points of agreement. Wilopo, the General Chairman of Constituent Assembly who himself was a P.N.I. leader, pointed to the absolute necessity "to produce a compromise, a resultant of parallelogram of strength (*paralelogram gaya*) within trends which existing in our society."[46] "Both Islam and Panca Sila desire that our nation be happy," Soewirjo said, "is it impossible to find the points of meeting?"[47] Wongsonegoro suggested that an *ad hoc* committee be established as a compromise committee, consisting of 10 members, the Islamic and the "Panca Sila" side each being represented by 5 members.[48] Takdir Alisyahbana proposed that:

> In this council probably we may decide to submit the matter to a Preparatory Committee of the Constitution to arrange a compromise formula, where both of the different and confronting sides would bring their sacrifices.[49]

In its third session — that was the 59th meeting — of November 11, 1957, the Constituent Assembly formed the *Panitia Perumus tentang Dasar Negara* (Formulating Committee on the Basis of the State), consisting of 18 members representing all groups in the Assembly.[50] In the Plenary Session of the Constituent Assembly of December 6, 1957, the Formulating Committee reported five main conclusions. Among 13 points of the third main conclusion was a concrete proposal for a new compromise formula:

> The State of the Republic of Indonesia is based upon the desire to form a socialistic society whose members believe in God Who is Absolutely One, in the sense that the social justice and equally-spread prosperity shall be guaranteed, and in which the Mercy of God the Beneficent the Merciful, according to Islam, Christianity, Catholicism, and other existing religions in our country may be known.
>
> The further bases are: the unity of the nation which is given shape by the qualities of the *gotong-royong* (mutual help), humanitarianism, nationalism and democracy (*kerakyatan*) which is guided by the inner wisdom in the unanimity arising out of deliberation amongst representatives.[51]

In his speech at the Assembly's session of May 6, 1959, A. Kahar Muzakkir gave us some important accounts concerning the work and the final result of the Constituent Assembly until that time:

> I have the experience that, as usual, our General Chairman of the Assembly is really a gentlemen of truth in his feelings. On the closing day of the Preparatory Committee of the Constitution on February 18, 1959, I kept in mind his closing words at the closing session of the Committee on that day, clearly saying that the Constituent Assembly has finished 90% of its task.[52]

It is true in the words of Kuasini Sabil, a Perti member, that many of the problems solved were "the easy and light" ones and that the rest, regarding the Basis of State were the most difficult ones, which had been postponed as the last point on the agenda.

> But we should notice as well that no matter how difficult at first it may be, nevertheless the rest concerns two different opinions which can be united; and such a unity has already existed, as proven by the Constituent Assembly.[53]

If the Constituent Assembly had been given a fair chance to finish its task over the period of few more months, without any intervention from the outside, it would have succeeded in solving its problems and finishing its task to form the permanent Constitution of the Republic of Indonesia which would have been unanimously and wholeheartedly accepted, supported and sustained by all living groups in the Indonesian society.

NOTES

1. Letnan-General H. Soedirman is the President of *Pendidikan Tinggi Dawah Islam* (the Higher Education of Islamic Propagation). Not to be confused with Senior General Soedirman, who was the Commander of the Armed Forces during the physical revolution (died in 1949).
2. Quoted in Hasan Zaini Z., *Pengantar Hukum Tatanegara* (Bandung: Alumni, 1971), p. 63.
3. Harun Nasution, "The Islamic State in Indonesia: The Rise of the Ideology, the Movement for its Creation and the Theory of the Masjumi (M.A. Thesis, I.I.S McGill University, Montreal, 1965) p. 76.
4. Zaini, *Pengantar Hukum Tatanegara,* p. 63.
5. H. Muhammad Yamin, *Naskah Persiapan Undang-undang Dasar 1945* (Jakarta: Yayasan Prapanca, 1959) I, 110.
6. Prawoto Mangkusasmito, *Pertumbuhan Historis Rumus Dasar Negara dan Sebuah Projeksi* (Jakarta: Hudaya, 1970) p. 29.

7. Notonagoro, *Pemboekaan Oendang-oendang Dasar 1945* (Yogjakarta: Universitas Gajah Mada, 1956) p. iv. See also: Herbert Feith, *The Indonesian Election of 1955*. Interim Report Series, Modern Indonesian Project (Ithaca, N.Y.: Cornell University Press, 1962), p. 281.
8. Herbert Feith, *The Decline of Constitutional Democracy in Indonesia* (Ithaca, N.Y.: Cornell University Press, 1962), p. 281.
9. *Ibid.*
10. *Ibid.*
11. *Ibid.*, pp. 281–282.
12. *Ibid.*, p. 282.
13. *Ibid.*
14. See: Herbert Feith and Lance Castles (editors), *Indonesian Political Thinking 1945–1965* (Ithaca, N.Y.: Cornell University Press, 1970) p. 164.
15. Soekarno, *Negara Nasional dan Cita-cita Islam* (Jakarta: P.P. Endang, 1954), p. 44.
16. *Ibid.* Soekarno quoted Natsir's passage from *Islamic Review,* March, 1953. For the complete Natsir's speech read: M. Natsir, *Some Observations concerning the Role of Islam in National dan International Affairs.* Data Paper Number 16, Southeast Asia Program, Department of Far Eastern Studies, Cornell University (Ithaca, N.Y.: 1954).
17. M. Natsir, *Capita Selecta,* II (Jakarta: Pustaka *Pendis,* 1957), 144–150.
18. *Ibid.*, 149.
19. *Ibid.*, 148.
20. *Ibid.*, 150. It is obvious that Natsir does not consider Soekarno's "Panca Sila" as the official one; he only considers the Panca Sila created in the representative body.
21. Quoted in *Tentang Dasar Negara Republik Indonesia di Konstituante* (Bandung: Konstituante, 1959), II, 248.
22. *Ibid.*, 249.
23. Quoted in M. Natsir, *Islam sebagai Dasar Negara* (Bandung: Masyumi Faction in the Constituent Assembly, 1957), pp. 17–18. See also: Soekarno, *Panca Sila Dasar Falsafah Negara* (Jakarta: Panitia Nasional Peringatan Lahirnya Panca Sila (Juni 1945–1964), pp. 88–93.
24. S. Takdir Alisjahbana, *Indonesia in Modern World* (New Delhi: Office for Asian Affairs, Congress for Cultural Freedom, 1961), pp. 149–150.
25. See: "*Laporan Komisi* Konstitusi tentang Dasar Negara" (The Reports of the Committee of Constitution concerning the Basis of State), in J.T.C. Simorangkir and B. Mang Reng Say, *Konstitusi dan Konstituante Indonesia* (Jakarta: Soeroengan, n.d.), pp. 169–173; hereafter cited as Simorangkir, *Konstitusi.*
26. Alisjahbana, *Indonesia in Modern World,* pp. 151 – 152.
27. The various formulations of the Panca Sila are discussed in Chapter VIII.
28. *Dasar Negara,* II, 160.
29. *Ibid.*, III, 348–372.
30. Quoted in Natsir's address, *Ibid.*, 439.
31. Natsir, *Islam sebagai Dasar Negara,* p. 19.
32. *Ibid.*
33. See Chapter I, p. 22.
34. *Dasar Negara,* II, 190–191.
35. Notonagoro, *Pemboekaan,* p. 18.
36. Walter Bonar Sidjabat, *Religious Tolerance and the Christain Faith* (Jakarta: Badan Penerbit Kristen, 1965), p. 39.
37. *Dasar Negara,* II, pp. 159–160.
38. *Ibid.*, III, 46.
39. *Ibid.*, 41–42.
40. M. Natsir, "The Danger of Secularism" in Feith, *Political Thinking,* p. 218; Natsir, *Islam sebagai Dasar Negara.* p. 28.
42. Natsir, *Islam sebagai Dasar Negara,* p. 28.
43. *Dasar Negara,* II, 244.
44. *Ibid.*, p. 243.
45. B.J. Boland, *The Struggle of Islam in Modern Indonesia* (The Hague: Martinus Nijhoff, 1971), p. 85.
46. *Dasar Negara,* III, 365.
47. *Ibid.*, 40.
48. *Ibid.*, II, 298.
49. *Ibid.*, III, 41–42. In the same spirit, Firmansjah, an *I.P.K.I.* member, proposed the compromise. See: *Ibid.*, I, 39.
50. There were: Sajogja Hardjadinata, Enin Sastraprawira, H. Hoesein, Siswo Sudarmo, K.H. Sjukri, K.H.

Masjkur, A.S. Dharta, Achmad Astrawinata, J.C.T. Simorangkir, Amin La Engke, B. Mang Reng Say, S. Takdir Alisjahbana, Firmansjah, Baheramsjah St. Indra, Kuasini Sabil, Oei Tjoe Tat, Sjamsu Harya Udaya, Madomiharna.

51. Simorangkir, *Konstitusi,* pp. 182–185.
52. Yamin, *Naskah,* III, 41–42. It seems an exaggeration when Harun Nasution says that "in its two years of existence the Constituent Assembly produced nothing substantial. It became a forum of ideological debat." "Islamic State", p. 109. See, e.g., "Hasil Karya Konstituante Bandung" (The Results of the Constituent Assembly of Bandung), in J.T.C. Simorangkir and B. Mang Reng Say, *Tentang dan Sekitar Undang-undang Dasar* 1945 (Jakarta: Penerbit Djambatan, 1959), pp. 83–90.
53. Yamin, *Naskah,* II, 528.

The Shari'ah Law Courts in Malaya

ABDUL MAJEED MOHAMED MACKEEN

The development of the Shari'ah law courts in Malaya vis-à-vis the judicial organization in the country as a whole proceeded on significant lines which deserve our special attention here. While the courts of the qadi in the states of Malaya had, from the early years of the British administration, exclusive jurisdiction in respect of matters personally affecting the Muslims, especially matters of personal law, they remained an integral though distinct part of the system of civil and criminal courts prevailing in the state and in most cases[1] appeals could be made from them to higher courts of competent civil or criminal jurisdiction — a situation, one might have thought, conducive to a natural evolution of a unified courts system. This is what happened in the countries of the Middle East,[2] e.g. Egypt and Tunisia, where the Shari'ah courts were dissolved in 1955 and 1956 respectively and the administration of Shari'ah family law transferred to the national courts of the land. But events in Malaya moved in the opposite direction. In spite of the present relatively greater centralization of government and political authority in the Federation and in consequence of the rise of a unified system of civil and criminal courts, the Shari'ah law courts, adhering to a role defined in the prevailing constitutional system and functioning under aegis of the state legislatures, have crystallized into almost rival judiciaries with concurrent though restricted jurisdiction. Under the immediate impact of developments in the neighboring states of Malaya, Singapore too — where the Shari'ah law had often been administered in the ordinary civil courts by English judges — has with the introduction of the *Administration of Muslim Law Act, 1966* at last guaranteed the Shari'ah a permanent and independent place in the judicial structure of the Republic.

ORGANIZATION AND JURISDICTION

The only central judicial organ provided for in classical Islam for the administration of the Shari'ah law was not so much the "court" of the qadi as the "office" of the qadi and consequently legal treatises dealing with the subject usually spoke of the appointment to office of a qadi (*taqlīd al-qaḍā*)[3] rather than of the constitution of the court (*maḥkamah*). In line with the reorganization of the machinery of Islamic legal administration that had been taking place from the late 19th century onward in the states of Malaya and in Singapore as in the rest of the Muslim world, the several Enactments on the administration of Islamic law in Malaya provided for both the appointment of the qadis and the constitution of courts of the qadi and other judicial bodies as seemed necessary in the context. Based on the extent and nature of jurisdiction involved, the Islamic law courts in the states of Malaya[4] are presently organized into the following grades: the court of a qadi, the court of a

Excerpted from Abdul Majeed Mohamed Mackeen, *Contemporary Islamic Legal Organization in Malaya* (New Haven: Yale University Southeast Asia Studies Monograph Series no. 13, 1969), by permission of the author and the publishers.

chief qadi, and a court of appeal styled by different names[5] in the different states. Thus the *Administration of Muslim Law Act, 1966*[6] of Singapore provides, in elaboration of a precedent set in 1935 by Johore's *Muhammadan Marriage and Divorce Registration Enactment,* for appointment of qadis, and by implication for the constitution of courts too, according to different schools of law (*madhāhib*). Somewhat earlier Kelantan had provided for what was called the "court of the mufti" and vested it with appellate jurisdiction to "hear and determine appeals from any judgment or order of a Court of a Kathi in suit between Mohamedans."[7] No special courts have been created to administer pure customary law. At best, scope is provided for a concordat between the prescriptions of the Shari'ah law and "Malay custom" as recognized in the legal form of "*'ādah*" and treated in some states[8] as a source of law within the general framework envisaged in the Administration of Muslim Law Enactments; at worst, the term "Malay custom" appears to be virtually expunged from the corresponding or similar Enactments of other states[9] in an apparent refusal to recognize even the slightest suggestion for compromise in the spiritual ascendancy of the Shari'ah law.

The jurisdiction of a court of a chief qadi[10] extends throughout the state. In its criminal jurisdiction the court of a chief qadi tries offenses committed by a Muslim and punishable under the Enactment concerned, while in its civil jurisdiction the court may adjudicate, where Muslims are involved, upon the following matters:

(i) betrothal, marriage, divorce, nullity of marriage or judicial separation;
(ii) any disposition of, or claim to, property arising out of any of the matters set out in sub-paragraph (i) of this paragraph;
(iii) maintenance of dependents, legitimacy, guardianship or custody of infants;
(iv) determination of the persons entitled to share in the estate of deceased persons and such division of the shares to which such persons are respectively entitled to in accordance with Ilukum Shara' [sic];
(v) wills or death-bed gifts of deceased persons who professed the Muslim religion;
(vi) gifts *inter vivos,* or settlements made without consideration in money or money's worth, by a person professing the Muslim religion;
(vii) Wakaf [sic] or Nazar [sic]; or
(viii) other matters in respect of which jurisdiction is conferred by any written law.

The original jurisdiction of a court of a chief qadi, however, does not embrace matters which fall within the competence of a court of a qadi.

The jurisdiction[11] of a court of a qadi generally covers the same ground as that of the court of a chief qadi subject to restrictions as follows:

(a) in respect of territory, to prescribed local limits within the state;

(b) in respect of the nature of jurisdiction, to try criminal offenses which do not involve punishment beyond a stated maximum of imprisonment or extent of fine, and to hear and determine civil actions and proceedings which do not involve amount or value beyond a stated maximum or amount not capable of estimation in terms of money.

The court of appeal (the Appeal Committee in Perak) exercises appellate jurisdiction[12] in civil and criminal matters from the decision of a court of a qadi or of a chief qadi or in other cases for which leave to appeal is granted by the Appeal Committee; but there can be no appeal against decisions made by consent. The Appeal Committee may, in the exercise of its appelate jurisdiction in criminal and civil matters, confirm, quash, vary the sentence or decision appealed against, or order a retrial. The Enactments of the states of Malaya give no indication as to the question of finality in appeal cases but in Singapore the decision of the Appeal Board is final.[13]

No sphere in the administration of Islamic law in contemporary Malaya has been so deeply affected by legal modernism as that of the adjectival law which, with a few reservations, is based on current rules of procedure[14] and evidence[15] in force in the land. Of considerable interest are the diverse rules concerning representation in court proceedings; while some Enactments provide for a party to any criminal proceedings to appear in person and in any civil proceedings to be represented by "an advocate and solicitor or pleader"[16] others[17] lend only qualified recognition to such practice by the provision that no such person shall "have the right to appear" in any court of a qadi in representation of a party if such appearance "would be contrary to the principles of Muslim Law."[18] In two states,[19] however, provisions exist for a class of pleaders learned in the Shari'ah law — or what is in fact a reference to a body of Islamic lawyers, the *fuqahā'*, though they are not referred to as such in the Enactments concerned — to appear and plead on behalf of a party in a court of a qadi; the majlis in these states is charged with the duty of maintaining a register "of suitable persons who are competent in matters pertaining to Muslim Law."[20]

If the intention behind these provisions is to install the *fuqahā'* (who hitherto have been merely the learned exponents and custodians of the Shari'ah law) in the legal profession as practicing lawyers, it would indeed usher in a new era in the expansion of Islamic legal practice.

Provisions concerning evidence, a most controversial question in Islamic law, seem to be based on an eclectic principle which seeks to combine the provisions of the Shari'ah law relating to "the number, status, and quality of witnesses for evidence" with the guide rules of the Law of Evidence in force in the state without imposing an obligation to apply the latter strictly,[21] while at the same time admitting the validity both of evidence sworn on oath "in a manner binding upon Muslims"[22] and of evidence taken on affirmation. The Perak Enactment further provides[23] that in matters of practice and procedure in criminal and civil proceedings not expressly covered, the court shall take cognizance of the procedure governing the subordinate civil courts in such matters.

MALAY CUSTOMARY LAW

We have already indicated the divergent attitudes in the state Enactments on Islamic law toward Malay customary law (*adat melayu*) as implied by the inclusion or exclusion of reference to it as a source of law. The fact that some state Enactments contain no mention of Malay customary law does not, of course, mean that questions concerning the relationship between customary observances and Shari'ah law no longer exist for the Shari'ah law experts of the states concerned but does tend to show, one might perhaps conclude, a more positive development in the expansion of Islamic legal thought and an increased awareness of the impact of Islam upon local society. To judge, if at all, by the present rate of internal expansion, especially since Malaya attained independence in 1957, the clues are that more states will follow the lead and conceive of what is called in Malay *hukum shara* (i.e. Shari'ah law) as a broader entity embracing those valid elements of Malay custom capable of assimilation into the framework of Islamic law through the effective instrument of *fatwā,* for the sole purpose of which specially constituted committees exist in all states as a constituent of the majlis. In cases, however, of conflict involving a clash with the more fundamental doctrine of the substantive law which admits of no change, the stand taken — at any rate by those who have a say in the matter as spokesmen of the Shari'ah law — would be to force what they consider to be serious deviations from the norms of Islamic law to a total surrender, and this could be effected by making a ruling of the majlis binding on all Muslims resident in the state. We may cite the example of a bill[24] proposed in 1964 in Selangor, published in the state *Gazette,* but not passed, to change the title of the majlis from the "Council of Muslim Religion and Malay custom" to "Council of Muslim Religion, Selangor." It is indeed most instructive that of the states which do not reckon Malay customary law among the laws to be observed by the majlis, it was Negri Sembilan, the seat of the matrilineally organized society based on the perpateh tradition, where a furious debate[25] raged in 1951 over the proper realms of Malay customary law and Islamic law. While those with a vested interest resisted any changes in the customary notions of ancestral property (*harta pesaka*), the announced aim of the reformists to bring the customary law in this respect "into conformity with Islamic law"[26] served to illustrate the pattern of political agitation which can exert a pull on the whole fabric of traditional

Malay custom when it does not accord with Islamic legal concepts.

But even those states which must be considered somewhat outside the orbit of matrilineal society were confronted in the matter of succession to property by the customs of the matrilineal society and hence the inclusion in their Enactments of the reference to Malay customary law, the intention perhaps being to find a theoretical basis, where this was permissible, for indigenous rules in the concepts of Islamic jurisprudence.

The word for "custom" in Islamic legal nomenclature is *'ādah,* generally also referred to as *'urf*. Although custom *per se* did not succeed in becoming an official source[27] of Islamic law, it has functioned as a principle of subsidiary value[28] within the framework of the recognized sources. The role of custom in determining the application of the substantive law of the Shari'ah has, without implying any variation of the substantive law itself, been recognized by the classical manuals of the Shari'ah law. On this basis custom was not only assimilated into Islamic law but its binding nature was fittingly acknowledged in the maxim: "Custom ranks as stipulation." The guiding principles for resolving conflicts between customary practice and Shari'ah law have been laid down with great lucidity by the Shafi'i jurist al-Suyūtī (d. 1505) in the form of *qawā'id*[29] (rules or technical principles of positive law).

The author enumerates the following rules:

(1) Customs are reckoned only in so far as they show continuity of practice.

(2) Cases of conflict between customary practice and a doctrine of Shari'ah law shall be resolved in favor of the former in the absence of a definite Shari'ah rule (*hukm*), e.g. if x swears that he will not eat meat, he shall not be offending the oath if he takes fish although fish is called meat in the Quran (obviously a reference to Quran 16:14).

(3) Cases of conflict between customary practice and a Shari'ah rule shall be resolved in favor of the latter in the presence of a definite Shari'ah rule on the question in issue, e.g. if y swears that he will not marry, he shall be offending the oath only if he concludes a contract (*'aqd*) of marriage but not merely by having sexual intercourse (*wat'*).

(4) Between a general (*'āmm*) and a particular (*khass*) custom, the latter shall be valid only in so far as it is not of limited incidence, e.g. a custom limited to an individual as opposed to a group.

(5) Custom shall prevail in certain matters in respect to which the Shari'ah provisions are general and on which neither the doctrine of the law nor its phrases suggest any definitions.

These rules provide the basis on which the scope for integrating custom within the framework of Islamic law may be, and is in fact, exploited under the existing provisions of those Enactments which seek to control the development of Malay customary law together with the Shari'ah law. Malayan Islamic jurisprudence therefore stands midway between extreme Shari'ah puritanism and blind veneration of customary observances. By combining Shari'ah law, the statute law, and customary practice in a harmonious balance, it sets the pace for continuous expansion of the Shari'ah law.

It is disappointing to note that Taylor's description, "Muhammadan law as varied by local custom,"[30] gives an inadequate and probably misleading picture of the real situation obtaining in contemporary Malaya. In 1937 Taylor, a lawyer and a former member of the Malayan civil service, recorded and discussed a series of cases[31] on the distributions of property following dissolution of marriage among the Malays in different states of Malaya. The utter confusion that prevailed in the evidence of the expert witnesses called and the author's failure to appreciate the opinions of these witnesses against principles of Islamic jurisprudence led to his conclusion[32] that the qadis in Malaya when consulted often declared an adat rule to be Islamic law. In particular the proceedings in *Lebar vs. Niat*[33] and Taylor's commentary on it highlight the confrontation of modern law courts and lawyers less familiar with Islamic jurisprudence with a problem of much consequence in Malaya.

These two uncodified sources apart and barring the written laws in force in the state, the only other remaining "source" so to speak is the state Enactments[34] which provide for the administration of Islamic law and the constitution of the majlis in the states concerned;

but these state Enactments do not, strictly speaking, constitute a "source" of law but rather set out the machinery of legal administration and, to the extent that they embody siyāsah measures of some legal consequence, may be regarded as instruments of the positive law in the Malay sultanates. The two main spheres toward which the powers of the ruler to legislate on grounds of siyāsah were directed, as far as the administration of Islamic law in the states of Malaya is concerned, were those of the adjectival law instanced elsewhere[35] and penal law, the provisions of which, as we shall observe later, have, far from supplementing the rigorous sanctions of the classical Shari'ah law, replaced them.

APPLICATION AND INTERPRETATION

The Muslims in Malaya and Singapore are for all intents and purposes subject to the written law, both public and private, of the land with the reservation that in the case of private law affecting domestic relations they are governed by the provisions in the Enactments bearing on the administration of Islamic law. This in a sense also postulates the validity of a system of Islamic "public law" by declaring a special category of offenses[36] — arising out of such matters as matrimonial cases and the practice and propagation of Islam — cognizable by a court of a qadi in its criminal jurisdiction. While the criminal and civil jurisdiction of the Shari'ah courts is restricted only to Muslims[37] resident in the state concerned, the Enactments expressly provide that the provisions therein in respect of marriage and divorce, maintenance of dependents, and the offenses specified thereunder shall apply[38] only to persons professing the Muslim religion, with the additional clause, in the case of maintenance of dependents, that in the Federation of Malaya the *Married Women and Children* (Maintenance) *Ordinance* (1950) shall not apply.[39]

As remarked earlier, these Enactments are not intended to formulate and codify any fact of the Shari'ah law; all references to the substantive law, therefore, are generally couched in the phrase "in accordance with Muslim law,"[40] the interpretation of which is further restricted, on the basis of the doctrine of *taqlīd* (adherence to a school of law), to a particular school of law and to a particular kind of juristic opinion within the school concerned when naming the authorities to be followed[41] by the majlis and the Shari'ah Committee in their exposition of the law. It is provided[42] that in "making and issuing a ruling" the majlis and the Shari'ah Committee shall ordinarily follow the most approved juristic view (*al-qaul al-mu'tamad,* mistakenly rendered in the Enactments as "orthodox tenets") of the Shafi'i School (rendered as a "sect" in the Enactments). Astonishing enough are provisions of the Perlis *Administration of Muslim Law Enactment* (1964) which alone of all such Enactments on the subject states simply that the majlis and the Shari'ah Committee "shall follow the Quran and the Sunnah of the Prophet,"[43] omitting all reference to any of the established schools of Islamic law or the need to adhere to any of them. This is an innovation of unimaginable magnitude when compared with provisions of the corresponding Enactments in the other states for it means that at least one state among the states of Malaya has chosen to disregard — perhaps in a bid to stimulate a measure of creativity — the partisan tendencies in the historical development of Islamic legal thought and, by this open rejection of the doctrine of *taqlīd,* has come close to accepting, if not in fact accepted, the juristic views of Ibn Taimiyyah (d. 1283) who is generally reckoned the archenemy of "orthodox" Islam. My field investigations in Perlis in May 1966 revealed that prevailing practice in the state confirmed the construction of the provisions concerned.

The sources of Shari'ah law described elsewhere in this chapter relate in their entirety to the Shafi'i school of law and so in Perlis, where no official recognition is extended to the Shafi'i school or for that matter any school, these sources do not apply. The authorities in Perlis, it would appear, rely on such works as that of the Zaidī scholar Shaukānī's[44] (d. 1832) *Nail al-auṭār,* which contains a discussion of Sunni legal traditions (*ḥadīth*) forming the basis of Islamic law as structured in the different schools. A question addressed to the mufti as to the validity of this endeavor to initiate independent thinking in matters of law, i.e. to "open the door of *ijtihād*" (individual reasoning) that was closed long ago following the crystallization of the schools, elicited a curious counterquestion as to the validity of the assertion that the door had ever been closed.

Parallel with the consolidation of the Shari'ah law courts of Malaya into the exclusive judicial organs which they are today, the substance of the Shari'ah law itself, in so far as the provisions of the Enactments rely upon it, have so far escaped any form of codification or even any attempt to speculate on it. With the organization of the judicature in the Middle Eastern countries — especially Egypt and Tunisia — into a unified system of national courts, the need to provide ready access to the facts of law in comprehensive codes was inevitable.

The states of Malaya, however, do not yet seem to be ready for this kind of experiment for a number of reasons. There is something to be said in favor of leaving the Shari'ah law uncodified as it stands today in Malaya and of directing present effort toward more positive reforms in the quality and methods of Islamic legal education and in the training of competent personnel to administer the law with a greater awareness of their responsibility than now seems the case.

The criminal jurisdiction conferred upon the courts of a qadi and the sanctions prescribed for offenses provide an instructive feature in the application of contemporary Islamic law in Malaya. Being in essence a system of private law, Shari'ah law did not develop the notion of criminal law into an effective system of public law as it is understood in the modern world.

Crimes, as conceived in Shari'ah law, are not merely acts or defaults which imperil the interests of society but also include the commission of certain acts specifically forbidden[45] in the Quran such as illicit sexual intercourse (*zinā*), false accusation (*qadhf*) of illicit sexual intercourse, drinking of wine, theft, and highway robbery, all of which incur special sanctions (*ḥadd*) as provided in the Quran. They acquired the character of offenses not entirely on account of the religious authority behind them but also because they involved questions of individual liberty, injury, and property equally applicable to the general class of offenses known to Islamic law as *jināyāt*[46] (lit., offenses). Defaults of certain obligatory acts of religious worship such as prayer do not really amount to offenses for which specific legal sanctions are provided,[47] but in so far as they involve or affect the Muslim community as a whole their neglect is considered an offense punishable by *ta'zīr* (discretionary punishment which a qadi may award). The offenses punishable under the Enactments pertaining to Islamic law in Malaya may be broadly exemplified by the following enumeration: matrimonial offenses; illicit sexual intercourse; drinking of intoxicating liquor; neglect of certain religious obligations, e.g. nonattendance at mosques for Friday prayers or non-payment of *zakāt*; and unauthorized public teaching or preaching of religion.

The sanctions provided for such offenses are those that have been extensively modified by *ta'zīr*, which means all punishments must be in the form of imprisonment or monetary fine. Thus, where the sanctions in the classical Shari'ah law for illicit sexual intercourse or the drinking of wine were stoning to death or lashes respectively, the Enactments in Malaya prescribe imprisonment or fine for the former and a fine only for the latter.[48]

NOTES

1. See for example Perlis, *Courts Enactment* (1330 A.H.), sec. 7; and Kelantan, *Courts Enactment* (1925), sec. 3.
2. N.J. Coulson, *A History of Islamic Law*, (Edinburgh, 1964) p. 163.
3. Mawārdī, *Al-Aḥkām al-sulṭaniyyah* (Cairo, 1960), pp. 65f.
4. Singapore and Johore have provisions for the appointment of *qaḍıs* and *na'ib qaḍis*; Perlis provides for the appointment of *qāḍīs* and assistant *qāḍīs*.
5. In Perak, Selangor, Penang, Malacca, and Negri Sembilan it is called the Appeal Committee: in Pahang, the Religious Appeal Court; in Trengganu, the Shari'ah Appeal Court; in Kelantan, appeals are made to His Highness the Sultan-in-Council; Singapore has an Appeal Board.
6. Sec. 85 (4) (c) (ii).
7. Kelantan, *Courts Enactment* (1955), sec. 6.
8. In Perak, Perlis, Selangor, Kelantan, Pahang, and Trengganu.
9. In Penang, Malacca, Negri Sembilan, and Singapore.
10. Administration of Muslim Law Enactment, 1965 of Perak, sec 45(1) to (3) (hereafter cited as Perak Enactment).

11. Ibid., sec. 45 (4) (a) to (b).
12. Ibid., sec. 46.
13. Administration of Muslim Law Act 1966 of Singapore, sec. 54 (7), (hereafter cited as Singapore Act).
14. Malaya, *Rules of the Supreme Court* (1951).
15. Malaya, *Evidence Ordinance* (1950).
16. Trengganu Enactment (1955), sec. 31; also the Pahang and Penang Enactments. In Singapore a person may be represented in any proceedings.
17. Malacca, Kelantan, and Selangor.
18. Selangor, Administration of Muslim Law Enactment, 1952, sec. 50(ii), (hereafter cited as Selangor Enactment (1952).
19. Perak and Perlis.
20. Perak Enactment, sec. 51 (2). In Perak such persons are known as *peguam* Shari'ah (Shari'ah lawyers).
21. Perak Enactment, sec. 55 (1).
22. Ibid., sec. 55 (2).
23. Ibid., sec. 91.
24. *Administration of Muslim Law: Change of Title Majlis Enactment and Amendment* (1964).
25. P. E. Josselin de Jong, "Islam versus Adat in Negri Sembilan," *Bijdragen tot de taal-, land- en volkenkunde, 116* (1960), 159–203.
26. Ibid., 166.
27. J. Schacht, *An Introduction to Islamic Law,* (Oxford, 1964) p. 62.
28. Coulson, p. 143.
29. Al-Suyūṭī, *Al-Ashbāh wa 'l-Naẓā'ir* (Cairo, n.d.), pp. 102–09.
30. E. N. Taylor, "Malay Family Law," *Journal of the Royal Asiatic Society JRAS* (Malayan Branch), *15* (1937), 533f.; A. Ibrahim, *Islamic Law in Malaya* (Singapore, 1965), p. 147.
31. Taylor, pp. 15–68.
32. Ibid., pp. 9, 47.
33. Cited by Taylor, pp. 48–49.
34. Entitled *Administration of Muslim Law Enactment* in Penang, Malacca, Selangor, Negri Sembilan, Perak, and Perlis; *Council of Religion and Malay Custom and Kathis* [sic] *Courts Enactment* in Kelantan; *Administration of Islamic Law Enactment* in Trengganu; *Administration of the Law of the Religion of Islam Enactment* in Pahang; and *Administration of Muslim Law Act* in Singapore.
35. See Mackeen, *Islamic Legal Organization in Malaya,* pp. 42f.
36. Ibid., see Appendix II pp. 50–51.
37. Perak Enactment, sec. 45 (3) (a) and (b).
38. Ibid., secs. 137 (2), 147 (1).
39. Ibid., sec. 137 (1).
40. Ibid., sec. 129 (1). Variant English translations of the term *hukm shar'* (literally, Shari'ah law) have yielded "in accordance with Muhammadan law" (Kelantan), "in accordance with Islamic law" (Trengganu), "in accordance with the law of the Religion of Islam" (Pahang), etc.
41. Perak Enactment, sec. 42 (1). The adherence of the Shari'ah law courts to these principles of interpretation is implied but not specifically stated.
42. Ibid., sec. 42.
43. Perlis, *Administration of Muslim Law Enactment* (1963), sec. 7 (4).
44. Schacht, p. 227.
45. Ibid., p. 175.
46. Ibid., p. 184.
47. Ibid., p. 187.
48. The Shari'ah law did not provide for fines as a form of punishment; Schacht, pp. 176 – 207.

Problems in the Implementation of Sharī'a

CESAR ADIB MAJUL

What will give great pleasure to Muslims all over the world is the news that the Philippines has recently granted national recognition to the application of the personal laws of the *Sharī'a* to its Muslim minority. The Muslims in the Philippines are concentrated in the southern islands of the country. Numbering more than three million, they are divided into various ethno-linguistic groups who are, nevertheless, increasing mutual contacts due to greater communication facilities. Their youth are increasingly being represented in the various universities and colleges in Manila. With the coming of the Americans to the Philippines in 1898, the different Muslim ethnolinguistic groups, which were generally successful in their resistance to Spanish efforts of conversion and colonization, were slowly but surely integrated into the American colony. Nevertheless, they have kept a great deal of their customary laws and applied to themselves, in varying intensities the family rules of the *Sharī'a* as expressed in the *Shafi'ī madhhab*. These rules, as such, did not have national sanction, but the Muslims continued to get married and divorced along Islamic lines. However, many of them tended to follow the inheritance provisions of the customary laws which antedated the advent of Islam in their lands.

In the early fifties, many members of the local *'ulamā'*, especially those who had studied in some of the Islamic educational institutions in the Middle East, began to point out to their brother Muslims at home the need for gaining national recognition for *Sharī'a* personal rules in order to maintain the dignity and preserve the integrity of the Muslim community. Not long after, in the sixties, Muslim lawyers who were trained in the national laws supported this view of the *'ulamā'* on the principle of religious freedom. Not a few non-Muslim sociologists and liberal thinkers supported the same view, but their stand was based more on the need of the Philippines to make more operative and meaningful the emerging concept of cultural pluralism. The government, in response to all these, has actually recognized the validity of Muslim marriages by means of executive orders which specified the number of years within which such marriages could be performed. Pressure from Muslim politicians and government officials have led to the renewal of such executive orders. But many Muslim learned men and professionals felt that such orders were merely expedient or temporary measures, since they could not help but suspect that the government would ultimately cease to recognize such a validity in favor of a uniform system for all citizens. Actually, this action of government was due not so much to ill-will towards its cultural minorities as from an ignorance of the way of life of Muslims as well as a lack of sensitivity to the manner in which Muslims view and cherish their Holy Law.

Excerpted from Cesar Adib Majul, *Islam and Development: A Collection of Essays*, edited by Michael O. Mastura (Manila: Office of the Commissioner for Islamic Affairs, 1980), by permission of the author.

The Muslim secessionist movement in the early seventies in the Philippine South coupled with fears on the part of the generality of the Muslim population that some of their cherished values and institutions were in danger led the Philippine government for once to study seriously the various aspects of the problems confronting the Muslims as a religious and cultural minority. The New Society which was proclaimed in 1972, showed a sympathetic and genuine response to Muslim religious and social aspirations and declared that it was going a long way, as against the past, to satisfy them. On August 13, 1973, President Marcos signed Memorandum Order 370 creating a Research Staff to come up with a draft on a Proposed Code of Philippine Muslim Laws. The Staff completed its work and submitted the Draft to the President on April 14, 1974. Subsequently, on December 23, 1974, the President issued Executive Order No. 442 creating a Presidential Commission to Review the Code on Filipino Muslim Laws. It is significant to note that this Order stated that "the realization of the aspiration of the Filipino Muslims to have their system of laws enforced in their communities will reinforce the just struggle of the Filipino people to achieve national unity. . . ."

The Executive Order provided for eleven members: The Dean of the Institute of Islamic Studies, Philippine Center for Advanced Studies, University of the Philippines, who was to serve as Chairman, representative of the Supreme Court who was to be the Vice-Chairman, a representative of the Integrated Bar of the Philippines, a representative of the Department of Justice, a representative of the University of the Philippines Law Center, the Project Officer of the former Research Staff which prepared the draft, a representative of the Catholic Hierarchy, two reputed Muslims representing the Muslim laywers of the country, and two well-respected Muslim members of the *'ulamā'*. Out of the eleven members, seven were Muslims. However, one Muslim *'ālim* and the representative of the Catholic Hierarchy, who was abroad, did not participate in any of the sessions or activities of the Presidential Commission.

The idea of having representatives from different government legal institutions, some who happened to be non-Muslims, was meant to see to it that the Muslim personal laws to be codified fitted well within the Constitution of the country. It was also aimed at committing such government institutions to support the work of the Commission. The appointment of a Catholic to the Commission to represent the religious majority in the country, was probably intended to dramatize the fact that there was national unity behind the move to give the Muslims the legal right to be governed by the personal laws of the *Sharī'a*.

The Presidential Commission held various meetings with large groups of Muslim lawyers and the most prestigious members of the *'ulamā'* to help it as well as to get support for its work. On August 29, 1975 the Commission presented its Final Report and Draft of the Code to the President. This draft, with minor changes in the proposed number of *Sharī'a* Courts and the procedure for appeal was signed by the President into law as Presidential Decree No. 1083 on February 4, 1977, without a single amendment to any of the substantive provisions of the Code as prepared by the Commission.

The promulgated code now entitled "Code of Muslim Personal Laws of the Philippines" states in Article 2 what it proposes to accomplish. These are as follows: "(a) Recognizes the legal system of the Muslims in the Philippines as part of the law of the land and seeks to make Islamic law more effective; (b) Codifies Muslim personal laws; and (c) Provides for an effective administration and enforcement of Muslim personal laws among Muslims." A major characteristic of the Code is that it makes a distinction between "the legal system of the Muslims" (or *Sharī'a*) and those "Muslim personal laws" being codified. Moreover, the Code provides for "other applicable Muslim laws" which may be utilized but which are not stated at all in the Code. In other words, regarding Islamic laws, the provisions in the Code are not exclusive. Except for a few minor provisions regarding fines, the Code has nothing to do with penal or criminal law. Also, except for a provision on communal property and a few others on holidays and conversions to Islam, the Code does not deal with the other fields of law. Hence, Muslims, like all other citizens of the Philippines, are subject to laws of general application — provisions of the civil law not in conflict with the Code as well as the penal, commercial, tax, and other public laws.

Although generally influenced by the *madhhab Shafi'ī*, for this is the school that had generally been followed in the region of South East Asia, the Commission did not hesitate to utilize the technique of *takhayyur* when it decided to adopt some desirable provisions of the other schools so as to keep in step with modern tendencies of legislation in other Islamic countries. The Commission, too, showed sensitivity to the views of educated Muslim women, in the Philippines when in at least four articles (Articles 50–53), it took into consideration nearly all, if not all, of the different grounds stated in the four orthodox schools whereby a woman could petition the court for a judicial dissolution of her marriage, while adding a few more grounds. It also provided conditions to make it not so easy for a husband to acquire an additional wife to the detriment of the rights of a woman who is already his wife. It further institutionalized an arbitration committee to protect the rights of Muslim wives. All these as well as other provisions demonstrate, albeit modestly, that the Presidential Commission exercised some form of *ijtihād*. The Code will tend to universalize and systematize the inheritance laws of the Filipino Muslims in spite of their ethnic and linguistic differences. As a published document it will certainly help in the dissemination of Islamic knowledge and raise the educational standards of the Muslims.

Incidentally, the Code also provides for the position and office of a jurisconsult (*Muftī*) under the administrative supervision of the Supreme Court of the Philippines. The *Muftī*, who will need awesome qualifications, will be appointed by the President of the country.[1]

The promulgation of the Code into law has, nevertheless, brought at least two immediate problems which hopefully will be solved as early as possible. The first is that the government has not yet established the system of *Sharī'a* courts. This is an administrative matter, but it involves details referring to additional budgetary appropriation which can quite be a burden for a poor country like the Philippines. Another problem refers to the appointment of the judges and other court officials to take care of the details or registration, etc. The problem arising from the appointment of judges is that the vast majority of Muslim lawyers in the Philippines know the country's legal system but not the *Sharī'a* and Islamic juristic techniques. Moreover, some Muslim members of the *'ulamā'* though specialists in Islamic law, do not appear to be well versed in the national laws or possibly even the Philippine Constitution. Muslim lawyers have received their legal education from the universities of the Philippines, while many members of the *'ulamā'* have studied in the universities of Egypt and Saudi-Arabia. At present, Philippine Law does not allow a person to serve as a judge unless he is a lawyer who has been admitted to the bar or passed government examinations for the practice of law. A temporary solution or compromise to the above situation is to have a Muslim lawyer serve as judge with an *'ālim* attached to him or to the court to serve as a sort of *muftī* or consultant. This consultant should be a specialist in Islamic law. Possibly, in the future, these Muslim judges will be required to delve deeper into Islamic law by attending a course of regular lecturers or seminars. The advisers, too, will be encouraged to work for a law degree and pass the bar. The problem as to who shall be appointed as judges to the *Sharī'a* courts will then disappear. But this is all for the future.

To conclude, a major significance of this promulgated Code is that, for once, a sizeable portion of that aspect of the *Sharī'a* covering personal law is now part of the national laws of the Philippines. It is also significant that the Philippines is a predominantly Christian (at least 80%) country and the first country of its kind to have taken such a bold and imaginative step. This move of the Philippines reflects emerging tendencies not only in the Philippines but also in other countries as well. These refer to the acceptance of the legitimacy of cultural pluralism where different cultural groups all participate in the national processes and share in its benefits — without abandoning their cultural identity. What puts them together is loyalty to a wider community — that of the national community. There is certainly no real reason why commitments to a cultural or religious group cannot be consistent with, or complementary to, loyalty to the nation. Indeed, such a loyalty can increase in proportion to the recognition and protection of religious and cultural rights.

NOTES

1. For a more comprehensive discussion and analysis of the "Code of Muslim Personal Laws of the Philippines", see Esteban B. Bautista, "The Muslim Code: Towards National Unity in Diversity". Mimeographed copy published by the U.P. Law Center, Diliman, Quezon City, Philippines, 1977; and Cesar A. Majul, "The General Nature of Islamic Law and its application in the Philippines". Mimeographed copy published by the Institute of Islamic Studies, PCAS, U.P., Diliman, Quezon City, Philippines, 1977.

The Kyai, the Pesantren, and the Village: A Preliminary Sketch

M. DAWAM RAHARDJO

Because the *pesantren* is the institutionalised form of the teaching of the *kyai,* the personality tendencies inherent in the *kyai* are expressed in the development of the *pesantren.* The types of knowledge and the specialities taught at the pesantren evolve in step with the level and breadth of the *kyai*'s knowledge and the *santri*s' ability to study. Since the *madrasah* system came into being, the curriculum and syllabus of the *pesantren* has been standardised to some degree. The *madrasah* system was introduced into the *pesantren* in 1929, when *ustadz* Moh. Ilyas (who later became an *ulama* and Minister of Religion) became the *lurah pondok* in Tebuireng. At the present time, almost all *pondok,* with a few exceptions like the Tegalrejo and Lirboyo *Pondok* in Kediri) have adopted the *madrasah* system.[1] Nonetheless, some of the non-*madrasah* institutions have sections of their classes or levels which do not employ the usual methods. The division is usually made into basic (*ibtidaiyah*), middle (*tsanawiyah*) and higher (*aliyah*) levels. Some *pesantren,* like Krapyak, Lirboyo and Rejoso, have an even higher level called *takhazsus,* which is reserved for *santri* who wish to study special branches of learning such as the science of the Qur'an, *ilmu fiqih* and others. Tegalrejo has created seven separate levels. The highest is reserved for those who wish to study *ilmu tasauf.*[2]

Because of the hereditary character of *pesantren* ownership, the *kyai* out of consideration for his *pesantren*'s future will naturally look to his children. And, aside from his children, he may also look to his sons-in-law or prospective sons-in-law. Leadership of Tebuireng, for instance, is now in the hands of M. Jusuf Hasjim, the youngest son of *Kyai* Hasjim Asj'ari. Before him, leadership went successively to his brothers-in-law and brothers, one of whom was his brother-in-law, *Kyai* Baidhowie, the son-in-law of *Kyai* Hasjim. The principal of Rejoso *Pesantren* at present, *Kyai* Musta'in Romli, is the son of *Kyai* Romli Tamim, one of the *pesantren*'s founders. At Gontor, among those who are being groomed to become leaders of the *pesantren* are *ustadz* Subakir and Drs. Zaini, who are sons-in-law of K.H. Imam Zarkasji and K.H. Achmad Sahal, the present leaders and caretakers of the *pesantren.* The present leader of the Krapyak *Pesantren* is K.H. Ali Ma'sum, but final decisions on the *pesantren*'s affairs rest with the *ahlil bait* or family.

This situation naturally creates ways of thinking about responsibility for the continuity of the *pesantren*'s existence. The results of interviews with a number of respondents comprising *kyai, ustadz, santri,* the parents of *santri,* former pupils of *pesantren* and members of the public in the neighbourhoods of *pesantren* in Bogor (N=294) were extremely interesting. They produced the conclusion that between 63% and 83% of *kyai,* the parents of *santri,* alumni and the public were of the

Reprinted in abridged form from *Prisma* (1975), 32–43, by permission of the author and Lembaga Penelitian, Pendidikan dan Penerangan Ekonomi dan Sosial (LP3ES), Jakarta, Indonesia.

opinion that it was the descendants of the founder who had responsibility for the continuity of the *pesantren*. But, the *santri* and the *ustadz* tended to see the responsibility falling on the government or the community (50% of *ustadz* and 60% of *santri*). This response shows a fairly clear divergence between the ways of thinking of the older and younger generations in the *pesantren* environment.

The majority of *pesantren* combine the *weton* and *madrasah* systems. K.H. Wahid Hasjim, when he was principal of Tebuireng, introduced a mixed system, so that at that *pondok* at present there are two recognisable systems, the *'am* or *weton* system and the *nidhom* system (*harfiah* or literally means organisation) which is the same as the classical system. Together with the introduction of the *madrasah* system, a number of general subjects have also been introduced such as reading and writing using Roman characters, Indonesian, arithmetic, geography, natural science, English and so on. The introduction of these general subjects was clearly due to the influence of the Dutch educational system.[3] But these general subjects are of no more than a supplementary character. Usually at the *ibtidaiyah* level their proportion is no more than 60%. At the *tsanawiyah* level, it declines to 50% or 40% only. At the *aliyah* level it can decline to just 20%, while at the *takhassus* level, no general subject at all are taught.[4] A few *pesantren* have changed their *madrasah* status to state *madrasah* or 6 year *PGAN*. In this case, they follow the government curriculum (for *PGAN*s the proportion is 50:50).

Rejoso has adopted another style. In the *pesantren*'s vicinity, general high schools have been established using a system similar to that of the state secondary schools with the only difference that the *santri* of Rejoso are obliged to follow a *madrasah* education devoted exclusively to the study of religious knowledge. The *santri* must also attend *weton* teaching. It is difficult to understand how the *santri* of Rejoso can manage to follow so many lessons each day. But, in fact, there are many young people studying at two kinds of school, The Al Islam *Madrasah* at Solo is a *madrasah* which teaches religious knowledge exclusively for general school students who wish also to take courses at a religious school. Like Rejoso, the Babakan Ciwaringin *Pesantren* under *Kyai* Haririe combines scholastic and vocational schools (*SPG* and *STM*) with *sorogan* and *bandungan* system (the latter is the term used in West Java for the *weton* system).

A number of *pesantren* have now also adopted what is called "the vocational training". But this kind of training is in fact still very limited. What counts as vocational would be for example no more than (boy) scouting, co-operative and poultry husbandry. Education in scouting is a long-established feature of Gontor — it almost dates back to the *pondok*'s foundation in 1926 — and for that reason is very advanced. At Tebuireng, there is also scouting, but, unlike Gontor, where every *santri* is obliged to become a scout, only a portion of *santri* do so. Nonetheless, scouting, particularly for girls, is very well developed at Tebuireng, and they have one of the best groups in Jombang.

Pondok co-operatives, although not legally incorporated, exist at *pondoks* like Gontor, Tebuireng, Denanyar, Tambakberas and Tegalrejo. These co-operatives' function is primarily educational — although also economic in that they offer essential goods for the *pondok* at cheap prices (consumers' co-operatives) and are administered by the *santri* themselves in rotation. By operating these co-operatives, the *santri* can receive training in business, principles of economic organisation, financial administration and the spirit of mutual aid. Naturally the character of these co-operatives and their business is very simple. In Tebuireng, the volume of sales each day is between *Rp* 15,000 and *Rp* 25,000 while in Gontor, it has reached *Rp* 40,000 a day. In Gontor, there are three separate shops — one selling books and school equipment, one miscellaneous small goods and one food and medicines. In Tebuireng, the co-operative shop is a general store selling everything from rice to writing utensils and hair oil. The co-operatives at Tambakberas and Tegalrejo are similar.

Just recently, a number of *pesantren* have begun to try poultry husbandry with the assistance of the Department of Religion and the Department of Agriculture. But usually, only the principals of the *pesantren* (the family of the *kyai*) and not the *santri* themselves are engaged in animal husbandry. Tegalrejo is an exception. Tegalrejo in fact is not just developing poultry husbandry but also goat and milk cow raising. Of all the existing *pesantren,* except for Darul Falah in Bogor, Tegalrejo is foremost in the teaching of skills. There, study of skills is directly under old *Kyai* Khudhori. The skills taught include husbandry, agriculture, seed breeding and economic co-operation, craftsmanship and handicrafts.

In its teaching methods, Tegalrejo is a traditional *pesantren.* It does not offer general studies. But, in practical studies, like farming and business, it is far more advanced than other *pesantren* like Tebuireng or Rejoso. Under the leadership of *Kyai* Khudhori himself, the *pesantren* has at present already established a *Baitul Mu'awwanah* or *Badan Amalan Sosial* (Board of Social Services). It specialises in selling seeds (coconuts, vanilla, cloves and coffee), rice milling and even cultivation. The *Baitul Mu'awwanah* used its capital to grant interest-free loans to members of the public up to a total of *Rp* 25,000 a person with a repayment period not exceeding one year. The borrower does not pay interest but only "administration costs". All this business is conducted by the *santri* themselves. The *santri* are also obliged to save each month according to their means and may redeem their savings only at the end of the year or when their education is finished. This saving is conducted in conjunction with the consumer co-operative.

One interesting feature of Tegalrejo is the construction of dormitories, a meeting hall and a school building by the *santri* themselves assisted by carpenters and stone-masons. They studied and carried through the process of construction from the physical and financial planning to the workmanship. The *santri* also made equipment and accessories, wall decoration etc. themselves. It was all done in the course of studying and practicing artisanship and handicrafts. The capital also came from the *santri* from contributions of *Rp* 1,000 per year and loans from the co-operative. There was hardly any assistance from outside the *pondok,* except for voluntary contributions from a few donors in the *kabupaten* of Kedu. Nonetheless, these efforts at self-sufficiency have already resulted in a storeyed building that is quite impressive, especially by the standards of building existing in the vicinity of Tegalrejo.

The education in skills offered at Tegalrejo is very simple. It is not scientific, but based only on experience — in particular that of *Kyai* Khudhori himself. It is different from what is given at Darul Falah *Pesantren* which is supported by teachers from the *Institut Pertanian Bogor* (*IPB,* Bogor Agricultural Institute). But at Tegalrejo, there is no institute like *IPB* — indeed, even the local Agricultural Service hardly offers any assistance. In view of the environment and the personnel available, what has been achieved by Tegalrejo is quite impressive.

Unlike other *pesantren,* the Darul Falah *Pesantren* in Bogor has been purposely developed as a *takhassus pesantren* emphasising practical studies in farming and crafts. Religious study accounts for only 25.7% of all subjects (between 13 and 20 hours a week), although in principle the religious curriculum is regarded as the core of the whole education. Religious sciences which are usually taught at *madrasah* are also taught at Darul Falah from elementary sciences up to those levels regarded as advanced like *ilmu usul fiqih* or *balaghah* (literature). The remaining 74.3% consists of both theoretical and practical general studies, divided between farming (12.6%), technical (13.1%), sociology and economics (8.8%), natural sciences (10.6%), project activities (20.6%) and other subjects comprising Indonesian, English and physical education (8.6%). The number of subjects in each class (there are six classes or six years) are between 22 and 28 and during six years one would take 55 subjects. The hours of study in a week for each class are between 35 and 45 hours for theory and 16 to 23 for practical study. So, the proportion of theoretical to practical study is 70:30.

There is no doubt that the amount of religious study offered at Darul Falah is not very great, though it is hoped that this religious education will give the fundamentals and an adequate understanding of the basics of Islamic teaching. A graduate of Darul Falah is not expected to continue his studies at an institution of higher education, but directly to take the plunge into community life. Darul Falah seems to come close to the aim of religious education as defined by the criterion of *mu'amalah* or putting knowledge into practice. Clearly, after a grounding in the religious education of Darul Falah, graduates of the *pesantren* can be expected to spread Islam in its practical or scientific aspect through co-operation with religious experts.[5]

THE *PESANTREN* AND VILLAGE DEVELOPMENT

The *pesantren* can be classified as one form of village institution. Jay, for example, treats the *pondok pesantren* as a "boarding school" and a "corporate group" with an important role in the village setting of Mojokuto in Central Java. He discusses the position and role of the *kyai* as the "learned man" on a par with the figures of the *guru* (teacher) and the *dalang* (puppeteer), who have important influence in the formation of values in village society.[6] The government at present sees the importance of the *pesantren*'s role in the development of the village "bearing in mind that many of them are located in the rural areas." The Minister of Religion, A. Mukti Ali, who made that remark, has also said:

> the government is now endeavouring to ensure that the *santri* who graduate from the *pondok pesantren* or *madrasah* will be able to become true leaders or modernisers of rural society. This policy is part of the sphere of the rural development effort as a whole. *Pesantren* are not now regarded as isolated units but are part of the sphere of that effort.[7]

There are good reasons to link the *pesantren* to the rural areas especially in view of their location. However, it is also clear that the *pesantren* has no necessary direct function to perform for the surrounding society. Gontor, for example, though it is located in a remote village, has hardly any visible function in regard to the surrounding society. This extremely well-organised *pesantren* does not perform "extension service" for the villages in the area. The *santri* are absolutely forbidden to have social relations outside the walls of the *pondok*. Even activities like the Friday sermon are not undertaken. Only recently have the inmates of the *pondok* been asked to perform voluntary work (*kerja bakti*) to improve village infrastructure. Gontor is simply a religious teaching institution which has sited itself in the remoteness of a village. The *santri* come from other regions to study religion. It is likely that the *santri* come from trading or middle-level business families from towns such as Ponorogo, Solo, Pekalongan or Kudus. The development of the *pesantren* also does not stem from forces within the local community, but from funds originating in the towns. Gontor was built up from a traditional *pesantren* on the point of collapse. Subsequently, it seems to have developed, thanks to the aspirations of the town as is reflected in its classical system of education, its curriculum which is 50% general studies, its stress on teaching Arabic, English and, formerly, Dutch, and in the "intellectualist" cast of its whole education. Gontor firmly rejects the "vocational training".[8] The opinion of K.H. Imam Zarkasi, the intellectual director of Gontor, about vocational schools was expressed to Lance Castles in 1964.[9] In actuality, Gontor clearly does teach skills. Besides its co-operatives, its poultry husbandry and scouts' training, which are well-advanced, it is stated in its yearbook, *Warta Dunia,* that Gontor now has a *tile* factory, which "will further add to the *santris*' skills." But the primary aim of education at Gontor is to turn out "intellectual *ulama*", who will probably feel more at home in urban society.

In Gontor, we see an educational institution founded on the aspirations of the town and oriented to the urban community but located in the remote countryside. However, Gontor is not an instance of the phenomenon of *"le retour aux champs"* as Darul Falah, which is directed by men with town education and culture, would be. Are *pesantren* like Rejoso and Sabilil Muttaqien in Takeran which have general schools and classical education now taking an urban orientation? This question requires some consideration, because, when we recall the vertical development of the big Jombang *Pesantren,* the phenomenon of a shift in orientation to the town seems a real possibility. It is conceivable that the *pesantren* may some day divorce themselves from the surrounding community and its aspirations. The development of the towns which are increasingly swallowing up the areas where the *pesantren* are located may stimulate this change of aspiration. The *pesantren* of Jamsanen in Solo, Krapyak in Yogyakarta and Denanyar in Jombang have practically been swallowed up by the development of the town or at least urban culture. In fact the *pesantren* of Tebuireng and Rejoso, which are some distance from Jombang (between 5 and 10 kilometres at present) are already based on urban culture. The university of Darul Ulum (which has a political science faculty) has selected a site in the middle of the town.

Certainly, the location of the *pesantren* is not the only influence on its aspirations. Tebuireng, directed by M. Jusuf Hasjim, for example, now has plans for programs oriented to the village including some dealing with transmigration problems. The more youthful leadership of Mamba'ul Ma'arif *Pesantren* around the figure of Abdurrachman Wahid seems to be very conscious of the possibilities for the *pesantren* to apply a role in the community. In one of his essays,[10] he reminds us that the prospect for the *pesantren* should not be looked at only in terms of the three factors which have hitherto been the yardstick — physical infrastructure, pedigree and geographical situation. The prospect for the Denanyar *Pesantren*, in his opinion, depends also on the *pesantren*'s own capacity to respond to challenge and change in education, the formation of social values and socio-political developments — in fact on how the *pesantren* can meet the demands of the community. "The local community will undergo great changes if sustained economic growth occurs. These changes require a correct attitude from the Mamba'ul Ma'arif *Pesantren* itself based on detailed observation and planning. We have to decide what is to be our attitude to the development of skills, agricultural training, village co-operatives and so on.[11]

Linking the *pesantren* to the development of the village community is, of course, a relevant concern. Not only because *pesantren* are usually located in the rural areas, but also because *santri* usually come from farmers' families or from village families. Table 1 below illustrates the family background of *santri* in 8 small *pesantren* in Bogor.

TABLE 1 Number of *Santri* by Family Background at 8 *Pesantren* in Bogor (1973)

Family Background	*Male*	*Female*	*Total*	*%*
1. Farmer	560	53	613	65.56
2. Trader/Businessman	177	20	197	21.07
3. Civil servant/military	36	—	36	3.85
4. Private employee/labourer	43	—	43	4.60
5. Family of *kyai/ustadz*	35	1	36	3.85
6. Moslem notable	4	—	4	0.43
7. Family of *pesantren*	5	1	6	0.54
	860 (91.98%)	75 (8.02%)	935 (100%)	100.00

We can see from this table that the *pesantren* in Bogor are usually attended by youth from farming (65.7%) and trading and business background (21.0%). They also usually come from reasonably nearby areas. But, as regards *santris*' areas of origin, it should be noted as Jay mentions in his *Javanese Villagers*, that distant *pesantren* have greater drawing power for *santri* than *pesantren* close to their home areas. The reason is that youth tend to prefer to be separated from their parents when they "wander to seek science", while the parents themselves feel more certain that their children will study assiduously, if they are far from their parents. These reasons suggested by Jay are reflected in Table 2.

TABLE 2 Number of *Santri* at Rejoso, Jombang in 1967 by Area of Origin

Region	*Male*	*Female*	*Total*	*%*
1. Jombang	154	49	203	7.44
2. East Java (14 towns)	1,099	876	1,975	72.33
3. Central Java (4 towns)	328	178	506	18.54
4. West Java	30	16	46	1.69
Total	1,611	1,019	2,730	100%

The above table indicates that only 7.4% of the *santri* came from the area of Jombang itself. But, the fact that most *santri* come from far away should not necessarily prevent the *pesantren*'s orientation to its neighbourhood. In fact, Rejoso is well-known for being integrated with its village. Diverging from Gontor's principles, the *santri* of Rejoso in fact live together with the village community. The *pesantren* also has a working arrangement with stalls and shops which are run by the village community with the needs of the *pesantren* in mind. What is more, the village community and the *pesantren* together bear responsibility for the security, spiritual development and survival of the village as a whole.

As a rule, it can be said that the *pesantren* has great potential in the development of the village community not only in education and spiritual guidance and development, but also in fields relating to wordly problems. What happens will depend on whether or not there is a change of orientation in the *pesantren* itself. The fact remains that the *pesantren* is first of all a "religious school". If this religious basis disappears from the *pesantren,* the *pesantren* itself will also disappear. Indeed, if a *pesantren* comes to emphasise non-religious education, people begin to doubt whether the institution should still be called a *pesantren.* This is what happened with Darul Falah which put the stress of its education on agriculture. But, more thorough consideration suggests that in fact Dural Falah should still be regarded as a *pesantren.* First, because Darul Falah bases its existence on religion: it is just that the institution interprets religion from a practical (*amaliah*) point of view. Secondly, the day-to-day atmosphere on Darul Falah campus is totally religious. Moreover, Darul Falah's education puts emphasis on morals and character — something which is also the real aim of all *pesantren.*

The difficult problem of modernising the *pesantren* is probably very much dependent on the *kyai,* the "owner of the *pesantren*". The problem has been stated by Dr. A. Mukti Ali: "The prospects for modernisation of the system of teaching and education in the *pesantren* depends more on the willingness of the *kyai* to modernise and change."[12] In fact, modernisation does not just depend on the *kyai* but also on the community, and especially on the parents of the *santri.* A *kyai* may change orientation, but he may also be deserted by his followers. A *kyai* who wants to make reforms, then, must possess charisma, influence and sound knowledge.

Kyai Khudhori from Tegalrejo is a very attractive figure. His case shows how a traditional *pesantren* in a traditional community can carry through significant reform. Another question: to what extent is the *pesantren* capable of adapting to social change? Is the *pesantren* prepared to accept well-intentioned assistance from the government? Is the *pesantren* broad-minded enough to accept ideas for reform from other institutions? It is important in this regard to note the state of mind reached at Tebuireng under the direction of M. Jusuf Hasjim as reflected in the following:

> Some time ago, one section of the community thought of the *pesantren* as a world in itself with a closed attitude, rejecting whatever came from outside the *pesantren.* This view cannot be abstracted from the historical background against which the *pesantren* were founded as institutions for the education of cadres for the struggle against the colonial Dutch government. They adopted the principle of non-cooperation with the Dutch government with the aim of keeping their cadres immune to the penetration of the cultural, educational and other influences of Dutch colonial authority. This meant that almost everything emanating from outside the *pesantren* was inevitably suspected of being an attempt by the Dutch to penetrate the *pesantren.* But, since August 17, 1945, we have had to make the shift from non-cooperation to cooperation because, before the proclamation of independence, we were under foreign rule, but since then we have been under our own government.[13]

What has made Tebuireng's attitude towards reform possible is that it is now a *pesantren* strong enough to be able to protect its identity in the face of the problems of adaptation created by social change. The ability to adapt is very important for a *pesantren;* for, if it cannot adapt, it will lose its roots in the community. On investigation, the causes of the success of *pesantren* in the past, in fact, rested on the ability of the *kyai* and the institution of the *pesantren* to adapt to its environment. The ability to adapt later creates the power to bring about changes in the local community.

In fact, *pesantren,* large or small, can play a bigger role in their environments. Due to the influence of the *kyai,* the value of religion, the *pesantren* can muster the facilities around it, like instruction agencies, teachers and instructors, the community's agricultural land, government services and officers, for the sake of education. An influential *kyai* can, for example, make arrangements with farmers to have the *santri* participate in farm work as part of their studies. If a number of small *pesantren* in one district can work together, they can more effectively integrate with the community. Large *pesantren,* like Tegalrejo or Tebuireng, can act as coordinators of smaller *pesantren* in various activities.

If *pesantren* can work together, their activities can be organised more rationally and efficiently. For that reason, the Minister of Religion was correct when he said that teaching of skills can be introduced to *pesantren* without altering the existing curriculum. The problem, in the end, comes down to modernisation both in organisation and in the system of education and teaching. If the *pesantren* undergoes a change in orientation, it is proper that the decision to change should be made by the leadership of the *pesantren* itself. Outside parties, including the government, can give proposals or assistance, but standardisation of goals and of the system of education according to an outside party's conception, is clearly inappropriate. The uniqueness of the *pesantren* lies precisely in its diversity. This characteristic permits the flexibility very necessary to an institution which wants to play the role of an umbrella for various kinds of non-formal education.

NOTES

1. Kyai Khudori of Tegalrejo says that general subjects need not be taught in *pesantren* because almost all *santris* have completed *SD* (elementary school), *SMP* (Junior High School), *STM* (Technical High School) and so on.
2. Complete information on this question can be read in *Laporan Penelitian dan Seminar Pendidikan pada Perguruan Agama* (Report on the Investigation and Seminar on Religious Education) (*Departemen Agama RI,* 1970–1971) or *Laporan Survey Pesantren di Jawa Timur* (Report on the Survey on *Pesantren* in East Java) by students of the *Adab* Faculty, of Syarif Hidajatullah *IAIN,* Ciputat, Jakarta, 1967.
3. K.H. Moch. Ilyas who uses this concept at Tebuireng besides having a *pesantren* education, also completed studies at a H.I.S. (Dutch Elementary School). See the book *Sejarah Hidup KH Wahid Hasjim* (The Biography of KH Wahid Hasjim) by H. Abubakar Aceh.
4. *Ibtidaiyah* is roughly equivalent to the (6-year) elementary education, *Tsanawiyah* is roughly equivalent to the (3-year) lower secondary education. *Aliyah* is roughly equivalent to the (3-year) higher secondary education. And *takhassus* is semi-academic education after *Aliyah* and takes two years.
5. Some doubt exists whether Darul Falah is a true *pesantren* because of its curriculum and its classical system of education. On the other hand, because Darul Falah is under the direction of a *kyai* and its aim is also the fostering of Islamic teaching, others regard it as one type of *pesantren.*
6. Robert R. Jay, *Javanese Villagers,* (Cambridge, Massachussetts: The MIT Press, 1969), pp. 273–274 (on the *kyai)* and pp. 419–421 (on *pesantren*).
7. Harian *Kompas,* May 15, 1973.
8. This opinion was expressed by KH Imam Zarkasi when the writer visited Gontor with M. Jusuf Hasjim, the director of Tebuireng. But KH Imam Zarkasi also said that what was important was to "instill the entrepreneurial spirit", so that mastery of skills was not of paramount importance.
9. Lance Castles in his article "Notes on the Islamic School at Gontor," records the opinion of KH Imam Zarkasi, who said, among other things, that not one of the businessmen in Ponorogo at that time had been educated at a vocational school.
10. Abdurrachman Wahid, *"Prospek Pesantren Mamba'ul Ma'arif,"* (The Prospects for Mamba'ul Ma'arif Pesantren) in the book *Risalah Akhira Sanah,* 1972. (Note: Abdurrachman Wahid is the son of KH Wahid Hasjim, the well-known intellectual *ulama* from the *Nahdhatul Ulama Party).*
11. *Ibid.*
12. Dr. A. Mukti Ali, "Pembaharuan Sistim Pendidikan dan Pengajaran pada Pondok *Pesantren* dalam Rangha Merealisir Tujuan Pendidikan Nasional", ("Modernization of the System of Education and Teaching in the *Pesantren* in the Framework of Realising National Educational Goals"), statement to *Higher Religious Education Seminar* at Tugu, Puncak, June 1972.
13. From a brochure published by the leadership of the Tebuireng *pesantren* in 1973.

The Payment of Zakat Al-Fitrah in a Minangkabau Community[1]

UMAR JUNUS

Zakat al-fitrah (to be referred to as *fitrah*), compulsory alms to be given by every living Muslim during the fasting month and before the end of the prayer ending the fasting month[2] have to be given to one of the following: 1. poor men; 2. needy persons; 3. collectors of the *fitrah*; 4. those whose hearts are to be reconciled; 5. captives who are to be set free; 6. debtors who are to be set free: 7. fighters for the cause of Allah and 8. wayfarers (Al-Koran, Sûrah IX, At-Taubah, 60; see Mohammed M. Pickthall, 1953, 150).

The idea of the *fitrah* is to give these people the possibility of enjoying the feast celebrating the end of the fasting month.

Not in every community is this rule applied literally. Sometimes it is replaced by a new one, as can be seen in a community in the Minangkabau society, i.e. *Silungkang*, a village of around 10,000 people[3] located on the road between *Solok* and *Sawah Lunto* in the province of Sumatra Barat (= West Coast of Sumatra), Indonesia (see, Junus, 1964, 293).

This community has its own specific structure which differentiates it from its neighbours, as can be seen from the discussion below.

DATA

Ideally, every member of this community should give his *fitrah* to a certain person, i.e. the *pandito* of a *kampueng* to which he belongs (for the division of this community, see Junus, 294 ff). Sometimes but rather rarely, instead of to the *pandito*, one gives his *fitrah* directly to persons who belong to the categories mentioned above. Although it is not preferred, this is allowed because the obligation does not fall on an individual but on a *paruik*.[4] A *paruik* is under an obligation to encourage its members to give their *fitrah* to the *pandito*.

No account is taken of the place of a person's domicile, since he is always under the obligation of giving his *fitrah* to the *pandito* of his *kampueng*. Sometimes a member of a *paruik* may feel that he is obliged to pay the *fitrah* of another of the members of his *paruik* by giving it to the *pandito*.

This last phenomenon is changing, especially when many members live in a place remote from the village, as can be seen in Djakarta. They instead establish an office after the pattern of the *pandito* although the two are quite different in nature, as can be seen in the discussion of the structure of this community. The difference is either in function of this office or in the idea of founding this office. This office bears no name, and the officer is referred to as: *'injo nan djadi pandito awak disiko'* (he is substituting for our *pandito* here).

Some members of this community do not regard the founding of this office as an excuse for not sending their *fitrahs* to their

Reprinted from *Bijdragen tot de Taal-, Land- en Volkenkunde* Deel 122 4e Aflevering (1966), 447–454, by permission of the author and the Koninklijk Instituut voor Taal-, Land- en Volkenkunde, Leiden, The Netherlands.

real *pandito* in their own village. It is only for humanitarian reasons that they give their *fitrah* to the pseudo *pandito*, as the office is referred to here.

In conformity with Islamic law, it is the father who has to pay the *fitrah* of the wife and the children, not the mother's brother. Since the father does not belong to the same *paruik* and *kampueng* as the wife and the children, they do not all pay the *fitrah* to the same *pandito*. The father gives his *fitrah* to the same *pandito* as his sisters, his mother and his sister's children, while the wife and the children give theirs to the same *pandito* as his wife's mother, his wife's mother's brothers and his wife's brothers.

THE STRUCTURE OF THE COMMUNITY

The *Silungkang* community has the same general pattern as every community in Minangkabau is supposed to have. The descent is matrilineal,[5] the marital residence is uxorilocal in a sense rather different from what is usually meant by this. The term is understood here as meaning that the wife continues to live in her own home, while the husband lodges with her (family).

The community practices local endogamy. A male member is compelled to marry a woman of his own community. He can take a woman from another community as his co-wife, but he is not supposed to do that. If he did, he would be (very) unpopular in the community.

On the contrary, a woman is not, under any circumstances, supposed to take some one from another community for a husband. If she did, her *paruik* would unhesitatingly expel her from the *paruik*. Since the membership of this community is through the membership in a *paruik* she would thus be expelled from the community as well. She would neither be allowed to stay in the *nagari* (= village)[6] nor to visit it, until she divorced the husband.

All members, no matter where or under what conditions they live, do their best to behave as the rule mentioned prescribes. They have to keep their ethnic identity by keeping the marriage circle within themselves. This rule makes them different from the other groups where they live, although they mix with each other in every day interaction.[7]

Almost every member of this community is engaged in business, either as a merchant or as an owner of a handicraft manufacturing business. Although the present writer cannot give exact figures, most of them are merchants, a fact which explains why they have spread to places relatively far from their native village.

There are four kinds of merchants, classified according to where and in what way they live, i.e.:

i) the merchant who is either domiciled or conducts his business in his own village;
ii) the merchant who is domiciled in the village but conducts his business in other places and who is away from the village during the day-time or for several days a week;
iii) the merchant who is domiciled in another place, while the wife and the children continue to be domiciled in the village;
iv) the merchant who together with his wife and children is domiciled in another place.

For quite a long time, almost every member practiced either ii) or iii). Historically stated, ii) existed long before either iii) or iv) did.

It could be expected that a person would be away during the day-time or for several days a week or longer.

This raised the problem of who was going to take care of the social problems of his *paruik* during his absence. His family affairs are matters of great concern to him, and sometimes cannot wait until his return.

It is quite correct to say that everything is related to family affairs. Every one has to take care of the interest of his *paruik* without disturbing the interest of other *paruiks*. He has to keep his *paruik* in order, and keep it away from any harm. He has to arrange a marriage partner for any member of the *paruik*.

Marriage ceremony and burial are two important occasions in the community. Every one who has any relation with a *paruik* which conducts one of these two ceremonies has to participate in them. He holds a specific position depending upon what kind of relationship he has with the *paruik* concerned.

There are two groups in a marriage ceremony, each of which in turn can be subdivided into two. The first big group is *'sipangka'* (the hosts) which consists of *'nan punjo olek'* (the ones who have the party, the owners of the party), and an un-named group which can be labelled as 'the workers'. The other group is *'olek'* (the guests) which consists of *'olek'* and *'marapulai'* (the groom and his group).

The same division occurs also at burial except that there is no name for each group. There are 'the hosts', 'the workers' and 'the guests.'

The 'hosts' and *'nan punjo olek'* take the full responsibility for conducting these ceremonies. Any adult member of a *kampueng* where the ceremony takes place belongs to the host group, but members of the *paruik* concerned play the important roles.

Neither of these two ceremonies is the business of the *paruik* concerned alone. The whole *kampueng* is supposed to play an important role in them, as can be seen in the marriage procedure.

The question of marriage is not a matter between two *paruiks* concerned alone, although the decision to make a contract is theirs.

In a marriage ceremony they take no active part other than preparing and conducting it. It is their *kampuengs* who represent them in it.

Except for some recent innovations there are no paid workers in the community; especially this is so in the case of social affairs. Anyone who does hard work for his living and gets paid for it is unpopular, since its members like to be their own bosses. And if they do work for some one else, the relationship between the employer and the employee is as follows:

i) the employer is a relative or is regarded as such by the employee;
ii) the employee gets no payment for his service, although the employer provides him with food, clothes and a small allowance. Besides this, he gets a share of the profit earned over a certain length of time;
iii) the job, for the employee, is a matter of apprenticeship. After a certain length of time he tries to go into business of his own, i.e. after he has acquired enough money to buy the basic assets and a skill in business.

This system makes them dislike living on charity.

A man feels embarrassed if one of his relatives lives on charity. He has to do his best to support this fellow. Then, if some one is too poor to afford his or her living expenses, he or she is not supposed to receive any support except from relatives. But he is not in a position to receive any *fitrah* from his relatives, since he is regarded as a dependent.

The living standard of the people of this community is likely to be "higher" than that of most people of its neighbours. This can be seen by the diet, the clothes and so on they have. And this situation makes the people of this community feel that they are "superior" to the other people.

A *kampueng* is administered by two officers, *'datuek kampueng'* (*kampueng* chief) and *'pandito'* (Indonesian *'pendeta'* is its cognate). The *datuek kampueng* deals with problems such as the security of the *kampueng*, arranging marriage partners for members of the *kampueng*, arranging certain parties and generally preserving the interests of the *kampueng*. In other words he deals with the profane aspects of the social life.

In contrast to this, a *pandito* deals with the sacral aspects of the social life in a *kampueng*. He has to be a witness to the signing of a marriage licence, and to arrange the appointment with the village officer who issues marriage licences.

The *pandito* also conducts the burial of members of his *kampueng*. Unless the dead person is a woman, he must bathe the corpse, and cover it with winding sheets, conduct the prayer and supervise the ceremony of putting the body into the grave.

Neither of these officers receives regular payment for his services. And there is no property requirement for candidates for these two offices. These offices can be held by either a relatively rich man or a poor man.

A person appointed to one of these offices is elected for a time of indeterminate length. The election is based on the *gotong rojong* or consensus principle, since there is no balloting.

The main concern in appointing a man to one of the offices is not to choose some one who belongs to *lotjieh* (for *lotjieh*, see Junus, 296f).

The pseudo *pandito* office for the members of this community living in Djakarta has nothing to do with the linearity principle of descent. This pseudo office is for all members of the community living in Djakarta, although they belong to different *kampuengs* in Silungkang.

There is no election for this pseudo office since no one is officially appointed to it. The members come to regard some one as holding it because he does the jobs a *pandito* would do. He, the pseudo *pandito,* attends and conducts every burial. He is a religious man in the eyes of the members of this community. And they let him know whenever someone dies.

This situation makes him known as *"pandito"* and the people begin to give their *fitrahs* to him.

As a matter of fact, this *"pandito"* is relatively poor, since he has no business of his own; besides, he is quite old. Thus he is able to give his service any time the people need him.

This system is quite different in nature from the appointment of *pandito* in their village.

ANALYSIS

The neighbouring communities have the following characteristics:

a) they earn their living by way of agriculture, so they do not have to be far away from their villages regularly;
b) they have a rather fixed income provided by the soil, so that only a few people are really in a position to support other members of their *paruik*;
c) every member of a *paruik* is supposed to have the same income since the income is divided into equal portions;
d) they do not think that being a paid worker will make them unpopular;
e) they do not practice strict local endogamy in marriage, although they do prefer to marry some one from their own village;
f) there are no *'pandito'* in these villages, and the people give their *fitrahs* to the poor.

In contrast to this, Silungkang can be summarized as having the following characteristics:

a) they earn their living by trading, so they have to be far away from the village regularly;
b) they do not have fixed incomes and a person can become rich enough to support his *paruik*;
c) members of this society have become acquainted with many outsiders, but this does not affect their social system. They still practice their village customs, although they are living in a place remote from their native village;
d) wherever they live they continue to practice the local endogamy system in the sense of the community, i.e. they have to find a marriage partner among the members of this community;
e) there is an office called *'pandito'* to which the people give their *fitrahs*.

By comparing the situation in this and the neighbouring, the present author is able to make the following statements:

a) the way the people earn their living has an influence on the structure and the living standard of a society and the degree of wealth they have;
b) the structure of a society and its wealth have an influence on the method of the payment of *fitrah*;
c) the living standard of a society, as far as this sample is concerned, is a factor in forming the attitude of its members;
d) the attitude of a society towards other societies, as far as this community is concerned, is a factor in determining whether or not a society practices the endogamy system (within a certain community).[8]

CONCLUSION

The paper has answered the question as to why the distribution of the *fitrah* in this community deviates from what Islam prescribes. The deviation is due to the way the people earn their living.

Besides, the paper has proved that acquaintance with outsiders does not necessarily influence the social structure of a community, as P. E. de Josselin de Jong had also proved in Malaya (Josselin de Jong, 1956, 1952). This might be due to the way the members of the community deal with outsiders. They limit their dealings with the outsiders to business problems. And if some one tries his luck in a certain place he tries his best to be associated with some one who comes from his own village, often as an apprentice. This system makes them keep their ethnic identity wherever they live.

NOTES

1. The term 'community' is here understood in a rather loose way. It is primarily a matter of descent, unless especially indicated as a matter of locality.
2. It is considered preferable to distribute the *fitrah* after the sun sets on the last day of the fasting month, and it is compulsory to distribute it before the end of the prayer ending the fasting month. The *fitrah* may, however, be distributed during the fasting month.
3. The population mentioned here does not mean only those staying in this village. It is based on the descent principle, and includes both those living in the village and in other places.
4. There is no special name to refer to this group within this community. The term *paruik* is thus used here as a common term in Minangkabau as described by Josselin de Jong (1960, 12).
5. The descent is understood here to be based on the side a person affiliates with. The present author in this occasion takes no account of factors other than the grouping. This statement can not be interpreted as a denial of the existence of the double descent principle in this community as has been stated in another article (Junus, 1964).
6. *'nagari'* is understood here as having a territorial connotation.
7. It is interesting to study how the members of this community maintain their ethnic identity. It is quite different from what E. M. Bruner describes for a Batak community (E. M. Bruner, 1961).
8. The present writer would like to state that this is the main problem to be solved in finding a way to integrate those of Chinese descent into Indonesian society.

Administration of Waqf in the State of Kedah[1]

MOHD. ZAIN HJ. OTHMAN

This work, in short, deals with the principles of Islamic law relating to *waqf* which applies in the State of Kedah. As far as the State of Kedah is concerned, there is no law of *waqf* proper. Therefore to understand the law of *waqf,* one has to go to *Sh*afi'i law books (the works of *fiqh*).

However, in the absence of historical records no definite date can be given for the institution of *waqf* in the State of Kedah since it has been carried on since time immemorial. In colonial days, however, *waqf* was administered by the Land Office, and it was subsequently placed under the jurisdiction of the Department of Islamic Affairs.[2] It was officially handed over to this department on January 1st, 1965.[3] It may be assumed that the *waqf* came into existence upon the coming of Islam to the State of Kedah, approximately 531 A.H. 1133 A.D.[4]

As this department is still in the slow process of recompiling previous records obtainable from various sources, it is not possible to furnish here information which is as complete and detailed as would have been desirable.

As far is as known is no written history available on *waqf* in Malaya, and as far as the State of Kedah is concerned the relevant enactment deals only with the administration of *waqf*.

The following enactment was introduced to repeal the existing Muslim law and to make provisions for regulating Muslim Religious Affairs and to constitute a Council to advise the ruler in matters relating to the Muslim Religion in the state of Kedah. This Enactment was called the "Administration of Muslim law Enactment, 1962".

His Highness the *Sultan* is the Head of the Muslim Religion in his State,[5] and exercises spiritual and disciplinary authority including the prerogative of mercy over his subjects. For all practical purposes, Parliament has no power to legislate in relation to the Muslim Religion except to implement an international agreement, and even then the State Government must be consulted.[6] With the concurrence of both the Conference of Rulers and the Ruler of the State concerned, however, the *Yang Di Pertuan Agong*[7] may be empowered to perform any act, observance or ceremony ordinarily performed by the individual Ruler in his State. In all other respects, the jurisdiction of the Ruler is absolute. The power of the Federal Parliament to legislate as to personal or family law does not extend to Muslims, but Parliament may make special financial provision for Muslim Religious foundations.[8] Nevertheless, Parliament has no authority to legislate in respect of *waqf.*[9]

The Department of Islamic Affairs, formerly known as the *Majlis Ugama Islam,* deals with the administration of *waqf,* according to this Enactment,[10] for there is no law of *waqf*

Reprinted from *Islamica* (1981), 86–96, by permission of the author and Sarjana Enterprise, Kuala Lumpur, Malaysia.

proper. It is, therefore, to some extent, rather important to look at how this Department was constituted.

As far as this work is concerned, we shall deal with only those sections which relate to the question of *waqf*.

CONSTITUTION

There shall be a *Majlis Ugama Islam,*[11] Kedah to aid and advise His Highness in matters relating to the Muslim Religion in the State.[12]

The *Majlis* shall be a body corporate under the name of *"Majlis Ugama Islam,* Kedah", having perpetual succession and a corporate seal, and the said seal may from time to time be broken, changed and made as new as the *Majlis* sees fit, and, until a seal is provided under this section, a stamp bearing the inscription *"Majlis Ugama Islam,* Kedah" may be used as the corporate seal.[13]

The *Majlis* may sue and be sued in its corporate name.[14]

The *Majlis* may enter into contracts and may acquire, purchase, take, hold and enjoy movable and immovable property of every description, and subject to any written law affecting the same, may convey, assign, surrender and yield up, charge, mortgage, demise, reassign, transfer or otherwise dispose of, or deal with, any movable or immovable property vested in the *Majlis* upon such terms as the *Majlis* sees fit and in accordance with Islamic law.[15]

The *Majlis* shall have power to act as an executor of a will or as an administrator of the estate of a deceased Muslim or as a trustee of any trust.[16]

All rights, powers, duties and liabilities which were, immediately before the commencement of this Enactment, vested in or imposed on the *Majlis Ugama Islam* shall, on the commencement of the Enactment, be vested in or imposed on the *Majlis,* save in so far as may be repugnant to the terms of this Enactment.[17]

All property, movable and immovable, of whatever description, which, immediately before the commencement of this Enactment, was vested in the *Majlis Ugama Islam* for its public purposes shall, on the commencement of this Enactment, and without any conveyance, assignment or transfer whatever, vest in the *Majlis* for the like title, estate or interest and on the like tenure as the same was vested or held immediately before the commencement of this Enactment.[18]

His Highness may, by Order, vest in the *Majlis* any property, movable or immovable, which immediately before the commencement of this Enactment was vested in any person or authority within the State for the purpose of the Muslim Religion, or on trust for religious or charitable purposes for the benefit of persons professing the Islamic faith and, upon the coming into operation of any such order, the property to which such order relates shall, without any conveyance assignment or transfer whatever, but as regards immovable property subject to and upon registration, vest in the *Majlis* for the like title, estate or interest and on the like tenure as the same was vested or held immediately before the coming into operation of the order.[19]

The *Majlis* shall consist of the following:

(a) The President;
(b) The Secretary of the Department of Religious Affairs;
(c) The *Kathi Besar* (*Chief Qadi*)[20]
(d) The Registrar of Religious Schools;
(e) The Secretary of *Zakat Committee;*
(f) The Secretary of the *Bayt al-mal;*
(g) Five members of *'Alim Ulama* (learned Muslims) appointed by His Highness on the recommendation of the President;
(h) Five members appointed by His Highness on the recommendation of the Executive Council.[21]

FETUA (FATWA) COMMITTEE

His Highness may, after consultation with the *Majlis,* appoint a fit and proper person to be Chairman of the *Fetua Committee.* Notice of such appointment shall be published in the Gazette.[22]

There shall be a *Fetua* Committee of the *Majlis,* consisting of the Chairman, two other members of the *Majlis,* and not less than two or more than six other fit and proper Muslims (pious) who are not members of the *Majlis.*[23]

The members of the *Fetua Committee,* other than the Chairman, shall be appointed by His Highness for such period as he may deem fit and notice of every such appointment shall be published in the Gazette.[24]

The Chairman of the *Fetua Committee* shall preside at all meetings of the Committee.[25] In the absence of the Chairman of the Fetua Committee by reason of leave, sickness or other cause, His Highness may, on the recommendation of the *Majlis,* appoint another person to be Chairman in his place.[26]

The Chairman and the two other members of the Fetua Committee, one of whom shall not be a member of the *Majlis,* shall form a quorum.[27] Subject to the provisions of this Enactment, the *Fetua Committee* may regulate its own procedure.[28] The members of the *Fetua Committee* shall be deemed to be public servants for the purposes of the Penal Code.[29]

Any person may, by letter addressed to the Secretary, request the *Majlis* to issue a *Fetua* or ruling on any point of Islamic law. On receiving any such request the Secretary shall forthwith submit the same to the Chairman of the *Fetua Committee.*[30] The *Fetua* Committee shall consider every such request and shall answer it, unless in its opinion the question referred is frivolous or for other good reasons ought not to be answered. The Chairman shall then on behalf and in the name of the *Majlis* forthwith issue a ruling approved by the *Fetua Committee* in accordance therewith.[31] The *Majlis* may at any time of its own motion make and publish any ruling or determination.[32] If in any Civil Court any question of Islamic law falls for decision, and such Court requests the opinion of the *Majlis* on such question, the question shall be referred to the *Fetua Committee* which shall, for and on behalf and in the name of the *Majlis,* give its opinion thereon and certify such opinion to the requesting Court.[33]

Provided that in issuing any such ruling the *Majlis* and the *Fetua Committee* are ordinarily required to follow the orthodox tenets of the *Sh*afi'i school. If it is considered however that the following of such orthodox tenets will be opposed to the public interest, the *Majlis* or the *Fetua Committee* may, unless His Highness shall otherwise direct, follow the less orthodox tenets of the *Sh*afi'i school. Further if it is considered that the following of either the orthodox or the less orthodox tenets of the *Sh*afi'i school will be opposed to the public interest, the Majlis or the Fetua Committee may, with the special sanction of His Highness, follow the tenets of any of the Hanafi, Maliki or Hanbali schools, as may be considered appropriate, but in any such ruling the provisions and principles to be followed shall be set out in full detail and with all necessary explanations.[34]

However, any ruling given by the *Majlis,* whether directly or through the *Fetua Committee* in accordance with the foregoing provisions shall, if His Highness so directs, be published by Notification in the Gazette and shall thereupon be binding on all Muslims resident in the State.[35]

CONSTITUTION AND JURISDICTION

His Highness shall, after consultation with the *Majlis,* appoint a Chief *Qadi,* Kedah, and shall similarly appoint *Qadis* for such areas as he may prescribe, all such appointments shall be notified in the Gazette and, on the advice of the *Majlis,* may also from time to time grant letters of authority (tawliyah) to any Chief *Qadi* or *Qadi* and may be the terms of any such letter restrict the exercise of any powers which would otherwise be conferred on such Chief *Qadi* or *Qadi* by this Enactment.[36]

His Highness may by notification in the Gazette constitute a Court of the Chief *Qadi* for the State, and in the like manner, he may also constitute Courts of *Qadis* at such areas as he may deem fit, and may prescribe the local limits of jurisdiction of such Courts. The Court of the Chief *Qadi,* however, shall have jurisdiction throughout the State and shall be presided over by the Chief *Qadi.* Subject to the provisions of this Enactment, a Court of a *Qadi* shall have jurisdiction in respect of any civil or criminal matter of the nature hereinafter specified arising within the local limits of jurisdiction prescribed for it under the preceding section or, if no local limits are so prescribed, within the State, and shall be presided over by the *Qadi* appointed thereto.[37]

The Court of the Chief *Qadi* shall, in its civil jurisdiction, hear and determine all actions and proceedings in which all the parties profess the Islamic faith and which relate to *waqf.* Provided it shall not ordinarily try any offence or hear or determine any action or proceeding in respect of which any Court of a *Qadi* has jurisdiction.[38]

No decision of the Court of the Chief *Qadi*

or a *Qadi* shall affect any right of property of any non-Muslim.[39]

The definition of *waqf,* according to this Enactment is as follows:

(a) *Waqf 'am* (public) means a dedication in perpetuity of the capital and income of property for religious or charitable purposes recognised by Islamic law, the income of the property being paid to persons or for purposes prescribed in the *waqf.* Property, includes all estates, interests, casements and rights, whether equitable or legal, in, to or arising out of property, and things in actions.[40]

For anyone wishing to give away a piece of land or such like for purposes of *waqf* there are forms prescribed,[41] and in creating a *waqf* there are two methods:

(1) By declaring intention to set up *waqf* using the prescribed form and handing over the title deed to the Majlis.[42]

(2) It is provided that every *waqf khas* after the commencement of this Enactment, shall be void unless:

(a) His Highness shall have expressly sanctioned or validated it in writing, or

(b) It was made during a serious illness from which the maker subsequently died and was made in writing by an instrument executed by him and witnessed by two adult Muslims one of whom shall be a *Penghulu,*[43] *Pegawai Masjid,*[44] or a *Panglima,*[45] being in the same village as the maker, provided that if no *Penghulu, Pegawai Masjid* or *Panglima* is available any other adult Muslim who would not have been entitled to any beneficial interests in the maker's estate had the maker died intestate shall be a competent witness.

A *waqf* also shall be invalid if it is invalid under Islamic law. Nevertheless, whether or not made by will or death-bed gift, after the commencement of this Enactment, no *waqf* involving more than one-third of the property of the person making the same shall be valid in respect of the excess beyond such one-third except with the consent of the beneficiaries.[46]

Notwithstanding any provision to the contrary contained in any instrument or declaration creating, governing or effecting the same, the *Majlis* shall be the sole trustee of all *waqf* whether *waqf 'am* or *waqf khas* and of all trusts of any description creating any charitable trust for the support and promotion of the religion of Islam or for the benefit of Muslims in accordance with the Islamic law, to the extent of any property affected thereby wherever situated. All property affected by such trust of *waqf* shall be vested in the *Majlis.* The *Majlis* shall take all necessary steps to vest in itself for the like purposes any such property situated elsewhere than in the State.[47]

The income of the *waqf khas,* if received by the *Majlis,* shall be applied by it in accordance with the lawful provisions of such *waqf khas;* the income of every other *waqf* shall be paid to and form part of the General Endowment Fund or *Bayt al-mal,* which is vested in and administered by the *Majlis.* The capital property and assets affected by any *lawful waqf* shall not generally form part of the *Bayt al-mal,* but shall be applied in pursuance of such *waqf* and held as segregated funds. If however from lapse of time or change of circumstances it is no longer possible beneficially to carry out the exact provisions of any *waqf* the *Majlis* shall prepare a scheme for the application of the property and assets affected thereby in a manner as closely as may be analogous to that required by the terms of such *waqf* and shall apply the same accordingly; or the *Majlis,* may in such case, with the approval in writing of His Highness, decide that such property and assets shall be added to and form part of the *Bayt al-mal* or the General Endowment Fund. Again, if the terms of any *waqf* are such that no method of application of the capital property and assets affected thereby is specified, or it is uncertain in what manner they should be applied, the *Majlis* may direct that such capital property and assets shall be added to and form part of the General Endowment Fund. All instruments creating, evidencing or affecting any *waqf,* together with any documents of title or other securities relating thereto, shall be held and retained by the *Majlis.*[48]

It is provided that if, in the opinion of the *Majlis,* the meaning or effect of any instrument or declaration creating or effecting any *waqf* is obscure or uncertain the *Majlis* may refer the matter to the Fetua Committee for its opinion as to the meaning or effect thereof and the *Majlis* shall act in accordance with the opinion of such Committee or a majority thereof, unless His Highness shall otherwise direct.[49]

A fund is to be known as the General Endowment Fund, except as otherwise provided under the provisions of this Enactment, such Fund shall consist of all money and property, movable or immovable, which by Islamic law or under the provisions of this Enactment or rules made hereunder, accrue from or are contributed by any person or payable to the Fund. The said property as a whole shall be vested in the *Majlis* who shall administer all such money and property, in accordance with the rules made under this Enactment. Provided that any instruments of assets and funds invested in the *Majlis* may be sold, realised and disposed of, and they and the proceeds thereof may be invested, from time to time, in any investments authorised by any written law for the time being in force for investment of trust funds, on approval of His Highness, the *Majlis* may make rules for collection, administration and distribution of all property to the General Endowment Fund.[50]

ACCOUNTS

The *Majlis* shall cause full and true accounts of the General Endowment Fund to be kept and shall as soon as possible after the 31st December of every year issue and publish in the Gazette a report on the activities of the *Majlis* during the preceding year, together with a balance sheet of the General Endowment Fund, as at the 31st day of December, an income and expenditure account for the year and a list of the properties and investments of the General Endowment Fund indicating their cost, if bought, and estimated value as at the 31st day of December. Prior to the issue thereof such accounts shall be audited and certified by the Auditor General. A copy of the auditor's certificate shall be annexed to all copies of the report and accounts as issued.[51] The *Majlis* shall also prepare, issue and publish in the Gazette a list of all properties, investments and assets vested in the *Majlis* subject to any trust or *waqf*, and not forming part of the General Endowment Fund, such list shall be audited in the manner above set out.[52]

The *Majlis* shall prepare and submit to the Ruler in Council not later than the 31st day of October in each year estimates of all income and expenditure of the *Majlis*, including therein estimates of all property receivable and disposable in kind, in respect of the ensuing year. The Ruler in Council may approve or direct that such estimates be amended, such approval or amendment shall be published in the Gazette. The *Majlis* may at any time submit to the Ruler in Council supplementary estimates of expenditure in respect of the current year, or, at any time prior to the 31st March in any year, in respect of the preceding year, and it is subject to the same manner above mentioned. No monies shall be expended, or property disposed of in kind, save in accordance with such estimates as aforesaid and upon voucher signed by the President.[53]

All costs, charges and expenses of administering the property and assets vested in the *Majlis,* including the cost of maintenance and repair of any immovable property, the salaries and allowances of all servants of the *Majlis,* and the fees and allowances payable to any officer or member of the *Majlis* in respect of his services as such, shall be paid out of the property and assets of the General Endowment Fund. The *Majlis* shall appoint bankers to be approved by His Highness and may operate such account or accounts as may seem proper. Payments by the *Majlis* of amounts exceeding fifty dollars (Malaysian) shall be made by cheque. All monies received by or for the *Majlis* shall be paid into a bank account of the *Majlis* in the manner prescribed.[54]

MOSQUES

Notwithstanding any provision to the contrary in any written instrument, the *Majlis* shall be the sole trustee of all mosques in the State and every mosque, together with any immovable property on which it stands or appurtenant thereto and used for the purposes thereof, other than State land, shall without any conveyance, assignment or transfer whatever vest in the *Majlis* for the purposes of this Enactment unless the *Majlis* otherwise directs.[55] There are 391 mosques in the State as a whole, under the administration of the *Majlis.*[56] No person shall erect any mosque, or dedicate or otherwise apply any existing building as or for the purposes of a mosque, without the permission in writing of the *Majlis.* Under no circumstances shall such permission be given unless the site of the proposed new mosque has been, or will prior to the erection or dedication thereof be made a *waqf*. It is the responsibility of the *Majlis* to ensure that all mosques in the State are kept in proper state of repair and that the compounds thereof are maintained in a proper state of cleanliness. The *Majlis* may raise and apply, or authorise the raising and application of, special funds for the purpose of such repairs and maintenance, or may defray the necessary cost from the General Endowment Fund. It shall be the duty of the *Imam* promptly to inform the *Majlis* of any want of repair, and to effect or supervise any repairs as agent for and on behalf of the *Majlis*. No material alteration to the structure of any mosque shall be made without written permission of the *Majlis* and the *Majlis* may direct any Mosque Committee to keep the mosque for which it is responsible in a proper condition.[57]

The *Majlis* may for sufficient reason close or demolish any mosque and may, where any mosque has been demolished and it is not intended to build another mosque in its place, and it is in the opinion of the *Majlis* no longer possible to use such site for other religious purposes, sell and dispose of such site, the proceeds of such sale then shall be earmarked for the erection, maintenance or repair of mosques, and no other purposes. It shall have the power at any time to determine the boundaries of any *kariah (qaryah) masjid*[58] and to amend or alter such boundaries, and in case of any dispute, the matter shall ordinarily be referred to the Fetua Committee for its opinion. It shall also maintain a register bearing the names of the *pegawai masjid* of every mosque in the State, and it shall be their duty promptly to inform the *Majlis* of any vacancy or change in the particulars relating to their mosque. Upon knowing of vacancies or impending vacancies in the office of *pegawai masjid* in the State, the *Majlis* is to make enquiry for possible candidates for such appointments, and after due examination of the qualifications of such possible candidates, to select them and submit their names to His Highness with a recommendation that they shall be appointed to fill the vacancies in question.[59]

Every *pegawai masjid* shall hold office during the pleasure of His Highness and may be removed by him for such reasons as may seem good. It shall be the duty of the *Majlis* to bring to the notice of His Highness any disgraceful conduct on the part of any *pegawai masjid*, whether in relation to his duties as such or otherwise, and to make recommendations.[60]

Nevertheless, on approval of His Highness the *Majlis* may make rules for:

(a) the appointment of the *jawatankuasa kariah*,[61]
(b) prescribing the manner in which the members of a jawatan kuasa kariah shall be appointed;
(c) prescribing the duties and functions of a *jawatan kuasa kariah*.

The *jawatankuasa kariah* in conjunction with the local *pegawai masjid* shall:

(a) be responsible for the proper conduct and good order of the mosque and all Muslim burial grounds within their *kariah;*
(b) be responsible for the good conduct of the anak *kariah*[62] of the mosque in respect of the religion of Islam; and
(c) give due and prompt information to the *Majlis* of all matters arising in the kariah and requiring the attention of the *Majlis*.[63]

Whoever, in contravention of the provisions of section 105, erects any mosque, or dedicates or otherwise applies any existing building as or for the purposes of a mosque, without written permission of the *Majlis*, shall be guilty of an offence punishable with a fine not exceeding one thousand dollars, and the Court may, subject to any rights of any third party, order the person convicted to demolish the building.[64]

One has to bear in mind the word "mosque" means a building erected or used for the purpose of holding prayers (Friday prayer in particular or "Jumlah"), services and other ceremonies related to the religion of Islam, and includes a Surau (a house of prayer).[65]

So much in respect of the administration of *waqf* in the State of Kedah; as the general situation in other States in Malaysia has been touched upon by Ahmad Ibrahim.[66] In the absence of a complete survey, the following figures relating to *waqf* in the State of Kedah may be taken as representative of the general situation.[67]

The total area of land held under *waqf* in

Kedah is 2,098 *relong* 6 *jemba* 47 *kaki* (909 lots).[68] There are still *waqf* not yet registered; however, such registration is being carried out now, under the supervision of the Department of Religious Affairs.[69]

Lands held under *waqf* and planted with specified crops are as follows:

1	Sungai Pau	5 *relong* 039 *jemba* R/C.64 planted during July, 1966 with 1,200 coffee, 126 kapok (Latin: Ceiba) and 204 coconut trees.
2	Charok Pelandok	2 *relong* 236 *jemba* R/C.32 planted during July, 1966 with 94 kapok trees, during December, 1966, with 200 low coconut trees and during April, 1967, with 510 coffee trees.
3	*Shari'ah* Court and mosque area in Sik	R/C.49 commenced on 26th July, 1966, areas planted with 63 low coconut, 16 ordinary coconut and 4 *rambutan* trees.
4	Cemetery area, Sik Dalam	40 kapok trees planted on August 7th, 1966.
5	Telaga Batu	10 *relong* fully planted with rubber during August, 1966
6	Kampong Betong	R/C.25. 850 rubber trees planted during September, 1966.
7	Kampong Tua Tanah Hitam	Planted with 200 bud-grafted rubber trees during October, 1966.

Lands planted during 1967:

1	Tupal	R/C.31 20 *relong* and 300 *jemba* planted with 1,500 low coconut trees on 6th March 1967.
2	Cemetery area Teloi Dua	9 *relong* and 200 *jemba* planted with 186 low coconut trees on 6th March, 1967.
3	Cemetery area Bandar	Planted with 126 low coconut trees on 6th March, 1967.
4	Gulau Sok	Planted with 1,000 rubber trees on 15th April, 1967.

Lands cleared in 1967 and ready for planting:

1	Cemetery area Kemelong	1 *relong* 090 *jemba* will be planted with 1000 low coconut trees.
2	Kampong Bandar	9 *relong* 353 *jemba* R/C.39. will be planted with 800 low coconut trees.
3	Kampong Sena	3 *relong* 398 *jemba* R/C.23. will be planted with 200 low coconut trees.
4	Kampong Sok	15 *relong* 320 *jemba* R/C.29. will be planted with 1050 low coconut trees.
5	Padang Chichar	6 *relong* 057 *jemba* will be planted with 420 low coconut trees.
6	Kuala Jeneri	Will be planted with 150 low coconut trees.
7	Gajah Puteh	Will be planted with 100 low coconut trees.
8	Sidu Jeneri	14 *relong* 200 *jemba* R/C.16. will be planted with 800 low coconut trees.
9	Sik Dalam	5 *relong* 237 *jemba* will be planted with 200 low coconut trees.
10	Kampong Tua Namek	Will be planted with 50 low coconut trees.
11	*Durian Burong*	Will be planted with 114 low coconut trees.
12	Kuala Sok	11 *relong* will be planted with 150 low coconut trees.
13	Nami	Will be planted with 210 low coconut trees.[70]

INCOMES OF WAQF

Before 26th October, 1965, the incomes of *waqf* were governed by the State Treasurer. It was only when this became a statutory body that it came to be transferred to the *Majlis* (on the above-mentioned date). Since then up to 31st December, 1967, the total income of *waqf* in the State of Kedah was represented as follows:

Waqf savings	$5,212.26
Waqf 'am	4,094.74
Waqf khas	7,097.85
	$16,404.85

Estimates of Income and Expenditure 1969

Balance of income up to 1.1.1968	$112,277.62
Final Estimates of income 1968	50,000.00
Total	$162,277.62
Total incomes up to 1.1.1969	$162,277.62
Estimates of income 1969	49,500.00
Total	$209,777.62
Expenditure	162,500.00
Balance	$ 47,277.62

Estimates of certain expenditure 1969[71]

Co-operation for organising kindergarten	$ 20,000.00
Building for kindergarten	25,000.00
Plan to purchase some property	100,000.00
Total	$145,000.00

The following *waqf* is widely known in Kedah, for it has played and still plays a very important role there, e.g., several students have been awarded scholarships for higher education in Egypt at the University of Al-Azhar, out of the proceeds of such *waqf*, that is, a piece of land dedicated by Che' Gayah[72] on 10th *Jamad al-awwal*, 1359, the total area of the said land being 68 relong 439 jemba. In order to understand it better, the instrument and its translation are attached[73] which provide full details as regards the purposes for which such *waqf* was made.

It is estimated that the present yearly income is approximately 5,800/- Malaysian dollars. Income from the date of commencement of this *waqf* in 1360 A.H. up to 1367 A.H. without deducting expenses such as land rent, *ex-gratia* payments to persons(s) looking after the land and other miscellaneous items amounted to 104,304.21.

Expenditure not including land rent, miscellaneous items and *ex-gratia* payments:

1	Purchasing of *padi* land	33,703.00
2	Tables and chairs for students of college.[74]	3,764.50
3	Library	1,504.25
4	Scholarship[75]	10,680.37
5	Scholarship	8,307.54
6	Prayer mats (rubber)	600.00
7	Gestetner machine	800.00
8	Two school clocks	160.00
9	School bell	250.00
10	Donation for Muslim Welfare	200.00
11	Loan (for a student to further studies)	3,000.00
	Total	$ 70,969.66

From the above figures, although they are not up-to-date, it appears that *waqf* in Kedah were composed exclusively of lands. There are only two mosques under *waqf*, namely, the mosque at Akar Peluru and Gurun,[76] nevertheless, the *Majlis* is the sole trustee of all mosques in the State.[77]

As far as the institution of *waqf* in the State of Kedah is concerned, there is no evidence whatsoever to indicate whether this Department has been able to meet adequately the needs of those who should benefit by *waqf*. It is almost certain that there are a lot of known *waqf* in the State of Kedah including mosques and Muslim Cemeteries which have not been officially registered. Such *waqf* should be looked into seriously in order to be of benefit to the Muslims. As far as we are concerned, the mosques should become *waqf* by themselves whether they are registered or otherwise. Therefore, it is incredible that there are only two mosques under *waqf* in the State of Kedah.

Apart from the fact that the figures given above are not up-to-date, nothing too has been done to upkeep the institution of *waqf* as required by the Islamic law. The present paper must be considered merely a preliminary survey of the subject. Perhaps it will help to stimulate interest in the subject.

NOTES

1. Capital: Alor Star. Area: 3,600 sq. miles.
2. Correspondence, Bil: (43) dalm. Ugama (K) 9/65 Jld. 2, 12th June, 1968.
3. (53) dlm. Ugama (K) 9/65 Jld. 2, 16th July, 1968.
4. Jabatan Hal Ehwal Ugama, Kedah, letter of 6th July, 1969.
5. *The laws of the Constitution of Kedah incorporating all amendments up to the 21st June, 1962,* s. 39 (2)d.
6. *Malaysia Year Book,* 1964, p. 613; D.C. Buxbaum, *Family law and Customary law in Asia,* Martinus Nijhoff/the Hague, 1968, pp. 108–109.
7. King of Malaysia.
8. *Malaysia Year Book,* loc. cit.
9. *Ibid.*, p. 623.
10. Kedah No. 9, 1962.
11. Recently the *Majlis* has adopted this name instead of "Jabatan Hal Ehwal Ugama Islam" or Department of Islamic Affairs.
12. Kedah, *Administration of Muslim law Enactment,* No. 9, 1962, s.4.
13. *Ibid.*, s.5.
14. *Ibid.*, s.6.
15. *Ibid.*, s.7.
16. *Ibid.*, s.8.
17. *Ibid.*, s.9.
18. *Ibid.*, s.10 (1).
19. *Ibid.*, s.10 (2).
20. Means Chief *Qadi* of Kedah, appointed under section 39.
21. Kedah, *Administration of Muslim law Enactment,* 1962, s.11 (1).
22. *Ibid.*, s.35.
23. *Ibid.*, s.36 (1).
24. *Ibid.*, s.36 (2).
25. *Ibid.*, s.36 (3).
26. *Ibid.*, s.36 (4).
27. *Ibid.*, s.36 (5).
28. *Ibid.*, s.36 (6).
29. *Ibid.*, s.36 (7).
30. *Ibid.*, s.37 (1).
31. *Ibid.*, s.37 (2).
32. *Ibid.*, s.37 (3).
33. *Ibid.*, s.37 (4).
34. *Johore, Council of Religious Endowment,* (No. 2) 1949; *Kedah, Administration of Muslim law Enactment,* (No. 9) 1962; *Kelantan, Council of Religious and Malay Custom and Kathis Courts Enactment,* (No. 1) 1953; *Malacca, Administration of Muslim law Enactment,* (No. 1) 1959; *Negri Sembilan, Administration of Muslim law Enactment,* (No. 15) 1960; *Pahang, Administration of the law of the Religion of Islam Enactment.*

(No. 6); 1956; *Penang, Administration of Muslim law Enactment,* (No. 3) 1959; *Perak, Majlis Ugama dan 'Adat Melayu Enactment,* (No. 6) 1951; *Perlis, Administration of Muslim law Enactment,* (No. 3) 1964; *Selangor, Administration of Muslim law Enactment,* (No. 3) 1952; *Trengganu, Administration of Islamic law Enactment,* (No. 4) 1955, and Amendment, 1963.

35. *Ibid.*, s.38 (2).
36. *Ibid.*, s.39.
37. *Ibid.*, s.40–41 (1, 2).
38. *Ibid.*, s.41 (3.b.IV).
39. *Ibid.*, s.41 (5).
40. *Ibid.*, s.2 (1).
41. Owing to circumstances beyond control it has not been possible to reproduce specimen copies of the forms here.
42. Bil. (43) dlm. Ugama (K) 9/63 Jld. 2, 12/6/1968.
43. A *Penghulu* who is appointed in accordance with the *Penghulu* Scheme of Service of the State.
44. Assistant *Penghulu.*
45. This refer to the *Imam, Bilal* and *Siak* if any, for the time being.
46. Kedah, Administration of Muslim Law Enactment, 1962, S. 912.
47. *Ibid.*, ss.90 (2), 91.
48. *Ibid.*, ss.93, 94.
49. *Ibid.*, s.95.
50. *Ibid.*, s.89 (1, 3, 4).
51. I regret that no copies are obtainable despite all efforts to acquire them.
52. Kedah. *Administration of Muslim law Enactment,* No. 9, 1962, ss.96, 97 and 98.
53. *Ibid.*, s.99.
54. *Ibid.*, ss.100, 101 (1, 2).
55. *Ibid.*, s.104.
56. Jabatan Hal Ehwal Ugama Islam, Kedah, letter of 1st December, 1968.
57. Kedah, *Administration of Muslim law Enactment,* 1962, ss.104 (5 & 6).
58. *Kariah* and *kariah masjid* means the area prescribed by the *Majlis* in accordance with section 108 within which a mosque is situated.
59. Kedah, *Administration of Muslim law Enactment,* 1962, ss.107, 8, 9, 10 (1).
60. *Ibid.*, s.111.
61. Means a Committee of a *kariah masjid* appointed under rules made under section 113.
62. Means the person permanently or habitually resident in any *kariah masjid.*
63. Kedah. *Administration of Muslim law Enactment,* 1962, s.113.
64. *Ibid.*, s.159.
65. *Ibid.*, s.2 (1).
66. *Islamic law in Malaya,* Singapore. 1965, pp. 276–90.
67. The following information is given officially by the Department of Religious Affairs, Kedah (*Jabatan Hal Ehwal Ugama.* Kedah) in Malay, for which all correspondence is available for the author.
68. 1 *relong* = 484 *jemba:* 1 *jemba* = 64 sq. feet; 1 *kaki* = one foot.
69. *Jabatan Hal Ehwal Ugama,* Kedah, of 1st December, 1968.
70. *Jabatan Hal Ehwal Ugama,* Kedah, Bil. (43) dlm. Ugama (K) 9/65 Jld. 2., 12th June, 1968.
71. Jabatan Hal Ehwal Ugama, Kedah, 4th June, 1969.
72. Hajjah Rogayah binti Mohd. Yusuf, a house-wife, piety and generosity, very keen interest in charity, born in 1899 and died on 12th June, 1955 (May God bless her).
73. See Appendix B [in *Islamica* (Kuala Lumpur: Sarjana Enterprise, 1981)].
74. College stated in the *waqf* instrument.
75. Scholars' name have been made available to the author.
76. *Jabatan Hal Ehwal Ugama,* Kedah, of 1st December, 1968.
77. Kedah. *Administration of Muslim law Enactment,* 1962, s.104.

Modern Concept of Hajj Management: The Experience of Malaysia

AWANG HAD SALLEH

The English translation of the name ['Tabang Hajji'] is 'the Hajji fund'. Its actual name when first passed by the Houses of Parliament in 1962 was the Pilgrims Management and Fund Board. By another Act of Parliament in 1969, the name was changed to the Muslim Pilgrimage Control and Savings Corporation, absorbing into it the office of Hajj which was hitherto under the Ministry of Internal Affairs.

Objectives: The following are the objectives of the Corporation:

1. To enable Muslims to save for the Hajj or other purposes.
2. To enable Muslims, through their savings, to participate indirectly in investments in industries, commerce and real estates that are allowable under Islam.
3. To provide management, protection and assistance to the members performing the Hajj through the facilities and services of the corporation.

The Structure: The 'Lembaga Urusan dan Tabung Hajji' — the formal Malay name of the corporation — is directed by a board and managed by a Director-General as an executive head assisted by a deputy and other officials. In all the organisation has about 300 employees. Figure 1 is a simplified diagram showing its overall organisational structure.

Major Activities: Activities of the Tabang Hajji may be divided into three broad categories, namely: (1) savings; (2) investments; (3) Hajj services. Any Muslims may open a savings account with the corporation provided they are citizens and enrolled as members of the corporation. Table 1 indicates the number of depositors during the 1969–74 period.

Table 1: Number of Trading Hajji Depositions by Year During 1969–74

Year	Depositors
1969	48,082
1970	60,452
1971	73,264
1972	97,192
1973	125,194
1974	82,629

The total number of depositors as at 1 July 1976 was 266,723. The rate of membership growth is estimated to be at 5,000 persons per month. The amount deposited up to 1 July 1976 was M$ 191.5 million*. Out of this M$ 140 million has been withdrawn by members either for purposes of Hajj or for other purposes such as purchasing a house, land, etc. So far the corporation has put in M$ 68.5 million in various forms of investments. These are either in the form of shares or real estate or subsidising companies. The current market value of first stocks has been estimated at M$ 100 million, which is envisaged to

*Malaysia dollars

Reprinted in abridged form from Z. Sardar and M. A. Zaki Badawi (eds.), *Hajj Studies*, Vol. 1 (London: Croom Helm, 1979), pp. 73–86, by permission of the author and the publishers.

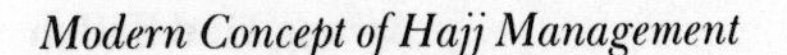

Figure 1: The Organisation Structure of 'Tabang Hajji'

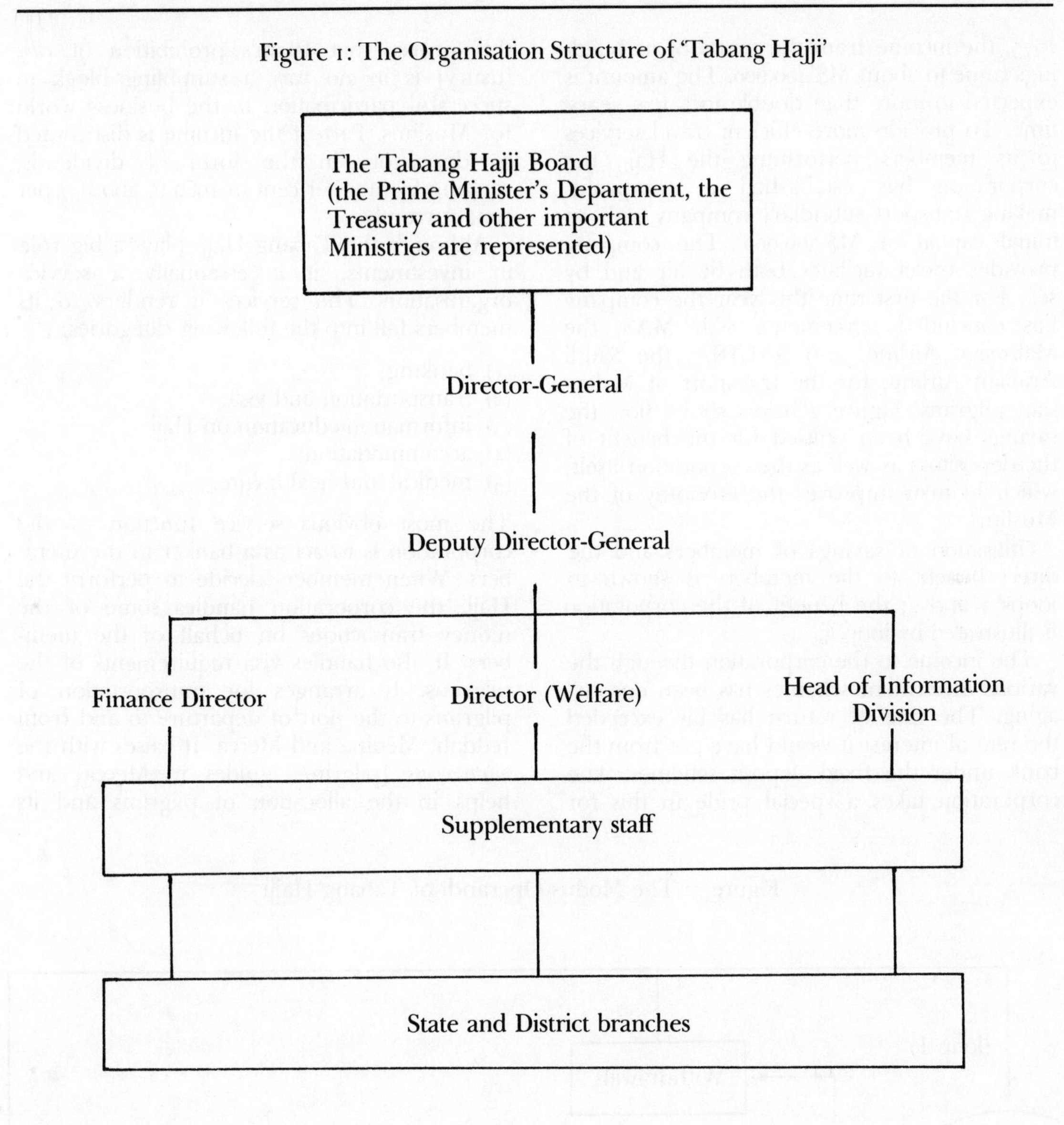

increase in value to M$ 150 million by 1980. The pattern of investment of the corporation at October 1976 is shown in Table 2.

Table 2: Investments by Tabang Hajji

Shares	M$ 66.3 million
Real Estate	M$ 5.2 million
Total	M$ 71.5 million

The Tabang Hajji has share holdings in more than fifty industrial ventures. To manage its 10,500-acre oil palm estate, the corporation created a subsiding company with an initial capital of M$ 10 million. The estate yielded an income of M$ 3 million in 1976.

The corporation has purchased lands and buildings in various parts of Malaysia. The amount invested in this form totalled about M$ 5 million. It has also purchased a building in Jeddah at a cost of about M$ 1 million. In

1975, the income from the rental of its buildings came to about M$ 400,000. The amount is expected to more than double in a few years' time. To provide more efficient travel services to its members performing the Hajj, the corporation has established a non-profit-making transport subsidiary company with an initial capital of M$ 500,000. The company provides travel facilities both by air and by sea. For the first time this year the company has concluded agreements with MAS, the Malaysian Airline, and SAUDIA, the Saudi Arabian Airline, for the transport of Malaysian pilgrims. Figure 2 below shows how the savings have been utilised for the benefit of the depositors as well as the corporation itself, which in turn improves the economy of the Muslims.

Utilisation of savings of members and the direct benefit to the members is shown in loops 1 and 2; the benefit of the corporation is illustrated by loop 3.

The income to the corporation through the various investment schemes has been encouraging. The rate of return has far exceeded the rate of interest it would have got from the bank under the fixed deposit schemes. The corporation takes a special pride in this for this proves that Islam's prohibition of *riba* [usury] is in no way a stumbling block to successful participation in the business world for Muslims. Part of the income is distributed to depositors in the form of dividends, ranging from 3 per cent in 1969 to about 7 per cent currently.

Although the Tabang Hajji plays a big role in investments, it is essentially a service organisation. The services it renders to its members fall into the following categories:

(1) banking;
(2) transportation and visa;
(3) information/education on Hajj;
(4) accommodation;
(5) medical and health care.

The most obvious service function of the corporation is to act as a banker to the members. When members decide to perform the Hajj, the corporation handles some of the money transactions on behalf of the members. It also handles visa requirements of the pilgrims. It arranges for transportation of pilgrims to the port of departure to and from Jeddah, Medina and Mecca. It liaises with the *mutawwafs* [pilgrims' guides in Mecca] and helps in the allocation of pilgrims and its

Figure 2: The Modus Operandi of Tabang Hajji

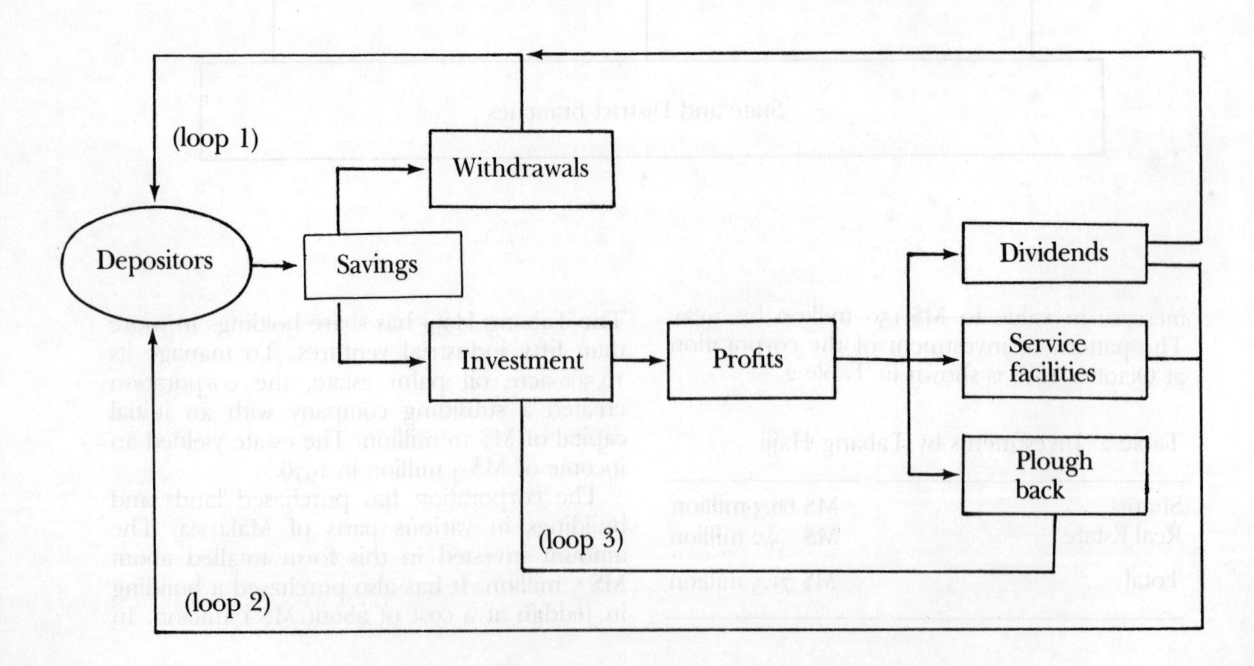

accommodation is available for rental to the pilgrims in Medina. In Mecca, the *Tabang Hajji* owns three buses, three ambulances and one van-cum-ambulance.

Lectures and information sessions giving information on Hajj are conducted for the benefit of the pilgrims. These are held at various local centres, during the few weeks preceding departure time for Mecca. Accommodation is arranged for the pilgrims at various points such as at port of departure in Malaysia, at Mecca and Medina. It accommodates pilgrims that have lost their way and therefore cannot return to the camps of their *mutawwafs*. These pilgrims are looked after until their respective *mutawwafs* have been found. This happens very frequently at Arafat and Muna. In difficult traffic situations in Muna, it is not uncommon for buses and taxis to simply leave the pilgrims at points convenient to the drivers. The Tabang Hajji plays host to these pilgrims while locating the camp sites of the *mutawwafs*.

The last, but in no way least, service offered by the Tabang Hajji is the medical one for the pilgrims. The medical mission was already in existence in 1952 prior to the formation of the Tabang Hajji. It was then under the Pilgrimage Control Board. When the Tabang Hajji was formed, the medical mission was placed under the Tabang Hajji by courtesy of the Ministry of Health, which lends its staff to the corporation for a period of three months or so. The work of the mission starts with a medical examination of the members of the Tabang Hajji applying to perform the Hajj. Members may not come to Mecca if they suffer from infectious diseases, insanity or if they should be at an advanced stage of pregnancy. The next stage of contact with the pilgrims is at Jeddah. The work begins with the arrival of the first group of pilgrims reaching *Madinatul-hujjaj* [the city of the Pilgrims]. With the departure of the pilgrims to Mecca or Medina, the medical mission breaks into three groups, one remaining in Jeddah, one going to Mecca, and the last one going to Medina. The three groups will combine again at Arafat and Muna. The whole mission then goes to Mecca before sending again another group to Jeddah to look after those in Jeddah prior to their departure for home.

Every year, almost every pilgrim seeks medical help. Last year, when there were 16,000 pilgrims from Malaysia, the Mission treated about 30,000 cases. On the average, each pilgrim was seen and treated twice. It seems that on the average 5 per cent of the patients are non-Malaysian pilgrims. The mission started its own hospital in Mecca in 1959. But surgical cases and cases of infectious disease are still referred to the Saudi Government Hospitals. The mission hospital now has 50 beds. Attempts are being made to increase them to 70.

The mission for the 1395 Hajj consists of one senior medical doctor (as head of the mission), eight doctors, two of whom are lady doctors, a few hospital assistants, eighteen nurses, sixteen male and nine female attendants, three drivers, one laboratory assistant, four dispensers, two X-ray technicians and three cooks — a total of 76 persons. The doctor-patient ratio this year works out to be about 1:400. This very favourable ratio is due to an unexpected fall in the number of pilgrims this year. Usually the ratio is around 1:1,000.

While on secondment to the Tabang Hajji, the members of the Medical Mission are paid their normal salaries by the Ministry of Health, while the Tabang Hajji pays all necessary travel and accommodation fees as well as various allowances. The government contribution in terms of salaries and medicine is said to be around M$1 million a year. Figure 3 shows a cycle of services provided by the Tabang Hajji to its member pilgrims.

That the concept of management of pilgrims through the Tabang Hajji has been well accepted is borne out by the following factors. First, as stated earlier, more and more Muslims become members and depositors of the Fund (see Table 1). Second, the number of pilgrims increases year by year, except for the 1975/6 season, when there was a drastic fall in number due to general international recession, the 50 per cent increase in fees, and general confusion over arbitrary allocation of pilgrims to *mutawwafs* by the Saudi authorities. Table 3 gives figures of Malaysian pilgrims performing Hajj through Tabang Hajji.

Another test of acceptability of the Tabang Hajji is the fact that a very high percentage of the Malaysian Hajjis have been members of

Figure 3: Services Rendered to Pilgrims by the Tabang Hajji

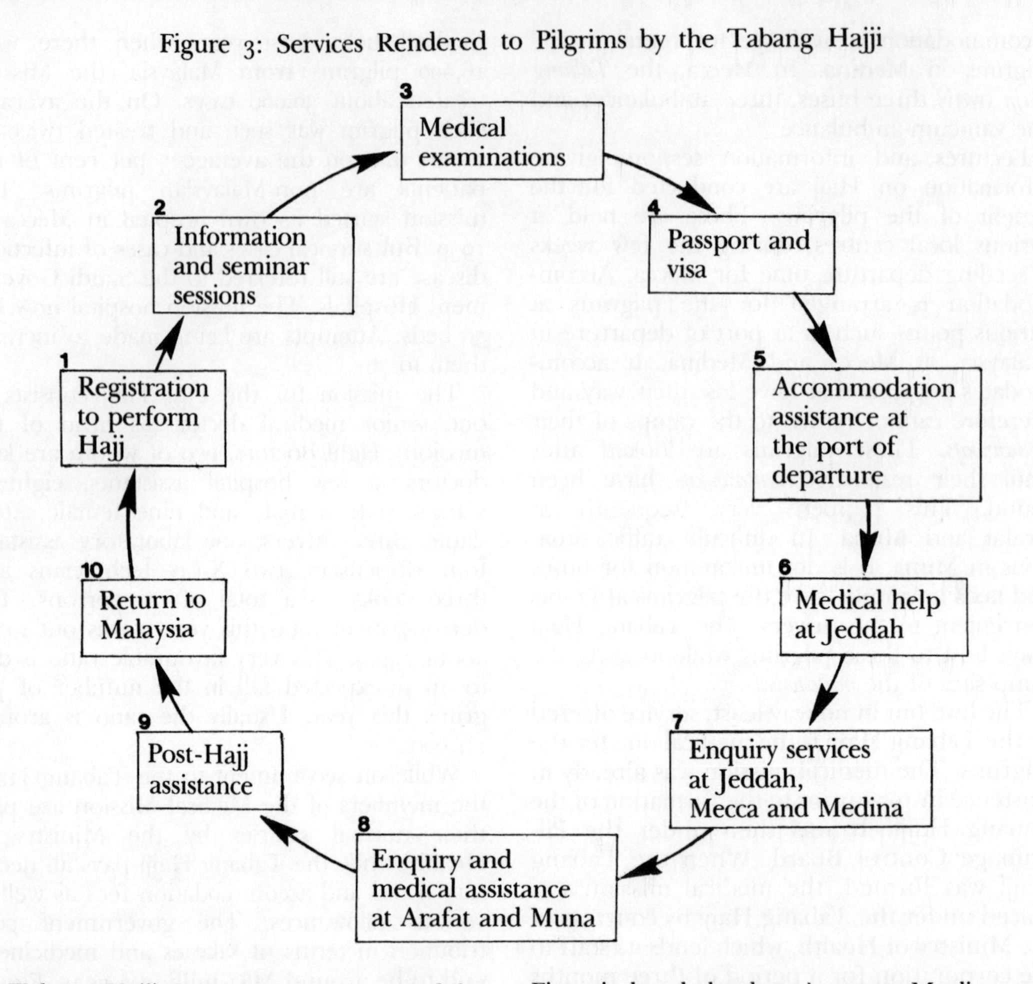

the Tabang Hajji. Last year 90 per cent of the total Malay pilgrims performed Hajj through Tabang Hajji. It is envisaged that in the near future all pilgrims will have to first enrol as members of the Corporation before they could be allowed to perform the Hajj. This is due to the Saudi government's proposed plan to allow pilgrims only through national government's sponsorship.

Direct and Indirect Contributions of the Corporation

The most direct beneficiaries of the Tabang Hajji scheme are, of course, the subscriber-pilgrims themselves. They receive a yearly bonus and they enjoy the Hajj-related Tabang Hajji services and facilities. However, through its various investment schemes, the Tabang Hajji has brought about other benefits to the Muslims of Malaysia as a whole. First, it has helped to increase Muslim property (real estate) ownership in Malaysia. Second, through its acquisition of properties, it provides employment to more Muslims in the country. These two further contribute to the fulfilment of the aspiration of the late Prime Minister of Malaysia who said, 'I hope we will continue to strive to rebuild a strong economic position among the Islamic communities of this country.' These, incidentally, also contribute to the realisation of the New Economic Policy of Malaysia, the two-pronged strategies of which are the eradication of poverty and the restructuring of society. Finally, the corporation has enhanced tremendously a sense of unity and purpose among the Muslims of Malaysia.

The Future

Judging from the trend in its brief past, the

Table 3: Number of Malaysian Pilgrims performing the Hajj through Tabang Hajji During 1970–6 Period by Method of Travel

	1970	1971	1972	1973	1974	1975
Sea	8,571	9,069	7,615	9,691	10,207	10,237
Air	1,131	1,581	2,780	3,292	5,159	5,498
Total	9,702	10,650	10,395	12,983	15,366	15,735

corporation will continue to play more effective roles as an Islamic agent of change. It will be able to provide greater and more efficient services to its members so as to make life much easier for the pilgrims.

Owing to the fact that it is still at a formative stage and that its services are meeting increasing demands, the corporation is facing development at a very rapid rate. In order for it not to lose its sense of direction, the corporation must now or in the very near future initiate evaluations of its policies, implementations and strategies. The time has also come for the corporation to set up its own research division. Without such evaluations the effectiveness of its mode of operation may be displaced by goals generated by purely economic motivation. A sense of balance must be preserved, especially between profit-motivated and service-oriented schemes.

Socio-Cultural Settings

The Religion of Java

CLIFFORD GEERTZ

Snouck Hurgronje, Holland's great Islamic scholar, wrote of Indonesian Islam as he found it in 1892:

> To follow up the image of the five pillars (of Islam), we might say that the pointed roof of the building of Islam is still mainly supported by the central pillar, the confession that there is no god but Allah and that Muhammad is the messenger of Allah, but that this pillar is surrounded with a medley of ornamental work quite unsuited to it which is a profanation of its lofty simplicity. And in regard to the other four, the corner pillars, it might be observed that some of these have suffered decay in the long lapse of time, while other new pillars, which according to the orthodox teaching are unworthy to be supports of the holy building have been planted beside the original five and have to a considerable extent robbed them of their functions.[1]

Hurgronje was referring specifically to Acheh in northern Sumatra, but his simile would have applied even more aptly to Java, where the pillars were scarcely visible among the buttresses. Aside from a conviction that they were Moslems and that to be a Moslem was in general a good thing, Hurgronje found among the inhabitants of tropical Indonesia little of the desert-dried Near Eastern monotheism he had (perhaps) known in Mecca, where he had lived, a Christian disguised as a Moslem pilgrim. Indonesians, he said, "render in a purely formal manner due homage to the institutions ordained of Allah, which are everywhere as sincerely received in theory as they are ill-observed in practice";[2] and a generation of scholars echoed him — in despair if they were Islamologists, in triumph if they were ethnologists dedicated to preserving native customs in their pristine beauty.

But Hurgronje was writing at the end of one era and the beginning of a new one. Twenty years after he wrote, Muhammadijah, a vigorously modernist Islamic society, was founded in Djokjakarta, the very center and climax of Hindu-Javanese culture, heralding what the Javanese call "the time of the organizations" and announcing the final arrival on the Indonesian social scene of the self-conscious Moslem, the man not only fond of his religion in theory but also committed to it in practice. The appearance of such a man was not as sudden an occurrence as it looked to some, surprised by signs of life in a religion they had long accounted lacking in either internal dynamism or in basic appeal to what they took to be "the Indonesian soul." Hurgronje, wiser than most and knowing that changes in the sphere of Islamic life and doctrine were taking place even in his time, warned his readers that these changes were so gradual that "although they take place before our eyes they are hidden from those who do not make a careful study of the subject."[3]

Islam came to Indonesia from India,

---

brought by merchants. Its Mid-Eastern sense for the external conditions of life having been blunted and turned inward by Indian mysticism, it provided but a minimal contrast to the mélange of Hinduism, Buddhism, and animism which had held the Indonesians enthralled for almost fifteen centuries. Although it spread — peacefully for the most part — through almost all of Indonesia in a space of three hundred years and completely dominated Java except for a few pagan pockets by the end of the sixteenth century, Indonesian Islam, cut off from its centers of orthodoxy at Mecca and Cairo, vegetated, another meandering tropical growth on an already overcrowded religious landscape. Buddhist mystic practices got Arabic names, Hindu Radjas suffered a change of title to become Moslem Sultans, and the common people called some of their wood spirits jinns; but little else changed.

Toward the middle of the nineteenth century the isolation of Indonesian Islam from its Mid-Eastern fountainhead began to break down. From the Hadhramaut, that barren ground of Moslem medievalism at the southern tip of the Arabian peninsula, came Arab traders in ever increasing numbers to settle in Indonesia and transmit their fine sense for orthodoxy to the local merchants with whom they dealt. And, with the growth of sea travel, Indonesians began to go on the pilgrimage to Mecca in such numbers that by the time Hurgronje lived there in the 1880's the Indonesian colony was the largest and most active in the entire city. "Here," he wrote, "lies the heart of the religious life of the East-Indian archipelago, and the numberless arteries pump thence fresh blood in ever accelerating tempo to the entire body of the Moslem populace in Indonesia."[4]

At the other end of these arteries, in Java, were rural Koranic schools in which the returning pilgrim taught, if not the content of Islam (for the most part neither he nor his peasant students could understand any Arabic, although they could chant it well enough), at least a sense for the austerity of its form and for the fact that it was different in spirit from the polytheistic mysticism to which the Javanese had been so long accustomed. Around these schools and around the mosques attached to them, a space for orthodoxy was cleared; and those who lived in this clearing — the *santris* — began to see themselves as minority representatives of the true faith in the great forest of ignorance and superstition, protectors of the Divine Law against the pagan crudities of traditionalized custom.

But even in this context the drift toward orthodoxy was slow. Up until about the second decade of this century the various Koranic schools located around the countryside remained independent, mutually antagonistic, mystically tinged religious brotherhoods in which a certain compromise was reached with the religious beliefs of the *abangans* on the one hand and the fears of the colonial government of an organized and socially conscious Islam on the other. It was in the towns, where continued contact with Hadhramaut Arabs, a developing merchant ethic, the growth of nationalism, and modernist influences from the Islamic reform movements of Egypt and India combined to produce a greater militancy among the explicitly Moslem, that Islam became a living faith in Indonesia.[5]

With the founding of Muhammadijah by a returned pilgrim in 1912, and the birth of its political counterpart Sarekat Islam ("The Islamic Union") in the same year, the awakened sense for orthodoxy spread beyond the towns to the villages. Conservative organizations arose to combat what they took to be dangerous departures from the more medieval Islamic doctrines in the programs of the modernist groups, but, details apart, the recognition that there was at last a true Islamic congregation in *Indonesia* — a genuine *ummat,* as Moslems call the community of true believers — was finally inescapable. Even those who had ignored Hurgronje's warning to make a close study of the subject could now see that Indonesian Islam had changed and that in almost every village and town in Java there was a group, often living in a separate neighborhood, commonly made up of petty traders and richer peasants, to whom Islam was no longer another mystic science among many but a unique, exclusivist, universalist religion demanding total surrender to a distant God and dedicated to an eternal struggle against the unbeliever.

Modjokuto, having been founded in the latter half of the nineteenth century, has a history lying almost entirely within this period in which a self-conscious Moslem community crystallized out from the more general *abangan* background. The great majority of its prewar trading class and much of its peasant population having been drawn through migration from the heavily Islamic areas of northern Java — Demak, Kudus, Gresik — where the Moslem tradition brought by the earliest traders never wholly died out, Modjokuto has experienced each phase of reform and counter-reform within the Islamic community in Indonesia during this century until today perhaps a third of the population — as a rough estimate — are *santris.* Grouped into their own neighborhoods (less so now than before the war, but still noticeably clustered), their own political parties, and their own social organizations, and following their own ritual patterns, this group represents a genuine variant of Modjokuto culture.

Santri versus *Abangan:* General Differences

Comparing the *abangan* and *santri* variants of the Modjokuto religious pattern, two very striking general differences, other than their differential evaluation of Islamic orthodoxy, are immediately apparent. In the first place, *abangans* are fairly indifferent to doctrine but fascinated with ritual detail, while among the *santris* the concern with doctrine almost entirely overshadows the already attenuated ritualistic aspects of Islam.

An *abangan* knows when to give a *slametan* and what the major foods should be — porridge for a birth, pancakes for a death. He may have some ideas as to what various elements in it symbolize (and as often he may not, saying that one has porridge because one always has porridge on such an occasion), but he will be little upset if someone else gives a different interpretation. He is tolerant about religious beliefs; he says, "Many are the ways." If one performs the correct passage rituals, one is not an animal; if one gives the *slametans* in the Fast, one is not an infidel; and if one sends a tray off to the "cleansing of the village," one is not a subversive — and that is enough. If one doesn't believe in spirits or if one thinks God lives in the sun, that's one's own affair.

For the *santri* the basic rituals are also important — particularly the prayers, the conscientious performance of which is taken by *santris* and non-*santris* alike to be the distinguishing mark of a true *santri* — but little thought is given to them; they are simple enough in any case. What concerns the *santris* is Islamic doctrine, and most especially the moral and social interpretation of it. They seem especially interested, particularly the urban "modernist" *santris,* in apologetics: the defense of Islam as a superior ethical code for modern man, as a workable social doctrine for modern society, and as a fertile source of values for modern culture. In the countryside the doctrinal aspect is less marked; there the *santri* ethic remains somewhat closer to the *abangan.* But even in the countryside a *santri* differs from an *abangan* not only in his self-declared religious superiority to the latter, but also in his realization, if only vague, that in Islam the main religious issues are doctrinal; and in any case the rural *santri* follows an urban leadership. For the *santri* the dimensions have shifted. It is not the knowledge of ritual detail or spiritual discipline which is important, but the application of Islamic doctrine to life. The kinds of *santris* vary from those whose difference from their *abangan* neighbors seems to lie entirely in their insistence that they are true Moslems, while their neighbors are not, to those whose commitment to Islam dominates almost all of their life. But, for all, a concern for dogma has to some extent replaced a concern for ritual.

One result of this difference of emphasis is that the curiously detached unemotional relativism that *abangans* evince toward their own religious customs, an attitude not entirely unlike that of the dilettante ethnologist collecting quaint customs among the heathen, tends to be replaced among the *santris* by a strong emphasis on the necessity for unreserved belief and faith in the absolute truth of Islam and by marked intolerance for Javanese beliefs and practices they take to be heterodox.

> I talked to Abdul Manan from the village (some distance away from Modjokuto) where we stayed for a while a few months back . . .

Asked him about *pundèns* (spirit shrines) there, and he said there is no one there with the same name as the one here — *mBah Buda* — just down the street from his place. People give *slametans* there just as here, in order to fulfill a vow that they would do so if cured and so on. He said he as a good Moslem doesn't believe in it, and said he proved this one dark night by taking the statue of a man that was there and carrying it off to the mosque and breaking it into pieces. Nothing happened, he said, which proves it was just a statue. He said there is a statue of an ox there now and people still go on holding *slametans* there as usual, but only those who are too stupid to know any better.

The second obvious way in which the *abangan* and *santri* religious variants differ from one another is in the matter of their social organization. For the *abangan* the basic social unit to which nearly all ritual refers is the household — a man, his wife, and his children. It is the household which gives the *slametan,* and it is the heads of other households who come to attend it and then carry home part of the food to the other members of their families. Even the *bersih désa,* the "cleansing of the village" ceremony, the closest thing to a public or super-household ritual that one can find within the *abangan* system, is but little more than a compound of separate *slametan* contributions from each of the village's households rather than a ritual of the village as a whole; it is food from separate kitchens brought together, rather than food from a common kitchen divided up. Aside from coming with their food, there is little that the participants are called upon to do, and the kind of large-scale religious ritual carried out by special clubs, fraternities, and associations one finds in, say, Melanesia, parts of Africa, or among the American Pueblos is quite foreign to the Javanese tradition. With the exception of Permai, a latter-day development indeed and largely politically inspired at that, there is nothing in *abangan* religious life which could even in the remotest sense be called a church or a religious organization, and there are no temples either. The Javanese peasant, who has so often been held to be a featureless cipher swallowed up in his social whole, actually holds himself rather aloof from it, keeping his thoughts to himself and willing to give others only what tradition assures him they are going to give back to him; and his religion shows it. There is no organic religious community, strictly speaking, among the *abangans:* in contemporary Modjokuto at least, there is only a set of separate households geared into one another like so many windowless monads, their harmony preordained by their common adherence to a single tradition.

For the *santri,* the sense of community — of *ummat* — is primary. Islam is seen as a set of concentric social circles, wider and wider communities — Modjokuto, Java, Indonesia, the whole of the Islamic world — spreading away from the individual *santri* where he stands: a great society of equal believers constantly repeating the name of the Prophet, going through the prayers, chanting the Koran.

Usman (a local Koran teacher, speaking to about twenty mostly illiterate peasants in a small, heavily *santri* village near Modjokuto on the occasion of the Prophet's birthday) gave as usual a series of unrelated commentaries on *hadiths* and Koranic passages. He started by saying, "The world is round, is it not, my brothers? You've seen it on the Nahdatul Ulama (one of the two major Moslem political parties) flag haven't you, and it is round, isn't it? Thus it is different times in different places, so that if it is evening prayer here, perhaps it is already morning prayer in Mecca, and further west in Cairo or Morocco it is already perhaps noon prayer, and there are all gradations in between, in Djokjakarta, in Djakarta, in Pakistan. There are three hundred million Moslems, my brothers, so that every minute of every day someone is saying *Muhammad ar-Rasulullah* (Muhammad, the Prophet of God), someone is saying it around this round globe. And this has been going on, my brothers, for 1,344 years. No one's name has been spoken so often as that of the Prophet, is it not true? If there is someone whose name has been spoken more often I would like to know who he is! We here in Sidomuljo, in a tiny village out in the corner of the countryside, are only a part of a great *ummat Islam;* in Modjokuto, in Djakarta, in Mecca, all over the world right now as we chant our prayers, Moslems just like us are chanting theirs."

Before the power and majesty of God all men are as nothing, and in their nihility they are equal. Cut off by an absolute gulf from direct experience of God and so restricted to the books of prophets, and especially to the Koran and the Hadith, for their knowledge of Him, mankind — a part now, the whole of it later — has bound itself into a legal community, defined by its adherence to a set of objective laws based upon the revelations God has seen fit to communicate to man. There are no priests, because no man is any closer to God or of any greater intrinsic religious worth than any other; but the law must be communicated, interpreted, and administered, and so there are teachers, judges, and officials, and schools, courts, and religious bureaucracies. It is the adherence to an objective, deductive, abstract law that defines a Moslem and defines the Moslem community; and, although in Java, as I imagine elsewhere, the greater flexibility of the inductive, relativistic, pragmatic customary law tends to be in practice more attractive to *santris* as well as *abangans* than the rigid beauties of the Koranic law, the sense for a concrete community regulated by an objective system of law is quite real in *santri* minds.

> We got on to Islam and he went over the usual business about the importance of the law as a compass, as a way of choosing between right and wrong. Admittedly, some people who don't know the law are good, but they don't have a sure guide and they may go wrong. Only those who have the Koranic law really can find their way safely through life to the afterlife. He read me a Koranic passage saying that the true Moslem is willing to labor and to sacrifice his money, his property, and all his personal resources for the good of society, to build mosques, schools, and so forth; and he said that this social conscience is obligatory to Moslems. It is like making a suit of clothes, he said. To make clothes that fit and won't fall apart the tailor needs to make measurements. For life, individual and social, we need measurements too, and there are in the Koran and the law.

This concern with the community means that, despite their tremendous interest in doctrine, Modjokuto Moslems never see their religion as a mere set of beliefs, as a kind of abstract philosophy, or even as a general system of values to which as individuals they are committed. Instead, they always conceive of it as institutionalized in some social group: the *santris* in their neighborhood, or all those they consider such in the Modjokuto area, or all Indonesian Moslems, or "the Islamic world." When they speak of Islam, there is almost always in the back of their minds a social organization of some sort in which the Islamic creed is the defining element. It may be a charitable organization, a woman's club, the village mosque committee, a religious school, the local office of the religious bureaucracy, or their political party at either the local, regional, or national level.

These two distinguishing features of the *santri* religious pattern — a concern for doctrine and apology and for social organization — crosscut one another to produce the internal structure of the Moslem community in Modjokuto. On the doctrinal level there is only one major distinction of importance, rather less marked now than it was in the years before the war: that between the "modern" (*modèren*) and the conservative or "old-fashioned" (*kolot*) variants of the creed. From 1912 almost until the war the conflict between those Indonesian Moslems who had been influenced by modernist Islamic reform movements originating in Cairo, Mecca, and, to a far lesser extent, in parts of India, and those who reacted against this influence, was indeed a sharp and bitter one. Today, this once entirely religious conflict has been transformed in part into a political one as the leaders of both groups have come to accept a general and watered-down version of modernism and have shifted their interest more and more towards the ever intriguing question of how they are going to get into power. But the old division still remains. Although many of the leaders of the "old-fashioned" group have abandoned the extreme reactionary position, many of the rank-and-file members have not; and the general distinction between modern *santris,* who accept the twentieth century with enthusiasm and see its complexities as but a challenge to be dealt with, and those who are at best resigned to it and its pitfalls for the pious, is still of fundamental importance within the Modjokuto *ummat.*

On the organizational side, Islam in Modjokuto is focused around four major social institutions: the Moslem political parties and their associated social and charitable organizations; the religious school system; that division of the central-government bureaucracy — largely under the Ministry of Religion — which is concerned with the administration of the Moslem law, the preservation of mosques, and other similar duties; and the more informal kind of congregational organization which focuses around the village mosque and the neighborhood prayerhouse. These four *institutional* structures interweave with one another and with the *modèren* and *kolot* ideological patterns to provide a complex framework for almost all the Moslem religious behavior which takes place in Modjokuto.

Prijaji versus *Abangan:* General Differences

Of course there are no sovereign courts in Java, and there have not been for centuries. The Dutch, however, not only drew their native administrators, teachers, and clerks from among the descendants of nobles and king but also permitted the two great courts of Djokjakarta and Surakarta to persist through the entire colonial period, having destroyed their military power and relieved their kings of any independent authority. Thus the cultural tradition persisted, grafted now to a progressively more rationalized colonial bureaucracy. The *prijajis* remained both the cultural leaders and, so far as the indigenous society was concerned, the political ones even though everyone was aware that the ultimate locus of power in the society had shifted into foreign hands. The gentry concern for etiquette, art, and mysticism continued, as did the peasant imitation of the forms they developed.

The *prijaji* religious orientation is more difficult to set off from the *abangan* than is the *santri,* because the change from a syncretic South Asian polytheism (or "animism," if "deity" is too elevated a term to apply to such as *ḍanjangs, ṭujuls,* and *ḍemits)* to a Mid-Eastern monotheism is rather greater than the shift from such a religion to a Hindu-Buddhist pantheism. The traits I shall discuss under *prijaji* are not confined to them. The *gamelan* orchestra and the *wajang* shadow-play, for example, could hardly be said to be absent from peasant life; but they are included in this context because their cultivation, the elucidation of their religio-philosophical meaning, and their most elaborate variations are found in a *prijaji* context; and because they have been pulled into and integrated with a general gentry style of life toward which the whole rest of the society, even the *santri* sector, to an extent and grudgingly, looks as the very model of civilized living.

Although the *prijaji* and *abangan* orientations, from the point of view of culture content, are in part but genteel and vulgar versions of one another, they are organized around rather different types of social structure and expressive of quite different sorts of values, a difference Cora Dubois has characterized, speaking of the entire Southeast Asian culture-area, as follows:

> Here was a class (the gentry) whose ethos was deeply at variance from that of the peasantry. It conceived of life in terms of hierarchy and power rather than in terms of simple communal democracy; in terms of privilege rather than mutual obligations; in terms of ostentation and aggrandizement rather than subsistence and communal obligations.[6]

Thus, as one traces *prijaji* patterns downward, they tend to shift in significance as they approach the *abangan* social context. Mystic practices tend to turn into curing techniques; a vague and abstract pantheism gives way to a vivid and concrete polytheism; a concern for individual religious experience is replaced by a concern for group religious reciprocality. And the corollary holds too: *abangan slametans* become *prijaji* formal banquets. In any case, although the *prijajis* and *abangans* have, in many ways, very similar world-views, and although they share many concrete items of religious belief and practice, the ethics which can be deduced from these underlying world-views and which the items are arranged to symbolize differ rather markedly.

NOTES

1. C. Snouck Hurgronje, *The Achehnese* (Leyden, 1906), p. 313.

2. *Ibid.* He also noted that "The [indigenous customs] which control the lives of the Bedawins of Arabia, the Egyptians, the Syrians, or the Turks, are for the most part *different* from those of the Javanese, Malays and Achehnese, but the relation of these [customs] to the law of Islam, and the tenacity with which they maintain themselves in despite of that law, is everywhere the same. The customary law of the Arabs and . . . of the Turks differ from the written and unwritten [customary law] of our Indonesians, but they are equally far removed from the revealed law, although they are equally loud in their recognition of the divine origin of the latter" (p. 280).
3. *Ibid.*
4. C. Snouck Hurgronje, *Mekka in the Nineteenth Century* (London, 1931), p. 291.
5. Actually, a more orthodox version of the Moslem creed has been characteristic of the peoples of the north coastal areas and of the small urban Javanese trading classes scattered throughout the larger and smaller towns all over Java since the conversion of the island to Islam in the fifteenth century. In these groups, where the mercantile tradition has also remained stronger, Islam has been rather less diluted with mystical and animistic elements than it was either in the great inland courts, such as those at Djokjakarta and Surakarta, or in the rice-plain peasant villages of the Solo and Brantas rivers, where syncretism was, and is, very strong. Thus the recent growth of Moslem orthodoxy in Java is, in part, a strengthening and widening of this persistent minority tradition, not a wholly novel development.
6. *Social Forces in Southeast Asia* (St. Paul, 1949).

The Religion of Java: A Commentary

HARSJA W. BACHTIAR

THE 'ABANGAN RELIGIOUS VARIANT'

In Dr Geertz's study it is reported that the Javanese acknowledge the existence of a distinct *abangan* religious variant or tradition. He observes that this particular religious variant is associated in a broad and general way with the village.

> The *abangan* religious tradition, made up primarily of the ritual feast called *slametan*, of an extensive and intricate complex of spirit beliefs, and of a whole set of theories and practices of curing, sorcery, and magic, ... is associated in a broad and general way with the Javanese village (Geertz 1960:5)

Although the author also associates the town proletariat, i.e. the urban lower classes, with the *abangan* religious variant, in another passage he definitely identifies the *abangan* religious variant with the peasantry.

> The *abangans* are Java's peasantry . . . . *Abangan* religion represents the peasant synthesis of urban imports and tribal inheritances, a syncretism if old bits and pieces from a dozen sources ordered into a conglomerate whole to serve the needs of an unpretentious people growing rice in irrigated terraces (Geertz 1960:229)

It may safely be concluded then that what is designated in the study as the *abangan* religious variant refers to what in common parlance would be called basic folk tradition, the tradition of the peasantry. The ritual core consists of *slametan*, or neighborhood feast, which is carried out to assure the psychological state of *slamet*, or the absence of emotional disturbance. With a complex of spirit beliefs and curing practices, the *abangan* religious variant represents 'a stress on the animistic aspects of the over-all Javanese syncretism,' the general religious system. It is a characteristic of the *abangan* people to be indifferent to doctrine and fascinated with ritual detail. Thus, in brief, is Dr Geertz's description of the *abangan* religious variant.

A closer scrutiny of the description, however, should yield the conclusion that perhaps the concept of *abangan* religious variant is in need of some drastic revisions. What does the term *abangan*, as understood by the Javanese, actually refer to? The term *abangan* is applied to people who are not concerned with religion. It has only meaning as the opposite of *santri*, or people who are involved, actively involved, with Islam. *Abangan* people, or *wong abangan* as the Javanese call them, means 'the red men,' as opposed to *wong putihan* or *wong kaputihan*, which literally means 'the white men' on account of the fact that those who are actively involved with the religion of Islam ordinarily are dressed in white. Those 'white men' who are affiliated with a theological school, *pesantren*, are called *santri*, a term which in common parlance is also used to refer to any religious person and therefore becomes a synonym of *wong putihan*. Non-religiosity, of

---

Reprinted in abridged form from *Madjalah Ilmu-Ilmu Sastra Indonesia* Vol. 5 (1973), 85–115, by permission of the author and the publishers.

course, need not be a characteristic of the peasantry; in fact, every village community has at least one prayer house, if not a mosque, where the prescribed Islamic Friday prayers are held. It is also not necessarily true that the religious in the village are limited to the wealthy peasants, as Dr Geertz implies when he qualifies his statement on the relationship between the *abangan* religious variant and the peasantry by his assertion that 'poorer peasants and town proletariat' are seen as typically *abangan*, or, for that matter, that the wealthy peasants are necessarily *santri*. There are many peasants who endeavor through all possible means to obtain enough funds to be able to make the pilgrimage to Mecca, the holy city of Islam.[1] After their return from this pilgrimage, they are usually regarded by their villagers as respected members of the community. The fact remains that before these *hadji*, for thus people who have made the pilgrimage to Mecca are called, succeeded to gather enough funds to be able to fulfill this Islamic precept, they may have been ordinary peasants. On the other hand, as might be expected, non-religious are also found among the urban people of every social category, including the nobility and the traders. Accordingly, it would be more accurate not to regard the so-called *abangan* tradition as the tradition of the peasantry or town proletariat.

It is thus argued here that *abangan* need not necessarily refer to 'basic folk tradition,' which is comprised of the cultural tradition of the common people, the wong *tjilik* (little men). In other words, it would be misleading to regard the cultural tradition of the peasantry as the *abangan* tradition.

As to the belief in animistic spirits, it is useful, and more in accordance with the facts, to make a clear distinction between 'folk belief' and Javanese religion (*agama Djawa*), although both involve the belief in spirits. 'Folk belief,'[2] which is manifested in the belief in a variety of spirits, malignant or beneficial, is, as has been noted previously, frequently regarded as superstition by those who adhere to the Javanese religion, especially by the sophisticated *prijaji*. Quite a number of these spirit beliefs are also found, although under different names, among other ethnic groups on some of the other islands of the Indonesian archipelago.

Since there are lower class *santri* people and since many *prijaji* people have been reared by lower class servants who were in a position to influence them, what is here designated as 'folk belief,' or animistic belief, is also common among those who Dr Geertz classifies as *santri* and *prijaji* people, although, quite naturally, they may not admit it.

The core of the *abangan* religious variant, we might recall, is, according to Dr Geertz, the *slametan* or communal meal. He distinguishes four main types of *slametan:* 1) those centering around the crises of life — birth, circumcision, marriage, and death; 2) those associated with the Moslem ceremonial calender — the birth of the prophet Muhammad, the ending of the Fast, the Day of Sacrifice, and the like; 3) those concerned with the social integration of the village, the *bersih desa* (literally: 'the cleansing of the village' — i.e. of evil spirits); and 4) those intermittent *slametans* held at irregular intervals and depending upon unusual occurrences — departing for a long trip, changing one's place of residence, taking a new personal name, illness, sorcery, and so forth. Such a classification, with the exception of those *slametan* that are related to the Islamic ceremonial calender, may suggest that the *slametan* is indeed associated with, if not the core of, the folk tradition as distinct from the *santri* and the *prijaji* tradition. But *slametan* are not exclusively held as a house affair, as Dr Geertz seems to suggest, but may also take place at the prayer house (*langgar*) or mosque. In former times, until not very long ago, the royal courts participated in *slametan* in a royal way.[3] Following Dr Geertz's logic, if the *slametan* is held at the mosque it should be an element of the *santri* religious variant; if it is held at the royal court it should be regarded as part of the *prijaji* religious variant, but since all participate in this particular type of ritual, *slametan* cannot actually be associated with any one of the three religious variants which Dr Geertz tried to describe. It is characteristic in this respect, that when a *prijaji* anthropologist offered a description of the life cycle rituals of the Javanese, 'especially of those on the higher social levels' since he is a participant of the culture of that class, his report turns out to be a description of a series of *slametan*, described as *adat* ceremonies (Cf. Koentjaraningrat 1957:19–63).

Perhaps one might be misled in thinking that the *santri* do not participate in *slametan* because of the fact that religious Moslems, *santri* people, may arrange to hold a *slametan* which, to make it more suitable to Islam, is offered as a *sedekah*, alms giving, considered to be a proper Islamic act.

As to *petungan*, or traditional calculation system, which Dr Geertz describes as a constituent part of the *abangan* religious variant, it should be noted that there are various kinds of *petungan*.[4] The simple type of *petungan* is more or less common knowledge and deals with rather ordinary situations which do not interest the more sophisticated Javanese. Weddings and other important endeavors, however, need more special care and accordingly use is frequently made of specialists in *petungan*, i.e. those who have specialized in knowledge about the calculation of propitious days. Thus, while ordinary people engage in *petungan* on their own, better situated people may make use of specialists which, of course, does not mean that they are not concerned with the proper timing of important endeavors. *Petungan* is, after all, regarded by the Javanese as a Javanese science.

Lastly, mention should be made of the fact that the belief in the supernatural powers of the *dukun*, or native curer, is not only limited to the lower class people, peasantry or urban proletariat. There are perfect examples of religious, and thus *santri*, and upper class, and thus *prijaji*, *dukun*, individuals who have mastered the knowledge to cure the sick by supernatural means.[5]

What, then, do the *abangan* people believe in? They may be atheists — one is reminded of the wide-spread and violent communist rebellion which occurred in the area of, or near, Modjokuto in 1948 — , agnostics, believers in animistic spirits, adherents of the Javanese religion, or Moslems who believe in God but who do not bother to be concerned with the more detailed aspects of that religion. They may put great emphasis on *adat* rituals, because a good Javanese is expected to be guided in his conduct by the Javanese *adat* prescriptions or merely because rituals are enjoyable, or they may not be interested in rituals at all.

It is, to conclude this discussion on Dr Geertz's *abangan* religious variant, true that *abangan* is understood by the Javanese to refer to an empirical social category — those who are not actively involved in the religion of Islam — but it is also true that Dr Geertz's description of it is rather misleading because, perhaps, of his assumption that the *abangan* tradition is identical with the 'folk tradition.'

THE 'SANTRI RELIGIOUS VARIANT'

To describe the '*santri* relgious variant' should be a more manageable task than to describe the *abangan* tradition, if there is really a distinct *abangan* tradition to be observed. In contrast to the *abangan* who are only identified, implicitly or explicitly, in a negative way — an *abangan* is a person who does not take Islam seriously — , the *santri* are identified with reference to more definite characteristics, to cultural patterns that are exclusively associated with the *santri*. These patterns, including a distinct system of beliefs, values, and norms, are, in fact, what is more known as the Islamic religious tradition.

The detailed description of the *santri* religious variant offered by Dr Geertz in his study may be summarized as follows: It is manifested in a careful and regular execution of the basic rituals of Islam, such as the five prescribed daily prayers, the Friday religious service in the mosque, the fast during the month of Ramadhan, and the pilgrimage to Mecca. It is also manifested in a whole complex of social, charitable, and political organizations, such as the Muhammadijah, Masjumi, and Nahdatul Ulama. Its values are anti-bureaucratic, independent, and equalitarian in nature. The *santri* themselves group into their own neighborhood, 'less so now than before the war, but still noticeably clustered.' And, lastly, 'it is fidelity in performing the prayers which, ultimately, defines a *santri*; *prijajis* and *abangan* almost never do them' (Geertz 1960:215).

Dr Geertz asserts very positively that in the Modjokuto social structure — in this matter it is suggested that Modjokuto represents Javanese society as a whole — the *santri* religious variant is associated with the market, the other two social-structural nuclei being the village and the bureaucratic government. Since the establishment of so positive a relationship between a distinct religious tradition and 'the market' may suggest the existence of an analogue between the '*santri* religious variant' in Java and Max Weber's spirit of Protentantism in Europe, a closer examination of the *santri* people, those who are considered to be *santri*, might be useful. The linkage between the *santri* religious variant and 'the market' is qualified by Dr Geertz as follows:

> Although in a broad and general way the *santri* subvariant is associated with the Javanese trading element, it is not confined to it, nor are all traders, by far, adherents of it. There is a storing element in the villages, often finding its leadership in the richer peasants who have been able to make the pilgrimage to Mecca and set up religious schools upon their return (Geertz 1960:5).

In a further passage, the *santri* who live in town rather than in the villages are even more positively identified: 'In town, most *santri* are either traders or small craftsmen, notably tailors (Geertz 1960:222). Such a statement strongly suggests the existence of a positive relationship between the *santri* religious variant, or tradition, and entrepreneurship, but does it reflect reality?

Dr Geertz's other data seem to indicate that in reality the *santri* constitute a more complex group of people. Is curious that the religious teachers, *kijaji*, and their students — the *santri* proper — , who are usually considered to constitute the nucleus of the *santri* people, are disregarded in favor of the traders who, if they are *santri,* are dependent on these religious teachers, orthodox or modern, for the formulation of the legitimate religious values and norms, the core of the *santri* tradition. Only when the *santri* are described in a more detailed manner, are the religious functionaries brought to the fore. Then it is noted that the orthodox religious teachers and their schools 'have formed, and to an extent still form, the nucleus of rural Islamic social structure' (Geertz 1960:180), or, plainly, the *santri.* In view of these diverse statements it is not very clear with whom the *santri* religious variant is regarded to be associated in Modjokuto, the traders or the religious teachers, the market or the mosque. Besides, as Dr Geertz observes himself, not 'all traders, by far' are adherents of the *santri* religious tradition.

Although Dr Geertz maintains that in the village the *santri* religious tradition is associated with the wealthy peasants, which obviously is in conformity with the assertion that in the urban areas the *santri* religious tradition is associated with the traders, the quotation cited above definitely states that there is a strong *santri* element in the villages, 'often finding its leadership in the richer peasants.' In other words, although the leadership among the *santri* in the village may be held by the wealth peasants, there are also ordinary peasants who are *santri.* Accordingly, the assertion that the peasantry, with the exception of the wealthy peasants, represents the *abangan* tradition while the wealthy peasants in the village together with the traders in town represent the *santri* tradition is a simplification which should be regarded as questionable.

Since active involvement with the religion of Islam, its beliefs, values, and norms, is the distinguishing property of the *santri,* it is reasonable to expect that among the Moslem population of Modjokuto the *santri* are found in every major social category, nobility and commoners, traders and peasants, young and old, the traditional and the modern, the educated and the uneducated, as it is also reasonable to expect *abangan* people in each of these categories. Actually, apart from those who are formally committed to the preservation, if not propagation, of Islam, such as mosque functionaries, religious teachers and students of the various religious schools, it is frequently difficult to identify a *santri.* Whether a person considers himself a *santri* or not a *santri* depends on the concept of *santri* this particular person holds: the term may be associated with a religious person, a person who regularly and dutifully observes the prescribed rituals, a student of a religious school, a person who has knowledge about the content of the Qur'an, a moralistic person, etc. Then, there is the matter of evaluation by other persons who may rest their evaluation on a concept of *santri* which differs from that held by the person evaluated. This, consequently, means that a person who regards himself to be a *santri* need not be regarded as *santri* by others, and the reverse, for there is really no uniform method of identifying a *santri.*There is no process of initiation which can be used as a marker; there is no formal membership. Thus, although it is relatively clear what the characteristics are of the *santri* religious tradition, it is frequently not very clear who are considered to be *santri.*

There are Javanese people who acknowledge the following distinctions among the *santri*: *santri leres,* or the religious and studious who reside at a religious school, *pesantren*, in order to pursue the knowledge being taught by the religious teachers; *santri blikon*, or those who are religious and knowledgeable but who disregard the observance of prescribed rituals; *santri meri,* or those who are not learned but strict in the fulfillment of the prescribed patterns of behavior expected of a *santri*; *santri blater,* or religious fanatics who may do more harm than good; and *santri ulia,* or those who regard it a real pleasure to be continuously involved in prayers and other religious prayers. Regarded by many as an oddity are the *santri birai* and *pasek dul,* members of devotional sects whose rituals involve sensual and sexual manifestations.

The *santri* need not be found grouped together to form a neighborhood, although clusters of houses occupied by *santri* people may be found in various locations of the town or country side, such as in the surrounding area of the mosque and the dwellings of the various religious teachers. The clusters of houses surrounding the mosque comprise what is known as *kauman* and the complex of dwellings of religious students surrounding the house of the *kijaji,* the religious teacher, as *pesantren.*

In the past, when villages were still parts of Javanese kingdoms, the villages were classified into ordinary villages, subject to regular taxation by the state, and 'free villages' (*desa perdikan*), not subject to taxation but responsible for the fulfillment of certain specified religious obligations. Some villages have acquired the status of 'free village' because they are the sites, or located near sites of holy places, such as the tomb of a great religious teacher; these villages are still known as *desa pekuntjen.* Some villages acquired this desirable status because religious schools, pesantren, were established within their territorial boundaries; and are, of course, known as pesantren villages. Some other villages became 'free villages' because their population were predominantly comprised of religious men; these villages are known as desa *keputihan-putihan*, or *mutihan* ('white villages'). All these villages may claim to be typical Javanese villages and so they are. However, it is more than obvious that the study of a *desa pekuntjen, desa pesantren,* or *desa keputihan* — the religiously oriented villages — may yield data about patterns of religious beliefs, values, norms and behavior that are quite different from data obtained in other villages.

It would not be necessary to elaborate on the characteristics of the *santri* religious variant since these characteristics are rather well known as the Islamic tradition.[6]

THE 'PRIJAJI RELIGIOUS VARIANT'

In a society where the prevailing normative system makes a clear distinction between the legitimate elite and the commoners, each of these social classes may be associated with a distinct religious tradition, one different from the other. If there is such a difference in religious tradition, each social class should manifest belief, value, and normative patterns that are exclusively associated with it. Since a particular religious tradition may be conceived as a syndrome, not all patterns need be unique, in the sense that they are not found in the other tradition, but some should certainly be so. There is a difference, however, between difference in kind and difference in development which should also be applied to the description and analysis of religion in communities such as Modjokuto. Differences in kind refer, of course, to phenomena which are distinctly different from each other without one being a stage of development of the other, while differences in development refer to the fact that one particular phenomenon differs from another because it is in a different stage of development but of the same kind. Difference in development, I suggest, should not be regarded as a criterium for the acknowledgement of the existence of a distinct religious tradition.

Dr Geertz assumes that the *prijaji,* the legitimate elite, manifest a distinct religious tradition designated as the 'prijaji religious variant' of the general religious system of Java.

> *Prijaji* originally referred only to the hereditary aristocracy which the Dutch pried loose from the kings of the vanquished native states and turned into an appointive, salaried civil service. This white-collar elite, its ultimate roots in the Hindu-Javanese courts of pre-colonial times, conserved and cultivated a highly refined court etiquette, a very complex art of dance drama, music, and poetry, and a Hindu-Buddhist mysticism. They stressed

> neither, the animistic element in the over-all Javanese syncretism as did the abangans, nor the Islamic as did the santris, but the Hinduistic . . (Geertz 1960:6)

In terms of the position of the *prijaji* in the Modjokuto social structure, Dr Geertz describes them as a white collar bureaucratic group who are, in terms of residence, town dwellers. In the past, they were supposed to be part of the 'court aristocracy,' a rather misleading portrayal.

The *prijaji,* who indeed comprise the traditional elite, are differentiated from the commoners by the possession of honorific titles which are ranked in accordance with a hierarchy of rights and duties. The titles are hereditary in a certain way: the children of a title holder have the right to possess a honorific title which is one rank lower than that of their father's, unless their father only possesses the lowest ranked honorific title in which case the children get the same title. Some of these titles, the lowest title being *Mas,* are *Raden, Raden Mas, Raden Pandji, Raden Temenggung, Raden Ngabehi, Raden Mas Pandji,* and *Raden Mas Aria.* The titles are usually placed, in the form of the initial letters of these titles, in front of the name of the title holder. These titles, then, serve as a means of identification.[7]

The honorific titles of the *prijaji* are not all 'court titles.' Some titles are or were obtained by virtue of appointment to an official position in the traditional patrimonial bureaucracies; these need not be 'court titles.' Some titles are held by virtue of being a member of the landed gentry; these titles are also not court titles. The possession of honorific titles is not limited to the male members of the legitimate elite, for the female members of the prijaji class are also in possession of titles, such as *Raden Roro, Raden Adjeng,* and *Raden Aju.* Accordingly, whether one is a true *prijaji* or only given the social prestige of a *prijaji,* although not actually a member of the *prijaji* class, depends on the possession of honorific titles. It is therefore a weakness of Dr Geertz's study not to have identified his informants by the possession or non-possession of honorific titles, especially considering the fact that an attempt is made to describe the *prijaji* tradition.

Members of the *prijaji* class are usually able to trace their genealogies to some illustrious persons in the recent, and sometimes distant, past. Reproductions of photos or paintings of these honored persons are usually put on display in the living room of the *prijaji* house. It is not unusual to have a visitor questioned by the mistress of the house about his genealogy to establish his position in the general genealogical scheme of the *prijaji,* in order to determine the proper rules of conduct in relation to that visitor. The *prijaji* class is, in contrast to the *abangan* and *santri* categories, a distinct social class. Non-*prijaji* members of the local elite, such as medical doctors, certain government officials, teachers, and military officers, may be regarded and treated as *prijaji* but with the awareness that they are not actually members of the prijaji class: they are regarded as *prijaji* by association, not by right.

If there is a *prijaji* religious tradition, distinct from the *abangan* and *santri* tradition, the tradition should be manifested by these honorific title holders. Dr Geertz's description of the '*prijaji* religious variant' is based on the assumption that the *prijaji* tradition and the *abangan* tradition were in the historic past two distinct subcultures, the *prijaji* tradition associated with the ruling elite and the *abangan* tradition associated with the ruled peasantry, which together comprised the sole constituent components of Javanese civilization, until the penetration of Islam brought about the existence of a third subculture, that of the *santri.* It is further assumed that the *abangan* religious tradition is essentially animistic while that of the *prijaji* more Hinduistic. The contrast is suggestive, but considering the facts is it legitimate? The answer depends very much on what Dr Geertz intended to describe. If he intended to describe the religious situation in Java when, some centuries ago, Hinduism had just been adopted by members of the ruling class, Dr Geertz's assumption may be right, although there is still a possibility that it is also not a true picture of the past. Historical studies have yielded information which indicate that ruling princes converted themselves to adherents of Hinduism in order to legitimize their authority, which implies that a substantial part of the population, of the peasantry that is, also believed in Hinduism of some sort. This applies also to the role of Islam in the historical past. If, on the other hand, Dr Geertz intended to describe the present situation, reality shows a more complex picture than Dr

Geertz seems to suggest by his classification and which even succeeded to be reflected in his descriptive material.

Briefly, the '*prijaji* religious variant' is described as follows: Its core consists of mysticism, aestheticism, and rank-consciousness. Great importance is attached to the difference between *lahir,* i.e. the external actions, motions, postures and speech of the individual, and *batin,* i.e. the inner or subjective life of the individual. Strict rules of etiquette, language forms, and classical art forms, like *wajang* (shadow play) and court dances, express and sustain the religious orientation of the *prijaji.* A distinction is also maintained between *alus* (refined) and *kasar* (coarse). Certain art forms that are associated with the *prijaji,* like the *wajang, gamelan* (a type of percussion music), *djoged* (court dance), *tembang* (a type poetry), and *batik* (wax and dye method of textile decoration), are regarded as *alus* in contrast to folk art forms, like *ludrug* (popular farce), *kledek* (female street dance), *djaranan* (paper horse dance), and *dongeng* (folktales) which are regarded as *kasar*. Mystical sects function as outlets for *prijaji* beliefs and practices. That, in short, is the content of the '*prijaji* religious variant,' which, it should immediately be noted here, is essentially a description of the characteristics of Javanese culture as a whole.

The necessary distinction between belief and knowledge is very relevant in any attempt to describe the 'prijaji religious variant,' since obviously the belief in a particular religion and knowledge about that religion need not necessarily go together. As the elite in Javanese society, the *prijaji* have more opportunity to acquire knowledge, traditional or modern, than have the commoners. Traditionally the *prijaji* are expected to be versed in literature and philosophy and to be trained in the classical arts. The traditional *prijaji* literature and philosophy consist of old and modern Javanese writings, and the great Hindu epics. The *prijaji* are expected, at least, to know something about them, for knowledge about these writings marks the true *prijaji*. They are therefore familiar, or are regarded to be familiar, with Javanese, Hindu, and Buddhist religious concepts, which may give the observer the impression that the *prijaji* tend to express their religious belief in Hindu terms.

The *prijaji* are trained to observe the proper forms of conduct in their behavior, patterns of conduct that are associated with the *prijaji.* They should be able to control themselves and not show their emotions. Self-control is considered to be a characteristic of the *ksatria,* which is, as has been suggested before, comparable to knighthood in medieval Europe. It may be associated with religious belief or not. There are quite a number of *prijaji,* particularly among the younger members, who are self disciplined but not conscious of religious beliefs in connection with this self-discipline. Obviously, in such a case self-control is not a reflection of spiritual force in Javanese minds but conformity to prescribed forms of conduct. Familiarity with Javanese and Hindu culture heroes are enforced by various art forms, like *wajang* and traditional dances.

Rather important, in getting an understanding of the *prijaji,* is the popularity of theosophy among them, which may explain certain patterns of thought among contemporary *prijaji.* In the last decades of the colonial period, theosophy was rather popular among Dutch intellectuals in Java. Lodges and clubs were established in various towns to discuss theosophical problems. Many *prijaji* became members of these groups because they had an opportunity to discuss the relationship between the religion of the Dutch members and their own and be on equal terms with these Dutch members. The more secular minded *prijaji* found the opportunity to be on equal terms with the Dutch in Rotary clubs. Otherwise, a strong distinction was maintained between the Javanese, the natives, and the Dutch, the colonialists. These theosophy groups have affected many *prijaji,* consciously or unconsciously, in their patterns of thought in regard to religious beliefs. Then, association with the Dutch themselves caused many a *prijaji* to be imbued with Dutch values, such as a great emphasis on cleanliness, and possessing a knack to rationalize the belief in non-Christian and non-Islamic beliefs in Western terms.

There are, then, a variety of religious beliefs among the *prijaji* instead of only one religious tradition which constitutes a variant of the general system of Javanese religion. There are, first of all, *prijaji* who are actively involved in the Islamic religion. They are the *santri prijaji.* They are usually elder persons. Their religiosity may express itself in mysticism or in a serious study of Islamic writings. In the historic past, prominent *prijaji* including ruling princes, had been *santri,* to mention only Sultan Agung and Prince Diponegoro. It is not implied here that the *santri prijaji* adhere to the Islamic tenets in their pure form. Secondly, there are *prijaji* who are not very much concerned with Islam. They are the *abangan prijaji.* Some of them are not concerned with religion at all; they may be atheists or agnostics, although it seems that there are not many of them. On the other hand, there are *prijaji* who are called *abangan* but who are really far from being irreligious. They may be adherents of the religion of their ancestors, *agama Djawa* or Javanese religion. Here again the religiosity of the believer in Javanese religion may express itself in mysticism of a sectarian or personalist type. The mystical sects described by Dr Geertz, belong to the category of Javanese religion sects for, although Islamic elements are part of the belief system of these sects, the core of their belief systems seems to be Javanese religion rather than Islam. Dr Geertz's unawareness of the distinctness of Javanese religion may explain the fact that, based on the existence of mystical sects led by *prijaji* teachers, mysticism is described as a characteristic of the *'prijaji* religious variant', not withstanding that some of these sects have a numerically large non-*prijaji* membership and that in the form of *tassawuf* mysticism is not uncommon among the *santri.* To conclude the roster, mention should be made of *prijaji* theosophists as discussed above.

It is my contention, then, that religious beliefs, values and norms of the *prijaji* are not essentially different from those that are found among the non-*prijaji*, but that, except perhaps in regard to Islam, the *prijaji* are more articulate in expressing their beliefs and values and, accordingly, possess a more developed, more sophisticated form of a religious tradition which, in more unpolished forms, is possessed by the commoners, the little men.

NOTES

1. Indonesia, including Java, has always been represented by the largest group of pilgrims at the annual religious rites at Mecca.
2. Studies about manifestations of animistic beliefs in Java include, among others, studies on 'superstition' among thieves. Cf. J.A.B. Wiselius (1872). R. Prawoto (1919). A Vergouw (1929). H.A. van Hien (1934). D.H. Meijer (1935), and J.E. Jasper (1935).
3. Cf. J. Groneman (1896), R.S. Tirtakoesoema (1932; 1933), T. Pigeaud (1932), and R.M. Noto Soeroto (1951–1952).
4. Cf. H.A. van Hien (1934), T. Pigeaud (1929).
5. Sosrokartono, a Javanese *prijaji* who was educated in Holland and a brother of Kartini, national symbol of Indonesian womanhood, practiced what is known as *dukun* knowledge. He became a well-known practitioner in Bandung where he died in 1951. His case is not unusual.
6. Cf. F. Fokkens (1877), L.W.C. van den Berg (1882; 1886), and Th. W. Juynboll (1903).
7. Cf. L.W.C. van den Berg (1902).

Javanese Terms for God and Supernatural Beings and the Idea of Power

KOENTJARANINGRAT

FAMILIAR AND UNFAMILIAR RELIGIOUS CONCEPTS

The Javanese people, particularly those who adhere to the Kejawèn religion,[1] have a system of belief in which all elements and concepts are dualistically viewed on the basis of various principles of differentiation, one of which utilizes the contrast between familiar and unfamiliar. Supernatural beings are therefore also divided into these two categories in this system, those associated with the early Javanese Hindu-Buddhist pantheon and mythology, i.e., the ancestral and local spirits, belonging to the familiar category, whereas the supernatural beings who are associated with Islam belong to the unfamiliar category.[2]

Kejawèn Unfamiliarity with Islam

The Kejawèn unfamiliarity with Muslim concepts, and particularly with Muslim supernatural beings is, of course, not difficult to explain. In contrast to the Hindu-Buddhist religious concepts which have influenced the indigenous Javanese religion probably from as early as the third or fourth century A.D., and which are therefore deeply rooted in the indigenous system of religious belief, Islam has affected the heartland of the Javanese civilization only quite recently, i.e., for about three centuries. After the fall of the capital of the Hindu-Buddhist Javanese empire of Majapahit in the Brantas Delta area, near the present-day Javanese city of Majakerta, in the early 16th century, the communities and principalities in the interior of Java, although not completely immune to Muslim influences, were apparently able initially to preserve their pre-Islamic Javanese cultural tradition.

My view of the Central Javanese attitude towards Islam differs from the picture drawn of the spread of Islam in Indonesia in general, and Java in particular, by a number of other scholars in the field of Indonesian studies, especially the American ones among them. One leading scholar, for instance, saw the process as one whereby a religion ". . . cut off from its centers of orthodoxy in Mecca and Cairo, vegetated, another meandering tropical growth on an already overcrowded religious landscape . . ." (Geertz 1960:125). The view that the kind of Islam that came to Indonesia (and hence also to Java) was one which, unlike the orthodox Islam from Mecca and Cairo, had picked up many mystical elements in Persia and India, and was therefore congruent with the contemporary Javanese traditional world view, is of course correct. The view that Islam in Java meandered seemingly uncontrolled, however, is very misleading.[3]

For the whole of the 16th century, Islam must still be regarded as the culture of foreigners, as it was the religion of the population of the ports and trading centers of Java's North Coast area, called by the Central Javanese the Pasisir Area. This population was, at least from the Central Javanese viewpoint, dominated by

Reprinted from R. Schefold et al. (eds.), *Man, Meaning and History. Essays in Honour of H. G. Schulte Nordholt* (Verhandelingen van het Koninklijk Instituut voor Taal-, Land- en Volkenkunde 89 [The Hague: Martinus Nijhoff, 1980]), pp. 127–139 by permission of the author and Koninklijk Instituut voor Taal-, Land- en Volkenkunde, Leiden, The Netherlands.

foreigners, such as Arabs, Persians, South Indians, and others. These foreigners had an unfamiliar way of life. Thus Islam was considered an alien religion at that period. And thus it did not "vegetate", an uncontrolled "meandering . . . growth" in Javanese society.

Even when, in the latter half of the 16th century Muslim influences from the north-eastern coastal region of Java succeeded in penetrating Java's interior owing to the emergence of a Muslim-oriented principality called Pajang, at the headwaters of the Solo River in Central Java, Islam must have continued to be considered alien, as there was not enough time to introduce it among the population of the area and to allow it to penetrate Central Javanese culture and tradition. The reason was that the people who brought Islam were unable to establish themselves long enough here, as in the last decade of the 16th century a rapidly emerging Central Javanese kingdom, Mataram, located to the west of Pajang, in the fertile basin of the Opak and Praga Rivers, in the middle of the Sumbing-Merapi-Merabu volcanic complex, succeeded in attacking Pajang and consequently in keeping the further political penetration of Islam under control.[4] This, however, did not prevent Mataram's ruler from paying lip-service to Islam, for the sake of maintaining good economic and political relations with Muslim powers outside Java.

With the rise of Mataram in the first half of the 17th century, and the simultaneous decline of the Javanese coastal ports during the same period, the opportunity for Islam to impress itself on the major centers of Javanese civilization by political force was also removed. So the majority of Javanese in the heartland of the Javanese civilization continued to view Islam as a remote and alien religion.

This situation lasted until the second half of the 17th century, when the political supremacy of Mataram declined as a consequence of internal quarrels over the succession. Its subsequent rulers became more and more dependent on the Dutch East India Company in Batavia, which often lent them military assistance to suppress rebellions of rival candidates for the succession and in return claimed large portions of Mataram's territory, which thus gradually passed into the hands of the Dutch in the course of the first half of the 18th century. In 1755 Mataram was divided into three small vassal states of the Dutch East India Company, and when in 1799 that company went into liquidation, these Javanese vassal states came under the direct control of the Dutch colonial government.

Socio-political instability then gave rise to cultural poverty and impotence and inability to resist a steadily advancing Muslim culture as Javanese intellectuals and poets at the Central Javanese courts, who had hitherto always set the standards of contemporary Javanese culture, were finally brought face to face with Islam.

THE ACCEPTANCE OF ISLAM

Muslim Missionary Activities in Rural Java

Moreover, the way in which some American scholars of Indonesian Studies visualize the process of the acceptance of Islam by the Javanese in the interior is very misleading. It is obviously inaccurate to assume that "after the fifteenth century, the [Javanese] rulers assumed Islamic titles, kept Islamic officials in their entourage, and added Islam to the panoply of their attributes" (Anderson 1972:58–59). Although the assertion by the same scholar that Islamization of the rulers of Java was superficial and that it "does not seem to have caused major alterations in their way of life and outlook" (Anderson 1972:59) is correct, Islam definitely did not spread rapidly in the interior of Java after the 15th century, and the Central Javanese rulers did not accept it, to add it "to the panoply of their attributes", without resistance.

Not until the period between the 17th and 18th century did Islam spread to the interior of Java. This started first in the rural areas as a result of the zeal of Muslim missionaries. The latter apparently made use of the pre-Islamic institution of the self-sufficient religious training community, consisting of a religious teacher, his family, and a few dozen of his students, who lived in a somewhat secluded spot away from the village community, near the edge of a forest. It appears that they converted the old pre-Islamic training communities into Muslim *pondhok pesantrèn* schools, which until today still form small, self-sufficient communities throughout rural Java. These consist of a compound with dormitories, workshops and a mosque, where a religious teacher and his students live, work, study and hold religious gatherings and ceremonies.

These communities, established along the main river valleys in the course of the second half of the 17th century and the first half of the 18th century, were the centers via which Islam penetrated the areas dominated by the Central Javanese courts. In the latter areas the predominantly pre-Islamic culture had thus far been able to survive.

Several of the best-known Muslim missionaries became canonized in Javanese folk belief. This popular belief in the semi-historical nine "apostles" of Islam, the Wali Sanga, according to Th.G.Th. Pigeaud probably developed in the 17th century (1967:150–152). The utterances and teachings of the most famous Muslim missionaries of that period must have been preserved for posterity by their students and their descendants. Their number was fixed at eight or nine, forming a kind of "Round Table of Saints", who were all contemporaries. The number nine was probably inspired by the Hindu-Javanese concept of the eight Lokapala deities guarding the eight points of the universe, with the ninth in the center.[5]

The congruence of Muslim mystical ideas with the contemporary general Javanese world view doubtless facilitated the institutionalization of the *pondhok pesantrèn* communities in the rural areas. However, there is ample evidence that the spread of mystical Islam in the course of almost two centuries even here did not take place without resistance.[6] Moreover, *pesantrèn* and *santri* communities seldom dominate a Javanese village community in its entirety, and usually isolate themselves as exclusive social units, rather than integrating into the larger community.

The Acceptance and Incorporation of Islamic Concepts in Court Circles

The process of the penetration of Islam into court circles seems to have met with even greater resistance. The integration of Muslim concepts and institutions into the Central Javanese court tradition seems to have occurred not until the second half of the 18th century.

Facing the advance of Islam from the rural areas and the imposition of Dutch political power from above, the Central Javanese court was unable to maintain its former isolation. Javanese intellectuals and poets of the second half of the 18th century, the guardians of the Javanese pre-Islamic cultural tradition, were obliged to accept Islamic concepts, and to incorporate them into the Central Javanese cultural tradition. This process has been studied by an Indonesian philologist, S. Soebardi, who among other things has edited and translated a number of manuscripts representing different versions of a long Javanese poem, the *Serat Cabolèk* (Bibliotheca Indonesica 10),[7] which was written by the court poet Yasadipura I[8] at the end of the 18th century. Soebardi has indicated a passage in the book which illustrates the resistance the spread of Islam met with, and how it was finally at the end of the 18th century that one of the aforementioned guardians of Central Javanese culture was obliged to give up his resistance to the advancing Muslim civilization. Yasadipura the elder, being well aware of the inability of the Javanese court tradition to resist the growing influence of Islam made a compromise in an effort to preserve at least the essence of Javanese cultural values and ideals. In the *Serat Cabolèk* he proposes the acceptance of Islam, on condition, however, that the Javanese consider the religion of Allah and the *shari'ah*, or Muslim law, only as a formal guide, or as a *wadhah* (container) for Javanese culture, while letting their inner spiritual life adhere to the essential values and ideals of Javanese culture, namely the search for spiritual purification and perfection, as well as the attainment of the Divine Unity, or the ultimate experience of the unity of Man and God. Soebardi has thus correctly pointed out the important fact that the ideas of poets such as Yasadipura I at the end of the 18th century prepared the way for the basically dualistic view of Kejawèn religion with respect to Islam. Islam had to be accepted, but only in its outward manifestation; the content and essence had to remain Javanese (Soebardi 1975:45–53). Although focused more particularly on the mystical tradition, Soebardi's analysis also sufficiently illustrates the general attitude of the Kejawèn Javanese towards Islam in the broader sense.

Another illustration of the way in which the Javanese have incorporated Islamic concepts into their court tradition is provided by the syncretic idea on the left- and right-hand lines in Javanese royal genealogies. The left-hand line (*alur pangiwa*), according to the Javanese conception of the cosmic order, constitutes the line linking the Hindu-Buddhist gods, the Pandawa heroes and Rama of the *wayang* epics, the nature gods, and the ancestral spirits, down to the Central Javanese kings; the right-hand line (*alur penengen*), on the other hand, comprises the holy *walis*. In the Javanese conception of history, the separation of the two lines occurred immediately after creation, but their original unity was re-established by a marriage of a member of the Central Javanese royal house with a descendent of the *walis* (Pigeaud 1967 I:151). In connection with this idea of the re-established unity between the *pangiwa* and *panengen* lines of descent, the 19th-century kings of Central Java instructed their court poets to write a history of the nine *walis* in which the unification theme was incorporated.

KINSHIP TERMS AND OFFICIAL TITLES

Kinship and Power Relations

The dualistic view which differentiates the Javanese Hindu-Buddhist religion from Islam is also reflected in the terms of reference or address and titles for God and supernatural beings. Javanese etiquette always requires the use of honorific terms or titles to refer to or address other people. The omission of such terms or titles (*njangkar*) is permissable only where a person is referring to or addressing another person whom he considers a very close friend or someone occupying a subordinate position.

In referring to or addressing superiors or equals with whom one is not on intimate terms these titles and terms are obligatory. In a like way the Javanese utilize honorific terms and titles to address or refer to God and supernatural beings in exclamations, prayers, or ordinary conversation. Different terms and titles are used for supernatural beings from the Javanese Hindu-Buddhist religion and for those of Islam, however.

The relationship of man to the Hindu-Buddhist gods, the heroes of the *wayang* epics, the nature deities, the ancestral spirits, and the spirits of local saints is conceived of by the Javanese as a relationship to senior but intimate kin, whereas the relationship to the Allah of Islam, to Muhammed, Allah's prophet, and to the other prophets, the *walis*, and the Muslim saints is considered as one to powerful but distant beings. Consequently the Javanese consistently use the kinship terms *hyang, éyang, kyai, nyai*, or *mbah* to refer to or address the deities or spirits, and the titles for kings or high officials, such as *gusti, kanjeng*, of *sunan*[9] to refer to or address Allah, the prophets, and the *walis*. The supreme eternal spirit of the universe, for instance, is called Sang Hyang Guru; the latter's destructive aspect is called Sang Hyang Bathara Kala; the spirit of the ocean is called Eyang Lara Kidul, or Nyai Lara Kidul; the local spirit of a particular area is called Mbah Untung, and so on. Allah, on the other hand, is called Gusti Allah; His prophet is called, or addressed as, Kanjeng Nabi Muhammad; the individual *walis* are called Sunan Kali Jaga, Sunan Bonang, Sunan Giri, Sunan Ngampel, etc.[10]

Muslim Supernatural Beings and Power

Although Islamic Supernatural beings have become integrated into the Javanese system of belief alongside the pre-Islamic ones, a distinction between the two categories thus is maintained by the difference in the terms of address. These have now become institutionalized in the Javanese language, and are uttered automatically in conversation and in exclamations. The question as to when these terms may have become institutionalized is difficult to answer, and requires a special study. It is obvious, however, that with these terms the Javanese associate Allah, the prophets and the saintly Muslim missionaries with high office, high rank, and power.[11]

THE JAVANESE IDEA OF POWER

At this point it may be appropriate to comment on the traditional Javanese idea of power as envisaged by a number of scholars of Indonesian Studies, especially B.R.O'G. Anderson in his well-known essay on the subject (1972). According to these scholars, the Javanese consider power as a concrete existential reality, which exists independently of its possible users. They maintain that, in contrast to Europeans, who consider power as an abstract secular aspect of a human relationship which has a heterogeneous source and no inherent limits and is morally ambiguous, the Javanese think of power as a homogeneous, constant, intangible, divine energy which animates the universe and is thus without inherent moral implications as such (Anderson 1972:4–8).

In my opinion, traditionally oriented Javanese, too, think of power in terms of an abstract quality, or an aggregate of abstract qualities, just as Europeans do. The difference lies in the fact that, unlike the Europeans, they attribute these qualities, which they call *kawibawan*, not to particular types of human relationship, but to specific persons. These qualities are the human qualities which are idealized by the majority of the members of society and which therefore have deep moral implications.[12] Three of these qualities are universal human virtues, and must therefore also be relevant in the European conception of power. For example, a human being who in the eyes of the people is just and righteous (*adil tan pilih sih*), possesses great wisdom (*wicaksana*), and is generous and bountiful (*bèrbudi tan pamrih*), possesses some of the important requirements which will enable him to become powerful. This obviously does not differ very significantly from the European conception of power as a human relationship whereby certain persons or groups of persons are obeyed by others willingly or unwillingly, due to their ability to dispense justice, to show exceptional wisdom, or to display great wealth.

Traditionally oriented Javanese, like Europeans, are well aware of the fact that the possession of physical strength (*patohan kadigdayan*), or the ability to mobilize and organize physical strength, constitutes a principal source of power. Early as well as more recent Javanese history provides ample examples of kings or other leaders planning or evolving rational strategies for the accumulation or organization of concrete physical strength, while the pursuit of power on the exclusive basis of the power of some magic heirloom or mysterious weapon, or through rigorous asceticism actually only occurs in legends, *wayang* stories and myths.

There is indeed one basic difference between the traditional Javanese and European conceptions of power which relates to the fundamental problem of the source of power. This in turn affects the way in which each conceives of the problem of the quest for power, the acquisition and preservation of power, and the problem of succession to positions of power. The Javanese of the time of the early as well as the more recent Javanese kingdoms and of the period of colonial domination regarded power strictly as a quality possessed by sacred kings, feudal lords and princes, authoritative foreign administrators and despotic high-ranking officials. They experienced it only in the form of arbitrary orders or instructions, which flowed downwards from the top. And they learned to accept the belief that the source of the power possessed by such extraordinary, foreign, or high-ranking persons was heredity, divine appointment, or some other incomprehensible, mysterious historical condition or event, which they had come to accept as decreed by fate.

Legitimation of power by means of democratic election is therefore irrelevant for traditionally oriented Javanese. For them power is an ascribed quality which is obtained through inheritance or by divine favour. Consequently the quest for power does not necessitate efforts to gain public support and approval, while the pursuit of popularity through public appearances, and so on, comes to constitute a hindrance rather than a useful means towards the acquisition of power. In traditional Javanese societies the power of a leader is enhanced by keeping aloof from the people, by remaining distant and hidden from view, or through the mere fact of being a foreigner. However, the image of a just and righteous, immensely wise, and exceptionally generous king, leader or high-ranking administrator requires a constant effort of preservation and intensification by means of the appropriate ceremonial acts and rites, wherein material objects, incantations, and acts symbolizing the qualities of power and authority play a key role.

In addition to the afore-said physical attributes which symbolize the profane aspects of power and authority, an important attribute that reinforces the rituals for the preservation and intensification of power, according to the traditional Javanese point of view, is magical energy (*kasektèn*). Although kings and leaders are believed to possess such magical energy, it is an error, however, to consider *kasektèn* as the main and most important source of power and authority, or, as Anderson has done in his above mentioned essay (1972:7–19), to identify *kasektèn* with power. Many Javanese individuals are considered to possess the same kind of *kasektèn* as that possessed by the legendary claimant to the throne Ken Arok, or by such legendary heroes as Arya Penangsang or Untung Surapati. And those who are believed to be able to accomplish extraordinary feats are not only respected individuals such as religious teachers, curers and *dhukuns*, but also the common folk dancers of Ponorogo (East Java), the *waroks*, and even thieves and criminals.[13] No Javanese, however, will regard the latter individuals as being in possession of the necessary power which will make them eligible for leadership, or potential just, wise, and generous kings.

CONCLUSION

The use of royal and official titles and terms of address and reference for Allah, the prophets, the saints who brought Islam to Java, and other supernatural and legendary Muslim figures has indicated that in the Javanese system of belief Allah and those other beings are conceived of as a king or as high-ranking officials. As a result they are attributed qualities which in the traditional Javanese conception support the components of power.

The Kejawèn Javanese unfamiliarity with Islam and Islamic concepts coincides with that very same traditional Javanese conception of power which implies unfamiliarity. Powerful individuals are attributed universal qualities such as justice, wisdom and generosity; they naturally also possess the major component of power, i.e., the ability to mobilize and organize physical force. Unlike the European concept of power, however, the traditional Javanese concept omits the component of public approval. Moreover, a king or leader should even avoid as much as possible exposing himself to the public, since this may taint his holiness and thus damage his charisma.

In European industrial democratic societies, public approval, rather than charisma, forms an important component of power. For here the main source of power is public support, rather than descent, divine appointment, or a particular sacred historical mission. The authority of the leader is legitimated by public election and legal procedures, rather than through ritual intensification. In Javanese traditional society such ritual intensification has to take place repeatedly; on such occasions sacred objects which symbolize authority occupy a central position.

In conclusion, the above discussion may be summarized in the following diagram, comparing the components of power and the required qualities of leaders according to the European and to the traditional Javanese concepts.

European Industrial Societies

	Components of power	*Required qualities of a leader*
Power	Public approval	Popularity
		Possession of rational capacity and intellectual expertise
		Embodiment of community norms and ideals
	Authority	Acquisition of legitimacy through legal procedures
	Authority / Charisma	Possession of the symbols of authority
	Charisma	Possession of spiritual qualities
	Power in the restricted sense	Ability to mobilize and organize physical strength

Javanese Traditional Society

	Components of power	*Required qualities of a leader*
Power	Charisma	Proper descent
		Divine appointment
		Having a sacred historical mission
		Possession of *kasektèn*
	Authority	Embodiment of community norms and ideals
		Acquisition of legitimacy through ritual intensification
		Possession of sacred symbols of authority
	Power in the restricted sense	Ability to mobilize and organize physical strength

NOTES

1. The term *Kejawèn* refers to the variant of Javanese Islam which in Indonesian studies is usually called the *Abangan* religion. The term *Kejawèn* or *Agami Kejawèn* more often used by the Javanese themselves, means 'Javanese religion' (from *Jawi* = Java; and *agami* = religion). The term *Abangan* was first used in an early article on Javanese customs, world view, and religion by a Dutch missionary, C. Poensen (1870:312). Here, however, the term *Bangsa Abangan* (Red People, or non-puritan Muslims) was used in contrast to *Bangsa Putihan* (White People, or puritan Muslims). C. Geertz was the first in academic circles to introduce the terms *abangan* and *santri* to designate the two variants of Javanese religion in his book on the subject (1960). At present the term *abangan* in many areas of Java, particularly Central Java, is a degrading term for Javanese who do not take Islamic doctrines and norms seriously. It can be used jokingly, but otherwise may offend people. The term *santri* formerly simply meant 'religious person'. Such religious persons used to take up residence in a particular ward of the town where the mosque was located. Subsequently communities of *santri* people living in particular wards developed, and came to be called *kauman*.
2. The Javanese conceptualization of Islam as an alien religion has also drawn the attention of another Dutch missionary, B.M. Schuurman, who in his dissertation *Mystik und Glaube in Zusammenhang mit der Mission auf Java* (1933), with special reference to Javanese mysticism, drew a distinction between a Javanese *einheimische mystische Strömung* based on the Hindu-Javanese religion, and a Javanese *ausländisch-geprägte Mystik* based on Muslim principles. See also the approving comments on this distinction in a lengthy review of the book by the Dutch mission advisor H. Kraemer (1934).
3. Moreover, the metaphor of an "overcrowded religious landscape" is hardly to be taken seriously. I wonder whether an "overcrowded religious landscape" really does exist in any culture at all.
4. For the history of Central Java in the 16th century, see De Graaf and Pigeaud's book on the history of the early Islamic states in Java (1974).
5. This concept is still preserved today in that of the *Debata Mawa Sanga,* the Nine Gods, in the Hindu-Dharma Balinese religion.
6. This part of the social history of the spread of Islam in rural Java requires a special study involving more specifically the intensive study of the 16th–18th century Javanese *pondhok pesantrèn* literature, supported by a deeper understanding of the world view and social structure of *pesantrèn* communities in particular, and of *kauman santri* society in general.
7. The *Serat Cabolèk* is a long poem consisting of 15 cantos (one of the manuscripts representing one particular version of the poem even comprising 23 cantos), each of which contains an average of 30.8 stanzas of 18–65 lines. One version of the poem totals 709 stanzas (Soebardi 1975).
8. Yasadipura I (died 1830 A.D.) was court poet during the reign of two Mataram kings, i.e., Paku Buwana III (1749–1788 A.D.) and Paku Buwana IV (1788–1820 A.D.). His son, Yasadipura II, was also a court poet, who has written such books as *Panitisastra Jarwa* (1819 A.D.).
9. *Hyang* means 'ancestor'; *éyang* is the Krama term for 'grandfather' or 'grandmother'; *kyai* means 'old man'; *nyai* means 'old woman'; and *mbah* is the Ngoko term for 'grandfather' or 'grandmother'.
10. *Gusti* is a term of address for a king or queen; *kanjeng* is a term of address for a regent; *sunan* is a title for a king.
11. This does not mean that the non-Islamic supernatural beings are less powerful than those associated with Islam; the non-Islamic supernatural beings are, however, more familiar, associated more with the day-to-day affairs of the Javanese family and household, so that communication with them assumes a less formal character.
12. Although the moral values and norms themselves naturally differ from those visualized by scholars such as Anderson and others.
13. A notorious criminal in the mountainous area of Celapar in South Central Java, where I did field work in 1958, boasted of having acquired *kasektèn* by rigorous asceticism in the same sacred spot (*pertapan*) as that where the local folk hero, Untung Surapati, is believed to have practised asceticism. According to local belief he must therefore have acquired the same *kasektèn* as that possessed by Untung Surapati. However, the local population did not regard him either as a hero or a leader.

Religion at the Village Level*

S. HUSIN ALI

RELIGIOUS BASIS

Close interactions and feelings of solidarity also arise among the villagers as a result of the common religious faith that they hold. Most of the villagers — in fact all the Malays — are Muslims. In Islam they have a religious as well as a cultural and social bond that holds them together. They strongly identify themselves with Islam to show that they are Malays. The feeling that normally prevails is found in expressions such as, 'We Muslims are all relatives, and we are in a big family'. Ideally of course the spirit of 'brotherhood-in-Islam' is shared among many.

Islam first began to spread among the Malays during the height of the Melaka kingdom in the fifteenth century. Since then it has penetrated extensively into many aspects of Malay life, to the extent that now the profession of Islam is almost inseparable from the acceptance of an individual as a Malay. Culturally speaking, the expression 'enter into Islam' (*masuk Islam*) is regarded as being synonymous with 'enter into or become Malay' (*masuk Melayu*). Legally, it has been embodied in the country's Constitution that by definition a Malay is someone who speaks the Malay language, practises Malay customs and professes Islam.

Ideologically, those who profess Islam believe that God (*Allah*) is supreme and that he is the ultimate source and cause of everything. The unity of God is an important doctrine of Islam, but it also tolerates the existence of other supernatural spirits, like the *syaitan* and *jinn* which are also the creation of God. Through the process of magic, man is able to 'tame' these beings and use them as agents of either good or evil. Their powers, however, are limited and they cannot have any effect unless God wills it.

Villagers often carry out their religious rituals on the basis of existing social units or institutions. One such unit is the family. The daily prayers and the fasting during the month of Ramadhan are done mainly at home. Often the reciting of these prayers are led by the father and followed by the wife and children. This collective prayer is practised as often as possible, especially in families where the father is quite old and religious, and it is believed that the virtues bestowed by praying together are much more than those obtained by praying alone. Again, during the fasting month, the breaking of the fast at sunset is normally looked forward to, especially by the younger children. Quite often sweet dishes are prepared, and the food served is normally much better than the usual dinner eaten at other times. When they break the fast they are together most of the time. In fact, during the fasting month the household members are closer together than usual, and among various households in the homesteads or neighbourhood, they normally exchange sweet dishes. When the wooden drum at the

---

Excerpted from S. Husin Ali, *Malay Peasant Society and Leadership*, (Kuala Lumpur: Oxford University Press, 1975), by permission of the author and the publishers.

mosque is beaten and the call to prayer is made to indicate that it is time for the breaking of fast, the members of the household will first of all take a date and then drink some beverage or other sweetened water. Then, quite often, they perform the evening prayer together, after which they sit down cross-legged around the food to have their dinner.

Another important institution is the prayer house (surau) and the mosque. Usually there is a small prayer house in a village, but there can be more than one if the village is sufficiently large. These prayer houses, like the mosques, serve mainly as religious centres; the only difference being that the Friday congregations are not held in them but in the mosques. The prayer house is constantly used by a few elderly people in the village to perform both their evening and night prayers. During the day the people are often involved with their own work, and so they seldom say their two afternoon prayers (*Zuhur* and *asar*) at the prayer house. By the evening, however, most of the them are already free and so they are able to gather together and perform their evening prayers (*maghrib*) at the prayer house. Some may even linger on and then recite the night prayers (*isyak*) collectively before going home. In between the two prayers they may read a chapter from the Quran or perform a kind of mystical ritual known as the *tahlil* in praise of God and the Prophet. In the course of this ritual, the participants utter repeatedly, 'There is no God but Allah' (*Lailaha illa Allah*), slowly at first before picking up speed. While doing so they move their heads or bodies sideways from left to right with each utterance, and have their eyes closed in full concentration. Besides these utterances, there are others in praise of the Prophet, and some verses of the Quran are also repeated together. Finally the leader of the ritual ends by reciting a prayer in Arabic to ask for blessing for the dead and protection and long life for the living. The tahlil is normally performed on Thursday nights, on the eve of Friday which is the day for the weekly congregation, and regarded therefore as the most blessed day of the week.

It is during the fasting month that the prayer houses and mosques are most often used. After breaking their fast, some of the people, adults as well as the children, and a few women, congregate at the prayer house or mosque. First they perform together the night prayer, led by the imam (literally a 'prayer leader'), and this is followed by what is known as the *tarawih* which is also a prayer, but performed only during the fasting month. The tarawih is performed at night, and is only commendable (*sunat*) and not compulsory (*wajib*) like the five daily prayers. There are more people participating in these prayers held in the fasting month than those carried out at other times of the year. After the tarawih most of the people go home, although some would stay behind, and together they read the Quran by turns prior to the performance of the tahlil. This goes on until about midnight when they return just in time for the late supper (*sahur*) which is also provided in some mosques.

In the Kangkong area there is only one mosque and there is no prayer house for the two villages. It is in this very mosque that most of the religious rites described above take place. At one time it used to be the focal point for villagers from both Kuala Kangkong and Permatang Kangkong, but after the occurrence of some political conflicts between the followers of the two political parties in the area, some of the villagers in Kuala Kangkong ceased to go to this particular mosque, and instead joined the congregation at the mosque in a neighbouring village. Since the mosque is rather far away, more and more of the villagers have begun to return to the one in Kangkong.

In Kerdau there are a number of prayer houses and mosques. The people in Pekan Kerdau have none of these and they normally join the Friday congregation at the mosque in Ketam or in Kuala Kerdau. There is a prayer house shared by the people of Kelibang and Guntung, but there is none for Macang Manis, Huma Luas and Kuala Kerdau. These last three villages share a common mosque situated in Kuala Kerdau, and in addition to the people from these three villages, those from Kelibang and Guntung also congregate here for their Friday prayers. The prayer leader for this mosque is also the headmen for Kelibang and Guntung. Parit and Peragap do not have their own prayer house, but there is one in Teluk Batu, and it is to this surau that most people in the three villages go.

There are also some, however, who go to the mosque in Kuala Kerdau. As for the Bagan area, there is a mosque at the end of Parit Besar, furthest away from the main road, and there are also two prayer houses situated near the roadside and around the middle of the village. The prayer house near the road holds evening prayers and also tahlil and tarawih, but the people around it join the rest of the village for Friday prayers in the mosque. There are also some others from Parit Bengkok, living at the furthest end of the village and away from the main road, who also join the Friday congregation at the mosque in Parit Besar. As for the rest of the people in Parit Bengkok, they perform their Friday prayers in a mosque that is by the roadside. There are at the same time two prayer houses in the village.

These prayer houses and mosques are not only used for religious purposes but also occasionally for meetings that are held to discuss village matters. There have been many occasions when the mosques and prayer houses have been used as a meeting place to elect the headman or penghulu. In fact they are also used by some villagers to discuss the need to carry out some rituals that are related to magical powers.

Although Islam is strongly entrenched in Malay society and culture, this does not mean that it has displaced the traditional beliefs. Traditional beliefs coexist with Islam is most of the villages. In traditional Malay beliefs, there are ghosts (*hantu*) and spirits (*jembalang, penunggu, semangat*). These supernatural beings are believed to reside in all things in nature—mountains, hills, seas, rivers, land, trees, rocks and so forth. In the daily activities of the people, due respect must be shown to them, otherwise they are capable of causing pain, suffering and disaster. Therefore if a person wants to go through a forest or climb a hill, for example, he has first of all to ask for permission by saying, 'Salutations venerable one, may I pass' (*Tabik datuk, saya tumpang lalu*); or if he wants to open up a piece of land, either for the construction of a house or for cultivation, it is necessary to pacify the spirits guarding the place or to drive them away. In the same way, evil spirits are driven away before the planting season, and due care must be taken not to upset the spirit or vital spirit (semangat) in the crop before harvesting, as this is believed to be responsible for bringing about good harvests.

Now from the ideological or doctrinal point of view, these spirits upheld in traditional beliefs fall outside Islam, for unlike the syaitan and jinn they are not mentioned in the Quran. Furthermore, the traditional spirits are believed at times to be the source of power and the ultimate cause of anything which occurs. Such a belief therefore runs counter to Islam because it encourages a form of polytheism (*syirik*). But in spite of this, the traditional belief systems still prevail, primarily because they are deeply embedded and they have defied many an attempt to uproot them. Also, the existence of the spirits has been rationalized by the acceptance of God as the final arbiter and that their powers are subject to the overriding power of the Almighty. Anything that happens is explained in terms of His power and will. A healthy body or a good harvest is not in the final analysis attributed to the power of things such as fertilizers or medicine, just as a bad harvest or illness cannot be attributed to the power of evil spirits or witchcraft. The fertilizer and medicine, like the spirits and witchcraft, are not the 'ultimate' but only the 'immediate' causes; they are mere agents whose effectiveness is subject to the power and will of God.

The belief in magic is related mainly to both the productive and protective aspects of the life of the people in the village. By the productive aspect is meant the process of economic production. At some stages of this production a number of rituals involving magical beliefs are still carried out by people individually or collectively in the hope of getting a better harvest or driving away pests and other evils that can cause damage or destruction to their produce. By the protective aspect is meant practices believed to protect people who have been inflicted by evil spirits. When Muslims resort to the help of the spirits through their mediums for curative or productive purposes, they are doing so simply as an 'attempt' (*ikhtiar*) to ward off any ill-fated consequences. This is in line with the doctrine that although man's fate is fundamentally predestined, he is free to make an 'attempt' in the hope that it may be changed. It is through such rationalization that ideologically the belief in traditional spirits is tolerated to some degree by many Muslims, although strict doctrinarians among them continue to insist that beliefs in spirits and the evil practices associated with them are non-Islamic.

With regard to rites, the position is slightly more complicated. There are rituals that can be said to be purely Islamic in nature, such as the daily prayers, fasting and pilgrimage. Of course it may be argued that even in these rites, particularly fasting and pilgrimage, their origins can be traced to the influences of certain pre-Islamic practices. When we say that these rites are purely Islamic in nature, it means that they have become an integral part of Islam. In these rites, the incantations uttered and the acts performed are regulated by the Islamic teachings, and they are followed rigidly according to the forms specified, without allowing themselves to be modified by any cultural influences.

At the other extreme, there are rites that are primarily if not entirely the product of traditional culture. Examples of these rites in the three communities studied are those relating to the planting and harvesting of crops, the opening of new residential sites and the protection of the villages from evil. They are related to the belief in the existence of different spirits, and distinctly belong to traditional sources quite unrelated to Islam. Today, they have, however, imbibed certain elements of Islam in their practices. The magicians who perform the rites normally begin by uttering 'In the name of Allah the Merciful and Compassionate' (*Bismillah ir-Rahman ir-Rahim*) which is a definite admission of the Omnipotence of God. The Muslim form of greeting is used, and praises to the Prophet are also invoked. Apparently in the rather lengthy incantations recited by the magicians during these rites, the Prophet and God, besides the spirits, are also invoked to give assistance. There are times when the Quranic verses are used as they are believed to have supernatural efficacy, and are regarded as effective means through which help can be asked for directly, not from the spirits but from God Himself. It is not surprising therefore that during some of these rites, religious men are often invited to conclude the ceremonies by saying prayers in Arabic. All these ritual practices therefore show not only the influence of Islam, but also the symbols of acceptance of God as the supreme being. As one person aptly sums it up, 'We are all human beings. We carry out all these rites only as an "attempt" (ikhtiar) to change our fate. But we submit everything to God, because He determines all.'

In contrast to the purely Islamic rites and those which are predominantly traditional, though displaying certain Islamic influences expressed mainly in the invocations, there are also many others that combine both these forms within the same rite. These rites can be placed in between the purely Islamic and traditional forms. Examples of these are found in the *rites de passage* and those related to hair-cutting, marriage and death.

There are several practitioners of traditional beliefs found in the rural communities. Some of these practitioners operate in specified areas; sometimes their activities cover a village and at other times areas beyond it. In Kangkong there are three practitioners who practise only within their own villages and the rites that they carry out often involve merely some of the members of the village. In Bagan, there are those who carry out rites involving only some of the members within the village, but there is also one individual who is sought after and who performs the rites in a wider area beyond that covered by Bagan itself. As for Kerdau, the situation is more well-defined. Besides the single practitioner who carries out these traditional rites in the whole area of Kerdau, there are also two others, one having jurisdiction over Kelibang and Guntung and the other presiding over Huma Luas, Macang Manis and Kuala Kerdau. Although the areas of 'jurisdiction' of these practitioners vary, some rites that they carry out are sometimes confined to the household, the neighbourhood, and at other times to the village. Of the rites that are applicable to the whole village, the best-known is that which protects the village (*membela kampung*). Such activities, like other religious practices, tend to bring into closer relationship members within the same village.

RELIGIOUS FUNCTIONARIES

Leading roles in religion are normally held by specialists in the field who act in various capacities. By religion here is meant both

Islam and the traditional belief system, and it follows therefore that there are also religious functionaries who play leading roles in the Islamic and traditional religions. Among the religious functionaries, besides those who specialize in either the practices of Islam or traditional beliefs, there are also others who combine their roles in both fields. The people who play leading roles in Islam are mainly the religious persons who are known by various names, such as *imam, lebai,* and *ustaz,* while those who play leading roles in traditional beliefs are known as *pawang* and *bomoh*. Their roles will be explained subsequently.

Among the villagers the most important criterion used for assessing whether a person is a good Muslim is whether or not he carries out the Islamic rituals. The majority of the villagers observe at least the daily prayers, the month-long fast during the month of Ramadhan and the payment of annual tithes (*zakat fitrah*) following the fasting month. Although as part of the Five Pillars of Islam they are considered to be obligatory, yet there are those who do not perform them, or perform them only irregularly. The social sanction on fasting seems to be more severe than that on praying. Not only is a person normally more strict with himself on fasting than praying, but also the attitude of the public and the religious authorities towards those who do not fast is more stern than to those who do not pray. For example, officials of the religious departments and also police officers are empowered to arrest and prosecute Muslims who are seen eating or drinking during the fasting month, but there is nothing similar that can be done to those who do not attend Friday prayers, and what is more those who do not perform the daily prayers. In spite of this, fasting is less strictly observed by the young than the old, especially the former who have undergone an English education and are without a firm religious foundation.

In fact, those who pray and fast during the times specified by Islam as 'compulsory' (wajib), and who in addition also observe the prayers and the fasts which are categorized as only 'commendable' (sunat), are regarded as highly religious and they earn the respect of the villagers. If they have also gone on a pilgrimage and have therefore become hajis, they often rise further in status. There are many religious persons of this type in the three areas studied.[1] They can easily be distinguished from other villagers for they normally wear white caps daily — even at home — and during Friday congregations, religious festivals (e.g. the *Id* to mark the end of the fasting month and that which commemorates the pilgrimage), or other auspicious occasions, such as the attending of marriage feasts. Some put on the cap of the *haji*, even though they may not have gone to Mecca. Those who have, including the imam, wear the loose frock-like dress (*jubah*) in addition to the cap during important functions. They also hold a rosary in their hands. All these are symbols that make them appear to be and recognized as being religious.

Among the broad categories of religious men, the most important one is the imam. There are two types of imam, one for the mosque and the other for the prayer house. The mosque is a more important institution for worship than the prayer house, and it is only in the mosque that the Friday prayers are held. Further, the imam of the mosque is an official appointed by the Government religious department, and is therefore a member of the religious hierarchy, while the imam of the prayer house is the choice of its members, especially the more respected ones, and is not absorbed into the same hierarchy. The mosque imam have to face certain qualifying examinations in order to be initially appointed and later to be promoted, and it is often the case that they are more knowledgeable on the rules and laws of Islam than the imam of the prayer houses. All these factors contribute to making the mosque imam more highly regarded than the imam of the prayer house.

The most important function associated with the imam is that of a prayer leader. However, just as the mosque and the prayer house are not only used for group prayers but also for other purposes, such as the giving of religious instruction and the holding of meetings to discuss religious and other village matters, so too the role of the imam is not confined solely to that of a prayer leader. Outside the mosque or prayer house, an imam may also be required to lead the *tahlil* associated with various types of rites, to say prayers at the end of religious as well as non-religious ceremonies, and also to give advice on matters pertaining to Islam. During marriages, some of the mosque imam are empowered by the religious department to solemnize and register them, and also to record divorces. Once a year, for the collection of the religious tithe (*fitrah*), he may be accredited as the chief collector or one of the 'collectors' (*amil*). He may also give regular instructions on certain fundamental aspects of the beliefs and practices of Islam.

The imam of the prayer houses and other religious people, such as the lebai and ustaz, do not lead the Friday prayers, although they may be invited to do so with other group prayers when the mosque imam is not present. They do not have the power to solemnize marriages, although they are often invited to be official witnesses. However, some of them give instruction on Islam in the mosque, prayer houses or in their own homes. It is these people who give such instruction who are normally termed by the villagers as ustaz. Some of them are also teachers in schools, such as the pondok school in Kangkong, the Arabic school in Kerdau and the religious school in Bagan, all of which give instruction on Islam. The lebai is regarded merely as a religious person, without having any specialized functions. In fact, the term 'lebai' itself is used generally for religious persons other than the imam and ustaz. Some of them teach the children to read the Quran in their homes.

The functions of these religious persons are mainly spiritual, being concerned with purifying the soul, so that it will not suffer in the after-world. For themselves, they are able to do this by 'fearing God and performing His bidding', and for others, they lead in certain rituals that need to be carried out within the commuity and also teach the fundamentals of the doctrines and practices of Islam. Thus they are more than just pious followers for they are also quite conscientious perpetrators of Islam at the village level. Most of them fulfil their functions 'for God' (*kerana Allah*) and not for money although occasionally some receive presents and alms for their services to others. Only the imam of the mosque and some religious teachers earn regular salaries from the Government.

As regards the main functionaries in the traditional belief system, they are known as the bomoh and the pawang. In fact, these terms do not refer to two different types of functionaries but they can be used interchangeably to refer to the same kind, the only difference being that in some areas pawang is more widely used and vice versa. Firth in his study of the Kelantan fishermen calls the bomoh 'spirit-medium healer' (Firth, 1966: 13). Perhaps his rendering of the term may be acceptable, subject to certain qualifications. It is true that the bomoh or pawang is in most cases a spirit-medium, but healing is only one of his functions, albeit the most important one. Associated with the power to heal is the power to cause affliction in the body or the heart of others; in other words the bomoh or pawang can also practise sorcery. Some of them may also act as diviners, specializing particularly in the prediction of the future and the tracing of lost or stolen property. The powers of sorcery and sometimes divination are ancillary to their curative powers. Finally, the bomoh or the pawang very often act as leaders or main performers of several rites associated with protective and productive activities such as have been described above. Most of these rites are waning; in fact they have even disappeared in some areas so that these traditional religious functionaries are left mainly with the work of healing. Although mainly a healer, they may possess many-faceted powers and functions. It may be more appropriate to consider the pawang and the bomoh simply as magicians as most of them derive their powers from spiritual sources.

In the three areas studied there are four persons who function as magicians: one in Kangkong, who specializes mainly in the healing of the sick and the tracing of lost property; one in Bagan who is known for his sorcery, healing and divining abilities; and two from Kerdau, one practising as a sorcerer, healer and diviner and the other one as a healer. All four of them also perform rites connected with protective and productive activities. They operate primarily within their village and among their neighbours, but the one from Bagan and one of the two from Kerdau operate in the villages as well although their activities are confined to the mukim.

The stories of how these magicians first obtained their skills are quite varied. The one from Bagan said that it took him a long time to become a magician. According to him, he was an apprentice to a famous magician in Java and after a considerable period he was asked to go away and to spend some time in a mountain cave as a hermit. One night, in a dream, an old man with a flowing white beard came before him, and this apparition told him that he had already obtained the necessary knowledge to practise as a magician. When he came out of his hermitage, he followed his teacher for some time after which the latter told him to go away and practise on his own. In contrast to this, two persons, one from Kangkong and the other from Kerdau, obtained their skill simply from their parents, who practised magic and whom they used to follow as assistants. They observed the different rites which were carried out, and learnt the various incantations. The one from Kerdau was able to practise on his own when his father was still alive, while the other started only a few years after the death of his father. As for the remaining one from Kerdau, he was neither an apprentice nor an assistant in the ways described above. It all started one day when he was possessed by a spirit, and spoke in a language that the villagers did not understand. From that day onwards he began to practise as a healer and also performed rites for both protective and productive purposes.

Besides these magicians, there are also others who are religious men, who act as healers and diviners. In the three areas studied, there are three persons, one from each area, who are the most prominent. The one from Kangkong is the elderly ex-imam, mentioned earlier as the person involved in the 'three digit' forecast. He is a healer as well as diviner. The one in Kerdau is the elderly ex-penghulu who is now an imam of the prayer house near his home; he functions primarily as a healer. As for the one in Bagan, he is an ex-teacher of a religious school and occasionally teaches Quran-reading to the young children of his neighbours. He is a healer, but is also sought after at times to trace lost or stolen property. All three claim that they depend entirely on the supernatural powers derived from the verses of the Quran: the incantations that they recite over drinking water to cure illnesses, and the inscriptions used in 'amulets' (*tangkal*) to drive away diseases and spirits from the persons who put them on. Two of them say they are helped by jinns of the Muslim kind. It is clear therefore that these people derive their magical powers not from the traditional magic but from Islam. As a result of this, and also the fact that they are considered to be religious men, they are rarely viewed disapprovingly, unless of course they start involving themselves in practices such as gambling which are forbidden by Islam.

Attitudes towards the magicians differ. The religious men — especially the mosque imam — tend to look down upon the magicians as individuals indulging in 'practices opposed to Islam'. Quite often these magicians are at pains to explain that they submit themselves to the power and will of God and to stress that by helping people in trouble or in pain, they are in fact giving their services 'for God'. They have never challenged the authority of the religious men who symbolize Islam at the village level and because of this they often respect the imam. Thus, the relationship between the religious men — the imam in particular — and the magicians is rather asymmetrical. The position of the imam is buttressed by his role within the hierarchy of Islam, which enjoys special status as the official religion of the country, while that of the pawang or the bomoh is considerably weakened by the disapproving attitude of the official religious authorities towards traditional magic, as will be explained presently.

The positions of the various religious functionaries depend a great deal on the general views of people on traditional beliefs and Islam. The traditional beliefs are fairly deeply rooted in the culture of the rural people who still have faith in the magicians. However there are two factors that tend to undermine the positions of traditional magic and magicians, namely, Islam and modernization.

As early as the turn of the century, modernists have tried to combat what they term as 'nonsensical beliefs' (*kepercayaan karut*) and they argued that beliefs in the supernatural other than God is anti-Islamic. However they were not effective and could not get the support of the religious departments and their officials whom they accused of being too conservative and also of perpetrating outdated 'innovations' (*bida'ah*) that are not consistent with the true form of Islam as upheld by the Quran and *hadith* (traditions). Nevertheless the religious departments and the officials, perhaps in their anxiety to prove themselves as the custodians of Islam, slowly made their voices heard against the 'non-Islamic practices', especially through the Friday sermons. However, they focused their attack mainly on the *puja pantai*, a ceremony popularly carried out by fishermen in the East coast of the country, mainly in the state of Kelantan, before the fishing season. A white buffalo is often sacrificed and then allowed to float into the sea to appease the sea spirits. After the War, several articles appeared, particularly in a daily Malay newspaper, the *Utusan Melayu*, condemning the ceremony as wasteful, besides being non-Islamic in nature. Then in the 1950s the political party PAS** which is Islamic in orientation also came out against it. When the party captured power in the state of Kelantan in 1959, it banned the ceremony, and since then it has never been known to be practised. This action had an effect on several religious departments in the other states and they were encouraged to take a more determined stand against similar ceremonies. In the three areas studied, in Bagan especially, the rites associated with productive activities exist mainly in the memory of old people. In Kerdau, the productive rites are still practised by a few, but the last known preventive rite was carried out in 1962. However, the rites that are associated with curative activities are still practised by magicians in the three areas.

The weakening or the disappearance of these rites has also been due to the process of modernization. Economic, technological and educational changes that are seeping into the rural society are slowly weakening some of the bases on which magic thrives. Looking at the three areas, it is seen that in Kangkong, where the main economic activity is rice-growing, traditional magic prevails to some extent in both economic production and medicine, although in the former it is confined only to rice and not to the rubber economy, while in Bagan, it remains almost entirely in medicine and is no longer apparent in the economic field of rubber production. In fact, in so far as the economy is concerned, there are hardly any magical practices associated with rubber in the whole country. Unlike rice, which is a crop closely linked with the traditional Malay way of life, rubber is a modern crop which came together with the spread of the money economy. The output of rubber is not as vulnerable to factors beyond the control of a peasant's knowledge and technology, like droughts, pests and diseases as is rice. There is a tradition of magic, associated with rice production, which peasants resort to in order to overcome natural difficulties but this, however, does not exist in the case of rubber.

Although certain rites have disappeared, it does not mean that the magicians have lost their roles in Malay society. It is true that the use of machines, fertilizers, insecticides, pills, injections and clinics has spread into some of the remotest villages. These have not, however, wiped out the magicians; they only supply the villagers with alternative means of solving their problems. There are times when the villagers combine the use of supernatural powers and science, but there are also other times when, as an 'attempt' (ikhtiar), they may turn to science after having failed with supernatural powers or vice versa. The spread of literacy and education has made some people sceptical of traditional magic and Islam. But most of them do not disbelieve totally in ghosts and spirits or in God. At times of great crises, there is in fact the tendency for them to revert to Islam and traditional beliefs. This was seen very clearly after the communal clashes referred to as the 'May Thirteenth Incident'. There was a sudden upsurge in the faith towards Islam and magic. Several magicians who suddenly came to the fore claimed the power to make people invincible, and the Malays from different walks of life and educational backgrounds began to turn to them. They have to participate in rituals, undergo certain tests, and also to perform the daily prayers regularly, for failure to do so will destroy their invincibility.

The influence of Islam is very strong among the rural people. Where Islam is strongly ensconced, and among groups that are religiously orientated, religious persons have a high standing in the public eye. In the three areas studied there are varying attitudes towards Islam not only in the different areas, but also among certain categories of people within the same area. Comparing the three, the impression gathered is that the people in Kangkong are generally more religious or at least more conscious about religion than those in Bagan, while the latter are generally more knowledgeable in Islam than the people in Kerdau.

Kangkong is in Kedah, and like the other padi-based states of Perlis and Kelantan which are also more predominantly settled by the Malays, the influence of modernization is least felt there. Islam enjoys a strong position and a large number of people who study religion, for instance in the Middle-Eastern countries, are from these areas. Also, the centres of pondok education are located here. Although Kangkong is only about ten miles away from Alor Star and about sixty miles from Penang, it has been relatively isolated for a long time. Until the road linking it with the state capital was opened in the late 1950s, very few people have really gone outside the village. There is a rather strong pondok school nearby and a good number of people have received their education there. Furthermore, the teachers in Kangkong have regularly been giving lessons on Islam in the local mosque. Above all, the elders of the most important lineage in Kangkong are religious men who have studied outside the village, some of them in the Middle East.

As for Bagan, though still essentially an agricultural area and based almost entirely on a cash economy, it is relatively accessible to Batu Pahat town about six miles away and Muar about twenty-eight miles away. Yet, when compared with Kerdau which besides rubber-growing depends on padi farming, and whose road communications linking it with the towns of Temerloh and Mentakab — both about eight miles away and dating only from 1959 — it is found that the people in Bagan generally feel more committed to Islam than those in Kerdau. There seems to be two main reasons for this. Firstly, in Bagan, as in the rest of Johore, religious education has been relatively well-organized for a long time. The Malay schools, which function in the morning, are converted in the afternoon into religious schools. Education is free, and schools and teachers are maintained by the Government. Almost all the children go to religious schools for up to six years, thus giving them some knowledge of Islam. Secondly, after World War II, there was an eruption of communal clashes in several parts of the country and Batu Pahat was one of the badly hit areas (Burridge, 1957). Bagan also experienced some clashes between the Malays and the Chinese. One of the effects of these clashes was that people began to turn more intensely to religion for identification as well as protection, just as many people have done after the May Thirteenth Incident. This intensity of feeling towards Islam is not apparent in Kerdau. Also, here as in the rest of Pahang generally, the system of religious education is not as widespread or well-organized. There is an Arabic school, but school-going children have to choose between this and the secular vernacular schools since all of them are held in the morning. Only a small number choose to go to the Arabic school.

Between the young and the old in each area there are also some perceivable differences in the way religion is generally regarded. Proportionately more young people are sceptical about magic and they are also more indifferent towards Islam than the older people. There is a tendency for some of these young people to ridicule some of the religious functionaries. A number of them seldom pray and sometimes they quite openly stay away from Friday congregations. There are also those who ignore rebukes and use the mosque or prayer house verandahs occasionally for playing cards. It is certain that new values and attitudes are influencing them. This being the case, it becomes more noticeable that among them religion is not considered a very important factor in determining leadership. Only those religious persons who are known to have some exceptional qualities and whose abilities extend beyond religion are looked up to and are given leading positions either in some communities or organizations. Otherwise the religious men will be confined only to carrying out the limited religious functions that may be required of them.

EDITORS' NOTE

* The three villages studied here are Kangkong which is situated on the coast of Kedah, Kerdau in Pahang, and Bagan in Johore.

** PAS. Parti Islam Se Malaya or Pan Malayan Islamic Party.

Rusembilan as a Moslem Community

THOMAS M. FRASER, Jr.

The Malay villager is seriously dedicated to his religion, but in spite of this puts certain basic Malay tenets before his Islamic precepts. The chief among these has to do with his treatment of women. In ordinary life there is no segregation of the sexes, women are not veiled, and there is a feeling of equality between men and women. If a woman seems to have a business sense superior to that of her husband, she will take over the handling of the family finances, and in one case a woman is listed in the official government census as being the head of the family.[1] For many years the rajas of Pattani were women.[2] Only when matters deal directly with the mosque and religion and when an unmarried girl has passed puberty does segregation of the sexes occur, and even here there is no feeling of disequality. In this connection, women may not hold office in the religious organization, although two women hajis have been among the most respected religious teachers in Rusembilan. Attendance at the mosque is not compulsory for them on Friday; when they attend, they are assigned a separate section, with a curtain between them and the men. They are separated from the men during *kenduri* or feasts, generally eating after the men in the kitchen of the feasting household. A postpubescent girl is kept carefully secluded in her parents' house until marriage, during which ceremony she wears the veil traditional with Moslem women, as well as a pair of very dark sunglasses. Innumerable relatively unimportant Islamic laws are ignored or openly contravened daily by the villagers: except for religious feasts, flesh is rarely slaughtered in accordance with the Koran; spirits and ghosts are of considerable importance to the villager, and he is constantly propitiating them; daily prayers are frequently omitted, and the bathing ritual is seldom carried out as prescribed by law.

To the villager of Rusembilan, the most important area of his religion is that of prayer and reading the Koran. Prayer, like any religious act of value, falls within two of the three categories of obligation defined by the Malay Moslem. The first of these categories, *wajib* (obligatory), includes all religious obligations that must be carried out, such as the five daily prayers (*sembayang lima waktu*), the observance of Ramadan, the fasting month (*bulan puasa*), and the *zakat* or alms to be contributed to the mosque for distribution to various classes of needy. The second category, *sunat* (commendable), includes those religious acts which, though not obligatory, are considered to be of great virtue, such as the addition of two extra prayers to the five which are *wajib*, continuation of fasting for six days beyond Ramadan,[3] and the haj or pilgrimage to Mecca. The third category, *harus* (proper), includes only acts which are of no religious value one way or another, but which are not specifically banned by the religion, such as

---

eating mutton on a feast day (rather than fish) because it is more valued.

The five daily prayers are required to be said by all adult men in the village, though on certain occasions, particularly when the men go out fishing, one or more of them may be omitted. The prayers (*sembayang*) include the following: *sembayang suboh* (dawn), *sembayang lohor* (midday), *sembayang asar* (afternoon), *sembayang maghrib* (evening), and *sembayang isha* (nightfall). In addition, two *sunat* prayers may be added: *sembayang loha* (forenoon) and *sembayang tahajud* (night). The time for each of these prayers is announced by the beating of drums at the mosque and the *balaisa*. Frequently, much of the prayer ritual is omitted, the supplicant simply performing the verbal portions of his prayer. Each prayer is supposed, however, to consist of certain definite elements. The supplicant stands *kiblat,* facing the direction of Mecca, and repeats a short prayer of aspiration or a specific request (*niat, hajat*). He then raises his arms and says several times the *takbir,* which consists of the phrase *Allahu akbar* (God is great). The supplicant now recites the *fatihah,* the opening verse of the Koran:

> In the name of Allah, the Beneficent, the Merciful.
> Praise be to Allah, Lord of the Worlds,
> The Beneficent, the Merciful.
> Owner of the Day of Judgment,
> Thee (alone) we worship; Thee (alone) we ask for help.
> Show us the straight path,
> The path of those whom thou hast favoured;
> Not (the path) of those who earn Thine anger nor of those who go astray.[4]

Following the *fatihah,* the supplicant performs the *rakaat* at least once. This consists of a prayer said standing erect, followed by a deep bow (*rukok*), full prostration (*sujut*), rising to the knees, and a repetition of the *sujut.*

The villagers usually think of their abbreviated form of prayer (with some of the ritual omitted) as the *hajat* and differentiate it from the full *sembayang.* Another form of prayer is the *donga* or *doa,* which is an informal petition to God, usually for some specific end, said in a standing position with raised palms. Some authorities see in this a suggestion of white or religious magic.[5]

Friday prayers (*sembayang jumaat*) in the mosque are *wajib* for men if forty or more male residents can be gathered at the mosque. If less than forty arrive at the mosque, the ordinary *sembayang lohor* is performed. When the Friday service is to be performed, a call to prayer is made by the *khatib,* who is accompanied by loud beating of the mosque drum. The *khotebah* is read by either the imam or the *khatib.* Although the *khotebah* may include an extemporaneous sermon, at Rusembilan it is ordinarily confined to readings in Arabic, followed by Malay translations from a book of passages from the Koran and sayings of the prophets. Passages are chosen as appropriate to the season of the year or the religious calendar, such as what to avoid and how to live virtuously during the fasting month. After the *khotebah,* the *sembayang lohor* is repeated twice, followed by the *shahadat* or confession of faith. People may leave after this, or they may remain in the mosque to read from the Koran or say additional prayers along with the imam. On leaving the mosque, the men *salam* with a double handclasp and ask each other for forgiveness and blessing. Usually, a large group of men remains on the porch of the mosque talking quietly of village matters until the imam and those who have remained inside with him have finished their prayers and are ready to return to the beach.

THE MOSQUE AND RELIGIOUS ORGANIZATION

According to strict usage, the mosque (*surau*) at Rusembilan is not a true mosque of general assembly (*masjid*). The *masjid* must be of permanent construction, such as stone or concrete, rather than wood. It must contain a lectern pulpit for the imam or the *khatib* and must to a degree be sanctified by avoiding such acts as smoking and loud, irreverent talking in and around it. The *surau* at Rusembilan fits none of these criteria, but the village is proud of it nonetheless as a place of worship, as many other villages in the area lack even this. The *balaisa* in Kampong Pata actually falls into the same category as the *surau* in Kampong Surau, but it is called *balaisa,* denoting an even less formal religious function than the *surau,* in order to maintain the significance of having one village mosque.

The mosque and the *balaisa* are cared for by the mosque committee, whose duty it is to look after the actual physical structures and to arrange for celebrations and feasts to be held there. The committee, made up of twelve men serving a four-year term, includes the imam, the *khatib,* and the *bilal* (muezzin). These three appoint the nine lay committeemen after consulting with other religious leaders in the community. The imam, *khatib,* and *bilal* are themselves appointed by the Moslem Religious Board (*Majalis Ugama*) of Pattani province from candidates suggested by the villagers. This board must notify the district officer of the choice and the date that the appointment is to be made in the village mosque. The actual appointment takes place right after the Friday service and is followed by a talk given by the district officer on the function of the government as well as religion in the villagers' lives. Other functions of the Moslem Religious Board include registration of the number of mosques and religious officials in the province, collection of the *zakat* or alms, and approval of the building of any new mosques in order not to have too many in a particular area. Frequently, this body is called upon to settle religious disputes or civil disputes involving Islamic law in the villages within the province. The board meets monthly with the governor and the district officers of the province to discuss matters dealing with both religion and administration, such as the government budget for building mosques and plans for joint Moslem-Buddhist prayers at civil functions.[6] Members of the Moslem Religious Board are chosen from men of wisdom and respect, usually hajis, by all the religious officials of the province.

The chairmen of the Moslem Religious Boards from all the provinces in Thailand having Moslem elements of population form an informal committee which is headed by a Moslem representative of the Thai national government, the *chakhul Islam.* He is supposed to be a wise and able man who will bring to the government's attention problems in the Moslem areas of the nation and actively work toward solutions of them. As he is appointed to his position by the political party in power, he is frequently no more than a spokesman for the government, whose duty is to explain to the Moslems of Thailand, through their Moslem Religious Boards, any government policy which seems to them to be counter to the interests of Islam.

NOTES

1. Government of Thailand, *Census BE 2499* (1956).
2. W. A. R. Wood, *A History of Siam,* Bangkok: Siam Bounakich Press, 1933, p. 167.
3. This is *wajib* rather than *sunat* if one has been forced to break the fast during Ramadan for any reason, for example, menstruation or illness.
4. Mohammed Marmaduke Pickthall, trans., *The Meaning of the Glorious Koran,* New York: New American Library, 1953, p. 31.
5. R. J. Wilkinson, *A Malay-English Dictionary,* 1, Tokyo: Daito Syuppan Kabusiki Kaiaya, n.d., 283.
6. Such joint Moslem-Buddhist civil ceremonies as the *Phud Mon Khon,* or blessing of the rice seed, are attended by Thai officials, a few Malay village officials, and a few Thai civilians.

What is a Malay? Situational Selections of Ethnic Identity in a Plural Society

JUDITH A. NAGATA

ETHNIC AND SOCIAL STRUCTURE OF GEORGE TOWN, PENANG

Material for the ethnic situational analysis which follows was gathered largely in the city of George Town, Penang.[1]

Until its incorporation into the Federation of Malaya in 1957, the status of Penang was that of a Straits Settlement, originally ceded to the British East India Company by the Sultan of Kedah in 1786. At the time of the initial British settlement there was no permanent population on the island, although the vacuum was quickly filled by various kinds of immigrants from the mainland of Malaya, the islands of Indonesia, or from India, Arabia, Thailand, China, and Europe. Because George Town was a port city, the early immigration was stimulated by trade and commerce. In 1970, George Town had a total population of 269,247 (Department of Statistics 1972:248) and is still known for its ethnic diversity. The present census breakdown is as follows:

Table 1. Ethnic composition of George Town, 1970.

Ethnic Group	Size of Population	Percentage
Malay	37,203	13.8
Chinese	192,701	71.5
Indian	35,690	13.3
Other	3,653	1.4
Total	269,247	100.0

Unfortunately, no finer breakdown (e.g., by Indonesian/Malay) or cross-tabulation by religion (Muslim/Hindu Indian) is yet available for the city as a whole.

The early politico-legal framework established by the British was essentially a form of indirect rule of the component ethnic communities. Thus the Chinese were administered through intermediaries known as *Kapitans China*, the Indians through *Kapitans Kling*, and the Malays through *penghulus* or traditional headmen. Later, there was a tendency by the British to administer all Muslims ("Mussulmans" or "Mohammedans") as a single category. The Chinese quickly established for themselves a tightly integrated community structure, replete with such corporate institutions as *kongsi* and secret societies. The Malays, Indians, Arabs, and various groups of Indonesians, such as the Boyanese, also had identifiable institutional structures and often tended to be residentially solidary, judging by accounts in the local newspapers of the time. While the *Jawi Peranakans* had no exclusive institutions, they were known as successful merchants, incumbents of certain clerical posts, the leading members of certain associations, and as the principal patrons of new mosques. Other institutions, especially those of a religious nature, such as mosque committees, death benefit societies, and more recently, religious associations, spanned

Reprinted in abridged form from *American Ethnologist* Vol. 1 No. 2 (1974), 331–350, by permission of the author.

the entire Muslim community regardless of ethnicity.

In the contemporary Muslim population of George Town it is still possible to define in institutional terms four fairly clear-cut ethnic communities. The Indians have a number of their own associations (regional, recreational, charitable, political, and a Chamber of Commerce) that use the epithet "Indian" in the title and define their activities as of purely Indian interest. All of these recruit their membership equally from Muslims and Hindus. Likewise the Arabs have an Arab League for recreation and death benefits, and there are also two or three residential communities *(kampongs)* whose land is endowed exclusively for those of Arab descent (in one case for *Syeds* and *Sharifahs* alone, known as *Kampong Syed).* Prior to Confrontation (1965–1966), the Indonesians, too, had a recreational association catering to Indonesian interests, but this was abolished by the Malaysian government as a subversive threat and is only just in the incipient stages of reforming itself under the leadership of a man whose father was Javanese-born. One particular Indonesian subgroup, the Boyanese, still maintains a distinct communal house residence (*pondok*) and organization; the Boyanese attempt to practice endogamy and are occupationally specialized, principally as grooms and horse-trainers at the turf club. Still other associations are labeled as "Malay," e.g., certain political, youth, and sports organizations and the Malay Chamber of Commerce, which are dedicated to Malay interests in their respective spheres. One of the earliest Malay organizations, the *Persatuan Melayu* (Malay Union), which was first formed in 1929 and is said by some to be the forerunner of UMNO, adopted as one of its major issues the question of the *Melayu jati* and the threat of invasion by the *Jawi Peranakans* (Roff 1967:242). So bitter was the debate, that a rival *Persatuan* was formed, drawing its membership from the ranks of the latter, although this eventually succumbed to the *Melayu jati.* Now there are no separate *Jawi Peranakan* associations, and it may be said that this is no longer a definable community, but only a category. Apparently the category is still meaningful, for a recently formed (1972) Petty Traders' Association raised exactly the same issue of the *Melayu jati* at its inaugural meeting. Finally, there is a plethora of interethnic Muslim associations, although in many cases the bulk of both leadership and membership tends to be identified with one ethnic group alone (e.g., the predominance of Indian Muslims in the religious organization, *Iqbal*).

It may be said provisionally that Islamic culture (as opposed to theology), in association with the *adat,* has created striking uniformities across ethnic lines. Furthermore, common association in some religion-based organizations has reduced the salience of ethnic boundaries and created the possibility of an identity overriding ethnicity.

SITUATIONAL VARIATION IN ETHNIC IDENTITY

Methodology. It should go without saying that the only way in which the notion of situational ethnic selection could initially be arrived at and tested was by intensive fieldwork of a participant-observation variety. Direct questions as to ethnicity (whether verbal or on questionnaires) can never elicit the complexity of the oscillation of an individual in social interaction, nor the spontaneity of his reactions in ethnic terms. Once asked to reflect consciously and rationally on ethnic affiliation, the dynamic aspect is lost. The fieldworker must therefore constantly be on the alert for verbal and other indications as to which reference group is being invoked in a given context and to work out the apparent inconsistencies independently.

The ethnic phenomenon in Penang is characterized by great fluidity in which the variables of culture (including religion), social institutions, and identity have different significance in different contexts. In this section examples will be given to illustrate some of the ways in which ethnic identity varies, and some of the factors which influence selection will be suggested.

There was a time, particularly in rural areas where the population was overwhelmingly and uniformly *Melayu jati* and relatively untouched by immigration, when any convert to Islam was said to *masok Melayu* ('become a Malay') (Freedman 1955:397). More sophisticated modern urbanites, however, recognize that, although few Malays are not Muslims, there are many Muslims who are not Malays, in other words, that ethnic and religious referents are mutually independent. The degree of independence, however, seems to vary according to the particular ethnic groups involved. It is significant that the traditional unity enshrined in the term *masok Melayu* operates much less readily for Chinese converts to Islam. Indeed, the concept of *sukubangsa,* which may be translated as "(sub-) ethnic group," is, in practice, usually restricted to the ethnic groups within Islam or to the indigenous (tribal) peoples of Malaysia, but is rarely applied to the Chinese. For Chinese, Indians, or Europeans, the term *bangsa* is more commonly used; this has the connotation of differences more extensive and basic than those between *sukubangsa.* The modern Muslim convert therefore does not automatically *masok Melayu* either in his own eyes or those of the Malay community, and this is particularly true in the case of Chinese converts. Factors other than religion or cultural criteria alone must be taken into account. Some of these clearly concern perception of position in the social system at large and the pressures for selection of one particular membership or reference group over another. The most important pressures involved in the selection of ethnic reference groups appear to be: (1) the desire to express either social distance or solidarity (comparative reference groups); (2) expediency, or the immediate advantages to be gained by a particular reference group selection on a particular occasion; and (3) consideration of social status and upward or downward social mobility (normative reference groups).

Social solidarity and social distance. This refers to cases in which individuals who on most occasions identify with one membership group temporarily reorient themselves and select a different (comparative) group of reference in accordance with the degree of affinity they wish to express in a given situation. Sometimes personal characteristics evoke *sukubangsa* or ethnic stereotypes which call for differentiation when they become relevant. For example, a lady who had repeatedly stressed that she, along with all the neighbors in her *kampong,* were Malay *(kita semua orang Melayu),* was vigorously cleaning her house in preparation for *Hari Raya Puasa,* the festival which celebrates the end of the fasting month. When I commented on her energy and industry, she remarked proudly that she is an Arab, and that "Arabs are not lazy like Malays."

In another case, a Malay urban *kampong* intensively studied by the writer experienced a serious crisis in which some of its land was threatened by an alien development company (Nagata 1972). Most of the *kampong* dwellers are typical of the urban Muslim population of Penang in general, and in other contexts claim various *sukubangsa.* In this case, however, the entire *kampong* suddenly became monolithically Malay and interpreted the projected development as a threat to "Malay interests." Furthermore, suspecting that the leaders of the Malay Chamber of Commerce were conniving at (and profiting from) the plan, the members of the *kampong* accused the latter of being proud and self-interested Arabs (*orang Arab yang sombong dan ikut kepentingan sendiri saja*) who exploit poor Malays. Predictably enough, in an issue involving a dispute with the Chinese, all the "Arabs" suddenly coalesce into Malays again. The same distinction also operates in reverse. That is, when the leaders of the Malay Chamber of Commerce were complaining that the Malays were backward because they objected to the proposed development plan, the significant groups were "we Arabs" and "those Malays." When the very same plan required the financial support of a MARA loan, however, the officialdom of the Chamber of Commerce was once more solidly Malay. Thus on this particular occasion, all *kampong*-dwellers were comparing themselves to, and wishing to share, the situation and concerns of the Malays, which resulted in a strong positive association with the latter as a reference group.

In the same *kampong,* those who lived in the front section near the mosque and main road, where the better quality houses are to be found, and who had a relatively higher representation in semiskilled, white collar, and professional jobs, would often claim to be Malays in contrast with those at the back, near the river, who are "laborers and hawkers and mostly *Kling.*" Needless to say, these categories do not coincide with those used on other occasions, e.g., a wealthy *Kling* entrepreneur from the front of the *kampong* who is proud of his *Kling* industriousness. Thus when questions of socioeconomic status and residential ranking become salient, a desire for positive association seems to arise, and the comparative reference group principle operates.

On an individual level, too, people will often project personal sentiments of association/dissociation in ethnic terms. Having previously identified a neighbor as a Malay "like all of us here," a *kampong* dweller would later admit to bad feeling between them over straying chickens and placement of fences, saying, "well, what can you expect, she's just a *Kling*." Sometimes speakers will identify themselves as D.K.K.* or Javanese, and in expressing dislike of another, make disparaging remarks about "those Malays." Identification of individuals against whom there is some negative feeling is frequently appended by an ethnic epithet different from the one currently being claimed by the speaker, whereas positive sentiments are more likely to generate common identification, e.g., "he's a Rawa (from Sumatra) and my grandfather was also from there, I'm a Rawa too."

Expediency. A second, and somewhat obvious factor influencing ethnic selection is expediency. The special position accorded to the Malays under the constitution and under the Second Malaysia Plan combine to make Malay ethnic status an attractive one now. Thus many Muslim entrepreneurs who aspire to loans from MARA or Muslim students who desire university scholarships are labeling themselves "Malay," although for other purposes they may still use other *suku-bangsa* terms. For all their claims about the unity of Islam, some Malays resent the competition of *Mamak Kling* (a term of real opprobrium) or "proud Arabs" for these scarce resources. On the other hand, one highly placed MARA** official is known to have said recently that he considers all Indian Muslims as Malays for purposes of special loans.

Many Arabs take advantage of an oscillating status for such purposes. Successful Arab businessmen, claiming *Syed* status and living in the exclusive *Kampong Syed,* are uniformly transformed into Malays in order to gain access to the special privileges. Other Arabs are prominent political leaders who similarly exploit their Malayness for party political purposes while disassociating themselves from the lack of political maturity of the Malay electorate.

Expediency may also reflect the requirements of current place of residence. There are a number of Indian Muslim businessmen, mostly in the import/export business, who literally lead double lives. Families and households are maintained independently in both India and Malaysia, between which they divide their time, either for a few months of each year or else every few years. In India, predictably enough, these individuals are Indian in every respect, while in Malaysia many associate with, marry into, and identify with the Malay community. Some of these men are Malaysia-born and Malaysian citizens, but they still maintain a social and cultural foothold in two distinct ethnic and national environments.

Concern with social status and social mobility. This is possibly the most important consideration of all and involves a perception (albeit often unconscious) of the relative status of different ethnic groups, at least in connection with a given issue, whether in conversation or action. Some implicit model of the broader social structure and of the position of groups in it will thus determine what norms are invoked and from which reference group the individual will identify and take his standards.

A typical example would be the manner in which the relative statuses of employer and servant are often expressed in ethnic terms. One woman, considered both by herself and by others to be *Melayu jati,* married an Indian Muslim whose family always identifies with the Indian community. The children of this marriage, who are classic examples of *Jawi Peranakan* or D.K.K., usually claim to be Malay. Indeed, for school purposes the children have dropped the distinctive Indian suffix from their name, and insist on using the Malay patronymic *bin/binte*[2] instead of the Indian "son of/daughter of" which appears on their identity cards. Two of their paternal parallel cousins, both of whose parents identify as Indians, have been adopted by the household under discussion and are also considered to be Malay. However, when pressed verbally by the fieldworker, they hedge and admit that they "might be considered D.K.K." or that they are "Indian but really Malay." In the household of the first family there is also a servant girl, of identical ethnic "mix" as the children of her employer, namely with an Indian father and a Malay mother and, by descent at least, "more" Malay than her employers' nephews. The girl normally speaks Malay, wears Malay dress, and considers herself Malay (in self-reference). Likewise, her employers have been heard to refer to her as "Malay" on more than one occasion. But one day, when the topic of conversation revolved around master/servant relationships in a discussion of the servant problem, the ethnic variability emerged quite distinctly. According to the employer, it is preferable to hire servants of a "different *sukubangsa* from one's own family," otherwise they will gossip to other members of the community about household affairs. The woman further supported her argument by invoking a common negative self-stereotype held by many Malays about themselves, namely that Malays are basically lazy and hence do not make good servants. On this occasion, therefore, she was aligning her own household (Malay), including the Indian cousins, in ethnic opposition to her servant, despite the objective cultural and social realities recognized in other contexts. As it transpired, in cases of servants, this pattern of ethnic differentiation was to be repeated several times. Malays appear to prefer employing non-Malay servants, but usually Muslims, and where this cannot be achieved, ethnic fictions like the one above are used. In a similar case, where it was impossible to consider the servant anything but a *Melayu jati,* it was her employer who temporarily switched her ethnic status, from being a Malay (her usual self-reference) to being "really Arab, you know."

Occupational reference groups frequently provide the salient distinction which causes a speaker or actor to identify with one group or another, because many common stereotypes about occupation and ethnicity exist. Indian Muslims are widely believed to be more successful as businessmen and traders than are the Malays, often because of their willingness to overcharge somewhat *(naik untong sedikit)* and other devious practices. In some cases, too, the unity implicit in having Islam in common disintegrates along ethnic lines, as when the Indians are accused of ignoring religious principles in their anxiety to make a quick profit, and in this respect they are even compared to the Chinese. Yet one individual, who had on many occasions freely admitted that he was a *Kling* (although he lives in a Malay *kampong*), and frequently speaks Tamil to his Indian paternal relatives and listens to Tamil radio, once the question of sharp business dealing is raised, quite explicitly dissociates himself from the *Klings* by stating emphatically that "we Malays are not like that, and that's the reason we can't compete with the Chinese." Others who also claim *Kling sukubangsa* in formal questioning will praise the *Kling* entrepreneurs for their ability to support one another and then proceed to include themselves in the common Malay negative self-stereotype by regretting that "we Malays can't do likewise."

A young shopkeeper, who is Malaysian-born and is wont to associate with Malays and refer to himself as such, was involved in a heated discussion on the problems of small businessmen. He offered the explanation that Malays do not know how to cooperate with one another and tend to quarrel (*tak tahu tolong menolong, biasa gadoh satu sama lain*), whereas the "Javanese like himeself" are more cooperative and therefore more successful.

Another factor which raises the question of relative status considerations is poverty. One woman who is from a prominent Arab *Syed* family and entitled to the honorific *Sharifah,* had married well beneath her (to a poor trishaw driver). At the time I knew her, she was considering applying for welfare, and she said that she never used her title "for I'm too poor to be a *Sharifah.*" But later, when a well-known Penang Arab leader died, she mentioned that "all we Arabs" had attended the funeral.

It is significant, as will be noted below, that Chinese Muslims seldom seem to participate in this easy flow from one ethnic group to another. It is clear that this is in no small measure due to rejection on the part of other Muslims, particularly in their capacity as

Malays, and almost certainly reflects the tensions of Malay/non-Malay relations in the broader economic and political spheres. This is the test of the limits of Islam's ability to create ethnic unity. For here, where social and structural distance is so much greater, even Islam tends to break along other institutional lines. Some of the Chinese Muslims now have their own association which exists independent of, and somewhat isolated from, other Muslim organizations, and this effectively maintains their distance and separation from Muslims in other ethnic groups. It remains a group unto itself, its members fully incorporated into neither the Islamic nor the Chinese community. The nature of the relationship between the Chinese and Malays as a whole therefore tends to force the individual with a foot in both to make a permanent decision in one direction or the other, as do most offspring of mixed Chinese-Malay marriages. Because a mixed marriage requires the conversion of the non-Muslim partner, and there is a high rate of rejection by the Chinese community of those who enter Islam, most of the latter become Malays and do not habitually revert to Chinese identity.

Thus the selection of ethnic reference groups can vary depending upon the perception of the relative ranking of ethnic groups within the wider social system, which then determines the oppositions being expressed.

It should be pointed out that this oscillation phenomenon is by no means a new one in the predominantly immigrant populations of the major port and urban settlements of Malaysia (and Singapore). The well-known chronicler of Malacca history and author of the *Hikayat Abdullah*,[3] Abdullah Munshi, was himself descended from a Yemeni Arab who migrated to India and married a Tamil. This man's son thereafter emigrated to Malacca, where he married a *Jawi Peranakan* and became the father of Abdullah. Abdullah himself, who spoke Malay, Tamil, and Arabic, would sometimes identify with the Indian and Arab communities (e.g., when mixing with the Indian soldiers in the Malacca garrison, where he learned his Tamil), but often declared, particularly when promoting the cause of Malay literacy, that "in spite of his mixed ancestry he always thought of himself as a Malay" (1849:32).

We may probably conclude, therefore, that the situational selection of ethnic identity, in which some factor of immediate relevance is equated with an ethnic status, is a long-continuing one, and bears no direct relationship to the length of residence of a group or individual in Malaysia. This pattern appears to contrast with the West African situation reported by Banton (1965) among urban tribal immigrants, where exclusiveness of tribal identity and membership is apparently maintained even within the broader ties of the Muslim community. In Freetown, according to Banton, even members of Muslim tribes act in a more exclusive and competitive fashion, such as in the construction of bigger and better tribal mosques, although there is a sense of communality among Muslim tribes which creates a cleavage between them and tribes who are not Muslims.

Finally, none of the many cases observed showed the remotest symptoms of personal insecurity or marginality arising from the lack of firm identity. On the contrary, such easy switching of ethnic identity seems to be of positive value in enabling the individual to avoid tensions due to inconsistencies of role expectations in any given set of circumstances. This is shown by the fact that few people are consciously aware of shifts in ethnic status either on the part of themselves or of others, and individuals do not appear to have problems of cordial relations and acceptance in either of the selected reference groups.

NOTES

1. The term "Penang" can refer either to the State of Penang, which includes the island and a portion of the adjacent mainland, to the island alone, or even just to the main urban settlement, more correctly known as George Town. Since all the fieldwork reported in this paper was conducted in the urban area, the primary focus throughout this paper is on the city of George Town, although it is believed that the findings are also valid in other towns and in some rural areas as well.
2. Arabic terms meaning "son of/daughter of" followed by the given name of the father, a device used by all Malays in lieu of a surname; thus Ahmad bin Abdullah, Ahmad son of Abdullah.

3. The *Hikayat Abdullah* (*The Story of Abdullah*) is a collection of reminiscences and astringent observations on both Malay and colonial life in the early nineteenth century, written by a scholar who moved freely in the circles of Raffles and other colonial administrators in Malacca and Singapore.

EDITORS' NOTE

* D.K.K. stands for darah ke-turunan Kling (of Kling descent).

** MARA is an acronym for Majlis Amanah Ra'ayat. It is an agency responsible for providing loans, training, insurance, trading contacts, and other assistance to aspiring Malay entrepreneurs.

The Kedayans

P. M. SHARIFFUDDIN

The Kedayans are a people with a common language and attitudes, who are distributed over a limited area of north-western Borneo along the coastal plain. In Brunei, they comprise about one quarter of the whole population of about 100,000 people. They also extend northwards along the coast and along the tidal stretches of the rivers as far as the Lawas district in the Fifth Division of Sarawak and across the Sabah border into the Sipitang district. There are also a number of Kedayans on Labuan Island, Sabah. Further south considerable numbers occur across the Sarawak border in the Miri district and as far down as the mouths of the Sibuti and Niah Rivers.

The Term "Kedayan"

Very little has been written about the Kedayans in any language. What little is published will be mentioned at the end of this paper. But wherever these people are referred to in any literature, they are nearly always called "Kedayan", with the spelling I have used here. However, as a matter of fact, in conversation, the sound is distinctly "Kadayan" here in Brunei. But it would only be confusing to adopt this spelling at the present stage, I suggest.

Whichever way we spell it, the term has no precise meaning in Brunei nowadays. Neither the Brunei Malays nor the Kedayans give any explanation for the term. It is simply accepted to describe these Muslim people who do not share the same descent and ancestry as the Bruneis (see following section for more on this origin aspect.)

It is very interesting that the late Sir Richard Winstedt's classical Malay Dictionary does give a meaning. He says it is Javanese Malay for "a Retainer". This also fits in with the usual version of these people's origin.

Kedayan Folklore

Where They Came From

It is a wide-spread belief among Kedayans that their people originated from Java. That they came to Brunei during the reign of Sultan Bolkiah who was nicknamed Nakoda Ragam. As a famed sea captain and voyager he became well-known to the peoples of the neighbouring countries including Java, Sumatra and the Philippines.

It is believed that when Bolkiah anchored at Java, he overheard stories about the wealth of Java and the rich produce of her soil. Brunei, though famous in name, was more backward in agricultural techniques than Java in those early times. It so happened that when Bolkiah landed on Java, he saw green fields of grass-bearing fruits — rice fields. Realising the importance of this crop to the people of Java, he began to understand what it would mean to his own people if they were to plant rice in Brunei. So Bolkiah looked for Javanese rice farmers who were ready to go and

Reprinted in abridged form from *Brunei Museum Journal* (1969), 15–23, by permission of the author and the Brunei Museum.

brought them to Brunei so that they might show his own people how to cultivate the crop.

Soon they arrived on the Brunei shores of what is known today as Pasir Jerudong and began planting rice. Presently a village formed around these fields and somehow these villagers were called Kedayans.

That was about five centuries ago. Jerudong District is still populated by Kedayans whose occupation is none other than farming (planting rice and other edible crops).

The Secret of the Tiger's Cave

Bukit Talanai, also known as *Sawang Rimau* (Tiger's Cave) is a small hill which was levelled recently in order to make a straight road from Brunei Town to Tutong. An old Kedayan legend connected with this site dates back to the time of our first story, to the reign of Sultan Bolkiah.

A certain Penglima, a descendant of the royal family, married to a beautiful Javanese woman, is believed to have resided at that time near Bukit Talanai. The Penglima, by virtue of his marriage to the Javanese woman, is considered to be an ancestor to the Kedayans.

To one side of Bukit Talanai, a large hollow — the Tiger's Cave — was known. Some people believed that this place was inhabited or made by tigers, while others thought that the Penglima himself had excavated it as an underground tunnel, so that he may be able to move secretly from place to place when he wanted to play tops (*bergasing*) or cock-fighting (*bersaong*), for he was a man of sport.

The tunnel was supposed to be very long, to reach from Talanai as far as Sinarubai, a place a few miles away. Unfortunately, the story can no longer be proved or disproved today! A similar story of a "Tiger's Cavern" is contained in the ancient handwritten *"Hikayat Negeri Brunei"* ("Stories and Records from Brunei").

Daily Life and Occupations

The Kedayans lead the simple life of farmers, planting rice, tapping rubber and keeping buffaloes and poultry on their small holdings. A farmer may own 3–4 acres on which he plants rice or fruit trees — and corn as an alternative to fruit trees. But rice is his main crop and food. Rubber is increasingly neglected. Hunting and fishing are practised whenever there is time away from farming.

Padi Cultivation

The Brunei Kedayan farm both wet and dry padi, generally one crop yearly. Double-cropping of wet padi would be difficult owing to shortage of water and inadequate methods of irrigation.

The farmer first selects a suitable place where the soil is fertile and then prepares for cultivation: felling and burning of timber, clearing and ploughing. As the ground is often too swampy for the use of a plough, it is prepared by yokes of two or more buffaloes, slowly puddling over the area to be planted, turning it into mud. Ridges are built as bunds round each plot of ground. Meanwhile the padi seeds are sown in nurseries.

The seedlings are planted by hand from the seed beds by the farmer and his family — very tiring work. In the following six months until harvest time the farmer inspects the fields daily to see that the crop is in good order and sufficient water is being supplied. When the plants bear grain the field is left to dry and the family will see to it that birds or mice do no damage. Scarecrows are erected. The fields are also supplied with elaborate systems of wires, ropes or vines from which sticks of bamboo, old tins and other simple rattles are suspended (*telinting*). A watcher controls the ropes which are tied to a lever from a shelter, setting the bamboo and the tins into motion to produce loud tinkling sounds scaring away the enemies of the crops.

Harvesting time (*musim mengatam*) is a happy, social period, specially when there is a good crop. The farmer fixes a day for the harvest and invites his neighbours to give him a helping hand. The crop is cut ear by ear with a sickle or hand-knife (*sabit*). People work in groups collecting the cut crop, thrashing and winnowing. Women remove the husks from the grain by pounding in wooden mortars (*lesong*) — though in many areas today a rice-mill is used.

Annual festival: Makan tahun

As soon as the harvest is completed, any Kedayan village will begin organising its annual festival (*makan tahun*) under the leadership of its headman (*penghulu*). An open hut (*taratak*) — large enough to accommodate all the villagers — is erected, financed by the community through subscriptions. Here people gather on the day of the festival, bringing along all kinds of food, as much as each family can afford to make from the produce of their farm. An Imam or Haji amongst them is asked to recite the prayers (*bacha-bacha*) while people sit down all around. When "amen" is quoted, food and drinks are shared out, including baked rice (*kelupis*), curry (*gulai kerbau*) and other specialities. What is not consumed on the spot is finally distributed equally to be taken home as a "share" (*champor*). The feast ends with a formal greeting and farewell (*jabat salam*) when everybody goes home.

Marriage

Marriage customs follow the Malay tradition. Agreement on the marriage is reached by the parents of the young people, often without their knowledge or consent. Presents and words of agreement (*menghantar tanda*) then follow. The relatives of the bridegroom go to the house of the bride to discuss the date and place of the marriage (*bersuroh*). The dowry (*berian*) — in form of money — is handed over to the parents of the bride.

Next the *berbedak* ceremony takes place: the bride and groom have their bodies anointed and rubbed over with rice powder (*bedak*, locally made). Then follows *berpachar* when the couple have their palms and soles anointed with henna (*pachar*). Now the Imam is called in by the families and guests to formally ask for the bridegroom's consent to marry in the presence of a witness (*wali*), a member of the bride's family. The marriage is considered official and legal once this ceremony (*membacha nikah*) is over.

But to finalise a wedding, *bersanding* is necessary. This takes place on the day following the *nikah* formality. Many guests are invited to take part on this happy day and be served with food and drinks. The young couple is beautifully dressed. The groom in rich Malay dress, usually a black sarong lined and woven with gold thread (*kain sungkit*), with gold *kris* tied to his waist and an embroidered *songkok* (*kupiah bepisnin*) instead of a cloth (*dastar*) on his head. The bride similarly wears a richly coloured sarong (*sutmaindra* or *jung sarat*) and a gold-embroidered blouse (*baju kurong*). She, as well as the groom, wear traditional golden bracelets (*gelang emas*) on arms and legs. Her hair is beautifully combed and a golden crown placed on the head. Sometimes a black beauty-spot (*tahi lalat, lit.* "fly-dirt") is fixed to one side of the cheeks to beautify her face.

Sacred Burial Places

The Kedayans pay homage (*berkaul*) at certain burial places that are considered sacred (*keramat*). People from around Sengkurong, Kilanas, Danau-Limau Manis and other villages go to Luba — the burial place of a late Sultan of Brunei now remembered as a saint. A family or group of people charter a large boat for transport to Luba, decorate it and turn out in their best attire. On arrival they seat themselves around the tombstone while an Imam or Haji reads extracts from the Koran (*bacha-bacha*). Heads of families then give out money to friends and relatives that are present (*bersedekah,* alms giving).

Each participant will now go forward, kiss the sacred tombstone and wish for favours (*ziarah*): a happy marriage, wealth, health, long life and so on. Women who wish for children will also take a bath in the river nearby while those wishing that they be clever, and those hoping that they have a good harvest kiss a small pebble and place it on the Sultan's tomb. They believe that if their pebble falls down from the tombstone their wishes will not be granted.

There are various sacred places (*keramat*) in Brunei, the tomb of "Dato Keramat" along the road outside Kampong Panchor, a village near Tutong and others at Subok, Kasat and other places close to Brunei Town.

Faith and Scepticism in Kelantan Village Magic

RAYMOND FIRTH

Earlier I have dealt very briefly (Raymond Firth, 1966, 122–5) with the part played by magic in the Kelantan fishing industry, particularly in placating sea spirits and in enabling master fishermen to 'meet with fish'. Whereas rice cultivators who celebrated the 'rice soul' tended to rely on their own resources, and master fishermen might perform some magic rites, Kelantan fishing has often been supplemented by magical aids of other kinds. Apart from general belief in the over-riding concept of the bounty of Allah, which might be granted or withheld at the will of the All-Mighty, help was sought from men of learning or holiness in the Muslim religious field, and from professional magicians (*bomoh*)[1] some of whom had no direct knowledge of the sea and fishing.

To illustrate local beliefs in fishing magic, including beliefs in its relation to Islam, I describe here a particular type of rite performed by a religious man (*orang lebai*), and its effect upon the local circle of fishermen. To set this in perspective I outline the general course of events in the fishing season of 1940, especially as seen by several master fishermen closely connected with this ritual. (For convenience I indicate the magical practitioner as B, and the master fishermen as L, M and P — cf. Firth, 1966, 109–111, 383, for some details of the fishing season and the receipts of L and M.)

I first consider the position of M. He was an intelligent man of long fishing experience who combined a rather self-consciously pious attitude towards Islam with a firm belief in spirits of the sea. With his dry, often subtle sense of humour and whimsical realism in discussing human relationships, his comments were among the most revealing offered to us. As the fishing season developed I noted several fairly distinct elements in his interpretation of success or failure. (The account is much compressed from my notebooks). Early in 1940 he like other fishermen was complaining about lack of success, and he had gone to a local holy man, To'Wali Awang of Bukit Merbau, to bless some rice he had taken, by stirring a finger in it. M spoke also of a net magician (*bomoh pukat*) living inland, whom local fishermen used. This man did not 'use *hantu*' but only the Kuran; he too uttered formulae over rice. M said he had called in this man a year or so before but without 'agreement' — he got no good catches as a result.

When M began to get good catches his first statement was in orthodox Muslim terms, for the bounty of Allah, expressed particularly through prayer and the blessing of the holy man. Early in February M got his new net ready and on his first day out he brought in the best catch of his village. I chaffed him about this, because the day before he had been very vague about making the traditional net offerings, and I thought he had not done these magic rites. I said 'But you didn't make

Reprinted in abridged form from W.R.Roff (ed.), *Kelantan, Religion, Society and Politics in a Malay State* (Kuala Lumpur: Oxford University Press, 1974), by permission of the author and the publishers.

the offerings!' He answered with a twinkle 'Made them — last night!' He had nine 'pious men' to perform the 'prayers of hope' (Firth, 1966, plate IIb) and one afterwards to make the offerings. For about a week he was very successful, and was elated, saying that other master fishermen would be very 'sick' at this outstanding performance; he likened their competition to cocks fighting and giving peck for peck. To draw him I said I supposed his success was due to his having had the fishing ground very much to himself, and to luck; he agreed, but added 'Tuhan Allah'. 'There it is — I think Tuhan Allah gives to me.' On another occasion he said 'Tomorrow, if Tuhan Allah grants, I shall get fish.' When he got a phenomenal catch, while many other nets got nothing, he said, obviously very pleased, that he was 'in agreement' — equivalent to being 'in luck'. He said that his success was due to To'Wali, the holy man, and hence to God. He added that six or seven fishing experts had gone to the holy man, but that he 'agreed' usually with only one or two. I asked why? He replied 'I don't know' but added with a laugh 'perhaps because if with all, they would all become rich, would all build tile houses, and the price of large boats would go up to $300!' But this idea that magical discrimination was necessary to avoid inflation was not meant very seriously. He said however that the arts of the holy man were often effective for only a week or so, instancing examples. (Note the pragmatic aspect of this: the chances are that one or two fishermen will have success, but their success will not continue for very long unless they have exceptional skill. What success that occurs can then be attributed to the immediate selective virtue of the holy man's blessing.)

Traditional folk ideas also played a considerable part in M's thinking about fishing. Towards the end of February I met him one evening with a ritual smear of rice paste on his forehead — he had just been dyeing his net according to his usual practice, weekly, with appropriate rites asking for blessing and the goodwill of sea spirits. As an instance of his magical belief, he said he had just met another expert who had just put ropes on his new net. 'I told him that he will probably get fish; a new net gets fish.' I asked if offerings would be made over it. He answered 'One must; if it is a new net, one must make offerings.' He went on to say that if it had been him he would not have put ropes on the net that day. Why, because it was Friday, the day one goes to mosque? No, because it was the 14th day of the 4th month (by local Malay reckoning). On the 4th, 14th, and 24th of the 4th month one should not do work on the net — nor also on the 3rd, 13th and 23rd of the 3rd month, and so on. The net would foul the lure, and break. 'But would you not go to sea?' I asked. 'Going to sea, that doesn't matter.' he replied. But he added that if it were for (ordinarily) the first time in a season, the opening day, he wouldn't. He quoted a colloquial saying which may be rendered as 'An ill-starred day, 'twill tear the net' — so old people said. Then he went on 'but if a *juru selam* has knowledge, a bit of revelation, it doesn't matter'. M was convinced that boat measurements could express relationships of good and bad fortune in fishing (Raymond Firth, 1966, 145), and inclined to believe that there were ways of injuring another man's net so that it wouldn't get fish. He told me that an *ubat* could be prepared by mixing hair of pig or tiger (both animals unmentionable at sea) with an infusion of *larak salah* (a medicinal plant, unidentified); if this were put in a kind of Siamese pot for keeping rice warm and secreted in the boat carrying the net, it would be prevented from getting fish. Such an *ubat* could cost $5 to $10 — a vast sum in 1940. He said that one fisherman alleged such magical interference with his net and so had not gone out to sea for a month; that a *bomoh* to whom he had gone for help refused to come, saying, "That is a net to which people have done evil'. Yet M was doubtful about the efficacy of much-vaunted talismans such as ambergris (Raymond Firth, 1966, 125). He distinguished between 'true' ambergris, which he described as the vomit of a large fish, and alleged ambergris from Mecca, which he had already used to no avail, and he held sceptically that while real ambergris was very dear that which people sold as such probably wasn't true anyway. Certain traditional taboos he categorically denied. I had been told that umbrellas should not be carried on a fishing boat. M argued that this was not correct. He said he took an umbrella himself in the rainy season, and suggested that I take one on my own boat; he said he had seen umbrellas occasionally on boats at Beserah in Pahang, and that when parties including women travelled to Semerak, Besut and other places they must have umbrellas against the midday sun. He added that people of the Perhentian islands, who were wise in all sea lore, brought umbrellas and even shoes with them when they came to the mainland. He certainly did not subscribe rigidly to a rule against mixing terrestrial with marine categories of objects. He was not without magical reservations. He said that one thing was prohibited on a boat, a certain kind of pandanus mat; if this was taken aboard a sailing boat there would be no wind. Yet even here he commented shrewdly, 'I think this is not true either — if it is taken in the season when there is plenty of wind, how will a mat stop it'?

With this critical intelligence and pious tendency, he might have been expected to reject the more purely magical rites connected with traditional *hantu*. Yet here he displayed an uncertainty, a swing in opinion, which showed his more orthodox and more sophisticated views to some extent at war with the strength of his involvement in his daily striving for fish and for reputation. He was no blind adherent of magic. Towards the end of the season, when fish were very scarce, P said 'There are no fish, so people are using *bomoh*.' Commented M caustically, 'When fish are plentiful *bomoh* don't matter; all men get fish'. But he also held that if fish were not in season then it was no good making offerings; the object of the offerings was to get men to 'meet with fish', not to conjure up fish out of nowhere. He said 'If I don't get fish for several days, and all other men are getting fish, *then* I make the offerings so that the sea spirits will be pleased, and I will meet with fish.'

The critical elements in M's judgement of the validity of magical performance emerged especially in his attitudes towards the practices of B, who while generally a minor scholar and teacher of religion, also served on occasion as *bomoh*. At an early stage in the 1940 season M had employed B to make the offerings for his net, and continued to give him alms as a kind of retaining fee. But M was clearly ambivalent about B's powers. He said at the start 'B is only a little skilled; he's not a man of the sea', and attributed his own net's success as much to the blessing of the holy man (who, however, was not a 'man of the sea' either!) When M heard that another fisherman, L, whom he did not rate highly was going to have B also make net offerings he was scornful — all the same, I think he won't get any fish; he is not skilled; if he makes the offerings today, tomorrow, he won't get above other people. You will be able to see; he's not skilled.' And he laughed and said 'We shall see'.

Now M's general estimate of L was about right, but in fact, whether through a spurt of enthusiasm generated by knowledge of the offerings or not, L's net did actually get a bumper catch the next day. This was generally attributed to the efforts of B. When next evening I asked M what he thought he replied 'I think B has magic power (*ada keramat*).' He said he thought that B was 'true' and skilled. Some days before, P, an old fishing expert and *bomoh*, had said to him that in making offerings to land spirits B was wrong; that one should invoke only sea spirits for fishing, and on the beach, not beside a house. Yet, M now thought, B was right: 'inland spirits can reach out to sea; sea spirits can reach inland.' However, M was much indebted to P, to whom he had been like an adopted son, and he added diplomatically 'when I am with P I follow him; when I am with B I follow him; I don't want to fight with them. But I think B is cleverer than P; I think B is *keramat*.'

Now this was a switch of opinion, as others too realized. Our servant Mamat, who had known B's father as a *bomoh besar*, and thought B himself was a clever *bomoh*, told me that four days previously M had said that he didn't trust B's performance. 'Now, he trusts!' (But P, with whom I discussed the matter, was still sceptical. His view was, let us wait and see; other nets for which B made offerings have got nothing as yet.)

A couple of days later M and I returned to the subject of fishing success. He held that only those master fishermen whose fathers had also been experts got fish. He quoted cases of men without ancestral heritage whose lack of success proved this. I asked why — do the dead watch over the sea? 'No, they don't come back,' he replied, but went on, 'I think they ask over there' — meaning that they intercede with Allah on behalf of their sons. He said that he himself went every Friday to the cemetery to ask his father, his mother and his dead child to make him rich and give him fish — he prayed to them. Their bones are in the grave, he said, but their spirits (he used the term *nyawa*) are yonder and have the shape of men. 'But do they hear?' I asked. 'People say they hear; if not, what is the good of going? It is simply work thrown away!' Then he came back to the subject of B. He said that about ten years before B had made offerings for one net, but no fish resulted, so he stopped. The net of M himself recently was the first net for which he had performed ritual since then. M then revealed that misleadingly he had told P — as indeed he had virtually told me too — that B had *not* made the offerings for him. He said he had told P, 'What is the good of getting him, a man of prayer, who doesn't go to sea . . . ?' He said that he had talked in this vein, but then towards midnight, when all men were inside their houses, he had the rites performed. Afraid that if it were generally known that he had had the magic done, but got no fish, people would chaff him and he would be ashamed, he had given a false impression.

M continued to oscillate in his attitude towards the validity of B's magical technique. When other master fishermen were successful and he himself was not he said 'It is not that I am unskilled, no; I think that no fish have been given to me'. He had lost confidence in B. Retrospectively, he thought that on the days when L got large catches it was because Tuhan Allah had wished to give him fish; even if B had not acted as *bomoh,* L could easily have got the fish. M backed this up by pointing to two other expert fishermen for whom B had made offerings, and who had caught no fish. In order to draw him my wife commented 'It is as Tuhan Allah wills'. He replied rather sharply 'As Tuhan Allah wills — but the men of Perupok [his competitors] get the bulk of the cash'. He admitted that some people might have special powers: one fisherman, previously markedly successful, had lost his wife by death, and had had few good catches since. M commented 'I think his wife was *keramat.*' But thinking of the non-success of others beside himself he said in resignation 'Tuhan Allah gives to all the same.' He hoped that people would speak of himself as good-omened, of blessed mouth, and then he would continue to get fish. About *bomoh* he said that people went from one to another, seeking success, and if they couldn't go themselves they sent their womenfolk far afield, as far as Ketereh or Pasir Mas, to get rice or water that had been blessed. However, though M himself got no further large catches, when some fishermen for whom B had made the offerings did very well he reverted to his opinion that B was *keramat.* He also pointed out that P had formerly acted as local *bomoh* for the nets, and was probably ashamed to see that another had been successful where he had not. He said 'perhaps the sea spirits like the offerings of B; perhaps they don't like the offerings of P.' And he added rather unfeelingly that P was an old man and perhaps he would die. M's belief in B's powers was further demonstrated when his eyes became very bloodshot from his work at sea. We put drops of acriflavin in them but he also consulted B, who said that he had been afflicted by sea spirits and recited a formula over them; he then refused more medicine, saying that he would see the effects of the formula first — though he consented to wear dark glasses which we gave him, saying that B had also advised them.

So here was an expert fisherman who, having a great amount of empirical knowledge of his craft, had also a set of beliefs of a mystical order, mingling Islamic concepts of the bounty of Allah with concepts of the power of sea spirits and the efficacy of human ritual to placate them. But he did not have a simple blind faith. He did not operate 'in obedience to the rules which the superstitious people have followed for ages' (Clifford, 1897, 148; also Skeat, 1900, 193). Doubt, suspension of judgement and even scepticism were mingled with his belief. A constant theme in his whole situation was his faith in the control exercised by the will of Allah over the destinies of men — this he never questioned. But a variable factor, in his judgement, was the degree to which the bounty of Allah was being accorded to him personally. Yet this was cross-cut by two other elements. One was the pragmatic nature of the situation: if it was the season when fish were normally absent, or if fish were present but the interference of another fisherman spoiled the shooting of his net, then he attributed his poor catch to these empirical factors and not to lack of Allah's favour. Nor were the rituals of magic, in his view, designed for such situations; they were for situations where fish were available but he was not getting them. The test in particular was where other fishermen were getting catches but he was not. This was where in his view offerings to spirits could be useful. But offerings in themselves could not remedy lack of fishing skill — hence his protests in the case of L. Yet if a *bomoh* were powerful enough (*keramat*) then he might overcome even relative lack of fishing skill, though only for a short time. Hence his concession that after all the performances of B *did* seem to give results. Note that his position was not quite that which anthropologists have generally recognized — where the efficacy of the ritual in general is not questioned but only the proficiency of individual practitioners. The position of M was more complex. The efficacy of the will of Allah was not questioned, but the efficacy of the arts of *bomoh* was subject to continual scrutiny — not just individual *bomoh,* but all *bomoh.* Only when empirical evidence seemed to indicate that they had produced results was he willing to concede their validity. But his alternation of faith and scepticism about the performances of *bomoh* did not mean that he lacked a general belief in the significance of magical forces. Apart from his free use of the concepts of *hantu* and of *keramat,* for instance, he recognized various rules of a mystical order, especially when backed by the authority of the elders. What he questioned was not so much the operation of mystical forces as the ability of men to cope with them. What did emerge very clearly with M was his tendency to retreat from faith in *bomoh* to faith in Allah — not at all the conventional picture of 'Malay first and Muhammedan afterwards' which is often offered in the older literature (e.g. Clifford, *loc. cit.).*

Another complicating element in M's attitudes was the problem of the extent to which modern changes had rendered old concepts and practices invalid. However, he did not seem as much bothered by this as did P, who as a *bomoh* of long standing had more of a vested interest in traditional matters. On one occasion P admitted with a laugh that while nets should be ritually sprinkled in order to get fish, as tradition dictated, nets which had not been sprinkled also took fish. He added, with a twist of his mouth, wryly, 'They don't understand, they haven't learnt, they don't know' — a kind of rather bitter 'ignorance is bliss' view.

The position of the *bomoh* B was also very interesting. He was a producer, not a consumer, of fishing magic; yet, a professedly religious man, he was operating with traditional local concepts of *hantu.* I was impressed by his apparent modesty and sincerity. He took the line that his role was to aid fishermen, not to substitute for them. 'Just to help', was his slogan. When L got his first phenomenal catch of fish B was sitting near by on the sand when the carrier boat came in. After the fish had been sold he asked me how much it fetched. When I told him he said 'Good!' So I asked him 'What if it had been a poor catch?' 'What about it, Tuan, I would help again.' His view was that his rites, if effective, helped to stop the fish from bolting the net, so that the fisherman had a fair chance to catch them.

B allowed me to be present when he performed his rites over the net of L; they began about 9 p.m. at the house where the net was kept, on the verandah. The master fisherman, who was also the major net owner, and four members of his crew constituted the group, apart from a few children on the outskirts. First the *bomoh* laid a cotton thread of three strands in the middle of some soft wax and moulded it to candle shape. A tray of conventional offerings had been prepared, and from it B took an egg, examined it close to his eye and then stuck the candle upright against it. He called for *beras kunyit* — rice with some shavings of turmeric root in it. Holding this in his hands and facing towards the sea (away from Mecca, in itself significant for a ritual address by a man of religious learning) he recited a long formula. From time to time he stirred the rice with his finger. (He was rocking slowly from side to side, a movement which I had noted he made also in ordinary conversation.) Most of the formula was inaudible, but occasionally he spoke more loudly, enabling me to hear what seemed to be characteristic phrases of the kind used by *bomoh*, addressed to *jinn* and *hantu* by name, and asserting that the reciter knew their origins. One of the principal spirits I heard addressed was Jinn Kuning, generally believed in Kelantan peasant circles to be very powerful. Then the *bomoh* passed the tray of offerings through incense smoke and recited another long formula.

The group then adjourned outside the house, on the earth below. A sail had been put up as a windbreak; the net remained on the verandah. I asked if I could see exactly what was to be done. B said 'Yes, but it is good if you keep ten feet away,' and I noted that part way through the rite he ordered one man who had inched forward to within about six feet to get back. At this stage the offerings were divided into three portions: i, for consultation; ii, for placing at the boats; iii, for throwing into the sea.

i. Consultation. The *bomoh* took a *parang* (short chopper) and with it dug a rectangular hole in the earth behind the sail screen. He stuck the parang in the soil at the side, then carefully slid the first portion of offerings on a banana leaf off the plate into the bottom of the hole. The top of the egg was broken with the parang and the egg added again to the offerings — having been opened for the spirits. The candle was lit from a lamp used hitherto to illuminate the scene, the lamp was extinguished, and the candle too was lowered into the hole. Then B, with knees apart, recited another formula, observing the flame the while. He sprinkled turmeric rice upon it, and also threw some of the rice up on to the net above, twice, part way through and at the end. Several times while the formula was being recited the flame died down, seeming as if it might go out, but then revived again.

ii. Boat offering. Immediately after, the rite over the boat took place. B sat in the boat, held rice paste in a brass bowl and recited a formula — a picturesque sight in the moonlight. The boat owner then sprinkled his boat with *ayer beluru* (medicated water, *beluru* being a large climbing plant, *Entada* sp., of which the bark has a pungent odour). B then sprinkled rice paste and burnt incense first under the bow and then under the stern of the boat. A similar rite was then performed for the carrier boat, used to bring catches of fish to shore. Each boat captain sprinkled his own boat with medicated water, one saying 'I just dare to do my own', as an indication of the awe with which the rite was viewed. The second portion of offerings was put by the sternpost of each boat.

iii. Then the *bomoh* went down to the sea and stood in the water up to his shins; there he cast away the third set of offerings, and so completed the rite.

The formulae used, and most of the offerings, seemed to be part of the common stock of *bomoh's* invocations and rites. But an idiosyncratic element, which was novel to the fishermen and which they did not pretend to understand, was the procedure with egg and candle, which seemed to involve very powerful spirits, needing special knowledge and confidence to control. Great interest was taken in the display and several fishermen came to discuss it with me. P emphasized that the results depended upon Allah and said 'I have had no teacher for this; I don't understand the meaning of it. The people who use it know.' But he and the others thought that the candle flame gave sign of the advent of *jinn* of various kinds. He contrasted with this the procedures of *juru selam* who used only excerpts from the Kuran as formulae, combined with smearing on rice paste. B himself took a very tentative attitude towards the efficacy of his rites. He was not sceptical about them, or cynical as M tended to be — it was rather that he seemed honestly to think that their outcome was uncertain. He said he was the only man in the Perupok area to perform rites in this way — which was confirmed by the fishermen. He said also that he used the same technique in cases of sickness, but only a little — if a patient was crazy or had swollen limbs. His knowledge of what to do did not go far.

In accounting for the validity of his performance B explained that his grandfather and his father had been *bomoh,* but that while he had had a little instruction from his father his *guru* had been To'Mamat of Kota Bharu and Sungei Besar, who had been a pupil of his grandfather. B said that he used primarily Jinn Tanah, the Earth Spirit, in his rites (hence the adjournment to the ground outside the house, and the pit dug in the ground). As against the opinion of P he held that according to the teaching of his own guru, the spirits of the sea could ascend on to the shore, and spirits of the inland could be effective at sea. Hence he performed his rite inland, with the earth as location, instead of on the seashore — though he also invoked Anah, Manah, Ganah[2] as spirits of the strand. He said that he had been told by his teacher not to invoke 'Sang Gano' (Sang Gana. cf. Cuisinier, 1936, 163n), lest being always present but called upon only occasionally he be angry and make people ill. But he did use Semar, (who, he said, originated in Mecca and was the first to become Haji — so in his view was obviously legitimate to invoke; this bears out Cuisinier [1936, 182n]). Of the candle rite B said that he judged by the flame whether the *jinn* were 'in agreement', whether they desired the appeal. He obviously felt that in invoking these *jinn* he was dealing with dangerous forces. So he refused to recite his formula to me; he said that without the flame he was afraid — he couldn't tell what their attitude was. With the flame one could tell 'a little' about how the spirits would be likely to react: if the flame was small and red, it was Jinn Merah; if small and white, then Jinn Puteh; if clear, then Jinn Kuning. When the flame burned up brightly this was a good sign; if it died down, this was a bad sign. As for egg offerings (to Jinn Tanah) he used these according to the stage of the rite. On the first night he used only one egg, on the second night he used two; should his efforts still be unsuccessful he continued, adding an egg each night until he reached a total of seven. There he stopped — if no results had been obtained by then he would hand the case over to another *bomoh,* since it would be an indication that the *jinn* were not willing to cooperate with him. He explained the unique nature of his rites locally by pointing out that his teacher gave his *ilmu* to only one son, and to himself, B, who was like a son to him, and that he had no other pupil to whom he handed it on.

Though I did not challenge his religious orthodoxy directly I am sure that he regarded himself as doing a morally and theologically respectable job, controlling and directing the *jinn* in the interests of hungry and suffering humanity. I did question him on the general issue. He said quite definitely that an *orang lebai* might be a *bomoh.* Those with 'knowledge' might have it of two kinds — of the Kuran and of the *bomoh* — and it was legitimate to use both if one had them. A religious man might 'blow' and make offerings. But he might not play the violin. Why not? Because the Prophet Muhammad didn't like it. Hence such a man couldn't conduct a *main puteri.* He himself could go into trance (*lupa*) but was embarrassed to do so. When I questioned whether the Imam and other dignitaries approved of religious men being *bomoh* he replied 'How can they be angry, when the Imam himself calls me in? When his son or his wife is sick, he called me; he has been two or three times to do so.' He said also that To' Guru Bachok, a highly respected Muslim teacher, had the attitude, if a person is sick the thing is to clear it up — implying that the end justified the means. B said too that even *main puteri* was tolerated by Islamic dignitaries, provided it was held for one of their relatives in another house than their own. I emphasize that what I am giving here is essentially the viewpoint of a local man justifying himself, and a viewpoint in 1940; it is not necessarily a 'correct' view from the standpoint of the religious authorities, and it is not necessarily a modern view. But it was certainly widely held in the Bachok area thirty years ago, with sincerity and a sense of moral commitment.

The admitted uncertainty as to his results which B showed was the very antithesis of a common stereotype of a magician, often represented as boldly confident in the validity of his rites. Some Kelantan *bomoh,* such as my old teacher To' Mamat Mindok, were quietly and firmly convinced of their powers. This was perhaps partly temperamental, partly a matter of field — for, in the end, sick people probably get well more often than mediocre fishermen catch fish! But B behaved as a man who had in his possession a powerful but dangerous tool of the accuracy of which he was not certain, but with which he was willing to experiment, convinced of the propriety of his intentions. He might almost be described as a 'reluctant magician'. He certainly seemed very far from wanting to claim the quality of being possessed of supernatural power, as had sometimes been said of him. Gimlette, one of the most careful students of Kelantan magic, wrote of 'the self-reliance of the *bomoh* and his sublime belief in his calling' (1929, 52). As a general statement this can pass, but it must not be taken as applying to every instance, and it is important to realize this in order to understand the interplay between the producer and the consumer of magic, and the nature of interpretations given to it.

NOTES

1. Variance in spelling and in meaning have been given to this term in the literature. Howison (1801, 100) has *boomo* (as doctor); Wilkinson (1903, 134) has *bomor* and *bomo;* and *bomoh* (1932, 150); Swettenham, (1905, 30) has *bomo*. Favre (1875, II, 226) gives only *bumu*, as elephant-hunter. Pak Che Mat once gave me *bo'omor* in what he seemed to think was high-class pronunciation. Like Gimlette (1913, 29; 1915, 2 *et seq*.: 1929, 18 *et seq*.; and Cuisinier (1936, 31 *et seq*.; 1957, 89) I have tended to favour *bomor* (1966, 122–4), which has also had official authority (State of Kelantan: Estimates, 1938, 23 — 'Bomor for H.H.') (cf. Gimlette, 1913, 31). I here follow the recent *Kamus Dewan* (1970).
2. According to To'Mamat Mindok [a teacher of magic], independently, these three, or alternatively Anah, Janah, Manah, were siblings, *hantu* of the water's edge, responsible for overturning boats as they came in; their father was Usemain Pari (c.f. Cuisinier, 1936, 183) and their mother Mak Sengaroh.

Folk Islam and the Supernatural

THOMAS M. KIEFER

The Tausug approach to death and the afterlife revolves around the concept of religious merit and its acquisition by man through the accumulation of good deeds and regular performance of ritual obligations. Religious merit has both an active and a passive dimension. As the result of man's active striving to acquire merit, it is called *karayawan,* literally "goodness". As a gift of God to man according to principles which only He can ultimately understand, it is called *pahala* (the passive dimension). In addition, *karayawan* in this context also implies a state of pleasure and happiness in the afterlife. Many of my informants explained the idea to me by describing heaven as analogous to a state of perpetual sexual orgasm. But the amount of *karayawan* one receives in heaven is directly proportional to the amount of *pahala* one has been given by God in return for good deeds.

For the Tausug heaven and hell are thought of less as physical places than particular states of being. *Sulga* (heaven) and *narka* (hell) are commonly used terms derived from Arabic, but quite often *karayawan* (state of goodness) and *kasiksaan* (state of suffering) are used instead. The pleasures of heaven and the pains of hell — which are vividly described in the Koran — are a source of much everyday imagery. One old man told me of two dreams during which his soul visited heaven briefly before returning to his sleeping body. In the first dream he went to heaven and saw his recently murdered son, sitting in a golden rocking chair and surrounded by beautiful women, food, and other pleasures. He was about to enter when his son said "Do not come in father . . . it will be a long time yet until you die." In the second dream he came to a bridge leading to the entrance to heaven crossing over a pit of fire. He saw that one of his distant kinsmen had fallen from the bridge and was being devoured by a crocodile as punishment for stealing a lantern from the mosque. Another woman was being punished for inducing an abortion: she had fallen into the fire, and a monkey was tugging ferociously at a bamboo tree which had sprouted from her vagina. A rapist was watching his penis being cut off; a blasphemer was having his tongue pulled out; and thieves were dragging their stolen goods through the fire. He was scared as he approached the bridge, but a helpful man told him to read the Koran. As he crossed he looked back to see many screaming people falling into the fire.

The Tausug conception of the afterlife is a mixture of orthodox Moslem ideas syncretized with older ideas common to many of the non-Moslem peoples of the greater Indonesian Archipelago, especially the idea of multiple souls. While no two religious leaders have exactly the same ideas of the subject, the theory of the afterlife described by one young religious leader can be taken as fairly typical.

Excerpted from Thomas M. Kiefer, *The Tausug, Violence and Law in a Philippine Muslim Society* (New York: Holt, Rinehart and Winston, Inc., 1972), by permission of the author and the publishers.

According to this man, the human person is divided into body and soul. The body is composed of proportions of the four cardinal elements: earth, air, fire and water; in addition, the body possesses the faculties of intelligence and feeling. Since the state of *karayawan* is primarily a sentient state, it follows that the religious merit given by God to man is attached solely to the body, not the soul. Only the body is capable of the free choice which leads to good or evil; the soul is good from the beginning.

The soul itself is actually composed of four souls. First is the transcendental soul which exists in heaven at all times, although it will occasionally visit the body when it is praying. God created one transcendental soul for each person, past, present, and future. It is totally good, does not suffer the punishments given to the body, and will eventually be reunited with the body in heaven. Second, there is the life-soul, sometimes associated with the blood. Before a child is born, it begins to attach itself permanently to his body, imperfectly at first, and does not leave until he dies, although it may wander during dreams. Third, there is breath, the real essence of life itself, which always remains while the person is alive, even while the life-soul may be temporarily gone. Finally, there is the spirit-soul which also wanders during dreams and which is the essence of a man's shadow.

When a man dies, all four souls are initially separated from his body. Since the source of all sin is the body and since all men have committed some evil deeds during their life, the bodies of all men (with the exception of a very few extremely pious individuals) go to hell. The time spent being tortured in hell varies with the number of bad deeds which have been recorded.

Eventually the ashes of the body leave hell and are sifted to separate the remaining good from the bad. The good goes to heaven and is reunited with the soul. The amount of pleasure felt by the body in heaven is proportional to the amount of good works the individual has performed in his lifetime. All Moslems eventually reach heaven, while Christian Filipinos are destined to remain in hell forever. Americans, according to one informant who was perhaps being tactful, go to an intermediate state between heaven and hell.

Once religious merit is acquired by an individual, God will not take it away again. Good behavior is always eventually rewarded, and bad behavior punished in a relatively direct and uncomplicated manner. There is little emphasis on faith, devotion, grace, or forgiveness, although similar ideas are not unknown to the Tausug.

One of the major differences between Tausug folk Islam and the stricter Islam taught by the Egyptian religious teachers in Jolo concerns the transference of religious merit from one individual to another. According to the Tausug, if one man is innocently killed or otherwise victimized by another, the accumulated religious merit of the killer is transferred to the victim, while the accumulated bad deeds of the victim are transferred to the killer. The uneven exchange of life is balanced by a compensating exchange of religious status in the afterlife; reciprocity in this world is balanced by a complementary reciprocity in the other world. Most Tausug fighters believe that if they die in battle they will be automatically "inside of *karayawan.*" These ideas are opposed by the foreign teachers, but given the great emphasis which Tausug place upon reciprocity and exchange in all aspects of their life, it is understandable that they are applied to religion as well.

When death comes, there is no public expression of grief on the part of kinsmen and friends; whatever people may feel in private, the acceptance of inevitable fate dominates the public aspects of Tausug funerals. There may be some crying on the part of close consanguine kin, but it is thought better not to do so. The only overt expression I observed of strong grief on the part of a male was a young father who began raving and aimlessly firing his rifle shortly after his three year old son died of dysentery. In cases of homicide the grief of the victim's close kin is usually hidden by sentiments of vengeance directed against the killer.

The body is taken immediately to the home of the deceased or the home of close kin. The body is thought to be both physically and ritually polluting and must be thoroughly cleansed by religious officials before internment through a series of bathings in ritually prepared water. Defecation must be removed from the anus, body orifices cleaned and plugged with cotton, and the body dressed in a loosely fitting white shroud.

On the evening before burial, ritual prayers are offered in Arabic for the deceased. Young women who are expert in reading the Koran are invited to read in an effort to increase the fund of religious merit and ease the pains of hell. The object of the recitation is to finish as much of the Koran as possible in one evening, and each woman begins reading in a different place at the same time in a deafening torrent of ritual chant. One week after the death a special seventh-day ceremony is held by the kinsmen of the deceased. A major feast is given and a prayer is offered for the dead. As on all social occasions of this kind, distant kinsmen, friends, and allies are invited and contribute to the cost of the occasion.

Burial usually takes place the afternoon following the day of death. A final version of the normal daily prayer is done on behalf of the dead by the priests. The body is carried down from the house on a bamboo stretcher and conveyed to the nearest cemetery where a grave has been prepared by hollowing out a niche in the earth from the sides of a pit. The body is placed facing Mecca, the niche is boarded up, and the pit filled with dirt.

Tausug believe that it is not merely being dead which is significant, but being dead and knowing it. Since the corpse is not totally devoid of feeling, it must be told that it is dead so that it will not persist in the delusion that it is merely dreaming. At the graveside a special ritual is read in Arabic, which is necessary in order to wake the dead up, tell him he is dead, and allow him to become adjusted to his new status. If this is not done properly the wandering soul of the dead will perhaps communicate with the living through dreams.

While in everyday behavior Tausug are quite unconcerned with the souls of the dead, two yearly rituals are conducted in each community to pacify them. In the month prior to Ramadan the ritual of *nispu* is held in the mosque on the full moon. A feast is given and prayers are offered on behalf of the souls in heaven and hell; if this was not done, it is said that the dead would curse the living. The souls are attracted by the smell of the food, and some people say that they also partake in the feast. Several days later the entire community turns out to the cemetery to clean the graves, remove weeds, and plant flowers. A prayer for the dead is offered by religious leaders, and the Koran is briefly read on each to ease the sufferings of the deceased and bring religious merit to the reader. This is followed by a communal feast in the graveyard.

Social anthropologists sometimes maintain that the religion of a society is a reflection of its social structure, that the ideas men have about life influence the ideas they have about death. Most Tausug believe that the fate of a man's body and soul in the afterlife depend at least partially on how well his surviving kinsmen perform the rituals on his behalf: prayers, reading the Koran, pouring water on the grave "to cool the body off," repeating the profession of faith over and over again, and others. Again the Egyptian teachers disagree, but they have had little success in changing belief outside the town. In a society where a man's death may often be the result of his obligations to his kinsmen and friends, it seems reasonable that these same kinsmen should be able to help him in turn after his death.

Another source of disagreement between traditional Tausug and the small percentage of Islamic modernists in the town concerns the importance given to private magic and esoteric knowledge as a means of obtaining a shortcut into heaven, bypassing the usual good works and ritual obligations. As indicated before, Tausug set very high ethical standards for themselves, yet consistently violate these standards in practice. The reason for this is partially a result of the same tendencies toward risk taking and stress seeking which operate in piracy and feuding. Just as a man can take a physical risk involving danger to his body, so he can also take an ethical risk involving exposure to the dangers of the afterlife and a punishing God. But the risk, like the risk of armed combat, is not "really" a risk if the person has the proper magical knowledge. It is for this reason that to an outsider it often seems as if the Tausug throw themselves into evil with a robust enthusiasm, and then regret their conduct later with as much enthusiasm, especially as they grow older and begin to see a day of reckoning. Tausug folk Islam is, perhaps, a form of adventure for the elderly.

Perspectives on Modernization

Three Major Problems Confronting the World of Islam

SAID RAMADAN

"Which, in your opinion, are the major problems of the Muslim world, the problems upon which the attention of the workers of Islam should be focused, and to the solution of which they should devote all, or the greater part of, their endeavours?" This was my question to my friend who has been working for Islam for the last thirty years. For a while he remained silent and then replied: "I consider three problems to be responsible for the disastrous state of affairs in the Muslim world: first, the failure to distinguish between what God laid down in His Book and the Tradition of His Prophet, and the elaborations derived therefrom by our legists; second, the plight of womenfolk in Muslim society; and third, the perversion of the meaning of "obedience to those in authority" to denote abject subservience and shameless acquiescence to rulers, regardless of the extent of the wrongs that they might commit and the injustices which they might perpetrate."

This observation was followed by a long discussion which centered upon these questions, with a view to the full appreciation of the importance of these problems, and the realisation of the need for earnest, unrelenting endeavour towards their solution. During this discussion, I found myself keenly responsive to the need for appreciation of the importance of these problems, and as my learned friend held forth on the subject, I had the feeling of a doctor's fingers probing sore spots. For these three problems do indeed occupy a pre-eminent position among those numerous maladies which afflict our body-politic. Moreover, these maladies are becoming chronic ones and as time passes we are getting used to them.

The first of these problems is our failure to distinguish between what has been laid down by God in His Book and the Tradition of the Prophet (Sunnah) on the one hand, and the elaborations on their basis by our jurists on the other hand. In deploring this failure, we neither wish to deny the value of the opinions of our Fuqaha nor to slight these venerable men in any way. On the contrary, we believe their work to constitute a great asset, a prized treasure of which we should feel proud. We believe that we should pore over the subtleties of their learning, and should derive the utmost benefit from it. What is necessary, however, is that we should at the same time be very clear about the following important points:

1. That the Quran and the Sunnah alone constitute the Shariah (Divine Law) of God which is binding on Muslims; that these two alone form the ideological and practical basis of life for the Muslim nation.

2. That there is nothing strange in the fact that disagreements exist among people with regard to the interpretation of certain Quranic verses, or the authenticity of certain

First published by the Islamic Centre, Geneva, January 1961 in Arabic, English, French, and German. Reprinted from *World Muslim League Magazine* Vol. 1 No. 4 (1964), 34–44, by permission of the author and the publishers.

Prophetic traditions of their rendering, so long as people do not abandon the use of their intellects. What is important is that these disagreements should remain subject to arguments based on the texts of the Quran and Sunnah, and that the opinions of particular schools of Muslim Law on controversial points should not, either owing to negligence or ignorance, be elevated to the point where they begin to be considered more authoritative than the texts of the Quran or Sunnah. Such a distorted view impairs our proper attitude towards the injunctions of God and His Prophet, as laid down in the Quranic verse:

> Judge between them by that which God hath revealed, and follow not their desires. [Surah al-Maida (5): 52]

Moreover, we should be careful that our attitudes on controversial points do not harden to such a degree that they prevent Muslims from applying their minds to the understanding of the Shariah, although the Shariah itself remains the criterion for all differences of opinion; and every generation of Muslims has an Ordinance from God to remain in direct and constant contact with the Shariah, as embodied in the Quran and the Sunnah:

> . . . and if ye have a dispute concerning any matter, refer it to God and the Messenger. [Surah An-Nisaa (4): 59]

Abandoning reference to the Quran and the Sunnah and attaching an exaggerated importance to the opinion of one's own school of law implies also the adoption of an unrighteous attitude towards our Fuqaha of past generations who, though they disagreed among themselves, did not claim infallibility for their opinions. Their disagreements were based on the texts of the Shariah available to them, and with regard to its interpretation. It never occurred to our Fuqaha, however, that they would become an impregnable wall preventing the radiation of the light of the Quran and the Sunnah, or that they would be depriving all other Muslims of the right to apply their intellects to the understanding of the Quran and the Sunnah. Imam Malik has epitomised his view on the question in these fine words:

> I am a human being. I can be right and I can be wrong. Examine every one of my opinions: accept those which conform to Quran and Sunnah; reject those which do not conform to Quran and Sunnah.

3. That the Shariah of God, as embodied in Quran and Sunnah, does not bind mankind in *mu'amalat* (worldly dealings) except by providing a few broad principles of guidance and a limited number of injunctions. The Shariah only rarely concerns itself with details. The confinement of the Shariah to broad principles and its silence in other spheres are due to divine wisdom and mercy. For the divine knowledge embraces human life in its totality: in all its spheres, in all stages of its development, and in all periods of human history. Now, God was not incapable of laying down, had He considered it good to do so, an injunction for every minor issue and a law for every new problem that might arise. The fact that the Shariah is silent on these points — and we should bear in mind that, as the Quran remarks, "God is not forgetful" — means only that the application of the general injunctions of the Shariah to the multifarious details of human life, and the confrontation of new problems according to the dictates of *maslahah* (public good) have been left to the discretion of the body of conscious Muslims. Moreover, if the Shariah has refrained from laying things down definitively in the form of clear-cut injunctions regarding matters about which God knew that people would disagree, and if it has not fixed regulations in respect of the problems which, of course, God knew would arise in human existence, all this is due to God's mercy, for he wanted comfort, not discomfort, for human beings, and breadth, not narrowness, in human life. The Quran has said:

> God desireth for you ease: He desireth not hardship for you. [Surah Al-Baqarah (2): 185]

The Prophet explained this by saying:

> God has enjoined certain prescriptions, so do not abandon them. He has imposed certain limits, so do not transgress them. He has prohibited certain things, so do not fall into them. He has remained silent about many things, out of Mercy and deliberateness, as He never forgets, so do not ask me about them.

The Prophet — peace be unto him — stressed this point repeatedly. Most illustrative of this basic characteristic of the Shariah, is his authentic saying:

> Leave me as long as I leave you. Too much questioning brought only disaster upon people before you. Only if I forbid your doing anything, then do not do it, and if I order you to do something, then try to do whatever you can of it.

Since God has granted this freedom, and has left a wide margin of choice open to human beings from sheer beneficence and mercy, it would be utter ingratitude and stark disregard for the spirit of the Shariah, to impose upon its ageless and merciful features the variety of rigorous regulations in matters of minor detail which have been formulated by our legists in the past. These interpretations and elaborations of the fiqh have been gradually misconceived as matters of indisputable validity, so much so that as soon as the word 'Shariah' is mentioned they come instantly to mind and impair the eternal freshness of divine revelation and the beauty and grace of divine mercy.

We who strive for Islamic regeneration should make it abundantly clear to people that: this is the Shariah — the lenient Shariah — embodied in the Quran and the Sunnah, and God binds you to this and nothing else. As for our juristic heritage, handed down to us by our great ancestors who earnestly endeavoured to interpret the Shariah in the face of continually new problems of life regarding which the Shariah had observed silence, in the light of *maslahah* (public good) and with a due regard for the circumstances of their age — while profiting from this heritage, our attitude towards the Shariah should nevertheless be the same as that of our ancestors. Following in their footsteps, we should apply our minds to understand it. We should also treat the circumstances of our epoch as they did theirs, and try to face our special problems in the light of *maslahah,* as they did. And bearing all this in mind, our recourse to the vast, rich fiqh heritage at our disposal should serve to strengthen our bonds with the Quran and the Sunnah, rather than prevent direct reference to these original sources. It should help us to apply the Quran, and the Sunnah to the circumstances in which we live in the same way as our ancestors did for their part. It is altogether unrealistic to seek from our legists of the past solutions to the problems of our own age — an age of which they could have no knowledge — or to impose upon ourselves regulations devised to fit circumstances which no longer exist. And it is altogether unworthy to abandon the use of our intellects to understand Islam (for it is that power of rational discernment, with which each one of us has been endowed, which makes us answerable to God) thereby reducing ourselves to the position of parasites, living perpetually on the fruits of labour bequeathed us by our ancestors — by their heavy intellectual toils, unrelenting efforts and patient endeavour.

It can be asked: "Where do you draw the line of demarcation between the Quran and the Sunnah, and the interpretations thereof of the fuqaha? Are the interpretations not the attempts of the fuqaha to arrive at the true intent of the Quran and the Sunnah?" These are certainly reasonable questions. The reply is that our desire to distinguish between the two does not mean that we wish to dispense with fiqh as such. On the contrary. All we want is for it to be clear that the texts of the Quran and the Sunnah are the true sources of guidance, the norms for our lives; that they alone constitute the Shariah which is binding upon us; that all opinions must be weighed with the Quran and the Sunnah as the criteria; that every human being after the Holy Prophet is fallible; that in every matter where there are no texts to bind us, the consideration of *maslahah* alone is binding; and that the precepts, for *maslahah* change with changing circumstances and ages — as earlier fuqaha have said: "Where there is *maslahah,* there is the path of God."

This distinction between the divine Shariah (as embodied in the Quran and the Sunnah) which is eternally binding, and the details opined in its light by the fuqaha should have a thoroughly healthy influence on contemporary Muslims, in a number of ways. It invests Islamic ideology with simplicity that should help cultivate deep in the hearts of Muslims genuine faith in their Lord and in their Prophet. It restores the clarity of the original message of Islam. It restores also the lustre to the Islamic ideology which it owes to the words of God and His Prophet. It provides a rallying-ground for all Muslims, notwithstanding the existence of various schools of thought among them. Moreover, it should keep Islam intact in its original broad and vigorous form, in a form which provides scope and ease for the human mind, and not discomfort and restriction.

It may also asked: "Do you want to make the Quran and the Sunnah a tool of any imposters who step forward to interpret them according to their whims and desires once the door for their interpretation is flung open?" The reply, obviously, is "No." For when we talk of 'opinions' in Islamic matters, we mean 'opinions' and not whims and desires, and we presume piety and godliness to be basic with regard to problems relating to Islam. Further, there is no harm in trying to devise sound rules, of a scientific as well as an administrative nature, which could effectively ensure specialisation in studies relating to the Shariah as embodied in the Quran and the Sunnah, just as is attempted by all legal systems the world over. Rather, it is our duty to ensure this. We shall thus have saved the Shariah from pollution by the whims and desires of false claimants to its interpretation. At the same time, however, we should try to ensure that specialisation does not lead to the creation of priesthood in Muslim society, and that the door remains open for the consideration of all opinions, whatever their sources, purely on the basis of their intrinsic worth.

The second problem is that of the position of womenfolk in Muslim society. In this regard also, as in regard to our social life as a whole, we are in a state of complete chaos, a hotch-potch of competing forces: the remaining Islamic influence, our inherited traditions and extraneous influences which have crept into our life as a result of the enveloping wave of blind imitation of the West. This has created a myriad of problems in Muslim society, among which deserving of special attention is the problem of womenfolk. This is not so merely because women constitute something more than half the community. It is particularly pressing because it is a problem which affects the family, the very basis of our social life, and because of the deep and inherent relationship that it has with those factors which make for the cohesion of our society. It is in fact a problem that affects in its ramifications most of the aspects of our national orientation.

It is strange that we Muslims should neglect the important position of women. The Shariah has placed such emphasis on it in connection with the lives of those great men whom God entrusted with high tasks and whom He chose as the recipients of His revelation — those noble souls ordained to deliver God's message to mankind. In the story of Moses it is his mother, Pharaoh's wife and the daughters of Madyan who constitute great figures. In the story of Jesus, his virgin and virtuous mother is a great pillar of the story. The principal in nobility and virtue among those who stood faithfully by the side of Muhammad in his apostolic mission was Khadijah, the compassionate and noble lady of Mecca. Indeed, the numerous verses of the Quran and the large number of prophetic traditions which speak of woman's status and of her rights and responsibilities, are quite sufficient to determine our attitude towards womanhood. The Holy Quran refers to the position of women in various ways. Sometimes it refers to their position while comparing it with the position of men in the sight of God and proclaims it to be one of complete equality:

> I shall not let the work of any worker, male or female, be lost. You issue from one another. [Surah al-i-Imran (3): 195]

On other occasions it mentions the rights and duties of women as akin to those of men before mentioning man's administrative leadership of the family:

> And they (women) have rights similar to those (of men) according to what is equitable, and men are a degree above them [Surah Al-Baqarah (2): 228]

On still another occasion we find Islam pointedly stressing gentleness and good behaviour in the treatment of women. Said the Prophet in his last address:

> I advise you to be good to women.

It is not my intention to discuss the position

of womenfolk in all its ramifications. What I have to say will be quite brief, but nevertheless of serious importance, for the time has come when we should be very clear on a number of questions relating to this problem and devote a good deal of our thought and attention to the solution thereof.

It should be very clear in our minds that woman, according to Islam, is intrinsically like her male partner. She is a human being endowed with the same essence of nobility which is shared by the whole human species. As far as human quality is concerned, men and women are absolutely alike:

> O mankind! Revere your Lord, Who created you from a single soul and from that created its mate, who thereafter brought forth a multitude of men and women. [Surah An-Nisaa (4): 1]

Moreover, each one, man as well as women, will be held responsible for his own individual self:

> . . . and every one of them will come to God, on the day of Resurrection, alone. [Surah Maryam (19): 95]

This means that those who either believe, or whose behaviour, reveals the unconscious concept, that woman is an inferior who has to be subjugated, that she is a servant who has to be commanded, and whose job is only to obey or that she is merely an instrument for the self-indulgence of man — such people require a radical reorientation of their attitude towards womankind. Such people, by clinging to such unhealthy ideas, or through their unhealthy conduct, are grossly distorting God given human nature and are killing potentialities of thought, feeling and vitality in their partners of life.

It should also be clear that the unbridled self-will of certain women in other societies, or of those of our own women who blindly imitate them, should not be countered by extremism on our part: by imposing on women what God has not imposed upon them, or by forbidding them what God has not forbidden. We should remember that women in the Western world began to lean in the wrong direction from definite causes, at least some of which were undoubtedly related to social injustices, under the deadweight of which women had languished for so long, imprisoned and ignorant, with no will or personality of their own. They revolted against this injustice — and this revolt was a completely natural and genuine one. Then they began to lean in the wrong direction, becoming stubborn and headstrong. The same type of injustice continues to have its strongholds in our own society, where there are still people, though very few, who are proud of the fact that since the wedding night when their wives were driven home, they have not seen the street once. There are still others who consider themselves entitled to beat their wives if they dare to disagree with their views and advance an opinion of their own. Again, there are those who spend year after year with their wives and daughters without sitting down to discuss a problem with them or attempting to make them share their views.

Who would claim that any of these has anything to do with Islam? On the contrary, it is Islam which elevated women to heights of prestige which have neither precedent nor parallel in human history. At a time when womanhood in the West was held in such a state of impurity that even a women's touch was an evil pollution of the Bible, Quranic manuscripts were held in the trust of the Lady Hafsa at Medina. At a time when the Romans held conferences to debate whether woman was a "person" or a "thing", Muhammad stood up to declare that "women are but the sisters of men" and to shatter the pre-Islamic era of darkness and injustice, so that a woman could argue with the Holy Prophet in the courtyard of the mosque and say: "I have been deputed to you on behalf of women!" Indeed, it was Islam which, for the first time, established the status of women as full-fledged members of human society and granted them the right to own whatever they earned, since the Quran proclaimed:

> Unto men of fortune from that which they have earned, and unto women of fortune from that which they have earned. [Surah An-Nisaa (4): 32]

Whatever standards of decency Islam has laid down in matters of dress and behaviour between men and women, they are all with the sole intention of ensuring the sanctity of the home and the inviolability of marital intimacy. Not one of these standards could ever imply an attitude directed towards humiliation of women as regards her social status or her role in her relationship with man. When a newly-married girl complained to the Prophet that her father had chosen her husband without consulting her, he immediately gave her permission to annul her marriage, to which she replied: "I have no personal objection to my husband and I accept him, but I wanted it to be known that a father has no right to impose a husband upon his daughter without her consent." In contrast to the then prevailing ignorance and plutocracy of tribal traditions, Muhammad enjoined the quest for knowledge, as an integral part of faith, for men and women alike. He praised highly the women of Ansar with:

> Blessed be those whose modesty never prevented them from seeking knowledge.

Far from being rough or rude, Muhammad's consciousness of women's tenderness and delicacy was so intense that even in the impelling harshness of the desert, he gently appealed to Anjashah, the caravan driver:

> O Anjashah, slow down a little, for thy camels are carrying glasses!

This is only a glimpse of Islam: thus, how could we possibly be justified in so grossly distorting it by all sorts of misconceived traditions and beliefs? What could be more unjust, whether to Islam or to ourselves, than to misrepresent as we do, or rather to deform, the beautiful features of Islam? And consider when? — at a time when we are encountering the movement of so-called progress and emancipation, which is advancing like a storm and wreaking havoc in our lives.

It is imperative to realise that the really weak points in our society are those which provide genuine cause for feminine revolt, which can subsequently take an extremist turn and ultimately lead to unbridled feminine self-will. If we are serious about resisting these unhealthy trends, it is our duty to call a stop where God has done so, and combat the deceptive misleading elements we are encountering by adhering to what God has laid down for us. We should neither depart from anything which God has decreed out of our weakness or compromise, nor add anything to it from extremism and severity.

These things are of relevance for all Muslims. But they are of particular importance to those who are actively devoted to the revival of Islam. I fervently wish that such people would put these ideas into effect: would stop at the point where the Shariah stops, and have the courage to proclaim and insist on what God has made binding on us and that alone. This is essential in creating a strong wall around whatever of virtue and purity remains in our society. It is to be hoped that by so doing the workers for the cause of Islam will have created a real barrier, one strengthened by the word of God and of His Prophet, against the sweeping, devastating storm which threatens Islam today. For, if matters are not clarified, and confusion is allowed to reign as it does today, if the good aspects are not separated from the bad, both in theory and by good example, the result of this confusion is bound to be this: the good elements will be mistaken for the bad, and both will be swept away by the rising storm. This will not be in the least surprising. For there is neither a divine code which is being sincerely adhered to, nor is there any social system based on experience and clarity of outlook, and God has not appointed a gendarme to regulate the conflicting traffic of good and evil.

A further consideration in this connection is that many of our women, like our men, do not possess an adequate knowledge of Islam. The picture of Islam they have deep in their minds is a confused and distorted one. It is the picture of Islam as it is practised in our countries. In addition to this, there is a dire absence of religious discipline among our people, while on the other hand there is the aggressive advance of moral laxity in our society, fully armed with formidable weapons: the attraction of the culture of our "colonial masters", which has cultivated deep down in the hearts of our young men and women an admiration for our "overlords" and their mode of life. It is armed also with the admiration of their civilisation sown in our hearts by the pioneers of this culture: magazines, radio broadcasts, films, etc. And above all, it is armed with temptations, the potential response to which has been planted by God in the nature of every man and woman as the Quran says:

> Decorated for mankind is love for joys (that come) from women. . . [Surah Al-i-Imran (3): 14]

All this requires that our collective attitude to the solution of this problem should be based on a full consideration of the magnitude of the impact of the cultural invasion of the West on those who are exposed or have fallen victim to it. This should be borne in mind particularly when the problem requiring a solution concerns women, for with women the emotional factors are predominant. Hence, leniency itself is not enough. The approach to reform should be based on a careful distinction between what is good and what is bad. Moreover, we should not begin by condemning people for lacking honour and decency by falling into some of the widespread errors, for instance, the violation of limits in matters of dress, etc. For not every unveiled woman is a bundle of vices and immodesty, nor is every veiled woman a paragon of virtue and piety!

I do not want what I am saying here to be underestimated, for incautious accusations against people and harshness in rendering advice have most seriously damaged the cause of Islam among women. This has unfortunately created a gulf between those who work for Islam and many basically good women. I have countless practical instances of this, although our sisters can recount many more. A large number of them, young and old, whose reactions against wrong traditions or clumsy approaches first put them in firm opposition to Islam and its workers, have subsequently become among the best champions of the cause once they were approached in a proper, understanding and decent manner.

The third problem is the degeneration of the construction put on the Quranic expression "obedience to those in authority among you" to mean abject acquiescence to rulers, however wrong or unjust they might be. This is a malady which has afflicted the Muslim body-politic during the long centuries of our history. Most of our *ulama* and self-made priests, have, unfortunately, neglected coming to grips with the problem, although it was imperative for various degrees of reason. It was imperative to bring Muslims to a correct understanding of their religion. It was also essential to remind them of their duty to give proper advice to the ruler who commits a wrong-doing and to correct him. Instead, many of these *ulama* were themselves instrumental in intensifying the abject spirit of acquiescence to tyrants and in making silence legitimate in the face of their injustices and extravagant blunders, either from fear of punishment or desire for royal patronage, or unconcern for Muslim affairs. This malady, therefore, became deep-rooted in the body-politic, and Muslims gave up the practice of this commandment of their Lord:

> And whose affairs are decided by counsel among themselves. [Surah Ash-Shura (42:35)]

This negative attitude and unconcern proved factors of appreciable assistance to despots in strengthening their tyrannical authority. An error, if it is left uncorrected, aggravates and recurs; and injustice, if not resisted, leads its perpetrators to excesses and consolidates the foundations of tyranny.

It is, moreover, surprising that all those who neglected to enlighten Muslims regarding their duty to fight against the unjust until he returns to the paths of justice, as well as those who, either because they were swayed by their own desires or because of their lack of concern for Muslim affairs, have helped in the consolidation of the authority of tyrants, all these people have tried to seek invalid support in the Quranic verse:

> O ye who believe! Obey God, and obey the messenger and those of you who are in authority. [Surah An-Nisaa (4): 59]

They have done this in spite of the fact that most of our learned ancestors such as Ibnu Abbas, Mujahid, Ata, Alhasan Albasry and Abul-Aliah, had interpreted the Arab term: "those in authority," to denote the authority of their knowledge of Islam, rather than to mean the temporal rulers irrespective of what they possess of such knowledge. This interpretation is also supported by the content of the verse which reads:

> O ye who believe! Obey God and obey his messenger and those of you who are in authority, and if ye have a dispute concerning any matter refer it to God and the messenger. [Surah An-Nisaa (4): 59]

This means that obedience which has been ordained for believers is obedience of their Lord in respect of what He has laid down, and of His Prophet in respect of what the Prophet conveyed to mankind on behalf of God, and of the learned by virtue of the ordinance of God and His Prophet. The latter are to be obeyed in respect of whatever commandments of God and His Prophet they deliver to the people. And if there is any disagreement, then there is a reliable standard of judgment — Quran and the Sunnah, and not the desires of people or the whims and interests of any particular group or class. Even those who interpret "those in authority among you" to denote temporal rulers are aware that this verse has placed an obstacle in the way of despotism by rulers by stipulating that they shall rule in conformity with the injunctions of God and the teachings of the Prophet. Such people also know that the Prophet has said, as it is authentically reported:

> Verily obedience is (only) in good.

He is further reported in another authentic tradition to have said:

> No obedience in disobedience of God.

The despicable negative spirit which has disseminated this wrong concept of Islam can only be countered by spreading the right concept of Islam, and it is the duty of those who are working for Islam to make this a definite target of their endeavours. They should devote attention to it in speech, in writing and in all their efforts to provide a rightful guidance for suppressed Muslims.

For it is not right that in its battle against falsehood, Islam should remain deprived of the zeal and enthusiasm of millions of its followers, even though Islam is the religion whose Prophet proclaimed that the leader of the martyrs after Hamzah would be he who would stand up before an unjust ruler, would proclaim the word of truth, and be killed for proclaiming it. It is not right that there should persist this neglect in rectifying the mental attitude of the nation, and that the energies of people should be allowed to be wasted, with the result that active minorities in many Muslim lands have been able to entrench themselves in power and manoeuvre Islam and Muslims despite the fact that the broad mass of Muslim peoples are believers, though scattered and confounded, not knowing what to do; or perhaps they are aware of what should be done, but are not aware that God will hold them responsible for their omissions and inaction.

All this is not intended to arouse emotions. It is not empty sentimental talk. The truth of what we say can be verified if one simply takes stock of the elections in Muslim countries. This will show that the predominant majority of those who are apathetic when it comes to casting their votes consists of genuine believers who, out of sheer negligence and unconcern, are playing the role of disinterested observers in a battle which concerns their religion, their culture, and the most deeply cherished values of their life.

Conceptualizing Contemporary Islam: Religion or Ideology?

SHARON SIDDIQUE

An attempt to view Islam in Southeast Asia from an exclusively Southeast Asian perspective is dissatisfying for one basic reason. Most significant Islamic political, economic and social change originates not in Southeast Asia, but rather in the Middle East, Pakistan and the universities of Western Europe and the United States. Although Southeast Asian Muslims are participating members, they are not, as a general rule, prime movers in these developments. Moreover, reactions on the periphery are, to a certain extent, distortions of the centre. The rationalization for the generalizations which follow is thus that an attempt to conceptualize contemporary Islam is a prerequisite to a satisfactory understanding of contemporary Islam in Southeast Asia.

INADEQUACIES OF CONCEPT 'RELIGION'

The first problem is to find a theoretical construct which is adequate to the task of conceptualizing contemporary Islam. In this context, regarding Islam as merely 'religion' leaves unanalysed the political, economic, legal and perhaps social aspects of Islam as a religion. The dilemma here naturally does not lie with Islam, but rather with Western definitions and conceptualizations of religion. Most recent Western sociological conceptions of religion ultimately place the individual at the centre of analysis. They focus on the personal relationship between man and God. Even when attempts are made to deal with the broader concepts of the role of religion in society the importance of individual motivation is portrayed as paramount.

One of the most popular definitions of religion — a definition which has been utilized by many field ethnographers for religion in a non-Western context — is that of Clifford Geertz (1972:168):

> Religion is a system of symbols which acts to establish powerful, pervasive and long-lasting moods and motivations in men by formulating conceptions of a general order of existence and clothing these conceptions with such an aura of factuality that the moods and motivations seem uniquely realistic.

Geertz seems to imply that the individual manipulates — and is manipulated by — these religious symbols in order to make sense of the society in which he lives. Although this individual-oriented focus does allow for the construction of a triangular model of individual-religious symbolization-society, it seems, nevertheless, singularly inadequate to furthering our understanding of the dynamics of the contemporary Islamic resurgence.

Islam as a canonical system incorporates more than a sense of personal relationship between man and God — it also contains the formulation for a social, political and economic order — a formulation which, of course, has been open to various demarcated interpretations. Perhaps no other canonical religion —

Reprinted from *The Annual Review of the Social Sciences of Religion* Vol. 5 (1981), 203–222, by permission of the author and Mouton Publishers, a division of Walter de Gruyter Berlin.

certainly not the contemporary Christian milieu out of which the Western sociology of religion has sprung — is capable of generating, in anything like the same way of Islam, the sense of mission to direct the economic and political processes which is unleashed upon the social order. The most fundamental implication of the contemporary Islamic resurgence, therefore, is the active attempt to shape the entire social order into an ideological and canonically-inspired vision-of-reality.

One reason why the individual's relationship to his religion has generally been placed at the core of sociological religious theorizing is because the Christian fundamentalist revival is primarily an ethical revival — a call based upon the need for the individual to re-establish and/or strengthen his bond to God. This ethical revival, of course, has profound economic and political ramifications, but these implications radiate from the individual and his renewed role in revitalizing his society. I will argue that there is a fundamental difference in the way that the Islamic revival is perceived by its participants — and, therefore, in the way in which social scientists should conceive of it.

IDEOLOGY AS A SOCIOLOGICAL CONCEPT

Sociological theory regarding the concept of ideology has progressed in recent years, shedding forever, one hoped, the shroud bestowed by Mannheim in his struggle to evolve a value-free conception of ideology. Clifford Geertz has provided us with a succinct definition of ideology, published in 1964, which continues to serve as a valid general statement: Ideologies, he writes, are '. . . maps of problematic social reality and matrices for the creation of collective conscience' (Geertz, 1964:64). There appears to be a dynamic element in this definition which is essentially missing in his conceptualization of religion. He views an ideology as a three dimensional phenomenon — including sociological, psychological, and also cultural or conceptual elements.

Geertz focuses his attention on the *genesis* of an ideology. It is, he writes, 'a confluence of socio-psychological strain and an absence of cultural resources by means of which to make (political, moral or economic) sense of that strain, each exacerbating the other, that sets the stage for the rise of systematic (political, moral economic) ideologies' (Geertz 1964:64). His perspective is thus essentially *causal* in nature. Under what conditions, he asks, is an ideology generated?

The approach to the study of ideology, of '. . . maps of problematic reality', more relevant to our present concern with conceptualizing contemporary Islam, is *motivational* in nature, seeking rather to probe the mechanisms whereby ideologies are not only generated, but also perpetuated. This implies, in turn, a focus on those individuals, groups, organizations or communities which utilize a particular 'matrix for the creation of a collective consciousness' and which seek both to perpetuate and expand it. Such a focus allows a discussion of ideology at two levels: first at the descriptive level of delineating a 'map of social reality', and second at the level of implementation, of attempts to impose this map by attaining and maintaining power — be it political, economic or social.

The moment, however, that one begins to conceive of Islam as an ideology, a paradox is encountered. There is a contradiction, so to speak, between two ideological perspectives: one universalistic, and the other particularistic. The universalistic ideology of Islam is generated from canonical Islam and its orthodox commentaries, while the particularistic ideology of Islam is essentially a product of fragmented political realities. Islam, in this sense, is one Third-World ideology which immediately becomes one of several Third-World ideologies, or diverse 'maps of social reality' which chart the unknown and bewildering seas of technological development and modernization, but which are all drawn within the parameters of the universalistic matrix of canonical Islam. It must be stressed that these two perspectives are not merely complementary, nor does one simply generate the other. A universalistic ideology is by definition also a unitary, all-embracing ideology which can tolerate no internal contradiction. Thus diverse streams of ideological Islamic consciousness must be explicitly and vehemently denied, even as they are implicitly espoused.

UNIVERSAL ISLAM

At a high level of generalization there is certainly a 'map of social reality' to which all Muslims would subscribe. Politically there is the ideal of the world-wide *ummah* (community). Economically, there is the dedication to the establishment of an economic system founded upon social justice and redistribution of wealth — idealized in systems of *zakat* and *fitrah* (Muslim tithes payable after Ramadan) and *wakaf* (donation for a religious purpose). Legally, there is at least some acceptance of the *syariah* (Muslim legal code) as a template (to borrow a term from Geertz) of social organization, although the degrees to which this *syariah* would be actually implemented may differ. This universal ideology is based upon the fundamental tenet that Islam is *ad-deen* — that is, a complete way of life — both for the individual, and for the society. Moreover, this universalistic ideology is perceived as also universally applicable, transcending race, ethnicity, and linguistic and territorial boundaries.

A symbolic expression of this universalistic ideology is enacted each year during the *haj* (pilgrimage to Mecca). For the duration of the pilgrimage every Muslim is equal — divested (in theory at least) of his political, economic and social position and one before God. But just as the *haj* sustains the ethereal image of the universal ideological ideal, the dispersion on the final days of the pilgrimage — by jet, ship, limousine or camel caravan — symbolizes the fragmentary quality of international reality.

Perpetuating and propagating a universal ideology, however, requires more than a presentation of a 'map of social reality', and also more than a symbolic representation of this ideal. In order to sustain a successful contemporary universal ideology, at least three integrated prerequisites are necessary. First, an international clientele, composed not only of individuals and organizations, but also of nations; second, a network of supranational organizations which enable individuals, organizations and nations to lobby and coalesce, and third, an intellectual body of literature, created by a functioning elite, to feed the system with its ideas, rationales, plans, goals, etc.

INTERNATIONAL CLIENTELE

There are three hundred ethnic groups in the world today whose populations are wholly or partly Muslim. Of these three hundred, ninety-six groups have a population of over 100,000. These ninety-six ethnic groups, therefore, include more than ninety-two percent of the total world's Muslim population. These ethnic groups are dispersed in almost every country of the world, including thirty-six nations which have a majority Muslim population, with an additional five having close to 50% Muslim population (Weekes, 1978: Introduction). Thus this 'international clientele' is riddled with linguistic, ethnic, cultural, and — in contemporary times perhaps the most significant — national — divisions.

SUPRA-NATIONAL BUREAUCRACY

The emergence of the contemporary supranational bureaucratic infrastructure through which the international Islamic clientele can interact and express its solidarity can be traced to the creation of OPEC (Organization of Petroleum Exporting Countries). During the 1950s and 1960s there were relatively few international Islamic organizations. The most well-known was the Rabitah, founded by King Feisal of Saudia Arabia in the mid-1960s. Demoralized by ineffective attempts to put Israel on the defensive in the Middle-East, pan-Islamism seemed a dead issue. The establishment and stunning success of OPEC, eleven of the thirteen members of which are Muslim countries, provided both the moral and material endorsement to support the mushrooming of international Muslim organizations which has become one of the dominant features of contemporary Islam of the 1970s. Fuelled by petrodollars and inspired by OPEC's successful confrontation with the industrialized countries, international Islamic organizations were created in the political, economic, educational and social spheres. Politically the most important is the Islamic Conference, and its subsidiary, the Islamic Conference of Foreign Ministers. Economically, there has been some attempt to formulate an Islamic system of banking which deals with the dilemma caused by the Muslim condemnation of *riba* (interest). Such organizations as the Islamic Development Bank, the Islamic Development Fund, the Islamic Monetary Fund and the Islamic Institute of Research and Training have been grappling with the problem. Educational organizations are to be found in the many international Islamic youth organizations which are to be found on most campuses in the West where there are many Muslim students, as well as in the Middle East and Southeast Asia. Examples of such federations of student organizations are IIFSO (International Islamic Federation of Student Organizations). WAMY (World Assembly of Muslim Youth), and MSA (Muslim Students Organization of North America). Such organizations publish and disseminate large quantities of Islamic literature, much of it in English. Muslims have also been organizing other aspects of development from an Islamic perspective. This trend is witnessed by the founding of such organizations as an International Islamic News Agency, an Association of Islamic Capital Cities, an Islamic Chamber of Commerce and Industry, an Organization for Muslim Minorities and the Islamic Conference Committees for Economic, Cultural, and Social Affairs.

These and many other international Islamic organizations organize countless local, regional and international conferences and seminars, the deliberations of which are often published and widely disseminated. With the generous support of OPEC countries, they are able to experiment with development projects in many Muslim countries throughout the world. The degree to which these various programmes are actually implemented and to which a measure of success or failure can be ascertained is difficult to assess, for one reason because of their relatively recent implementation.

FUNCTIONING ELITE

One of the most striking characteristics of contemporary Islamic thinkers and writers is the fact that they are overwhelmingly non-European. This is significant because the contribution to internationally-oriented ideologies by non-Westerners has been nugatory in the past few decades. Islam, in this sense, is thus a Third-World ideology which seems to be providing Third-World Muslim thinkers with a vehicle with which to reassess their colonial past, to voice increasing dissatisfaction with the political-economic experimentations of the immediate independence period, and to formulate their own conceptualization of the future. After casting aside various 'isms', of which the most prominent are capitalism, communism and socialism, some Islamic intellectuals are beginning to formulate a manifesto of their own, the key point of which is the creation of an 'Islamic State' with all that this creation implies. This 'new' Islamic ideology is therefore, at the moment, intensely political.

It is not possible to discuss this fundamentalist literature in detail. However, the writings of such Muslim authors as Sayyid Qutb, Syed Abdul A'la Maududi, Dr. Muhamed Hamidullah, Said Ramadan, Abdul Hasan Ali Nadwi, Dr. Ali Shari'ati, M.H.K. Brohi, A.Q. Sufi, Hasan Banna, Maryam Jamellah and Khurshid Ahmad serve as examples. Publications of these authors are widely disseminated in English — and, of relevance here, also in Malay translations — by such organizations as the Islamic Council of Europe, and the International Islamic Federation of Student Organizations.

UNIVERSALISM VS. PARTICULARISM

In sum, Islam as a universal ideology has a certain coherence, a certain unity and also a certain ideological reality. And yet one has only to survey the bewildering inundation of literature on Islam to realize that there is certainly also much squabbling going on within Islam, and that, to paraphrase the Indonesians, this unity also contains a great deal of diversity.

Viewing Islam from the perspective of a universal ideology allows us to consider why this diversity is generally denied, or at least only reluctantly acknowledged. Universal Islam maintains an international ideology of unity, while Third-World Islam provides a possibility for constructing a typology of this diversity. The key to understanding this diversity of Islam as a Third-World ideology is dependent on examining the Islamic implications of the concept of nationalism. Third-World nations are new nations, most having gained independence only after the Second World War. A struggle to resolve, on the one hand, the Western concept of the nation-state and its accumulated colonial legacies and, on the other, the increasing pressure to concede to the demands of the 'new' ideology of supranational unity of the Islamic *ummah,* has provided one of the most intense struggles of the era. It is a struggle, however, which has been largely under-estimated until quite recently. In a sense, the smell of oil is in danger of deadening our sensitivities. Although it is true that petro-dollars have fuelled the contemporary resurgence of Islam, it is equally important that scholars utilize the perspective of hindsight to attempt a reassessment of the origins of this movement in the immediate pre- and post-independence period. I return to this point in the final section, in the context of Islamic resurgence in Southeast Asia.

SECULARISM, FUNDAMENTALISM AND MODERNISM

It is necessary at this juncture to construct some sort of rough typology of this diversity of Islamic political ideology as it seems relevant to Southeast Asia. The focus for the construction of these ideal types would therefore be the orientations on the role of Islam in a Muslim state (i.e., an independent nation whose majority population is Muslim). Here, I borrow from a scheme developed by Humphreys (1979) who discusses Islamic alternative ideal types under the classifications of 'secularist', 'fundamentalist', and 'modernist'. Although Humphreys lists several 'critical foci' of political orientation, for our present discussion of Southeast Asian Islam, two seem most relevant: first, restrictions on the religious affiliation of the ruling political elite, and second, provisions for the sources of public laws.

Underlying the *secularist* position is the belief that it is possible to separate the religious and political spheres of life. This is accomplished by relegating the 'religious' to the private sphere of individual spirituality, and excluding it from the public arena of politics, administration and law. Put simply, this means that 'the church' (i.e., organized religion) can and should be separated from the state. This is a position, of course, which has been borrowed from the West along with the Western nation-state model of parliamentary democracy. As one would expect, the secularist ideal type makes no provision for the religious faith of political leaders being a criterion for their election. Appropriate sources of public law are also seen as deriving from legislated acts of the elected parliament. Politics and religion, it is argued, belong to different spheres (Humphreys, 1979:10).

In the context of Islam, the *fundamentalist* ideal type has at least three important components: first, a call to return to the original inspirational sources of the Quran and the Sunnah, second, a campaign against all deviations away from the path portrayed in the Quran and the Sunnah, and third, a resolute attempt to make this holistic approach relevant to the modern world by rejecting Western political models based on a separation of 'church' and state, and by a rejection of 'secularist' economic models such as capitalism, communism, and socialism. Although Humphreys does not explicitly enumerate these three components, his view of the implications of Islamic fundamentalism is nonetheless of relevance to our discussion. Islamic fundamentalism according to Humphreys insists that all positions of authority be filled by Muslims, and moreover, Muslims who are sufficiently versed in the Quran and the Sunnah to be capable of implementing its principles. Regarding public law, the *syariah* is regarded as the sole source of law in both private and public spheres (Humphreys, 1979:6).

The *modernist* ideal-type ideology is much more ill-defined than the secularist and fundamentalist ideal-type alternatives. In one sense the modernist position represents a compromise between a traditional Islamic and a modern Western nation-state model which was inherited by most contemporary Muslim countries. According to Humphreys, modernism is in a dilemma regarding the identity of the political elite. It '. . . appreciates the concept of equal citizenship, but it also wishes to create a state in which specifically Muslim values underlie citizens' rights and duties' (Humphreys, 1979:10). A common solution to this dilemma might be to require that the head of state be a Muslim, but to accede to non-Muslim citizens the right to serve as parliamentarians and cabinet members. Modernism faces the same dilemma regarding appropriate sources of public law. Again, a compromise solution is usually offered: materials from the *syariah* are used as far as possible, but this position is liable to criticism because it '. . . requires an admission that it is legitimate to rip these out of their original context and apply them in new ways' (Humphreys, 1979:10).

CONTEMPORARY MUSLIM STATES

If one surveys the governments in the forty or so Muslim states in existence today, most of them appear to conform most closely to the modernist ideal-type model. States in which the fundamentalist ideal has been implemented are conspicuously lacking, although one might point to the diverse attempts in Iran, Saudi Arabia, Libya, and Pakistan. Thus, measured in terms of political power those states most closely conforming to the modernist ideal-type seem to be in the majority, while the fundamentalists have not as yet achieved political dominance in many countries.

It is equally evident, however, that the fundamentalist position dominates the burgeoning literature of the contemporary Islamic revival. A possible reason for this is most clear when one returns to our former discussion of the ideology of universal Islam. The fundamentalist position as described above is most congruent with the universal ideal. Fundamentalism has captured the attention of increasing numbers of the international Islamic clientele, and has also succeeded in expanding its influence through the vehicles of international Islamic organizations. Finally, proponents of a fundamentalist position are the main contributors and disseminators of the current flood of literature connected with this Islamic resurgence.

This observation leads us to an interesting paradox: why is fundamentalist Islam becoming increasingly significant in the international (or supra-national) context, while it continues to fail in capturing political power in Muslim states? Or put in the reverse, why is the modernist position increasingly being put on the defensive, but at the same time, succeeding in retaining and consolidating political power in individual Muslim states? One possible explanation for this, it seems to me, is the respective success and failure to harness the force of what Jansen has termed 'positive nationalism' (Jansen, 1979:128).

In an insightful analysis, Jansen provides an explanation for the strengthening of the antagonist dichotomy between Muslim fundamentalist on the one hand, and Muslim secular nationalists on the other. Referring to the historical context, he points out that during the fight for independence from colonial rule in most contemporary Muslim countries, nationalism was expressed in an essentially negative sense. 'Negative nationalism united *against* something (i.e., colonial rule) and it was thus possible to suspend fundamental differences concerning what one was *for* (Jansen, 1979:127).

Jansen contrasts this 'negative nationalism' with what he terms 'positive nationalism'. Jansen lists several reasons for the fundamentalist rejection of 'positive nationalism': first, it divides mankind into smaller, mutually antagonistic units, second, it splits up the *ummah* and third, it '. . . has established a "new object of worship", the materialist nation, destructive and incompatible with the "nationalism of divine principles" decreed by God in Islam' (Jansen, 1979:128). Thus, to the degree that fundamentalism remains faithful to the universalist Islamic ideal, it must reject the realities of particularistic, 'positive' nationalism. One can conclude, therefore, that fundamentalists pay a heavy price for their inability to come to ideological terms with 'positive nationalism' — political power in their respective Muslim countries continues to elude them.

CONTEMPORARY ISLAM IN SOUTHEAST ASIA

Southeast Asian Muslims are participating, if peripheral, members of the international Islamic community. Limiting our discussion to the five ASEAN states of Malaysia, Indonesia, Thailand, Philippines and Singapore, the first two have Muslim majority populations, while the latter three have significant Muslim minorities. With the increase in literacy, and the increase of available literature — as witnessed for example by the number of titles in both English and Malay/Indonesian on sale in bookshops in Kuala Lumpur and Jakarta — the worldwide Islamic resurgence is making itself felt. In general, the Islamic revival movements, which are usually categorized under the rubric 'dakwah' (which means to call to Islam) movements, appear to be urban-centered and youth-oriented.

Many diverse international Islamic organizations have an impact on Southeast Asian Muslims. One of the most influential is the Islamic Conference whose first Secretary-General was Tunku Abdul Rahman, former Prime Minister of Malaysia, and various of its subsidiary committees. The Conference of Islamic Foreign Ministers, for example has played a mediating role between the rebel MNLF (Moro National Liberation Front) and the Marcos regime in attempting to resolve the nine year separationist struggle in the Southern Philippines.

In addition to diplomatic services, the international Islamic organizations have also played increasingly important financial and educational roles in the region. Organizations such as WAMY (World Assembly of Muslim Youth) and IIFSO (International Islamic Federation of Student Organizations) are active at a regional, and also national level. Rabitah, the Saudi-based Muslim missionary organization has funded several projects for PERKIM (a Malaysian missionary organization founded by Tunku Abdul Rahman in 1960), and also missionary activities in other ASEAN countries.

Although there has been some bilateral aid between Middle Eastern and ASEAN countries, such financial aid has made relatively little impact. Also, although there has been much talk of Muslim economic solidarity, little real foreign aid and investment has been forthcoming. This is due, in part, to a reluctance by recipient governments to accept such funds. The Malaysian and Indonesian governments, for example, keep a close check on internal religious movements which receive funding from outside the country. There have also been frequent but unconfirmed reports that some Middle East petro-dollars (primarily Libyan and Syrian) have been converted into arms and aid for the Muslim separatist movements in Thailand and the Philippines.

The contemporary Islamic resurgence in Malaysia and Indonesia has another important component to which our overview of nationalism has allowed access. There is currently a move, on the part of some Malaysian and Indonesian fundamentalists it seems, not only to align themselves with the international Islamic movement, but also to assess their own past. And in this context it is the immediate pre- and post-war period that is being re-examined.

In Indonesia this reassessment of the post-war relationship between the secular nationalists and the Islamic nationalists centres on a re-evaluation of the evolution of the Jakarta Charter and its relationship to the 1945 Constitution, as well as the evolution and meaning of the Pancasila (national ideology). According to Saifuddin Anshari, for example, there were significant concessions to the Islamic nationalists at crucial first-draft stages of the Jakarta Charter which were subsequently dropped in the final version. Saifuddin discusses four changes proposed by Soekarno which were made in the original version of the Jakarta Charter, and argues that their deletion from the final draft fundamentally altered the extent of Islamic influence in the evolving Indonesian nation-state structure (Saifuddin Anshari, 1979:30). Indonesia thus evolved into a self-declared secular state — of sorts. Although Islam is not recognized as the official religion of the country, the first principle of Pancasila exhorts a belief in Tuhan Yang Maha Esa, The One God. The legal system in Indonesia is also not based on the *syariah*, but rather is primarily a legacy of the Dutch colonial era. No constitutional provision is made for to require that any elected leader be of a particular religious persuasion.

The reassessment in Malaysia concerns the role of the Malay-Muslim Islamic-oriented nationalists, particularly during the post-war pre-independence period (1945–1957). This involves a re-examination of such organizations as the MATA and the Hizbul Muslimin, the genesis of PAS, and the Islamic ideological formulations of its first presidents, particularly Burhanuddin al Helmy. According to one author, Burhanuddin al Helmy embodied both streams of Malay-Muslim opposition to UMNO rule, that is, the Islamic and the 'leftist' (Kamaruddin Jaafar, 1980). According to the 1957 Constitution, Islam is the religion of the state. The administration of religious law in the Constitution is mentioned only in connection with the fact that it is a state, and not a federal, perogative. There are, however, strict restrictions on the jurisdiction of these state *syariah* courts, and public law is based on a western legal system inherited from Great Britain. Regarding provision for the religious affiliation of the political elite, only the Prime Minister is required to be of the Islamic faith.

The specific direction that this growing momentum towards an emphasis on the quality of the role of Islam in these two nation-states is difficult to predict. If one refers to the immediate post-war situation in Malaysia, it becomes increasingly obvious that a reassessment of the period allows us to view much more accurately the conflict which was generated between moderate and more fundamentalist-oriented nationalists — a conflict which saw the moderate Malay-Muslim nationalists emerge triumphant. An explanation for this victory of the modernists in the construction of the modern nation-states at a conceptual level can be found in the ideological paradox described above. The modernists were successful because they could explain the nation-state structure in terms of compromise. Modern nation-state structures, they argued, could compromise with the universal Islamic ideal. The fundamentalists, on the other hand, had a conceptual problem in appealing, and in being relevant to, particularistic nationalistic tendencies, while attempting, at the same time, to resist compromising the universalistic Islamic ideal to which they were conceptually committed.

The momentum of the universalistic ideology leads to calls — successful or not — for changes in the nation-state structure. This was clear during the formation of Malaysia and Indonesia after World War II. The decade of the 1970s has seen a re-opening of the question of the relationship between Islam and nation-state structure in Malaysia and Indonesia, and this can be expected to continue and intensify in the next decade. In Malaysia, the more Islamic-oriented political party, PAS (Islamic Party) and also various dakwah organizations, most notably ABIM (Muslim Youth Movement of Malaysia) have been lobbying the government and the general Malay-Muslim public for a more fundamentalist interpretation. In Indonesia, too, there is an alternative Islamic party, the PPP, and a growing group of young Islamic intellectuals who are assessing political and economic development strategies in Islamic terms.

A basic arena in which to view this confrontation will be found in debates on interpretations of articles of the constitution, and conceptualizations of national ideological formulations such as Pancasila and the Malaysian Rukunnegara. A key question will be whether the modernists will succeed in maintaining their position, or whether they will be forced increasingly to opt for more fundamentalist perspectives, or at least conciliatory positions. Two important indicators will be, first, changes in the religious affiliation requirements of the political elite, and, by extension, changes in the system of participatory parliamentary democracy, and second, the moves toward the implementation of *syariah* law, which carries the corollary of fundamental changes in the presently constituted legal systems which are based essentially on western legal traditions. Thus, the attempt, largely influenced by Muslim fundamentalists, to view Islam as a universalist ideology, has an important corollary: a reassessment of the Islamic ideological construction to state formation in post-war nation-building. This synthesis, which is still very much in process, will be a force to be reckoned with in the next decade.

Finally, in the context of conceptualizing Islam in Southeast Asia, there is an important countervailing dichotomy which will also play an increasing role in influencing the development of the fundamentalist modernist equation: the majority-minority question. There are two manifestations of this, first, the Muslim majority versus non-Muslim minority (as in the case of Malaysia and Indonesia) and second, the Muslim minority versus a non-Muslim majority (as in the case of Thailand, the Philippines and Singapore). The most significant factor to note with regard to the former is that the struggle between the modernists and the fundamentalists is not being carried out in a vacuum: the economic and political significance of the non-Muslim minority is an important variable. In keeping with the emergence of particularistic ideologies we should expect that various nationalist models would arise, and that these models would be perceived as being unique to the particular national circumstances in which the Muslim groups find themselves. One key element in these models with reference to Malaysia and Indonesia is the need to rationalize a role for the large non-Muslim minorities. A particularistic Islamic ideology must be constructed which can accommodate the diversity of population composition. No ready-made models exist outside of Southeast Asia, and so this development of a particularistic ideological model is very much in process. There seems to be a tendency, however, on the part of Muslim reformers in both countries to stress universalistic ideals of mankind, and such causes as social justice, land reform and corruption-free government, which, transcending the concerns that affect only Muslims, embrace problems which confront all citizens of the nation-state irrespective of religion and ethnicity. It is emphasized that the concerns of the Islamic *ummah* are the concerns of the *ummah* of mankind.

The basic question for Muslim minorities in non-Muslim states, on the other hand, is to what extent a distinct Muslim identity in the universalistic sense can be maintained, and how much assimilation to a dominant nation-state pattern will prevail amongst Muslim nationals. Within the context of Singapore, the Philippines and Thailand, the dominant pattern takes into consideration two factors of relevance — one linguistic, and the other ideological. In Thailand, Thai is the dominant language and Buddhism forms the basis for the national ethos. In the Philippines it is Tagalog which is the dominant language and Catholicism which forms the dominant component of the nation-state ethos. In Singapore the policy is to preserve a multilingual balance within a secular nation-state ethos.

In Malaysia, the presence of a large Chinese and Indian, non-Muslim minority, and, in Indonesia, the presence of Christian and Hindu-Buddhist minorities pose practical, if not ideological problems to fundamentalist innovators. In Thailand and the Philippines the concentration of Muslim minorities in the southern geographical regions of these nations has led to problems of state integration. These problems have been aggravated in the 1970s, since at least some of the Muslim leaders participate in the international Islamic resurgence and see in it an alternative model to national integration into a non-Muslim state. Singapore's small size, and its ambitious public housing projects have led to a physical integration of the (largely Malay) Muslim community. A National Council of Islamic Affairs has been set up to cater amongst other things, to the administration of the country's mosques and religious schools. In addition there is a *syariah* court to register and administer Muslim marriage, divorce, adoption, property and inheritance disputes. In Thailand and the Philippines there also appears to be a trend to provide some autonomy in such matters as religious education and the administration of civil religious law. Assuming that this trend continues and that the Muslim religion in these three states is not repressed, but allowed to function in limited spheres, a separation of state and religion is of course inevitable. The central question for these Muslim minorities then becomes to what extent, and with what consequences, is assimilation and integration into a larger nation-state ethos going to affect them, and the way in which these consequences will be accepted and interpreted.

To some extent, such development will be determined by the fact that this majority-minority question is intimately related to the position of the Malay-Muslim people in Southeast Asia. Malay-Muslims, in various permutations, are found from Southern Thailand to the Southern Philippines. The perceived status of the Malay-race as the indigenous race of the archipelago, and their geographical distribution transcending the boundaries of the present nation-states, may also lead to the emergence of a certain regional Muslim identity. Indeed, the recent formation of RISEAP (Regional Islamic Organization of Southeast Asia and the Pacific), with headquarters in Kuala Lumpur, heralds, perhaps, a regional ideological perspective which will complement both the national and universalistic ideological perspectives dealt with in this discussion.

Minangkabau and Modernization[1]

M. G. SWIFT

Anyone who has studied Indonesia could hardly fail to form the impression that the Minangkabau are a special people. In most fields of modern endeavour Minangkabau have been prominent, either as individuals or as a group. Stereotypes of the Minangkabau emphasize their initiative and striving, whatever other qualities may also be attributed to them, and these qualities do seem to set them apart from other Malaysian peoples.[2]

In business, especially as traders, the Minangkabau reach into most areas of Sumatra and Malaya, and can even be found playing an important role in more distant parts of Indonesia. Minangkabau themselves like to refer to the way Chinese were not able to dominate local trade in Minangkabau, a marked contrast to the situation in most other parts of the archipelago.

We can indicate the importance of the Minangkabau in politices by citing a few famous names such as Hatta, Sjahrir, Tan Malaka, M. Natsir, and Chaerul Salleh, who between them, significantly I think, cover most of the Indonesian ideological spectrum. Modern Indonesian literature of the pre-revolutionary period also owed a great deal to Minangkabau authors, and even now, when the early predominance has been lost, there still remain some talented Minangkabau writers.[3] The Minangkabau administrator is naturally not as obvious as the writer or the politician but even so these people provided disproportionately large numbers of the Civil Service, ranging from lowly primary school teachers and medical assistants upward.

In religion the Minangkabau are famous for their devotion to Islam, and like to refer to their country as the *serambi Makkah* (the verandah of Mecca) although the Achehnese would certainly dispute their claim to the honour. Minangkabau are best known for their contribution to the Islamic fundamentalist reform movement, but, as I will argue later, this does not mean that traditional orthodoxy lost its supporters in Minangkabau.

Paradoxically, despite their achievements in all these modernizing fields, the Minangkabau are equally well known for, and equally proud of, their devotion to their traditional matrilineal social arrangements (*adat*).

My interest was attracted to the Minangkabau by the contrast between their reputed qualities and those I had observed among the Malays of Negri Sembilan (Swift, 1965). These people trace their historical origin to Minangkabau, and still preserve a social system closely comparable to the Sumatran original. In Malaya I had been concerned with the differential economic success of Malays and Chinese, something too familiar to warrant further elaboration here. Systematic comparison between Malays and Chinese involves such a range of social and cultural variables as to appear unmanageable, while it seemed

Reprinted from L.R. Hiatt and C. Jayawardena (eds.), *Anthropology in Oceania: Essays presented to Ian Hogbin* (Sydney: Angus and Robertson, 1971), pp. 255–267 by permission of the publishers.

that the broadly similar cultural base would give a more controllable Malay/Minangkabau comparison. In this paper the Malays remain my implicit base for understanding Minangkabau, although I have not attempted a systematic comparison. I refrain from this because my short stay in Minangkabau merely allowed me to form impressions and gather isolated facts. Now I am endeavouring to organize these impressions and these facts, aided by further information gathered from the literature, as a preliminary to further fieldwork in Sumatra, or, failing that, as a goad to other interested students of the Minangkabau to state their own understanding of the issues.

The main question is: What is there about these people that has carried them so far and so successfully? This specific question can be related to more general problems of economic development and cultural change. For example, the Minangkabau invite comparison in some respects with the minority business communities, such as the Marwari in Bengal and the Syrian in West Africa. Is the initiative and economic success of such peoples to be explained simply by their special position as minority groups, or must one look for distinctive qualities in the values and social organization of particular minorities to explain their economic success? Another question, most recently posed by Geertz (1963), is whether Reformist Islam plays an ideological role in economic activity comparable to that which has been claimed for the Protestant Ethic. I would not venture a general answer to this question, especially as it has been posed specifically for Java, but will offer some thoughts on the Minangkabau situation later in this paper.

The first step in explaining the success of the Minangkabau in modernizing fields is to explain their migration, for most of their exploits occur outside the home area. A natural poverty of resources would provide a powerful incentive for people to migrate, and might even explain their acquiring habits of drive and hard work. We may discount this explanation for two reasons. Firstly, while Minangkabau would now be hard-pressed to support all the people who in some sense belong there (that is, if all the Minangkabau were to come home), and while the living standards of those resident there now, in some villages almost entirely women, children and the aged, depend very much on outside remittances, these conditions would not have applied when the migratory pattern was first established. The pressure on land now so evident in the core area of Minangkabau reflects population growth as much as the inherent limited supply of land. Secondly, a "reaction of poverty" argument would not explain the characteristically temporary nature of the *merantau*[4] migration, ranging from the seasonal search for work of the craftsman, and the *merantau pipit* of the poor peasant seeking work harvesting rice, to the career-long migration, interspersed with home leave, of the civil servant. Poverty in Minangkabau would equally favour the establishment of permanent agricultural settlements outside the area. It is true that Minangkabau have spread from the heartland into neighbouring areas of Sumatra such as Acheh Barat, Singkel, Pasisir Barus, down the Indragiri and other east-coast rivers, and even as far afield as Malaya, but the *merantau* pattern of temporary migration still remains characteristic.

As a first step in our search for another explanation of the migration pattern let us consider the apparent contrast between the devotion of the Minangkabau to tradition and their modern strivings. Tradition is a complex concept with many nuances of meaning — here I wish to distinguish three dimensions of the term.

The first dimension of tradition refers to *adat* status differences. While I am quite prepared to concede to local experts that there were marked variations in this regard between the two *laras* (a major traditional territorial division) of Koto Piliang and Bodi Djaniago, and between the *darat* (highlands) and the *pasisir* (coast), it seems to me that in both the semi-mythical past and the colonial period all Minangkabau areas were marked by pronounced status differences which embraced not merely matters of prestige ranking, but also, by control of clan lands, economic differentiation as well (Josselin de Jong, 1951). These status differences existed even within clan and subclan groups, distinguishing the real sisters' sons of high-ranking men (*kemanakan*) from the low-ranking members of the clan who were merely "sisters' sons beneath the knee" (*kemanakan di-bawah lutut*). The majority of modern Minangkabau are not attached to this form of tradition, and I believe it was this area of privilege which was the main concern of the various large *adat* conferences, even if other matters, such as Islamic law and matrilineal inheritance, appear to have loomed larger in the discussions. Although *adat* privilege plays an important part in the novels of the pre-war period, normally as an evil force thwarting the course of true love and justice, it is hard to find any reference to status differentials in modern discussions by Minangkabau authors of *adat*, which is rather treated as a form of aboriginal democracy, implicitly or explicitly more suited to Indonesia than forms borrowed from the West.

In so far as these *adat* privileges persisted into fairly recent times the reason was Dutch support of, and reliance on, traditional chiefly elements.

Adat status differences provide an important element for the solution of our problem. One factor in the *merantau* pattern is the search by less-privileged Minangkabau for status to compensate for their ascribed inferiority at home. My experience in Minangkabau leads me to the tentative conclusion that people who were in a privileged position under traditional arrangements were less inclined, by and large, to exert themselves in any of the areas of modern endeavour. I frequently met people who had been successful in modern occupations gleefully describing the stupid ignorance of chiefly families, their comic arrogance in trying to maintain their out-moded superiority, and, best of all, the occasions when such people, confronted by the modern world, were reduced to pleading for assistance from those they affected to despise. Schrieke (1957) reported conflict between *nouveaux riches* and chiefly people in the 1920s; even today, at least in the villages, this type of conflict, and memories of it, still affect the quality of interpersonal relations.

I do not go so far as to say that the *merantau* pattern can be understood solely as a status-group matter. Minangkabau competitiveness is so pervasive that even well-placed individuals are motivated to achieve and assert themselves, but I do feel that they are more likely to find a suitable arena within traditional social arrangements than the ordinary man.

A second important dimension of tradition refers to the cultural exclusiveness of the group, symbolized in shared values and patterns of behaviour, which in one sense express the superiority of the group, and in another are felt to explain it.

The Minangkabau have strong in-group sentiments and feelings of superiority to other groups. One expression of this is their attachment to cultural forms free of association with the disliked aspects of tradition. A complex of individually trivial traits, such as the dress of Minang women, the *lagu minang* modernizations of traditional Minang songs, the Minangkabau dialect, food, the *saluang* verse form, give a distinctive flavour to what is, at root, merely a variant of a much more widespread culture. The triviality of these items of the Minang way of life make them common ground for all Minangkabau; more precise expressions of Minangkabau superiority also express the internal differentiation of this complex society. One area may emphasize that a particular Padri leader, or (formerly) a close associate of Sukarno, or a well-known writer (one can go on) is, or was, a local boy, while another area will have a different set of heroes. Some people prefer to emphasize the presumed greatness of Minangkabau in antiquity, hinted at by archaeological relics, others prefer the greatness of Islamic education in Minangkabau, the famous reformers who taught there or came from there, and the role of the Padri in fighting the Dutch. One village recounts the names of high-ranking administrators who have come from it, another tells of the important part played by their men in the trade of some part of the *rantau*. These expressions of more local pride, and of class and ideological differentiation, qualify but do not contradict the more widespread sentiment of the general superiority of Minangkabau to other peoples.

These feelings and their associated cultural expressions are relevant to the migration pattern. Minangkabau in the *rantau* can occasionally call on the help of their fellows when in need; sometimes the Minangkabau community in the *rantau* may form itself into an association, led perhaps by the local schoolmaster or some other prestigious figure. In expressed values people show a strong feeling for the rightness of co-operation between Minang. But this point should not be overemphasized. A strong sense of group superiority, aided by the persistence of a variety of traditionally validated cultural forms, can give rise to practical expressions of Minang solidarity. Nevertheless, the struggle of the Minangkabau is an intensely individual one, and mutual superiority to non-Minang does not prevent Minang competing with each other. I would suggest, however, that these superiority feelings can be powerful psychological supports for the often isolated and not especially popular Minangkabau making his way in the *rantau,* and even, hesitatingly, that this may be a point of comparison with the accommodation of the Jewish and the Chinese trader isolated in stronger, but secretly despised, host communities.

A final relevant dimension of tradition refers to the organization of the matrilineal extended family, the property owning unit in traditional society. Here we find tradition providing a set of special obstacles to economic activity in Minangkabau and a set of motives for concentrating economic activities in the *rantau,* while using the wealth thus gained for kinship and prestige ends in Minangkabau; such goals being reinforced by the continuing cultural involvement mentioned in discussion of the second dimension of tradition.

In the area where I lived the people were grouped by *nagari,* a territorial unit, and within each *nagari* divided into four clans under a number of chiefs, paramount among whom was the *Dato Puchok.* Each clan was divided into subclans (*kampuang*), and each subclan less precisely into a number of matrilineal extended families. Within the subclan there was a well-distributed knowledge of how the various subgroups were related, but little co-activity beyond the expression of concern by making visits at times of life crises. The corporate group was the extended family, comprising the children and grandchildren of one woman, not necessarily alive, but only recently dead if not. Members of this group held property in common, had a hereditary right to certain clan and subclan offices and ideally lived together in one *adat* house (*rumah gadang*). Because of the extent of migration there was little opportunity for the group members to come together, but they were continually in contact through letters, messages and visits. There was a very lively concern with common interests, especially the increase in property held by the female members of the group and the education of the young. This was assuming that things were going well. Some less fortunate groups were more concerned with raising help from members in the *rantau* for distressed members stuck at home, or in finding ways out of the various problems which arose from the P.R.R.I. (Revolutionary Government of the Republic of Indonesia) rebellion, perhaps fixing a "screening" clearance so that a man might be re-employed or his pension be paid, or, failing that, finding a niche for him in the *rantau.*[5]

Apart from education, groups which had some members prospering were particularly busy with two operations: building houses or acquiring ricefields. Both of these are aspects of the traditional obligation to provide for the female and infant members of the group — they are certainly not innovatory economic activities.

Both endeavours were complicated in western Sumatra in 1962–3. With houses, the first question was the style, a matter of some sociological import. In Minangkabau only the traditional *adat* house is graced by the word *rumah* (which in other places is synonymous with house). A sign of a group's prosperity and regard for custom is the members' ability to maintain a large *adat* house in good repair on the appropriate site. However, such houses are not comfortable, and many people, especially those who have made money in the *rantau,* preferred to build modern bungalows, and even to build outside the traditional boundaries of the *nagari.* This meant, according to the chiefs, that their houses only qualified as *dangau* (sheds) and could not be used for ritually correct ceremonies.

I heard several discussions of this problem, but in the event no one spent much money on an *adat* house. One reason for this is the unwillingness of those who have made the money to accord status to *adat* superiors who are class inferiors, or, indeed, even to be reminded of such unpleasant issues, and this would be unavoidable in the context of an *adat* house. A further point is that building an *adat* house would mean losing an opportunity to assert one's status by the *nouveau riche* standards of the new bourgeoisie (O.K.B.),[6] as one might by building a house in modern style. People still recognize traditional obligations towards their kin, and find the status increment involved worth the expense, yet they are clearly selecting from the corpus of traditional rules those elements they will follow and those they will ignore.

In the same way that men spend a lot of money building houses for their sisters and mothers (and to a much lesser extent for their wives; nuclear family investments would normally be made outside Minangkabau where the affairs of the family would be freer from *adat* "interference") they also make large payments acquiring land. These transactions were very complex, especially as the confused state of modern land tenure was made worse by the then threatened implementation of the Agraria laws.[7] In most of Minangkabau, certainly in the rural area where I lived, land cannot be bought and sold, nor is it individual property. Transfers take the form of mortgages which require the consent not only of the individual currently holding the property but of all the entitled kin group and the local administrative authority. It might happen, and I was told of cases where it had, that a remote member of the pledging group might turn up years later claiming that, since he was not consulted or given a share of the pledge money, the agreement was invalid and both land and money should be returned. Partly because of a desire for secure possession, but also because of the effects of inflation, people acquiring land endeavoured to get the owners and the *wali negri* (local council chairman) to accept a form of agreement which would permanently transfer the land, sale in fact if not in name, but were unable to do so, nor would it have been clearly legal had they done so. Another favoured way of avoiding the dangers of inflation was to make the agreement in terms of rice rather than money.

The confusion of the contemporary legal position is partly an inheritance from the colonial arrangement of leaving some aspects of the law to the operation of *adatsrecht* (custom law) while retaining the administrative power to overrule or replace the *adat* authorities if their decisions were unsatisfactory. Difficult enough to operate decades ago, the dual system has collapsed in the face of continuing social change, and as yet no realistic alternative has been found for the regulation of affairs in this sensitive area, charged with emotions of local patriotism, involving varied vested interests and further complicated by the pervasive deterioration in Indonesian administration which would make it difficult to implement an extensive administrative programme even if firm political decisions could be made.

The rights and duties of *adat* are nowadays no less confused. People are generally agreed that the rules are still valid, but quite opposed positions can be justified in terms of one *adat* rule or another, or of some more or less well attested past agreement which may or may not apply to the current generation. The upper reaches of the *adat* hierarchy no longer function effectively even at *nagari* level, and cannot give authoritative rulings on disputes at the extended family level — for example, on where the bounds of the owning group are. Some offices are not filled, others have two hostile incumbents; where the offices are filled the chiefs possess no sanctions beyond their personal prestige, which may be limited indeed. Despite this, the notion of chiefly authority is there to complicate extended family disputes.

Local administration is also little help in clarifying property matters. The wise *wali negri* merely says that he cannot interfere in *adat* matters which are the province of the kin elders (*nenek mamak*). Even if he should try to assert himself, he possesses no sanctions to impose a settlement beyond the general expectation that, if the occasion arises, he will make himself disagreeable to people who thwart him, say in forcible grain sales, or the distribution of cheap rationed goods. People who do not like the *wali's* decision can always appeal to higher grades of the hierarchy, or simply hang on hoping that he will be replaced at the next election.

At the time when I observed some of these transactions the whole province was suffering from the aftermath of the P.R.R.I. rebellion. This certainly made things worse in many ways, but even if one were to assume maximum efficiency the land system would still be confused by the partial retention of traditional rules in a very changed society.

Tree crops (for many decades the main source of native wealth in Sumatra) are not normally planted on ricefields or to any significant extent on house-sites, but rather are grown on newly cleared scrub and jungle land. It is then possible to adopt new rules for land devoted to commercial crops, while retaining traditional rules for the traditional productive assets and activities. This is what occurred in Negri Sembilan, the matrilineal area of Malaya, where the British decided the local controversy about whether rubber holdings were subject to traditional rules by pronouncing that they were private property held on title from the state. In Minangkabau, on the other hand, unoccupied land is the property of the *nagari*. It may be used for cultivation by any member, but the land cannot be permanently alienated. In principle it can be used for the cultivation of tree crops; the trees are the property of the planter, but he has only insecure possession of the land, especially in the light of the long life of the rubber tree. This helps to explain why there has been relatively little rubber-planting in the central area of Minangkabau, especially when contrasted with the Malay areas of the east coast, and why what little rubber there is is so old and neglected. Many rich Minangkabau own rubber, but in the *rantau* under private property rules.

This third dimension of tradition bears on our problem in another way. The "matrilineal puzzle" acquires a special emphasis in Minangkabau. The usual stress is on the potentiality for conflict which exists between brother/uncle and husband/father in a matrilineal system. In Minangkabau I would stress the opposing demands of wife and children and mother/sister/sister's children. Ideally a man will meet both sets of demands, but they can naturally come to have overtones of jealous competition going beyond claims for help in meeting objective needs. The traditional socio-political system lent its weight to kin rather than nuclear family claims, with frequent divorce as the corollary. The decline of the traditional political system, and the general modernization of the society, have redressed the balance without substantially lessening the absolute legitimacy of matrilineal claims. Talking to Minangkabau at home and in the *rantau* I formed a strong impression of the pressures which matriliny places on a man in this society. On the one hand it requires exertion so that the demands can be met, and also makes periods in the *rantau* a welcome relief from daily pressure. On the other hand their varied emotional commitments prevent most men from making a complete break with the homeland.

At this point, the matter of emotions having been raised, it would be well to pause briefly and discuss Minangkabau personality and the possibility that their modal personality is characterized by a highly developed achievement motive or similar feature. I broach this matter even though I know that a satisfactory discussion of it would require an analysis of child-rearing patterns, feeding, toilet-training and so on and even though I have little more than impressions to offer. My limited observation is that Minangkabau children are brought up very much as are Malay children with presumably similar consequences for the early implicit moulding of their personalities. Child handling is permissive in both societies with obvious differences from child to child following from factors such as parental personality, birth order, and the presence or absence of father and grandparents. Where I see a difference between Minangkabau and Malay emerging is in the messages about the nature of life and of a worthwhile person which the child receives when it can understand. The Minangkabau is left with little doubt that the worthwhile person competes and succeeds. The Malay child, as I have argued elsewhere (Swift, 1965), is taught that there is little relation between effort and reward. These impressions cannot masquerade as a substitute for a competent technical analysis, yet I have no doubt in some way a substantial proportion of socialized Minangkabau acquire highly competitive personalities, very strongly motivated to individual success in a range of culturally defined contexts.

The ideal used to be that the Minang male went away to the *rantau*, frequently, if married, leaving his wife and children with her kin. Every year, at the Fasting Month, he would return, bringing a lot of money and presents to make a fine display until the *Hari Raya* (*Id 'ul Fitri*) celebrations were over, when he would go to the *rantau* again to make more money for next year. Radjab has given us an eloquent account of how he, as a boy too young to *merantau,* was moved by this display, and from this we can derive a major clue for understanding the whole pattern. Migration is a temporary phase in a status game which is really played in the home village. An appreciation of the *merantau* pattern, and hence of the fortunes of the Minangkabau people in modern Indonesia, requires that we understand both the pressures which lead Minangkabau to migrate, and their intense continuing involvement with the home area, the arena for the status game.

While I was in Minangkabau no one returned who could avoid it, and as we approached the Fasting Month people spoke with nostalgia of the old days when people would have been returning for their annual visit. The new pattern was for the wealthy to support their relatives in pleasanter parts of Indonesia, perhaps Medan, the dollar-area of Riau, or one of the cities of Java. The post-rebellion troubles would provide an immediate explanation of this state of affairs, but I think it may also be a sign of a new development — that Minangkabau settle in the *rantau* and allow their home ties to lapse. I certainly formed this impression talking to Minangkabau in Malaya, and to others who have had long careers in Medan or Java. In some cases their children cannot even speak the Minangkabau dialect, and show a distinct impatience with the nostalgia of the older generation. One would expect ethnic (*suku*) loyalties to lessen in this way as nations develop, and it would not be surprising if the *merantau* pattern were to change. But for the present signs remain signs, and the *merantau* pattern retains much of its characteristic form.

A further question which the economic anthropologist should certainly pose relates to the role of kinship ties in the organization of activity in the *rantau.* Are traditional ties redefined and put to new purposes, lending their legitimacy to new types of relationships, and perhaps giving the Minangkabau a competitive advantage against other peoples who do not have such ties? At first glance this seems a reasonable expectation when we contrast the unilineal corporate groups of Minangkabau with the ramifying kindreds of the Malay and Javanese, but I did not in fact find kinship bonds providing a set of ties that could be put to important use, nor the discipline of the kin group underwriting the discipline of the enterprise. The young Minangkabau is entitled to support and assistance from both his uncle (*mamak*) and his father when he first begins an enterprise. The potential administrator or professional man will get his education paid for, and the right contacts made to get him a job; the young trader may be given a small stock in trade, or begin work at a kinsman's store. But the young Minangkabau is competing with kinsmen as well as outsiders and wishes to succeed on his own, so whatever the enterprise he typically soon breaks out of the early relationship of dependence.

An important support for the *merantau* migration pattern is the devaluation of agriculture as an occupation. I cannot imagine the honoured landowner — who has successfully pursued peasant agriculture to the point where he has enough land rented to others not to need to work it himself, who has been to Mecca, and who has generally become an influential village personality — being regarded in Minangkabau as one who has had a model career, which he certainly would be by some Malay and Javanese youths. One expression of the strong traditional status differences was the saying that there are four varieties of people (*orang empat djenis*) and people of no standing (*orang ta'berdjenis*). These latter were peasants. A modern version of the saying I heard (the first has by no means lost currency) is that there are four occupations: official, merchant, craftsman, and peasant. Only failures are peasants; to work the land implies either that one lacked the initiative and ability to go to the *rantau,* or that one went and failed.

Dutch colonialism and a general economic and administrative development presented a people who already possessed a strong motivation to competitive success with many new opportunities and a minimizing of some traditional obstacles. A cultural pattern that was already present became a dominating theme of the culture. An impressionistic survey of fields where Minangkabau have done well and those where they have made little mark suggests that the former have been areas suited to individual initiative not demanding large-scale organizational ability. Writing is such a profession. In politics the success of Minangkabau has been more a matter of individual careers as intellectual spokesmen or fixers rather than as effective controllers of organizations. In the bureaucracy the Minangkabau climbs the ladder as an individual according to rules made by others. Some Minangkabau have done well in bureaucratic careers but they appear most prominent in low to middle-rung positions, providing a major source of civil servants for surrounding areas of Sumatra. In Minangkabau who are traders this same individualism appears. In Malaya the Minangkabau are confined to operations where the Chinese are ruled out, where competition is intense and returns are small. The typical career seemed to involve coming over from Sumatra as a young man, with nothing specific in mind, beyond the determination to do one's best in what was, in fact, a limited field of opportunity.

Post-war Sumatra has seen a number of groups emerge into prominence. It is the Achehnese rather than Minangkabau who have grasped control of former foreign-owned rubber estates around Medan. Various groups of Batak have also found profitable niches for themselves, using their patrilineal groupings in their adjustment to the modern situation and apparently being prepared to sublimate individual competition to group advantage to some extent. I suggest that the intense competitiveness of the Minangkabau is such that success as part of a group is not satisfying for the personality and cultural drives involved. I see the genius of the Minangkabau as most suited to a quick perception and grasping of short-term opportunity, best exemplified in the world of petty trading. This may be seen in the commercial skill with which they reacted to the breakdown of their provincial economy. Great initiative went into smuggling and evading the restrictions of the "guided economy", an impressive skill was shown in keeping vehicles on the road, and in devising handcrafted substitutes for goods which would previously have been imported. Nevertheless, despite the high price of foodstuffs, few turned to producing them, rather people tried to get into trading in such goods. It seems to me that this reaction is very much in line with the competitive individualism and distinctive cultural values which have been attributed to the Minangkabau in this essay.

Now I will briefly discuss the issue of Reformist Islam and the ideology of economic activity. I do not attribute an important role to this factor in explaining the emergence of the Minangkabau as a significant group in one phase of Indonesian history. Since the discussion of this issue now derives from Geertz's work I will introduce some of his terms. In the first place Minangkabau is a *santri*[8] society and culture. Cultural stratigraphy can clearly identify folk, Hindu, and Muslim elements in Minangkabau culture, but these do not identify *aliran*[9] in modern Minangkabau. Migration and the military occupation have brought large numbers of *abangan*[10] to the area, and the wholesale involvement of Minangkabau in the P.R.R.I. rebellion and the subsequent "screening" of government employees have meant a substantial influx of Javanese *prijaji*-type[11] civil servants, but Minangkabau remains a Muslim society where the main tensions are between tradition and modernity. Trading and rational accumulation were legitimate enough activities in Minangkabau culture, as indeed they are in any form of Islam which has access to the Middle East, whether reformist or traditional.

A further point is that I was unable to discern any close correlation between a man's occupation and his religious position, and it is also important not to overestimate the extent to which the Reformers came to dominate Minangkabau. They were not in any case a united group, and while people of a generally Reformist orientation have come to dominate the literature, traditional practices are still often followed in Minangkabau, albeit with a certain hesitation.

But while I am arguing against any direct and special connection between Reformist Islam and Minangkabau economic activity, there is another sense in which the Reformist slogan "Back to the Koran and Hadith" is important for all forms of modernization.

Traditional Islam emphasizes the religious significance of minor details in everyday life so that at times it seems as if the pious live their whole lives accumulating merit in a quite arithmetical way, adding so much for this detail and subtracting so much for that. Such precise rules can be a great hindrance to a man trying to make his way in a profession not foreseen by traditional Islam. Islamic Reform introduces a new criterion of moral judgement. A man makes reference to the Holy Book and the traditions of the Prophet rather than blindly adhering to the opinions of medieval legists as handed down to his own religious teachers (*taklid buta*). The conscience of the individual becomes more important than the old received view, and the assumption is made that whatever is not strictly forbidden is permitted. In this way Islamic Reform enables a person to make a gradual adjustment to the ways of modern society without any need for a traumatic rejection of religion and his emotional stance as a devout Muslim.

Let me conclude with a brief summary. If the question is, why do Minangkabau strive? — the answer must be given in terms of the dynamics of personality formation and the cultural patterns which direct individual efforts towards competitive achievement in a variety of contexts. But understanding a particular case also means taking account of the historical circumstances, and the more general ecological situation. Here I would note the restricted home environment, to which people have a strong emotional attachment. This attachment is related to the persistence of a rich local culture, which makes ties with the homeland valuable. Here there seems a contrast with the situation reported for Javanese rural "suburbia".

In the past, temporary migration and achievement in the *rantau* offered some escape from the tight status restrictions of the homeland, and the role of religious leader seems to have offered mobility to a few. The Dutch colonial period opened up a much wider range of opportunities for individual status improvement. Economic change increased trading opportunities, and the Minangkabau had an aptitude for trade which some local peoples lacked. There was also a wide range of entirely new positions directly or indirectly connected with the growth of administration and the spread of Western enterprise. The Minangkabau were willing to fill these positions and spoke a dialect of Malay, the official language of the Dutch administration; also, because of a local tradition of religious education, some individuals were literate in Malay. I think it should also be noted that the Minangkabau were pacified relatively early, and so were available to take advantage of the colonial opportunities in a way that some other peoples were not.

From the general viewpoint of economic development I can see only limited lessons to be drawn from the Minangkabau case. We can derive some confirmation of the importance of an achievement orientation in successful modernization, with a less clear rider on the dangers of too much competitive individualism. The special position of the Minangkabau I see as being as much a result of a unique constellation of historical circumstances as a matter of their special qualities. While I am sure their special aptitudes will continue to serve them well in the new Indonesia it is difficult to see them ever regaining their special position as a group now that so many other peoples have joined them on the modern stage.

NOTES

1. Fieldwork and other research for this paper were made possible by the generosity of the Wenner-Gren Foundation, the Research Centre for Economic Development and Cultural Change, University of Chicago, and the University of Sydney.

   I have not tried to document every point in this essay. I merely list the main sources for my understanding of Minangkabau. This seemed appropriate since in most cases I am indebted to books for general impressions rather than points of detailed information. I have included these books in the consolidated list of references at the end of this volume; they may be identified by their Indonesian-language titles. Instead of listing all the famous Balai Pustaka novels, I refer readers to Mokhzani's (1960) thesis.

2. Malaysia is here used in its culture area sense, not to mean the Federation of Malaysia.
3. For example, the works of A. A. Navis and Nurdin Jacub cited in the references.
4. *rantau:* narrowly, this means the "colonial" areas of Minangkabau expansion, while more widely, and in this discussion, it means the outside world where the Minangkabau goes to seek his fortune, *merantau:* temporary migration in search of wealth.
5. Mossmann (1961) gives a first-hand account of the 1958 "Colonels' Revolt" of the Revolutionary Republic of Indonesia.
6. *Orang Kaya Bahru:* literally, newly rich people. The initials, O.K.B. pronounced Okahbah, became a word in their own right during the period of flagrant corruption and profiteering in the midst of general economic difficulty.
7. Harsono (1961). In most of Minangkabau these agrarian reform laws had not even begun to be applied; but had they been, they would have threatened the structure of Minangkabau social organization by their provision that all land be converted to private title, and that all mortgaged land should revert free to its owner after seven years, a special threat in the light of the large sums paid at mortgages which were intended by the mortgagers to be permanent transfers. This was the only issue on which I read explicit criticism of the Government in the Padang press, despite military rule and guided democracy.
8. *santri:* a life-style stressing Islam.
9. *aliran:* social movement cum political party.
10. *abangan:* syncretic peasant life-style.
11. *prijaji:* Hinduistic/aristocratic life-style. On this and the preceding three foot-notes cf. Geertz (1960).

Malayism, Bumiputraism, and Islam

CHANDRA MUZAFFAR

The Universalism of Islam is an open proclamation to everyone — Muslim and non-Muslim alike — that communalism is totally alien to the spirit and philosophy of Islam.

This proclamation is particularly relevant in a society like ours. It is unfortunate that over the decades Islam in Malaysia has come to be seen in communal perspectives. 'Communal' in this context does not mean mere association with a particular community. It is perhaps unavoidable that in a situation where all Malays are Muslims, Islam will be perceived as a Malay religion by both Malays and non-Malays. As long as there is sufficient awareness that Islam does not belong exclusively to the Malays and that there are millions upon millions of non-Malays who are also Muslims, no one can say that such a perception is in itself communal.[1]

What makes the prevailing attitude towards Islam communal is the tendency to link the religion with what I shall call *Malayism* and *Bumiputraism* when it is apparent that both the premises of these two almost identical 'isms' and their implications have nothing to do with Islam. By Malayism I mean that whole philosophy that argues that, *as the indigenous community,* the Malays have certain political, economic and cultural rights that distinguish them from the non-indigenous communities. Bumiputraism rests upon the same premise except that it also encompasses indigenous non-Malay, non-Muslim communities whose interests may, at certain points, conflict with those of the Malays.[2] A clear instance would be the political pre-eminence of the Malays which is not just pre-eminence in relation to the non-indigenous communities but also pre-eminence in relation to the non-Malay, non-Muslim indigenous communities.[3]

Since both Malayism and Bumiputraism are founded upon the notion of an indigenous people, let us consider this factor from the point of view of Islam. The Islamic Party of Malaysia (PAS) has all along demanded the "restoration of Malay sovereignty" primarily because of the indigenous status of the community.[4] What is important to us is that its demand has invariably been presented in the name of Islam. Even a cursory analysis of PAS's philosophy will reveal that its insistence upon Malay political pre-eminence, Malay economic pre-eminence and Malay cultural pre-eminence have been articulated as a way of protecting the integrity of Islam.[5]

Now Islam does not recognise an indigenous — non-indigenous dichotomy as the basis of any social system. If terms like indigenous (Bumiputra) and non-indigenous (non-Bumiputra) are used merely as descriptions of categories within the population which have emerged as a result of the evolution of the Malaysian nation, it would not be altogether

---

Excerpted from Chandra Muzaffar (ed.), *Universalism of Islam* (Penang: Aliran, 1979), by permission of the author and the publishers.

antithetical to Islamic principles. For then the categories concerned would be of historical rather than social relevance. But since the PAS argument is that public life should be conducted on the basis of an indigenous — non-indigenous dichotomy one would be right in describing it as an un-Islamic stance. There are three important reasons for saying so. Firstly, it is seldom realized that by distinguishing the indigenous community from the non-indigenous communities one is, in fact, dividing the Muslims since there are Muslims who are non-bumiputras just as there are bumiputras who are non-Muslims. Islamic teachings are opposed to any covert or overt attempt to divide Muslims. This is borne out by the importance attached to the very well-known principle in Islam that "the Believers are but a single Brotherhood, so make peace and reconciliation between your two contending brothers".[6] Lest this idea of Muslim unity is misunderstood it must be stressed that Islam does not advocate an obscurantist sort of unity without considering the ethical foundations of that unity. As proof, it is stated in the Quran that "Allah will not leave the Believers in the state in which ye are now until He separates what is evil from what is good".[7] Dividing non-indigenous Muslims from indigenous Muslims in matters relating to politics, economics, education and culture is certainly not a case of separating evil from good! Secondly, even if all Bumiputras were Muslims and all non-Bumiputras non-Muslims, it would still be wrong to differentiate between the two groups in employment, education and other similar areas where the paramount consideration should be the welfare of the human being. The Quran itself prohibits such discrimination.[8] The constitution of Medina formulated by Prophet Muhammad (May peace be upon him) provided equal rights and responsibilities to Muslims and non-Muslims alike.[9] Illustrious Caliphs in early Islam like Abu Bakar, Omar and Ali took great pains to ensure that their non-Muslim citizens were well looked after. According to the 8th century Hanafi jurist, Abu Yusuf, the second Caliph Omar even fixed special pensions for the non-Muslims living in Damascus.[10] Thirdly, by placing the whole Bumiputra — non-Bumiputra dichotomy at the centre of things one has, in a sense, elevated ethnicity and ancestry to a level which is repugnant to genuine Islamic values. One of the hadiths (sayings of Prophet Muhammad) reminds mankind that "there is no pride whatsoever in ancestry; there is no merit in an Arab as against a non-Arab nor in a non-Arab as against an Arab".[11] What is at the kernel of Islam is not ethnicity or ancestry but the unity of God. And the one most significant implication of that unity is the unity of the whole of mankind. The Quran for instance, observes, "O mankind! We created you from a single pair of a male and a female, and made you into nations and tribes, that ye may know each other, not that ye may despise each other. Verily, the most honoured of you in the sight of Allah is he who is the most righteous of you".[12] This concept of unity is in fact linked to the idea of equality within the human community as suggested in sura Al-i-Imran: 195.[13] In other words, the very endeavour to sustain and strengthen ethnic dichotomies like the indigenous—non-indigenous distinction amounts to a denunciation of the central principle of Islam itself — the principle of the unity of God or *Tauhid*.

Obviously then, PAS cannot justify Bumiputraism by using or misusing Islam. Of course it is not just PAS that advocates Bumiputraism. It is, as we know, the whole basis of public policy formulation. However, in all fairness to the UMNO-led government which is responsible for this, it must be recognised that it does not justify Bumiputraism in the name of Islam.[14]

That Bumiputraism cannot be defended from an Islamic point of view is something that very few Muslims in Malaysia are aware of. Even where there is some awareness, there doesn't seem to be a willingness to articulate such a view in public. This is true of almost all Muslim groups in the country including those who argue that PAS is un-Islamic and that they represent pure, pristine Islam. That is why I have never believed for one moment that the tremendous interest in Islam manifested in recent years by educated youths and others who are part of the urban environment reflects the emergence of a genuine Islamic consciousness.[15] To establish this point, I shall undertake a brief analysis of the so-called 'rising tide of Islam' of the seventies. I hope to show that Islam in Malaysia is still clothed in communal garb; that Muslims in Malaysia have yet to understand what the universal spirit of Islam means in reality.

It is no mere coincidence that this 'Islamic tide' has risen in the seventies. For the seventies has seen the emergence of the Malay community as a significant component of the urban environment, especially the Kuala Lumpur environment.[16] It is estimated that by 1980, 32 per cent of the urban population would be Malay.[17] In a society where ethnic consciousness is pervasive, Malays who have just become part of a largely non-Malay milieu are bound to develop an awareness of their ethnic background which may not have been there when they were amongst their own ethnic kind in the rural areas. One can argue that even in societies where ethnic consciousness is not as pervasive, a first generation community in a somewhat alien setting is expected to manifest a similar psychological response. A sense of insecurity, a feeling of suspicion, of distrust, are some of the accompanying elements of this increased ethnic awareness. Islam provides a useful channel for the expression of this awareness since it touches the life of an ordinary Malay in a thousand different ways. No other cultural symbol of the Malay community can be as effective. The Malay language expresses only one dimension of Malay identity and besides, since 1970, it has become increasingly the language of social communication of non-Malays as well.[18] It cannot therefore be used as an avenue for expressing 'Malayness'. But Islam on the other hand, as it is understood here, can be used as the rationale for dressing in a certain way, staying away from certain groups, avoiding certain places and, most of all, adhering to certain beliefs and ideas. More specifically, this explains why some Muslim women in colleges and universities, firms and factories — more than their counterparts in the padi-fields and rubber smallholdings — are so concerned about dressing in the 'proper Islamic way', about avoiding male company, about staying away from cinemas and so on. It also explains, I suppose, why there is so much concern among certain Muslim circles in the cities about whether 'tanggung halal' signs displayed in some non-Muslim eating shops are genuine or not.[19]

What all this shows is that as a reaction to the non-Malay, non-Muslim dominated urban environment, certain segments of the urban Malay community are seeking to carve out a distinctive identity, establish a separate ethnic presence. As I have tried to explain, this search is not the outcome of a sudden realisation of what it is to be a Muslim in terms of dress or social intercourse; rather it stems from a feeling of deep insecurity that compels the individual concerned to protect his 'Malayness'. This is why he chooses only those elements from Islam which will help him maintain his separateness, his distinctiveness. After all, an Islamic identity is much more than dress forms or modes of social intercourse. Is not a Muslim also defined on the basis of his commitment to truth and justice, his readiness to fight oppression and corruption, his willingness to help the poor, the weak, his capacity for charity, for kindness? There are numerous verses in the Quran that support such an idea of a Muslim identity. One such verse says, "And show him the two highways? But he hath made no haste on the path that is steep. And what will explain to thee the path that is steep? — It is freeing the bondman; Or the giving of food in a day of privation, To the orphan with claims of relationship, Or to the indigent down in the dust. Then will he be of those who believe and enjoin patience, (constancy & self-restraint) and enjoin Deeds of kindness and compassion. Such are the Companions of the Right Hand".[20] Another verse says, "Seest thou one Who denies the Judgement (to come)? Then such as the (man) Who repulses the orphan (With harshness). And encourages not the feeding of the Indigent. So woe to the Worshippers Who are neglectful of their Prayers. Those who (want but) to be seen (of man) But refuse (to supply) (Even) neighbourly needs."[21]

Of course, defining the identity of a Muslim in terms of his kindness to the poor will not serve the purpose of maintaining a separate identity since kindness like compassion is a sentiment, a value, which any human being, Muslim or non-Muslim, Malay or non-Malay, is capable of. If, on the other hand, one emphasises dress or food or various rituals which are specific and exclusive to the religion, one would be highlighting forms and practices which others cannot share.

Thus, one would be able to sustain a Muslim — non-Muslim dichotomy which at the emotional-psychological level equals a Malay — non-Malay, a Bumiputra — non-Bumiputra dichotomy.

So far, I have shown that the interest in Islam in the seventies is closely aligned to the crystallization of ethnic consciousness in a new urban environment. Insecurity has been suggested as one of the propelling forces behind this consciousness. There is, however, another psychological force which is also at work at the same time — a force which superficially at least appears to contradict the feeling of insecurity we have just analysed. The political climate of the seventies with its emphasis upon Malay interests and aspirations in the economy, in politics and in the cultural life of the nation, has bestowed various Malay groups with a sense of confidence about the legitimacy of their demands.[22] Confidence of this sort derived from an overall political situation where the Malay position is undoubtedly strong and powerful can, of course, co-exist quite happily with insecurity generated by a specific urban environment where the Malay position is neither strong nor powerful as yet. It is because there is this confidence that Malay groups are more vocal than ever before in demanding an Islamic administration based upon the Quran and the Sunnah (the way of the Prophet), Islamic laws, an Islamic economic system, an Islamic education system, indeed, a total Islamic society.[23] There are a number of things about these demands which must be noted. Firstly, as I have mentioned, the stronger Malay political position — an ethnic phenomenon — is at the root of these demands. Secondly, like the obsession with dress and rituals, the interest in Islamic laws cannot possibly evoke any empathy from the non-Muslims since Islamic laws are also, on the whole, very specific to the religion. It would have been different if the concern was with fighting exploitation or ensuring self-reliance — goals which are highly cherished in Islam — since they have an appeal that transcends religious boundaries. The emphasis given to Islamic laws and Islamic administration only helps to underline the differences that exist between Muslims and non-Muslims and, by implication, Malays and non-Malays. In that sense, it reveals the true character of the whole agitation for an Islamic state. Thirdly, if it were a genuine Islamic movement inspired by a genuine Islamic consciousness there would have been an increasing endeavour to study and analyse the structure and content of an Islamic society in Malaysia. This is particularly important in our context because the non-Muslim segment is a little more than half of the total population. How this large number of non-Muslims would fit into an Islamic society, what their rights and roles would be, what responsibilities they would share with the Muslims, how they would relate to an Islamic legislature or judicial system — all these and a number of other issues should have been debated and discussed in depth and detail. The fact is there has been no such effort. This lack of interest in the position and status of the non-Muslims among the so-called 'Champions of Islam' of the seventies is no different from the total lack of concern for the non-Muslims and non-Malays exhibited by PAS in the fifties and sixties. It is because there isn't this concern, that no Muslim group in the country has taken up cudgels on behalf of the non-Muslim poor. Yet, the humanitarian ideals which lie at the heart of Islam, the noble examples of the Prophet Muhammad (May peace be upon him) and the great Caliphs which I had alluded to earlier, would demand such a response. Once again, this negative attitude of various Muslim groups exposes the real nature of their political struggle. It is just another way of preserving Malayism. To understand this better, one has to compare the situation here with the attitudes that prevailed among Islamic groups in Indonesia from the thirties right up to the sixties. In spite of a smaller non-Muslim population, leaders of the Masyumi, in particular, like Muhammad Natsir, spent so much time and effort elucidating the rights and responsibilities of non-Muslims in the Islamic state they envisaged for Indonesia.[24] One of their more important intellectual commitments was the quest for common principles that could unite Muslims and non-Muslims — a commitment which conforms with Qurannic ideals.[25] In this connection, no Muslim group in Malaysia has ever bothered to embark upon such a mission, though, at the level of social philosophy, there are many outstanding similarities between Islam and aspects of Chinese culture and Hindu thought.[26] The reason is, of course, obvious. It is because Islam is seen from a communal angle — not a universal perspective. Finally, one would have thought that those who seek to establish an Islamic state would first examine critically the ideas, beliefs and attitudes of the Muslim community itself, in order to discover if these are elements which need to be jettisoned in the endeavour to create a genuine Islamic spirit. Apart from the occasional blast at some insignificant ritual like Mandi Safar or puja ceremonies,[27] Muslim groups have maintained an embarrassing silence in relation to more fundamental ideas and attitudes within Malay society. These are ideas and attitudes which need to be rectified in the interest of Islam. One such important idea which I have already analysed is the whole notion of Bumiputraism. If the post-70 Muslim movement was genuinely Islamic it would have at least attempted to show Muslims how a concept based upon ethnicity and ancestry — or upon residence and territory if you like — does not synchronize with Islamic values. The willingness to live with Bumiputraism, and worse still, defend it at times, shows that the real spirit of Islam has not crystallized. After all, Islam is a religion which has even questioned nationalism — let alone the perpetuation of communal dichotomies within a nation. Muhammad Iqbal, one of the greatest Muslims of this century, argued that territorial or racial nationalism was foreign to the spirit of Islam. As one writer on Iqbal put it, "He (Iqbal) was convinced now that it would be a tragically retrograde step if the Muslim World began to try to remedy its frustrations by replacing the global Islamic sentiment by aggressive nationalism of the Western type. He conceived of Islam as a universal religion which envisaged all humanity as a unity. But the Islam of his time had become narrow, rigid and static. He conceived of life as evolutionary and dynamic. He came to the conclusion that a fossilized religious dogmatism could not generate an outlook that would lead to the self-realization of individuals and communities".[28]

NOTES

1. There is this awareness, though non-Malays who become Muslims are sometimes referred to as people who have "masuk Melayu" (become Malays). "Masuk Melayu", however, need not be interpreted literally; it could simply mean those who have adopted the religion of the Malays.
2. These communities would be the Kadazans, Ibans, and others of East Malaysia in the main and some of the Orang Asli of West Malaysia.
3. In both Sabah and Sarawak, for instance, the Chief Ministership and certain other important political offices are held by indigenous Muslims, though non-Muslim indigenous communities are numerically stronger in both states. For a fuller discussion of politics in these states, see K.J. Ratnam and R.S. Milne, *New States in a new nation,* (Frank Cass, London, 1974).
4. See 'Amanat Yang di-Pertuan Agong PAS Ulang Tahun 1958' in *Cenderamata Pembukaan Bangunan PAS Kelantan & Kongres PAS ke 13.*
5. For a detailed analysis see my *Protection of the Malay Community: A study of UMNO's position and Opposition Attitudes,* (MS. Sc thesis, Universiti Sains Malaysia, 1974).
6. See A. Yusuf Ali, *The Holy Quran,* Text, Translation and Commentary. (Sh. Muhammad Ashraf, Lahore, Pakistan, 1972), sura al-hujurat: 10.
7. *Ibid,* sura Al-i-Imran: 179.
8. *Ibid,* sura Baqara: 272.
9. For a discussion on the Constitution of Medina, see Zainal Abidin Ahmad, *Piagam Nabi Muhammad* s.a.w., (Bulan Bintang, Djakarta, 1973).
10. See Sayyid Abdul A'la Maududi, *The Islamic Law & Constitution.* (Iṣlamic Publications Ltd., Lahore, Pakistan), p. 312.
11. *Ibid,* p. 159.
12. A. Yusuf Ali, *The Holy Quran, op. cit.,* sura Hujurat: 13.
13. *Ibid.* In commenting upon that sura Yusuf Ali notes, "In Islam, the equal status of the sexes is not only recognised but insisted on. If sex distinction which is a distinction in nature, does not count in spiritual matters, still less of course would count artificial distinctions such as rank, wealth, position, race, colour, birth, etc.," p. 175.

14. For the UMNO leadership as a whole, Bumiputraism is apparently justified on its own basis. Some analysis of this is available in my 'The New Economic Policy & the Quest for National Unity,' *Fifth Malaysian Economic Convention,* (Malaysian Economic Association, 1978).
15. Two points, however, must be made. Firstly, there are without any doubt a number of Muslim youths who understand genuine Islamic principles. See, for instance, Anwar Ibrahim's (President, Angkatan Belia Islam Malaysia ABIM) view, *Bintang Timur,* 1st March 1979. Secondly, the world-wide interest in Islam among young Muslims has also had some bearing upon the Malaysian situation but I do not consider it a crucial factor.
16. This is due to both the rural-urban drift which has been on since Merdeka and the New Economic Policy (NEP) which *inter alia* emphasises Malay participation in commerce and industry.
17. See, *The Star,* 20th March, 1979.
18. This is partly due to the implementation of Malay as the main medium of education since 1970.
19. The crucial word here is 'halal' (legitimate). 'Halal' signs therefore refer to foods that Muslims are allowed to eat. There has been a great deal of discussion about this in *Utusan Malaysia* and *Utusan Melayu* in the last 2 years or so.
20. See A. Yusuf Ali, *The Holy Quran, op. cit.,* sura Balad: 10–18.
21. *Ibid.,* sura Ma'un: 1–7.
22. The genesis of this whole atmosphere is discussed in my 'Some Political Perspectives on the New Economic Policy', *Fourth Malaysian Economic Convention,* (Malaysian Economic Association, 1977).
23. The development of these demands finds some mention in my *Dominant Concepts and Dissenting Ideas on Malay society & Malay rule from the Malacca period to the Merdeka period,* (Ph.D. thesis, University of Singapore, 1977).
24. See various parts in Muhammad Natsir, *Capita Selecta, I, II,* (Pustaka Pendis, Djakarta, 1957).
25. The Qurannic call for common principles is contained in sura Al-i-Imran: 64 – 66.
26. For some discussion of common values, see my 'Values in the Education System', (*New Directions,* Singapore, March 1976).
27. 'Mandi Safar' is a sort of purification bath confined mainly to Muslim groups in Malacca. It is pre-Islamic in origin and has some roots in Hindu custom. One of the better known puja ceremonies was the puja conducted for fishermen going out to sea. It was once popular in Kelantan. The former PAS government banned it.
28. See Khalifah Abdul Hakim's 'Renaissance in Indo-Pakistan: Iqbal', in M.M. Sharif, (ed), *A History of Muslim Philosophy,* Vol. Two, (Otto Harrassowitz, Wiesbaden, 1966), p. 1619.

Muslim Ideological Responses to the Issue of Modernization in Indonesia

MUHAMMAD KAMAL HASSAN

MUSLIM VIEWPOINTS: A CROSS-SECTION

In order to show in detail the varying emphases, attitudes and reasoning which constitute the "Muslim perspective," I propose to survey the most representative statements of the Muslim elite concerning the issue of modernization, covering the period 1966 to 1973. Presentation of the whole spectrum of the Islamic response will, I believe, make for a better assessment of Muslim position(s) and the quality of its thought content.

Chronologically, the first non-polemical and self-critical essay on the problem of modernization by a Muslim intellectual in New Order Indonesia was, most probably, that of Dr. Deliar Noer[1] entitled *"Ummat Islam dan Masalah Modernisasi"* (The Muslim Community and the Problem of Modernization).[2] In his view, modernization does not pose a theological problem because the essence of modernization conforms to the social teachings of Islam. A modern society, he says, "is not only not contradictory [to Islam]; it should even be realized by Muslims. At least, they should assist in its actualization and fulfilment."[3]

Modernization, according to Deliar Noer, demands that Indonesians; (a) be forward looking, not backward looking; (b) possess a dynamic and active attitude, not one of "waiting"; (c) pay particular attention to time; place emphasis on rationality, not feelings or assumptions; (e) develop an open attitude toward the thoughts and products of scientific significance; (f) give priority to a person's achievements, not his ascribed status; (g) give greater attention to the immediate, the more concrete and the more mundane problems; (h) commit themselves to goals which transcend the goals of the group.[4]

The crucial question he asked was "Can Indonesians acquire those modernizing qualities?" The culture-bound obstacles in Indonesia's transitional society posed serious problems, but they had to be surmounted if the goals of modernization were to be achieved. Islam taught the equality of man in the sight of God and also the principle of individual accountability for one's actions. But could Muslims realize these teachings in society? Muslims shouldered a greater responsibility than others not only because they were required to be "a mercy to all mankind", but also because of their numerical superiority in Indonesia. Noer said;

> We received this land of Indonesia as a trust from Allāh. Therefore we have to take good care of it and utilize it well, so that we may bequeath it to our sons and the future generations as something whose form and content are better than when we inherited it from our fathers.[5]

Muslim modernists, Deliar Noer reminded them, must come to grips with the internal problems of the Muslim community, such as the tradition of blind adherence to medieval

---

Excerpted from Muhammad Kamal Hassan, *Muslim Intellectual Responses to "New Order" Modernization in Indonesia* (Kuala Lumpur: Dewan Bahasa dan Pustaka, 1982), by permission of the author.

constructs, the predisposition of some to Sufi practices, the exclusive devotion of some to a legalistic outlook and the preoccupation of others with the struggle for political power.[6] The question they would have to answer was, "How can our *ummah* act, function, and acquire the attitudes of a modernizing agent in facing the demands of time, if we truly claim our teachings to be forever modern?"[7]

According to Deliar Noer, it was what he called "democratic modernization" that Indonesia needed most. By this he meant a state of affairs in which education was made accessible to all citizens of all social classes; equitable distribution of income existed; and free elections were held. He feared, however, that the possibility of the growth of "undemocratic modernization" would hamper such a development.

The more popular type of Muslim response to the issue of modernization is embodied in the defensive attitude characteristic of polemical writings. This attitude reveals the overriding concern with the influence of cultural values of "Western" origin which accompanies the process of modernization. The attitude is primarily an emotional reaction to the secular intelligentsia's argument that modernization implied Westernization.[8] A second common Muslim attitude is one that views modernization as encompassing all forms of non-religious philosophical systems, while Islam is seen as an alternative system of meaning which is capable of delivering mankind from the morass of existential problems. From this perspective the phenomenon of "modernization" stands for the predicaments of contemporary civilization to which men like Bertrand Russel, Arnold Toynbee or Albert Schweitzer have addressed themselves.[9]

An example of the first type of Muslim attitude is contained in an article entitled *"Sekali Lagi Modernisasi"* (More on Modernization) written by Omar Hashem.[10] This young pamphleteer sought to explain what he considered to be the "spirit of Western culture" to coreligionists so that they would not become prey to its negative aspects in their zeal to modernize. He asserted that between the extreme poles of what Spengler termed the "Faustian spirit" of Western culture and the *"magische Seele"* of the Orient, the Qur'ān advocated an *"ummatan wasatan"* (a middle community).[11] The Qur'ān declares in another place:

> It is not righteousness that ye turn your faces to the East and the West; but righteous is he who believeth in Allāh and the Last Day and the angels and the Scripture and the Prophets; and giveth his wealth for love of Him, to kinsfolk and to orphans and the needy and the wayfarer and to those who ask, and to set slaves free; and observeth proper worship and payeth the poor-due.[12]

Islam rejected, said Hashem, the hedonistic aspects in Western culture as much as it frowned upon the kind of Oriental asceticism which inhibited normal bodily needs. It postulated the view that man was a unity of spirit and body whose respective needs were equitably met, thus preserving his inner equilibrium.[13] In the face of the powerful attraction of the outer trappings of modern Western civilization, the Muslim was enjoined to exercise great moral restraint. He ought not to be blind, however, to the positive aspects of Western civilization, such as the cultivation of science and learning.

> That Islamic civilization was enriched by various elements of alien culture could not be denied, and Muslims . . . are proud of it. Islam holds the innate spiritual disposition of man, regardless of his religion, in high esteem, and believes that every creature is subjected to the "way of God" [*sunnatullāh*], the law of cause and effect.[14]

The Muslim attitude towards knowledge, said Hashem, could be seen in Dr. Sigrid Hunke's book, *Allah's Sonne uber dem Abendland* (Frankfurt: Fischer Bucherei, 1965), in which it was said:

> Every Muslim, male or female, is commanded by Muhammad to seek knowledges as a religious obligation. 'Seek knowledge from the cradle to the grave,' he said. 'One who seeks knowledge is in a state of worshipping Allah.' He repeatedly ordered his followers to follow this path. 'Study and contemplation are equal of fasting; seeking knowledge is equal to prayer!' Understanding His creation and His majesty enables the Muslim to appreciate his Creator. To Muslims knowledge lights the way of faithful men — even though that would take them as far as China. The Prophet showed his followers the way which

> transcended national boundaries. Those who cultivated knowledge (in fact) glorified God. Allāh's wisdom came from God and would ultimately return to Him. Therefore 'seek it from wherever it may come from!'[15]

In Hashem's view, the Muslim who "condemns knowledge is really not a Muslim."[16] There were no Muslim scholars who pronounced progress or knowledge to be forbidden, such that "Muslims had to abandon their Islamicity for the sake of the shaky slogan of 'modernisasi' ".[17]

There were two types of sciences which Muslims had to confront; the exact and the social sciences. The social sciences were not free from the subjectivism of the investigator, and therefore should be approached with extreme caution.[18]

> Sciences which are based on facts . . . such as the exact sciences, must be acquired by Muslims . . . . In the social sciences and Western philosophy, however, Muslims should be critical, and in these areas they should not imitate like a monkey or repeat like a parrot . . . .[19]

There was no alternative for Muslims but "to acquire knowledge through the world-view of *tauhid* [Ar. *tauḥīd*, the doctrine of Islamic monotheism], and to strive for the well-being of mankind, which is one".[20]

In *"Agama, Modernisasi, dan Mahasiswa"* (Religion, Modernization and University Students), Mohammad Amien Rais, a student leader, reviewed the opinions which upheld the "absolute necessity of modernization or renewal" and considered them as highly commendable in view of the sufferings of the Indonesian people.[21] In the effort to bring an end to the people's misery, students belonging to the "1966 Generation" had a vital role to play as "agents of modernization". The will to develop among Indonesian students of all shades of opinion had to be sustained or else the process of renewal would stagnate, said Rais. Admitting that modernization "has become a national consensus", he regretted, however, that there existed some selfish elements in Indonesia who wanted to use the idea of modernization for their particularistic political goals.

> The PMKRI [*Pergerakan Mahasiswa Katolik Republik Indonesia* — Catholic Students Organization of Indonesia], for instance, in its Members' Deliberating Council held in Bandung last month adopted 'modernization' as its national program. But, in addition to that, it categorically stated that in order to accomplish renewal in Indonesia, the state should not manage matters pertaining to religion. This statement implied insistence on the abolition of the Department of Religion and its divisions . . . . The motive behind PMKRI's attitude is simple; that is, to hit the Muslim community (whose toleration has been excessive) which forms the majority of the population.[22]

He urged, in conclusion, that modernization should be carried out through a simultaneous and integrated program of moral, psychological, social, political and economic reconstruction. He warned that Indonesians should be wary of the political exploitation of "modernization", which in the end would weaken the importance of religion in Indonesian society.

> Even in the Old Order period, religion was considered as a 'fundamental element in Nation and Character Building' (albeit as lip service), but why is it that in the New Order era religion appears to be an object of triviality and is discredited? Where will Indonesia be driven?[23]

Professor H.M. Rasjidi, professor of Islamic law at the University of Indonesia, revealed in a speech delivered at the 1967 Inter-Religious Consultation, the widely shared suspicion of Muslim leaders toward concepts such as "modernization", "religious tolerance", "human rights", "progress" which were being peddled in Indonesian society as convenient tools of religio-political ambitions. He said, *inter alia:*

> The missionaries then said: 'Oh, we really came to Indonesia in order to modernize the Indonesian people who are lagging behind in education and various other spheres of life'. The Dutch colonial government replied: 'In order to become modern one does not have to be a Christian'. Such were the words of Snouck Hurgronje. In fact it is not only in Indonesia that Islam is compatible with modernism; everywhere else it is not only not incompatible with, but itself contains the principles of modernism.
>
> Finally the missionaries looked for another excuse; they claimed that they came to Indonesia because they were motivated by

the mission of humanitarianism. They wanted to ease the hardships of the Indonesian peoples, who are poor, hungry and sick. The Dutch government at that time replied: 'Fine ... [but do not] influence the school children, and the poor who are given treatment, to become Christians'.

I said earlier that as a result of the success of the West in the pre-World War II period, they [i.e. the Westernized Indonesians] developed feelings of 'the arrogance of cultural superiority' whereby they considered everything coming from the West as the best; the rest should be discarded. Among the terms they propagated were 'modernism' and 'toleration' ... Just now we heard that word [modernism] being mentioned by Dr. Tambunan as being a Christian mission. This gives the impression that that which is un-Christian is not modern .... When the people in Iran and in the Middle East began to wear trousers and neckties, people said those nations had begun to be modern .... In short, the Christian mission represented progress, implying that what is non-Christian is unprogressive.

* * *

But the word 'modern' is used by the Christians mainly as means of enticing people to discard Islamic qualities. When we are about to enter the month of fasting, there are people who say that fasting impedes progress and the efficiency of labor. Let us be 'modern' and forget fasting.[24]

The Christian-Muslim polemic was carried on by Saadoeddin Djambek, a reformist essayist, in his article on "Knowledge, Modernization and Secularism".[25] He exemplified popular Muslim sentiment when he said:

On the one hand Muslims are being urged to implement secularization, but they are expected to keep their mouths shut when non-Muslim groups pursue their unnegotiable objectives [with reference to the Christian stand in the 1967 Inter-Religious Consultation] in expanding and strengthening their religion at the expense of Islam. This is done allegedly in the name of fundamental human rights ... But it seems that these fundamental rights belong only to those outside Islam. When Muslims begin to defend their interests, suddenly those rights vanish into thin air.[26]

He also criticized those who charged or insinuated that Islam impeded modernization. The essence of modernization, in his view, involved the making of all means of procuring the needs of life easy and amenable. The Qur'ānic support for this idea could be found in *Sūrahs* XIV: 32; XIV: 33; XVI: 12; XVI: 14; XXII: 65; XXXI: 20; and XXXXV: 12–13. It was evident from these verses, he said, that the earth's treasures and resources were meant to be used for the continuous improvement of living conditions. The view that Islam was opposed to the idea of modernization was, therefore, based on ignorance of Islamic teachings. "It is Christianity", he contended, "which became involved in the question of religion obstructing modernization in Europe, because it used to suppress the growth of modern sciences".[27]

The issue of modernization was also seen as a part of a new strategy of the ex-colonialists. This view is best represented by Hamka (Hadji Abdul Malik Karim Amrullah) the venerable reformist Islamic scholar. In his opinion, the policy of direct political subjugation had now been replaced by a more subtle method of maintaining economic and political interests.[28] Behind the economic and technical aid which former colonial masters were extending to the newly independent states, lay a sinister plan to ensure that the new nations continue to be dependent on the advanced nations. To that end, the minds of the formerly subjugated peoples were being exposed to new concepts — modernization being one of them — as weapons of cultural warfare. Muslims living in their newly independent countries were facing this trial, and Indonesia was by no means spared from this economic and political design.[29]

"What is now called 'modernization' ", said Hamka, "is but camouflage for a big plan aimed at removing Islamic influences from our hearts so that we shall willingly become the tail-end of nations which are considered advanced. ..."[30] To him true modernization meant the "transformation of a colony to an independent nation, of feudalism to democracy, of an agrarian society to an industrialized one".[31]

In the preceding survey I have tried to show the different emphases in viewpoint of concerned Muslims as they saw the issue of modernization from their respective vantage points. The attempt at a comprehensive examination of the many-sided problem was made first of all by the chairman of HMI, Nurcholish Madjid in *Modernisasi Ialah Rationalisasi Bukan Westernisasi* (Modernization is Rationalization, Not Westernization) (Bandung: Mimbar Demokrasi, 1968), and later by Drs. Sidi Gazalba[32] in *Modernisasi Dalam Persoalan: Bagaimana Sikap Islam?* (Modernization in Question: What is Islam's Attitude?) (Jakarta: Bulan Bintang, 1973). In these two publications, the different facets of the problem of "modernization" are given a fuller treatment. Like their colleagues, Nurcholish Madjid and Sidi Gazalba too are concerned with the semantic, cultural and religio-political, rather than the practical aspects of the problem.

NURCHOLISH MADJID'S VIEWPOINTS PRIOR TO 1970

According to Madjid, intellectual leader of the largest and most important Muslim university students' organization, HMI (whose chairmanship he held for two consecutive terms from 1966–1972), a simplified definition of modernization is "that which is identical, or almost identical, with rationalization".[33] It involves "a process of overhauling outmoded thought and action patterns which are not rational, and replacing them with new ones which are rational. This is for the achievement of maximum utility and efficiency".[34] This process is based on the application of the latest findings and discoveries in the sciences. Since scientific knowledge is the result of human understanding of objective laws governing nature, its application to life will render the latter more rational and, therefore, modern.[35]

"To a Muslim", he declares, "modernization is an imperative — indeed, an absolute obligation. Modernization as interpreted in the preceding paragraph constitutes a command and a teaching of God".[36] This standpoint is derived from the following premises which are deduced from specific Qur'ānic verses:

1. Allāh created the whole universe not in vain but for a sacred purpose. (Qur'ān, XVI: 3; XXVII: 28).
2. Allāh administers the universe through His laws (i.e., Ar. *sunnat Allāh*) which are fixed. (Qur'ān, VII: 54; XXV; 2).
3. The universe is good, beneficial and in harmony. (Qur'ān, XXXII: 7; XL: 3).
4. Man is commanded by God to study and investigate the laws that operate in nature, (Qur'ān, X: 101)
5. Allāh created the universe for the benefit, welfare and happiness of man as an act of mercy from Him. (Qur'ān, XXXV: 13).
6. With the explicit command that man use his mind fully, God dislikes anything that impedes the development of thought, particularly in the form of sterile conservatism. (Qur'ān, II: 70.)[37]

Madjid then goes on to say that "modernization means thinking and working in accordance with the true and inherent laws of nature".[38] To be modern is, therefore, to be scientific; it also means to be dynamic and progressive for the process of man's discovery of objective universal truth usually threatens the *status quo*. He recognizes that although it is incumbent to modernize, modernity itself possesses a relative nature because it is circumscribed by the factors of time and space. "Only that whose essence is truly absolute is permanently modern, and only God possesses that attribute". So modernity lies in the process of discovering relative truths in the forward movement toward the absolute Truth (God), this being the ultimate goal of man's life.[39]

This relativism makes possible a continuous process in man's progress, a process which is in harmony with his inborn *hanif* (Ar. *ḥanīf*) nature — a nature Nurcholish Madjid describes as that which "seeks and yearns for Truth".[40] A Muslim, in Madjid's view, ought to be the "one most aware of his relative nature since he is, after all, a weak and humble creature of God." By the same token, a Muslim should be most reluctant to cling tenaciously to "human truths" as though they are absolute truths. He is ever ready to accept new truths from other people. The Prophet himself said that wisdom was the lost property of believers [*"al-ḥikmah ḍallat al-mu'minīn"*] wherever they find it, they should gather it unto themselves. Madjid arrives at the conclusion that, aside from its immediate and practical benefits, modernity has a more profound meaning, namely as man's approach to the Absolute (God). It will bring the man of faith nearer to God and will develop in him the quality of God-consciousness and the fear of God.[41] The pursuit of exact sciences, argues Madjid, will also bring the practitioner to a profound religious experience. To support his contention, he adduces the testimony of Einstein on what constitutes the center of true religiosity.

> The most beautiful and most profound emotion we can experience is the sensation of the mystical. It is the sower of all true science. He to whom this emotion is a stranger, who can no longer stand rapt it awe, is as good as dead. To know that what is impenetrable to us really exists, manifesting itself as the highest wisdom and the most radiant beauty which our dull faculties can comprehend only in their most primitive forms — this knowledge, this feeling is at the center of true religiousness.[42]

In his comments on the idea championed by secular groups and the military elite, that Indonesian modernization should be realized through the institutionalization of "program-orientation" in the political sphere, thereby bringing an end to ideology, Madjid reflects basic predispositions of the Muslim leadership. He emphasizes the necessity of ideology and the indispensability of religion as conditions of purposeful national existence. There are groups in Indonesia who do not share this view, says Madjid, but it is their right to disagree. The first principle of *Pantja Sila,* Belief in the One True God, not only underlies but gives meaning to the rest of the *Silas,* viz. "nationalism," "democracy," "humanitarianism," and "social welfare." Unless the theistic foundation is preserved and strengthened, the nation will find itself in the grip of non-religious "isms" and trends such as secularism (which includes humanism, liberalism and communism) and Westernization, both of which may disguise themselves under the cloak of "modernization".

Fearing the rise of secularism in New Order Indonesia, Madjid is most emphatic in his rejection of all its forms. The separation of Church and State implies that "God has no right to administer worldly affairs".[43] This contradicts the Islamic concept of *tauḥīd* which implies oneness of His spheres of jurisdiction and sovereignty, whereas secularism, "of a less consistent nature", says Madjid,

> will induce us to subscribe to the belief that religious life is a private matter, i.e. it functions only to connect man with his God. (This is *ibadat* [Ar. *'ibādah,* worship] in a restricted sense). In facing worldly problems it will lead us to approach and solve them by measures and considerations of an entirely different nature . . . . Islam does not recognize any separation between religion and politics, because Islam — as explained by Islamic savants — is *Aqidah* [Ar. *'aqīdah,* creed]; *Sjari'ah* [Ar. *sharī'ah,* Divine Law or Code of Life] and *Nizam* [Ar. *niẓām,* system, organization] at one and the same time . . . . In short, anyone who has a deep knowledge of Islam will discover that Islam does not recognize a separation between mundane matters and other-worldly matters.[44]

The secularists, Madjid asserts, offer rationalism as the approach to the solution of worldly matters. This stems from their conviction that man, unaided by divine guidance, has the ability to solve all his worldly problems thanks to his reason. Islam demands the use of reason, but denies that reason alone would suffice for the needs of man in his journey towards Truth. At best, the exercise of reason will lead man to the discovery of relative truths, while the absolute can only be acquired through revelation. He quotes Einstein as saying that "the realization that our whole knowledge of the universe is simply a residue of impressions clouded by our imperfect senses makes the quest for reality seem hopeless" in order to lend support to his contention.[45]

He goes on to show that the liberal humanism of secularists is indeed a form of religion. Julian Huxley's statements to that effect are cited to prove his points. From Archie J. Bahm's *The World's Living Religions* (New York: Dell Publication Co., 1964), Madjid surveys the list of works on humanism given therein and argues that:

> Humanism is none other than an effort of Western man to arrive at new values of life, after the religions which were known there could no longer hold their own in the face of scientific developments and man's intellectual prowess. And now, as A.J. Bahm says, Humanism has become a common religion of Western civilization.[46]

In its claim, which is also shared by the materialists, that "the universe is self-existing" and that life's values are not necessarily found in a supernatural source but in man himself, humanism is not much different from atheism. While Islam is the antithesis of atheistic philosophies, it favors modernization in the sense of rationalization, and that, too, has to be further qualified. The proper field of the operation of rationalization is the concrete, such as in the agricultural system, communications, the process of production in factories, and the like. In concrete and materially-related matters, man can draw generalizations based on objective observation, but when faced with human problems, he tends to be subjective. To arrive at objective truths about non-material concerns, man needs a transcendent source of knowledge. Indonesian modernization, properly defined, is "rationalization supported by moral dimensions arising from the principal basis of faith in the One Supreme God [the first principle of *Pantja Sila*]".[47] This implies a rejection of Westernization on account of the latter's inherent secularism. But that does not mean, however, that "we reject true knowledge and science including technology, even though they originated in the West or, for that matter, from the communists, because knowledge and technology cannot be said to be the monopoly of the West".[48]

Turning to another secular philosophy, liberalism, Madjid maintains that from the Islamic point of view, it has to be combatted. Islam esteems the ideal of individual freedom in liberalism but does not envisage unbridled freedom because of its potentially disastrous social consequences. Islam upholds individual freedom, but teaches that freedom is limited by the freedom of other individuals. Thus the Islamic injunction of *al-amr bi'l-ma'rūf wa'n-nahy 'an al-munkar* (enjoining what is right and forbidding what is wrong)[49] and social responsibility in Islam, go hand in hand with individual freedom. Capitalism, for instance, is incompatible with Islam because it leads to inequity, exploitation and social injustice. Communism, on the other hand, preaches equality and denies individual freedom, but in practice equality does not exist. "The dictatorship of the proletariat," says Madjid, "is in reality the dictatorship of party bosses and managers".[50] The fact that each system adopts some features of the other shows the inherent weakness of both. This is only to be expected since both are based on secular intellectual premises.[51]

From this point on, Madjid tries to show that there is ample evidence in the present and from the colonial past to justify Indonesian Muslim apprehension of the adverse effects of Westernization (secularism being its most characteristic manifestation) on the national identity defined by the unique ethico-cultural values which inform the *Pantja Sila*. "Are there really efforts to direct modernization towards Westernization?" he asks rhetorically. The Old Order, he says, had offered a good example of how national interests might be deftly manipulated and subverted by elements (i.e. Indonesian communists) whose real motives were inimical to Indonesia's national goal as prescribed by and enshrined in her state ideology and the Constitution of 1945. Indonesia in the New Order, on the other hand, can be said to be in a critical period of transition in which caution and vigilance are called for because there exist certain groups who would like to see the government implement their concepts of social change so that the nation may be brought into their particularistic spheres of interest.[52]

Madjid argues that as a result of Dutch Islamic policy, shaped by the views and recommendations of Christian Snouck Hurgronje, Adviser on Arabian and Native Affairs, Indonesia inherits a Westernized and secularized ruling class.[53] Snouck's "basically low esteem for Islam,"[54] and his conviction that a modern Indonesia would have to be a Westernized Indonesia in which Dutch culture acted as a liberator of the natives from the "narrow confines of the Islamic system" while Western education served as "the surest means of reducing and ultimately defeating the influence of Islam in Indonesia",[55] had detrimental effects on Islam and the Muslims in Indonesia.[56] For one thing, the Westernized elite, with some exceptions, developed a strong dislike for anything Islamic, and Muslim leaders became the object of a cynicism and arrogance stemming from a sense of cultural superiority.[57]

In the search for national identity, independent Indonesia has to come to grips with the cultural legacy of what Madjid calls "Snouckism" in the disoriented political elite and intellectuals who have been uprooted from their native value systems. To preserve Indonesia's cultural identity, Madjid contends that there is no need to look to extraneous sources; Indonesia's indigenous heritage is a rich reservoir of those cultural values conducive for preserving her national character. The most obvious of these value systems is the Islamic. For a long time Islam served as a focal point of national unity and a symbol of protest against colonial rule. Islamic movements of political as well as social orientations are, therefore, absolutely necessary to an Independent Indonesia.[58] Madjid's remarks here are in reference to the political remodelling that was under way in 1968, and the growing demand on the part of New Order radical secularists for the overhaul of the party system. He also stressed the vital role which Muslim student organizations will continue to play in "removing the duality of being Islamic and [at the same time] being educated, so that those Muslim scholars who emerge later will be those in whom Islamicity and intellectuality are integrated".[59]

Modernization in the Indonesian case, Madjid continues, should not entail the end of ideology, because life is not possible without a set of beliefs, ideas, attitudes and convictions. Moreover, to uphold an ideology — provided that it is in harmony with the constitution — is in keeping with the principle of the right to believe in one's convictions. Even those who propagate the abandonment of ideology do subscribe, consciously or unconsciously, to a philosophy of one sort or another. In his views,

> Their conviction is Secularism, or Pragmatism, or Humanism, since all are [mutually] compatible. Did not William James write Pragmatism, *A New Name for Some Old Ways of Thinking*? Did not Horrace Kallan write *Secularism Is the Will of God,* and Charles Francis Potter, *Humanism, A New Religion?*[60]

Muslims, Madjid claims, do not reject the ideas of "program-orientation" or pragmatism as long as they are derived from the existing ideological frames of reference of their respective groups. Otherwise the rule of expediency — that "the end justifies the means" — will prevail. The so-called "intellectual group" is advocating the abandonment of ideology because it is afflicted by *"Islamophobia"* — the deeply ingrained fear and suspicion of the political power of Islam which can be traced back to the biases of colonial government. Its motive does not spring out of a genuine and objective belief in the efficacies of "program", but rather in the shrewd political calculation that only through the abolition of ideology can the power of Islam be contained, making it easier for non-Islamic groups to attain their political objectives. "Anyone", says Madjid, "who is courageous enough to be honest with himself will admit that the present difficulties are due to the fact that minority groups which do not enjoy the popular support of the people are playing too big a role, while the majority group is being obstructed from playing their decisive role. The role it is playing does not correspond to its majority position".[61] In a democracy the will of the majority prevails, but in Indonesia, where a truly representative government has yet to materialize, there is a likelihood that "certain groups who are presently occupying highly advantageous positions" will take the opportunity of the present transitional period to win their strategies exactly as the Communist Party (PKI) did during Sukarno's regime.[62]

Turning to his coreligionists, Madjid points to a fundamental weakness which has hampered their cause: their inability to formulate their religious experience and values in a language that is understood by the common people of today. Consequently, many people fail to grasp the essence of Islam, and when this ignorance is compounded with the sentiment of *"Islamophobia"* the result is that many nominal Muslims become opponents of Islam. More efforts should be expended on "what should be done" than "what ought to be".[63] Muslims have to admit that they are not yet capable of integrating *imam* [Ar. *īmān,* faith, belief], from which they derive normative values, with *ilmu* [Ar. *'ilm,* knowledge, science] which yields practical operational guidelines in life. He appeals to the Islamic political leadership to give more attention to the younger generation of Muslims for they are the heirs of the *ummat's* [Ar. *ummah,* community, nation] legacy. The younger generation, on their part, should have the courage to reformulate the traditional teachings they inherit in a way that conforms to the truths and living realities of life.[64]

SIDI GAZALBA'S VIEWPOINTS

Sidi Gazalba, being the college teacher that he is, presents a more elaborate and text-book-like exposition of the issue than Nurcholish Madjid, but like the latter his aim too is to remove prevailing misconceptions and confusion in the minds of both Muslims and non-Muslims surrounding the subject of modernization. In so doing, "Indonesians would perchance discover what exactly is in the best interest of Indonesia".

He defines modernization simply as a process of renewal and change leading to that which is "more-effective" and "more-efficient". By using the instruments of science and technology, man would be able to develop "a more peaceful social life, a more prosperous economic life, a philosophical life more capable of discovering the truth about existence, and a religious life more acceptable to the mind".[65]

Westernization, however, is the transmission and implantation of Western cultural forms in Indonesian society. Sidi Gazalba sees Western culture as characterized by individualism in social life, pragmatism and capitalism in economic life, and the principle of "the end justifies the means" in political life. "Hedonism", "utilitarianism", and "vitalism" color its ethical philosophy. Its world-view is secular and anthropocentric, and its attitude to life is materialistic. Under such circumstances, the Christian religion has lost, in the West, its social relevance, and the majority of people are virtually agnostics. Secularism likewise provides the basis of education.

To Gazalba, the Westernization process in Indonesia was and is, however, aligned with "Christianization". To argue this point, he cites several passages from the writings of S.M. Zwemer, Martin Hartmann, A.W.F. Idenburg, Arnold Toynbee, D. Julius Richter and Snouck Hurgronje.[66] Both Westernization and Christianization must therefore confront strong Islamic opposition.

As an illustration of how confused popular images of modernization and Westernization are in Indonesian society, Gazalba provides picturesque examples of what constitutes modernity for a young man, a girl, a man-in-the-street, a lady and a city mayor. The case of the mayor is a sarcastic criticism of Jakarta's modernization under the pragmatic governorship of strong-willed Major General Ali Sadikin. As a typical example of present-day Islamic resentment of the cultural aspects of modernization, as symbolized in the development of Jakarta, this vignette deserves a full translation:

> Mr. Mayor, do you want to modernize your city? Then make it into an imposing metropolis. How are you going to finance it? Well, all kinds of ways may be tried, even that which is religiously forbidden. After all, the end is good. Legalizing gambling and the profits from this provide a good source of revenue to support its budget. Increase the number of cinemas, and do not prevent them from showing pornographic and sadistic films. That way the movie houses will make large profits, part of which will naturally flow into the city's coffers. Night clubs, massage parlors and steam-bath facilities should be available in every corner of the city. Prostitution is but another step [in the development] of night clubs, massage and steam-bath parlours. So you should localize prostitution. But does not localization imply legalization? Well, there's nothing we can do about it. A modern city should have all the amenities proper to it; besides, should we not provide pleasant services for tourists? O how modern your city would be if you could also build drive-in theaters in which viewing couples could avail themselves of 'modern' freedom while enjoying pornographic films and, at the same time, committing immoral acts in their automobiles. There should be amusement parks where couples can enjoy unrestricted freedom. There should be casinos and public gambling! .... Market places should be 'upgraded' even though each time they are being modernized, foreign businessmen take over the places of those whose ethnic background is the same as Mr. Mayor's .... Beauty contests earn for your city a good name, so organize them more frequently. The street peddlers seeking 'a mouthful of rice'... must be chased out. Order the police to go after them. Don't these street peddlers mar the modern image of your city? What about the *betjas* [pedicabs]? They obstruct modern traffic. Free the streets of the city of these *betjas*. But then, wouldn't that deprive the *betja*

> drivers of their means of livelihood? There's nothing we can do about that. Why did they become *betja* drivers and not drivers of modern vehicles? Tourists not only bring in revenue, they also lend international status to your city.... Ah now! Do not be old-fashioned; we have to be international minded! When will we ever progress if 'this is forbidden and that is forbidden'? Cities possess a modern life-style which certainly cannot be compared to that of the country. What is not acceptable in the rural areas should be allowed in the city if you want to modernize your city.[67]

Gazalba goes on to say that Indonesia has to be modern in order to free itself from the shackles of traditional culture — isolationism, cosmocentrism, backwardness, irrationality. Indonesian society has to change from *Gemeinschaft* to *Gesellschaft,* from dependence on nature to dependence on science and technology. The characteristics of modern man as defined by the Harvard sociologist, Alexander Inkeles, such as "openness to change and innovation", "democratic", "orientation to the present and the future", "involvement in planning and organization" and "belief in his ability to control nature" should, Gazalba says, become the traits of modern Indonesians.[68] Muslims could regain their previous leadership in the development of scientific learning, he assures his readers, if they are willing to free themselves from the obscurantisms of traditional culture rooted in pre-Islamic background.

Misconceptions regarding the essence of modernity is further complicated by misconceptions concerning the nature of Islam itself. In colonial Indonesia Islam came to be identified with the term *"religie"* (religion) which describes the personal and private relationship between man and God. The meaning of Islam was narrowed down to worship proper, while the other dimension of Islam — "the relationship between man and man" was forgotten. This misconception led to neglect of mundane concerns for the sake of man's social and material wellbeing. As a result, Indonesian Muslims (as with other Muslim communities) were dominated and controlled by a nation materially and technologically superior than they. Islam signifies wellbeing in this world (*dunyā*) and in the hereafter (*ākhīrah*), therefore Muslims should maintain this equilibrium by giving due attention to their earthly needs and the promotion thereof.[69] "Islam", says Gazalba, "embraces *'ibadah* and *mu'amalah* [Ar. *mu'āmalah,* social relations], religion and culture". He goes on:

> The principles governing religion were completely revealed, fully clarified, interpreted, explained, and exemplified by the Prophet, Muhammad. Compared to the [Qur'ānic] verses concerning *mu'āmalah,* those concerning *'ibādah* are fewer in number. Their object is the hereafter. The essence of *'ibādah* is the relationship between man and God. It is immutable in nature. The character of man's relationship with God is not subject to change, in as much as man is a creature and God is the Creator. The hereafter which is the object of religion proper is likewise not subject to change.... So there can be no change as far as religion proper is concerned. There can be no renewal in that dimension.[70]

On this last point there is a consensus of opinion among both principal segments of the Muslim community, the traditionalist and the reformist.[71] Innovation in the sphere of worship proper [*'ibādah*] is blasphemous "because it would alter the status of man, God, and the relationship between the two...."[72] As far as principles governing culture [*kebudayaan* which he distinguishes from religion, *agama*] are concerned, Gazalba maintains that God did not reveal them in detail: only general precepts were given. Echoing the opinions of many reformists, Gazalba says:

> The major part of the Qur'ān and the *Sunnah* deals with culture....
>
> Why are the laws concerning social life, economics, politics, science, technology and system of thought given in the form of general principles only? And how should these principles be implemented? The answers to these questions are given by *ijtihād* [Ar. *ijtihād,* exercise of independent reasoning within the framework of scriptural guidelines].
>
> Islamic scholars always teach that Islam is in accord with the true nature of man *fiṭrah* [Ar. *fitrah*]. This means that adherence to Islamic teachings is in fact being in conformity with *fiṭrah.* Man's *fiṭrah* yearns for peace and happiness; Islam regulates life in order to realize peace and happiness.... Man incline to social interaction; Islam lays down regulations for this. Man desires to have

mates and families; Islam commands marriage and the establishment of families.

* * *

> The quality of change is also a characteristic of *fitrah*.... Now, the Qur'ān and *Sunnah* address themselves to the proper growth of Man's humanity [or *fiṭrah*]. Change, which is inherent in man's nature, is dealt with by the third source of Islamic law, namely *ijtihād*.[73]

Ijtihād, which Muhammad Iqbal described as "the principle of movement" in Islam, is similarly defined by Gazalba, as with all pro-*ijtihād* Muslim thinkers, as the intellectual instrument which enables the *ummah* to decide the manner and form of response to changing modes of living. Modernization, being a form of change insofar as it does not impinge on matters of worship and injuctions of the Qur'ān and *Sunnah,* belongs to the realm of *ijtihād.*[74] It will be the task of *ijtihād* to determine what kind or aspect of "progress" is truly in the best interest of man.

Gazalba regrets that some aspects of Muslim behaviour have contributed to the anti-Islamic propaganda that Islam impedes progress. The conservatives' reluctance to liberalize the use of *ijtihād* have made Muslim communities backward because they have turned their backs on the law of change. Their errors, Gazalba pleads, should be construed not as the "error of Islam, but as the mistakes of man". If after recognizing this distinction, there are groups which still persist in spreading the propaganda that Islam impedes modernization, "then they have an axe to grind. There are political ambitions which they want to fulfil. There is the ambition of another religion wishing to alter the religious map of Indonesia".[75]

The major problems concerning the question of modernization are, in Gazalba's analysis, related to problems endemic to the state of transition from traditional agrarian to a modern industrial society; inertia of Islamic thought due to syncretism of pre-Islamic beliefs in Indonesia; perpetuation of acculturation of Western values in independent Indonesia; and the direction of developmental efforts.[76]

Gazalba argues that the agrarian social system underlying Indonesian rural society has remained basically unchanged "in spite of the advent of Islam, which at the outset was an urban phenomenon. Interrupted by Western colonial intervention, Islam was unable to affect fundamental changes in the traditional character of the indigenous social structure. The *desa* (village) way of life, although modified later by the inroads of urbanization, industry, education and other changes which Western rule brought to Indonesia, remains to this day a powerful determinant of the behavior pattern of the average Indonesian.[77]

Gazalba contends that the authentic teachings were not able to influence the traditional social systems sufficiently to assist in creating the mental prerequisites of modernity. The central Islamic thesis that God created the physical world in order that man, by studying nature, would utilize it for his own welfare, and that it is a form of ingratitude to God not to benefit fully from the bounties of nature, was not grasped by the average Muslim, since the principal emphasis was on the rituals of worship. Newly-won converts to Islam, Gazalba says, needed a longer period of exposure to Islamic education to appreciate fully and then to manifest in their lives Islamic social teachings. They would then be better equipped to realize the exalted status of man as God's *"khalīfah fi'l–arḍ"* ("Vicegerent on earth")[78] who has been commissioned to promote the spiritual as well as the material well-being of mankind. Islamic education was in its initial stage when the aggressive forces of colonialism appeared on the scene, and in its wake followed the spread of the Christian Gospel. Thus internal impediments and external obstruction arrested the purification and deepening of the Islamic consciousness among the Muslim masses.[79]

In agreement with Nurcholish Madjid, Gazalba believes that the acculturation of Western socio-cultural values continues to exert a powerful influence in the moulding of Indonesian identity and in charting the political destiny of the nation. From the Islamic angle of vision, this cultural drift is not a necessary concomitant of modernization. If those who are at the helm of national affairs allow the Westernizing trend to dominate the development effort, then Indonesia would be replaced by a "Western nation made up of Indonesians".

As far as the Muslim community is concerned, it is in desperate need of a "re-Islamization" which will clean it from syncretism, expose it to the unalloyed teachings of the Qur'ān and Sunnah so that the causes of its anti-modernization stance would disappear. According to Gazalba,

> Nine out of ten Indonesians should be Islamized again. Many within the *ummah* are ignorant of 'what Islam is'. They do not know that seeking knowledge is obligatory and that *ijtihād* as the principle of change is the third source of Islamic law. In the formal profession of a religion they are Muslims, but in their cultural life they are still living in a state of isolation, depending on nature, static and with minimum to vague differentiation. Their social life is still characterized by collectivism, *Gemeinschaft,* mutual aid, uniformity, conservatism, sacred leadership and relationships, slight differentiation in personal wealth, the use of wealth to gain social esteem, and closed social interaction. That is why they dislike and even oppose modernization. Thus, without they being conscious of it, they are a hindrance to development.[80]

Gazalba concludes that "re-Islamization" of Indonesian Muslims, whereby the true values of knowledge and social change in the Islamic scheme of things is properly understood, is indeed an ally of modernization. They are, moreover, complementary.[81] On the other hand, Indonesian Christians are relying on the process of Westernization as part of an anti-Islamic strategy. Genuine modernization, particularly its penchant for rational thought, will, in the opinion of Gazalba, have adverse effects on Christian religion, particularly if it means exposing Christian dogma to rational analysis. The decline of Christian practice in the modernized West, culminating in the "Death of God" movement, is proof of this. Gazalba reasons:

> Modernization is grounded in scientific knowledge. The scientific method of thinking is rational and is based on logical premises. When a Christian thinks rationally and logically about culture, and is prompted to do the same in religious matters, he will be forced to contradict his religion, which is non rational and contrary to logic. The alternatives he has to choose from are: either to cease such thinking in religious matters or to continue at the cost of losing his religion. The result? Religion becomes mere custom.[82]

CONCLUSION

From the preceding survey of Muslim viewpoints, beginning with the realistic and scholarly attitude of Dr. Deliar Noer and ending with the polemical and defensive posture of Drs. Sidi Gazalba, it is possible to conclude that the modernization debate has borne on two broad issues, one pertaining to Islam as a theological proposition, and the other to Islam in terms of its cultural-political "scope" in Indonesia.[83]

As far as the first implication is concerned, it is the Muslim consensus that Revelation does not stand in the way of appropriating the beneficial developments of modernity, the advancements in natural sciences and technology, and the efficient techniques of production, organization and administration which modernization requires. It also provides the spiritual motivation for involvement in all efforts aimed at the amelioration of the human condition. The Qur'ānic idea of Man as God's Vicegerent who, equipped with the divine gift of the faculty of reason, is entrusted with the proper utilization and management of the God-given resources of nature "made subservient to man", provides the strongest scriptural support for development — the human endeavour to raise living standards.[84] Political insubordination, economic backwardness, ignorance and neglect of worldly matters due to a one-sided concern for spiritual life are regarded as conditions which detract from the elevated status of Allāh's trusteeship on earth.

Traditional cultural values which survived the formal profession of elementary Islam are pointed out as the real impediment to much desired social change. The representatives of a religious conservatism which blends into the social fabric of a syncretist culture are blamed for perpetuating the *status quo.*[85] Nevertheless, if "re-Islamization of Muslims" is pursued, the attitudinal impediments to modernization will be minimized and the image of Islam will have been vindicated.

The modernist's deductive logic, however, may at times be carried to extremes, as in Nurcholish Madjid's assertion that the process of rationalization is a movement toward the Absolute, as though there is no risk of the reverse happening. He saw in Einstein's remark concerning "the center of true religiosity" the highest testimony to the inherent harmony between faith in metaphysical propositions and scientific empiricism, because the latter is seen as merely seeking to discover the immutable *sunnat Allāh* embedded in the physical universe. He would not, presumably, go so far as to identify Islam with Einstein's "religion" or Allāh with Einstein's "God".[86]

The modernists' advocacy of "rationalization" and the great value attached to science and technology too should not be mistaken for an unreserved support of the "scientific outlook".[87] What they have in mind is the application of the findings and techniques of science to the practical affairs of man in the form of technology. What they see is the vast opportunity offered by the advancement of human knowledge for the betterment of man's material life, whether in manufacturing, transportation, communications, agriculture or medicine. The chief concern, however, is with the influence of what is felt to be the crass materialism and secularism of "Western" culture.

Nurcholish Madjid and Sidi Gazalba do no more than repeat the claim of the Reformist Movement that if *ijtihād* were restored to its proper place in Islamic thought, the Muslim community would be equipped with the instrument to surmount the problems of adjustment to new developments in human society.[88] As to the question of the precise relationship between *ijtihādī* adjustments — assuming for the sake of argument that the problem of defining, organizing and institutionalizing *ijtihād* in a national state not based on Islamic ideology were to be solved — and secular thought which underlies contemporary development in the economic, political, social, administrative, technological and other aspects of national life, Muslim spokesmen have little to offer.

Their primary purpose has been either to convince their political opponents or their own followers that Islam, as a set of beliefs and insights into the nature and purpose of the universe and of man's role and destiny in it, does not impede "the systematic, sustained and purposeful application of human energies to the rational control of man's physical and social environments".[89]

It is obvious that the greatest concern of Muslim spokesmen has been with the political implications of the modernization issue, because this affects the "scope" of Islam in Indonesian national life. From the Muslim perspective, it is not with modernization as such that Muslims have to come to grips, but with the direction modernization takes; that is, the particular orientation and value system of the proponents of modernization among the ruling elite and those in close contact with the centers of the decision making process. Westernization, the alleged goal of the secular and Christian elites, would destroy, the Muslims have claimed, the religious basis of Indonesian identity. Islam, on the other hand, as the religion of the majority of Indonesians and a major motivating force in Indonesian resistance to colonialism, should continue to be one of the chief sources of national values. Besides, Islam has been the staunchest ideological enemy of communism in modern Indonesian history. It would serve as a bulwark against future attempts of the communists to make a political come-back.

As far as the *Pantja Sila* is concerned, it is the Muslim's contention that once secular philosophies and values become entrenched in the socio-political system, thanks to the liberal policies of the present regime, the cornerstone of *Pantja Sila* and the only ideological concession therein to Islamic aspiration —Belief in The One True God— will become another empty slogan.

What seems to be at stake is the compromise of an Islamic symbol whose meaning content is feared to be undergoing a process of reformulation at the hands of anti-Islamic elements aligned to the power elite. Already the scope of Islam has suffered with the growing secularizing political orientation at the center of political power; a further deterioration would be difficult to bear. As far as the declining force of Islam in the lives of its adherents is concerned, it is perceived as a problem of Islamic education, and is to be tackled as an internal matter. Both "scope" and "force" are affected by political decisions of the ruling elite, but it is the former that is most vulnerable to hostile political policies. It is also the most visible indicator of Islam's declining influence in society due to external obstruction. This is because

Current military Islamic policy is based upon the policy conceived and implemented by the eminent Dutch Islamologist, Snouck Hurgronje, during the opening years of the 20th century, and continued by Sukarno and Suharto. Hurgronje differentiated between the religious and political desires of Islam. He advised the Dutch colonial government to encourage Islamic religious activities, while proscribing attempts by Islam to develop a powerful political base. Sukarno was able to divide Muslim ranks — rewarding Nahdatul Ulama [the traditionalist Islamic party] with many non-critical patronage positions, while pushing Masjumi [the reformist Islamic party] beyond the limits of acceptable opposition and eventually dissolving it. A docile Islam was what was desired; an Islam concerned with the fulfilment of religious and ethical obligations but one which would remain uninvolved in the struggle for political influence. The efforts of the military and secular groups to limit Islam's political power has been at the price of increasing bitterness among modernist ranks.[90]

In sum, the real issue behind the "modernization debate" is not the substantive and pragmatic questions relating to the process of modernization, but the ideological orientation of the modernizing elite. Muslim political frustration has indeed colored their perception of the issue, but since the self-proclaimed modernizers belonged to socio-political forces which have been vying with the Muslim groups for a bigger share of political power, their advocacy of modernization, program-orientation and renewal became highly suspect and was understood largely in terms of a struggle for religiopolitical hegemony.

NOTES

1. He obtained his Ph.D. at Cornell University in 1963. In the late 1950's he became the chairman of HMI (Muslim Students' Association). An admirer of former Vice-President Hatta, he was involved in the latter's effort to establish a *Partai Demokrasi Islam* in 1966–1967. He was serving as dean of Jakarta's teacher's college until late 1974, when he was removed from office and barred from teaching because of some critical remarks contained in the text of a speech he was not allowed to deliver.
2. *Api,* No. 3 (October, 1966), pp. 7–10.
3. *Ibid.,* p. 10.
4. *Diskusi Tjibulan,* (June 20–22, 1969), p. 13.
5. *Api, op. cit.,* p. 9.
6. *Diskusi Tjibulan, op. cit.,* p. 12.
7. *Api, op. cit.,* p. 10.
8. The view that modernization has to pattern itself on Western models is best illustrated in the statement of a young economist from the University of Indonesia, Drs. Dorodjatun Kuntjoro Jakti. He said:
   "For me modernization cannot but be like what obtains in the West which manifests itself in building, bridges and all the existing technological advancements. I cannot visualize the manifestation of modernization which is evolved from within. If there are people who could present the picture of modernization *a la* the Orient, I might change my opinion." *Kami,* May 24, 1973.
9. An example of this perspective is "Islam dan Modernisasi," written by Wadjiz Anwar, L. Ph. which appeared in *Pandji Masyarakat,* Nos. 128, 129, 130 (June–July, 1973). Since it belongs to the genre of philosophical writings which do not have any relevance to the religio-political situation in Indonesia, I have excluded it from my survey.
10. *Pembina,* (July, 1968), pp. 8–10.
11. Qur'ān, II: 143. For English translation of the Qur'ān, I have used in most instances Mohammed Marmaduke Pickthall's *The Meaning of the Glorious Koran* (New York: Mentor Books, n.d.).
12. *Ibid.,* II: 177.
13. *Pembina, op. cit.,* p. 9.
14. *Ibid.*
15. Quoted in *Pembina, op. cit.,* pp. 0–10.
16. *Ibid.,* p. 10.
17. *Ibid.*
18. *Ibid.,* p. 9.
19. *Ibid.,* p. 10.

20. *Ibid.* Hashem has since become a medical doctor but continues to show interest in Islamic activities.
21. *Suara Muhammadijah,* No. 16 (August, 1967), p. 8ff.
22. *Ibid.,* p. 10.
23. *Ibid.,* p. 26.
24. "Usaha Mengkristenkan Indonesia dan Dunia," *Suara Muhammadijah,* Nos. 1–2 (January, 1968), p. 3ff.
25. "Ilmu Pengetahuan, Modernisasi dan Sekularisme," *Mertju Suar,* July 15, 1968.
26. *Ibid.*
27. *Ibid.*
28. *Panji Masyarakat,* No. 125 (April, 1973), p. 6.
29. *Ibid.*
30. *Ibid.*
31. *Panji Masyarakat,* No. 29 (April, 1968), p. 2.
32. A well-known reformist writer now teaching in a Malaysian university.
33. *Modernisasi Ialah Rationalisasi Bukan Westernisasi,* p. 5. See also Boland, *op. cit.,* p. 221; Samson, "Islam and Politics," pp. 293–7.
34. *Modernisasi,* p. 5.
35. *Ibid.*
36. *Ibid.,* p. 6.
37. *Ibid.,* pp. 6–9.
38. *Ibid.,* p. 99. The concept of *Sunnat Allāh* is derived from Qur'ān, XXXIII: 38, 62; XXXV: 43; XXXXVIII: 23.
39. *Modernisasi,* pp. 9–10.
40. The idea of *hanīf* is found in Sūrahs II: 135; III: 67; VI: 79, 161, XVI: 120, 123; XXX: 30; XCVIII: 5.
41. *Modernisasi,* p. 11.
42. Lincoln Barnett, *The Universe and Dr. Einstein* (New York: Time Inc., 1957), p. 100.
43. *Modernisasi,* p. 16.
44. *Ibid.,* pp. 17–8.
45. Quoted in *ibid.,* p. 20.
46. *Modernisasi,* p. 25.
47. *Ibid.,* p. 25.
48. *Ibid.*
49. Qur'ān, III: 104, 110, 114; IX: 71, 112; XXII: 41.
50. *Modernisasi,* p. 26.
51. *Ibid.*
52. *Ibid.,* pp. 28–9.
53. *Ibid.,* pp. 30–3. On the study of Dutch Ethical Policy and some of its social and political consequences, see Robert van Niel, *The Emergence of the Modern Indonesian Elite* (The Hague and Bandung, 1960).
54. Harry J. Benda, *The Crescent and the Rising Sun: Indonesian Islam Under the Japanese Occupation 1942–1945* (The Hague and Bandung, 1958), p. 28; see pp. 9–31 on Indonesian Islam and the foundations of Dutch Islamic policy. Cf. Alfian, "Islamic Modernism in Indonesian Politics: The Muhammadijah Movement During the Dutch Colonial Period (1912–1942)," (unpublished doctoral dissertation for the University of Wisconsin, 1969), pp. 33–45.
55. See Benda, *Crescent,* pp. 26–7.
56. *Modernisasi,* p. 33. Cf. Deliar Noer, "The Rise of the Modernist Muslim Movements in Indonesia 1900–1942," (doctoral dissertation for Cornell University, 1963), pp. 31–2.
57. *Modernisasi,* p. 34. For an insight into the problem of Indonesia's national identity, see J.D. Legge, "Indonesia's Search for Identity," in Legge, *Indonesia* (New Jersey: Prentice-Hall, Inc., 1964), pp. 170–3.
58. *Modernisasi,* pp. 36–7.
59. *Ibid.,* p. 37.
60. *Ibid.,* p. 38.
61. *Ibid.,* p. 39.
62. *Ibid.,* p. 40. On the Party, see Donald Hindley, *The Communist Party in Indonesia 1951–1963* (Berkeley: University of California Press, 1964); van der Kroef, *The Communist Party of Indonesia, Its History, Program and Tactics* (Vancouver: University of British Columbia, 1965).
63. *Modernisasi,* p. 41.
64. *Ibid.,* p. 42.

65. Gazalba, *Modernisasi Dalam Persoalan: Bagaimana Sikap Islam,* p. 18.
66. *Ibid.,* pp. 26–28.
67. Gazalba, *Persoalan,* pp. 33–4. *Time's* report on Jakarta's development, in its April 2, 1973, issue is revealing:
"Faced with a critical shortage of housing, schools, roads and jobs, the governor of Jakarta . . . undertook and unorthodox rescue program three years ago. To curb the population crush, he closed the city to unauthorized new residents; to increase tax revenues, he opened it up to gambling and other forms of pleasure. Now called *kota maksiat* ('sin city') by angry Moslems, Jakarta offers horse racing, dog racing, jai alai, lotteries, 24-hour casinos and slot machine parlors with one-armed bandits imported from Nevada. Three thousand Balinese women staff some 30 massage parlors, and 6-foot-tall Australian strippers bump and grind around a circuit of 36 glittering nightclubs."
68. *Persoalan,* pp. 35–7.
69. *Ibid.,* pp. 40–2.
70. *Ibid.,* p. 46.
71. See "Modernisasi Tak Boleh Rombak Soal Ibadat dan Akidah," *Abadi,* June 17, 1970.
72. *Persoalan,* p. 46.
73. *Ibid.,* pp. 46–8.
74. *Ibid.,* pp. 49–51.
75. *Ibid.,* p. 58.
76. *Ibid.,* p. 82.
77. *Ibid.,* pp. 76–7.
78. See Qur'ān, II: 30; VI: 165; X: 14; XXXV: 39; XXVII: 62.
79. *Persoalan,* p. 77. These points were reiterated by Gazalba in a number of interviews I had with him in Jakarta in 1973.
80. *Persoalan,* p. 87.
81. *Ibid.,* p. 90.
82. *Ibid.*
83. The term "scope" is used by Geertz to mean "the range of social contexts within which religious considerations are regarded as having more or less direct relevance." It is contrasted with "force" which means "the thoroughness with which such a pattern is internalized in the personalities of the individuals who adopt it, its centrality or marginality in their lives." Clifford Geertz, *Islam Observed* (New Haven: Yale University Press, 1968), pp. 111–2.
84. In a similar effort to show the religious motivation for development, the Islamic scholar Al-Bahay Al-Kholi inferred from the Qur'ānic verse "and He revealed iron, wherein is mighty power and (many) uses for mankind," (LVII: 25) that Allāh wanted man to exploit the mineral resources of the earth, implying that industrialization is in conformity with the will of God. See Donald Eugene Smith (ed.) *Religion, Politics, and Society in the Third World* (New York: The Free Press, 1971), p. 207.
85. In Benda's word, "Indonesian reformism battled against four opponents simultaneously. In the first place, it attacked the formalism of Islamic orthodoxy embodied in the *santri* [devout Javanese Muslim] civilization of rural Indonesia, as well as the animistic and Hindu-Buddhist 'impurities' of village Islam, by insisting on a religion purified from scholasticism and mysticism and yet compatible with everyday life." Benda, *Crescent,* p. 48.
86. In Lincoln Barnett, *The Universe and Dr. Einstein,* Einstein, whose philosophy of science has sometimes been criticized as materialistic, is reported to have said:
"My religion consists of a humble admiration of the illimitable superior spirit who reveals himself in the slight details we are able to perceive with our frail and feeble minds. That deeply emotional conviction of the presence of a superior reasoning power, which is revealed in the incomprehensible universe, forms my idea of God." Barnett, *The Universe,* p. 101.
87. See Geertz, "Religion as a Cultural System," in D. Cutler (ed.), *The Religious Situation* (Boston: Beacon Press, 1968), p. 668.
88. For a systematic critique of Islamic reformist thought, see Malcolm Kerr, *Islamic Reform* (Berkeley: University of California Press, 1966); see also Bellah, "Islamic Tradition and the Problems of Modernization," in *Beyond Belief* (New York: Harper & Row, 1970), pp. 146–66; H.A.R. Gibb, *Modern Trends in Islam* (Chicago: University of Chicago Press, 1947); W.C. Smith, *Islam in Modern History* (Princeton: Princeton University Press, 1957); Nadav Safran, *Egypt in Search of Political Community* (Cambridge, Mass.: Harvard University Press, 1961).
89. Definition of modernization according to Benjamin Schwarts in "Factors in the Process of Modernization in Asian Countries," *Asian Affairs,* Vol. 59, (February, 1972), p. 41. He defines modernization as

the process of rationalization in his "Modernization and the Maoist Vision: Some Reflections on Chinese Communist Goals," *Dissent*, (Spring 1974), p. 239.

90. Samson, "Islam and Politics," pp. 229–30.

The Issue of Modernization among Muslims in Indonesia: From a Participant's Point of View

NURCHOLISH MADJID

By way of introduction let me present a few remarks about my personal involvement with the issue of modernization among Muslims in Indonesia. In 1963, after my first two years of college, I started participating in the activities of the *Himpunan Mahasiswa Islam* (Islamic Student Organization, HMI), the largest student organization in Indonesia. In 1967 I was elected president, the first and so far the only president who did not come from a secular university. In 1969, to the surprise of many people, I was reelected president of the HMI. Again, I was the first and so far the only person who was elected twice. In addition to my active practical involvement with the issues, I wrote in 1969 a small book entitled *Nilai-nilai Dasar Perjuangan* (The Basic Values of Struggle) which became the ideological manual for members of the organization. This booklet was based on our experiences in Indonesia and on my personal observation and encounters with political groups in the Middle East during a three-month visit in 1968.

In the early years of the 1970s *pembaharuan* (modernization), which had always been a controversial issue in Indonesia, began to be discussed with an intensity much greater than before — especially among Muslims. Sukarno himself spread the notion of Islamic modernization in his famous *Surat-surat dari Ende* (Letters from Ende) which he wrote while exiled by the colonial administration. In 1962 as the *Muhammadiyah* commemorated its fiftieth anniversary, Sukarno made the issue of "Islamic rejuvenation" the theme for his speech in front of the thousands who filled the huge Senayan Sport Palace. At that time Sukarno introduced the slogan "*Menggali Kembali api Islam*," (Recultivate the spirit of Islam). In reality, however, Sukarno did not have the modernization of Islam or its reformation as his central concern; what he was interested in was religion and its relationship to the formation of the Indonesian nation. Sukarno, I think, was looking for something in Islam which could be used to support his concept of nation building through never-ending revolution. He also wished to unite the Muslims with the nationalists and the communists, under the umbrella of *Nasakom*, i.e., Nationalists, Religionists, and Communists.

The issue of Islamic modernization, or modernization at large, gained a new impetus after Sukarno with the emergence of the New Order. This era of the Indonesian nation, under the political leadership of the Indonesian Army, has afforded opportunity to test the validity of a concept of nation building opposite to that of Sukarno's: namely, nation building through economic development. This development has carried with it many implications, the most important of which is modernization. Modernization, in turn, involves controversial issues such as a pragmatic

Reprinted from Gloria Davis (ed.), *What is Modern Indonesian Culture?* Papers in International Studies, Southeast Asia Series No. 52 (1979), pp. 143–155, by permission of the author and the Center for International Studies, Ohio University, Athens, Ohio, U.S.A.

approach to problems (rather than the ideological one of the Old Order); rationalization, and, above all, secularization of the nation.

During this period Mochtar Lubis and Rosihan Anwar, the two most prominent journalists of the Indonesian press, were among those who argued strongly for notions of modernization in their respective daily newspapers, *Indonesia Raya* and *Pedoman*. The Indonesian Muslim groups were extremely hostile towards the ideas of pragmatism, rationalism, and secularism. They were especially sensitive to secularism, which they condemned as "infidel" or *kafir*. Therefore, the articles of Mochtar Lubis and Rosihan Anwar were read with deep suspicion by the Muslims, and criticized severely. At first, I too was one of those Muslims who criticized Mochtar Lubus and Rosihan Anwar, (even though indirectly), and I did so in a series of articles in the student weekly magazine *Mimbar Demokrasi* published in Bandung.

THE GENERATION GAP AND THE IDEA OF ISLAMIC REFORM

The battle for Islamic reform became much more involved after my presentation of a working paper entitled "The Necessity of Reforming Islamic Understanding and the Problem of Islamic Integration" on January 2, 1970. The occasion was a meeting of *Halal bi halal*, or the "Idul Fitri Party" which had been organized by the four most important organizations of young Indonesian Muslims: HMI (Islamic Student Organization), PII (Islamic Movement for Indonesian Secondary School Students), Persami (Indonesian Muslim Scholars Association) and GPI (Muslim Youth Movement). Despite the fact that these organizations consistently emphasized their independence in practical political matters, people have always considered them as natural successor organizations to the *Masyumi* party which was dissolved during the Sukarno regime.

The meeting was initially sponsored by the activists of the PII under the leadership of Utomo Dananjaya and Usep Fathuddin the president and the secretary general, respectively, and it took place in their headquarters. The sponsors decided that in this particular meeting of *Halal bi halal* there would be free discussion about matters concerning contemporary Islam in Indonesia, instead of the lengthy boring speeches containing nothing other than political demagoguery. Dr. Alfian was the man originally approached by the PII leaders and asked to write a working paper to be presented for discussion. But he declined, and the sponsors approached me as his substitute. I agreed promptly after their assurance that the gathering would be a closed and limited one.

It turned out that their understanding and mine about what constituted a closed and limited meeting differed considerably. I expected that the meeting would be attended by no more than a dozen representatives from each organization, and that there would be no publication of any kind. My understanding about closed and limited meetings was based on my experience in the HMI during the time of the Old Order when we were confronted with the threat of communists and were forced to work semi-secretly. But my friends from the PII understood a meeting to be special, or closed and limited, if no one was invited other than members of the organization. The number of those attending did not matter very much to them. And thus, the meeting at which I made my controversial presentation was attended by hundreds, and my paper was printed and distributed among the audience. I was surprised by this but could not do anything about it; any protest on my part would have been taken the wrong way by my PII colleagues. Besides, I was deeply concerned to keep my energetic friends motivated to participate in activities that could bring about the break-down of the traditional social order.

As was to be expected, my paper was leaked to outsiders, and a copy of it reached the enthusiastic journalists of *Indonesia Raya* who then published it in the following Sunday edition. Because of this, I became a big question mark in the Muslim community which became very suspicious of me and my friends. It was rumored that I was part of a conspiracy against the Muslim community, a conspiracy organized by the PSI (Socialist Party of Indonesia) which had always been considered an advocate of Westernization and secularization. The accusation was quite logical, because it was, after all, *Indonesia Raya*, the newspaper of the socialist journalist Mochtar Lubis, which had enthusiastically publicized the discussion.

It is interesting that the PII leaders were

the sponsors of the controversial meeting since the PII had long been considered closer to the conservative *Masyumi* party than the HMI or Persami. PII members had always enjoyed the title of the "Cadres of *Masyumi*," or more broadly the "Cadres of Umma," and they felt they were more loyal to the *Masyumi* than any other young Muslim group. Promoting such a controversial activity as this particular meeting was taken as a sign of disillusionment of PII leaders with their elder patrons in the *Masyumi*.

The HMI, on the other hand, already had a reputation as recalcitrant in the eyes of the *Masyumi* leaders. Its foundation was somewhat controversial and at least at the beginning, the *Masyumi* establishment was a little unhappy with the emergence of the HMI in Yogyakarta in 1947. The reason for this was that they wanted to have only one organization for all Indonesian Muslim youth and that was to be the GPII (Indonesian Young Muslim's Movement). Dissatisfied with the performance of the GPII (especially since it could not meet the particular needs of university students) Lafran Pane, a student of Gajah Mada University, and his friends, in cooperation with the students of STI (the Islamic High School), founded the HMI. From the beginning, the HMI had continuous conflicts, major and minor, with the *Masyumi* leadership. The situation became very dramatic in 1953 when the president of the HMI, Dahlan Ranuwihardjo, organized a large meeting in the hall of the University of Indonesia in Jakarta to discuss the two prevailing concepts about the nature of the Indonesian republic: namely, whether it should become a national state or an Islamic one. To the great surprise of the Islamic-state proponents in the *Masyumi*, the resolution of the discussion was in favor of Sukarno's concept; the HMI, or at least its president, Dahlan Ranuwihardjo, preferred the national state. (Sukarno was invited to come to the discussion and he attended it enthusiastically.)

From that time on, the gap between the Muslim older generation, as represented by the *Masyumi*, and the younger one in the HMI, began to widen. When Deliar Noer and Ismail Hassan Murareum presided over the HMI, an attempt was made to bridge this gap, but the reconciliation between the two generations was never complete. In the final analysis, both Deliar Noer and Ismail Hassan were almost as critical of the leadership of *Masyumi* as their predecessors; and in fact, those two presidents of the HMI often identified themselves more closely with Dr. Mohammad Hatta, a stout Muslim nationalist, than with the *Masyumi* leaders.

A more important conflict between the *Masyumi* and the HMI developed during the Old Order period. At that time the HMI had been so successful in recruiting members among Indonesian students that the Department of Higher Learning estimated that 32 per cent of all Indonesian students were members of the HMI; 40 per cent were not affiliated with any student organization; and the remaining 28 per cent belonged to various other student organization of which the most important were the nationalist-leftist *Gerakan Mahasiswa Nasional Indonesia* (Indonesian National Student Movement, GMNI), and the communist *Consentrasi Gerakan Mahasiswa Indonesia* (Indonesian Student Movement Concentration, CGMI). Because political initiatives generally came from the communists in those days, it was in the interest of communist propaganda to disseminate the notion that the HMI was closely related to the *Masyumi* an organization which they considered counter-revolutionary and which had been dissolved by the Sukarno regime. Thus communist propaganda held that the HMI was a reactionary and counter-revolutionary student organization which had no right to exist on Indonesian soil. This was inconsistent with the fact that the *Masyumi* from the beginning had been the arch-enemy of the communists. The years 1964 and 1965 were times when the communists launched a major campaign to "*Ganyang HMI!*" (Crush HMI!) which created hard times for its members. Indeed, in some cases communist pressures were almost unbearable; terrors, intrigues, intimidations, insinuations, and other forms of psychological warfare were experienced by members of the HMI.

It seems to me that one of the many possible motives behind the escalated communist fight against the HMI was the fact that this organization had managed to stand in the way of communist control of university students. The communists had been able to dominate almost all social and political fields at that time; the journalists (PWI), the trade unions (SOBSI), the artists (LEKRA), the farmers

(BTI), the youths (*Pemuda Rakyat*, which dominated the *Front Pemuda*, the high school students (IPPI), and so forth. Therefore it was no surprise that the communists tried at all costs to eliminate the HMI from the Indonesian political arena. But thanks to protection by the Indonesian Army and the support of the late General Ahmad Yani, the HMI was never outlawed and even Sukarno himself seemed little persuaded by the communist propaganda.

But the HMI had to pay a high price for this leniency; that is, its leaders were forced to follow a policy of accommodation with prevailing political positions, i.e., to revolutionism and "*Manipol*" (Political Manifesto) for the sake of the survival of the organization. This policy of accommodation became an area of severe conflict between the leaders of the HMI and of the *Masyumi*, with some of the latter accusing the HMI of giving up its Islamic ideology and surrendering to the communist-inspired Sukarno regime. In fact, leaders of the HMI had talked with leaders of the *Masyumi* prior to their decision on the policy of accommodation and requested their advice. This happened in 1963 in a meeting at the home of a *Masyumi* leader who was under house arrest at the time. This meeting brought about a showdown between the two Muslim generations in which the *Masyumi* leaders bluntly condemned the policy of the HMI.

The leaders of the HMI worked for the survival of the organization at almost any cost because of their belief in its potential for the future. Furthermore, if the HMI had been outlawed, thousands of its members would have been banned from the universities, and hundreds of alumni who once had belonged to the HMI would have lost their jobs. But the leaders of the older generation in the *Masyumi* did not appreciate these reasons and, they argued, that it would be better to have martyrs for an ideology than to practice hypocrisy. Of course the leaders of HMI were of the opinion that there was nothing hypocritical about the policy of accommodation; in fact, they viewed it as a tactical and strategic measure — a neccessary evil. They further said that sacrificing a potentially powerful organization for the mere sake of heroism and martyrdom was irrational and too costly. This conflict was important in enlarging the already widening gap between the two factions. The younger generation continued to see the older generation as irrelevant and out of date, and the latter deplored the increasing ideological disaffection of the young.

When I was elected president of the HMI in 1966, the *Masyumi* leaders held out new hope for the HMI. Even though I was chosen at the expense of their candidate. Their hope was based upon the simple fact that I come from a very religious family of *Masyumi* members, and more importantly, that I had been educated in a religious institution, the *Institut Agama Islam Negeri* (State Islamic Institute, IAIN). They were not entirely wrong in their expectations: I was strongly inclined towards them, and I tried to bring as many of their ideas to the HMI as possible. I even tried to reconcile the former leaders of the HMI with the leaders of *Masyumi* but I was not successful. The prejudices on both sides were insurmountable.

At first I was on the side of the *Masyumi* in almost everything. I joined the *Masyumi* intellectuals to fight the issue of secularization discussed by Mochtar Lubis and Rosihan Anwar. Most importantly, I joined the *Masyumi* leaders in their effort to rebuild their party. But after a short time, we from the HMI realized that rehabilitation was impossible. The *Masyumi* had been accused of promoting separatist activities, and supporting the rebellion of the *Darul Islam-Tentara Islam Indonesia* (Darul Islam-Indonesian Islamic Armed Forces, DI-TII) armed factions and of the *Pemerintah Revolusioner Republik Indonesia* (Revolutionary Government of the Republic of Indonesia, PRRI). These insurgencies were detrimental to the army and apparently army leaders simply could not forget the bitter experiences of their campaign to subdue them. Besides, the *Masyumi* by stressing the idea of an Islamic state, stood in sharp contrast to the endeavor of the army to bring about a national state. Therefore, the army did not support any effort to bring the *Masyumi* back into legal and formal political activity.

Quite aware of these facts, my colleagues and I in the HMI sponsored the idea of founding a new political party. The basic idea was to create a *Masyumi* faction under a new name. This idea was agreed to by the ruling military regime, but rejected by the *Masyumi* leaders.

They argued that their political party had not been guilty of any unpatriotic activities, and that, after all, they had fought uncompromisingly against Sukarno and the communists. And since Sukarno and the communists had now proved to be in the wrong, the *Masyumi* was automatically in the right. Therefore, they argued, they deserved the right to revive their political party. The *Masyumi* failed to think politically because they presupposed a well-established rule of law. Reality did not conform to their expectations, however, and the existing political parties did not support the idea of *Masyumi* rehabilitation.

The argument over either rehabilitating the *Masyumi* or founding a new political party was so arduous, and the discussion took such a long time (more than one year), that when agreement was finally reached, the new party came into existence too late and, therefore, did not become effective. The new political party, under the name of *Partai Muslimin Indonesia* (Parmusi) failed to attract the mass of the former members of the *Masyumi* because *Masyumi* leaders were not at the head of it. In fact, the army stood in the way of allowing *Masyumi* leaders to take leading positions in the new political party. This occurred, I think, because at the time when Parmusi emerged (early 1968), the army was no longer badly in need of social and political support from the members of the dissolved *Masyumi* — the army already had such support from the other groups which were safer to them ideologically.

The experiences brought us to the conclusion that the *Masyumi* leaders suffered from inflexibility, almost dogmatism, in practical considerations. There were serious questions as to what really lay behind their way of thinking. Was it due to their conception of conservative Islamic ideology? Was it because of political-psychological conditions resulting from continuous pressure upon them by the Sukarno regime? Or was it simply general inability on the part of the older generation to deal with the up-and-coming generation? As the president of the HMI, I was especially concerned with this latter problem. Thanks to my social and educational background, I had easy access to *Masyumi* circles. And in spite of my deep involvement in student activities and aspirations, I was quite aware of the worlds which kept the two generations apart.

In October 1968, I visited the United States as a student leader, sponsored by the Council for Leaders and Specialists (CLS) in Washington. More impressive, however, was my visit to several Middle East countries (Turkey, Lebanon, Syria, Iraq, Kuwait, Saudi Arabia, Sudan, and Egypt) on my way back from the United States. My curiosity about models of Islamic ideology led me to arrange meetings with numerous authorized people in these countries. We had very interesting discussions, and I obtained some very important reading materials, including the outlawed books of Hassan al-Banna, the prominent leader of the Muslim Brotherhood of Egypt.

I returned to Indonesia in January 1969. In March of the same year I went to the holy places (Mecca and Medina) at the invitation of the government of Saudi Arabia. At the time, I was the head of ten leaders of the HMI who were performing the *haj* (pilgrimage). After my return to Jakarta, I dedicated my time to writing my version of Islamic ideology. The result was the booklet which I mentioned earlier, *Nilai-nilai Dasar Perjuangan* or NDP. This small book was a summing up of all my learning and experience about the ideology of Islam. Two months later, in May 1969, the ninth national convention of the HMI at Malang approved my booklet as the guiding manual for ideological orientation of members of the HMI.

I was inspired to write this manual by three facts. The first was the absence of comprehensive and systematic reading in Islamic ideology. We had become fully aware of this shortcoming during the time of the Old Order when we had been in continuous ideological battle with the communists and the nationalists-leftists and were badly in need of a weapon to counter their ideological offensive. At that time we had to make do with the Cokroaminoto's *Islam dan Sosialisme,* which after a short time we found inadequate. The second reason for writing was my envy of the young communists who were provided by the party with a manual called *Pustaka Kecil Marksis* (Marxist Small Reader), known as PKM. The third was that I was deeply impressed with Willy Eichler's small book *Fundamental Values and Basic Demands of Democratic Socialism,* an ideological reformulation for the *Sozialdemokratische Partei Deutschlands* (German Social-Democratic Party, SPD) of West Germany.

My book gained considerable acceptance among Muslims beyond HMI members, and especially among young intellectuals. Although many of its ideas advocated reform or change in existing Islamic understanding in Indonesia, their presentation used familiar symbols and expressions, so that most of the readers were satisfied.

This relatively calm situation did not change until I made my controversial address on January 2, 1970. As I have said, I made this presentation because I expected a special, closed meeting with free discussion among the leaders of four young Muslim organizations. There was a strong reaction against my use of such controversial terms as "secularization," "desacralization," "liberalization," "socialism," and so on. Of course, I was quite aware of the danger of publicly referring to these points. As a matter of fact, some of my adversaries suggested that I "repent" and apologize to the Muslim community. This I could hardly have done. Despite my knowledge that the approach was wrong, I firmly believed that the purpose was right.

TOWARDS THE FUTURE

At the first stage, the discussion of modernization was limited to young Muslims in the four organizations I mentioned. But contrary to public impression, we always insisted that the discussion involve only individuals who did not necessarily represent the views of the organizations they came from. This was to keep the discussion free and open, and not to convert it into a rigid and doctrinaire session. The issue had become the concern of almost all young Muslims and, as was to be expected, members of the HMI were at the forefront of the discussion, followed by members of the PII.

In the following stage, the discussion involved almost everybody from both the old and the young generations. Besides oral reactions in the form of *tabligh* (religious) speeches and Friday prayer sermons, two books became available to counter or comment on my ideas about *pembaharuan* or reformation. The first, entitled, *Pembaharuan Pemikiran Islam* (Reform of Islamic Thinking), contains my paper and three comments or reactions from representatives of organizations other then the HMI. This book was published by the Islamic Research Center in 1970. The second book, entitled *Koreksi terhadap Drs. Nurcholish Madjid tentang Sekularisasi* (Correction to Drs. Nurcholish Madjid about Secularization) was written by Professor Dr. H. Rasyidi, and contains his sharp and critical analysis of my ideas. It was published in 1972 by the well-known publishing house Bulan Bintang whose manager was a member of the *Masyumi.*

Three things appeared to me to trigger Professor Rasyidi's strong comment and a bitter reaction to my ideas. The first was the violent discussion organized by the leaders of the HMI and of the PII in August 1972. This discussion occurred in my absence, since I was on a visit to several Asian countries and the sponsors had not given me notice about the discussion beforehand. As a matter of fact, my absence at the discussion — which was the first to be arranged with the older generation like Professor Rasyidi present — led some participants to suspect me of and even accuse me of being a coward. The second incident was my further elaboration on the idea of secularization in a bulletin which my friends and I published in 1972. The name of the bulletin was *Arena.* The third was my presentation on October 30, 1972 at the prestigious Taman Ismail Marzuki (an auditorium in Jakarta), the theme of a talk being *Menyegarkan Faham Keagamaan di Kalangan Ummat Islam Indonesia* (Refreshing Religious Understanding Among Indonesian Muslims).

But in the final analysis, Professor Rasyidi's correction showed his deep concern about Islam in Indonesia and emerged from his genuine eagerness to "save" the younger Muslims in that country. (His book is dedicated to Muslim students.) However, I do not agree with most of his corrections and comments. For one thing, some of them are too personal. Upon the advice of another respected Muslim leader, Abdul Ghaffar Ismail, however, I have never responded to Professor Rasyidi in written material. We had come to the conclusion that such a response would invite long-term polemics which might be too costly in social and political terms.

Looking back at our experiences, I wished

that I had never committed such a tactical blunder as that manifest in my speech on January 2, 1970. It was socially too expensive, and we suffered almost irreparable damage to our reputation within the Muslim community. If I were able to go back in time, I would follow my previous methods, i.e., *penetration pacifique,* the "smuggling method" of introducing new ideas. This is what I did when writing the above-mentioned book *NDP*.

But time heals all wounds, and my friends and I have managed to surmount the difficulties and have begun to regain our reputation for trustworthiness within the community. This has happened without any change in our commitment to social change or *pembaharuan.* After all, the *Masyumi* leaders themselves still serve as our inspiration. Indeed, we still believe that the leaders of that dissolved political party are the best men in our country. Their lives are examples to many youth. They are the people who have successfully combined the best elements of the two world-outlooks: Islam and Westernization, or more safely, modernization. From Islam they learned piety and God-fearingness; and from the West they came to appreciate ideas such as democracy, human rights, and rule of law. Generally they learned these things in a much better way than most other Indonesians. They are the people whom history will acknowledge as the most honest and trustworthy in Indonesia, and I am of the opinion that their ethics are most needed in developing economic policy.

Nothing is too surprising in these facts. Besides their sincere dedication to the cause of Islam, the old *Masyumi* leaders were among the few Indonesians who were given the privilege of the highest level of education during the colonial era. For this reason they are counted among the first generation of Indonesian intellectuals. Seven of the ten most prominent of them were graduates of the prestigious *Recht Hogere School* (RHS) in Jakarta: Mohammad Rum, Yusuf Wibisono, Kasman Singodimedjo, Sjafruddin Prawiranegara, Prawoto Mangkussamito, Assaat, and Burhanuddin Harahap. At their head is Muhammad Natsir, who never had a higher education, but has demonstrated admirable intellectual capacity. Professor Dr. H. Rasyidi, who specialized in Islamic religion, was educated at the Al-Azhar University, then at the Sorbonne: and Sukiman, a medical doctor, is one of the students who founded the *Perhimpunan Indonesia* (Indonesian Association) in Holland and pioneered the struggle for Indonesian independence. Sukiman is also the Muslim leader who for the first time managed to successfully unite all Muslim forces under one political party, the *Masyumi.* That unity fell apart shortly after he left its top leadership.

Besides those secularly educated people, the *Masyumi* has many other types of leaders; most important of the latter are the *kiyahis* (teachers) or the *ulamas* (Islamic scholars). But these men only had a secondary role in the leadership of the party. Indeed, Muslims virtually identified the *Masyumi* party with Dutch-schooled leaders and that was one of the main reasons why the more *ulama*-oriented faction of Indonesian Muslims, that is the *Nahdhatul Ulama,* were not "at home" in the *Masyumi* federation and why they left it in 1952.

For this reason the bitter reaction of *Masyumi* leaders to my ideas about modernization came as something of a surprise. After all, the members of the HMI were university students and the natural heirs to *Masyumi* leadership. They were Muslims who were closest to the *Masyumi* in ways of thinking, those most likely to appreciate their aspirations. But there were two points on which the younger generation disagreed. The first was the idea of the so-called *Negara Islam* (Islamic state). It is a necessary belief of Muslims that their religious teachings inspire them in all activities in this world, including those related to state or political matters. But to advocate an Islamic state in *Masyumi*'s terms sounded too formalistic and inflexible. The second difference was manifest in the unbending attitude of the *Masyumi* towards practical political problems. This inflexibility seemed to lead them to see everything in black and white; that is, along the concepts of *halal* and *haram,* acts which are *allowed* or *forbidden* in Islamic teachings. We considered this to be too much religious interference in day-to-day practical affairs. In fact, had the leaders of *Masyumi* been more flexible and relativistic at that time, their political position would be much better now; and the implementation of the government's development policy would have been backed by people of the utmost honesty and trustworthiness.

Unfortunately the time has gone when *Masyumi* leaders themselves heeded the *hadith* (the sayings of the Prophet): "In religious matters, you have to ask me. But in secular matters, you have better knowledge than me." The *kiyahis* and *ulamas* were men to be consulted on religious matters, but the *Masyumi* leaders, thanks to their modern educational background, should have known more about political affairs than their religious teachers did. And that was one of the most important notions that we, the younger generation, wished them to realize. But it turned out, to our great sorrow, that the terms we chose for the discussion were too strong for our purposes. Even in the most advanced countries like the United States the terms secularism and secularization are still emotional and controversial; something which we tended to forget.

In retrospect, therefore, it is possible to find many points of weakness on our part, both in the ideas we propagated and in the methods we used. No doubt these experiences opened our eyes and helped us mature, but at the same time they helped us to realize that the process of regaining our strength will be a very slow one. Some reasons for this are worth mentioning here. The first is, that we, the younger Muslim generation, particularly the HMI "establishment" including current members and the alumni, are not regarded as first class intellectuals in Indonesia. This is unlike the case of the *Masyumi* leaders in the early years of independence, or the position of the younger generation in political groups which have not suffered severe generational conflict. The growth of Islamic intellectualism was severely interrupted and damaged by the political disaster which fell upon *Masyumi* in the 1950s and 1960s. This intellectual discontinuity, in turn, has had a great deal to do with the inability of emerging Muslim intellectuals to regain political initiatives comparable to those of the *Masyumi* in its heyday. The members of HMI, even the alumni, are still too inexperienced and are still denied the wisdom of the more experienced older generation.

The second reason for our slow pace is that even among the younger generation of the nation as a whole, the HMI does not play an important role in national politics. Two things, at least, are responsible for this. One is that the HMI, at the national level, declined to take a prominent position in the organizational hierarchy of the *Kesatuan Aksi Mahasiswa Indonesia* (Indonesian Student Action Front, KAMI), despite the fact that the HMI was the largest student organization represented. This policy was adopted so that the youthful KAMI would not become an easy target for communists. The formal leadership of the group was given to the presidents of two of the best protected student organizations, that is, the Islamic PMII and the Catholic *Perhimpunan Mahasiswa Katolik Republik Indonesia* (Catholic Students' Association of the Republic of Indonesia, PMKRI). But this policy was followed at the expense of the reputation and popularity of the HMI among more radical Muslims, including members of the HMI themselves. Their response was to create the *Komando Strategi Mahasiswa* (Strategic Student Command, Kostram), which was then a rival organization to the KAMI in which HMI elements dominated the leadership. The national board of the HMI refused to recognize Kostram and subsequently the new organization dissolved.

But those things do not stand by themselves. There is a reciprocal relationship between those facts and the fact that the HMI has persistently remained independent in political matters. The HMI has always refused to affiliate with any official political groups (i.e., the government sponsored Joint Secretariat of Functional Groups, Golkar; the Muslim Development Unity Party, PPP; or the predominantly nationalist/Christian Indonesian Democratic Party, PDI). This has meant that even in the Islamic PPP, the HMI is underrepresented — compared with the NU's PMII, for example. Trapped by its insistence on independence, and alienated from the first generation intellectuals as represented in the *Masyumi*, the HMI is driven to perpetuate its own. From the 1950s on, the HMI began to have alumni in sizable numbers. In the 1960s the number of alumni grew rapidly, and in the first half of the 1970s there were thousands who belonged to this category. Under their organization *Korps Alumni HMI* (KAHMI), they constitute the senior members of the HMI establishment, from whom the younger members seek orientation and protection.

These emerging intellectuals might be lacking in maturity and hence lacking in quality compared with those in other social and political groups in Indonesia, but numerically they are larger than any other intellectual group and their influence is strongly felt in student governments in almost all universities of the country. Dr. Deliar Noer, one of the former presidents of HMI, is well aware of the growing strength of that student organization and is very optimistic about its future. In fact, he used to say that even if the HMI did not do anything except maintain its existence and continue its activities in "leadership training," the future still would be bright for its supporters.

The time will come when the HMI, the most important representative of the younger generation among Indonesian Muslims, will have built its pyramidal establishment and younger Muslims will have gained a true sense of self-confidence. This psychological condition is, I think, a precondition for working and thinking positively and constructively; both for the Muslim community, and for the Indonesian people at large. With self-confidence, modernization can be transformed from a slogan or topic of controversy, into a reality.

Abbreviations of Journals

AA — *American Anthropologist.*

AES — *Archives Europeennes de Sociologie.*

BEFEO — *Bulletin de l'Ecole Française d'Extrême Orient* (Bulletin of the French School of the Far East).

BJ — Bibliotheca Javanica published by the Koninlijk Bataviaasch Genootschap van Kunsten en Wetenschappen.

BKI — *Bijdragen tot de Taal-, Land- en Volkenkunde* published by the Koninklijk Instituut voor Taal-, Land- en Volkenkunde.

BSOAS — *Bulletin of the School of Oriental and African Studies.*

CIS — *Cahiers Internationaux de Sociologie.*

CJHSS — *The Ceylon Journal of Historical and Social Studies.*

CSSH — *Comparative Studies in Society and History.*

IG — *De Indische Gids.*

JMBRAS — *Journal of the Malayan Branch of the Royal Asiatic Society.*

JRAI — *Journal of the Royal Anthropological Institute of Great Britain and Ireland.*

JRAS — *Journal of the Royal Asiatic Society of Great Britain and Ireland.*

JSAH — *Journal of Southeast Asian History.*

JSBRAS — *Journal of the Straits Branch of the Royal Asiatic Society.*

KT — *Koloniaal Tijdschrift.*

SIAH — Schriften des Instituts für Asienkunde in Hamburg.

TBB — *Tijdschrift voor het Binnenlandsch Bestuur.*

TBG — *Tijdschrift voor Indische Taal-, Land- en Volkenkunde* published by the (Koninlijk) Bataviaasch Genootschap van Kunsten en Wetenschappen.

TNI — *Tijdschrift voor Nederlandsch-Indië.*

VKI — *Verhandelingen van het Koninklijk Instituut voor Taal-, Land- en Volkenkunde.*

Bibliography

Abdul Karim. *Social History of the Muslims in Bengal.* Dacca: Asiatic Society, 1959.
Abdul Majeed Mackeen. *Contemporary Islamic Legal Organization in Malaya.* New Haven: Yale University Southeast Asia Studies, 1969.
Abdul Majid bin Haji Zainuddin, Haji. *The Malayan Kaleidoscope.* Kuala Lumpur, 1935.
Abdullah bin Abdul Kadir, Munshi. *Hikayat Abdullah.* Annotated translation by A.H. Hill. Kuala Lumpur: Oxford University Press, 1970.
Abdullah Alwi Haji Hassan. "Islam di Singapura: Satu Pengenalan". In *Islamika I*, edited by Lutpi Ibrahim. Kuala Lumpur: Sarjana Enterprise, 1981.
Abdullah Zakaria b. Ghazali. "Islam dan Politik Anti-Penjajahan di Trengganu". In *Islamika II*, edited by Lutpi Ibrahim. Kuala Lumpur: Sarjana Enterprise, 1983.
Abdurrachman Wahid. "Prospek Pesantren Mamba'ul Ma'arif" (The Prospects for Mamba'ul Ma'arif Pesantren) . *Risalah Akhira Sanah* (Jakarta), 1972.
———. "Dakwah Islam dan Masalah Internasional". In *Dakwah Islam dan Perubahan Sosial,* edited by Amrullah Achmad. Yogyakarta: Prima Duta Yogyakarta, 1983.
———. "The Islamic Masses in the Life of State and Nation". *Prisma,* no. 35 (March 1985).
Aboebakar Atjeh, Haji. *Pengantar Ilmu Tarekat dan Tasauf.* Kota Bharu, Kelantan: Pustaka Aman Press, Sdn. Bhd., 1981.
———, ed. *Sedjarah Hidup K.H.A. Wahid Hasjim dan Karangan Terslar.* Djakarta, 1957.
Abu Bakar Hamzah. "Al-Imam and Politics". In *Islamika II,* edited by Lutpi Ibrahim. Kuala Lumpur, Sarjana Enterprise, 1983.
Ace Partadiredja. "Dakwah Islam Melalui Kebutuhan Pokok Manusia". In *Dakwah Islam dan Perubahan Sosial,* edited by Amrullah Achmad. Yogyakarta: Prima Duta Yogyakarta, 1983.
Ahmad Ibrahim. *Islamic Law in Malaya.* Singapore: Malaysian Sociological Research Institute, 1965.
———. "The Position of Islam in the Constitution of Malaysia". In *The Constitution of Malaysia, Its Development: 1957:1977,* edited by M. Suffian Hashim et al. Kuala Lumpur: Oxford University Press, 1978.
———. "Islamic Law in Malaysia". *Journal of Malaysian and Comparative Law — Jernal Undang-Undang,* 1981.
———. "Overview of Islamic Laws". *Syariah Law Journal,* November 1984.
Ahmad Syafi'i Ma'arif. "Islam and Nationalism in Indonesia". *Mizan* 1, no. 3 (1984).
Alatas, Syed Hussein. *Modernization and Social Change.* Sydney and London: Angus and Robertson (Publishers) Pte. Ltd., 1972.
———. *Kita Dengan Islam, Tumbuh Tiada Berbuah.* Singapore: Pustaka Nasional Pte. Ltd., 1979.
al-Attas, Syed Muhammad Naguib. *Some Aspects of Sufism as Understood and Practised Among the Malays.* Singapore: Malaysian Sociological Research Institute, 1963.

al-Attas, Syed Muhammad Naguib. *Rànīrī and the Wujūdiyyah of 17th Century Acheh.* Singapore: Malaysian Branch of the Royal Asiatic Society, Monograph III, 1966.

———. *Preliminary Statement on a General Theory of the Islamization of the Malay-Indonesia Archipelago.* Kuala Lumpur: Dewan Bahasa dan Pustaka, 1969.

———. *The Mysticism of Hamzah Fansuri.* Kuala Lumpur: University of Malaya Press, 1970.

Alfian. "Islamic Modernism in Indonesian Politics: The Muhammadijah Movement during the Dutch Colonial Period (1912–1942)". Ph.D. dissertation, University of Wisconsin, 1969.

———. "The Ulama in Acehnese Society". *Southeast Asian Journal of Social Science* 3, no. 1 (1975).

Algadri, Hamid. *C. Snouck Hurgronje, Politik Belanda terhadap Islam dan Keturunan Arab.* Jakarta: Sinar Harapan, 1984.

Ali, A. Yusuf. *The Holy Quran, Text, Translation and Commentary.* Lahore: Sh. Muhammad Ashraf, 1972.

Alisjahbana, S. Takdir. *Indonesia in the Modern World.* New Delhi: Office for Asian Affairs, Congress for Cultural Freedom, 1961.

Allamah Sayyid Mohammed Husayn Tabataba'i. *Sh'ite Islam.* London: George Allen & Unwin, 1975.

"Amanat Yang di-Pertuan Agong PAS Ulang Tahun 1958". In *Cenderamata Pembukaan Bangunan PAS Kelantan & Kongres PAS Ke 13.*

M. Amien Rais. "International Islamic Movements and Their Influence Upon the Islamic Movement in Indonesia". *Prisma,* no. 35 (March 1985).

Amrullah Achmad. "Dakwah Islam dan Perubahan Sosial". In *Dakwah Islam dan Perubahan Sosial,* edited by Amrullah Achmad. Yogyakarta: Prima Duta Yogyakarta, 1983.

———, ed. *Dakwah Islam dan Perubahan Sosial (Seminar Nasional dan Diskusi Pusat Latihan, Penelitian dan Pengembangan Masyarakat — PLP2M).* Yogyakarta: Prima Duta Yogyakarta, 1983.

Andaya, B.J.W. *Perak, the Abode of Grace: A Study of an Eighteenth Century Malay State.* Ithaca: Cornell University Press, 1975.

Andaya, Barbara Watson and Virginia Matheson. "Islamic Thought and Malay Tradition: The Writings of Raja Ali Haji of Riau (ca. 1809–ca. 1870)". In *Perceptions of the Past in Southeast Asia,* edited by Anthony Reid and David Marr. Kuala Lumpur: Heinemann Educational Books (Asia) Ltd., 1979.

Anderson, B.R.O'G. "The Idea of Power in Javanese Culture". In *Culture and Politics in Indonesia,* edited by C. Holt, B.R.O'G. Anderson, and J. Siegel. Ithaca: Cornell University Press, 1972.

Anrooiji, H.A. Hijmans. "Nota omtrent het rijk van Siak". *TBG* XXX (1885).

Anshari, E. *Kritik atas Faham dan Gerakan 'Pembaharuan' Drs. Nurcholish Madjid.* Bandung, 1973.

Anwar Ibrahim. "Islam — Penyelesaian Kepada Masalah Masyarakat Majmuk". Kuala Lumpur: ABIM, n.d.

H. Aqib Suminto. *Politik Islam Hindia Belanda.* Jakarta: LP3ES, 1985.

Arce, Wilfredo, F. *Before the Secessionist Storm: Muslim-Christian Politics in Jolo, Sulu, Philippines, 1961–62.* ISEAS Occasional Paper, no. 73. Singapore: Maruzen Asia, 1983.

Archer, R.L. "Muhammadan Mysticism in Sumatra". *Journal of the Royal Asiatic Society — Malayan Branch XV.* Part II.

Arnold, T.W. *The Preaching of Islam.* London, 1913.

Asip F. Hadipranata. "Dakwah Islam dan Masyarakat Industri". In *Dakwah Islam dan Perubahan Sosial,* edited by Amrullah Achmad. Yogyakarta: Prima Duta Yogyakarta, 1983.

Atho Mudzhar. "Religious Education and Religious Harmony in Indonesia". *Mizan* 1, no. 2 (1984).

Awang Had Salleh. "Modern Concept of Hajj Management: The case of Malaysia". In *Hajj Studies*, edited by Z. Sardar and M.A. Zaki Badawi. Vol. 1. London: Croom Helm, 1979.

Aziz Ahmad. *An Intellectual History of Islam in India.* Edinburgh: Edinburgh University Press, 1969.

———. *Studies in Islamic Culture in the Indian Environment.* Oxford: Oxford University Press, 1969.

Azizan bin Abdul Razak. "Conflict Resolution: Personal Law System, Civil Law System and Muslim Schools of Law (Madahib)". *Syariah Law Journal,* November 1984.

Bachtiar Effendi. "Politics and the Student Movement". *Mizan* 1, no. 3 (1984).
Bagley, F.R.C., trans. and ed. *Ghazālī's Book of Counsel for Kings (Nasīhat al-Mulūk).* London: Oxford University Press, 1964.
Al-Bahist. "Kronik dan Komentar Islam". *Gema Islam* I, no. 8 (May 1962).
———. "Kronik dan Komentar Islam". *Gema Islam* I, no. 11 (15 November 1962).
Bahm, Archie J. *The World's Living Religions.* New York: Dell Publication Co., 1964.
Bakker, S.J., J.W.M. "De Godsdienstvrijheid in de Indonesische Grondwetten". *Het Missiwerk,* 4 (1956).
Balandier, G. "Messianisme et nationalisme en Afrique Noire". *CIS* XIV (1953).
Banton, Michael. "Intertribal Relations Among Immigrants in a West African City". In *Urbanization and Migration in West Africa,* edited by Hilda Kuper. Berkeley: University of California Press, 1965.
Bautista, Esteban B. "The Muslim Code: Towards National Unity in Diversity". Mimeographed. Quezon City: U.P. Law Center, 1977.
Bellah, Robert. "Islamic Tradition and the Problems of Modernization". In *Beyond Belief.* New York: Harper and Row, 1970.
Benda, Harry J. "Christiaan Snouck Hurgronje and the Foundations of Dutch Islamic Policy in Indonesia". *The Journal of Modern History* 30 (1958).
———. *The Crescent and the Rising Sun: Indonesian Islam under the Japanese Occupation 1942–1945.* The Hague and Bandung: W. van Hoeve, 1958.
———. "The Structure of Southeast Asian History: Some Preliminary Observations". *JSAH* III, no. 1 (1962).
Benda, J. *The Treason of the Intellectuals.* Translated by R. Aldington. New York: W.W. Norton & Co., 1969.
Berg, L.W.C. van den. "De Mohammedaansche geestelijkheid en de geestelijke goederen op Java en Madoera". *TBG* XVII (1882).
———. "Het Panislamisme". *De Gids,* IVth Series, Vol. LXIV (1900).
———. "De Mohammedaansche Vorsten in Nederlandsche-Indië". *BKI* VI, no. 9 (1901).
———. *De Inlandsche Rangen en Titels op Java en Madoera.* 's-Gravenhage, 1902.
———, ed. and trans. *Minhāj al-tālibīn.* 3 vols. Batavia, 1882–84.
Birch, W. de G. de. *The Commentaries of the Great Alfonso Dalboquerque.* London: Hakluyt Society, 1880.
Bodrogi, T. "Colonization and Religious Movements in Melanesia". *Acta Ethnographica Academiae Scientiarum Hungaricae.* Vol. II, 1951.
Boland, B.J. *The Struggle of Islam in Modern Indonesia.* The Hague: Martinus Nijhoff, 1971.
van den Bosch, A. *The Dutch East Indies: Its Government, Problems and Politics.* Berkeley/Los Angeles: University of California Press, 1944.
Bousquet, G.H. "Introduction à l'ètude de l'Islam Indonésian". *Revue des études Islamiques,* 1938.
Bousquet, G.H. and J. Schacht, *Selected Works of C. Snouck Hurgronje.* Edited in English & French. Leiden: E.J. Brill, 1957.
Boxker, C.R. "Francisco Vieira de Fibueiredo, A Portuguese Merchant-Adventurer in South East Asia, 1624–1667". *VKI* 52 (1967).
Brown, D.E. *Brunei: The Structure and History of a Bornean Malay Sultanate.* Monograph of the Museum Journal 2, no. 2(1970).
Bruger, D.H. "Het B.B. op Java". In *Gedenkboek van de Indologen Vereniging van Ambtenaren bij het Binnenlands Bestuur in Nederlands-Indië.* Utrecht, 1956.
Brugmans, I.J. *Geschidenis van het onderwijs in Nederlandsch-Indië.* Groningen: 1938.
Bruner, E.M. "Urbanization and Ethnic Identity in North Sumatra". AA 63 (1961).
Bucknill, J.A.S. "Observations upon some coins obtained in Malaya . . .". *JMBRAS* 1 (1923).
Burridge, K.O.L. "Race Relations in Johore". *Australian Journal of Politics and History* 2(1957).

Bustanul Arifin. "The Administration of Shariah Laws in Indonesia". *Syariah Law Journal,* November 1984.
Buxbaum, D.C. *Family Law and Customary Law in Asia.* The Hague: Martinus Nijhoff, 1968.

"Cambodia — Land of Islam". *Sud Est Asie,* March 1981.
Casparis, J.G. de. *Prasasti Indonesia,* II. Bandung: A.C. Nix and Co., 1956.
Cenderamata Muktamar Senawi Ke 8. Angkatan Belia Islam Malaysia, 18hb–20hb Sya'aban 1399/13hb–15hb. Universiti Kebangsaan Malaysia, Julai 1979.
Clifford, Hugh. *In Court and Kampong.* London: Grant Richards, 1897.
———. *Studies in Brown Humanity.* London: Grant Richards, 1898.
Coedès, G. "Les inscriptions malaises de Crīvijaya". *Bulletin de l'Ecole Française d'Extrême Orient* (Hanoi) XXX (1930).
Cortesão, A., ed. *The Suma Oriental of Tomé Pires.* London: Hakluyt Society, 1944.
Coulson, N.J. *A History of Islamic Law.* Edinburgh: University of Edinburgh, 1964.
———. "The Concept of Progress and Islamic Law". *Quest,* n.d.
Cowan, H.J.K. *Dē "Hikayat Malem Dagang".* 's-Gravenhage, 1937.
———. "Bijdragen tot de kennis der geschiedenis van het rijk Samoedra-Pase". *TBG* LXXVIII, 1938.
Crawfurd, John. *History of the Indian Archipelago.* 3 vols. Edinburgh: University of Edinburgh, 1820.
Cuisinier, Jeanne. *Danses Magiques de Kelantan* (Travaux et Memoires de l'Institut d'Ethnologie) XXII. Paris: Institut d'Ethnologie, 1936.
———. *Le Théatre d'Ombres à Kelantan.* Paris: Gallimard, 1957.
———. "La guerre des Padri 1803–1838–1845". *Archives de sociologie des religions* IV, no. 7 (1959).

Dagh-register, gehouden int casteel Batavia vant passerende daer ter plaetse als over geheel Nederlandts India. 's-Hage, 1896–1931.
Dahm, Bernhard. "Sukarnos Kampf um Indonesiens Unabhängigkeit". *SIAH* XVIII 1966.
———. "Religion and Resistance in Colonial Southeast Asia". *Spectrum,* January 1971.
Dalrymple, Alexander. "Essay towards an account of Sulu". *Journal of the Indian Archipelago and Eastern Asia* (Singapore) III (1849).
Damais, L-Ch. "Études javanaises: I, les tombes musulmanes datées de Trālājā". *BEFEO* 48 (1957).
———. "L'épigraphie musulmane dans le sud-est asiatique". *BEFEO* 54 (1968).
Danois, Jacques. *Period of Resurrection.* UNICEF, May 1980.
M. Dawam Rahardjo. "The Kyai, the Pesantren and the Village: A Preliminary Sketch". *Prisma,* 1975.
———. "Pembaharuan Pemahaman Islam". In *Dakwah Islam dan Perubahan Sosial,* edited by Amrullah Achmad. Yogyakarta: Prima Duta Yogyakarta, 1983.
———. "Islam, Sailing Between Two Reefs: Socialism and Capitalism". *Prisma,* no. 35 (March 1985).
Deliar Noer. *The Modernist Movement in Indonesia, 1900–1942.* Singapore/Kuala Lumpur: Oxford University Press, 1973.
———. "Diperlukan Pendekatan Bukan Barat Terhadap Kajian Masyarakat Indonesia". In *Penelitian Agama, Masalah dan Pemikiran,* edited by Mulyanto Sumardi. Jakarta: Sinar Harapan, 1982.
Deventer, M.L. van. *Geschiedenis der Nederlanders op Java.* 2 vols. Haarlem, 1886–1887.
Dhavamony, M. *Love of God, according to Saiva Siddhanta.* Oxford: Oxford University Press, 1971.
Dijk, C. van. *Rebellion under the Banner of Islam; The Darul Islam in Indonesia.* The Hague: Martinus Nijhoff, 1981.
Dion, M., trans. and ed. "Sumatra through Portuguese eyes: excerpts from Joao de Barros, Decadas da Asia". *Indonesia* (Ithaca N.Y.) 9 (1970).

Djajadiningrat, R.A.H. *Critische Beschouwing van de Sadjarah Banten*. Thesis, Leiden, 1913.
Djamour, Judith. *Malay Kinship and Marriage in Singapore*. New York: Humanities Press, 1963.
Djohan Effendi and Moeslim Abdurrahman. "Pertumbuhan Islam di Pemukiman Baru". In *Penelitian Agama, Masalah dan Pemikiran*, edited by Mulyanto Sumardi. Jakarta: Sinar Harapan, 1982.
Dobbin, Christine. *Islamic Revivalism in a Changing Peasant Economy, Central Sumatra, 1784–1847*. Scandinavian Institute of Asian Studies Monograph Series, no. 47. London and Malmö: Curzon Press, 1983.
Draguhn, Werner. *Der Einfluss des Islams auf Politik, Wirtschaft und Gesellschaft in Sudostasien*. Mitteilungen des Institut für Asienkunde, no. 133. Hamburg: Institut für Asienkunde, 1983.
Drewes, G.W.J. *Drie Javaansche Goeroe's. Hun Leven, Onderricht en Messias-prediking*. Leiden: E.J. Brill, 1925.
———. "Sech Joesoep Makasar (van Banten, later aan de kaap)". *Djawa* VI (1926).
———. "Indonesia: Mysticism and Activism". In *Unity and Variety in Muslim Civilization*, edited by Gustav E. von Grunebaum. Chicago: University of Chicago Press, 1955.
———. "New Light on the Coming of Islam to Indonesia?" *BKI* 124, no 4 (1968).
Drewes, G.W.J., ed. and trans. *Een Javaanse primbon uit de zestiende eeuw*. Leiden, 1954.
———. *The Admonitions of Seh Bari*. The Hague: Martinus Nijhoff, 1969.
Drewes, G.W.J. and Poerbatjaraka, eds. "De mirakelen van Abdoelkadir Djaelani". *BJ* (Batavia) VIII (1938).
DuBois, Cora. *Social Forces in Southeast Asia*. St. Paul: University of Minnesota Press, 1949.
Dumont, L. *Homo hierarchicus: the caste system and its implications*. London: Oxford University Press, 1972.
Dzulkifli bin Mohd. Salleh, ed. *Hikayat Merong Mahawangsa*. Kuala Lumpur: Dewan Bahasa, 1973.

Eerde, J.C. van. "De adat volgens Minangkabausche bronnen". *Wet en Adat* I/II.
Eisenberger, J. *Indië en de bedevaart naar Mekka*. Leiden, 1928.
Emerson, Rupert. *Malaysia: A Study in Direct and Indirect Rule*. New York, 1937.
Emmet, D. "Prophets and Their Societies". *JRAI* LXXXVI 1956.

Fatimi, S.Q. *Islam Comes to Malaysia*. Singapore: Singapore University Press, 1963.
Favre, P. "A journey in Johore". *Journal of the Indian Archipelago* III (1849).
———. *Dictionnaire Malais-Français*. 2 vols. Paris: Maisonneuve et Cie, 1875.
Federspiel, H.M. "The Military and Islam in Sukarno's Indonesia". *Pacific Affairs* 46, no. 3 (1973).
Feith, Herbert. *The Decline of Constitutional Democracy in Indonesia*. Ithaca, N.Y.: Cornell University Press, 1962.
———. *The Indonesian Election of 1955*. Interim Report Series, Modern Indonesia Project. Ithaca, N.Y.: Cornell University, 1971.
Feith, Herbert and Lance Castles, eds. *Indonesian Political Thinking 1945–1965*. Ithaca, N.Y.: Cornell University Press, 1970.
Firth, Raymond. *Malay Fishermen: Their Peasant Economy*. 2nd ed. London: Routledge & Kegan Paul, 1966.
———. "Faith and Skepticism in Kelantan Village Magic". In *Kelantan, Religion, Society and Politics in a Malay State*, edited by W.R. Roff. Kuala Lumpur: Oxford University Press, 1974.
Fokkens, F. "De priesterschool te Tagalsari". *TBG* 24 (1877).
Francis, E. *Herinneringen uit de levensloop van een Indisch ambtenaar van 1815 tot 1851*. 3 vols. Batavia, 1856–1860.
Francis, E. "Korte Beschrijving van het Nederlandsch grondgebied ter Westkust van Sumatra". *TNI* II (1839).

Fraser, Thomas M., Jr. *Rusembilan: A Malay Fishing Village in Southern Thailand.* Ithaca: Cornell University Press, 1960.
Freedman, Maurice. "The Chinese in Southeast Asia". In *Race Relations in World Perspective*, edited by Andrew Lind. Honolulu: University of Hawaii Press, 1955.
Funston, N.J. *Malay Politics in Malaysia. A Study of the United Malays National Organisation and Party Islam.* Kuala Lumpur: Heinemann Educational Books (Asia) Ltd., 1980.
———. "Malaysia". In *The Politics of Islamic Reassertion*, edited by Mohammed Ayoob. London: Croom Helm, 1981.
Furnivall, J.S. *Netherlands India: A Study of Plural Economy.* London: Cambridge University Press, 1944.

Gazalba, Sidi. *Modernisasi Dalam Persoalan: Bagaimana Sikap Islam?* Jakarta: Bulan Bintang, 1973.
Geertz, Clifford. *The Religion of Java.* New York: The Free Press of Glencoe, 1960.
———. *Peddlars and Princes. Social Change and Economic Modernization in Two Indonesian Towns.* Chicago: University of Chicago Press, 1963.
———. "Ideology as a Cultural System". In *Ideology of Discontent,* edited by D. Apter. New York: The Free Press, 1964.
———. "Religion as a Cultural System". In *The Religious Situation,* edited by D. Cutler. Boston: Beacon Press, 1968.
Gericke, J.F.C. and T. Roorda. *Javaansch-Nederlandsch handwoordenboek.* Revised edition, edited by A.C. Vreede and J.G.H. Gunning. 2 vols. Amsterdam and Leiden, 1901.
Gibb, H.A.R. *Ibn Battuta's Travels in Asia and Africa 1325–1354.* London: Routledge, 1929.
———. *The Modern Trends in Islam.* Chicago: University of Chicago Press, 1947.
———. *Mohammedanism.* New York: Oxford University Press, 1962.
Gibb, H.A.R. and H. Bowen. *Islamic Society and the West.* Oxford: Oxford University Press, 1957.
Gibb, H.A.R., trans. and ed. *The Travels of Ibn Battuta A.D. 1325–1354.* Cambridge: Hakluyt, 1958.
Gimlette, J.D. "Some Superstitious Beliefs Occurring in the Theory and Practice of Malay Medicine". *JSBRAS* 65 (1913).
———. *Malay Poisons and Charm Cures.* London: J. & A. Churchill, 1915 (3rd ed., 1929).
Gobée, E. and C. Adriaanse, eds. *Ambtelijke adviezen van C. Snouck Hurgronje, 1889–1936.* 3 vols. 's-Gravenhage, 1957–1965.
Goitein, S.D. *Studies in Islamic History and Tradition.* Leiden: Brill, 1968.
Goldhizer I. *Muslim Studies* II. Translated by Barber and Stern. Albany: State University of New York Press, 1971.
Gonda, J. *Sanskrit in Indonesia.* New Delhi: 1973.
Gowing, Peter G. "Moros and Khaek: The Position of Muslim Minorities in the Philippines and Thailand". *Southeast Asian Affairs 1975.* Singapore: ISEAS, 1975.
Graaf, H.J. de. "De opkomst van Raden Trunadjaja". *Djawa* 20 (1940).
———. *De Geschiedenis van Indonesië.* 's-Gravenhage, 1949.
———. "Gevangenneming en dood van Raden Truna-Djaja, 26 Dec. 1679–2 Jan. 1680". *TBG* 85, no. 2 (1952).
———. "De regering van Sultan Agung, vorst van Mataram, 1613–1645, en die van zijn voorganger Panembahan Séda-ing-Krapjak 1601–1613". *VKI* 23 (1958).
Graaf, H.J. de and Th.G.Th. Pigeaud. "De Eerste Moslimse Vorstendommen op Java. Studiën over de Staatkundige Geschiedenis van de 15e en 16e Eeuw". *VKI* LXIX (1974).
Groneman, J. "De Garebeas te Ngajogyakarta". *BKI* 46 (1896).
Grunebaum, Gustave E. von. *Modern Islam: The Search for Cultural Identity.* Berkeley: University of California Press, 1962.
———. *Medieval Islam.* Chicago: Chicago University Press, 1971.
Guariglia, G. *Prophetismus und Heilserwartungs-Bewegungen als völkerkundliches und religionsgeschichtliches Problem.* Horn-Wien, 1959.
Gullick, J.M. "The Malay Administrator". *Merdeka Outlook,* no. 1 (May 1957).

Hadiwijono, Harun. *Man in the Present Javanese Mysticism.* Baarn: Bosch and Kenning, 1967.
Hamka. *Ajahku: Riwayat Hidup Dr. Abd. Karim Amrullah dan Perdjuangan Kaum Agama.* Djakarta, 1950.
———. *Adat Minangkabau Menghadapi Revolusi.* Djakarta, 1962.
———. *Prinsip dan Kebijaksanaan Da'wah Islam.* Kuala Lumpur: Pustaka Melayu Baru, 1981.
Harsja W. Bachtiar. "The Religion of Java: A Commentary". *Madjalah Ilmu-Ilmu Sastra Indonesia* 5 (1973).
Hasan Muarif Ambary. "Pendekatan Arkeologi Dalam Penelitian Agama di Indonesia". In *Penelitian Agama, Masalah dan Pemikiran,* edited by Mulyanto Sumardi. Jakarta: Sinar Harapan, 1982.
Hasjmy, Ali. *Hikayat Prang Sabi mendjiwai Perang Atdjeh lawan Belanda.* Banda Atjeh [Acheh]: Pustaka Faraby, 1971.
Hasselt, A.L. van. *Volksbeschrijving van Midden Sumatra.* Leiden, 1882.
Herinneringen van Pangeran Aria Achmad Djajadininggrat. Amsterdam/Batavia, 1936.
Hidayat Nataatmadja. "Dakwah Islam di Masa Datang". In *Dakwah Islam dan Perubahan Sosial,* edited by Amrullah Achmad. Yogyakarta: Prima Duta Yogyakarta, 1983.
Hien, H.A. van. *De Javaansche Geestenwereld.* 3 vols. Batavia, 1934.
Hill, A.H., ed. "Hikayat Raja-Raja Pasai". *JMBRAS* XXXIII (1960).
Hindley, Donald. *The Communist Party in Indonesia, 1951–1963.* Berkeley: University of California Press, 1964.
Hodgson, M.G.S. *The Venture of Islam.* Chicago: Chicago University Press, 1974.
Hollander, J.J. de. *Hundleiding bij de beoefening der land -en volkenkunde von Nederlandsch Oost-Indië.* 2 vols. Breda, 1861–64.
Hooker, M.B. *A Concise Legal History of South-East Asia.* Oxford: Clarendon Press, 1978.
———, ed. *Islam in South-East Asia.* Leiden: E.J. Brill, 1983. 983.
Hooykaas, C. *Over Maleise Literatur.* Leiden: E.J. Brill, 1947.
Howard, E.C. *Minhaj et Talibin.* London, 1914.
Hourani, A.H. and S.M. Stern, eds. *The Islamic City.* Oxford: Oxford University Press, 1970.
Howison, James. *A Dictionary of the Malay Tongue.* London: Arabic and Persian Press, 1801.
Humphreys, R. Stephen. "Islam and Political Values in Saudi Arabia, Egypt and Syria". *Middle East Journal* 33, no. 1 (Winter 1979).
Hunke, Sigrid. *Allah's Sonne über dem Abendland.* Frankfurt: Fischer Bucherei, 1965.
Husin Ali, S. *Malay Peasant Society and Leadership.* Kuala Lumpur: Oxford University Press, 1975.
———, ed. *Kaum, Kelas dan Pembangunan Ethnicity, Class and Development — Malaysia.* Kuala Lumpur: Persatuan Sains Sosial Malaysia, 1984.

Ibn Khaldun, Abu Zaid Abd, and Rahman. *The Muqaddimah: An Introduction to History.* 3 vols. Trans. F. Rosenthal. London: Routledge & Kegan Paul, 1958.
Ibrahim A. Ragab. "Islam and Development". In *Islamika II,* edited by Lutpi Ibrahim. Kuala Lumpur: Sarjana Enterprise, 1983.
Ibrahim Engku Ismail, Engku. "Sumbangan Islam dalam Bidang Perubatan". In *Islamika II,* edited by Lutpi Ibrahim. Kuala Lumpur: Sarjana Enterprise, 1983.
Ibrahim Yaacob. *Sekitar Malaya Merdeka.* Djakarta? 1957.
Idris, Mohammad Isa. "Persoalan pemuda remadja kita sekarang". *Gema Islam I,* no. 8 (15 May 1962).
Iftikhar Ahmad Ghauri. "Kingship in the Sultanate of Bajapur and Golconda". *Islamic Culture* XLVI (1972).
Imam Munawwir. *Kebangkitan Islam dan Tantangan-Tantangan yang dihadapi dari masa ke masa.* Surabaya: Bina Ilmu, 1984.
Indonesia, Angkatan Darat, Pusat Islam, *Pedoman Agama Islam untuk TNI.* Djakarta, 1962.
Indonesia, Angkatan Darat, Komando Mandala, Rawatan Rohani Islam. *Shalot Dalam Tugas Tempir, Pembebasan Irian Barat.* Djakarta, 1962.

Indonesia, Angkatan Darat, Pusat Rawatan Rohani Islam. *'Idul Fithri dan Zakat Fithrah*. Djakarta, 1964.
Tk. Ismail Yakub. "Dakwah Islam dan Kepastian Hukum". In *Dakwah Islam dan Perubahan Sosial,* edited by Amrullah Achmad. Yogyakarta: Prima Duta Yogyakarta, 1983.
Ismuha. "Lahirnja 'Persatuan Ulama Seluruh Atjeh' 30 Tahun yang Lalu". *Sinar Darussalam* 14 & 15 (1969).

Jansen, G.A. *Militant Islam*. London: Pan Books, 1979.
Jasper, J.E. "Het animisme op Java". *Indische Gids* 57 (1935).
Jay, Robert R. *Javanese Villagers.* Cambridge, Massachusetts: The MIT Press, 1969.
Johns, A.H. *Rantjak di Labueh: A Minangkabau Kaba.* Ithaca, N.Y.: Cornell University, Southeast Asia Program Data Paper No. 32, 1958.
———. "The Role of Sufism in the Spread of Islam to Malaya and Indonesia". *Journal of the Pakistan Historical Society* IX (1961).
———. "Sufism as a Category in Indonesian Literature and History". *JSAH* II, no. 2 (1961).
———. "Muslim Mystics and Historical Writing". In *Historians of South East Asia,* edited by D.G.E. Hall. London: Oxford University Press, 1963.
———, ed. and trans. *The Gift Addressed to the Spirit of the Prophet*. Canberra: ANU Press, 1965.
———. "Islam in Southeast Asia: Reflections and New Directions". *Indonesia* XIX (April 1975).
———. "Islam in Southeast Asia: Problems of Perspective". In *Southeast Asian History and Historiography: Essays Presented to D.G.E. Hall*, edited by C.D. Cowan and O.W. Wolters. Ithaca, N.Y.: Cornell University Press, 1976.
Jones, R. "Ten conversion myths from Indonesia". In *Conversion to Islam*, edited by N. Levtzion. New York: Holmes and Meier, Inc., 1979.
Jones, Sidney. "The Contraction and Expansion of the 'Umat' and the Role of the Nahdatul Ulama in Indonesia". *Indonesia,* no. 38 (October 1984).
Josselin de Jong, P. E. de. *Minangkabau and Negri Sembilan: Socio-Political Structure in Indonesia.* Leiden: Eduard Ijdo, 1951.
———. "De visie der participaten op hun cultuur". *BKI* 112 (1956).
———. "Islam versus Adat in Negri Sembilan". *BKI* 116 (1960).
Juynboll, Th. W. *Handleiding tot de Kennis van de Moehammedaansche Wet, volgens de leider der Sjafi'itische school.* 4th ed. Leiden: Brill, 1930.

Kahin, George McT. *Nationalism and Revolution in Indonesia.* Ithaca, N.Y.: Cornell University Press, 1952.
Kamarudin Jaffar. "Malay Political Parties: An Interpretative Essay". *Southeast Asian Affairs 1979.* Singapore: ISEAS, 1979.
———. *Dr. Burhanuddin al Helmy, Politik Melayu dan Islam.* Kuala Lumpur: Yayasan Anda Pte. Ltd., 1980.
———. "Brothers in Progress: The Role of the Islamic Secretariat in Muslim World Development". In *Islamika I,* edited by Lutpi Ibrahim et al. Kuala Lumpur: Sarjana Enterprise, 1981.
Kamus Dewan. Kuala Lumpur: Dewan Bahasa dan Pustaka, 1970.
Kartini, Raden Adjeng. *Letters of a Javanese Princess*. London, 1921.
Kassim Ahmad. *Kisah Pelayaran Abdallah*. Kuala Lumpur: Oxford University Press, 1964.
———. *Hikayat Hang Tuah*. Kuala Lumpur: Oxford University Press, 1968.
Kempe, J.E. and R.O. Winstedt. "A Malay Legal Digest Compiled for 'Abd al-Ghafur Muhaiyu'd-din Shah, Sultan of Pahang 1592–1614 A.D. with undated additions". *JMBRAS* XXI (1948).
Kerr, Malcolm. *Islamic Reform*. Berkeley: University of California Press, 1966.

Kessler, C.S. "Islam, Society and Political Behaviour: Some Comparative Implications of the Malay Case". *British Journal of Sociology* 23 (1972).
———. "The Politics of Islamic Egalitarianism". In *Humaniora Islamica II*, edited by H.W. Mason et al. 1974.
———. *Islam and Politics in a Malay State: Kelantan 1838–1969*. Ithaca, N.Y.: Cornell University Press, 1978.
Keyzer, S. *Précis de Jurisprudence Musulmane par Abou Chodja*. Leiden, 1859.
Khalid Hussain, ed. *Taj us-Salatin*. Kuala Lumpur: Dewan Bahasa dan Pustaka, 1966.
Khalifah Abdul Hakim. "Renaissance in Indo-Pakistan: Iqbal". In *A History of Muslim Philosophy*, edited by M.M. Sharif. Vol. 2. Wiesbaden: Otto Harrassowitz, 1966.
Kiefer, T.M. *The Tausug, Violence and Law in a Philippine Muslim Society*. New York: Holt, Rinehart and Winston, Inc., 1972.
Klerck, E.S. *History of the Netherlands East Indies*. Rotterdam: 1938.
Klausner, C.L. *The Seljuk Vizirate, A Study of Civil Administration 1055–1194*. Cambridge: Centre for Middle Eastern Studies for Harvard University, 1973.
Köbben, A.J.F. "Profetische bewegingen als uiting van sociaal protest". *Sociologisch Jaarboek* XIII (1959).
Koentjaraningrat, R.M. *A Preliminary Description of the Javanese Kinship System*. Yale: Yale University Press, 1957.
———. "Javanese Terms for God and Supernatural Beings and the Idea of Power". In *Man, Meaning and History, Essays in Honor of H.G. Schulte Nordholt, VKI* 89, edited by R. Schefold et al. The Hague: Martinus Nijhoff, 1980.
Koentowodijoyo. "Dakwah Islam dalam Perspektif Historis". In *Dakwah Islam dan Perubahan Sosial*, edited by Amrullah Achmad. Yogyakarta: Prima Duta Yogyakarta, 1983.
Kraemer, H. *Een Javaansche Primbon uit de Zestiende Eeuw*. Leiden, 1921.
———. "Geloof en Mystiek, Naar aanleiding van 'Mystik und Glaube' door B.M. Schuurman". *De Opwekker* LXXIX (1934).
van der Kroef, J.M. "Prince Diponegoro: Progenitor of Indonesian Nationalism". *Far Eastern Quarterly* 8 (1949).
———. *The Communist Party of Indonesia, Its History, Program and Tactics*. Vancouver: University of British Columbia, 1965.
"Kursus Dinas Imam Militer". *Gema Islam* I, no. 12 (15 July 1962).

Lambton, A.K.S. "Quis Custodiet Custodes: Some Reflections on the Persian Theory of Government". *Studia Islamica* V (1956).
———. "The Internal Structure of the Saljuq Empire". In *The Cambridge History of Iran*. Cambridge: University of Cambridge, 1958.
———. "Justice in the Medieval Persian Theory of Kingship". *Studia Islamica* XI (1962).
Landon, K.P. *Southeast Asia: Crossroads of Religions*. Chicago: University of Chicago Press, 1947.
Lanternari, Vittorio. *The Religions of the Oppressed; A Study of Modern Messianic Cults*. New York, 1963.
"Laporan Survey Pesantren di Jawa Timur". Report by students of the Adab Faculty of Syarif Hidajatullah IAIN, Ciputal, Jakarta, 1967.
"Laporan Penelitian dan Seminar Pendidikan pada Perguruan Agama". Departemen Agama, Djakarta, 1970–71.
Legge, J.D. "Indonesia's Search for Identity". In *Indonesia*, edited by J.D. Legge. New Jersey: Prentice-Hall, Inc., 1964.
Lev, D. *Islamic Courts in Indonesia: A Study in the Political Basis of Legal Institutions*. Berkeley: University of California Press, 1972.
Liaw Yock Fang. *Undang-undang Melaka*. The Hague: Martinus Nijhoff, 1976.
Lienhardt, G. *Divinity and Experience*. Oxford: Oxford University Press, 1967.
Lombard, Denys. *Le Sultanat d'Atjéh au temps d'Iskandar Muda, 1607–1636*. Paris: École d'Extrême-Orient, 1967.

Low, J. "Kedah Annals". *Journal of the Indian Archipelago* III (1849).
Ludjito, A. "Mengapa Penelitian Agama?" In *Penelitian Agama, Masalah dan Pemikiran*, edited by Mulyanto Sumardi. Jakarta: Sinar Harapan, 1982.
Lutfi, Ahmad. "Kewajipan Ulama Islam". *Seruan Ashar* I, no. 5 (February 1926).
Lutpi Ibrahim et al., eds. *Islamika I, Esei-Esei Sempena Abad Ke-15 Hijrah*. Kuala Lumpur: Sarjana Enterprise, 1981.
———. *Islamika II*. Kuala Lumpur: Sarjana Enterprise, 1983.

van der Maaten, K. *Snouck Hurgronje en de Atjeh Oorlog*. Leiden, 1948.
Mabbett, I.W. *Truth, Myth and Politics in Ancient India*. New Delhi, 1972.
Macciolchi, Maria Antonietta. "Cambodia — with the Survivors of the Genocide, if Any". *Noevel Observateur*, 12 Sept. 1981.
Mackeen, A.M.M. *Contemporary Islamic Legal Organization in Malaya*. New Haven, Conn.: Yale University Southeast Asia Studies, 1969.
Macpherson, C.B. *The Political Theory of Possessive Individualism: Hobbes to Locke*. London: Oxford University Press, 1962.
Mahfodz Muhamed. "Undang-undang Jinayah Islam: Kedudukan dan Pelaksanaannya Dalam Enakmen Pentadbiran Undang-Undang Islam di Malaysia". In *Islamika II*, edited by Lutpi Ibrahim et al. Kuala Lumpur: Sarjana Enterprise, 1983.
Majul, Cesar Adib. *Muslims in the Philippines*. 2nd ed. Quezon City: U.P. Press, 1973.
———. "An Analysis of the Genealogy of Sulu". Paper prepared for a Filipino Muslim History and Culture Seminar — Workshop Department of History, College of Arts and Sciences, University of the East, Manila, 20 Oct. 1977.
———. "The General Nature of Islamic Law and its Application in the Philippines". Mimeographed. Quezon City: Institute of Islamic Studies, 1977.
———. *Islam and Development*. edited by Michael O. Mastura. Manila: Office of the Commissioner for Islamic Affairs, 1980.
H. Mahmud Yunus. *Sejarah Pendidikan Islam di Indonesia*. 2ed. Jakarta: Mutiara 1979.
Malaysia, Department of Statistics. *1970 Population and Housing Census of Malaysia: Community Groups*. Kuala Lumpur: Government Printer, 1972.
Marsden, W. *History of Sumatra*. London, 1783.
———. *A Dictionary of the Malayan Language*. London, 1812.
———. *A Grammar of the Malay Language*. London, 1812.
Marrison, G.E. "Persian Influence on Malay life". *JMBRAS* XXVIII (1955).
Marx, K. "A Contribution to the Critique of Hegel's Philosophy of Right: Introduction." In *Critique of Hegel's Philosophy of Right*, edited by K. Marx. Trans. and ed. by J. O'Malley and A. Jolin. Cambridge: Cambridge University Press, 1970.
Mastura, Michael O. Datu. *Muslim Filipino Experience, A Collection of Essays*. Manila: Ministry of Muslim Affairs, Philippine Islam Series no. 3, 1984.
———. "The Administration of Muslim Personal Laws in a Muslim-Minority Country". *Syariah Law Journal*, November 1984.
Matheson, V. and A.C. Milner. *Perceptions of the Haj, Five Malay Texts*. Singapore: ISEAS, 1984.
Mattulada. "Penelitian Berbagai Aspek Keagamaan Dalam Kehidupan Masyarakat dan Kebudayaan di Indonesia". In *Penelitian Agama, Masalah dan Pemikiran*, edited by Mulyanto Sumardi. Jakarta: Sinar Harapan, 1982.
Maududi, Sayyid Abdul A'la. *The Islamic Law & Constitution*. Trans. and ed. by Khurshid Ahmad. Lahore: Islamic Publications Ltd., 1955.
Mawardi. *Al-Ahkām al-sultaṇiyyah*. Cairo, 1960.
Maxwell, W.E. "The Laws and Customs of the Malays with Reference to Land". *JMBRAS* XIII (1884).
Maxwell and Gibson. *Treaties and Engagements Affecting the Malay States and Borneo*. London, 1924.

McVey, Ruth. "Faith as the Outsider: Islam in Indonesian Politics". In *Islam in the Political Process*, edited by James P. Piscatori. Cambridge: Cambridge University Press, 1983.

Meijer, D.H. "Bijgeloof in dienst van de politie en m'sdadigers". *Djawa* 15 (1935).

Meilink-Roelofsz, M.A.P. "Trade and Islam in the Malay-Indonesian archipelago". In *Islam and the Trade of Asia*, edited by D.S. Richards. Oxford: Oxford University Press, 1970.

———. *Asian Trade and European Influence in the Indonesian Archipelago between 1500 and about 1630.* The Hague: Martinus Nijhoff, 1962.

"Mengenang: Seorang Pembela Rakyat dan Tokoh Perjuangan Nasional Tig Zaman". *Harian Mimbar Umum*, 24 October 1974.

"Menudju Da'wah Islamyah jang Lebih Sempurna". *Gema Islam* I, no. 8 (15 May 1962).

Mills, J.V.G., ed. *Ma Huan: Ying Yai Sheng-Lan.* Cambridge: Cambridge University Press, 1970.

Milner, A.C. "Islam and Malay Kinship". *Journal of the Royal Asiatic Society of Great Britain and Ireland* 1 (1981).

———. *Kerajaan: Malay Political Culture on the Eve of Colonial Rule.* Tucson: University of Arizona Press, 1982.

Mitsuo Nakamura. *The Crescent Arises over the Banyan Tree*. Yogyakarta: Gadjah Mada University Press, 1983.

Moeslim Abdurrahman. "Contoh-contoh Usulan Penelitian Agama: Posisi Berbeda Agama Dalam Kehidupan Sosial di Pedesaan". In *Penelitian Agama, Masalah dan Pemikiran,* edited by Mulyanto Sumardi. Jakarta: Sinar Harapan, 1982.

Mohamad Abu Bakar. "Kebangkitan Islam dan Proses Politik di Malaysia". Kertaskerja untuk Persidangan Antarabangsa Pengajian Melayu. Universiti Malaya, 8–9 September 1979.

———. "Islam dan Hubungan Antarabangsa: Sekitar Masakini Scenario Masa-depan". In *Islamika I*, edited by Lutpi Ibrahim et al. Kuala Lumpur: Sarjana Enterprise, 1981.

———. "Idea Kemajuan Dalam Pemikiran dan Perjuangan Golongan Funda-mentalis Islam". In *Islamika II*, edited by Lutpi Ibrahim et al. Kuala Lumpur: Sarjana Enterprise, 1983.

———. "Islam, Etnisiti dan Integrasi Nasional". In *Kaum, Kelas dan Pembangunan — Ethnicity, Class and Development, Malaysia*, edited by S. Husin Ali. Kuala Lumpur: Persatuan Sains Sosial Malaysia, 1984.

Mohamad Abu Bakar, Amarjit Kaur and Abdullah Zakaria Ghazali, eds. *Historia, Essays in Commemoration of the 25th Anniversary of the Department of History*. University of Malaya, Kuala Lumpur: The Malaysian Historical Society, 1984.

Mohamed Arief. "Ethics and Economics in Islam". In *Islamika II,* edited by Lutpi Ibrahim et al. Kuala Lumpur: Sarjana Enterprise, 1983.

Mohd. Mokhtar bin Shafi. "Maududi dan Pemikirannya dalam Dakwah Islam". In *Islamika II*, edited by Lutpi Ibrahim et al. Kuala Lumpur: Sarjana Enterprise, 1983.

Mohd. Nor bin Ngah. *Kitab Jawi: Islamic Thought of the Malay Muslim Scholars*. Singapore: ISEAS, 1982.

———. "Muslim Political Thought: Theory of the Caliphate or Imamate". In *Islamika II*, edited by Lutpi Ibrahim et al. Kuala Lumpur: Sarjana Enterprise, 1983.

Mohamed Sanusi. "The Role of the Mufti in the Administration of the Court System." *Syariah Law Journal*, November 1984.

Mohd. Taib Osman. "Raja Ali Haji of Riau: A Figure of Transition or the Last of the Classical Pujanggas?" In *Bahasa Kesusasteraan dan Kebudayaan Melayu: Essei-Essei Penghormatan Kepada Pendita Za'aba.* Kuala Lumpur: Dewan Bahasa dan Pustaka, 1976.

———. "Islamization of the Malays: A Transformation of Culture". In *Tamadun di Malaysia*. Kuala Lumpur: Persatuan Sejarah Malaysia, 1980.

Mohd. Zain Othman. "Administration of Waqf in the State of Kedah". In *Islamika I,* edited by Lutpi Ibrahim et al. Kuala Lumpur: Sarjana Enterprise, 1981.

Mokhzani bin Abdul Rahim. "Credit in a Malay Peasant Economy". Ph.D. dissertation, University of London, 1973.

Moment Verslag Congres ke-28 Muhammadijah di Medan. Jogjakarta: Muhammadijah, 1939.

Moquette, J.P. "De oudste Mohammedaansche Inscriptie op Java, n.m. de Graafsteen te Leran". *Handelingen van het eerste congres voor de taal-, land- en volkenkunde van Java*. Weltevreden/Jakarta, 1921.

Mossmann, James. *Rebels in Paradise: Indonesia's Civil War*. London: Jonathan Cape, 1961.

Mubyarto. "Islam dan Keadilan Sosial". In *Dakwah Islam dan Perubahan Sosial*, edited by Amrullah Achmad. Yogyakarta: Prima Duta Yogyakarta, 1983.

Muhammad Kamal Hassan. *Muslim Intellectual Responses to "New Order" Modernization in Indonesia*. Kuala Lumpur: Dewan Bahasa dan Pustaka, 1982.

Muhammed 'Aziz Ahmad. *Political History and Institutions of the Early Turkish Empire in Delhi*. Lahore, 1949.

Mühlmann, W.E., ed. *Chiliasmus und Nativismus. Studien zur Psychologie Soziologie und Historischen Kasuistik der Umsturzbewegungen*. Berlin, 1961.

Mujeeb, M. *The Indian Muslims*. London: 1967.

Mukti A. Ali. "Pembaharuan Sistim Pendidikan dan Pengajaran pada Pondok Pesantren dalam Rangha Merealisir Tujuan Pendidikan Nasional". Statement to Higher Religious Education Seminar. Tugu, Punchak, June 1972.

Mulyanto Sumardi, ed. *Penelitian Agama, Masalah dan Pemikiran*. Jakarta: Sinar Harapan for Departemen Agama Republik Indonesia, 1982.

Mustafa Mahmood. *Islam vs Komunisme dan Sosialisme*. Kota Bharu, Kelantan: Sharikat Dian Sdn. Bhd.

Muzaffar, Chandra. "Protection of the Malay Community: A Study of UMNO's position and Opposition Attitudes". M.Sc. thesis, Universiti Sains Malaysia, 1974.

———. "Values in the Education System". *New Directions* (Singapore), March 1976.

———. "Dominant Concepts and Dissenting Ideas on Malay Society & Malay Rule from the Malacca Period to the Merdeka Period". Ph.D. thesis, University of Singapore, 1977.

———. "Some Political Perspectives on the New Economic Policy". Fourth Malaysian Economic Convention, Malaysian Economic Association, Kuala Lumpur, 1977.

———. "The New Economic Policy & the Quest for National Unity". Fifth Malaysian Economic Convention, Malaysian Economic Association, Kuala Lumpur, 1978.

———. *Protector?* Penang: Aliran, 1979.

———, ed. *Universalism of Islam*. Penang: Aliran, 1979.

Nabil Subhi ath-Thawil. *Kemiskinan dan Keterbelakangan di Negara-Negara Muslim (Al-Hirman wat-Takhalluf fi Diyar al-Muslimin)*. Translated by Muhammad Bagir with an introduction by Jalaluddin Rahmat. Bandung: Mizan Press for Yayasan Tunas Bangsa, 1985.

Nabir bin Haji Abdullah. *Maahad il ihya Assyariff Gunung Semanggol 1934–1959*. Kuala Lumpur: Jabatan Sejarah, Universiti Kebangsaan Malaysia, 1976.

Nasir Tamara. *Revolusi Iran*. Jakarta: Sinar Harapan, 1980.

Nagasura T. Madale, ed. *The Muslim Filipinos: A Book of Readings*. Quezon City: Alemar-Phoenix Publishing House, Inc., 1981.

Nagata, Judith. "Social Perspectives of an Urban Village in a Malayo-Muslim Community". *Western Canadian Journal of Anthropology* III, no. 2 (1972).

———. "What is a Malay? Situational Selections of Ethnic Identity in a plural society," *American Ethnologist* I, no. 2 (1974).

———. *The Reflowering of Malaysian Islam: Modern Religious Radicals and Their Roots*. Vancouver: University of British Columbia Press, 1984.

Nasution, Harun. "The Islamic State in Indonesia: The Rise of the Ideology, the Movement for its Creation and the Theory of the Masjumi". Unpublished Master's thesis, McGill University, Montreal, 1965.

Natsir, Muhammad. *Islam sebagai Dasar Negara*. Bandung: Fraksi Masyumi dalam Konstitoante, 1957.

Natsir Muhammad. *Capita Selecta II*. Jakarta: Pustaka Pendis, 1957.
———. "Oleh-oleh" dari Algiers: Prof. Bousquet tentang "Testamen Prof. Snouck Hurgronje dalam teori dan praktek", *Capita Selecta*. Bandung/The Hague: Pustaka Pendis, 1955.
———. *Some Observations concerning the Role of Islam in National and International Affairs*. Data Paper Number 16, Southeast Asia Program . Ithaca, N.Y.: Department of Far Eastern Studies, Cornell University, 1954.
Am Muchlis (pseud. M. Natsir). *Islam dan Akal Merdeka*. Tasikmalaja: Pusat Pimpinan Persatuan Islam Bagian Penjiaran, 1947.
Nicholson, R.A. *Studies in Islamic Mysticism*. Cambridge: Cambridge University Press, 1921.
———. *The Mystics of Islam*. London: Routledge and Kegan Paul, 1975.
van Niel, Robert. *The Emergence of the Modern Indonesian Elite*. The Hague and Bandung: W. van Hoeve, 1960.
Niemann, G.K. *Inleiding tot de kennis van den Islam, ook met betrekking tot den Indischen Archipel*. Rotterdam, 1861.
Nieuwenhuijze, C.A.O. van. "Samsu'l-din van Pasai". *Bijdrage tot de kennis der Sumatraansche Mystiek*. Leiden, 1945.
———. *Samsu'l-Din van Pasai*. Leiden: E.J. Brill, 1945.
———. "Moslims leven en Indonesische levenssfeer". *Wending* 4, no. 140 (1949).
Nik Abdul Aziz bin Haji Ṇik Hassan. *Islam di Kelantan*. Kuala Lumpur. Persatuan Sejarah Malaysia, 1983.
Nizami, K.A. *Some Aspects of Religion and Politics in India during the Thirteenth Century*. Aligarh, 1961.
———. *Studies in medieval Indian history and culture*. Allahabad, 1966.
Noto Soeroto, R.M. "Wat is Sekaten?" *Indonesie* XII, no. 5 (1951–52).
Notonagoro. *Pemboekan Oendang-oendang Dasar 1945*. Yogyakarta: Universitas Gajah Mada, 1956.
Nurcholish Madjid. *Modernisasi Ialah Rationalisasi Bukan Westernisasi*. Bandung: Mimbar Demokrasi, 1968.
———. "The Issue of Modernization Among Muslims in Indonesia: From a Participant's Point of View". In *What is Modern Indonesian Culture*? edited by Gloria Davis. Papers in International Studies, Southeast Asia Series no. 52. Athens, Ohio: Center for International Studies, 1979.
———. "An Islamic Appraisal of the Political Future of Indonesia". In *Prisma*, no. 35 (March 1985).
———, ed. *Khazanah Intelektual Islam*. Jakarta: Yayasan Obor Indonesia, 1984.

O'Kane, J., ed. *The ship of Sulaimān*. London: Routledge and Kegan Paul, 1972.
Olthof, W.L., ed. and trans. *Babad Tanah Djawi in Proza: Javaansche Geschiedenis*. 2 vols. 's-Gravenhage: Martinus Nijhoff, 1941.
Omar Farouk. "The Muslims of Thailand". In *Islamika I*, edited by Lutpi Ibrahim et al. Kuala Lumpur: Sarjana Enterprise, 1981.
Overbeck, H. "The answer of Pasai". *JMBRAS* VII (1933).

Panuti, H.M. Sudjiman. *Adat Raja-Raja Melayu*. Jakarta: Penerbit Universitas Indonesia, 1983.
Parker, E.H. "The Island of Sumatra". *The Imperial and Asiatic Quarterly Review* (3rd series) IX (1900).
Paterson, H.S. "An Early Malay Inscription from Trengganu". *JMBRAS* XI (1928).
Peacock, James L. *Rites of Modernization*. Chicago: University of Chicago Press, 1968.
Pickthall, Mohammed Marmaduke, trans. *The Meaning of the Glorious Koran*. New York: New American Library, 1953.
Piekaar, A.J. *Atjeh en de Oorlog met Japan*. 's-Gravenhague/Bandung: van Hoeve, 1949.
Pieris, Ralph. *"The Cultural Matrix of Development"*. *CJHSS* V, no. 1, 2 (1962).
Pigeaud, Th. G. Th. *Javaansce uichelarij en Klassifikatie. In Feestpundel, uitgeven door het Koninklijk Bataisaasch Genootschap van Kunster en Westersch appen bij gelegenheid van zijn 15C jarig bestaan, 1779–1928*, II (1929).

Pigeaud, Th. G. Th. "Garebeg Moeloed Tahoen dal 1863". *Djawa* 12 (1932).
———. *Java in the Fourteenth Century: A Study in Cultural History*. 3rd. ed. 5 vols. The Hague: Martinus Nijhoff, 1960–63.
———. *Literature of Java: Catalogue Raisonné of Javanese Manuscripts in the Library of the University of Leiden and Other Public Collections in the Netherlands*. Vols. I–III. The Hague: Martinus Nijhoff, 1967.
Pijper, G.F. *Fragmenta Islamica. Studiën over het Islamisme in Nederlandsch-Indië*. Leiden: E.J. Brill, 1934.
———. "De Ahmadyah in Indonesie". *Bingkisan Budi*. Collection of articles presented to Dr. P. S. van Ronkel. Leiden: E.J. Brill, 1950.
Piscatori, James P., ed. *Islam in the Political Process*. Cambridge: Cambridge University Press, 1983.
Pistorius, A.W.P. Verkerk. "De Priester en zign invloed op de samenleving in de Bovenlanden". *TNI*, 1869.
Poensen, C. "Iets over Javaansche Naamgeving en Eigennamen". *Mededeelingen vanwege het Nederlandsche Zendelinggenootschap* XIV (1870).
Polem, Panglima T.M.A. *Memoir (Tjatetan) T.M.A. Panglima Polem*. Kutaradja: Alhambra, 1972.
Prawoto Mangkusasmito. *Pertumbuhan Historis Rumus Dasar Negara dan Sebuah Projeksi*. Jakarta: Hudaya, 1970.
Prawoto, R. "Dievenbij geloof op Midden Java". *TBG* 58 (1919).
Prins, J. "Adat-Law and Muslim Religious Law in Modern Indonesia". *Welt des Islams* I (1951).

Radin Soenarno. "Malay Nationalism, 1900–1945". *Journal of Southeast Asian History* I, no. 1 (March 1960).
Raffles, T.S. *The History of Java*. 2 vols. London, 1830.
Raja Chulan bin Hamid. In *Misa Melayu*, edited by R.O. Winstedt. Singapore: Methodist Publishing House, 1919.
Rasjidi, H.M. *Koreksi terhadap Drs. Nurcholish Madjid tentang Sekularisasi*. Jakarta: Bulan Bintang, 1972.
Ratnam, K.J. "Religion and Politics in Malaya". In *Man, State and Society in Contemporary Southeast Asia*, edited by Robert O'Tilman. New York: Praeger Publishers, 1969.
Ratnam, K.J. and R.S. Milne. *The Malayan Parliamentary Election of 1964*. Kuala Lumpur: University of Malaya Press, 1967.
———. *New States in a New Nation*. London: Frank Cass, 1974.
Ravaisse. "L'inscription coufique de Léran à Java". *TBG* 65 (1925).
Reid, Anthony. *The Contest for North Sumatra: Atjeh, The Netherlands and Britain 1858–1898*. Kuala Lumpur/Singapore: Oxford University Press, 1969.
———. "The Islamization of Southeast Asia". In *Historia*, edited by Muhammad Abu Bakar, Amarjit Kaur and Abdullah Zakaria Ghazali. Kuala Lumpur: The Malaysian Historical Society, 1984.
Reid, Anthony and David Marr. *Perceptions of the Past in Southeast Asia*. Singapore: Heinemann Educational Books (Asia) Ltd., for the Asian Studies Association of Australia, 1979.
Rétif, A. "Aspects religieux de l'Indonésie". *Études*, 1954.
Riboud, Marc. "Second Death of Angkar". *Paris-Match*, 12 Feb. 1982.
Ricklefs, M.C. "Six Centuries of Islamization in Java". In *Conversion to Islam*, edited by N. Lertzion. New York: Holmes & Meier Publishers, 1979.
———. "A Consideration of Three Versions of the Babad Tahah Djawi, with excerpts on the fall of Madjapahit". *BSOAS* 35, part 2 (1972).
———. *Jogjakarta under Sultan Mangkubumi, 1749–1792: A History of the Division of Java*. London, New York, Toronto, Kuala Lumpur: Oxford University Press, 1974.
Ricklefs, M.C. and P. Voorhoeve. *Indonesian Manuscripts in Great Britain: A Catalogue of Manuscripts in Indonesian Languages in British Public Collections*. Oxford: Oxford University Press, 1977.

Ridder de Steurs, H.J.J.L. *De vestiging en uitbreiding van Nederlanders ter Weskust van Sumatra*. 2 vols. Amsterdam, 1849.
Ringgren, H. "Some religious aspects of the Caliphate in Sacral Kingship". *Contributions to the Central Theme of the VIIIth International Congress for the History of Religions*, Rome, April 1955. Leiden: E.J. Brill, 1959.
Rinkes, D.A. *Abdoerrauf van Singkel, Bijdrage tot de kennis van de mystiek op Sumatra en Java*. Heerenveen: Hepkema, 1909.
———. "De maqam van Sjech 'Abdoelmoehji'". *TBG* LII (1910).
Roff, William R. "Kaum Muda-Kaum Tua: Innovation and Reaction amongst the Malays, 1900–1941". In *Papers on Malayan History (Journal of South East Asian History)*, edited by R.G. Tregonning, 1962.
———. "The Malayo-Muslim World of Singapore at the Close of the Nineteenth Century". *Journal of Asian Studies* XXIV (1964).
———. *The Origins of Malay Nationalism*. Kuala Lumpur: University of Malaya Press, 1967.
Ronkel, Ph.S. van. "De invoering van ons Strafwetboek ter SWK naar aanteekeningen in een Maleische handschrift". *TBG* 46 (1914).
———. "Het Heiligdom te Oelakan". *TBG* 56 (1914).
———. "Inlandsche getuigenissen aangaande de Padri-oorlog". *IG* 71 (1915).
———. *Rapport betreffende de Godsdienstige verschijnselen ter Sumatra's Westkust*. Batavia, 1916.
———. "Een Maleisch getuigenis over den weg der Islam in Sumatra". *BKI* 75 (1919).
Roolvink, R. "The answer of Pasai". *JMBRAS* XXXVIII (1965).
———. "The Variant Versions of the Malay Annals". *BKI* CXXIII, no. 3 (1967).
Roorda van Eysinga, P.P. *Voorlezingen over Kolonisatie door Nederlanders in Nederlandsch Indië*. Haarlem, 1856.
Rosen, L. "The Negotiation of Reality: Male-Female Relations in Sefrou, Morocco". In *Women in the Muslim World*, edited by L. Beck and N. Keddie. Cambridge: Harvard University Press, 1978.
Rosenthal, E.I.J. *Islam in the Modern National State*. Cambridge: Cambridge University Press, 1965.
Rozhan bin Kuntom. "A General Survey of Muslim Religious Schools in Malaya". Thesis, University of Malaya in Singapore, 1957.

Saadoeddin Djambek. "Ilmu Pengetahuan, Modernisasi dan Sekularisme". *Mertju Suar*, 15 July 1968.
Sadka, E. *The Protected Malay States, 1874–1895*. Kuala Lumpur: University of Malaya Press, 1968.
Safran, Nadav. *Egypt in Search of Political Community*. Cambridge, Mass.: Harvard University Press, 1961.
Said, Mohammed. *Atjeh Sepandjang Abad*. Medan, 1961.
Said Ramadan. *The Three Major Problems Confronting the World of Islam*. Geneva: Islamic Studies Centre, 1961.
Saifuddin Anshari. *The Jakarta Charter of June 1945*. Kuala Lumpur: ABIM, 1979.
Saleeby, Najeeb M. *The History of Sulu*. Manila: Filipiniana Book Guild, Inc., 1963.
Salim, Haji Agus. "De sluiering van de vrouw". Reprinted in *Djedjak langkah Hadji A. Salim: Pilihan Karangan Utjapan dan pendapat beliau dari dulu sampai sekarang*. Djakarta, 1954.
Samson, Allan A. "Islam in Indonesian Politics". *Asian Survey* 8 (1968).
———. "Indonesian Islam since the New Order". In *Political Power and Communications in Indonesia*, edited by K.D. Jackson and L.W. Pye. Berkeley: University of California Press, 1978.
Sartono Kartodirdjo. *The Peasants' Revolt of Banten in 1888. TBG*, Vol. 50. 's-Gravenhage: Martinus Nijhoff, 1966.
Sastri, K.A. Nilakanta. *A History of South India*. Madras, 1966.
Schacht, J. *An Introduction to Islamic Law*. Oxford: The Claredon Press, 1964.

Schimmel, A. *Mystical dimensions of Islam*. Chapel Hill: University of North Carolina Press, 1975.

Schrieke, B.J.O. "Bijdrage tot de bibliografie van de huidige godsdienstige beweging ter Sumatra's Westkust". *TBG* LIX (1919–21).

———, ed. *The Effect of Western Influence on the Native Civilizations of the Malay Archipelago*. Batavia, 1929.

———. "The Educational System in the Netherlands Indies". *Bulletin of the Colonial Institute* (Amsterdam) II (1938–39).

———. *Indonesian Sociological Studies: Selected Writings of B. Schrieke, Part I*. The Hague and Bandung: van Hoeve, 1955.

———. *Indonesian Sociological Studies: Selected Writings of B. Schrieke, Part II, Ruler and Realm in Early Java*. The Hague and Bandung: van Hoeve, 1957.

Schuurman, B.M. *Mystik und Glaube in Zusammenhang mit der Mission auf Java*. Dissertation Zürich, 1933.

Schwartz, Benjamin. "Factors in the Process of Modernization in Asian Countries". *Asian Affairs* 59 (February 1972).

Seddik Taouti. "The Forgotten Muslims of Kampuchea and Viet Nam". *Journal, Institute of Muslim Minority Affairs* 4, no. 1 & 2 (1982).

Sennett, R. *The Fall of Public Man*. Cambridge: Cambridge University Press, 1977.

Sidjabat, W.B. "Penelitian Agama: Pendekatan dari Ilmu Agama". In *Penelitian Agama, Masalah dan Pemikiran,* edited by Mulyanto Sumardi. Jakarta: Sinar Harapan, 1982.

Siegel, James T. *The Rope of God*. Berkeley and Los Angeles: University of California Press, 1969.

Safie bin Ibrahim. *The Islamic Party of Malaysia, Its Formative Stages and Ideology*. Pasir Puteh, Kelantan: Nuawi bin Ismail, 1981.

Shariffuddin, P.M. Dato. "The Kedayans". *Brunei Museum Journal*, 1969.

Shaw, W.W. and Mohd. Kassim Haji Ali. *Malacca Coins*. Kuala Lumpur: Muzium Negara, 1970.

Shellabear, W.G., ed. *Sejarah Melayu, or the Malay Annals*. Singapore: The Malaya Publishing House, 1950.

Siddique, Sharon. "Conceptualizing Contemporary Islam: Religion or Ideology?" In *Annual Review of the Social Sciences of Religion* 5 (1981).

Sidjabat, Walter Bonar. *Religious Tolerance and Christian Faith*. Jakarta: Badan Penerbit Kristen, 1965.

Simorangkir, J.C.T. and B. Mang Reng Say. *Konstitusi dan Konstituante Indonesia*. Jakarta: Soeroengan, n.d.

Simorangkir, J.C.T. and B. Mang Reng Say. *Tentang dan Sekitar Undang-undang Dasar 1945*. Jakarta: Penerbit Jambatan, 1959.

Skeat, W.W. *Malay Magic*. London: Macmillan & Co., 1900.

Smith, Donald Eugene, ed. *Religion, Politics, and Social Change in the Third World*. New York: The Free Press, 1971.

Smith, W.C. *Islam in Modern History*. Princeton: Princeton University Press, 1957.

Snouck Hurgronje, C. *Mekka in the Latter Part of the 19th Century*. Leiden: E.J. Brill, 1931. (English translation of the Dutch original, first published 1888).

———. *The Achehnese*. Leiden: E.J. Brill, 1906.

———. *Verspreide Geschriften*. Vols. I–IV. Boon and Leipzig: Kurt Schroeder; Leiden: E.J. Brill, 1923–27.

Soebardi. "Santri-Religious Elements as Reflected in the Book of Tjentini". *BKI* 127, no. 3 (1971).

Soebardim S. *The Book of Cabolek: A Critical Edition with Introduction, Translation and Notes*. Biblioteca Indonesica 10. The Hague: Martinus Nijhoff, 1975.

Soedirman, Brig. Gen. "Chotbah 'Idulfithri, March 18, 1961 dilapangan SESKOAD, Bandung". *Gema Islam* I, no. 4 (1 March 1962).

Soedjatmoko. *Etika Pembebasan, Pilihan Karangan tentang: Agama, Kebudayaan, Sejarah dan Ilmu Pengetahuan*. Jakarta: LP3ES, 1984.

Soekarno. *Negara Nasional dan Cita-cita Islam*. Jakarta: P.P. Endang, 1954.

Soekarno. *Panca Sila: Dasar Falsafah Negara*. Jakarta: Panitia Nasional Peringatan Lahirnya Panca Sila Jun: 1945–1964, 1964.

Stapel, F.W., ed. *Geschiedenis van Nederlandsch Indië*, Vol. V. Amsterdam, 1939.
Stoddard, L. *The New World of Islam*. London, 1921.
Sudjono, Brig. Gen. Dr. "Dharma Bhakti TNI AD sebagai alat revolusi dalam mentjapai Masjarakat Socialis Indonesia Pantjasila". *Karya Wira Jati* IV, nos. 13–15 (January–July 1964).
Sudjoko Prasodjo, et al., eds. *Profil Pesantren, Laporan Hasil Penelitian Pesantren Al-Falak dan Delapan Pesantren Lain di Bogor*. Jakarta: LP3ES, 1974.
Surin Pitsuwan. *Islam and Malay Nationalism: A Case Study of The Malay-Muslims of Southern Thailand.* Bangkok: Thai Khadi Research Institute, Thammasat University, 1985.
Al-Suyūṭi. *Al-Ashbāh wa'l-Naẓā'ir.* Cairo, n.d
Sweeney, P.L.A., ed. "Silsilah Raja Raja Berunai". *JMBRAS* XLI (1968).
Swettenham, Sir Frank A. *Vocabulary of the English and Malay Languages*, Vol. 1. 5th ed. Shanghai: Kelly & Walsh, 1905.
Swift, M.G. "Minangkabau and Modernization". In *Anthropology in Oceania: Essay presented to Ian Nogbin,* edited by L.R. Hiatt and C. Jayawardena. Sydney: Angus and Robertson, 1971.

S. Takdir Alisjahbana. "Islamic Thought and Culture in Southeast Asia". *Mizan* 1, no. 1 (January 1984).
Talmon, Yonina. "Pursuit of the Millennium. The Relation between Religion and Social Change". *AES* III (1962).
Taufik Abdullah. "Adat and Islam: An Examination of Conflict in Minangkabau". *Indonesia* 2 (1966).
———. *Schools and Politics: The Kaum Muda Movement in West Sumatra (1927–1933).* Ithaca: Modern Indonesia Project, Cornell University, 1971.
Taufik Abdullah and Sharon Siddique, eds. *Islam and Society in Southeast Asia.* Singapore: ISEAS, 1986.
Taylor, E.N. "Malay Family Law". *JMBRAS* 15 (1937).
Teeuw A. and D.K. Wyatt, eds. *Hikayat Patani*. The Hague: Martinus Nijhoff, 1970.
Tentang Dasar Negara Republik Indonesia dalam Konstituante II. Bandung: Konstituante, 1959.
Thrupp, Sylvia L., ed. "Millennial Dreams in Action: Essays in Comparative Study." *CSSH* (The Hague) Supplement II, 1962.
Tibbetts, G.R. "Early Muslim Traders in South-East Asia". *JMBRAS* XXX (1957).
Tirtakoesoema, R.S. "De viering van de Malem Selikoer, dal 1863, Dinsdagavond, 17 Januari 1933, te Jogjakarta". *Djawa 13* (1983).
Tirtakoesoema, R.S. "De viering van de Garebeg Moeloed dal 1863 in Jogjakarta (18 Juli 1932)". *Djawa* 12 (1932).

Umar Junus. "The Payment of Zakat al-Fitrah in a Minangkabau Community". *BKI* 122, no. 4 (1966).
Umar Khayam. "Dakwah Islam dan Kebudayaan". In *Dakwah Islam dan Perubahan Sosial*, edited by Amrullah Achmad. Yogyakarta: Prima Duta Yogyakarta, 1983.
Untung Iskandar. "Dakwah Islam dan Lingkungan Hidup". In *Dakwah Islam dan Perubahan Sosial*, edited by Amrullah Achmad. Yogyakarta: Prima Duta Yogyakarta, 1983.

van de Velde, J-J. *De godsdienstige, rechtspraak in Nederlandsch-Indië, staatsrechtelijk beschourd.* Leiden, 1928.
Vergouw, W.G. "Animisme in het Javaanarche dievenwereld". *Koloniale Studien* 13 (1929).
Vermeulen, W.H. "Oost-Indië in het Nederlandse parlement, 1891–1918". In *Schets eener parlementaire geschiedenis van Nederland,* edited by W.J. Welderen Rengers and C.W. de Vries. The Hague: Martinus Nijhoff, 1955.
Veth, P.J. *Java geografisch, etnologisch, historisch*. 3 vols. Haarlem, 1875–82.
Vlekke, B.H.M. *Geschiedenis van den Indischen Archipel, van het Begin der Beschaving tot het Door breken der Nationale Revolutie*. Roermond-Maaseik: J.J. Romen and Zonen, 1947.

Vreede, A.C. *Catalogus van de Javaansche en Madoereesche handschriften der Leidsche universiteits-bibliotheek*. Leiden, 1892.
Vredenbergt, J. "The Haddj: Some of its features and functions in Indonesia". *BKI* CXVIII (1962).

Waal, E. de *Onze Indische Financiën, Nieuse roeks aanteekeningen,* Vol. I. 's-Gravenhage, 1876.
Wadjiz Anwar, L. Ph. "Islam dan Modernisasi". *Pandji Masjarakat,* nos. 128, 129, 130 (June–July 1973).
Wan Salim Hj. Mohd. Nor. "Sumbangan Ibn Taimiyah terhadap Kebangkitan Pemikiran Islam". In *Islamika II,* edited by Lutpi Ibrahim et al. Kuala Lumpur: Sarjana Enterprise, 1983.
Weekes, Richard, V., ed. *Muslim Peoples, A World Ethnographic Survey.* Westport, Connecticut: Greenwook Press, 1979.
Wertheim, W.F. *Indonesian Society in Transition: A Study of Social Change.* The Hague/Bandung: van Hoeve, 1959.
———. *East-West Parallels: Sociological Approaches to Modern Asia.* The Hague: van Hoeve, 1964.
Westenik, C. "Iets over land en volk van Minangkabau". *KT*, 1912.
Widengren, G. "The Sacral Kingship of Iran". In *The Sacral Kingship, Contributions to the Central Theme of the VIIIth International Congress for the History of Religions, Rome, April 1955.* Leiden: Brill, 1959.
Wilkinson, R.J., general ed. *Papers on Malay Subjects, History.* Pts. III and IV. Kuala Lumpur, 1907 and 1909.
———. *A Malay-English Dictionary.* London: MacMillan and Co., 1959.
Winstedt, R.O. "Kedah Laws". *JMBRAS* VI (1928).
———. "Sejarah Melayu". *JMBRAS* XIV (1938).
——— and Josselin de Jong, P.E. de. "The Maritime Laws of Malacca". *JMBRAS* XXIX (1956).
———. "A History of Classical Malay Literature". *JMBRAS* XXXI(1958).
———. *The Malays: A Cultural History.* London: Routledge & Kegan Paul, 1972.
Wiselius, J.A.B. "Iets over het geesterdom en de geesten der Javanen". *TBG* 4 (1872).
Wolters, Oliver. *The Fall of Srivijaya in Malay History.* Ithaca: Cornell University Press, 1970.
———. "Khmer 'Hinduism' in the Seventh Century". In *Early South East Asia: essays in archaeology, history and historical geography,* edited by R.B. Smith and W. Watson. New York and Kuala Lumpur: Oxford University Press, 1979.
Wood, W.A.R. *A History of Siam.* Bangkok: Siam Bounakich Press, 1923.
Worsley, P.M. "The Analysis of Rebellion and Revolution in Modern British Social Anthropology". *Science and Society* XXI (1961).

Yahya Muhaimin. "Dakwah Islam dan Partisipasi Politik". In *Dakwah Islam dan Perubahan Sosial,* edited by Amrullah Achmad. Yogyakarta: Prima Duta Yogyakarta, 1983.
Yamin, H. Muhammad. *Naskah Persiapan Undang-undang Dasar 1945.* Jakarta: Yayasan Propanca, 1959.
Yusuff Quardhawi. *Islam "Ekstrem", Analisis dan Pemechaannya, (As-Shahwah Al-Islamiyah Bainal Juhul wat-Tatharruf).* Translated by Alwi A.M. Bandung: Mizan Press, 1985.

Za'ba. "Recent Developments in Malay Literature". *JMBRAS* XIX, Pt. 1 (February 1941).
Zainal Abidin Ahmad. *Piagam Nabi Muhammad s.a.w.* Djakarta: Bulan Bintang, 1973.
Zaini Z. Hasan. *Pengantar Hukum Tatanegara.* Bandung: Alumni, 1971.
Zamakhsyari Dhofier. *Tradisi Pesantren, Studi tentang Pandangan Hidup Kyai.* Jakarta: LP3ES, 1982.
———. "Contemporary Features of Javanese Pesantren". *Mizan* 1, no. 2 (1984).
Zamanhuri Hj. Shamsuddin, ed. *Koleksi PKPIM, Simposium Pendidikan Islam.* Kuala Lumpur: PKPIM, 1979.

Zanen, A.J. van. *Voorwaarden voor mattschappelijk lijke ontwikkeling in het central Batakland.* Leiden, 1934.

Zoetmulder, P.J. *Pantheisme en monisme in de Javaansche soeloek-litteratuur.* Nijmegen: J.J. Berkhout, 1935.

———. "Die Hochreligionen Indonesians". In *Die Religionen Indonesiens,* edited by Waldemar Stohr and Piet Zoetmulder. Stuttgart, 1965.

———. "The Wajang as a Philosophical Theme". *Indonesia*, no. 12 (October 1971).

———. *Kalangwan: A Survey of Old Javanese Literature.* The Hague: Martinus Nijhoff. 1974.

——— and W. Stohr. *Les religions d'Indonesie*. Paris: Payot, 1968.

NOTES ON THE COMPILERS

Datuk Ahmad Ibrahim is currently holding the post of Shaikh Kulliyyah of Laws at the International Islamic University of Malaysia in Kuala Lumpur. His publications include *Family Law in Malaysia and Singapore* (1978); *Legal Education in Malaysia* (1980); *Islamic Law in Malaya* (1965); and *Law and Population in Malaysia* (1977).

Sharon Siddique is a Senior Fellow at the Institute of Southeast Asian Studies, Singapore. Her publications include (with Nirmala Puru Shotam) *Singapore's Little India: past, present and future* and (with Taufik Abdullah, co-editor) *Islam and Society in Southeast Asia* (forthcoming).

Yasmin Hussain was formerly associated with the Institute of Southeast Asian Studies where she was a Research Associate from 1984 to 1985.